The Essential
Summa Theologiae

SECOND EDITION

The Essential
Summa Theologiae

A READER AND COMMENTARY

Frederick Christian Bauerschmidt

Baker Academic
a division of Baker Publishing Group
Grand Rapids, Michigan

© 2005, 2021 by Frederick Christian Bauerschmidt

Published by Baker Academic
a division of Baker Publishing Group
PO Box 6287, Grand Rapids, MI 49516-6287
www.bakeracademic.com

First edition published by Brazos Press 2005.

Printed in the United States of America

Library of Congress Cataloging-in-Publication Data
Names: Thomas, Aquinas, Saint, 1225?–1274, author. | Bauerschmidt, Frederick Christian, commentator.
Title: The essential Summa theologiae : a reader and commentary / Frederick Christian Bauerschmidt.
Other titles: Summa theologica. Selections. English
Description: Second edition. | Grand Rapids : Baker Academic, a division of Baker Publishing Group, [2021] | Includes bibliographical references and index.
Identifiers: LCCN 2021018992 | ISBN 9781540960061 (paperback) | ISBN 9781540964205 (casebound) | ISBN 9781493429059 (ebook)
Subjects: LCSH: Thomas, Aquinas, Saint, 1225?–1274. Summa theologica. | Catholic Church—Doctrines. | Theology, Doctrinal.
Classification: LCC BX1749 .T515 2021 | DDC 230/.2—dc23
LC record available at https://lccn.loc.gov/2021018992

Baker Publishing Group publications use paper produced from sustainable forestry practices and post-consumer waste whenever possible.

22 23 24 25 26 27   7 6 5 4 3 2

For Stanley Hauerwas, fellow hillbilly Thomist,
and
Trent Pomplun, Texan Scotist

Contents

Introduction

How to Begin with a Text for Beginners

Thomas Aquinas's *Summa theologiae* is undoubtedly a great work of theology.[1] Indeed, it is the only volume of anything like dogmatic or systematic theology among Britannica's Great Books of the Western World series. If there is a work of theology that needs no introduction, this is it. Moreover, Thomas himself says that he is writing it to aid those who are instructing "beginners" (*incipientes*), so it seems as if anyone ought to be able to sit down with the first article of the first question and work their way through it on their own.

But recalling my own initial attempts, now many years ago, to read Thomas, as well as my experience of attempting to teach Thomas, it seems evident to me that Thomas's theology is not immediately accessible. This may be because "beginners" in the thirteenth century were smarter than beginners today, or because Thomas misread his audience, or (what seems to me most likely) because Thomas never actually meant for beginners to read the *Summa*, but rather saw it as a guide for teachers, so that their pedagogy would have a reasonable structure. But whatever Thomas's original intention, the *Summa* has become a "great book" that people want to read—or want their students to read—despite the difficulties it may present. This is why I came up with the idea of a selection of key texts from the *Summa* accompanied by a running commentary that would explain terms, provide historical background, outline the shape of arguments, and make connections between different areas of Thomas's thought. My primary desire was to make it possible for those who are beginners in the thought of Thomas Aquinas, or even beginners in theology in general, to read him fruitfully.

---

1. *Summa theologiae* is "Summary of Theology." It is also called the *Summa theologica* or "Theological Summary."

But this book was also born out of a desire to help people read Thomas Aquinas differently. I hope this book will show that there is much of interest in Thomas that for many people remains unknown because it remains unread. Many people think they know what is important in Thomas's *Summa theologiae*: his proofs for the existence of God and perhaps what he has to say about natural law. While these things certainly are important, focusing on them exclusively distorts our image of what Thomas is up to in the *Summa*. He himself describes the *Summa* as an exercise in *sacra doctrina*, which is sometimes translated as "sacred doctrine," but which I think is better rendered as "holy teaching." This is an activity that is first and foremost God's activity of self-revelation through the prophets, the apostles, and preeminently through Jesus Christ. It is secondarily our human activity of passing on that revelation through teaching, which involves not simply rote repetition but a kind of critical reflection by which we seek to understand how to hand on this teaching faithfully.

So in this book I hope not simply to introduce the *Summa theologiae*, but to introduce it in such a way that its character as "holy teaching" is manifest.

Thomas's Life and Times

When studying some theologians, it seems crucial to understand their lives in order to understand their thought. If one wants to study Augustine, for example, his *Confessions* would seem the logical place to start, not least because his account of his own conversion illuminates the struggle between sin and grace—the earthly and the heavenly cities—that is at the heart of his theology. But not so with Thomas Aquinas. His writing displays little of the passion of Augustine: the tone is measured, the language without rhetorical flourish—reduced to essentials for the sake of clarity. One interpreter, presumably paying Thomas a compliment, went so far as to say that he "is hardly an 'author,' or even a 'man,' but rather a channel connecting us directly with intelligible truth" (Sertillanges 1932, 109). When confronted with a direct channel to intelligible truth, one is likely to be far more interested in the truth revealed than in the channel's family history. Thus have some viewed Thomas.

But I think this view of Thomas is mistaken. His life, while lacking the drama of Augustine's, is still important for understanding his work. More specifically, although one could remain ignorant of the pious anecdotes that surround Thomas without much loss in understanding his theology, some knowledge of the context in which he lived, taught, and wrote is crucial. Even if Thomas's theology is one for the ages, one cannot properly understand that theology if one does not understand its author's place within his own age.

For those seeking a full presentation of Thomas's life, Jean-Pierre Torrell's (1996) biography remains the authoritative text. For those who want something briefer, Simon Tugwell (1988) provides an excellent short biography in the introduction to his *Albert and Thomas: Selected Writings*. For those who want to know only the most essential information, I offer the following.

Youth

Thomas Aquinas was born around the year 1225 at the Aquino family castle in Roccasecca, midway between Rome and Naples, in what was then the Kingdom of the Two Sicilies. Thomas was the eighth of nine children born to Landulf and Theodora d'Aquino. Landulf was a minor noble, described in the necrology of the monastery at Monte Cassino as a "knight." Thomas was born at the beginning of a time of conflict between Emperor Frederick II and a series of popes,[2] which caused problems for his family, since his father was a vassal of Frederick and their lands lay on the border between imperial and papal lands.

It was customary for the youngest son of a noble family to be offered for service to the church, and so, around the age of five (ca. 1230/31), Thomas was taken to live at the famous Benedictine monastery of Monte Cassino (which was nearby) as what was called a "child oblate." This may sound a bit callous to us, but it was a common practice in the Middle Ages, not unlike sending a child to boarding school. *Oblatio* is different from *professio* (i.e., becoming a monk) in that it does not involve solemn vows. Thomas would have eventually been able to decide for himself if he wanted to profess vows, but it is not unlikely that his family hoped he would one day become abbot of the monastery, which would be a suitably important role for the son of a noble family. But Monte Cassino was a contested territory between the emperor and the pope, and in 1239 Frederick's troops took it over, turned it into a fortress, and began expelling the monks. Thomas probably left about this time, with a recommendation from the monks to his family that he should go study at the University of Naples.

Around the age of fifteen Thomas entered the *studium generale* at Naples to study the liberal arts and philosophy (not theology). Universities were a relatively recent educational innovation, and this one had been founded by Frederick II with the idea of training men to serve the emperor in various

---

2. Honorius III, Gregory IX (who excommunicated Frederick at least twice), and Innocent IV (who declared Frederick guilty of heresy and tried to depose him as king).

official capacities. The education offered in Naples was broader and more secular than in some of the other universities. Thomas would have studied the seven "liberal arts"—what Vergerius called "those studies . . . which are worthy of a free man." These were divided into the word-focused *trivium* (grammar, rhetoric, and logic) and the number-focused *quadrivium* (arithmetic, geometry, astronomy, and music) and were the basis for any higher study, whether in law, medicine, or theology.

At Naples, Thomas encountered two new phenomena that would profoundly influence him and that are crucial for understanding him and his times: the writings of Aristotle and members of the Order of Preachers, more commonly known as the Dominicans.

Aristotle

Though separated from Aristotle (385–323 BC) by 1500 years, Thomas encountered his works as something newly arrived on the intellectual scene. Boethius, in the sixth century of the Christian era, had conceived a plan to translate all the works of Plato and Aristotle into Latin, so that they would remain available to a Western Europe rapidly losing its intellectual ties with the Greek-speaking East. He had gotten only as far as translating Aristotle's *Posterior Analytics*, a work on logic, when this plan was cut short. Boethius ran afoul of Emperor Theodoric and was executed in 524. As a consequence, until the twelfth century most of the works of Aristotle were lost to the West. His logic was available in Boethius's translation, but no one had firsthand knowledge of his works of natural science, metaphysics, or ethics.

During the twelfth century works by Aristotle and by Arabic philosophers commentating on his work began to be translated into Latin, and in the thirteenth century intellectual engagement with those works began in earnest. This was a revolutionary event. Rather quickly, the Western intellectual world was introduced to a body of thought offering a comprehensive interpretation of the world. Most disturbing was the fact that this interpretation seemed to have no need for Christian revelation. Christianity had long before made a kind of peace with Platonic thought (e.g., in St. Augustine and, in a very different way, in the anonymous Syrian monk who wrote under the name Dionysius the Areopagite), but Aristotle contradicted Plato on many points and seemed to call into question the harmony of natural and supernatural wisdom. For example, Christians had long before appropriated Plato's notion of a realm of "forms" as a way of speaking of the Christian notion of divine ideas in the mind of God. Aristotle, however, conceived of "form" as existing not in a transcendent realm but immanently in particular things. In this and many other cases, Aristotle's departure from Plato seemed to threaten established Christian doctrine. And it did not help Aristotle's case that his work arrived accompanied by commentaries and paraphrases done by Muslim infidels.

Because of the threat that Aristotle seemed to pose to faith, the teaching of his scientific and metaphysical works was banned at many universities, most notably at the University of Paris (the full Aristotelian corpus finally became an official part of the curriculum at Paris sometime between 1252 and 1255, though it was undoubtedly read and taught unofficially before this). But this ban was not in effect at Naples, and it was here that Thomas first studied Aristotle—not only his logic and ethics but also his scientific and metaphysical works. Later, in his formation as a Dominican, Thomas continued to study Aristotle under Albert the Great, and later in life he wrote several commentaries on the works of Aristotle. To anyone who has read Thomas, it is clear that Aristotle's philosophy is one of his chief tools for solving intellectual puzzles, though he not infrequently ends up making that tool do jobs for which it was never designed.

The Order of Preachers

Dominic Guzman was born in Spain around 1170 and died in 1221. He founded the Order of Preachers in 1215 to combat heresy—specifically, the Cathar or Albigensian heresy in southern France—through preaching. The Dominicans were part of a broadly based and diverse movement known as the *vita apostolica*, which sought a return to the kind of life depicted in the book of Acts: a shared life of preaching, prayer, and poverty. Along with the Franciscans (founded around the same time by Francis of Assisi), the Dominicans were *mendicants*: rather than living off income from property and manual labor, like traditional monastics, they supported themselves by begging. Freedom from income-generating property allowed them to minister in cities, which were undergoing a revival. The mendicant orders emphasized active service and were not strictly contemplative—again, differentiating them from traditional monastics. Because of their emphasis on preaching, the Dominicans also emphasized education, establishing houses of study at major universities, along with their own network of institutions for educating Dominican friars.

Just as Aristotle's works presented a new way of proceeding intellectually, the mendicant orders presented an innovative form of religious life, one that responded to recent developments such as the rise of universities and the revival of urban life. As such, they were the object of much suspicion. The Dominicans had founded a priory in Naples in 1231, though only two friars were in residence when Thomas arrived (Frederick II had kicked most of the mendicants out of his realm). One of these friars, John of San Giuliano, inspired in Thomas a desire to join the Dominicans and live their life of prayer and study in the service of preaching.

We are not sure when exactly Thomas joined the Dominicans, though it was probably early in 1244,[3] and it touched off the most obviously dramatic event in his life. His family was not thrilled at his interest in the Dominicans, who seemed to them a bunch of scruffy upstart radicals, and certainly not the kind of group with which the son of a nobleman should associate. Thomas's family no doubt still harbored the hope that he would someday become the abbot of Monte Cassino.

The friars, foreseeing trouble, decided Thomas should get out of Naples, so they sent him first to the Dominican community at Santa Sabina in Rome and then on to either Bologna or Paris (scholars differ as to his destination). His mother, seeking to talk some sense into him, just missed him in both Naples and Rome.[4] Thereupon she sent a force, which included his brother Rinaldo, to intercept him and take him to the family castle in Roccasecca, so they could persuade him to adopt a more conventional path than that of a Dominican friar. His family kept him under a sort of house (or castle) arrest for about a year, during which time he is said to have memorized the Bible and studied the *Sentences* of Peter Lombard. John of San Giuliano was able to visit him. Thomas also engaged in discussions with his sister Marotta that eventually led her to become a Benedictine nun. His brothers, frustrated with their lack of progress, smuggled a prostitute into his room to dissuade him from his chosen path, but Thomas kept her at bay with a burning stick, with which he then inscribed a cross on the wall of his room. This scene indicated, at least to his mother, that the case was hopeless. According to legend, she supplied him with a rope that he used to climb out the window of his room to the ground below. Torrell (1996, 11) thinks "the truth is no doubt more prosaic" (i.e., they simply let him go).

Legend tends to exaggerate the conflict between Thomas and his family, and it is clear that later in life he had good relations with them; but it *is* important to remember that his decision to join the Dominicans, like his interest

---

3. Tugwell (1988) inclines toward an earlier date (1242/43), which would indicate a fuller period of formation for Thomas prior to the events that were to follow.

4. The *Vita* of Thomas by Bernard Gui (in Foster 1959, 25–58), written in the early fourteenth century, tells the story slightly differently, perhaps in order to put Thomas's family in a better light. In Bernard's version, Theodora was thrilled that Thomas was joining the Dominicans and went to Naples to congratulate him. The Dominicans, misunderstanding her motive in coming to Naples, secreted Thomas away, thus arousing the ire of his mother.

in Aristotle, was seen as something radical. Thomas has come to be seen by so many as the standard-bearer for theological orthodoxy and intellectual conformity that it is worth noting his association with two movements that in his day were seen as dangerously nonconformist.

Student

Upon his release by his family, Thomas first went back to Naples, but then his movements become difficult to track. Apparently the Dominicans sent him to study first in Paris (1245–48) and then in Cologne (1248–52), where he was ordained a priest in 1250/51. In both places he studied with the Dominican theologian Albert the Great, who used the philosophy of Aristotle extensively. Apparently, neither Albert nor Thomas's fellow students were particularly impressed with him at first. Tall and somewhat stout,[5] Thomas never spoke much and often seemed lost in his own thoughts. His fellow students referred to him as the "dumb ox." Albert, however, recognized fairly quickly Thomas's great intellectual gifts and took a special interest in him. Eventually, his fellow students also came to recognize Thomas's gifts and depended upon him to help them understand Albert's lectures. One of Thomas's earliest works, *On the Principles of Nature*, is thought to be something like a study guide to Aristotle's natural philosophy that Thomas prepared for his fellow students.

In 1251/52 Thomas went to Paris as a *baccalarus sententarium*—roughly equivalent to a doctoral student. As the title suggests, his job was to lecture on the *Sentences* of Peter Lombard. Lombard's text was a collection of quotations that represented conflicting authoritative opinions (which is what *sententia* means) from Scripture and the church fathers on a host of topics. Lombard (ca. 1100–1161) put these conflicting opinions into something like a coherent structure and often added his own resolutions. The *Sentences* became the standard theology "textbook" for medieval universities. Thomas spent his time lecturing on the *Sentences* and composing those lectures into a commentary, which would serve as the functional equivalent of a modern dissertation and become the first of his comprehensive summaries of Christian doctrine, the *Scriptum super libros Sententiarum* or *Commentary on the Sentences*.

Thomas was a good student because he was inquisitive and, like all truly inquisitive people, open minded (though not, perhaps, in our modern sense). He read voraciously in a time when books were hard to come by (he once

---

5. Though probably not, as some have claimed, obese. Like all Dominicans, Thomas would not ride a horse, traveling by foot on his various journeys. If one takes into account all of Thomas's travels, it becomes apparent that he got plenty of exercise—much more so than modern-day academics.

said he would give the whole city of Paris for a copy of John Chrysostom's commentary on Matthew). He sought truth wherever he could find it, including in Muslim and Jewish and ancient pagan sources. But his fundamental understanding of truth was shaped by his identity as a Christian. Those who disagreed with the Christian faith were worth listening to, but the goal was always the vindication and deeper understanding of Christian truth.

Teacher and Preacher

In the spring of 1256 Thomas incepted as a master of theology (*magister in sacra pagina* or "master of the sacred page"), which involved a two-day disputation on four questions as well as an inaugural lecture on a passage of Scripture. Once Thomas was a magister, his job was threefold:

Legere: to lecture/comment on Scripture. This task was a significant part of Thomas's responsibilities. From the texts that survive, we know that Thomas lectured on the Old Testament books of Isaiah and Job as well as the first fifty Psalms. Among the New Testament books, lectures on the Gospels of Matthew and John and on the letters of Paul (including Hebrews) survive. Thomas's role as a commentator on Scripture is worth underscoring since for him this is at the heart of his intellectual enterprise. Indeed, one might say that the whole point of studying the fathers of the church—and even Aristotle—is to understand Scripture better.

Disputare: to participate in disputations, which were, along with the lecture, one of the chief ways of teaching in the medieval university. In a disputation, a question (e.g., "Is any further teaching required besides philosophical studies?") was proposed; a group of students would first present arguments and citations of various authorities for the "no" side; then another group of students would present arguments and authoritative citations for the "yes" side. The next day the master would offer his own position, resolving the conflicts between the various authorities and responding to the specific arguments. A number of these disputations are preserved in edited form, and Thomas uses a modified form of the disputation to structure his arguments in the *Summa theologiae*.

Predicare: to preach. Thomas was, after all, a member of the Order of Preachers. But a reader of the *Summa theologiae*, or one of his commentaries on Aristotle, might find it difficult to imagine what one of Thomas's sermons would have been like. We have transcripts of a number of Thomas's sermons, which indicate that he shied away from high-flown speculation in his preaching, which he often did in his native Neapolitan dialect. His early biographer Bernard Gui notes, "To the ordinary faithful he spoke the word of God with singular grace and power. . . . Subtleties he kept for the Schools; to the people he gave solid moral instruction suited to their capacity; he knew that a teacher must always suit his style to his audience" (in Foster 1959, 47).

In addition to these official duties, Thomas wrote on a variety of topics. It is noteworthy that many of the works for which he is best known—specifically, his two *Summae* and his commentaries on Aristotle—were works he accomplished in his "spare time." In 1259, he was given Reginald of Piperno as a *socius*: what we might call today a research assistant. Reginald became important to Thomas in helping him carry out the vast amount of work he took on. Among other things, apparently, Reginald had to remind Thomas to eat, since Thomas often forgot to do so. During this time in Paris, Thomas began writing his second comprehensive work of Christian doctrine, the *Summa contra Gentiles*.

The habits Thomas formed as a magister in Paris between 1256 and 1259 in many ways defined the rest of his life, which he lived according to the relatively ordered pattern of lecturing to classes, conducting disputations, preaching, reading, writing/dictating, and praying. His world was primarily an academic one. He spent many years in Paris at the university, but he never learned French, since this was the language of the marketplace, whereas Latin was the language of the university. Thomas rose early, said Mass, attended another Mass, and then spent the rest of the day working.

Between spring 1259 and fall 1268, Thomas was in Italy, mainly teaching Dominicans. In Rome (beginning in 1265) he was the regent master of the Dominican *studium* (house of studies), where he was given free rein to develop his own ideas about how theologians were to be trained. During this time he finished the *Summa contra Gentiles* (1264) and soon after began the *Summa theologiae* (1266). No doubt, his experience at the *studium* in Rome prompted him to think about how one should proceed in teaching theology, and the students he had in mind were quite possibly the kind of men he was teaching at the *studium* in Rome: those preparing for pastoral ministry as Dominican friars.[6]

In 1268 Thomas returned to Paris as a regent master. It is possible that he was sent back to Paris to address the brewing controversy between the arts faculty and the theology faculty. The arts faculty, which instructed the students

---

6. This is Torrell's view (1996, 144–45), based on the arguments made by Leonard Boyle (1982).

in the liberal arts prior to more advanced study, was much enamored of Aristotle, particularly as interpreted by the Arabic philosopher Averroes. The theology faculty remained suspicious of the Aristotelians. They were willing to employ Aristotle's philosophy for certain purposes, but they suspected that the arts faculty was more Aristotelian—or in fact Averroist—than they were Christian.

Thomas had been critical of the so-called Averroists on a number of issues; yet, despite his disagreements with them, he was highly admired by many of the philosophers on the arts faculty—no mean achievement for a theologian, even in Thomas's day. His reputation was more mixed among the theologians, many of whom, particularly the Franciscans, accused him of being a closet Averroist and of holding something like a "double-truth" view of the relationship between philosophy and theology (i.e., the view that something could be true philosophically but not theologically, and vice versa). This charge would not go away quickly. The secular masters (i.e., those theologians who did not belong to the Franciscans or the Dominicans or any other religious order) disliked Thomas because he was a mendicant, and mendicants, as noted, were thought to be dangerous innovators.

While in Paris, Thomas continued work on the *Summa theologiae* (the *secunda pars*) and began working on commentaries on the works of Aristotle. In addition, he delivered his lectures on the Gospel of John, which are widely considered one of his masterpieces; he also wrote numerous smaller works. In 1272 he was once again sent to Naples, where he was to set up a *studium*, again with freedom to organize it as he wished. Here he delivered his lectures on Paul's Letters and continued work on his Aristotelian commentaries and on the *tertia pars* of the *Summa theologiae*.

Silence and Death

While celebrating Mass on December 6, 1273 (the feast of St. Nicholas), Thomas underwent some sort of extraordinary experience. After Mass, he did not set to work, as was his habit, but returned to his room. Reginald tried to get him to work, but Thomas said, "Reginald, I cannot, because all that I have written seems like straw to me." Thomas seemed as if he were in a daze—something different from his usual abstracted state. A few days later Reginald pressed him about the problem, and Thomas replied, "All that I have written seems to me like straw compared to what has been revealed to me."[7]

---

7. From Bartholomew of Capua's testimony at Thomas's first canonization inquiry (in Foster 1959, 110).

What happened? Scholars differ. Thomas had been working at an incredible pace and was undoubtedly under a certain amount of stress, both physically and mentally. Clearly Thomas experienced more than a simple mental breakdown, because the historical sources emphasize his physical weakness after this event. Some scholars have speculated that it was something like a stroke. But was this simply a psychological/physical event, or was there a spiritual component? Thomas's remark about "what has been revealed to me" seems to indicate a spiritual experience. Simon Tugwell notes that Thomas had just finished the section of the *Summa theologiae* dealing with the sacrament of the Eucharist, and whatever it was that happened occurred while he was celebrating Mass (Tugwell 1988, 265). Thomas had always had a strong devotion to Christ as present in the Eucharist, and perhaps he was granted some extraordinary insight into this mystery, an insight that made him unwilling or uninterested or unable to continue writing.

Some people wish to see in the words "All that I have written seems to me like straw" Thomas's repudiation of his own writing. However, Tugwell suggests a different interpretation: "'Straw' is a conventional image for the literal sense of scripture, which is worth having, even if it is only a beginning. Words can lead us to reality. But if Thomas had, in some way, peered beyond faith and glimpsed something of the reality to which the words of faith point, of course the words would lose their appeal. They had served their purpose" (Tugwell 1988, 266–67).

Although he had ceased his scholarly work, Thomas was still a friar in service to the church. So when in February 1274 he was summoned to attend the Council of Lyon, which was seeking to reunite the Eastern and Western churches, he set out, despite his physical weakness. While traveling, he hit his head on a tree branch and was unable to continue. He was taken first to the nearby house of one of his sisters and then, at his request, to the nearby Cistercian monastery at Fossanova, where he died on March 7.

The Character of Thomas's Thought

I make no pretense that the comments that accompany this selection of texts from the *Summa theologiae* represent anything like a "neutral" interpretation of Thomas. I have tried to make comments that will help the reader understand Thomas, but I, like all interpreters, have my biases. So I will spell out here what I take to be characteristic of Thomas's thought, noting where I differ from other interpreters.

First, I take Thomas to be a theologian through and through. Though philosophically astute, Thomas does not think of himself as a philosopher.

Indeed, he reserves the title "philosopher" for non-Christian lovers of wisdom. Thomas, by contrast, is a master of the sacred page—an interpreter of Christian Scripture who is willing to use whatever tools are at hand, including philosophical ones, to bring out the meaning of God's revelation. Thus the image some people have of Thomas as a philosopher who wrote a bit of perfunctory theology is prima facie incorrect. The more sophisticated view that there is within Thomas's theology a philosophy that can be detached and stand on its own is, to my mind, equally wrong. It is true that, for Thomas, things can be known about God apart from divine revelation, but he never tries to construct a system of thought out of those things, since he sees them as radically inadequate to true human flourishing.[8] And even when writing his commentaries on Aristotle, Thomas is always writing in service of the Christian faith.

Second, on a related point, I take Thomas's relationship to Aristotle to be a complex one, inadequately described as that of disciple to master. Thomas is surely an admirer of Aristotle and a brilliant commentator on his writings. He thinks Aristotle more useful for Christian theology than Plato (of whom he has, at best, secondhand knowledge), not least because Aristotle helps him focus on and analyze the concrete particular existing thing, which for him fits well with the Christian ideas of creation and incarnation. But Thomas is *not* an Aristotelian in at least two senses. First, his strong interest in Aristotle must be balanced by the fact that he draws upon a wide range of thinkers, including the two very different forms of Neoplatonic Christian theology represented by Augustine and by Dionysius the Areopagite, both of whom are pervasive influences on Thomas's writings. Second, although he finds Aristotle useful for his theological purposes, he is willing to change Aristotle both when the latter conflicts with divine revelation and when Thomas judges him to be philosophically mistaken. The common view that Thomas's reconciliation of Christian revelation with Aristotelian philosophy is one of his great achievements is true, in a sense, but we must always keep in mind that Thomas accomplishes this reconciliation only through a fundamental transformation of Aristotle.

Third, whereas some scholars think of Thomas as someone who thinks that we can know quite a lot about God, I take him quite seriously when he says that we can know more easily what God is not than what God is. For Thomas, God's essence—what God is—is ungraspable by created intellects,

---

8. It can appear in the first three books of the *Summa contra Gentiles* that Thomas does try to build a system out of what we can know of God apart from revelation. But for an argument that this is not the case, see Hibbs (1995).

and his theology always proceeds with this fact in mind. God's essence is ungraspable not because God hides from us, but because when we turn our minds to God there is too much offered to our understanding. We get a sense of this excess in Thomas's words to Reginald: "All that I have written seems to me like straw compared to what has been revealed to me." As Joseph Pieper (1999, 38) puts it, "He is silent, not because he has nothing further to say; he is silent because he has been allowed a glimpse into the inexpressible depths of that mystery which is not reached by any human thought or speech."

Fourth, I do not take Thomas to be someone who thinks that the ungraspability of God's essence consigns us to silence. In Christ, God has given us a language to speak, by which we can speak truly about God, even if the concepts to which our words refer are inadequate to the truth we seek to articulate. Some interpreters have taken the fact that Thomas's discussion of Christology is deferred to the third part of the *Summa theologiae* as an indication of a lack of interest on his part. This is, I think, too wooden a reading of the structure of the *Summa*. But whatever opinion one holds about the structure of the *Summa*, careful attention to the actual content that fills that structure reveals that Christ pervades the entire work. Indeed, the whole point of the *Summa* is to help us learn to follow Christ by teaching us the truth that God has revealed in Christ.

Reading the *Summa*

The format of the *Summa theologiae* can appear confusing at first, but once you grasp how Thomas proceeds, it is in fact a model of clarity.

The *Summa* is structured in three "parts." The *prima pars* (first part) concerns God and creation. The *secunda pars* (second part) concerns human action and is subdivided into a theoretical treatment of human action (the *prima secunda*, or first half of the second part) and a detailed examination of human virtues and vices (the *secunda secunda*, or second half of the second part). The *tertia pars* (third part) concerns Christ: his person and work, the continuation of his work in the church through the sacraments, and his second coming and the consummation of creation (though this eschatological section was never written). There are numerous theories about the significance of the structure of the *Summa*; although such theories can be illuminating, they should not distract us from its actual content.

Each part contains numerous "questions," which are further subdivided into "articles." Your reading of Thomas will be greatly helped if you understand how he proceeds in these articles.

As mentioned above, the articles of the *Summa* grow out of a medieval teaching practice known as "disputation." The pattern of the disputation was as follows:

- A question, or thesis, is put forward.
- Objections against the thesis are offered by students and other masters (these can be quite numerous).
- Counterobjections that speak for the thesis are offered by students and other masters (these also can be quite numerous).
- The master (usually the next day) offers a response outlining his own position.
- The master replies to any of the objections that remain.

If we look at any of Thomas's collections of disputed questions (e.g., *On Truth* or *On the Power of God*) we can see that these disputations could become quite unwieldy. After all, some students talk even when they have nothing to say; and so too in the disputed questions some of the objections and counterobjections are quite repetitive, and others are of dubious value. In the *Summa*, Thomas refines this form, boiling it down to its essentials:

- He states the thesis in the form of a question.
- He raises objections against the thesis—usually two or three, but occasionally more.
- He offers a counterposition, introduced by *sed contra* (on the contrary), which is almost always reduced to a single counterpoint and usually cites a biblical passage or other authority, instead of making an argument.
- He gives his own response, introduced by *respondeo* (I answer)—usually inclined toward the *sed contra*, but not always.
- He marshals replies to each of the initial objections.

We might note a few key points about reading an article. First, it is never enough to read the *respondeo* alone, since Thomas sometimes makes his most important point in the replies to the objections. Second, the objections are not "straw men." Of all the possible objections, Thomas chose those he thought most convincing. Often an objection is at least half of the way, and sometimes three-quarters of the way, to the truth. Third, we should not presume that the *sed contra* is Thomas's position. On occasion it misses the truth as much as the objections, albeit in a different direction. Finally, we should note how this structure, based as it is on the disputation, is dynamic. There is always an argument that is moving forward through objection and counterobjection. Indeed, we should think of the *Summa* as a vast, extended discussion of the truth of the Christian faith, a discussion we are invited to join.

Note on the Second Edition

Because the first edition of this work, under the title *Holy Teaching: Introducing the "Summa Theologiae" of St. Thomas Aquinas* (2005), proved useful to people teaching Thomas Aquinas, I have had the good fortune to be able to produce this second edition. Let me note some of the changes and additions from the first edition.

First, the content is expanded, primarily with material from the *secunda pars*. In part this is in order to make the book more useful for those who want to focus on Thomas's moral teachings. But mainly it is because in the intervening fifteen years I have come to understand better what Thomas is doing in the *Summa*. My original desire was to redress somewhat the bias against the explicitly theological elements of Thomas—his writing on the Trinity or Christology, for example. What I have come to see is that the second part of the *Summa* is just as theological as the first and third parts, and in a sense the first and third parts exist to give a capacious theological context for the second part, which was crucial for preparing Dominican friars for their ministry of caring for souls through the sacrament of penance.

So I have tried to select texts that will give an accurate, if not exhaustive, picture of how Thomas thought about human action—what makes it good and what makes it bad. The selections from the first half of the second part contain key elements of what modern philosophers might call Thomas's "action theory": the end-oriented or teleological nature of human action, the nature of the will and its freedom, the role of virtue and law in guiding human acts, and the role of God's grace. From the second half of the second part, which is structured around the cardinal and theological virtues, I have chosen one or more general questions on each virtue, along with some questions that show how what Thomas thinks about these virtues plays out in terms of practical questions, ranging from the toleration of heretics to the licitness of war to economic justice.

Second, I have identified for each article one or more key secondary readings, in part as an attempt to show my own intellectual indebtedness. I have tended to choose sources that have informed my own readings, but in some cases I have chosen readings that disagree with my interpretations, and some that disagree with one another, in order to initiate readers into the vast and sometimes fractious world of Aquinas interpretation. When at all possible, I have chosen secondary readings in English.

Third, Thomas changed his mind on a number of questions, and so have I. The commentary on all articles has been revised, and I hope the changes reflect my growth in understanding Thomas over the past fifteen years. Most of what I said in the first edition I stand by, but I have also come to a deeper understanding of how Thomas was not a unique beacon of truth in the thirteenth century; he was rather a member of a community of scholars who had their differences, but who also agreed on much. I have softened some of my judgments regarding those who disagreed with Thomas and become more aware of how much he took from predecessors and contemporaries, and I hope the commentary reflects this.

I too have lived as a member of a community of scholars, and like Thomas I have taken much from them. As was the first edition, this book is dedicated to Stanley Hauerwas, who showed me what it means to have a passion for teaching theology. But Stanley must now share that honor with his fellow Texan, Trent Pomplun, from whom I have learned much in the past two decades about theology and life.

Some Technical Matters

Text and the translation. The translation has been thoroughly revised from the first edition and is much more my own work, though I must acknowledge the debt I owe to the various English and French translations I consulted: the early twentieth-century translation by Laurence Shapcote (widely available online, usually identified as translated by "Fathers of the English Dominican Province"); the collaborative translation edited by Thomas Gilby (Cambridge, 1964–72); the as-yet incomplete translation of Alfred Freddoso (https://www3 .nd.edu/~afreddos/summa-translation/TOC.htm); and the various volumes published in French by Cerf under the imprint *Éditions de la Revue des Jeunes*. The Latin text upon which the translation is based is that of the Leonine edition, though in a few places that I note I prefer readings from earlier editions.

Citations. The *Summa theologiae* itself is cited by part, question, and article, so that 3.24.2 means third part, question twenty-four, article two. In referring to the reply to an objection, I use "ad," plus the number of the objection, so that 3.24.2 ad 1 means third part, question twenty-four, article two, reply to objection one. Because the second part of the *Summa* is itself divided into two "halves," references to this part begin with an additional numeral to designate the "half"; thus 1–2.5.1 means the first half of the second part, question 5, article 1. For other works by Thomas, I have noted standard divisions including parts, books, chapter, articles, and so on that should be clear to anyone consulting those works.

My annotations to Thomas's text appear as footnotes that are numbered sequentially within each question. In other words, as you move from one of Thomas's questions to the next, you will see that the numbering of the annotations starts over again with the numeral 1. Cross-references between notes thus rely on the same method of citation just described, although only the part and question number are required. For example, if I say "see 2–2.19 note 5," I mean "see the second half of the second part, question 19, note 5." When I refer to texts from the *Summa theologiae* that are contained in this volume, I add the word "above" or "below" (as appropriate).

I have tried to fill out all of Thomas's citations using the common English title of each work (except where the work is better known by its Latin title; for example, Augustine's *De Trinitate*) and to give the book and chapter divisions as they appear in most editions. Thomas typically cites the Bible according to the Vulgate, which in some cases (particularly the Psalms) has different chapter and verse numbering from modern Bibles. In these instances, the citations have been changed to conform to the New Revised Standard Version of the Bible, though the quotations themselves are translated from the Vulgate. In the case of Aristotle's works, I have also included the column number of the Berlin edition, which can greatly aid in locating texts in different translations. Unless otherwise indicated, quotations of ancient and medieval sources appearing in the notes have been taken from the translations listed in the "Ancient and Medieval Sources" section of the bibliography. Perhaps I should also note that Thomas refers to Aristotle as "the Philosopher," just as he refers to St. Paul as "the Apostle" and to Peter Lombard as "the Master."

PROLOGUE TO THE
Summa theologiae

Because the teacher of catholic truth[1] ought not only to instruct the advanced but also to enlighten beginners, since according to the Apostle, "As unto little ones in Christ, I gave you milk to drink, not solid food" (1 Cor. 3:1–2), the intention we set before us in this work is to treat whatever pertains to the Christian religion in a way suited to the instruction of beginners.[2]

For we have considered how newcomers to this teaching have been greatly hindered by what is written in various places, partly on account of the multiplication of useless questions, articles, and arguments. It is also because the things they need to know are not passed on according to the order of the subject matter, but according to what is required for commenting on a book or what is produced by the occasion of an academic debate. Finally, it is also because frequent repetition produced distaste and confusion in the minds of hearers.[3]

1. Note that Thomas here addresses "the teacher of catholic truth." This suggest that Thomas intended the *Summa* to be, rather than a textbook for students, something like a guide for instructors: a model for how to shape theological inquiry, as well as a sourcebook of important authorities and arguments that a teacher would consult when lecturing or conducting disputations.

2. There has been much debate over what Thomas means by *incipientes* (beginners). A growing consensus holds that his intended audience was those who were teaching students in the various provincial centers of study (i.e., *studia*) of the Dominican order, students preparing not for teaching careers but for pastoral ministry (see Boyle 1982). Thomas began writing the *Summa* while teaching not at a university but at the *studium* of Santa Sabina in Rome, and the innovative and detailed treatment of moral theology in the second part may suggest such a pastoral orientation. He clearly does not mean, however, those with no theological knowledge whatsoever.

3. We can infer what Thomas has in mind here. We know that theological instruction in medieval universities and *studia* took primarily two forms: lectures that commented on the books of Scripture or on Peter Lombard's *Sentences*, and "disputations" in which students and faculty debated specific theological questions (see the introduction to this book). It is perhaps these two forms of instruction that Thomas means when he says the things students need to know "are not passed on according to the order of the subject matter, but according to what is required for commenting on a book [i.e., of Scripture] or what is produced by the occasion of an academic debate [i.e., the disputation]." Thomas's

Striving to avoid these and other such faults, we shall try, trusting in God's help, to pursue whatever pertains to this holy teaching, as briefly and clearly as the subject matter allows.

---

point seems to be that in both these cases topics are taken up as they arise rather than presented in an orderly fashion, in which one question presumes and builds upon what has come before.

THE FIRST PART

Question 1:

The Nature of Holy Teaching

1.1.1[1]
Is any further teaching required besides philosophical studies?

It seems that, besides philosophical studies [*philosophicas disciplinas*], there is no need to consider any further teaching [*doctrinam*].[2]

1. A human being ought not to seek to know what is above reason, for, according to Sirach (3:21), "Seek not the things that are too high for you." But what falls under reason is sufficiently treated in philosophical studies. It therefore seems superfluous to consider any other teaching besides philosophical studies.

2. Teaching can be concerned only with things that exist, for nothing can be known except what is true, which is convertible with what is.[3] Everything that exists is treated in philosophical disciplines, even God: thus there is a part of philosophy called "theology," or "divine science" [*scientia divina*], as is laid

1. On this article, see White (1958); Marshall (2005).

2. *Philosophicae disciplinae* might be translated as "the philosophical disciplines," referring to areas of philosophy such as logic or ethics or metaphysics. I have translated it as "philosophical studies" in order to include both the activity of accomplished philosophers and that of students of philosophy. *Doctrina* does not refer primarily to a proposition that one is expected to adhere to (what we today normally mean by a "doctrine") but to an activity: the activity of teaching. This is significant because Thomas here is not asking about the legitimacy of some set of propositions but rather about the legitimacy of a particular kind of teaching activity. Thomas's question is whether one needs to engage in teaching apart from the teaching associated with philosophy. In other words, do we need theology or, as Thomas calls it, *sacra doctrina* (holy teaching)?

3. Like virtually all medieval thinkers, Thomas presumes what in technical language is called "the convertibility of the transcendentals," which refers to those perfections that necessarily accompany existence—such as goodness, truth, and unity—and therefore transcend the genera and species that divide beings into different kinds. So inasmuch as something exists, it is good, true, and one. And the more perfectly the existence of something is realized, the better, truer, and more unified it is. The point of the objection is that because being and truth are "convertible," philosophy, which in metaphysics deals with "being," is all you need for truth.

out by the Philosopher in his *Metaphysics* (6.1, 1026ᵃ).⁴ Therefore, beyond philosophical disciplines there is no need to consider any further teaching.

On the contrary: It is written in 2 Timothy 3:16, "All divinely inspired Scripture is useful to teach, to reprove, to correct, to instruct in righteousness." Divinely inspired Scriptures do not pertain to the philosophical disciplines, which are acquired through human reason. It is useful, therefore, that beyond philosophical studies there should be another sort of knowing [*scientia*], which is divinely inspired.⁵

I answer: It was necessary for human well-being [*ad humanam salutem*] that there should be a divinely revealed teaching beyond the philosophical studies investigated by human reason.⁶

First, because humanity is directed to God as to an end that surpasses the grasp of its reason.⁷ According to Isaiah (64:4), "Eye has not seen, O God, without you, what things you have prepared for those that love you."⁸ But the end must first be known by people who are to direct their intentions and actions to that end.⁹ And so it was necessary for the well-being of humanity that certain truths that exceed human reason should be made known by divine revelation.

---

4. The point of the objection here is that philosophers *also* inquire after God's existence and nature (Aristotle, "the Philosopher," being a prime example of this), and therefore philosophical inquiry is sufficient for understanding God.

5. On what Thomas means by *scientia*, see 1.1 note 17, below.

6. Aquinas sees the purpose of holy teaching as first and foremost soteriological—i.e., directed toward the salvation of human beings. This salvation involves both healing the effects of sin and fulfilling the potential of human nature in a way that surpasses the demands of that nature (see 3.1 note 20).

The Latin *salus* has a wider range of meanings than the English word "salvation." The root meaning of *salus* is "health" or "well-being," and although it certainly can, and in this specific case probably does, refer to the ultimate well-being of eternal life with God—i.e., salvation as we ordinarily conceive it—it is not restricted to this meaning. If one takes *salus* in the more restricted sense of eternal life with God, then Thomas can be understood to be saying that human reason is sufficient to secure this-worldly well-being, but that we need a truth beyond what reason can give us—the special teaching by God known as revelation—in order to attain eternal life. Put differently, he would be saying that reason suffices for natural fulfillment, but revelation is necessary for *super*natural fulfillment. However, if one takes *salus* in the broader sense of human well-being or flourishing, then Thomas would seem to be saying that a knowledge of divine truths beyond reason contributes to flourishing in all areas of human life, not simply in our religious or spiritual lives. Both interpretations can find support in the text of Thomas. Many debates over the proper interpretation of Thomas, especially in the last century, have revolved around this and related questions. Of particular relevance is the question of the relationship between divine grace and human nature (see note 28 in this question and all of 1–2.109.2, below).

7. This statement expresses some of the basic principles of Thomas's thought (and, indeed, of all Christian, Jewish, and Muslim theology)—namely, that God is (1) the goal or purpose (i.e., the "end") of our existence and (2) beyond our capacity to fully comprehend.

8. Thomas is here conflating Isa. 64:4, which reads "those who wait for him," with 1 Cor. 2:9, which reads "those who love him."

9. You cannot be said to be acting to obtain a particular goal unless you have at least *some* knowledge of the goal. If I went to college but did not know that the college awarded degrees upon successful

And even regarding those truths about God that human reason *could* have discovered, it was necessary that human beings should be taught by a divine revelation. For the truth about God discovered by reason would be available only to a few, and even then after a long time, and with the mixing in of many errors.[10] But humanity's whole well-being, which is in God, depends upon the knowledge of this truth. Therefore, in order that the salvation of human beings might be brought about more fittingly and more surely [*convenientius et certius*], it was necessary that they should be taught divine truths by divine revelation.[11]

It was therefore necessary to have, beyond philosophical studies investigated through reason, a holy teaching learned through revelation.[12]

Reply to 1: Even if things too lofty for human knowledge may not be sought by someone through reason, nevertheless, once they are revealed by God, they must be accepted through faith.[13] Therefore the text continues, "For many things are shown to you above human understanding" (Sir. 3:23). And in this holy teaching consists.

Reply to 2: Disciplines are differentiated by the various aspects under which things are known. The astronomer and the physicist may both prove the same conclusion—for instance, that the earth is round[14]—but the astronomer does

---

completion of the course of study, then one would not normally say that obtaining a degree was the goal of my going to college. For more on what Thomas means by acting for a goal or end, see 1–2.1.1, below.

10. Thomas does believe that we can know *some* things about God simply by using our human reason, but he also thinks that such knowledge is quite minimal and that it can be had only by very smart people who have a lot of time for thinking about such things. And even when they have arrived at some genuine truths about God (e.g., that God exists), they will still be wrong about many other things about God (e.g., that he requires human sacrifices or that he has no knowledge of the world). Thomas seems to derive this particular way of putting things from the twelfth-century Jewish philosopher Moses Maimonides (see *Guide of the Perplexed* 1.1.34).

11. Some manuscripts read "more widely and securely" (*communis et securius*). It is also worth noting here that when Thomas says revelation is "necessary," he does not mean that God is in any way obliged to reveal himself to human beings. Rather, he means that given the divine purpose of saving humanity—not only the clever and leisured but also the dull and busy—it was fitting that God teach human beings. On this use of "necessary," see Thomas's discussion in 3.46.1, below.

12. Thomas's view, therefore, is that divinely revealed teaching is necessary both (1) because some mysteries of faith are beyond human discovery and also (2) because some things about God could only be discovered with great difficulty. This view is articulated centuries earlier by Augustine in his *Confessions* (6.5.7), where he speaks of his discovery of the need to believe what cannot be demonstrated, "whether this was because a demonstration existed but could not be understood by all or whether the matter was not one open to rational proof."

13. In response to the first objection, Thomas points out that the discipline of theology is not simply a matter of human seeking, because it is based not on what *we* think about God but on what God has revealed about himself. At the same time, the human response of faith is a human intellectual act and is therefore subject to further intellectual exploration or, as St. Anselm (ca. 1033–1109) put it in his *Proslogion*, "*fides quaerens intellectum*" (faith seeking understanding).

14. Contrary to current popular opinion, educated medieval people knew that the world was round. As early as the sixth century BC the Greek philosopher Pythagoras argued for a round earth, and almost

this by means of mathematics (i.e., leaving aside matter), while the physicist does this by means that take matter into account. In this way, nothing prevents those things that may be learned from philosophical studies, insofar as they can be known by natural reason, from also being taught to us by another discipline, insofar as they are known by the light of revelation. Therefore the theology that pertains to holy teaching is of a different kind than that which is considered as a part of philosophy.[15]

1.1.2[16]
Is holy teaching *scientia*?[17]

It seems that holy teaching is not *scientia*.

---

no educated person after this thought that the earth was flat. The widespread belief that Christopher Columbus was the first to "prove" the roundness of the earth apparently originated with the novelist Washington Irving in the nineteenth century.

15. Sometimes what makes one kind of knowledge different from another is not so much the knowledge itself as it is the *means* by which the knowledge is obtained. Thomas's point is that philosophy and theology might lead us to the same bit of knowledge (e.g., that there exists a first mover of the universe), but they are still distinct ways of pursuing knowledge, since in the case of philosophy we believe something because human reason tells us, whereas in the case of theology we believe something because God tells us.

16. On this article, see White (1958); Marshall (2005).

17. Medieval debates over the "scientific" status of theology took on a particular urgency in the thirteenth century as the Latin West began to assimilate the writings of Aristotle, who, in his *Posterior Analytics*, mapped the terrain of *epistēmē* (translated in medieval Latin as *scientia*) as the highest and most certain form of knowledge. There was a wide diversity of views on the place of theology in relation to *scientia*, and Thomas's view was by no means normative.

I have chosen to leave the word *scientia* untranslated in order to remind readers that in Aristotelian and medieval usage *epistēmē/scientia* meant something quite different from its modern English cognate "science." Loosely translated, it simply means "knowledge," in contrast to "opinion" or "faith," and could include a wide range of inquiries. More precisely, however, *scientia* names the result of a process by which unknown things are deduced from known things; as Thomas says, "The meaning of *scientia* consists in this: that from things known, necessary conclusions about other things are drawn" (*Commentary on Boethius's "De Trinitate"* 2.2 [my trans.]). Normally *scientia* proceeds from premises or "first principles" to certain conclusions; we might think of how a proof in geometry works (see note 18, below). *Scientia* therefore differs from our modern notion of science, in which knowledge is based on experimentation and the gathering of evidence, not on deduction from things already in evidence.

It is also important to note that, in order to have true *scientia* of something, it is not enough to accept it as true; one must also grasp *why* it is true. Thus, to use an example from geometry, in order to have *scientia* of the Pythagorean theorem it is not enough to memorize $a^2 + b^2 = c^2$; one must also grasp how the proof works. Thomas contrasts *scientia* in its normal sense with both faith and opinion. Unlike opinion, it is certain of what it holds true (because its conclusions "follow of necessity"); and unlike faith, it involves a process in which reason gives assent to something that it "sees"—as when, after struggling to understand the Pythagorean theorem, one says, "Ah, *now* I see!"—whereas faith involves assent to what is not seen.

In addition to referring to the knowledge that one possesses, *scientia* can also have the sense of a body of knowledge, or what we today might call a "discipline." This is the primary meaning it has in 1.1.8, below.

1. Every *scientia* proceeds from self-evident premises.[18] Holy teaching, however, proceeds from articles of faith that are not self-evident, since they are not accepted by all, "for not all have faith," as it says in 2 Thessalonians (3:2). So holy teaching is not *scientia*.

2. *Scientia* is not about particular things.[19] But holy teaching discusses particular things, such as the deeds of Abraham, Isaac, and Jacob and the like. Therefore, holy teaching is not *scientia*.

On the contrary: Augustine says in *De Trinitate* (14.1.3), "To this *scientia* alone belongs that by which saving faith is brought forth, nourished, protected, and strengthened." This pertains to no *scientia* except holy teaching. Therefore, holy teaching is *scientia*.

I answer: Holy teaching is *scientia*. But we must bear in mind that there are two kinds of *scientiae*.[20] There are some that proceed from premises known by the natural light of intelligence, such as arithmetic and geometry and the like; there are some, however, that proceed from premises known by the light of a higher *scientia*, the way that optics proceeds from premises known through geometry, and music from premises known through arithmetic. It is in this second way that holy teaching is *scientia*, because it proceeds from premises known by the light of a higher *scientia*—namely, the *scientia* of God and the blessed.[21] Therefore, just as the musician trusts in the premises handed on by the mathematician, so holy teaching trusts in premises revealed by God.

18. The objection is that, if *scientia* is to be taken as certain knowledge, it must begin from truths that no one could deny (what Thomas calls premises or "first principles"). Thus, in geometry we might begin from the truth that a whole is always bigger than its part (which is self-evident to anyone who knows the meaning of "whole" and "part"); and in philosophy we might begin with the truth that a statement cannot at the same time be both true and not true (which is self-evident to anyone who knows the meaning of "true" and "false"). If someone will not grant these premises, then they have no access to geometric or philosophical truth. The objection here is that in theology there are no premises that everyone accepts, as is evidenced by the fact that not everyone has faith.

19. See Aristotle, *Metaphysics* (7.15, 1039^b). The objection expresses the common medieval view that genuine knowledge is first and foremost a knowledge of universals (such as "humanity" or "triangularity") and not of concrete particulars ("this human being" or "this triangle"). This is in part because *scientia* is about conclusions following of necessity from a set of premises, and contingent particulars are by nature nonnecessary. The difference between "opinion" and *scientia* is the difference between knowing the ratio of sides to hypotenuse in a right triangle because you measured them and knowing it because you grasp the Pythagorean theorem.

20. Here Thomas makes a move that we see him make again and again: he points out that we use the word *scientia* in at least two ways and that the answer to this question lies in properly distinguishing them. Thomas pays close attention to our use of language and frequently resolves questions by sorting out linguistic confusions. For example, he distinguishes various ways in which we use terms like "necessity," "comprehension," and "temptation."

21. Thomas points out that not all forms of inquiry proceed from self-evident premises. Some forms (like geometry and mathematics) do, but others (such as optics and music) begin from premises established by a "higher" (i.e., logically prior) *scientia* (cf. the reply to obj. 1). Thomas calls the latter forms of inquiry

Reply to 1: The premises of any *scientia* either are self-evident or can be traced back to what is known by a higher *scientia*, and the latter, as we have said, are the premises of holy teaching.

Reply to 2: Particular things are discussed in holy teaching not because it is concerned with them principally, but rather they are introduced both as examples for our lives, as in moral *scientiae*, and in order to establish the authority of the men through whom divine revelation, on which Holy Scripture or teaching is based, has come down to us.[22]

1.1.8[23]
Does this teaching prove anything through argumentation?[24]

It seems this teaching does not prove anything through argumentation.

1. Ambrose says in his book *On the Catholic Faith* (1.13.84), "Away with arguments where faith is sought." But in this teaching especially faith is sought, for it is said in John (20:31), "These things are written that you may believe." Therefore holy teaching does not prove anything through argumentation.

2. If it is a matter of argument, the argument is either from authority or from reason. If it is from authority, it does not seem to fit with the dignity of this teaching, since according to Boethius a proof from authority is the weakest sort of proof.[25] But if it is from reason, this does not seem to fit with the goal of this teaching, since, according to Gregory (*Sermon 26*, in *Homilies on*

"subaltern" *scientiae*. So, for example, although music is based on premises derived from mathematics, a musician may be a perfectly fine musician without having a firm grasp (i.e., *scientia*) of the premises of mathematics. What Thomas is saying is that theology is based on premises that are self-evident only to God and the blessed (those who behold God face-to-face in heaven). Just as the subaltern *scientia* of music must "borrow" knowledge from mathematics, so too the *scientia* of theology "borrows" knowledge from God's own self-knowledge, which is revealed in sacred Scripture. One point to note here is that the higher *scientia* acts as an "authority" for the lower.

Thus from the perspective of God and the blessed, *sacra doctrina* is *scientia* in the normal sense (see note 17, above); for human beings in this life it is *scientia* only in the sense of a subaltern *scientia*.

22. Here Thomas accepts the objection's presumption that *scientia* is concerned with the eternal and unchanging, not the contingent and historical. The *scientia* of holy teaching is primarily concerned with God, who is eternal and unchanging. However, in a secondary sense the *scientia* of holy teaching *also* knows those historical events by which the identity of God has been revealed in the world—such as the deeds of Abraham, Isaac, and Jacob. As Thomas goes on to argue in 1.1.4, theology is a practical inquiry (i.e., one concerned with human action) as well as a speculative inquiry (i.e., one concerned with truth).

23. On this article, see White (1958); Marshall (2005).

24. Thomas here asks a question that echoes questions asked in our own day: Isn't it pointless to argue about theological questions? Don't different people simply have different beliefs? Is there any way to decide between conflicting claims about the nature of God? Isn't it all a matter of opinion? As we shall see, Thomas's answer to the last question, in particular, is an emphatic "no." In saying that *sacra doctrina* is "argumentative" he is saying that it uses its own sorts of evidence in order to arrive at truths about God.

25. See Boethius, *In Ciceronis Topica* 1 and *De topicis differentiis* 3.

the Gospels), "Faith has no merit where human reason offers proof from experience." So holy teaching does not prove anything through argumentation.[26]

On the contrary: It says in Titus (1:9) that a bishop should "embrace that faithful word that is in accord with our teaching, that he may be able to exhort in sound teaching and to convince the unbelievers."

I answer: In the same way that other *scientiae* do not argue in proof of their premises but argue from these premises to demonstrate other truths in these *scientiae*,[27] so too this teaching does not argue in proof of its premises, which are the articles of faith, but rather from them it goes on to prove something else. In this way the Apostle in 1 Corinthians (15:12) argues from the resurrection of Christ to prove the general resurrection.[28]

Keep in mind, regarding philosophical *scientiae*, that lower *scientiae* neither prove their premises nor debate with those who deny them, but leave this to a higher *scientia*. The highest of them, metaphysics, can debate with one who denies its premises only if the opponent will concede *something*. But if he concede nothing, it is impossible to have a debate with him, though one can answer his objections.[29]

26. The objection states that arguments are based either on (1) authority ("you should have open-heart surgery because your cardiologist recommends it") or (2) reason ("if all human beings are mortal and Socrates is a human being, then Socrates is mortal"). Since arguments from authority are generally taken to be fairly weak (they work only if the person accepts the authority invoked), and since theology deals with things that surpass human reason, theology should not proceed by way of argumentation.

27. Note that in most of this article *scientia* has the sense of what we today would call a "discipline"—a body of knowledge that is arrived at by starting from certain presuppositions and proceeding from them in certain ways in order to reach new conclusions.

28. As we have seen in the previous article, Thomas says that every *scientia* presumes certain premises or "first principles," which it does not seek to prove, but which it uses to prove other things. So, for example, physics presumes certain mathematical laws that it does not attempt to prove. We do not generally think that this makes physics a doubtful matter. Similarly, theology presumes certain premises, which Thomas calls "the articles of faith" (more or less equivalent to the statements found in the creed, understood as summarizing the essential teachings of Scripture). It does not attempt to prove these articles of faith but uses them to prove other things, as Paul uses the resurrection of Christ to prove our resurrection from the dead ("Now if Christ is proclaimed as raised from the dead, how can some of you say there is no resurrection of the dead?" [1 Cor. 15:12]).

29. "Lower" or "subaltern" *scientiae* can appeal to a "higher" or "prior" *scientia* to prove their premises (e.g., physics can appeal to mathematics), but the highest *scientiae* cannot prove their starting premises. For example, how could one "prove" that a whole is always bigger than one of its parts? Such premises have a compelling obviousness about them that makes proof unnecessary—indeed, attempts to prove them only engender a debilitating skepticism. Thus in the case of metaphysics, which Thomas takes to be the highest of the philosophical disciplines, one cannot even get started on a metaphysical argument (such as "what is the nature of reality?") if one is arguing with a person who will not grant such basic premises as the difference between "true" and "false." In other words, there are some people who are so stubborn or obtuse (Aristotle compared them to vegetables; see *Metaphysics* 4.4, 1006ᵃ) that you will not only never convince them, but you cannot even really engage them. We typically call this "arguing in bad faith," meaning that one is not really interested in seeking the truth of the matter under discussion. If an

Therefore Holy Scripture, having no *scientia* above it,[30] debates with one who denies its premises by using arguments, so long as the opponent admits at least some of what is obtained through divine revelation. In this way we argue with heretics from the authoritative sources of holy teaching, and by one article of faith we can argue against those who deny another.[31] To be sure, if our opponent believes nothing of what is divinely revealed, there is no longer any way of proving the articles of faith by reasoning, but only of answering his objections, if he has any, against faith.[32] Since faith rests upon infallible truth, and it is impossible to demonstrate what is contrary to truth, it is clear that the proofs produced against faith are not demonstrations, but are arguments that can be answered.[33]

Reply to 1: Although arguments from human reason cannot serve to prove what is held on faith, nevertheless, this teaching argues from articles of faith to other truths, as has been said.

Reply to 2: It belongs especially to this teaching to argue from authority, since the premises of this teaching are obtained through revelation. So we should believe on the authority of those to whom the revelation was made. Nor does this take away from the dignity of this teaching, for although the argument from authority based on human reason is the weakest, yet the argument from authority based on divine revelation is the most effective.

---

intellectual opponent rises above the vegetative level and will grant the law of noncontradiction, even if they do not grant other premises, one can argue with such a person on an ad hoc basis—refuting the specific objections that they raise.

30. Here Thomas is using "Holy Scripture" interchangeably with "holy teaching" (*sacra doctrina*), as a way of naming that authoritative body of knowledge that God shares with humanity through divine revelation to prophets and apostles.

31. If someone acknowledges at least some of the premises of *sacra doctrina* (i.e., the "articles of faith") then one can argue with them in order to reasonably prove another article. For example, since both Jews and Christians accept the prophetic writings in Scripture as divine revelation, a Christian might reasonably argue with a Jew over the question of whether Jesus was the Messiah whose coming was foretold in the Prophets. Likewise, one can debate with Christian heretics who accept some Christian beliefs but reject others. Thus in the debates over the doctrine of the Trinity in the fourth century, the argument between St. Athanasius and his opponent Arius took the form of a debate over which view fit better with other Christian beliefs.

32. In the case of those who completely reject the premises of *sacra doctrina*, the options for reasoned argument are more limited, though not as limited as with someone who rejects the principle of noncontradiction. If someone rejects the divine revelation contained in Scripture entirely, then you are not going to get far in a theological argument with them. What Thomas thinks you *can* do, as long as they are arguing in good faith, is to answer their objections on an ad hoc basis—that is, show them how their objections do not disprove Christian claims about God.

33. A Christian should be confident that even if it is not possible to rationally convince someone of the truth of Christianity, he or she can reasonably answer any objections that are raised, since it is *impossible* to offer a genuine demonstration of something untrue, and Christian revelation is based on the highest truth, God.

Nevertheless, holy teaching makes use even of human reason, not of course to prove faith, since this would take away the merit of faith, but to make clear other things that are handed on in this teaching. Since therefore grace does not take away nature but perfects it, natural reason should serve faith in the way that the natural inclination of the will aids charity. Thus the Apostle speaks in 2 Corinthians (10:5) of "bringing every understanding into captivity to the obedience of Christ."[34] And so holy teaching makes use also of the authority of philosophers in matters where they were able to know the truth through natural reason,[35] in the way that Paul quotes a saying of Aratus in Acts (17:28), "As some also of your own poets said, 'we are God's offspring.'"[36]

Nevertheless, holy teaching makes use of these authorities only as inessential and probable arguments. But it properly uses the authority of the canonical Scriptures in making necessary arguments. The authority of other church teachers [doctorum ecclesiae] may properly be used in arguing, though only as probable. For our faith rests upon the revelation made to the apostles and prophets who wrote the canonical books, and not on the revelations—if there are any—made to other teachers.[37] Therefore Augustine says in a letter

34. In replying to the objection about the inadequacy of human reason to argue about divine things, Thomas states what is often taken to be one of the key premises of his thought: "Grace does not take away nature but perfects it." In addition to the natural capacities with which God endows us, God also acts graciously in ways that go beyond our natural capacities—in miraculous acts, in taking flesh in Christ, in the gifts of faith, hope, and love, etc. But according to Thomas, this acting in excess of our natural capacities does not override those capacities but fulfills them in the very act of exceeding them. Thus, to use Thomas's example, our will desires certain things by nature—food, sex, and so on—and grace does not destroy our willing but perfects it by making us desire God with the love that Christians call caritas (charity), which allows us to orient our other desires toward the attainment of what we ultimately desire. Likewise, we know certain things by the exercise of our natural capacity for knowing (i.e., reason). We can also know things through God's revelation, which does not contradict human reason but brings it to a fulfillment beyond itself by orienting all knowledge toward the end of knowing God (i.e., "taking every thought captive"). So what we know through faith does not contradict what we know through reason, but goes beyond it. One might even say that in the act of faith we do not become unreasonable, but in fact become more reasonable, through coming to know truths that exceed our reason.

35. Thomas reserves the term "philosophers" exclusively for pagan thinkers.

36. Aratus was a Greek poet from the third century BC. In the book of Acts, Paul is depicted quoting from his astronomical treatise Phenomena.

37. In ranking authorities, Thomas grants the views of pagan thinkers a certain authority, but of the lowest sort. Having Aristotle on your side adds rhetorical force to your argument. But as Thomas sees things, it does not prove anything (though the rational cogency of one of Aristotle's arguments might). Next would come the views of the "doctors"—those Christian teachers (doctores) whose views have been widely accepted by the church. But their authority can establish only the probability of something being true, and, like the views of the philosophers, they are not of final authority. Finally comes the authority of Scripture, which is supreme—resting, as it does, on the revelation given to the prophets and apostles. Arguments based on the authority of Scripture can attain a certainty that arguments based on the authority of philosophers and theologians cannot.

The reference to "the revelations—if there are any—made to other teachers" points to the distinction between what would come later to be called "public revelation" and "private revelation." When Thomas

to Jerome (*Epistle 82*, 1), "I have learned to hold only those books of Scripture that are called canonical in such honor as to believe their authors have not erred in any way in writing them. . . . But other authors, whatever may have been their holiness and learning, I read in such a way as not to deem everything in their works to be true merely on account of their having thought or written it."

1.1.10[38]
Can one word in Holy Scripture have several senses?

It seems that in Holy Scripture one word cannot have several senses: historical or literal, allegorical, tropological or moral, and anagogical.[39]

1. A multiplicity of senses in one scriptural text gives birth to confusion and deception and detracts from an argument's strength. A multiplicity of propositions produces no good arguments, but only leads to a number of fallacies.

---

speaks of "revelation," he generally does not mean personal insight granted by God but, rather, the truth that God has communicated through the prophets and apostles, and which is now contained in the canonical Scriptures.

38. On this article, see Baglow (2004); Prügl (2005).

39. Having discussed theological authority, Thomas now turns to consider the highest authority: Holy Scripture. During the Middle Ages, Christians generally thought of Scripture as having a fourfold meaning or "sense." A word or sentence or story has its literal or historical sense, which is simply what the words mean; it might also have a spiritual sense. This spiritual sense can be subdivided into three: the typological or allegorical sense, which refers to how things in the Old Testament point forward to their fulfillment in the New Testament and, by extension, the church; the tropological or moral sense, which refers to what a passage might teach us about our spiritual lives; and the anagogical sense, which refers to what a passage has to say about our ultimate destiny.

To clarify the matter, we might consider the word "Jerusalem." Its fourfold sense could be taken to be as follows:

literal:	a city in Palestine
typological / allegorical:	the church
tropological / moral:	the soul
anagogical:	heaven

Imagine that you are Thomas Aquinas, sitting in church with your fellow Dominicans and chanting the Psalms. You sing Ps. 137:5: "If I forget you, O Jerusalem, let my right hand wither!" You know that on a literal level "Jerusalem" refers to the city in Palestine and that for the writer of the psalm it was imperative to remember that city because it was the political and religious center of Israelite identity, where sacrifice was offered to God in the temple. But for you as a Christian it might not seem imperative to remember that city, because Jesus's offering of himself on the cross has made the sacrifice of animals unnecessary. Yet you are praying this psalm, so presumably it means something that you would actually want to say to God. And so, on the spiritual level, you can take "Jerusalem" to mean the church, the living temple in which God is worshiped through the Eucharist; or you can take it as a reference to your soul, which you must remember and care for, lest you wither and die spiritually; or you can let the word direct your mind to heaven—the eternal vision of God—which must be the constant goal of your life. This range of meaning makes it possible for a Christian like Thomas to give voice to his prayer through the words of the psalm.

Holy Scripture, however, ought to be effective in showing the truth without any fallacy. Therefore, in Scripture one word should not convey several senses.

2. Augustine says in *On the Usefulness of Believing* (3.5) that "the writing called the Old Testament has been handed on to us with a fourfold meaning: namely, according to history, according to etiology, according to analogy, and according to allegory." Now these four seem completely different from the four mentioned above, so it does not seem fitting to explain the same word of Holy Scripture according to the four senses spoken of above.

3. Besides these senses, there is the parabolical, which is not included among these four.[40]

On the contrary: Gregory says in his *Moral Reflections on the Book of Job* (20.1.1), "Holy Scripture, by the manner of its speech, transcends every *scientia*, because in one and the same sentence, while it describes a fact, it reveals a mystery."

I answer: The author of Holy Scripture is God, in whose power it is to signify not only by words (as a person also can do) but also by things themselves.[41] So while in every other *scientia* words refer to things, this *scientia* is distinctive in that the things referred to by words also themselves refer to things.

The first kind of referring, in which words refer to things, pertains to the first sense: which is the historical or literal. The kind of referring, however, in which things referred to by words also signify other things, is called the spiritual sense, which is based on and presupposes the literal sense.[42]

This spiritual sense has a threefold division. As the Apostle says in Hebrews (10:1), the Old Law is a prefiguration of the New Law, and the New Law itself, as Dionysius says in *The Ecclesiastical Hierarchy* (5.2), "is a figure of future glory."[43] Further, in the New Law, whatever deeds are done by [Christ] our head are signs of what we should do. Accordingly, insofar as things of the Old Law signify things of the New Law, there is the allegorical sense. Insofar as the things done in Christ, or in the things [in the Old Law] that prefigure Christ, are signs of what we should do, there is the moral sense.

40. By "parabolical" Thomas seems to mean the same thing as "metaphorical" (see the example given in the reply to this objection).

41. God speaks to us not simply through words but through things and events. Thus, for example, through King David and the events surrounding him God speaks to us of Christ. One might say that historical events have God as their "author" and so are a form of divine speech.

42. Here Thomas clarifies the rationale for the distinction between literal and spiritual meanings. The "literal sense" is how *words* refer to *things* (e.g., how the word "Jerusalem" is a "sign" pointing to the city in Palestine). The "spiritual sense" is how *things* refer to *other things* (e.g., how the city of Jerusalem is a "sign" pointing to the church or the soul or heaven).

43. When Thomas speaks of things being "figures" of other things, he means something like "foreshadowing." In this way, the animal sacrifices of the Old Covenant are "figures" of the sacrifice of Jesus on the cross.

And insofar as those things that are in eternal glory are referred to, there is the anagogical sense.

Since surely the literal sense is that which the author intends, and since the author of Holy Scripture is God, who comprehends all things at once by his intellect, it is not unfitting if, even according to the literal sense, one word in Holy Scripture should have several senses, as Augustine says in the *Confessions* (12.31.42).[44]

Reply to 1: The multiplicity of these senses does not produce equivocation or any other kind of multiplicity, because, as was said, these senses are not multiplied because one word refers to several things, but because the things referred to by the words can themselves refer to other things.[45] So in Holy Scripture no confusion results, for all the senses are based on one—that is to say, the literal. Only from this sense can any argument be drawn, and not from those spoken allegorically, as Augustine says in his letter to Vincent the Donatist (*Epistle 93*, 8.24). Nevertheless, nothing of Holy Scripture perishes on account of this, since nothing necessary to faith is contained under the spiritual sense that is not elsewhere handed on clearly by the Scripture in its literal sense.[46]

Reply to 2: Three of these—history, etiology, and analogy—all pertain to the literal sense. "History," as Augustine himself explains (*Epistle 93*), is when something is simply recounted; "etiology" is when its cause is assigned, as when the Lord gave the reason why Moses allowed the putting away of wives—namely, on account of the hardness of men's hearts (Matt. 19:8); "analogy" is when the truth of one text of Scripture is shown not to contradict the truth of another. Allegory, among the four, stands by itself for the three spiritual senses. Thus Hugh of St. Victor includes the anagogical under the allegorical sense, laying down in chapter 3 of his *Sentences* three senses only—the historical, the allegorical, and the tropological.[47]

44. The literal sense is related to the intention of the speaker. If I use the word "Alexandria" intending to refer to a city in Egypt and you take me to be referring to a city in northern Virginia, then you have misunderstood me. However, God can intend to say an infinite multitude of things with the same word or event, even on the literal level. When Thomas is presented with two equally plausible literal interpretations of a passage of Scripture, he is often quite happy to say that both meanings were intended by God.

45. If the word itself had multiple meanings, this would be a case of equivocation; but the multiple sense of Scripture is not based on the multiple meanings of words, but on the multiplicity of meanings of the things and events to which the words refer.

46. Nothing is said by means of a spiritual meaning that is not elsewhere said by means of a literal meaning. So, for example, "Jerusalem" in Ps. 137 cannot be taken allegorically to signify the city of Paris, since Scripture nowhere assigns salvific importance to the city of Paris.

47. See Hugh of St. Victor, *De scripturis et scriptoribus* 3; cf. Hugh of St. Victor, *On the Sacraments of the Christian Faith* 1.prologue.4.

Reply to 3: The parabolical sense is contained under the literal, for words can refer to something both properly and figuratively. Nor is the literal sense the figure of speech itself, but that which is referred to by the figure. When Scripture speaks of God's arm, the literal sense is not that God has such a bodily member, but that God possessed what is signified by this member—namely, operative power.[48] From this it is clear that nothing false can ever underlie the literal sense of Holy Scripture.

48. Thomas's point is that the spiritual meaning of a text is *not* the same thing as the metaphorical meaning. In fact, a metaphorical meaning is a *literal* meaning, because it is a case of words referring to things and not of things referring to things. Although metaphorical statements do not refer to things in the same *way* as nonmetaphorical statements, they are still cases of "literal" reference. Thus, in the example Thomas gives here, the words "God's arm" refer to a thing—God's power to act. In our Jerusalem example, the word "Jerusalem" refers *literally* to the city, which in turn refers *spiritually* to the church or the soul or heaven.

Question 2:

The Existence of God

1.2.1[1]
Is the existence of God self-evident?

It seems that the existence of God is self-evident.[2]

1. Things are said to be self-evident to us when knowledge of them is naturally in us, as is clear in the case of first principles. As John of Damascus says in the beginning of his book (*On the Orthodox Faith* 1.3), "Knowledge of the existence of God is naturally implanted in all." The existence of God is therefore self-evident.

2. Things are said to be self-evident when they are grasped as soon as the meaning of their terms is grasped, which the Philosopher, in his *Posterior Analytics* (1.3, 72^b), says is true of the first principles of demonstration. So when one knows what a whole is and what a part is, it is immediately known that every whole is greater than its part. But as soon as the meaning of the word "God" is understood, it is seen that God exists. For this word means that thing than which nothing greater can be meant. What exists in reality and in the mind, however, is greater than what exists only in the mind. Therefore, since God exists in the mind as soon as the word "God" is understood, it also follows that he exists in reality, and so the existence of God is self-evident.[3]

---

1. On this article, see White (1956, 35–61); Gilson (1960, 46–52); Dewan (2012).

2. It is helpful to think of this article and the one immediately following as something like bookends between which Thomas wants to position our natural knowledge of God's existence. In essence, Thomas argues in these two articles that God's existence cannot be a premise or first principle, but it can still be known based on what humans can observe of the world.

3. This objection gives a succinct presentation of what is sometimes called the "ontological argument" for God's existence, which says, in essence, that if "God" is defined as "that than which no greater thing can be conceived," then God must necessarily exist, since a perfect being that existed only in one's mind (which even an unbeliever would admit) would not be the greatest thing that could be conceived, since we can conceive of a perfect being who exists in the mind *and* in reality. This argument is most famously

3. The existence of truth is self-evident, for whoever denies the existence of truth grants that truth does exist. This is because if truth does not exist, then it is true that truth does not exist, and if something is true, then truth exists. God, however, is truth itself, according to John (14:6): "I am the way, the truth, and the life." God's existence is therefore self-evident.[4]

On the contrary: No one can think the opposite of what is self-evident, as the Philosopher makes clear in the *Metaphysics* (4.3, 1005ᵇ) and *Posterior Analytics* (1.10, 76ᵇ) concerning the first principles of demonstration. But the opposite of the proposition "God is" can be thought, for according to the psalm (53:1), "The fool said in his heart, 'There is no God.'" Therefore, it is not self-evident that God exists.[5]

I answer: A thing can be self-evident in one of two ways: on the one hand, it can be self-evident in itself, though not to us; on the other hand, it can be self-evident to us as well as in itself. A proposition is self-evident when the predicate is included in the meaning of the subject. Thus "a human being is an animal" is self-evident since "animal" is contained in the meaning of "human being."[6] If everyone knows what the predicate and subject terms are, then the proposition will be self-evident to everyone, as is clear with regard to the first principles of demonstration, the terms of which are common things that

---

associated with the *Proslogion* of St. Anselm. Although Aquinas does not name Anselm here, he clearly has Anselm in mind, and names him explicitly in the parallel discussion in the *Disputed Questions on Truth*.

It is worth noting that Anselm's *Proslogion* takes the form of a prayer addressed to God, and thus it seems unlikely that Anselm thinks of himself as offering a "proof" of the existence of God in the sense of a demonstration that could take someone from atheism to assent. Rather, he is probing the logic of the term "God," undertaken within the context of faith and prayer, trying to show how God as the highest good includes within himself all perfections, including the perfection "existing."

4. This objection offers the standard refutation of various forms of skepticism and relativism—namely, if I say that nothing can be known with certainty, this sounds like something I am certain about. It then goes on to claim that if it is self-evident that truth exists, then it is also self-evident that a highest truth exists, and this is God. A form of this argument can be found in Augustine's writings (e.g., *Against the Academics* 3.11.25; *Confessions* 7.10.16).

5. As a simple matter of fact, the mere existence of atheists would seem to settle the question of whether God's existence is self-evident—unless one wished to hold that atheists are all, for some unknown reason, lying about their state of unbelief. Why discuss the matter further? It is good to bear in mind that in discussing this question Thomas is speaking of propositions or statements, which consist of a subject and a predicate. So when he asks whether the existence of God is self-evident, what he is really asking is whether the truth of the statement "God exists" is immediately and necessarily grasped by those who hear it in the same way as, for example, the statement "a whole is bigger than its parts." Another way to put this same point would be to ask whether God's existence can serve as a first principle for human *scientia*, where *scientia* is taken in its normal sense (see 1.1.2, above). As we shall see in the body of this article, Thomas's answer will be "no," but he is also interested in exploring *why* this is the case.

6. Thomas, following Aristotle, defines human beings as "rational animals" (i.e., animals capable of reasoning). So "a human being is an animal" is a self-evident proposition since its predicate term, "animal," is contained in the definition of the subject term ("human beings").

no one is ignorant of, such as "being" and "nonbeing," "whole" and "part," and similar things.[7] If, however, there are some who do not know what the predicate and subject terms are, the proposition will be self-evident in itself, but not to those who do not know the meaning of the proposition's predicate and subject.[8] Therefore, it happens, as Boethius says in the book *On the Hebdomads* (1), that some mental concepts are commonplace and self-evident only to the learned, such as "things without bodies do not have locations."

I say, therefore, that this proposition, "God exists," is in itself self-evident, since the predicate is the same as the subject, for God is his own existence, as will be shown later (1.3.4). Because we do not know what God is, the proposition is not self-evident to us,[9] but needs to be demonstrated by means of things that are more evident to us, though less evident by their nature—namely, God's effects.[10]

Reply to 1: A general and confused knowledge that God exists is naturally implanted in us inasmuch as God is the ultimate happiness [*beatitudo*] of human beings.[11] For human beings naturally desire happiness, and what is naturally desired by people must be naturally known to them. This, however, is not to know absolutely that God exists, just as knowing that someone is approaching is not the same as knowing that Peter is approaching, even though it *is* Peter who is approaching; for there are many who imagine that the perfect good of humanity, which is happiness, consists in riches, and others in pleasures, and others in something else.[12]

Reply to 2: Those who hear this word "God" may not understand it to signify something than which nothing greater can be thought, since some have

7. Thomas seems to think that a grasp of some concepts (e.g., "whole" and "part") is so basic to the human form of life that we can safely presume that all human beings possess it.

8. Here it is helpful to remember that Thomas is talking about the structure of propositions. The basic distinction on which this article turns is that between something self-evident in itself and something self-evident to us. A proposition can be self-evident in itself, even if some do not recognize it as true, so long as the predicate forms part of the definition of the subject. A human being, therefore, is self-evidently an animal, even if someone mistakenly thinks that human beings are, say, angels instead. This understanding, of course, presumes that definitions are somehow written into the fabric of reality and are not simply conventions.

This point is important in order not to misinterpret what follows. Thomas's point is *not* that God's existence is evident to God but not to us (though this is true), but that the proposition "God exists" is in itself a self-evident proposition, though it is not evident to us. Thomas is not making a claim about God's self-awareness, but about the status of a proposition.

9. "God exists" cannot be self-evident to us in the way that "human beings are rational animals" is because we do not have a definition of "God" in the way that we do for "human beings." This is perhaps Thomas's real concern here: to ensure that we do not think that we can conceptually grasp what it is for God to be God in the same way that we can grasp other objects.

10. See the next article.

11. The Latin *beatitudo* can mean either "blessedness" or "happiness," and might loosely be translated as "fulfillment." See 1–2.3.8 note 2, below.

12. In other words, although everyone pursues happiness, not everyone identifies that happiness as "God." Therefore, the proposition "God exists" would not be self-evident to such a person.

believed God to be a body.[13] Yet even granting that everyone understands this word "God" to signify what was just said—namely, something than which nothing greater can be thought—it does not follow that they understand what the word signifies to exist in reality, but only as grasped by the mind. Nor can it be argued that it exists in reality unless it is granted that there in fact exists something than which nothing greater can be thought, which is what is *not* admitted by those who hold that God does not exist.[14]

Reply to 3: The existence of truth in general is self-evident, but the existence of a first truth is not self-evident to us.[15]

1.2.2[16]
Can it be demonstrated that God exists?

It seems that the existence of God cannot be demonstrated.[17]

1. It is an article of faith that God exists. Something that is a matter of faith, however, cannot be demonstrated, because a demonstration causes knowledge [*scire*], while faith is about things that are unseen, as is clear from the Apostle in Hebrews (11:1).[18] Therefore it cannot be demonstrated that God exists.

13. A material being (i.e., a "body"), because it is perishable, is inferior to a spiritual being, which is imperishable. So someone who holds God to have a body (as some Stoics did) would not conceive of God as that than which no greater could be conceived, since it is possible to conceive of a nonbodily being.

14. Thomas here makes the point that there can be no necessary passage from mental existence to actual existence unless one already admits that there is a highest actual being. Thomas's rejection of the so-called ontological argument is related to a distinction he makes in his early work *De ente et essentia* between the essence of a thing (*what* it is) and the existence of a thing (the fact *that* it is). The actual existence of a thing is something different from its definition; we can have a definition of a unicorn or the current king of France without there actually existing a unicorn or a current king of France. The existence of unicorns or French kings must be demonstrated. In other words, the so-called ontological argument seems to be begging the question of whether the highest being is necessarily one in which essence and existence are identical. Although Thomas thinks that God in fact *is* that than which no greater can be thought *and* that God's essence is identical with his existence, he also thinks that these are things that must be demonstrated (for the latter argument, see 1.3.4, below).

15. Thomas agrees that the skeptical denial of all truth is self-refuting, but does not see this as entailing the acceptance of a *highest* truth.

16. On this article, see White (1956, 35–61); Gilson (1960, 52–60); Dewan (2012).

17. It is worth noting that by *demonstratio* Thomas means a chain of syllogistic reasoning by which one moves from certainly held premises toward a conclusion that will be of equal certainty. He does not think that this exhausts what we might call "natural knowledge of God." Indeed, he seems to think that demonstrations for God's existence account for a relatively small slice of such natural knowledge. Some believe in God because of moral convictions about the absolute nature of goodness, or because of an aesthetic sense of the coherence of nature, or because of a kind of informal reasoning process (what Aristotle called an *enthymeme*) that produces an inclination to assent to God's existence. None of these is what Thomas means by *demonstratio*, and though they do result in a kind of knowledge of God, it is not *scientia* strictly speaking.

18. On the relationship between *scientia* and "seeing" see 1.1 note 17.

2. The middle term of a demonstration is that which something is [*quod quid est*].[19] But we cannot know what God is, but only what he is not,[20] as John of Damascus says (*On the Orthodox Faith* 1.4). We cannot, therefore, demonstrate that God exists.

3. If the existence of God were demonstrated, this could be only from his effects. His effects, though, are not proportionate to him, since he is infinite and his effects are finite, and there is no proportion between the finite and infinite. Since a cause cannot be demonstrated by a nonproportionate effect, it seems that the existence of God cannot be demonstrated.

On the contrary: The Apostle says in Romans (1:20), "The invisible things of God are clearly understood through things that are made."[21] But this would not be the case unless the existence of God could be demonstrated through the things that are made, for the first thing we must know of anything is whether it exists.

I answer: Demonstration is of two sorts. One is by means of the cause and is called *propter quid*, and this is to argue from what is prior in an absolute sense.[22] The other is by means of the effect, and is called a *demonstratio quia*, and this is to argue from what is prior relative to us,[23] for when the effect of something is better known to us than its cause, we proceed from the effect to knowledge of the cause. And from every effect the existence of its proper cause can be demonstrated, so long as its effects are better known to us, for granting that the effect exists, the cause must preexist, since every effect depends upon its cause. The existence of God, therefore, inasmuch as it is not self-evident to us, can be demonstrated from those effects that are known to us.

19. What Thomas here calls a "middle term" (*medium*) is the term that is found in both premises of a syllogism but not in the conclusion. It is the mechanism that enables the process of inference from premises to conclusion. A classic example, with the middle term italicized, would be the following:
   Socrates is a *man*.
   All *men* are mortal.
   Therefore, Socrates is mortal.
Note that the middle term—"man"—tells us what kind of thing Socrates is.

20. Thomas echoes this statement of John of Damascus in 1.1.9: "It is clearer to us what God is not than what God is. Therefore, likenesses drawn from things farthest away from God make us have a truer estimate of the God who is above whatever we may say or think of God." Many of the things we attribute to God are in fact disguised *negative* statements about God: God is omnipresent (meaning that God is *not* confined to a particular location, the way that we are), God is eternal (meaning that God's life is *not* lived within the stream of time, the way that ours is), etc.

21. Romans 1:19–20 is frequently invoked by Thomas to support the claim that we can know God by observing the world because the world is an effect of which God is the cause.

22. *Propter quid* might be translated as "on account of which" and refers to arguments that move from a known cause to an unknown effect. We might call this a demonstration of *why* something is the case.

23. *Demonstratio quia* might be translated as a "demonstration *that*"—in other words, a demonstration that moves from a perceived effect to the existence of an unperceived cause. A cause, by its very nature, is prior to its effect: there must be fire in order for there to be smoke. But we may know the effect before we know the cause: we see the smoke on the horizon.

Reply to 1: The existence of God and other similar things that can be known about God by natural reason, as Romans says (1:19), are not articles of faith but preambles to the articles. For faith presupposes natural knowledge just as grace presupposes nature and perfections presuppose something that can be perfected.[24] Nevertheless, nothing prevents something that in itself is capable of being demonstrated and known from being accepted as worthy of belief by someone who cannot grasp its demonstration.[25]

Reply to 2: When demonstrating a cause by means of an effect, it is necessary to use the effect in place of the definition of the cause in order to prove the existence of the cause, and this is especially so in the case of God. For in order to prove the existence of anything it is necessary to accept as a middle term "what the word means," and not "what it is" [*quod quid est*], for the question "what is it?" is subsequent to the question "is it?"[26] Now the words used for God are established based on his effects, as will be shown later (1.13.1); consequently, in demonstrating the existence of God from his effects, we can take for the middle term what is signified by this word "God."[27]

Reply to 3: From effects not proportionate to a cause, it is not possible to have perfect knowledge of that cause. Yet from any effect the existence of the

---

24. See 1.1 note 34.

25. In this response to the objection Thomas distinguishes the *articuli fidei* from the *praeambula fidei*. The articles of faith (see 1.1 note 28) cannot be known apart from revelation, whereas the preambles of faith *can* be known simply by observing the world. However, two things should be noted about these preambles: the knowledge they give us is limited and defective (see 1.1 note 10 and 1.12 note 6), and some people—indeed, many—come to know the content of these preambles (e.g., God's existence) not through the exercise of natural reason but through the teaching of revelation. And, of course, those who come to know God's existence through revelation know it differently from those who know it through the exercise of natural reason: those who know God's existence through reason know simply *that* God exists, but those who know God through revelation know, at least implicitly, all that revelation teaches about God.

26. Here Thomas is anticipating the distinction between essence and existence discussed in the notes to 1.3.4, below.

27. Thomas's point here is that in arguing for *why* something is the case, one needs a definition in the middle term of the demonstration. Thus, Socrates is mortal because he is a man and because all men are mortal. However, in arguing *that* something is the case, it is necessary merely to have an effect of that thing in the middle term. So, if we knew that people identified the cause of unrest among the youth of Athens as "Socrates," but had no idea what this "Socrates" was, we might still validly argue:

"Socrates" is the cause of unrest among the youth of Athens.
The youth of Athens are restless.
Therefore, "Socrates" exists.

Thus a demonstration of God's existence might go something like this:

"God" is what the world's cause is called.
The world exists.
Therefore, God exists.

This simply gives the basic form of a *demonstratio quia*. It remains to be argued that the world's cause (i.e., "God") is something distinct from the world itself, and this is what Thomas does in the next article.

cause can be clearly demonstrated, as we have said above, and so from the effects of God it is possible to demonstrate his existence, though from them we cannot perfectly know God as he is in his essence.[28]

1.2.3[29]
Does God exist?[30]

It seems that God does not exist.

1. If one of two contraries is infinite, the other would be completely destroyed. By the word "God" is understood something of infinite goodness. If, therefore, God existed, no evil would be found. Evil, however, is found in the world. Therefore God does not exist.[31]

2. What can be accomplished through a few principles is not to be done by many. If we were to suppose that God did not exist, it seems that everything we see in the world could be accomplished by other principles, for all natural things can be traced back to nature as a principle, and certainly all

---

28. See note 14, above, and 1.12 note 5.

29. On this article, see Gilson (1960, 60–94); Kenny (1969); McCabe (1987, 2–9); Wippel (2000, 442–500); Kerr (2002, 52–72); Bauerschmidt (2013, 91–107).

30. This article contains what have come to be called the "five ways" by which Thomas demonstrates the existence of God. It is important to have a sense of what Thomas is and is not doing in this article. He wishes to demonstrate that what we know about the world still leaves us with the question "Why is there anything at all?" and that the answer to that question is what people commonly call "God." This is, in a sense, a fairly modest project. Thomas is simply trying to show that the question "Why?" is legitimate not simply in reference to this or that thing, but in reference to *everything*; and it is legitimate because it is a question that has an answer (in the way that a question like "Is Duluth Tuesday?" does not). When we ask why there is anything at all, we may not know the answer, but we use "God" (that is, the God who can be known by the exercise of our natural reason) as something like the placeholder for whatever that answer might be. Of course, Thomas also thinks that reason can go on to discern of God such attributes as "simplicity," "eternity," and so forth, and some of these attributes are already implicit in the five arguments in this article. Thomas does *not* think, however, that what he is doing in this article is proving the existence of the Christian God. Rather he is pointing to features of the world that indicate that the world cannot account for its own existence. Thomas does this not to prove to the atheist that God exists (though an atheist *may* be convinced by what Thomas says) but to show that the normal way in which people use the word "God"—as the first cause of the world—is not nonsensical; indeed, this usage fits with and makes sense of our observation of the kind of world we live in.

I should also point out that the arguments Thomas offers in this article are fairly skeletal. One finds more fully fleshed-out forms of some of them in works like the *Summa contra Gentiles*. The arguments are likewise not strictly original to Thomas; they all draw heavily from the Greek philosophical tradition, both Platonic and Aristotelian, as well as from Arabic philosophy, and Thomas likely presumes some familiarity with these traditional arguments.

31. At first glance this objection seems to be the rather jejune one of "How can there be a good God when there is so much suffering in the world?" A second glance reveals that the objection is somewhat more subtle than that. The objector points out that "God" is usually taken to mean a being of infinite goodness. Yet if God is *infinite* goodness, then this would leave no "room" for evil in the world. But there is evil in the world; therefore, there cannot be a being of infinite goodness.

purposeful things can be traced back to human reason or will as a principle. There is therefore no need to suppose God's existence.[32]

On the contrary: Exodus (3:14) shows God saying, "I am who am."[33]

I answer: The existence of God can be proved in five ways.

The first and most obvious way is the argument from change [*motus*].[34] It is something certain and widely agreed upon that some things in this world are changing. But whatever changes [*movetur*] is changed [*movetur*] by something else.[35] For nothing changes unless it has potential to become that into which it changes, whereas something changes [something else] inasmuch as it is actual, since to change is simply to lead something from potentiality to actuality. Nothing can be led from potentiality to actuality, however, except by something in a state of actuality, in the way that something actually hot, such as fire, makes wood, which is potentially hot, to be actually hot, and thereby moves and changes it.[36] Now it is impossible for the same thing to

32. This objection echoes another commonly encountered modern objection to God's existence: for every individual thing in the world science can find a cause—that is, a reason why it exists. God is therefore a superfluous proposition, very much in the way he is for certain modern Darwinians.

The objections in this article are best understood if taken together. The first says that the existence of an infinite God would overwhelm a finite world, in effect leaving no room for anything that is not God (e.g., evil). The second says that since everything in the world can be accounted for by some finite thing, there is no room for an infinite God. Thomas's response to both of these objections is implicit in his conception of the relationship between God and the world: it is a mistake to think of God as an "object" that competes for room with the other objects that make up the world.

33. This is God's reply to Moses when he inquires after God's name. Étienne Gilson referred to this reply as "the metaphysics of Exodus."

34. *Motus* is often translated as "motion," but might also mean, at least in this context, "change." Thomas follows Aristotle (*Categories* 14, 15^a) in seeing at least three distinct sorts of *motus*: (1) any alteration or qualitative change, (2) a change of size, and (3) a change of location. Only the last of these is what we would normally call "motion" in English. Though this first argument is often referred to as the "argument from motion," Thomas's intention seems to be to speak of the wider phenomenon of change.

35. The Latin word *movetur* is the passive form of the verb *movere* and can mean either the intransitive "changes" (as in "the child changes into an adult") or the passive "is changed" (as in "the child's diaper is changed by her father"). Thomas's use of the passive form introduces some ambiguity into his argument, and perhaps prejudices him somewhat toward the view that whatever changes (*movetur*) is changed (*movetur*) by something else. I have translated it according to my own sense of what best fits the particular context.

36. Thomas draws his account of change from Aristotle: a thing changes by becoming actually something that it is potentially. So, to use Thomas's example, a piece of wood is potentially on fire; for it to burn is for it to actualize that potential. How then is it that some things come to actualize one particular potential rather than another (after all, a piece of wood is also potentially a club or a table)? Something that has *already* actualized that potential must act upon them. Thus wood (potential fire, but also potential club or table) burns because it comes into contact with a flame (actual fire). With respect to its potential to burn, a burning piece of wood is said to be actual or "in act."

One might object that this works in the case of wood coming to be on fire, but seemingly not in the case of wood becoming a table; after all, the potential of wood to become a table is not actualized by something that is itself a table, but by a carpenter. In the case of an artifact like a table, however, the actualized idea

be actual and potential at the same time and in the same respect, but only in different respects. For example, what is actually hot cannot at the same time be potentially hot; rather, it is at that point potentially cold. It is therefore impossible that something should, with regard to the same thing and in the same way, be both what is changed and what causes change or that it should change itself.[37] Therefore, whatever changes must be changed by something else. If what causes change is itself changing, then this also must be changed by something else, and that by yet another.[38] This cannot go on indefinitely, since then there would be no first cause of change [*primum movens*] and, consequently, no other cause of change, because secondary causes of change do not change things unless they are changed by the first cause of change, like a stick that moves only because it is put in motion by a hand.[39] Therefore it

---

of a table in the mind of the carpenter is the prerequisite for the actualization of the wood's potential to be a table. We might say that the carpenter is, in a special sense, like a table inasmuch as the carpenter has the idea of a table in mind.

37. In other words, nothing changes itself; it is always changed by something else. Things do not really spontaneously combust; they burn because something acts upon them. Were they to change themselves, they would have to be simultaneously *potentially* something and *actually* that same thing, which is contrary to the law of noncontradiction (see 1.1 note 29). In the *Summa contra Gentiles* Thomas argues, fairly elaborately, that when a thing might seem to change itself, it is in fact one *part* of a composite thing changing another *part*. He does not seem to feel the need to make this argument here.

38. Here Thomas points out that this account of change is true of *everything* in the world. Everything changes, and nothing changes itself. One might ask, however, whether Thomas has really demonstrated this claim. Wood burning and wood being made into a table are examples that support the claim, but what about helium rising? Is something acting upon helium to make it realize its "upward" potential? Examples like this may at least make contestable the claim that all change is accounted for by something with a realized potential acting upon something with an unrealized potential. Thomas might answer that most phenomena of change are not accounted for by a simple one-to-one causal chain; rather, a network of causal forces is in play in the case of helium rising that might escape our capacity to identify and characterize. But what he thinks is obvious is that *some* set of causal forces are involved.

39. It is misleading to think of Thomas's argument here in terms of a "chain" of movers stretching back through time until we get to God, who is at the end of the chain as prime mover. This would be a case of what Thomas calls "causes ordered *per accidens*," which he acknowledges could in theory be infinite. In his discussion of whether the idea of "creation" necessarily implies a beginning in time (1.46.2), Thomas makes it clear that he does not think of God as terminating a series of accidentally ordered causes. He says that what we mean by "creation" is a relationship of existential dependence (i.e., a creature's existing depends upon the activity of its creator), which does not necessitate that the creator be temporally prior. Rather, Thomas is thinking here of causes ordered "*per se*," by which he means causes acting in concert, ordered not temporally but logically, in terms of their dependence on one another. Thus, to use Thomas's example (which he takes from Aristotle), the hand that moves the stick that moves the stone has a logical and causal priority over the stick, even though it acts at the same time as the stick.

Thomas denies the possibility of an infinite regress of causes because, in effect, he thinks that "Why?" is an appropriate question to ask about the world *as a whole*. To grant the possibility of an infinite regress would be in effect to say that the question "Why is there something rather than nothing?" (which is the way that the seventeenth-century philosopher Leibniz formulated the issue) is a nonsensical question. The unmoved mover is not to be found at the end of a chain of causes, but in the answer to the question,

is necessary to arrive at some first cause of change, which is not changed by anything else, and this everyone understands to be God.[40]

The second way is from the nature of an efficient cause.[41] For we find in the things we perceive that there is an order of efficient causes. Yet we do not find, nor could we find, anything that is the efficient cause of itself, for in that case it would be prior to itself, which is impossible. Now in efficient causes it is not possible to go on to infinity. This is because in every ordered series of efficient causes the first is the cause of the intermediate cause, and the intermediate is the cause of the last cause, whether there are many intermediate causes or only one. But to take away the cause is to take away the effect; therefore, if there were no first cause among efficient causes, there would be no last cause, nor any intermediate cause. If efficient causes were to go on infinitely, however, there would be no first efficient cause, neither would there be a final effect, nor any intermediate efficient causes—all of which is plainly false. It is therefore necessary to posit some first efficient cause, to which everyone gives the name God.[42]

The third way is taken from possibility and necessity, and it goes like this: we find some things that have the possibility of existing or not existing, since they are found to be generated and to corrupt, and consequently have the

---

"Why is there a chain (or, perhaps better, network) of causes at all?"—the point at which causal questioning stops. In other words, the reason for there being an actual world rather than simply a potential world must be found outside the world, in something that is itself in no need of being actualized, in a being that is, as Thomas will put it, "pure act"—completely actualized existence. Thomas does not think the chain of causes *is* of infinite length, but he believes that it is only possible to know this because of divine revelation: "*In the beginning* God created the heavens and the earth." So for the purposes of his arguments here, the notion of temporal beginning is bracketed.

40. Each of the five ways concludes with a statement like this. Sometimes readers object: "Wait a minute. How does he know that God is the unmoved mover and not something else?" Thomas is not, in this context, particularly invested in what people *call* this uncaused cause, as long as they recognize that many people—indeed, most people—would call such a being "God."

41. An "efficient cause" is an "agent"—i.e., something that acts so as to bring about some effect. In modern thinking, this is typically what we mean when we say that something is a "cause." Thomas, however, has a much richer vocabulary of causation than we do, one taken over from Aristotle. In addition to efficient causality, there is also "material causality," or that matter from which something is made; "formal causality," or the character of a thing by which it is what it is (see 1.12 note 2); and "final causality," or the goal or purpose of something (see note 58, below). Thus a table has a carpenter as its efficient cause, wood as its material cause, "tableness" as its formal cause, and being used for meals (or some other activity) as its final cause.

42. The similarities between this second way and the first one should be obvious. In fact, what is less obvious is how it is *different* from the first way. Étienne Gilson (1960) argues that Thomas enriches Aristotle's four causes by distinguishing between Aristotle's "moving cause," which is the reason for something that exists undergoing change, and an "efficient cause" strictly speaking, which is the reason for something beginning to exist at all. On Gilson's reading, the first way still operates within the Aristotelian understanding of God as the cause of change in things, whereas the second way moves to a more specifically Christian understanding of God as the cause of the existence of things.

possibility of existing or not existing.[43] But it is impossible for everything to be like this,[44] for what has the possibility of not existing will at some point in time not exist, and if everything has the possibility of not existing, then at some time there would have been nothing existing.[45] But if this were true, even now there would be nothing in existence, because that which does not exist only begins to exist through something already existing. So if at one time nothing was in existence, it would have been impossible for anything to have begun to exist, and thus even now nothing would exist—which is obviously false.[46] Therefore, not all beings are merely possible; there must be something with necessary existence. Now every necessary thing either has its necessity caused by something else or it does not. It is impossible, though, to go on indefinitely regarding necessary things that have their necessity caused by another, as has been already proved in regard to efficient causes.[47] And

43. At least some (if not all) of the things we encounter in the world have a *contingent* existence: they can come into existence and pass out of existence.

44. This translates the text as found in the Piana edition (1570) of the *Summa*: "impossibile est autem omnia quae sunt, talia esse." The Leonine edition, which is the standard modern edition, reads "impossibile est autem omnia quae sunt talia, semper esse," which might be translated, "but it is impossible for something like this always to exist." The Piana version of the text is about the need for a noncontingent, necessary being in order to account for the existence of a contingent universe, whereas the Leonine version links contingency to having a limited length of temporal duration. Thomas's understanding of "necessary existence" is indebted to the Arabic philosopher Ibn Sina (Avicenna), who conceives of necessary and contingent existence not simply in terms of temporal duration—with necessary beings existing always and contingent beings sometimes existing and sometimes not—but in terms of necessary existence being "existence through itself" and contingent existence as "existence through another." So something exists necessarily if it owes its existence to nothing outside of itself; something exists contingently if it owes its existence to another. Even if something that owed its existence to another happened to exist always, its existence would still be contingent and not necessary. For Thomas's use of this understanding of necessity, see note 47, below. For Ibn Sina's account of necessity and contingency, see *The Metaphysics of "The Healing"* 1.6.

45. Thomas is sometimes accused at this point of falling into what is called "the quantifier shift fallacy." This is the logical error found in arguing, for example, that if *every*one loves *some*one then there must be *some*one that *every*one loves. This is a fallacy because, between the premise and the conclusion, the quantifiers "every" and "some" shift their position and therefore their scope. So, the criticism goes, Thomas is arguing that if *every*thing does not exist at *some* time, then there is *some* time when *every*thing does not exist. This would indeed be an invalid argument.

Thomas's argument, however, seems to be something different. Given an infinite amount of time (which we should presume if we are not presuming Genesis's account of creation; if we were presuming the Genesis account of creation then we would have no need to demonstrate God's existence), all possibilities would at some point be realized. But if everything is contingent, and therefore has the possibility of not existing, then at some point the possibility of every contingent thing not existing would have been realized and at that point there would have been nothing. This argument, whatever one thinks of it, does not seem to fall prey to the quantifier shift fallacy.

46. See the first two ways: whatever comes to be has a cause (which must be some existing thing). But if at some point nothing existed, then there would be no causes to bring about existence.

47. Thomas grants the possibility that there may be things in this world that have necessary existence (e.g., angels and heavenly bodies) in the sense of not passing out of existence, but he says that they would

so one must posit the existence of something that is necessary in itself, not receiving its necessity from another thing, but rather causing the necessity of other things. This is what everyone speaks of as God.[48]

The fourth way is taken from the gradations to be found in things.[49] For one finds among things that some are more and some are less good, true, noble, and so forth.[50] But "more" and "less" are said of different things insofar as they approach, in their different ways, something that is greatest, as in the case of something being hotter insofar as it approaches what is maximally hot.[51] Therefore there is something that is truest, something best, something noblest, and, consequently, something that is most fully in being, for those things that are truest are most fully in being, as it says in the *Metaphysics* (2.1, 993^b).[52] It is said in the same book that the maximum in any genus is the cause of everything in that genus, in the way that fire, which is maximally hot, is the cause of all hot things.[53] There is thus something that is to all beings

---

still have a "caused" necessity—that is, even though they might not pass out of existence, their existence would still be derived from something else and therefore might not have been. Here his debt to Ibn Sina's understanding of necessity as a thing existing "through itself" (see note 44, above) is evident, allowing Thomas to distinguish God's necessity from the "necessity" of beings of infinite duration.

48. I.e., there must be something that lacks the possibility of nonexistence because it exists through itself. But if everything in the world has the possibility of nonexistence (as Thomas thinks it does), then something that lacks that possibility must not be an object in our world (i.e., it must be what people call "God").

49. Thomas's fourth demonstration does not obviously follow the pattern of the previous three and seems, despite its citation of Aristotle, to be more Platonic in character (Thomas himself connects this sort of argument with "the Platonists" in his *Commentary on the Gospel of John* prologue.5). Specifically, it trades upon the Platonic idea that particular things are what they are by virtue of participation in an ideal exemplar or "form," with a variety of degrees of participation establishing a kind of hierarchy of beings.

50. In this context, "good" refers not to moral goodness, but to what might be called metaphysical goodness—i.e., desirability. So the claim here is that in the world as we experience it some things are more desirable than others. Likewise, "true" refers not to the truth or falsity of statements, but to the capacity of things to be understood: some things are more readily grasped by the intellect than others. It is not entirely clear what Thomas means by "noble" in this context, though some have suggested that it means "fully actual" (see note 36, above), which would reflect Thomas's understanding of reality as a hierarchy structured according to ever-more-intense realizations of the act of existing.

51. Thomas claims that our judgments about degrees of goodness, truth, etc. seem to have built into their logic the notion of that which is "highest" or "greatest" or "best." He doesn't offer an argument for this claim, and perhaps thinks it so obvious as to be a kind of first principle of thought.

52. See 1.1 note 3, on the concept of "transcendentals." The notions of a maximum degree of desirability or intelligibility or actuality are rooted in the idea of a maximum degree of being.

53. Thomas makes here what to us is the not entirely intuitive claim that whatever is highest in a particular category is the ultimate cause of all things that fall into that category, and so there must be a highest being that accounts for the being of everything else. The specific example of fire is probably not much help here, and Thomas's claim might be more convincing if restricted to the transcendentals. For example, according to the Platonic notion of participation, things are good to the degree that they share in the form of goodness, and in this sense the form of goodness can be said to be the cause of all lesser instances of goodness.

[*entibus*] the cause of their existence [*esse*],[54] goodness, and every other perfection. And this we call God.[55]

The fifth way is taken from the governance of things.[56] We see that some things that lack awareness—that is, natural bodies—act so as to obtain a goal. This is evident from their acting always, or nearly always, in the same way, so that they obtain the best result.[57] Thus it is plain that they do not achieve their end by chance, but by intention.[58] Whatever lacks awareness, however, cannot move toward an end unless directed by something that *is* aware and intelligent, the way an arrow is directed by the archer. Therefore, there is something intelligent by which all natural things are directed to their end, and this we call God.[59]

54. On the significance of *esse*, see 1.3 note 2.

55. By the end of the fourth way, Thomas is back to the notion of God as cause—not simply of this thing or that thing but of *everything* in its totality: "something that is to all beings the cause of their existence, goodness, and every other perfection."

56. At first glance, this argument might seem to resemble the so-called "argument from design" made famous at the beginning of the nineteenth century by William Paley in his *Natural Theology*. Paley used the analogy of finding a watch and extrapolating from this to the existence of a watchmaker to argue that the cosmos displays such intricacy of design that one is warranted in presuming the existence of a cosmic designer. One difference between Paley and Thomas is that, whereas Paley's watch image suggests a God who *assembles* things too complex for nature alone to produce, Thomas presents a God who *guides* or governs the universe, leading all things to their end in God. Paley's view is, we might say, a mechanistic one, whereas Thomas's is a providential one.

57. Thomas thinks that if the functioning of things were merely random, then we would not see the regularity that we do in nature. Fire, for example, would sometimes heat things and sometimes not. But this is clearly counter to our experience.

58. To possess a particular nature is to be oriented toward a particular goal. As just noted, the nature of fire is to heat things, and so we might say that the activity of fire is oriented toward heating. We might likewise say that trees, by nature, perform photosynthesis, so that the activity of the tree, such as growing leaves in the spring, is oriented toward photosynthesis; photosynthesis is the point (goal/end/purpose) of growing leaves. This view of a thing's activity as oriented toward a goal is what is commonly referred to as a "teleological" view of the world. The goal-orientation of a thing's activities is one way of accounting for those activities, and so Thomas, like Aristotle, speaks of there being "final causes"—the goal of an action in some sense causes that action to occur.

59. Thomas is well aware that it can seem strange to speak of fire as having the purpose of heating or a tree having a purpose for growing leaves. We should note, however, that there are two different ways in which we might speak of a thing having a purpose or a final cause: first, we might say that the purpose of an arrow is to hit a target; second, we might say that in shooting an arrow my purpose is to hit a target. The arrow and I have "purpose" in different senses. As an intelligent being, I can do things "on purpose"; an arrow is not an intelligent being, therefore it cannot. It is the archer who gives the arrow its purpose and who directs it to its goal. A tree is also unintelligent. Then who or what intelligent being guides the tree in fulfilling its purposes?

Today we might answer that the evolutionary process of natural selection is a sufficient explanation for the appearance of purpose in things lacking intelligence. The apparent nonrandomness of nature is simply the outworking of random mutations that give evolutionary advantages in a given environment. Thomas knows nothing of evolutionary theory, of course, but his concept of "secondary causes" (see note 61, below) would seem to give him the capacity to account for it. Moreover, as Thomas's concluding

Reply to 1: As Augustine says in the *Enchiridion on Faith, Hope, and Love* (11), "Since God is the highest good, he would not allow any evil to exist in his works, unless his omnipotence and goodness were such as to bring good even out of evil." This, therefore, is part of the infinite goodness of God: that he should permit evil and out of it bring forth good.[60]

Reply to 2: Since nature works for a determinate end under the direction of a higher agent, it is necessary that whatever is done by nature must be traced back to God as its first cause. Similarly, whatever is done purposefully must also be traced back to some higher cause that is not human reason or will, since these can change or fail. For, as was shown, all things that are changeable and fallible must be traced back to a first principle that is by its very nature unchanging and necessary.[61]

---

sentence in this argument suggests, in the end he is not asking about the purposiveness of this or that being, but the purposiveness of what we could call the evolutionary process itself—i.e., not why this or that thing seems to have purpose, but why the entire system of the universe has purpose.

A modern version of Thomas's fifth way might be found in so-called "fine tuning" arguments, which point to the narrow range of possibilities allowing for the emergence of life in the universe—e.g., if the force of gravity had been slightly weaker or stronger, then stars like the sun could not have formed—as suggesting intelligent purpose at work in the universe. Note here that Thomas has taken us a bit beyond the first four ways, which have simply demonstrated God as a universal cause. In the fifth way, Thomas shows God to be an *intelligent* cause, in the sense of being a cause that acts with purpose.

60. Like Augustine, and the Christian tradition generally, Thomas understands evil to be not a substance, but rather *privatio boni*—an absence of goodness. God can allow evil to "exist" because it has no positive being that could in any way "compete" with God.

61. The reference is to the body of the article. Thomas here refers to the distinction between "primary" and "secondary" causes that underlies not simply the five ways but his vision of created existence as a whole. For Thomas, God is the primary cause of every creature, but affirming this does not mean that creatures are not themselves genuine causes. Thomas is aware, through the writings of Moses Maimonides, of Islamic theologians who, seeking to emphasize the sovereignty of God, deny genuine causality to creatures. When, for instance, fire appears to be burning something, it is God who is causing the thing to burn, and the fire is merely serving as an "occasion" for God to act. A famous account, though not necessarily an endorsement, of the view of these Muslim theologians can be found in Al-Ghazali's *The Incoherence of the Philosophers*, discussion 17.5–6. To Thomas's mind, rather than enhancing God's power, this view detracts from it, suggesting that God cannot cause there to be creatures that are themselves genuine causes. For Thomas, because God is not an object alongside other objects within the universe, God's causality is not in "competition" with the causality of creatures, so it is entirely possible—indeed, it is normally the case—that something can be caused entirely by God and entirely by created causes. For Thomas's discussion of this, see *Disputed Questions on the Power of God* 3.7 and *Summa contra Gentiles* 3.69.

Question 3:

The Simplicity of God

1.3.4[1]
Are essence and existence the same in God?

It seems that essence and existence are not the same in God.[2]

1. On this article, see Gilson (1960, 113–48); Davies (2010); Kerr (2002, 73–96); Stump (2012).

2. Much of what Thomas thinks about the nature of divinity finds its foundation in this article. A great deal hangs on understanding the distinction between "existence" (*esse*) and "essence" (*essentia*). Throughout this article it is important to keep in mind Thomas's understanding of that distinction. In contrast to Aristotle (and drawing on Ibn Sina and Moses Maimonides), Thomas recognized that *what* something is differs from the fact *that* it is. In making this differentiation, Thomas calls the fact of a thing's existence its *esse*—a noun that he forms out of the verb "to be" and that we might translate as "existing" or "existence." This act of existing is distinct from the *kind* of thing something is.

Ibn Sina's way of making this point is to say that *esse* is an accidental property of things—that is, a quality that a thing might or might not possess, without changing what it is. Thus, Aaron is bearded, but being bearded is not part of the meaning of "Aaron," so he could cease to be bearded without changing what it means to be Aaron. Beardedness, therefore, is an accidental property of Aaron. Likewise, existence is not part of the meaning of "Aaron," as is witnessed by the fact that Aaron no longer exists, yet what it means to be Aaron is unchanged.

Though in one place (*Quodlibetal Questions* 2.2.1) Thomas adopts Ibn Sina's language of *esse* as an "accident," he is on the whole unhappy with this way of putting the matter, since Aaron's existence is not really like Aaron's beard, for if Aaron ceased to be, he would most certainly cease to be Aaron. Therefore Thomas says in another place (*Quodlibetal Questions* 12.4.1) that *esse*, "strictly speaking" (*proprie loquendo*), is not an accident. Still, Thomas recognizes that Ibn Sina has made a crucial distinction between a thing's essence and the fact of its existence: like an accidental property, existence is not contained within something's essence. Therefore we speak of *esse* in created beings as if it were an accident, even though it is in fact the very "actuality" of created beings. Even things that are unchanging have their existence "accidentally," in the sense that their unchanging existence is not given with their essence but depends on something else (see 1.2 note 47).

In this article Thomas argues that the distinction between essence and existence, while true of everything in the world, *cannot* be true of God if God is the cause of the world. The shorthand way of denoting the unity of essence and existence in God is to speak of God's "simplicity." By divine simplicity Thomas means, first, that God is not composed of form and matter (see 1.12 note 2). This, however, is also true of the angels, since they are pure form without matter (see 1.50.1, below). God's simplicity is more radical, since even the angels—like every created thing—consist in the *possibility* of existing or not existing, to which their *actual* existence is something added (since they might not have existed). God, however, has

1. If this were so, then nothing would be added to the divine being. But existence to which no addition is made is existence-in-general [*esse commune*], which is predicated of all things. From this it follows that God is the being-in-general [*ens commune*] that can be predicated of everything.[3] But this is false, according to the book of Wisdom (14:21), "They gave the name that cannot be shared to wood and stone." Therefore God's existence is not his essence.[4]

2. As said above (1.2.2), we can know whether God is, but we cannot know what God is. So God's existence is not the same as what he is—that is, his quiddity or nature.[5]

---

the radical simplicity of purely actual existence, since God does not have the possibility of not existing because he exists through himself.

It is also worth noting here that Thomas distinguishes not only between *esse* and *essentia* but also between *esse* (the act of "being") and *ens* (this or that particular "being" or "entity" or "individual"). All created beings "have" *esse* by virtue of being an entity, whereas God "is" *esse*, without being an entity alongside other entities. At the same time, God, like an individual entity, does have a kind of "uniqueness" inasmuch as God is God and everything else is not God, since it is created by God. There is a sense therefore in which God transcends even this distinction between *esse* and *ens*. For this reason, we must think and speak of God both abstractly—like a Platonic form—and concretely, like a particular entity. So we say that God is divine, but also divinity itself; God is good, but also goodness itself. Thomas writes in 1.13.1: "Because God is both simple and subsisting [i.e., existing independently], we attribute to him both abstract terms, to signify his simplicity, and concrete terms, to signify his subsistence and perfection, although both these kinds of terms fail to express his way of being, since our intellect does not know him in this life as he is." Eleonore Stump (see note 1, above) compares this to the way in which, in quantum physics, light appears to be both a wave and a particle.

3. To "predicate" (*praedicare*) is, most simply, "to say," though in Thomas's usage it has the more specific meaning of the act of affirming something of something else. Thomas calls the things that might be affirmed of something "predicates" and groups them into ten categories (see Aristotle, *Categories* 1[b]):

- substance ("Thomas is a human being.")
- quantity ("Thomas weighs two hundred pounds.")
- quality ("Thomas has blond hair.")
- relation ("Thomas is older than Sophia.")
- place ("Thomas is in Paris.")
- time ("Thomas was born in 1224.")
- position ("Thomas is standing.")
- possession/state ("Thomas is wearing a blue shirt.")
- acting on ("Thomas loves Sophia.")
- being affected by ("Thomas is loved by Sophia.")

Thus we would say that being in Paris is predicated of Thomas under the category of "place," while being a human being is predicated of him under the category of "substance." It might be noted that all of the categories apart from "substance" are "accidents"—i.e., incidental properties that do not alter the fundamental identity of a thing (see the previous note).

4. The point of this objection is that beyond the existence that all things share, each thing must have an essence (i.e., the specific way of being that makes a thing what it is); otherwise we could not distinguish different sorts of beings. If God had no essence added to, and therefore specifying, his existence, then he would not be an individual distinct from the being-in-general shared by creatures, and thus we would end up with pantheism—the view that "God" is simply a word for the sum total of all things.

5. Thomas speaks of God's "quiddity" (from the Latin *quid*, meaning "what") as a way of speaking about God's essence or definition. If God's existence and essence were identical and if, as Thomas maintains, we cannot know God's essence, then we also could not know of God's existence. But Thomas's point in

On the contrary: Hilary says in his *On the Trinity* (7.11) that in God "existence is not an accidental quality, but subsisting truth." Therefore what subsists in God is his existence.

I answer: God is not only his own essence, as shown in the preceding article (1.3.3), but also his own existence.[6] This can be shown in multiple ways.

First, whatever is in something apart from its essence must be caused either by the constituent principles of that essence, like a property that follows from the species (in the way that an ability to laugh belongs to a human being, being caused by the essential principles of the species), or by something external (in the way that heat is caused in water by fire).[7] If, therefore, the existence of a thing were different from its essence, its existence would have to be caused either by something external or by the essential principles of the thing itself. It is impossible, however, for something's existence to be caused solely by its essential principles, for nothing can be the sufficient cause of its own existence, if its existence is caused.[8] Therefore something in which its existence differs from its essence must have its existence caused by another.[9] This, however, cannot be said of God, because we say God is the first efficient cause.[10] So it is impossible that in God his existence should be other than his essence.

the five ways is to show that we *can* know of God's existence. Therefore, so the objection goes, since we can apparently know God's existence but not God's essence, the former must be distinct from the latter.

6. Think of the question "What is x?" If we replace "x" with anything in our world, we can answer the question without any mention of x's existence. For example, if asked "What is a human being?" we can reply, "A rational animal." We cannot not reply, "A rational animal that exists," since "rational animal" is a true definition of human beings whether or not any human beings are in existence. If this were not the case, then the statement "There were no human beings twelve million years ago" would be meaningless (see also the discussion of Aaron and his beard in note 2, above). However, if we are asking about God, the necessary cause of the contingent world, then our answer must be, "God is *esse*." In other words, unlike every being that is caused, in God there is no distinction between *what* he is and the fact *that* he is, and this is what we mean by "necessary existence."

7. Thomas here is distinguishing between ordinary accidents and "proper accidents." To take the example Thomas offers: Human beings are not defined by their capacity for humor (though Thomas does see complete humorlessness as a vice; see 2–2.168.4). At the same time, the ability to laugh is caused by the essential constitution of a human being, which is to be a rational animal. Other intelligent beings, such as angels, do not laugh, not least because one needs a body in order to laugh, and human beings (according to Thomas) are the only embodied intelligent beings. Other animals do not laugh because they do not possess reason and thus cannot understand jokes. So a proper accident like the ability to laugh is caused by the constituent elements of what it is to be human. Other accidents are externally caused: I am hot or cold because of the ambient temperature; I am fat or thin because of the food I take into my body; I am in Paris or Pomona because of my spatial location; etc.

8. Existence is not a part of the definition of any created thing; even more, it cannot be derived from that definition, as the ability to laugh can be derived from the definition of human beings as rational animals, for a particular thing's essence exists only because that thing exists.

9. See the third of the five ways (1.2.3, above).

10. In other words, if "God" is the answer to the question of why the world as a whole exists, then "to be" (*esse*) is not something caused in God by another, nor something derived from God's definition; rather, *esse* must itself be the definition (essence) of "God."

Second, existence is what makes every form or nature actual; goodness and humanity are not spoken of as actual unless they are spoken of as existing. Therefore existence must be related to an essence other than itself in the way actuality relates to potentiality.[11] Since in God there is no potentiality, as shown earlier (1.3.1), it follows that in him essence does not differ from existence.[12] Therefore his essence is his existence.

Third, just as what is on fire but is not fire itself is on fire by participation, so too what has existence but is not existence itself is a being by participation.[13] God is his own essence, as was shown earlier (1.3.3).[14] If he is not his own existence, then he will be a being by participation and not by nature [*per essentiam*]. He will therefore not be the first being—which it is absurd to say. Therefore God is his own existence and not merely his own essence.[15]

Reply to 1: The phrase "something to which no addition has been made" can be understood in two ways.[16] In one way, its definition may preclude any addition—the way the definition of an irrational animal is "that which is *without* reason." In another way, we may understand something to have nothing added to it inasmuch as its definition does not require that anything should be added to it—the way "animal," in a general sense, does not include reason, because "to have reason" is not part of the general definition of "animal"; but neither is "to lack reason" part of the definition.[17] And so "existence without addition" in the first sense is the divine existence and "existence without addition" in the second sense is existence-in-general [*esse commune*].

11. Thomas is drawing an analogy between existence and essence on the one hand and actuality and potentiality on the other (see 1.2 note 36). An essence is not something, but only a potential something. Existence actualizes a potential existence to be an actually existing thing. This, rather than substance and accident (see note 2), is Thomas's preferred mode of speaking of the distinction between existence and essence.

12. If God is the total cause of there being something rather than nothing, then it follows that God's own existence is not in need of actualization by anything. This fact makes God's existence radically free from all possibility of becoming: as Thomas is wont to put it, God is "pure act" (*actus purus*). This notion of God as *un*caused is something different from the notion developed by early modern philosophers such as Descartes (1596–1650) and Spinoza (1632–77) that God is *self*-caused (*causa sui*).

13. There is a difference between being fire itself and being "on fire." Using Thomas's vocabulary, we would say that something that is on fire is not fire itself, but fiery "by participation." Similarly, things that "have being" but are not being itself are beings by participation. See 1.2 note 49, above.

14. The Piana edition (1570) of the *Summa* reads simply, "Deus est" (God exists).

15. If God were a being by participation, then his existence would be derived from something else, which would involve us in yet another infinite regress.

16. Or we might say, "There are two senses in which a thing can be said not to have a distinguishing feature."

17. A definition may *exclude* distinguishing features, or it may simply *not include* them. "God" excludes any further specification beyond "existence itself," while "creation," taken as a whole, simply does not include any further specification, though all creatures do in fact have further features that distinguish them from one another. For more on this point, see the next article.

Reply to 2: "To be" [*esse*] can be used in two ways. In the first way, it means the act of existence [*actum essendi*]; in the second way it means the composition of a proposition, which the mind devises by joining a predicate to a subject. Taking "to be" in the first sense, we can understand neither God's existence nor his essence. In the second sense, however, we know that this proposition that we form about God when we say "God is," is true. And this we know from his effects, as was said above (1.2.2).[18]

---

18. Thomas notes here two ways in which *esse*, in its various grammatical inflections, is used in human discourse. One is to speak of the concrete actuality by which a thing exists as what it is (its "act of existence"), and of God's existence in this sense we have no knowledge in this life. The other is the use of *esse* in the formation of propositions, such as "the cat *is* on the mat" or "Socrates *is* mortal" or "the planet Uranus *exists*." In this sense we can know—for instance, by means of arguments like those found above in 1.2.3—that the proposition "God exists" is a true one, not in the sense of knowing what sort of existence God has, but in the sense of knowing that the subject "God" can (indeed must) be joined to the verb "exists." So you might say that we can know that God exists without knowing what "exists" entails in the case of God, though we might know what it does *not* entail (e.g., spatial or temporal location, materiality, etc.).

Question 12:

Knowledge of God

1.12.12[1]

Can God be known in this life by natural reason?

It seems that by natural reason we cannot know God in this life.

1. Boethius says in *The Consolation of Philosophy* (5.4) that "reason does not grasp simple form." God, however, is a supremely simple form, as was shown earlier (1.3.7).[2] Therefore natural reason cannot arrive at knowledge of him.

2. No soul understands anything by natural reason except by the use of an image [*phantasmate*], as is said in [Aristotle's] *De anima* (3.7, 431ᵃ). But we cannot have an image of God because he is nonbodily. God, therefore, cannot be known by us through natural knowledge.

3. Knowledge that is had through natural reason is shared in by both the good and the bad, since they share in a nature. Knowledge of God, though, belongs only to the good, for Augustine says in *De Trinitate* (1.2.4), "The weak eye of the human mind is not fixed on that excellent light unless purified by the justice of faith." Therefore God cannot be known by natural reason.

---

1. On this article, see Rocca (2004, 3–74).

2. In speaking of "simple form," Thomas presumes the Aristotelian view that things generally have a "composite" existence made up of "matter" and "form" (this view is sometimes referred to as *hylomorphism*, from the Greek words *hylē* ["matter"] and *morphē* ["form" or "shape"]). The form is the essential structure of the thing that allows us to identify it as the *kind* of thing it is (when we see a cow, we can know it as a cow because it has the "form" of a cow), whereas the matter is what differentiates *this* thing from *that* thing (the cow Bossy is different from the cow Belle because they are made up of different matter). God is not material (i.e., he is "nonbodily") and therefore has an existence that is "simple" rather than composite (i.e., composed of matter and form). The next objection develops this further and states that natural human reason is incapable of grasping form unless it encounters it in a particular material thing (we can only know "cowness" by encountering an actual cow). See 1.45 note 17. God is *supremely* simple because not only is God not composed of matter and form, but, further, in God essence and existence are identical. See 1.3, above.

On the contrary: It is written in Romans (1:19), "What is known of God"—namely, what can be known of God by natural reason—"is shown forth in them."

I answer: Our natural knowledge begins from the senses.[3] Therefore our natural knowledge extends as far as it can be led by perceptible things.[4] But our mind cannot be led by perceptible things so far as to see the divine essence, because perceptible creatures are effects that do not equal the power of God as their cause. From the knowledge of perceptible things, therefore, the whole power of God cannot be known, and consequently his essence cannot be seen.[5] But because they are his effects, dependent upon their cause, we can be led from them so far as to know of God whether he exists [*an est*] and to know of him what necessarily befits him as the first cause of all things, surpassing all the things caused by him.[6]

Hence we know of his relationship with creatures, so that he is the cause of them all; and we know that creatures differ from him, so that he is not any of the things that are caused by him; and we know that this is not attributed to him on account of any defect in him, but because he surpasses all things.[7]

3. The view that "our natural knowledge begins from the senses" is one of the ways in which Thomas is a follower of Aristotle, rather than Plato (who believed that we possessed a certain innate or inborn knowledge). For a discussion of how we derive knowledge from our senses, see note 11, below.

4. I have translated Thomas's term *sensibilis* as "perceptible" rather than as "sensible," which has misleading connotations of "practical" or "down-to-earth" in modern English.

5. Up to this point Thomas is basically agreeing with the objections: given that our minds know by means of observing material things, they are unsuited to knowing God, who is immaterial.

6. Here Thomas begins to disagree with the objections, or rather he introduces a distinction that clarifies the objections. He distinguishes between knowing *that* something is [*an est*] and knowing *what* something is [*quid est*] (cf. 1.2 note 14). Since the world is caused by God, it can yield the kind of knowledge of God that an effect can give us about its cause. We say, "Where there's smoke there's fire," but we don't say, without further evidence, "Where there's smoke there's a forest fire." Smoke is an effect of fire, so smoke allows us to say *that* a fire *exists* as the cause of the smoke, but it does not allow us to say *what* the fire is: how the fire started; what kind of fuel is burning; how long it has been burning; and, above all, what fire itself is. In other words, an effect cannot provide us with a definition of its cause. Were we to draw our definition of fire from smoke, we would define it as a "smoke-producing thing." This is clearly not an adequate definition of fire, omitting as it does the fact that fire is hot, it consumes combustible material, and so on. Similarly, the world allows us to say *that* God is but not *what* God is.

7. The world is capable of telling us (1) the kind of relationship that God has with it—that of a cause to its effect; (2) that, as the world's cause, God is not himself a part of the world (since nothing causes itself); and (3) that God's not being part of the world is a sign of his perfection and transcendence.

In everything that Thomas says about God it is important to remember that he thinks we have a better grasp of what God is not than we do of what God is. Thomas says a great many things about God, but it is important to recognize how often these are negative statements about God: God is omnipresent (meaning that God is not confined to a particular location, the way that we are), God is eternal (meaning that God's life is not lived within the stream of time, the way that ours is), etc.

This is not *much* knowledge of God, but Thomas wants to maintain that it is *genuine* knowledge of God and that it gives us sufficient conceptual purchase to affirm of God such things as goodness, infinity, immutability, eternity, and unity.

Reply to 1: Reason cannot grasp simple form so as to know what it is [*quid est*]; but it can know whether it is [*an est*].

Reply to 2: God is known by natural knowledge through the images of his effects.

Reply to 3: The knowledge of God's essence, because it is by grace, belongs only to the good;[8] but the knowledge of him that is through natural reason can belong to both the good and the bad. Therefore in his book of *Retractions* (1.4), Augustine says, "I do not approve what I said in prayer, 'God who wills that only the pure should know truth.' For it can be answered that many who are not pure can know many truths"—that is, by natural reason.

1.12.13[9]
Can a higher knowledge of God be attained by grace than by natural reason?

It seems that a higher knowledge of God is not attained by grace than that which is attained by natural reason.

1. Dionysius says in his *Mystical Theology* (1) that the best union with God in this life is union with him as something entirely unknown. He says this even of Moses, who nevertheless obtained a certain excellence in the knowledge attained by grace. Now to be united to God while not knowing what he is [*quid est*] also occurs through natural reason. Therefore God is not more fully known to us through grace than through natural reason.

2. We can arrive at knowledge of divine things through natural reason only through sense images [*phantasmata*], and likewise with the knowledge given by grace. Dionysius says in *The Celestial Hierarchy* (1.2) that "it is impossible for the divine rays to enlighten us unless they are veiled within the covering of many sacred veils." So we cannot know God more fully by grace than by natural reason.

3. Our intellect clings to God by the grace of faith. Faith does not seem to be knowledge, however, for Gregory says that things that are not seen "are possessed by faith, and not by knowledge" (*Sermon 26*, in *Homilies on the Gospels*). Therefore a more excellent knowledge of God is not imparted to us by grace.

---

8. It is important to remember that, for Thomas, we are good because God gives us grace; God does not give us grace because we are good. Thomas's point here is *not* that knowledge of God's essence—that is, the knowledge of *what* God is that the saints have in heaven—is a reward bestowed upon the good, but rather that it is a gift of grace.

9. On this article, see Niederbacher (2012).

On the contrary: The Apostle says in 1 Corinthians (2:8, 10), "God has revealed to us though his Spirit" that which "none of the princes of this world knew," these being, as the gloss explains, the philosophers.[10]

I answer: We have a more perfect knowledge of God by grace than by natural reason. This is clear from the following. The knowledge that we have by natural reason requires two things: sense images [*phantasmata*] derived from perceptible objects and a natural intellectual light [*lumen naturale intelligibile*], by whose power we draw intellectual conceptions [*intelligibles conceptiones*] from them.[11]

In both of these, human knowledge is assisted by the revelation of grace, for the intellect's natural light is strengthened by the infusion of gratuitous light. Also, as in the case of prophetic visions, images are sometimes divinely formed in the human imagination, to express divine things better than is done by those images that we receive from perceptible objects. And sometimes perceptible things, or even voices, are divinely formed to express some divine meaning, as in the case of [Christ's] baptism, when the Holy Spirit is seen in

10. When Thomas refers to the "gloss," he is speaking of explanatory notes on scriptural texts that were originally written either between the lines or in the margins of Scripture. These notes began as simple one-word definitions of unfamiliar terms but grew into more elaborate commentaries that sought to explain the literal sense of the text. These commentaries were sometimes separated from the scriptural text and became books in their own rights. The most common of these glosses was known as the *Glossa ordinaria*. Tradition ascribed the compilation of this text to Walafrid of Strabo (849), though most modern scholars doubt his authorship and see the *Glossa* as accumulating over several centuries, beginning in the ninth century and culminating in the twelfth, being assembled by the students of Anselm of Laon (d. 1117). We might think of glosses as ongoing works in progress, a kind of medieval Wikipedia.

11. Two points to note here. First, here and elsewhere, I translate intelligible as "intellectual" or, sometimes, "knowable" rather than as "intelligible," which is used in many translations of Thomas. This is primarily because in modern usage the word "intelligible" is normally contrasted with "unintelligible" and could mean either readily grasped by the mind or capable of being grasped through the senses—as in a transcription of a recording that reads [unintelligible] in those places where the transcriber could not make out what the speaker was saying. This latter sense in particular is not what Thomas means by a thing being intelligible. For him, "intelligible" is associated exclusively with intellectual processes, thus my translation of intelligible as "intellectual," even though this word is also used to translate *intellectualis*.

Second, in understanding Thomas here it is helpful to have some idea of how he thinks we normally know things. To greatly simplify: the senses receive images of things (i.e., *phantasmata*). From these images, reason (or "intellect's natural light") draws (or "abstracts") that essential structure of things that Thomas (following Aristotle) calls the "form" (see note 2, above). Here Thomas calls this structure an "intellectual conception"; more commonly, he calls it the "intellectual species" (on other uses of "species," see 1.75 note 6 and 3.63 note 4). This intellectual species is then imprinted or "impressed" on what Thomas calls the "passive" or "possible" intellect, which is the mind's potential for knowing. This is analogous to the way in which matter receives form, actualizing in it a particular potential.

The translation, here and elsewhere, of *phantasmata* as "sense images" may be slightly misleading, since we associate "image" with the sense of sight, whereas *phantasmata* would seem to include sound or taste or smell or touch "images" as well.

the shape of a dove, and the voice of the Father is heard: "This is my beloved Son" (Matt. 3:17).[12]

Reply to 1: Although by the revelation of grace we cannot in this life know of God "what he is" [*quid est*], and so are united to him as to one unknown, we nevertheless know him more fully inasmuch as more and greater effects of his are demonstrated to us, and inasmuch as we attribute to him things known by divine revelation, which natural reason cannot reach, such as God being three and one.[13]

Reply to 2: The stronger the intellectual light is in human beings, the more excellent the intellectual knowledge they have, whether from images received from the senses in the natural order or from those divinely formed in the imagination. Thus through revelation given through images a fuller knowledge is received by the infusion of divine light.

Reply to 3: Faith is a kind of knowledge, since the intellect is directed by faith to something knowable. This direction to an object, though, does not proceed from the vision of the one who believes, but from the vision of the one who is believed. So inasmuch as faith falls short of seeing, it falls short of the knowledge that belongs to *scientia*, for *scientia* directs the intellect to something through the vision and understanding of first principles.[14]

---

12. God gives us a knowledge that exceeds our normal knowledge in three ways: (1) sometimes he strengthens reason's natural capacity (as in the case of the saints who see God in heaven, but also in certain special cases in this life); (2) sometimes he forms sense images (*phantasmata*) in our minds (as when a prophet is given knowledge of some distant or future event); and (3) sometimes he makes things themselves convey divine knowledge to us, through miraculous oracles. An example of the last might be Numbers 22, when God causes Balaam's donkey to speak.

13. In this life, even with the aid of revelation, we cannot have knowledge of *what* God is. But Thomas maintains that revelation still gives us a greater knowledge of God because it gives us a greater knowledge of his effects—specifically, those effects that constitute the history of salvation.

14. For Thomas, faith is something like "opinion," inasmuch as its object remains unseen, at least by us. But it is also like *scientia* in the certainty with which we hold to that unseen object of knowledge. One believes or has faith in a situation in which one cannot "see" the truth between two alternatives. As Thomas says in his *Disputed Questions on Truth* (14.1), in such a situation, the intellect "is determined by the will, which chooses to assent decisively and precisely to one of the alternatives on account of something that, while insufficient to move the intellect, is sufficient to move the will, inasmuch as it seems good or fitting to assent to this alternative. And this is the situation of the believer" (my trans.). Faith, contrasted with opinion, is when that which moves the will is God's grace.

Thus, faith is inferior to natural "vision" (in the sense of the knowledge derived from the process described in note 11, above) if we approach it from the perspective of *how one knows*. It is clearly better to know about cows from having actually encountered cows than it is to know about them from a trustworthy authority. However, if we approach faith from the perspective of *what is known*, then it is superior to the kind of vision we have in this life, since our natural vision can know only natural things, whereas faith can know God. It is better to know God through faith than to know a cow through vision. The saints in heaven, of course, have it best of all, since they know God through "vision."

Question 13:

Words for God

1.13.3[1]

Can any word be applied to God in its literal sense?

It seems that no word is applied literally [*proprie*] to God.[2]

1. All words that we apply to God are taken from creatures, as was said earlier (1.13.1). But words said of creatures are spoken of God metaphorically, as when we say that "God is a rock," or "a lion," or something similar. Therefore words used for God are used in a metaphorical sense.

2. No word can be said literally of something if it is more truly denied of it than predicated of it.[3] Yet all words such as "good," "wise," and the like are more truly denied of God than predicated of him, as is clear from Dionysius in *The Celestial Hierarchy* (2.3). So none of these words are said of God in their literal sense.

3. Names of bodies are not said of God except metaphorically, since he is nonbodily. All words of this sort imply some kind of bodily condition, for they imply time and composition and similar things that are bodily conditions. Thus all such words are applied to God metaphorically.

On the contrary: Ambrose says, in *On the Catholic Faith*, that "there are some words that clearly express a property of divinity, and some that express the clear truth of the divine majesty, but there are others that are said of God

---

1. On this article, see Rocca (2004, 291–352).

2. Though *nomen* can mean "name," I typically translate it in this question as "word" or "term," since Thomas is here clearly thinking not only of proper nouns but also of any word used to describe or identify God. Also, Thomas frames his question of whether any words are said of God "properly" (*proprie*), which in this context means "with its own meaning" or, as we would say, "literally." Note that this is something different from the literal sense of scripture (see 1.1.10, above), which for Thomas includes metaphorical statements.

3. On predication, see 1.3 note 3.

metaphorically, by way of likeness."[4] Therefore not all words are spoken of God metaphorically; there are some that are spoken literally.

I answer: As was said before (1.13.2), we know God from the perfections that flow from him to creatures, perfections that are in God in a more eminent way than in creatures.[5] Our intellect, however, grasps them as they are in creatures and signifies them by words in a way that accords with how it grasps them.[6] Therefore, as to the words we apply to God, there are two things to consider: the perfections themselves that are signified [*perfectiones ipsas significatas*]—such as goodness, life, and such things—and the word's way of signifying [*modum significandi*].[7] With regard to what is signified by these names, they belong properly to God—indeed more properly than they belong to creatures—and are spoken primarily of him. But with regard to their way of signifying they are not literally said of God, for they have a way of signifying that is applicable to creatures.[8]

Reply to 1: Some words signify these perfections flowing from God to creature things in such a way that the imperfect manner in which creatures share in the divine perfection is itself included in the very meaning of the word, in the way that "stone" signifies a material being. Words of this kind cannot be

---

4. The *sed contra* is apparently quoting Peter Lombard's *Sentences* (bk. 1, dist. 22, ch. 1), which gives a very loose paraphrase of Ambrose's *De fide* (*On the Catholic Faith*; also known as *De Trinitate*) 2.prologue.2. Ambrose's text reads in the original, "There are evident indications showing the essential characteristics of divinity; there are expressions of the likeness of the Father and the Son; and there are those that clearly express the unity of the divine majesty" (my trans.). Ambrose here speaks of the "likeness" of the Father and Son, whereas the text transmitted through Lombard seems to take "likeness" as referring to metaphorical language, which is how Thomas uses it.

5. By "more eminent" Thomas means "more perfect." His argument here is not unrelated to what he argues in the fourth way (see 1.2.3, above) concerning how that which most perfectly possesses a quality such as goodness or being is the cause of the goodness and being of those things that participate in it.

6. In other words, we learn to use our repertoire of "perfection terms"—terms such as "good," "living," and so on—in our everyday encounters with good things and living things.

7. Here Thomas notes a distinction between *what* our words signify (the *res significata*) and *how* our words signify (the *modus significandi*). Verb tenses provide an example of this distinction. In the statements "he ran," "he runs," and "he will run" the same thing (*res*) is spoken of—the act of running—but it is spoken of in three different ways (*modi*): as something past, as something present, and as something future. Likewise with nouns and adjectives: whether we say "he is good" or "he possesses goodness" we are speaking about the same thing, but in the first instance it is signified concretely as a quality ("good"), and in the second instance it is signified abstractly as a thing ("goodness").

8. Terms we apply literally to God refer truly to God as the *res significata*, but according to the *modus significandi* of creatures. Thus a statement such as "God is good" is quite literally true, because there is something true of God that our word "good" is aiming at; but when used of God, our word "good" signifies in the same way that it does when we use it of creatures, since we acquire our repertoire of perfection terms in *this* world, which is a created world. Note, however, that Thomas also says that even though we acquire our repertoire of perfection terms from our interaction with creatures, those creatures themselves derive their perfections (i.e., their goodness, their life, etc.) from God, and in that sense our perfection terms are *more* truly applied to God than they are to creatures.

applied to God except in a metaphorical sense. Other words, however, signify these perfections absolutely, without this mode of sharing being included in their meaning—for example, "being," "good," "living," and so on. Such words can be said literally of God.[9]

Reply to 2: Dionysius says that these sorts of words are denied of God because what the word signifies does not befit God in the way that word signifies it, but in a more excellent way. Therefore Dionysius also says that God is above all substance and all life (*The Celestial Hierarchy* 2.3).

Reply to 3: These words that are said literally of God imply bodily conditions not in the thing signified by the word, but as regards their way of signifying. But those that are said of God metaphorically imply a bodily condition in the thing itself that is signified.[10]

1.13.5[11]
Is what is said of God and of creatures said of them univocally?

It seems that the things said of God and creatures are said of them univocally.[12]

9. Here Thomas shows how to distinguish metaphorical language about God from properly true language about God. Although a statement like "God is my rock and my redeemer" clearly says something positive about God, it cannot be a true statement because, although a rock shares in the perfection of existence that flows from God to creatures, it shares in it in an imperfect way (i.e., in a way that falls short of God's existence). We might say that imperfection is built into a word like "rock." In a statement such as "God is good," however, the word "good" does not itself imply any creaturely imperfection—even though we acquire the term from imperfect creatures—and it therefore is used literally and not metaphorically.

10. A metaphorical statement about God speaks of God as if God were a creature (usually by implying materiality), whereas a literal statement about God speaks of God in a way derived from created things.

11. On this article, see Rocca (2004, 77–195).

12. This is one of the most pored-over articles in the *Summa*. Some people see it as a (if not *the*) linchpin in Thomas's thought, wherein he establishes his "doctrine of analogy." My own inclination is to say that the importance of analogy for Thomas should not be *understressed*, but neither should it be *overstressed*. The notion of analogical uses of *language*, along with the notion of *causes* that are analogically related to their effects, is important for Thomas as he tries to articulate how it is possible to say true things about a God who exceeds our capacity for comprehension. In creation, God imparts to us an existence that *shares* in God's own existence while also being fundamentally *different* from God's existence (since our existence has a source outside of us, whereas God's does not). Although our language about God is manifestly inadequate to the task we give it, it is at the same time not entirely false, because it is a language that can speak truthfully about a world that shares in some way in God's own existence.

In this article, as so often in the *Summa*, Thomas is concerned with what we can *say*—with what true statements we can make. True statements are made by joining a subject with an appropriate predicate, which is what Thomas calls "predication" (see 1.3 note 3). But the truth of statements is inseparable from the truth of things, so when we judge a statement to be true, we are not simply saying something about language, but about things. What is peculiar in our statements about God is that we can know that our statements are true without knowing, in a comprehensive sense, the thing about which we are speaking.

1. Everything equivocal is traced back to the univocal, just as the many are traced back to the one.[13] For if the word "dog" is said equivocally of the thing that barks and of the thing that lives in the sea, it must be said of something univocally—that is, of all barking things—otherwise we go on infinitely. But we find some agents that are univocal and agree with their effects in both terminology and definition, in the way that a human being generates another human being. There are some agents that are equivocal, such as the sun causing heat while being itself hot only in an equivocal sense. Therefore it seems that the first agent, to which all other agents are traced back, is a univocal agent. And thus what is said of God and creatures is predicated univocally.[14]

2. There is no observable likeness among equivocal things. Since creatures have a certain likeness to God according to Genesis (1:26)—"Let us make the human being to our image and likeness"—it seems that something univocal can be said of God and creatures.

3. It is said in the *Metaphysics* (10.1, 1053ª) that a measure is homogeneous with the thing measured. But, as it says in the same place, God is the first measure of all beings. Therefore God is homogeneous with creatures. Thus something can be said univocally of God and creatures.

On the contrary:[15] Whatever is predicated of various things under the same word but not according to the same meaning [*ratio*] is predicated equivocally.

13. A term is used univocally when it has the same precise meaning in reference to different things. Thus, in saying "the knife is sharp" and "the sword is sharp," we are using "sharp" in exactly the same way. We might also note that the quality of "sharpness" is brought about in the same way: through honing the blade.

A term is used equivocally when it has a different meaning when used in reference to different things. Thus, in the statements "the knife is sharp" and "the note is sharp," the word "sharp" has two different meanings, and the quality of sharpness is brought about in two different ways: in the former case by honing the blade and in the latter case by raising the pitch by (if you're playing a stringed instrument) increasing tension on the string.

14. A univocal agent is one that produces something essentially like itself: in the example given here, a human being produces a human being. An equivocal agent is one that produces something different (in various respects) from itself: in the example given here, the sun produces heat while not being itself hot. This is not a particularly helpful example, of course, since we know that the sun is in fact hot. Perhaps a better example might be that the sun, while being an orb, causes the creation of helium, which is not round. An even better example would be that, while human beings are univocal causes of other human beings, they are equivocal causes of things like ships and sculptures.

The objection argues that if God is, as Augustine put it, "the cause of all causes" (*City of God* 5.8), then God is an agent that produces something essentially like itself (i.e., a cause producing a cause), and therefore we speak of God univocally.

Note that the term "analogy," which Thomas will introduce in his response, is itself used analogously when applied to both language and causes.

15. In this article the *sed contra* breaks with Thomas's usual practice of offering only one counter-objection. As becomes apparent in the rest of the article, this is because Thomas is inclined to agree *neither* with the objections (which argue that our language about God is ultimately univocal) *nor* with the *sed contra* (which argues that our language about God is simply equivocal).

But no word is fitting for God when said with the same meaning it has when it is said of creatures. For instance, in creatures "wisdom" is a quality, but not in God.[16] Varying the genus changes the meaning of something, since the genus is part of the definition. And the same reasoning applies to other terms.[17] Therefore, whatever is said of God and of creatures is predicated equivocally.

Further, God is more distant from creatures than any creatures are from one another. Now the distance of some creatures from one another makes any univocal predication of them impossible, as in the case of those things that are not in the same genus. It is therefore even less the case that anything can be predicated univocally of God and creatures; rather, everything is predicated equivocally.

I answer: It is impossible for something to be predicated univocally of God and creatures. For every effect that is not equal to the power of its efficient cause receives the likeness of the agent not according to the same nature [*ratio*] but in a measure that falls short. Thus, what is divided and multiplied in the effects is in the agent simply and in a unified way; for example, the sun, by the exercise of one power, produces multiple and various forms in all inferior things.[18] In the same way, as said in the preceding article, all perfections existing in a divided and multiple manner in created things preexist in a united manner in God.

If, therefore, any term pertaining to perfection is applied to a creature, it signifies that perfection according to a meaning distinct from other perfections. For instance, when this term "wise" is said of a human being, we signify some perfection that is distinct from a human being's essence and power and existence and from all similar things. But in applying this term to God, we do not intend to signify anything distinct from God's essence or power or existence.[19] And so this term "wise," said of a person, in some way circumscribes and encompasses the thing signified, but not when it is said of God, when the thing it signifies remains uncomprehended and exceeding the meaning of the word.[20] So it is clear that this term "wise" is not said of

16. See 1.3 note 2.

17. In other words, if you have two different kinds of things, the same word must be used equivocally when applied to both. Thus we use the word "sharp" equivocally in the sentence, "Threatened with a sharp knife, the singer produced a sharp note."

18. Again, the sun is not a particularly helpful analogy. Perhaps a better example would be how a human being, through the single power of the intellect, can produce a variety of computers that each can reproduce some, but not all, of what the intellect can accomplish.

19. Thus far, Thomas's argument agrees with that of the first *sed contra*.

20. This second argument against univocity bears some resemblance to the second *sed contra*, though here Thomas's emphasis is on God's excess rather than God's distance. This will be important when he argues for the possibility of analogical speech about God.

God and human beings according to the same meaning [*ratio*]. And the same reasoning applies to other terms. Therefore no term is predicated univocally of God and of creatures.

Neither are such terms purely equivocal, as some have said.[21] Because if this were so then nothing could be known or demonstrated about God from creatures, for the reasoning would always fall into the fallacy of equivocation.[22] Such a view is not only contrary to the philosophers who prove many things about God but also contrary to what the Apostle says in Romans (1:20): "The invisible things of God are clearly seen by being understood through the things that are made." So it must be said that such words are said of God and creatures according to analogy—that is to say, according to proportion.[23]

Words are used analogically in two ways: either because many things have a proportion to one thing, in the way "healthy" is said of both medicine and urine in relation and in proportion to the health of a body, with one being a cause and the other a sign;[24] or from one thing having a proportion to another, in the way "healthy" is said of both medicine and an animal, since medicine is the cause of health in the animal body.[25]

In this way some things are said of God and creatures analogically, and not in a purely equivocal nor in a purely univocal sense. For we cannot speak of

21. For example, the Jewish philosopher Moses Maimonides (see *Guide of the Perplexed* 1.51–60).

22. In the fallacy of equivocation, we fail to recognize that the same word can have different meanings. So we might fallaciously argue that because a knife is sharp and poses a physical danger, so too a sharp note can cause physical (as opposed to aesthetic) harm. If a term such as "good" applied to God and creatures in a purely equivocal way, then we could never argue from the goodness of creatures to the goodness of God.

23. As becomes apparent in the remainder of this article, it is misleading to take "proportion" as a strict definition of "analogy" as Aquinas uses it (though in fact the Greek word "analogy" does mean "proportion"). The general form that analogies take is something like "A is to B as C is to D," and mathematical proportions can certainly be fit into this general analogical form; for example, "2 is to 4 as 3 is to 9." However, it is difficult to see what proportion is involved in an analogy like "a knife is to a steak as an axe is to a tree." In fact, not only is it clear that not everything that Thomas means by analogy is encompassed in proportion, but the case of analogy that he is concerned with here, the analogical application of human language to God, is one in which, strictly speaking, there can be no proportion, because God is infinite and there can be no proportion between finite and infinite. So here we might simply take "proportion" to mean that there is some ordered relationship that makes analogy possible, not that such a relationship can be expressed in an algorithm.

24. Medicine and a urine sample are both described as "healthy" because they are both related to the health of the body: medicine as a cause of it and urine as a sign of it (though today we might be more likely to speak of a "healthy diet" than "healthy medicine"). This is a case where the analogical use of the term "healthy" for both medicine and urine is made possible by their relationship to a third thing, the body, from which the primary meaning of "health" is drawn.

25. Whereas the first type of analogy involves the relationship of two uses of a term by virtue of their relationship to some third thing, in this second type we simply have two uses of a term related by virtue of the relationship of one thing to another.

God except from creatures, as was said earlier (1.13.1).[26] So whatever is said of God and creatures is said according to some relation of the creature to God as its principle and cause, in which the perfections of all things preexist in the most excellent way.[27]

This way of sharing meanings lies between pure equivocation and simple univocity. For in analogies the meaning is neither identical, as it is in univocals, nor totally different, as in equivocals. Rather, a term that is said in multiple ways signifies various proportions to some one thing. Thus "healthy" applied to urine signifies the sign of an animal's health, and applied to medicine it signifies the cause of that same health.

Reply to 1: Although in predications the equivocal must be traced back to the univocal, in actions the nonunivocal agent necessarily precedes the univocal agent.[28] For the nonunivocal agent is the universal cause of the whole species, as in the case of the sun being the cause of the generation of all people.[29] A univocal agent, however, is not the universal efficient cause of the whole species (otherwise it would be the cause of itself, since it is contained in the species), but is a particular cause of this individual, which it constitutes as

26. When Thomas says "in this way" (*hoc modo*), he might be saying here that the analogies involved in using human language to speak of God are only of the second type, because there is no third thing apart from God and creatures that relates the two. Most translations seem to presume this, rendering *hoc modo* as "in this latter/second way." Thomas returns, however, to the "medicine–urine" example (i.e., the first kind of analogy) at the end of his response, to illustrate the different *modi significandi* involved in analogy. So "in this way" might well be referring collectively to both forms of analogy.

27. God is the cause of creatures; therefore, language about creatures can be applied to God. But when we use those terms that imply perfection (e.g., "one," "good," "true," etc.), we use them more properly in speaking of God than we do in speaking of creatures, since God is the source of those perfections as we find them in creatures.

28. Here Thomas distinguishes between the relationship of the univocal and the nonunivocal (i.e., the equivocal or analogical) with regard to language ("predications") and with regard to causes ("actions"). Although it is true (as obj. 1 states) that in the case of language the nonunivocal use must be traced back to a univocal use (otherwise it would be impossible to say what a word means), this is not true in the case of causes.

It is important to remember that, for Thomas, all effects are *in some sense* like their causes. The contrast drawn in the objection is between univocal and equivocal causes, but for Thomas there can be no *purely* equivocal cause. In the case of the example given in the objection, the sun is not something entirely different from heat, since the sun is, in fact, hot. Or, to use a different example, while the shipbuilder and the ship do not share a common genus, one being a rational animal and the other a water vehicle, they do at the very least share being actually existing things. So when Thomas is speaking of a nonunivocal agent in this reply, he is not speaking of a purely equivocal one but of an analogical one, and this is perhaps what later Thomists mean by the "analogy of being" (a phrase Thomas himself never uses). Cf. note 33, below.

29. The example Thomas uses here (perhaps drawn from Aristotle's *Physics* 2.2, 194[b]) is confusing, since we do not normally think of the sun as a "cause" of the human race. But one must certainly agree that while the sun by itself does not produce human beings, without the sun there would be no human race.

a member of the species.[30] Therefore the universal cause of an entire species is not a univocal agent, and the universal cause comes before the particular cause.[31] But this universal agent, while it is not univocal, is nevertheless not altogether equivocal, because then it could not produce its own likeness. Rather it can be called an analogical agent, in the same way that in speech everything univocal is traced back to one first term that is not univocal but analogical—that is, "being."[32]

Reply to 2: The likeness of the creature to God is imperfect, because it does not even represent God as a member of the same genus as itself, as said earlier (1.4.3).[33]

Reply to 3: God is not a measure that is proportioned to things measured, so it is not necessary that God and creatures should be in the same genus.

The arguments to the contrary show that these terms are not predicated univocally of God and creatures, but not that they are predicated equivocally.

30. Univocal agents can cause only this or that particular thing belonging to the same class as themselves; they cannot cause the whole class of things because they would then be their own cause. Thus a human being can be the univocal cause of another human being, but not of the entire category "human being."

31. Because a species is logically prior to its individual members, and because only a nonunivocal agent can be the cause of a species, nonunivocal agents are logically prior to univocal agents.

32. Thomas returns here to the analogy between causes and language. Whatever we affirm in our language involves a logically prior affirmation of some sort of being. For example, consider the statements "The president *is* in the White House" and "The president *is* a human being." But note that Thomas says this most basic use of language is itself analogical, since it is not exactly the same thing to be a human being and to be in a particular location. Presumably, I could change my location without ceasing to be me, whereas I could not cease to be a human being without ceasing to be me.

Thinking of the link between being and language in terms of God as the analogical cause of creaturely existence, we can say that although God's existence and our existence are not entirely dissimilar, they are no more similar than the use of "is" in the statements "The president is in the White House" and "The president is a human being."

33. God and creatures do not share a category, not even that of "things that exist," since God is the *analogical* cause of the existence of creatures and the cause of a category cannot itself be contained in that category (see note 30, above). Indeed, as Thomas notes in several places, God is not contained in any category whatsoever—"Deus non est in genere" (see 1.3.5 and *Disputed Questions on the Power of God* 7.3)—which means that God is no "kind" of thing.

Question 27:

The Procession of the Divine Persons

1.27.1[1]

Is there procession in God?

It would seem that there cannot be any procession in God.[2]

1. Procession signifies outward movement. But in God there is nothing movable or external, so neither is there any procession.

2. Everything that proceeds is different from that from which it proceeds. In God, however, there is no opposition [*diversitas*], but supreme simplicity.[3] Therefore in God there is no procession.

3. To proceed from another seems incompatible with the idea of a first principle. But God is the first principle, as shown above (1.2.3). Procession, therefore, has no place in God.

On the contrary: Our Lord says in John (8:42), "From God I proceeded."

I answer: Divine Scripture uses words that pertain to procession in relation to divine realities.[4] This procession, however, has been understood in different ways.

Some have understood this procession in the way that an effect proceeds from its cause. This is how Arius took it, saying that the Son proceeds from the Father as his first creature and that the Holy Spirit proceeds from the Father and the Son as the creature of both. On this view, neither the Son nor

---

1. On this article, see McCabe (2002, 36–53); Emery (2007, 51–77).

2. "Procession" (*processio*) means "coming-forth," whether it be a person coming forth from her house or a thought coming forth from one's mind. *Processio* also has connotations of the English word "process," meaning an activity that issues in a result, which is not unrelated to the idea of "coming-forth," since the result "comes forth" from the person or thing engaged in the activity.

3. On "simplicity," see 1.3 note 2. In this context, the Latin word *diversitas* implies a kind of contrast or opposition.

4. Here Thomas seems to be thinking of the terms "son" (i.e., one who "comes forth" from his parents) and "spirit" (i.e., the Latin *spiritus*, which means "air" or "breath" that "comes forth" from the lungs).

the Holy Spirit would be true God.[5] This is contrary to what is said of the Son in 1 John (5:20), "That . . . we may be in his true Son; this is true God." Of the Holy Spirit it is also said in 1 Corinthians (6:19), "Do you not know that your members are the temple of the Holy Spirit?" But only God can have a temple.

Others understand this procession in the way that a cause proceeds to an effect, inasmuch as it either moves it or imprints its own likeness on it. This is how Sabellius took it, saying that God the Father himself is called "Son" inasmuch as he takes on flesh from the virgin, and he is likewise called "Holy Spirit" inasmuch as he sanctifies the rational creature and moves it to life.[6] Such an interpretation is repudiated by the words of our Lord, however, speaking of himself in John (5:19), "The Son cannot do anything of himself," as well as many other passages, in which it is shown that it is not the Father himself who is the Son.

Careful consideration shows that both of these opinions took "procession" to mean movement toward something external, and therefore neither posited procession as existing in God himself.[7] Every procession always involves some sort of action: just as there is an outward procession corresponding to action directed toward external matter, so too there is an inward procession corresponding to action remaining within the agent.[8] This latter kind of action is clearest in the case of the intellect, the action of which—that

5. The fourth-century theologian Arius held that the Son or Word who was incarnate in Jesus of Nazareth was a being that came forth from God in the same way that any other creature came forth; though the Word was the first and greatest of God's creatures, it was still a creature and thus essentially different from God. The Council of Nicaea's adoption of the term *homoousious* (which might be translated as "consubstantial" or "coessential") to describe the relation of the Word to the Father was intended as a refutation of Arius's view. Though the status of the Holy Spirit was not an explicit point of controversy at Nicaea, Thomas correctly surmises that Arius's view of the Word as a creature would also apply to the Spirit.

6. Sabellius was a Christian theologian of the third century who seems to have promoted the view that the Father, Son, and Spirit spoken of in the New Testament were simply three different "names" or "modes of appearing" of the one God. Thus when God is in heaven we call God "Father"; when God is incarnate in Jesus we call God "Son"; and when God is present to the church we call God "Spirit." One way of putting the matter is to say that for Sabellius the names "Father," "Son," and "Spirit" refer to how God relates to the world, not to relations within God.

7. In Thomas's writings, the names of Arius and Sabellius are often paired in order to illustrate the two principal errors one can make regarding the Trinity: either overstressing (Arius) or understressing (Sabellius) the difference between the Persons. On Thomas's use of opposed heresies to describe a doctrinal position, see 2–2.11 note 3, below.

8. Thomas is searching for a suitable analogy by which he can speak of an action of "coming-forth" that does not imply that what comes forth is essentially different from that from which it comes forth. The errors of Arius and Sabellius both stem from their inability to conceive of a genuine coming-forth that does not entail such a difference. Sabellius, to maintain the unity of God, denies that the coming-forth of the Son and Spirit is anything more than a way of expressing different modes of God's action in

is, understanding—remains within the one who understands. Whenever we understand, by the very fact of understanding something comes forth within us [*procedit aliquid intra ipsum*] that is a conception of the object understood, a conception coming from our intellectual power and proceeding from our knowledge of that object.[9] This conception is signified by the voice and is called the "word of the heart" [*verbum cordis*], signified by the word of the voice.[10]

Since God is above all things, what is said of God should not be understood according to the mode of the frailest of creatures—namely, bodies—but according to the likenesses of the greatest of creatures, which are intellectual substances, though even the likenesses derived from these fall short in the representation of divine things.[11] "Procession," therefore, is not to be understood from what it is in bodies, whether movement from one place to another or the action of a cause in its external effect, the way heat from something hot makes something else hot. Rather it is to be understood along the lines of an intellectual emanation—that is, like a mental word that remains within oneself. It is in this sense that the catholic faith posits procession in God.[12]

---

the world, whereas Arius, to maintain the genuineness of the coming-forth, says that the Son (and, by implication, the Spirit) is different in being from the Father.

One way of thinking about what Thomas means by "the act remaining within the agent" is to think in terms of transitive and intransitive verbs. A transitive verb has an object that "receives" its action ("The man hit *the dog*"), whereas an intransitive verb does not ("The man thought"). Both kinds of verb involve action, but the action of the intransitive verb remains "within" the one doing the action.

9. The analogy that Thomas finds most appropriate is one that he takes from St. Augustine: "And so you have a kind of image of the Trinity: the mind itself, and also its knowledge, which is its offspring and its word about itself, and, third, its love; these three are one and also one substance" (*De Trinitate* 9.12.18 [my trans.]). Thomas's emphasis on a coming-forth that remains in the agent, however, is somewhat different from Augustine's interest in how the analogy reconciles threeness and oneness.

10. The use of the term *verbum cordis* (word of the heart) suggests that, for Thomas, thinking is structured in a way analogous to language. This is reflected in his view that the word *intelligere* (understand) comes from *intus legere*—to read within (see 2–2.8.1; *Disputed Questions on Truth* 1.12). To know something is to have a concept of it, which is something like having a word for it. Further, it is *only* by means of its concept that we know something, even though it is the thing itself that we know, and not simply our conception of it.

11. We should always speak of God in analogies drawn from the highest creatures, while still recognizing that God infinitely surpasses even the most exalted of creatures. Thus, despite the trinitarian names "Father" and "Son," we should draw our understanding of "coming-forth" not from biological generation but from the spiritual generation that occurs in the soul when a concept ("the word of the heart") is formed. At the same time, we must recognize that God's eternal generation of the Word infinitely surpasses even the mind's generation of a concept.

12. At first glance, it might appear that here Thomas is elevating his particular way of understanding the "coming-forth" of the eternal Word—as analogous to the formation of a "mental word" or concept—to the status of dogma (i.e., a teaching that *must* be believed by the faithful). But in fact, Thomas is not saying this. Rather, he thinks that the analogy between eternal Word and mental concept is simply one possible

Reply to 1: This objection is based on the kind of procession that is movement from one place to another or involves action directed toward external matter or an external effect. But this kind of procession does not exist in God, as has been said.

Reply to 2: What proceeds by way of outward procession must be different [*diversum*] from that from which it proceeds. But what proceeds interiorly by means of an intellectual process is not necessarily different; indeed, the more perfectly it proceeds, the more it is one with that from which it comes. For it is clear that the more a thing is understood, the more intimately the intellectual conception is joined to the one who understands, and the more they are one, since by this act of understanding the intellect is made one with the object understood.[13] Thus, since the divine understanding is the limit of perfection, as said above (1.14.2), the divine Word is necessarily perfectly one with that from which he proceeds, without any kind of opposition [*diversitate*].

Reply to 3: To proceed from a principle so as to be something outside and opposed to that principle is contrary to the idea of a first principle; but to proceed by an act of intellect that is intimate and without opposition is included in the idea of a first principle. For when we say that the architect is the "principle" of a house,[14] the architect's concept of what he is going to make is included in this idea of "principle"; and if the architect were the *first* principle of the house, it would be included in the idea of the *first* principle. God, who is the first principle of all things, stands in relation to created things as the architect does to fabricated things.[15]

---

way (though perhaps the *best* possible way) of understanding what *is* a dogma of the church (defined at the Council of Nicaea in AD 325)—namely, that the Father brings forth the Son in such a way that the Son, while being distinct from the Father, shares fully in the Father's divinity.

13. Here Thomas is displaying the particular aptness of an intellectual process as an analogy for understanding procession in God. He notes that although the coming-forth of one material thing from another necessarily implies a distinctness of being (e.g., a woman producing a child is giving birth to someone distinct in being from herself), this is not the case in the coming-forth of a concept from the mind. In fact, the more perfect the intellectual process is, the more closely the concept will resemble what it is that the mind knows. Thus in knowing a cow, the mind receives the "intellectual species" of the cow and thus takes on the form of the cow without actually becoming a cow. In the bringing forth of the concept of the cow, the more closely that concept resembles the intellectual species that the mind has taken on, the more perfect this process of concept generation is. See 1.12 note 11.

14. "Principle" is used here in the sense of "source" or "starting point" or "originator."

15. The force of the objection is that first principles are not derived from anything else; if the Son proceeds from the Father, then he cannot be the first principle of creatures; but if he is not the first principle of creatures, then he is not God. In replying to this objection, Thomas holds to his analogy of intellectual procession. When an architect conceives of a house, we can properly speak of the house as deriving either from the architect or from the architect's conception of it, because the architect's conception is not something external to the architect's identity.

1.27.3[16]
Does any procession exist in God besides that of the Word?

It would seem that no other procession exists in God besides the generation of the Word.[17]

1. The same reason given for another procession would apply to yet another and so on to infinity, which is unfitting. We should therefore stop with the first and hold that there is only one procession in God.

2. In every nature is found only one way of communicating its nature. This is because operations derive unity and diversity from their results.[18] But procession in God is only by way of communication of the divine nature. Since, therefore, there is only one divine nature, as was shown earlier (1.11.4), it must be granted that only one procession exists in God.[19]

3. If any procession other than the intellectual procession of the Word existed in God, it could only be the procession of love, which is by the operation of the will. Such a procession, however, cannot be anything other than the intellectual procession, because in God will is the same as intellect, as was shown earlier (1.19.1).[20] Therefore in God there is no procession other than the procession of the Word.

On the contrary: The Holy Spirit proceeds from the Father, as is said in John (15:26), and is other [*alius*] than the Son, according to the same gospel (14:16): "I will ask my Father, and he will give you another [*alium*] Advocate."[21] Therefore, there is another procession in God beyond the procession of the Word.

I answer: There are two processions in God: the procession of the Word and another.

16. On this article, see McCabe (2016, 269–90); Emery (2007, 51–77).

17. Here Thomas is pursuing the analogy of human intellect in attempting to understand the Trinity, asking whether this analogy can provide us with a way of thinking about the procession of the Holy Spirit by analogy with a *second* "coming-forth" that remains within the rational agent, one that is distinct from the intellect's production of the concept.

18. The objection is that we judge two processes ("operations") to be the same if they issue in the same results. If we are talking about the process of a nature sharing or communicating itself, there can be only one such process because there is only one result. Thus when fire shares its nature with water (i.e., by heating it up), we have the single process called "heating." Any instance of fire communicating its nature is called "heating."

19. The only way there could be more than one process of self-communication of God's nature (i.e., more than one procession in God) would be if there were more than one divine nature, which would entail there being more than one God, since God *is* his nature.

20. This objection is, in essence, the same as the second objection in 1.27.1: How can the multiplicity of procession in God be reconciled with the idea that God is radically simple?

21. "Paraclete" (in Greek, *paraklētos*) means "advocate" or "comforter" and is a name the Gospel of John gives to the Spirit.

To see this clearly, one must bear in mind that there is no procession in God except according to an action that is not directed to anything external, but remains in the agent itself. In an intellectual nature such action is the action of the intellect and the action of the will. The procession of the Word is understood along the lines of an action of the intellect. The operation of the will within us involves also another procession, the procession of love, by which the object loved is in the lover, in the same way that by the conception of the word the thing spoken of or understood is in the one who understands.[22] Thus beyond the procession of the Word there is posited another procession in God, which is the procession of love.

Reply to 1: It is not necessary to go on to infinity in the divine processions. For the procession that is within an intellectual nature terminates in the procession of the will.[23]

22. The intellect has two operations of "coming-forth": knowing, which is an act of the intellect, and loving, which is an act of the will. But there seems to be a difficulty with this second kind of coming-forth, since we generally think of love involving something external to our will, something outside of us that draws us to itself. Thus love does not seem to be a coming-forth that remains within God. However, we might note (as Thomas does here) that just as through knowing something we virtually "become" what we know (see note 13, above), so in loving we virtually "become" what we love. In loving, we love the object as we apprehend it—that is, as it is *in* us. This would seem to account for how the operation of love in God can be a coming-forth that remains within God.

But there is still a problem. Although we know something by having a conception of it within our mind, we generally think that something has gone wrong if we love our idea of something rather than the thing itself. Indeed, Thomas does not think that our becoming what we love involves the generation of a "thing" in us at all (or at least nothing beyond the conception of it that our intellect has formed); rather it is what he calls "an impulse and movement toward an object" (1.27.4). In discussing this question in his *Compendium of Theology*, Thomas says, "The act of loving reaches its perfection not in a likeness of the beloved (in the way that an act of understanding reaches perfection in a likeness of the object understood); rather the act of love reaches its perfection in a drawing of the lover to the beloved person" (1.46).

The solution to this difficulty for Thomas is that the operation (or "breathing forth") of love in God is not a matter of God's love being drawn by something "external"; rather, it is the love of the Father (who is God) for the Son (who is God). The generation of the Son is the Father's knowing of his own divine nature, and the breathing forth of the Spirit is the impulse of love that comes forth from the Father and the Son in that act of knowing.

23. This rather curt reply anticipates what Thomas will say in 1.27.5. It is important to remember that Thomas does not think that by analyzing human reason he can prove that there is procession in God. Even if one accepts that both God and humans are intellectual beings, it does not follow that God's activity of knowing is the same as the human activity of knowing. We have no reason to think that God needs to generate a concept in order to know. What Thomas is trying to do is simply to find an analogy that can help us understand what we already accept on the basis of revelation—namely, that from the beginning there exists a Word that is with God and that is God, and that the Spirit that descended upon the Word-made-flesh and now makes the saints holy also comes forth from God. So if the objector *could* somehow demonstrate that human intellectual operations involve more than two "comings-forth," this would in no way disprove the Trinity; it would simply indicate that the analogy of human intellectual processes limps even more badly than was originally thought.

Reply to 2: Whatever exists in God is God, as was shown above (1.3.4), which is not the case with other things. Therefore the divine nature is communicated by whatever procession is not external, but this does not apply to other natures.[24]

Reply to 3: Though will and intellect are not different in God, nevertheless the meaning of will and intellect is such that the processions belonging to the action of each exist in a certain ordered relationship. For there is no procession of love except in an ordered relationship to the procession of the Word, since nothing can be loved by the will unless it is conceived in the intellect. So in this way we see a certain ordered relationship of the Word to the principle from which it proceeds, though in God the substance of the intellect and the concept of the intellect are the same. So too, though will and intellect are the same in God, nevertheless, there is still a distinction of order between the procession of love and the procession of the Word in God because the very meaning of love is that it comes forth [*procedat*] only from the conception of the intellect.[25]

24. This response is perhaps somewhat less than satisfactory. Thomas does not really answer the objection's claim that one nature equals one process of self-communication; he simply responds that this is not true in the case of God, referring back to the claim that anything "in" God *is* God—that is, shares the divine nature. Thus he seems entirely to beg the question (i.e., presumes what he sets out to prove) of whether there is a second procession in God. However, to understand what he is doing here, we should note two characteristics of Thomas's trinitarian theology that are implicit in this response.

First, Thomas *never* tries to prove that God is triune (see 1.32.1, below); this is something that he accepts on the basis of faith. Such an assumed starting point is not, however, question-begging, since Thomas is not trying to "prove" anything. Further, Thomas's response questions the objection's assumption that the analogy of a nature communicating itself can serve as a source of information about the number of processions in God. It cannot; only Scripture can give us that information.

Second, like the previous response, this response underscores the point that we should not push our analogies too far in speaking and thinking about God's nature. As much as the processions of the Word and Spirit are like a created being communicating its nature to something else (e.g., fire heating water), we cannot require these processions to conform to the communication of a created nature in every way. As the Fourth Lateran Council (1215) stated, "No likeness can be expressed between creator and creature without implying a greater unlikeness" (2).

25. The Latin word *ordo* can have the sense of "relation"—placing things in a certain order is a matter of giving them a particular set of relations to one another. What Thomas seems to be saying in this response is that he is willing to grant that because of divine simplicity (see 1.3 note 2) God's intellect and will are not things distinct from God's existence (in doctrinal terms, the Son and Spirit are both *homoousious* or of "one substance" with the Father). However, God's thinking and willing *do* have a certain relationship to each other that allows them to be distinguished from each other. Thus, when Thomas says that "there is no procession of love except in an ordered relationship to the procession of the Word," we could paraphrase him as saying that the procession of the Son and that of the Spirit are different because they are related in different ways to their origin: the Son proceeds from the Father as his image (just as the concept arises from the intellect's knowledge of itself), and the Spirit proceeds from the Father and (or through) the Son (just as the will must be moved by the concept of what attracts it). So the two cases of coming-forth (Son and Spirit), along with that from which they come forth (Father), are all the same "substance" (i.e., God), but they differ as the different terms of their different relations. See 1.36 note 11.

Question 29:

The Divine Persons

1.29.4[1]
Does this word "person" signify relation?

It would seem that in the case of God this word "person" does not signify a relation, but a substance.[2]

1. On this article, see Emery (2007, 78–127).
2. In the Latin West the vocabulary used to express trinitarian faith, dating at least from the writings of Tertullian (ca. 150–ca. 240), is that God is one *substantia* and three *personae*. In this article, Thomas is trying to relate what he has said in questions 1.27 and 1.28 about Father, Son, and Spirit as "relations" with this traditional theological vocabulary of the Western church, where they are called "Persons." As we shall see, the language of three Persons raises some significant theological difficulties, yet Thomas is unwilling to abandon the language, hallowed as it is by centuries of use. However, he will clarify that, when used in the case of the Father, Son, and Holy Spirit, "person" means "relation."

This is an extremely complex article, but the problem it addresses is not all that esoteric. Christians generally say that they believe in a "personal God," by which they mean a divine being that is distinct from the world, characterized by knowing and willing, and to whom they can relate in an interpersonal way. God is not simply an "impersonal" force. At the same time, the Christian tradition has used the word "person" as a way of expressing the distinction and relatedness among the Father and the Son and the Holy Spirit—the three "Persons" of the Trinity. But this seems to be a confused (and confusing) use of language: Is God a "person," or is God three "Persons"? Here Thomas is trying to sort this out.

All of the objections really turn on the same issue: if the Father, Son, and Spirit are "Persons," does this not entail their being three distinct substances (that is, three distinct "somethings"), and not simply relations? A complicating factor in this question is that the Latin word used for the unity of God—*substantia*—translates into Greek as *hypostasis*, the word used in the East for the distinctness of Father, Son, and Spirit. Both words literally mean "that which stands under." So when Greek-speaking Christians heard Latin-speaking Christians say that God was one *substantia*, they heard this as a denial that Father, Son, and Spirit were really distinct; in other words, they heard echoes of the Sabellian heresy (see 1.27 note 6). This mistaken impression could seem to be exacerbated by Thomas's claim that the Persons of the Trinity were "merely" relations of origin.

The notion of "relation" itself presents a further difficulty. Thomas conceives of a relation not as something "between" two entities, but—at least in the case of a "real" relation (see 3.1 note 10), which Thomas holds the Persons of the Trinity to be—as something that an entity possesses. In other words, "relation" is a property that exists in things, and not something that arises between them. In this understanding, Thomas follows Aristotle, for whom "relation" was one of the ten "categories" (see 1.3 note 3).

1. Augustine says in *De Trinitate* (7.6.11), "When we speak of the Person of the Father, we are speaking of nothing other than the substance of the Father . . . for 'person' is said with reference to himself, and not the Son."

2. The question "What?" refers to essence.[3] But, as Augustine says in the same place (*De Trinitate* 7.4.7; cf. 5.9.10), when we say "there are three who bear witness in heaven, the Father, the Word, and the Holy Spirit,"[4] and it is asked, "Three what?" the answer is, "Three Persons." Therefore "person" signifies essence.

3. According to the Philosopher in the *Metaphysics* (4.7, 1012[a]), what is signified by a word is its definition. The definition of "person" is "an individual substance possessing a rational nature," as stated earlier (1.29.1).[5] "Person," therefore, signifies substance.

4. "Person," in the case of human beings and of angels, does not signify a relation but rather something absolute.[6] Therefore, if in God it signified a relation, it would be said equivocally of God and of human beings and angels.

On the contrary: Boethius says in his *De Trinitate* (6) that every word pertaining to the Persons signifies relation. But no word pertains to the Persons more than this word "person" itself. Therefore this word "person" signifies relation.

I answer: A difficulty arises concerning the meaning of this word "person" in the case of God because, in contrast to the nature of the words pertaining to the essence, it is predicated plurally of the three,[7] nor does it refer to another in the way that words that signify a relation do.[8]

Because of this some have seen "person," taken absolutely by virtue of its basic meaning, as signifying the divine essence, as is the case with the words "God" and "wise"; but in order to meet heretical objections a council decreed

The difficulty is that "relation" is normally an accidental property of things, which cannot be the case with God, who is supremely simple and therefore has no accidents.

3. See 1.12 note 6.

4. This is the so-called "Johannine comma," which in the West during the Middle Ages was taken as an authentic part of the first letter of John (coming at 5:7). It is now apparent that this verse, which appears nowhere in Greek manuscripts, was a gloss on the text that found its way into the text itself. One should also note that Augustine's remark from *De Trinitate* about "three what?" makes no reference to the Johannine comma, though Thomas makes it sound as though it does.

5. This definition of "person," taken from Boethius (*De duabus naturis* 3), was a standard one in the Middle Ages. In the course of this article, Thomas takes this standard definition and modifies it significantly.

6. For "something absolute" read "a substance."

7. The "words pertaining to the essence" would be such terms as "goodness" or "wisdom" or "power." We do not say that God is "three goodnesses," even though the Father, Son, and Spirit are all in fact good. We do, however, say that God is "three Persons." On "predicated," see 1.3 note 3.

8. In other words, the Son can be "the Son" only because of his relation to the Father, which is implied in the word "Son" itself. But the word "person" has no such implication.

that it was to be taken in a relative sense,[9] and especially when used in the plural (as when we say, "three Persons") or when used with the addition of a distinguishing adjective (as when we say, "one is the Person of the Father, another of the Son," and so on). Used in the singular, however, it may be taken as either absolute or relative.

But this does not seem to be a satisfactory explanation, because if "person," by virtue of its proper meaning, expresses nothing but the divine essence, it follows that when we speak of "three Persons," the sophistry of the heretics would not have been silenced; instead, they would have been given an even greater opportunity to quibble.[10]

For this reason others said that "person" signifies in God both the essence and the relation. Some of these said that it signifies the essence directly [*in recto*] and relation indirectly [*in obliquo*], since "person" means something like "in itself one" [*per se una*], and oneness pertains to the essence.[11] To say that something is "in itself" [*per se*] implies relation indirectly, for the Father is understood to be in himself distinct from the Son on account of relation.[12] Others, however, have said the contrary: it signifies relation directly and essence indirectly,[13] since in the definition of "person" the term "nature" is mentioned indirectly.[14] This latter view came nearer to the truth.

9. In discussing this issue in his *Disputed Questions on the Power of God* 9.4, Thomas specifies that the council he is referring to is the Council of Nicaea, though it is difficult to find a place in the documents of Nicaea that corresponds to the view described here. In this same discussion, he also identifies one of the unnamed *quibusdam* (some) of the previous sentence ("some have thought") as Peter Lombard (see *Sentences* bk. 1, dist. 25).

10. Lombard and others claimed that the Council of Nicaea decreed that "person" be used in a peculiar way when one is speaking of the Persons of the Trinity, in order to respond to the threat of Arianism. Thomas says that such a peculiar use of language, imposed by a conciliar *fiat*, would not have been an effective answer to the heretics. Thomas recognizes that when we speak of God we must use our ordinary way of speaking in peculiar ways, but apparently if a particular use of language is *too* peculiar (so as to be entirely equivocal), it causes confusion among the faithful and ridicule from unbelievers. What Thomas wants to show is that the Council of Nicaea is not simply *inventing* a new use of the word "person" (i.e., "hypostasis") but is discovering a meaning of "person" that was implicit all along in our way of using the word.

11. Various figures have been suggested as among those Thomas is thinking about here: the twelfth-century theologians Simon of Tournai, Gilbert of Porrée, and Alan of Lille and the thirteenth-century theologian Alexander of Hales.

12. This view holds that if one takes unity—being a unique "something"—to be the key to the meaning of the word "person," then it is clear that the divine essence is "a person," since God's nature is unique. At the same time, the distinctness of Father, Son, and Spirit implies relation indirectly since their uniqueness is rooted in their relatedness, specifically each not being the other. As it is sometimes put, everything that is true of the Father is true of the Son and Spirit, except that the Father is neither the Son nor Spirit.

13. William of Auxerre (thirteenth century) is sometimes suggested as one who holds this view.

14. Thomas is referring to the Boethian definition of "person" as "the individual substance of the rational nature" (and he is using "nature" and "essence" interchangeably). He is pointing out that the definition does not speak of the nature itself, but of something belonging to the nature. Therefore "person" applies to a

To resolve this question, we must consider that something may be included in the meaning of a narrower term that is not included in the broader term, the way "rational" is included in the meaning of "human being" and not in the meaning of "animal."[15] So it is one thing to ask the meaning of "animal," and another to ask the meaning of "the human animal." Similarly, it is one thing to ask the meaning of this word "person" in general, and another to ask the meaning of "divine person."[16] For "person" in general signifies the individual substance of a rational nature. An individual, however, is that which is in itself undivided and distinct from others. In any nature, therefore, "person" signifies what is distinct in that nature, so that in a human nature it signifies *this* flesh and *these* bones and *this* soul, which are the sources of human individuality and which, though not belonging to the meaning of "person" in general, nevertheless do belong to the meaning of a particular human person.[17]

No distinction is made in God, however, except by relation of origin, as stated earlier (1.28.3).[18] Relation in God is not like an accident in a subject; it is the divine essence itself. Thus it is subsistent just as the divine essence subsists. Just as "godhood" [*deitas*] is God, so too divine "fatherhood" [*paternitas*] is God the Father, who is a divine Person.[19] Therefore "divine Person"

---

nature only indirectly, while it applies to what shares in the nature (i.e., the relations) directly. As Thomas notes, he thinks this view is closer to the truth.

15. Thomas here presumes the definition of human beings as "rational animals," so the category "human beings" is a narrower subcategory of the broader category of animals-in-general. What makes the subcategory narrower is that it includes more in its definition (i.e., the attribute "rational").

16. Thomas's point is that the specification "human" is not simply something added to a generic meaning of "animal" but modifies "animal" in such a way that it has a new meaning. Human animality is something different from animality in general. Likewise, the meaning of "person" when said of a divine Person is different from the generic meaning of "person."

17. Included in the generic meaning of "person" are those things that distinguish a person from other members of its class. In the case of human beings, for example, what makes one human person distinct from another is that he or she consists of this *particular* flesh, these *particular* bones, this *particular* soul, and so on; no other human person shares these particulars. Just as the qualifier "rational" is part of the definition of human beings but is not part of the definition of the broader category "animals," so too being constituted by these particulars is part of what it means to be this *particular* human being, but it is not part of what it means to be a human being in general.

The larger point here is that "human nature" is not a person; only particular instances of human nature are persons. Thus "human person" means this or that particular person, distinguished from other persons by being made of particular bones and flesh and soul. So although the particulars that make me who I am are not part of the definition of "person," since one can be a person without having *my* particular bones and flesh and soul, the definition of "human person" does require that one have *some* particular bones and flesh and soul; otherwise he or she would not be distinct. See 1.75.4, below.

18. See 1.27 note 25. The Persons in God, unlike human persons, are not distinguished by bones and flesh. They are distinguished by their relations of origin.

19. The barbarism "godhood" is an attempt to find a way of rendering *deitas* that would show its parallel with *paternitas*. It is important to follow Thomas's thinking here carefully. Although the relations are something distinct from one another, they are not distinct from all that it means to be God (i.e., "the divine

signifies a relation as subsisting. And this is to signify relation in the manner of a substance, and such a relation is a hypostasis subsisting in the divine nature,[20] although what subsists in the divine nature is nothing but the divine nature itself.[21]

Thus it is true to say that this word "person" signifies the relation directly, and the essence indirectly—but it does not signify the relation inasmuch as it is a relation, but inasmuch as it is signified in the manner of a hypostasis.[22] It likewise signifies the essence directly and the relation indirectly, since the essence is the same as the hypostasis. For "hypostasis" in God means what is distinct by virtue of a relation, and so relation, as such, enters into the definition of "person" indirectly.

We can also therefore say that this meaning of "person" was not clearly perceived before it was attacked by heretics, so "person" was used like any other absolute term. But afterward, "person" was adapted to stand for something relative, since it lent itself to that signification. So "person" stands for something relative not only from use and custom, as the first opinion says, but also from its own meaning.[23]

---

essence"); therefore, what is true of the divine essence is true of them as well. One of the things that are true of God is that God is "simple" (see 1.3 note 2), so just as *deitas* is not distinct from God, *paternitas* is not distinct from the Person of the Father. Thus the Person of the Father *is* the relationship of fatherhood.

20. On "hypostasis," see note 2, above.

21. Once again, since the relations are distinct from one another but not from the divine essence, they share fully in everything that the divine essence is. One of the things that the divine essence is is "subsisting." Thus the divine Persons are what Thomas terms "subsistent relations"—things constituted by and existing as their mutual relations. Just as "human person" means "human nature subsisting as particular bones, flesh, and soul," so "divine Person" means "the divine nature subsisting as a relation." And just as a human person is distinct insofar as he or she subsists in the particulars of this flesh, these bones, and this soul, so too are the divine Persons distinct insofar as they subsist in the particular relations of Father, Son, and Spirit.

It might also help to note that here Thomas is employing his distinction (see 1.13 note 8) between *what* is signified (*res significata*) and the *way* it is signified (*modus significandi*). Though the Persons are not different from the divine nature, because God is supremely simple, we speak of them as if they were accidents because our way of speaking about relations is taken from creatures, in which relations are accidental.

22. We cannot apply the word "person" to just any relationship, but only to those relationships of origin that are the Father, Son, and Spirit, because only those relations, by virtue of their identity with the divine essence, are subsistent. For example, if I am next to a tree, I have the relationship of being alongside the tree. But that "alongsideness" is not identical with my essence; if I move away from the tree, the "alongsideness" ceases to exist without changing who I am. In the case of God, however, the relations are hypostases that are identical with God's essence.

23. Here Thomas is trying to account for how the meaning of "person" as "that which makes a distinct instance of a nature" was overlooked for so long. The oversight was the result of the emphasis on the element of subsistence (i.e., independent existence) rather than on distinctness. But once we use the word "person" to mean "divine Person," we see that it can mean a relationship, so long as that relationship is not simply an attribute of something distinct (as "alongsideness" can be an attribute of mine so long as I am alongside the tree) but is itself something distinct.

Reply to 1: "Person" is said regarding the thing itself and not another, because it signifies a relation, not in a relation-like way, but in the manner of a substance that is a hypostasis. It is in that sense that Augustine says it signifies the essence, since in God essence is the same as the hypostasis, because in God there is not difference between "what he is" and "that whereby he is."[24]

Reply to 2: "What" sometimes asks about the nature expressed by the definition, as when we say, "What is a human being?" and we answer, "A mortal rational animal." Sometimes it asks about the subject [*suppositum*], as when we ask, "What swims in the sea?" and answer, "A fish." So to those who say, "Three what?" we answer, "Three Persons."[25]

Reply to 3: In the case of God the individual—that is, distinct and incommunicable substance—includes the idea of relation, as explained above.

Reply to 4: A different meaning of a less common term does not produce equivocation in a more common. Although "horse" and "ass" have their own proper definitions, nevertheless the word "animal" is used univocally in both cases because the common definition of "animal" applies to both. So although relation is contained in the meaning of "divine Person," but not in the meaning of "angelic person" or of "human person," it does not follow that the word "person" is used equivocally. But neither is it used univocally, since nothing can be said univocally of God and creatures, as was shown above (1.13.5).[26]

---

24. In a human person, what I am—that is, a specific human being—is something different from that which makes me human—that is, my human nature. In the case of the divine Persons, on the other hand, what they are—Father, Son, and Holy Spirit—is identical with what makes them divine—that is, the divine nature or essence.

25. When we ask "what?" sometimes we give the name and ask about the nature ("What is a fish?") and sometimes we give the nature and ask about the name ("What do you call that thing that swims in the sea?").

26. Language used about both God and creatures is analogical. Here the meaning of "person" in both cases fits the Boethian definition, "the individual substance of the rational nature," but in the case of creatures, persons are individuated either by matter (human beings) or by species (angels), whereas in the case of God the Persons are distinguished by their relations.

Question 32:

Knowledge of the Trinity

1.32.1[1]

Can the Trinity of divine Persons be known by natural reason?

It would seem that the Trinity of divine Persons can be known by natural reason.

1. Philosophers came to the knowledge of God only by natural reason, and yet we find in them many sayings about the Trinity of Persons.[2] Aristotle says in *On the Heavens and the Earth* (1.1, 268ª), "Through this number"—namely, three—"we bring ourselves to magnify the one God, whose attributes surpass all things created."[3] And Augustine says in his *Confessions* (7.9.13), "There"—that is, in the Platonic books—"I read, not in these words but with the same meaning, and suggested by many and various reasons, that 'in the beginning was the Word, and the Word was with God, and the Word was God,'" and so on, in which words the distinction of Persons is conveyed. It says, moreover, in a gloss on Romans 1 and Exodus 8, that the magicians of Pharaoh failed in the third sign—that is, as regards knowledge of a third Person, which is to say, the Holy Spirit—and so they at least knew two of the Persons.[4] Likewise Trismegistus says, "The monad begot a monad, and reflected upon itself its own ardor,"[5] by which the generation of the Son and procession of the Holy

---

1. On this article, see Emery (2007, 1–35).

2. The first objection offers examples of pagan thinkers who write in ways that sound as if they have knowledge of the Trinity. The point is that if these pagans knew of the Trinity, they must have done so by the exercise of their natural reason, since the Trinity was not revealed to them.

3. The objection quotes the translation of Gerard of Cremona (1114–87), who was working from Arabic and did not accurately represent what Aristotle actually wrote (i.e., "We make further use of the number three in the worship of the gods"). This article was probably written at some point prior to the fall of 1268. William of Moerbeke's far more accurate translation of *On the Heavens and the Earth* did not appear until 1271.

4. On "glosses," see 1.12 note 10.

5. "Hermes Trismegistus" was supposedly the author of the third-century "hermetic books," which represented a fusion of Platonism, Stoicism, and Eastern religions.

Spirit seem to be indicated. Therefore knowledge of the divine Persons can be obtained by natural reason.

2. Richard of St. Victor says in the book *De Trinitate* (1.4), "I believe without doubt that probable and even necessary arguments can be found for any explanation of the truth."[6] So even to prove the Trinity of Persons some have brought forward reasons based on the infinite goodness of God, who communicates himself infinitely in the procession of the divine Persons.[7] Some, however, argue from the principle that "no good thing can be joyfully possessed without partnership."[8] Augustine, however, proceeds to manifest the Trinity of Persons by the procession of the word and of love in our own mind, a way that we have followed above (1.27.1 and 3).[9] Therefore the Trinity of Persons can be known by natural reason.

3. It seems superfluous to pass on to human beings that which cannot be known by human reason. But it should not be said that the divine teaching of knowledge of the Trinity is superfluous. Therefore the Trinity of Persons can be known by human reason.

On the contrary: Hilary says in *On the Trinity* (2.9), "Let no one think to reach the sacred mystery of generation by one's own understanding." And Ambrose says, "It is impossible to know the secret of generation. The mind fails, the voice is silent" (*On the Catholic Faith* 1.10). But the Trinity of Persons in God is distinguished by origin of generation and procession, as is clear from what is said earlier (1.30.2). Therefore, since a person cannot know and understand something for which no necessary reason can be given, it follows that the Trinity of Persons cannot be known by reason.[10]

I answer: It is impossible to arrive at knowledge of the Trinity of divine Persons by natural reason. For, as shown above (1.12.4, 11, 12), human beings cannot arrive at knowledge of God by natural reason except from creatures,

---

6. The second objection offers examples of Christian thinkers who tried to show the necessity of God's triunity through the use of natural reason. On the whole, medieval theologians, with the possible exception of Peter Abelard, did not try to demonstrate the Trinity in such a way as to convince those who did not already believe in it. Rather, beginning from faith in the Trinity, they tried to discover "necessary reasons" why God *must* be triune. As we shall see, for Thomas, even this more modest task causes reason to step beyond its proper limits.

7. This sort of argument, based on the "self-diffusiveness" of the Good, can be found not only in Richard's *De Trinitate* but also in Bonaventure's *Itinerarium* 6.2.

8. In his *Disputed Questions on Truth* 10.13, obj. 6, Thomas identifies Boethius as the source of this quotation, though it in fact comes from Seneca's sixth epistle.

9. As the objection points out, Thomas himself uses this analogy to explore the Persons of the Trinity (see articles 1.27.1 and 3, above). The objection seems to presume that, beginning from our knowledge of our faculties of memory, reason, and will, we can argue that God is necessarily three in one.

10. For the sense in which *scientia* involves knowledge of conclusions flowing necessarily from premises, see 1.1 notes 17 and 21, above.

while creatures lead us to the knowledge of God in the way that effects lead to their cause. By natural reason, therefore, we are able to know of God only what is necessarily applicable to him as the source of all beings, and we have cited this fundamental principle in discussing God earlier (1.12.12). The creative power of God, however, is common to the whole Trinity, and therefore it pertains to the unity of the essence, and not to the distinction of the Persons.[11] So by natural reason we can know of God what pertains to the unity of the essence, but not what pertains to the distinction of the Persons.[12]

Whoever, then, relies on natural reason to prove the Trinity of Persons takes away from faith in two ways. First, with respect to the dignity of faith itself, which is that it is concerned with invisible things that exceed human reason. Thus the Apostle says in Hebrews (11:1) that "faith is of things that appear not." Second, with respect to the usefulness of drawing others to the faith. For those who, trying to prove the faith, bring forward reasons that are not cogent are subject to the ridicule of unbelievers, since they suppose that we rely on such arguments and that we believe on account of them.[13]

Thus we must not attempt to prove what belongs to faith, except through authorities to those who receive them. As regards others, it suffices to prove that what faith teaches is not impossible.[14] Therefore Dionysius says in *On the Divine Names* (2.2), "If someone wholly resists [divine] utterance [*eloquiis*], he will be far off from our philosophy. . . . If, however, he considers the truth of the utterance"—that is to say, Holy [Scripture]—"we too follow this rule."

Reply to 1: The philosophers did not know the mystery of the Trinity of the divine Persons by its properties, which are paternity, sonship, and procession,[15] for according to the Apostle's words in 1 Corinthians (2:6), "We speak the

---

11. Here Thomas invokes the theological principle that, with regard to the world, the Trinity always works as a unity; it is the Trinity that creates, redeems, and sanctifies the world, not one or the other of the Persons of the Trinity. Behind this principle is the notion that the Persons of the Trinity are not simply three "functions" of God (e.g., creating, redeeming, and sanctifying), nor are they a divine "division of labor"; rather, they are a communion of love that acts out of the plentitude of the shared life of the Persons as a unity in our world.

12. Natural reason knows God by arguing from effects to their cause. But the effects of God in the world are brought about by the Persons of the Trinity acting as one; therefore all we can know about God from the world is that God is a unity, not that God is triune. Knowledge of the Trinity must come to us through God's self-revelation in Jesus Christ.

13. In other words, if you use reason to prove something that cannot be proved by reason, you end up looking stupid and you and your beliefs will be mocked.

14. As we saw earlier (see 1.1 notes 28 and 32), you can prove things to those who grant your first principles but not to those who do not. Thomas does think, however, that you can show people who do not grant your first principles that your views are not impossible. This is what Thomas does with the Christian doctrine of the Trinity: he shows that it is not an *un*reasonable belief, even if it is a belief at which one cannot arrive through reason alone.

15. See 1.36 note 11.

wisdom of God, which none of the princes of the world know"—by which he means, according to the gloss, the philosophers. Yet they knew some of the essential attributes appropriated to the Persons, such as power to the Father, wisdom to the Son, and goodness to the Holy Spirit, as will be made clear later.[16]

So, when Aristotle said, "By this number," and so on, we must not understand this to mean that he applied a threefold number to God, but that he wished to say that the ancients used the threefold number in their sacrifices and prayers on account of some perfection residing in the number three.

In the Platonic books we find "In the beginning was the word," not meaning by "word" the Person begotten in God, but the ideal pattern (*ratio idealis*) of things by which God made everything, and which is appropriated to the Son.[17] And even if the Platonists knew things appropriated to the three Persons, yet they are said to have failed in the third sign—that is, in the knowledge of the third Person—because they deviated from goodness, which is appropriated to the Holy Spirit, because knowing God "they did not glorify him as God," as said in Romans (1:21). Or perhaps, since the Platonists asserted the existence of one primal being whom they also declared to be "father of the whole universe," they consequently asserted another substance beneath him that they called "mind" or the "father's intellect," in which were the ideas of all things, as Macrobius relates in his *Commentary on the Dream of Scipio* (1.2).[18] They did not, however, assert the existence of a third separate substance that might correspond to the Holy Spirit. Moreover, we do not assert in this way that the Father and the Son differ according to substance, which was the error of Origen and Arius, who followed the Platonists in this matter.[19]

What Trismegistus says—"Monad begot monad," and so on—does not refer to the generation of the Son, or to the procession of the Holy Spirit, but to the production of the world. For one God produced one world on account of his love for himself.

16. Despite things that sound like Christian trinitarian belief in their writings, pagan philosophers did not know the Trinity itself. Thus, for example, though they knew that God possessed power, wisdom, and goodness, they did not attach or "appropriate" those divine attributes to distinct divine Persons. On Aquinas's understanding of trinitarian "appropriations," see 1.39.7, below.

17. In Greek, the term *logos* can mean both "reason" and "word." The Platonists knew that God possessed reason, but they did not conceive of this as a distinct Person (i.e., the Word) within the Godhead.

18. Macrobius was a Latin Neoplatonist writer of the fifth century.

19. Thomas suggests that, lacking divine revelation, the best the Platonic philosophers could have done regarding the Trinity was something approximating the views of Arius (see 1.27 note 5, above). Indeed, he says it is because Arius thought of the Son and the Spirit in a Platonist manner that he fell into error. Western medieval theologians generally thought Origen held something like the view of Arius, though modern scholarship shows that the matter is a good deal more complicated, and in many ways Origen anticipates later trinitarian orthodoxy.

Reply to 2: Reason is brought to bear on things in two ways. In one way, it is used for the purpose of furnishing sufficient proof of some fundamental premise, as in natural *scientia*, where reasons are brought forth that are sufficient to prove that the movement of the heavens is always of uniform velocity. In the other way, reasons are brought forth not as furnishing a sufficient proof of a fundamental premise but as confirming an already established premise by showing the congruity of its results, in the way that the theory of eccentrics and epicycles is considered as established in astronomy because the visible appearances of the heavenly movements can be explained by it. But it is not as if this reasoning were sufficient as proof, since some other theory might explain them.[20] In the first way, we can prove that God is one, and similar matters. In the second way, reasoning leads to showing forth [*manifestationem*] the Trinity; that is, assuming the Trinity to be true, it is shown to be congruent with reason. We must not, however, think such reasoning sufficient to prove the Trinity of Persons.[21]

This becomes evident when we consider each point. The infinite goodness of God is shown forth also in creation, because to produce from nothing is an act of infinite power. For if God communicates himself by his infinite goodness, it is not necessary that an infinite effect should proceed from God, but simply that according to its own mode and capacity it should receive the divine goodness.[22] Likewise, when it is said that "no good thing can be joyfully possessed without partnership," this holds in the case of one person who is imperfect in goodness and therefore, in order to have the goodness of complete happiness, needs to share in someone else's good. Nor is the image in our intellect sufficient to prove something about God, since intellect is not found univocally in God and us. Therefore, Augustine says in his commentary on John (*Sermon 27, 7*, in *Homilies on the Gospel of John*) that by faith we arrive at knowledge, and not the other way around.[23]

20. Thomas makes his point with yet another distinction: reason can be used to demonstrate a fact, or reason can be used to show that a fact we have accepted on some other basis can be made to fit with what we know through reason. The astronomical specifics of "eccentrics" and "epicycles" (circles that have their center on the circumference of other circles), by which ancient astronomers such as Ptolemy attempted to explain what they observed in the heavens, are not particularly significant to the point he is making, except inasmuch as they are part of a theoretical account intended to cast light on something established on the basis of empirical observation.

21. Reason can "manifest" or show forth the harmony or congruence of Christian trinitarian faith with what reason can tell us about God, but it cannot *demonstrate* that faith. Put another way, reason cannot discover the land of trinitarian faith, but it can help us explore that land once it is discovered. This is the kind of use to which reason is put in arguments from "fittingness" (see 3.1 note 2).

22. Against views like those of Richard of St. Victor, Thomas claims that creation would be a sufficient sharing of God's goodness, so that one need not posit "otherness" in God.

23. In other words, the objection has misread Augustine's intent in offering an analogy for the Trinity drawn from the human mind.

Reply to 3: There are two reasons why the knowledge of the divine Persons was necessary for us. In one way, it was necessary for thinking correctly about creation. By saying that God made all things by his Word, we exclude the error of those who say that God's production of things was necessitated by his nature. When we say that in him there is a procession of love, we show that God produced creatures not because he needed them, nor because of some other extrinsic cause, but on account of love of his own goodness. So Moses, after saying, "In the beginning God created heaven and earth" (Gen. 1:1), added, "God said, 'Let there be light'" (Gen. 1:3), to show forth the divine Word, and then said, "God saw that the light was good" (Gen. 1:4), to show confirmation of divine love, and likewise in the other works of creation.

In another way, and chiefly, it was necessary for thinking correctly about the salvation of the human race, accomplished by the incarnate Son and by the gift of the Holy Spirit.[24]

24. Thomas thinks knowledge of the Trinity adds two things to our knowledge of God. (1) It shows us that God was in no way compelled to create the world: God was not "lonely" and in need of something to love; rather, the world is an overflow of the love shared by Father, Son, and Spirit. (2) It shows us that in our salvation through Christ and the Holy Spirit it is truly God himself who saves us. The doctrine of the Trinity is not some esoteric bit of information about the inner life of God; rather, it is a necessary backdrop to a proper understanding of God's two great acts on our behalf: our creation and our re-creation through Christ and the Spirit.

Question 36:

The Person of the Holy Spirit

1.36.2[1]

Does the Holy Spirit proceed from the Son?

It would seem that the Holy Spirit does not proceed from the Son.[2]

1. According to Dionysius (*On the Divine Names* 1), "We must not dare to say anything concerning substantial divinity beyond what has been divinely expressed to us by holy utterance." In Holy Scripture we are not told that the Holy Spirit proceeds from the Son, but only that he proceeds from the Father, as is clear in John (15:26): "The Spirit of truth, who proceeds from the Father." The Holy Spirit, therefore, does not proceed from the Son.

2. In the creed of the Council of Constantinople we read, "We believe in the Holy Spirit, the Lord and giver of life, who proceeds from the Father; with the Father and the Son adored and glorified." So in no way should

---

1. On this article, see Emery (2007, 269–97).

2. The issue here is one that has contributed to the split between the Eastern and Western churches. The creed promulgated by the Council of Constantinople in 381 (commonly called the "Nicene Creed") reads, "We believe in the Holy Spirit, the Lord, the giver of life, who proceeds from the Father, who with the Father and the Son is worshiped and glorified." At a local council in Toledo, Spain, in 589, the word *Filioque* ("and the Son") was first added to the phrase "proceeds from the Father." Over the course of the Middle Ages this usage spread throughout the Western church and was adopted in Rome (which was originally not inclined to accept it) around the year 1000. The *Filioque* became a point of theological controversy between East and West in 867 when Photius, the patriarch of Constantinople, accused the Western church of unwarranted innovation leading to a host of theological difficulties. Photius argued that the claim that the Father and Son together were the source of the Spirit was equivalent to saying that the divine essence, which the Father and Son share, was the source of the Spirit. But since the Spirit shares the divine essence no less than the Son and the Father, this would mean that the Spirit was the source of his own procession (*Mystagogy of the Holy Spirit* 6). Further, Photius saw the *Filioque* as a denigration of the Spirit, writing in a letter to the bishops of the Eastern church, "By the *Filioque* teaching, the Holy Spirit is two degrees or steps removed from the Father, and thus has a much lower rank than the Son." In his view, the *Filioque* was not simply bad theology; it was heresy.

it be added in our creed that the Holy Spirit proceeds from the Son, and those who added such a thing appear to be deserving of condemnation (*anathema*).[3]

3. John of Damascus says (*On the Orthodox Faith* 1.8), "We say the Holy Spirit is from the Father, and we name him the Spirit of the Father, but we do not say the Holy Spirit is from the Son, yet we name him the Spirit of the Son." Therefore the Holy Spirit does not proceed from the Son.

4. Nothing proceeds from that in which it rests.[4] But the Holy Spirit rests in the Son, for it is said in the legend of Blessed Andrew, "Peace to you and to all who believe in one God the Father, and in his one Son our only Lord Jesus Christ, and in the one Holy Spirit, proceeding from the Father and abiding in the Son."[5] Therefore the Holy Spirit does not proceed from the Son.

5. The Son proceeds as the Word. Yet in us our breath [*spiritus*] does not seem to proceed from our word.[6] Neither, then, does the Holy Spirit proceed from the Son.

6. The Holy Spirit proceeds perfectly from the Father. It is therefore superfluous to say that he proceeds from the Son.

7. It is said in the *Physics* (3.4, 203[b]) that "to exist [*esse*] and to be possible [*posse*] do not differ in things that are perpetual," and much less so in God. But it is possible for the Holy Spirit to be distinguished from the Son, even if he did not proceed from him,[7] for Anselm says in his *On the Procession of the Holy Spirit* (1), "The Son and the Holy Spirit, to be sure, have their existence from the Father, though in different ways: one being born and the other by proceeding, so that they are thus distinct from each other." And after this he says, "For even if for no other reason were the Son and the Holy Spirit distinct, this alone would suffice." Thus the Holy Spirit is distinct from the Son, without existing from him.

---

3. As much at issue as the question of the *Filioque* itself was the question of the authority of the Western church to make an addition to the creed without consent of the Eastern church. The objection quotes the Nicene-Constantinopolitan Creed of 381 in its original form and notes the anathemas (i.e., condemnations) leveled against those who would add to it.

4. In other words, "coming-forth" and "remaining" appear to be contradictory.

5. The legend of Blessed Andrew is found in Migne, Patrologia Graeca 2:1217.

6. The objection is drawing on the fact that in Latin (as also in Greek and Hebrew) the same word means both "spirit" and "breath." Therefore, the point is that just as our breath *accompanies* our words and does not *originate* in them, so too the Spirit *accompanies* the Word but does not *originate* in him.

7. Since God is pure act (see 1.3 note 12), the objection argues, if something is possibly true of God, then it must be actually true; and since the distinct coming-forth of the Spirit is *possible* without the Spirit coming forth from the Son, this distinct coming-forth must be *actually* the case. The objector goes on to cite Anselm in support of the view that the distinction between "birth" and "proceeding" is sufficient to make possible the distinction between the Son and the Spirit.

On the contrary: Athanasius says, "The Holy Spirit is from the Father and the Son, neither made nor created nor begotten, but proceeding."[8]

I answer: It is necessary to say that the Holy Spirit is from the Son. For if he were not from him, he could in no way be personally distinguished from him, which is clear from what has been said earlier (1.28.3; 1.30.2). It cannot be said that the divine Persons are distinguished from one another on account of anything absolute, because it would follow that there would not be one essence of the three, since everything that is said of God in an absolute sense pertains to the unity of essence. So it must be said that the divine Persons are distinct from one another only by the relations.[9]

But the relations can only distinguish the Persons inasmuch as they are opposites. This is clear from the fact that the Father has two relations: one by which he is referred back to the Son, and the other to the Holy Spirit. Yet these, because they are not opposites, do not make two Persons, but pertain only to the one Person of the Father. If therefore in the Son and the Holy Spirit there were found only the two relations by which each was related to the Father, these relations would not be opposites of each other, just as neither of the two relations by which the Father is related to them would be opposed. So it would follow that, just as the Person of the Father is one, the Person of the Son and of the Holy Spirit would also be one, having two relations that are opposites of the two relations of the Father.[10] But this is heretical, destroying faith in the Trinity. Therefore, the Son and the Holy Spirit must be related to each other by opposite relations.

In God the only relations in opposition to one another are relations of origin, as proved earlier (1.28.4). Now opposite relations of origin are to be understood in the sense of a "source" [*principium*] and "what is from the

---

8. Here Thomas is quoting not Athanasius himself but the so-called Athanasian Creed, which is a Latin composition that dates from a time later than Athanasius, probably the late fifth century.

9. As mentioned before (1.29 note 2), Eastern Christians have tended to read statements such as "It cannot be said that the divine Persons are distinguished from one another on account of anything absolute" and "The divine Persons are distinct from one another only by the relations" as implying that the Father, Son, and Spirit are not *really* distinct and that the Persons are *merely* relations. This, however, is certainly not what Thomas means. Thomas's point is that the Father, Son, and Spirit are constituted as distinct precisely *through* their relatedness, not *in spite of* it.

10. Here Thomas is addressing the issue raised in the seventh objection, which claims that the Son and Spirit are sufficiently distinct because of their different ways of coming-forth from the Father: the former by being begotten or born and the latter by being breathed-forth or proceeding. For Thomas, these two ways of coming-forth are insufficient to establish the distinction between the Son and Spirit; rather, these two ways of coming-forth are sufficient to establish only the distinction of Son and Spirit from the Father, because these ways say nothing of the relation of origin that the Son and Spirit have with regard to *each other*. If the Son and the Spirit are indistinguishable apart from the word used to describe their coming forth, then we have at best some sort of quasi-Sabellianism, in which the Son and Spirit differ in name only (see 1.27 note 6).

source" [*quod est a principio*]. We must therefore conclude that it is necessary to say either that the Son is from the Holy Spirit, which no one says, or that the Holy Spirit is from the Son, as we profess.[11]

Furthermore, this is in harmony with the order of the procession of each. For it was said earlier (1.27.2, 4; 1.28.4) that the Son comes forth in a manner like that of the intellect, as Word, but the Holy Spirit comes forth in a manner like that of the will, as love. Now love must proceed from a word, for we do not love something unless we grasp it by a mental conception. In this way it is likewise clear that the Holy Spirit proceeds from the Son.

The very order of things teaches this same truth.[12] For nowhere do we find that several things proceed from one thing without any relation [*ordine*] to one another, except in those that differ only by their matter, as is the case when one knife maker produces many knives distinct from one another materially, but having no relation [*ordinem*] to one another.[13] In things in which

11. Thomas is referring back to an earlier discussion (1.32.2–3) in which he treats the five *notiones* or abstract concepts by which we know the relations that are the Persons of the Trinity. He describes these "notions" as follows: "The divine essence is signified as *what*; and the Person as *who*; and the property as *whereby*" (1.32.2); so the subsistent relations are "whos," and the abstract concepts are those things "by which" the subsistent relations are conceived of as distinct. We might see these notions as ways of speaking of the actions by which the Persons originate in relation to one another: "unbegottenness" (*innascibilitas*), which is the Father's being-without-origin (for Thomas, not an originating act, but something like a non-originating non-act that is logically entailed by the other notions); "fatherhood" (*paternitas*), which is the Father's act of originating the Son as his likeness; "sonship" (*filiatio*), which is the Son's act of coming forth from the Father; "shared breathing-forth" (*communis spiratio*), which is the Father and Son's shared act of originating the Spirit; and "coming-forth" (*processio*), which is the Spirit's act of coming forth from the Father and Son. Notice that all of these notions except *innascibilitas* refer to origination, either as the one who produces or the one who is produced. And this relatedness in terms of origination must be expressed in terms of mutually exclusive notions.

So the relationship between the Father and the Son is known by two opposed notions: *paternitas* and *filiatio*: within the same relationship, one cannot be both father and son (though, of course, someone's son could in turn become someone else's father). Likewise, the relationship between the Father and the Spirit is known by two opposed notions: *spiratio* and *processio*—one cannot be both the breather and the breath that comes forth. It is these oppositions that enable the Persons to be known as distinct.

Thomas's specific point here is that the notions *filiatio* and *spiratio*, while indeed *different* notions, are not *opposed* notions, because they do not describe a "producer" but two things that are produced. So if the Son and Spirit are to be known as distinct from each other, then there must be a notion by which one can be known as the producer of the other. Thomas's solution is to say that the Father and the Son are both known by the notion *spiratio* or, more properly, *spiratio communis* (shared breathing-forth). The Spirit proceeds from the Father *and* the Son—as the creed declares once the *Filioque* has been added to it—and so Son and Spirit are distinct from each other as "producer" and "produced."

He notes that the difficulty could also be solved if the Spirit were understood as the producer of the Son. But, he goes on to say, there is no precedent for this notion in Scripture or tradition.

12. In this paragraph and the following one, I translate the various forms of *ordo* sometimes as "order" and sometimes as "relation" (see 1.27 note 25). In the latter case, I have put the Latin in parentheses.

13. Even if the knife maker could produce two knives that were identical to each other, they would be different inasmuch as they would be made out of different matter and therefore could not occupy the

there is not simply a material distinction, we always find that some relation [*ordo*] exists in the many things produced. Thus the beauty of the divine wisdom is displayed in the order of creatures produced. If therefore from the one Person of the Father two Persons proceed, the Son and the Holy Spirit, there must be some relationship [*ordinem*] between them, and no other relationship can be assigned to them except the order of their nature, by which one is from the other. So it is not possible to say that the Son and the Holy Spirit proceed from the Father in such a way that neither of them proceeds from the other, unless we posit a material distinction in them, which is impossible.[14]

The Greeks themselves recognize that the procession of the Holy Spirit has some relation [*ordinem*] to the Son, for they concede that the Holy Spirit is "the Spirit of the Son" [*Spiritum Filii*] and is from the Father "through the Son" [*a Patre per Filium*]. And some of them are said to concede that he is "from the Son" [*a Filio*] or "flows from him" [*profluat ab eo*], but not that he proceeds. This refusal seems to come either from ignorance or from impudence. Because if one thinks about this correctly, one finds that "procession" is, out of all the terms used to denote any sort of origin, the one of widest application, for we use it to describe origin of any kind. Thus we say that a line proceeds from a point, a ray from the sun, a stream from a source, and likewise in everything else. Therefore, if one grants that the Holy Spirit originates in *any* way from the Son, we can conclude that the Holy Spirit proceeds from the Son.[15]

---

same place at the same time. So their distinctness comes not from how they stand in relation to each other, but from the fact that they are composed of different matter.

14. Material things can be distinguished by their matter; nonmaterial things, such as angels and God, must be distinguished from one another by the order or relationship (*ordo*) that they have with one another. In the case of the angels' relationship to one another or the angels' relationship to God, this order is one of greater and lesser perfection. As Thomas puts it in his *Disputed Questions on the Power of God* 10.5, "In nonmaterial things, which cannot be multiplied through material differences, it is impossible for there to be plurality except through some kind of order. Thus in nonmaterial created substances there is an order of more-and-less-perfect, by which one angel is more perfect in nature than another." On the nonmateriality of the angels and the implications of this, see 1.50.1, below.

But this obviously cannot be the case with the Persons of the Trinity, since no one Person shares more perfectly in the divine nature than another. In this article of the *Summa*, Thomas leaves this loose end untied, but in the disputed question he continues, "Since it is impossible for there to be an order of [greater and less] perfection in God (as the Arians proposed, saying that the Father is greater than the Son, and both are greater than the Holy Spirit), we must conclude that a plurality of divine Persons can be understood only according to the relationships of origin—that is to say, the Son being from the Father and the Holy Spirit from the Son." The order is not one of greater or lesser perfection, but of origin.

15. Thomas accuses his opponents of verbal quibbling, noting that they grant that the Spirit somehow originates from the Son yet they balk at the word "proceeds." His point is that "originate" and "proceed" are, in everyday usage (e.g., in geometry), synonyms. Thus although Thomas is willing to make a distinction between the ways in which the Spirit proceeds from the Father and from the Son—the Spirit proceeds

Reply to 1: We should not say anything about God that is not found in Holy Scripture either explicitly or implicitly [*vel per verba vel per sensum*]. Although we do not find it said explicitly in Holy Scripture that the Holy Spirit proceeds from the Son, we do find it implicitly, above all where the Son says in John (16:14), speaking of the Holy Spirit, "He will glorify me, because he shall receive from what is mine [*de meo*]."[16] Also, it is a rule of Holy Scripture that whatever is said of the Father ought to be understood as applying to the Son, even if an exclusive term is added,[17] except in cases in which the Father and the Son are distinguished from each other by opposite relations. Thus when the Lord says in Matthew (11:27), "No one knows the Son except the Father," the idea of the Son knowing himself is not excluded. Therefore when we say that the Holy Spirit proceeds from the Father, even if it is added that he proceeds from the Father alone, the Son would not be at all excluded by this, because the Father and the Son are not opposed to each other in being the source of the Holy Spirit, but only in the fact that one is the Father and the other is the Son.

Reply to 2: In every council a creed has been formulated on account of some error condemned in that council. Subsequent councils are not making a different creed but are explaining what was implicitly contained in the first creed by some addition directed against heresies arising at that time. Thus in the decision of the Council of Chalcedon it is said that those who were

---

from the Father *through* the Son (1.36.3)—he maintains that this distinction does not constitute a denial that the Spirit proceeds from Father and Son together, as *unum principium* (1.36.4).

Thomas is perhaps being a bit unfair to his opponents. What he dismisses as mere verbal quibbling in fact reflects a real difference between the Greek and Latin languages. Medieval theologians may have had an insufficient understanding of the semantic difference between the Greek *ekporeuesthai* (meaning specifically "to issue forth as from an origin") and the Latin *procedere* (meaning more generically "to move forward" or "to come forth"), which is more akin to the Greek *proienai*. In recent ecumenical dialogues between Roman Catholic and Orthodox theologians, it has been argued that both the Orthodox condemnation of the *Filioque* and the Roman countercondemnation were based on a failure to recognize that the Latin tradition used one word (*procedere*) where the Greek tradition used two (*ekporeuesthai*, for the Spirit's coming forth from the Father, and *proienai*, for the Spirit's coming forth from the Son). This has undeniably been one factor in the mutual incomprehension between East and West, though greater clarity on terminology does not itself resolve the difference.

16. It may not be immediately apparent how this verse supports the *Filioque*. In his *Commentary on the Gospel of John* (16.4.2115), Thomas clarifies his point somewhat, noting that the preposition *de* "expresses consubstantiality along with a relation of origin." So, according to Thomas, when Christ says that the Spirit receives "from" (*de*) what is his and then says that what is his is "all that the Father has" (John 16:15), Christ is saying implicitly (*quantum ad sensum*) that he, along with the Father, is the source of the Spirit's divine essence.

17. In other words, even if "alone" or "only" is added. In interpreting a passage such as John 17:3—in which Christ prays to the Father, "That they may know you, the only true God"—Thomas says that "such a way of speaking is not to be taken too literally, but it should be piously expounded, whenever we find it in an authentic work" (1.31.4).

gathered together in the Council of Constantinople handed down teaching concerning the Holy Spirit, without suggesting that there was anything lacking in the teaching of their predecessors who had gathered together at Nicaea, but clarifying against heretics what those predecessors had meant.[18] Because at the time of the ancient councils the error of saying that the Holy Spirit did not proceed from the Son had not arisen, it was not necessary for anything to be stated about this. Later on, when certain errors arose at another council convened in the West, the matter was explicitly defined by the authority of the Roman pontiff, by whose same authority the ancient councils were convened and confirmed.[19] But the truth was contained implicitly in the very fact that the Holy Spirit was said to proceed from the Father.

Reply to 3: The Nestorians were the first to introduce the error that the Holy Spirit did not proceed from the Son, as is clear from a Nestorian creed condemned in the Council of Ephesus. This error was followed by Theodoret the Nestorian[20] and several others after him, including even John of Damascus. On that point, therefore, his opinion should not be followed. Alternatively, it has been said by some that John of Damascus, while not professing the Holy Spirit to be from the Son, also does not expressly deny it by his words.

Reply to 4: That the Holy Spirit is said to rest or abide in the Son does not in fact exclude his proceeding from him, for the Son also is said to abide in the Father, while nevertheless proceeding from the Father. Also, the Holy Spirit is said to rest in the Son, either as the love of the lover abides in the beloved or in reference to the human nature of Christ, because of what is written in John (1:33), "The one on whom you shall see the Spirit descending and remaining upon him, this is the one who baptizes [in the Holy Spirit]."[21]

18. The original creed of the Council of Nicaea (325) ended abruptly with "And [we believe] in the Holy Spirit." The Council of Constantinople (381) added the familiar final lines of the so-called Nicene Creed: "The Lord and giver of life, who proceeds . . ." and so forth. Thomas's point is that, as the decree of the Council of Chalcedon (451) makes clear, the bishops gathered at Constantinople were in no way suggesting that the teachings of Nicaea were deficient, but were rather clarifying the implicit claim of the Spirit's divinity in response to new heresies that had arisen since the formulation of the creed of Nicaea.

19. The reference here is possibly to the so-called *Fides Damasi*, a creedal formula originating in southern Gaul, probably at the end of the fifth century, but attributed to St. Damasus, who was pope in the latter half of the fourth century. This document probably did not itself contain the *Filioque* in its original form; rather, the *Filioque* was added to it later, just as it was to the Nicene Creed. These historical matters aside, Thomas's point is that the church can modify authoritative creedal statements in order to address new errors that arise, without this constituting any sort of repudiation of prior creedal forms.

20. Theodoret of Cyrus, who in the fifth century accused Cyril of Alexandria of erroneously holding that the Spirit proceeded from the Son.

21. To say that the Spirit "rests" in the Son is not to deny that the Spirit comes forth from the Son. Note that in arguing this point, Thomas gives two possible explanations without feeling a need to choose between them.

Reply to 5: "Word" in God is not understood according the likeness of the vocal word, from which the breath [*spiritus*] does not proceed, for it would then be said only metaphorically.[22] Rather, it is understood according to the likeness of the mental word, from which love proceeds.

Reply to 6: The fact that the Holy Spirit perfectly proceeds from the Father not only does not make it superfluous to say he proceeds from the Son, but makes it absolutely necessary. For one power belongs to both the Father and the Son, and whatever is from the Father must be from the Son, unless it is incompatible with the property of sonship [*filiationis*]. For the Son is not from himself, although he is from the Father.[23]

Reply to 7: The Holy Spirit is distinct as a Person from the Son because the origin of the one is distinct from the origin of the other. But the difference of origin itself comes from the fact that the Son is only from the Father, whereas the Holy Spirit is from the Father and the Son. Otherwise the processions would not be distinct from each other, as shown above.[24]

---

22. Metaphors are comparisons with material things (see 1.13 notes 9 and 10). Therefore, if "spirit" were a reference to our breath, it would be a metaphor, and the statement "God is spirit" could not be literally true.

23. If the Trinity is truly "one God," then this God must exercise his power as a unity in all things; the only exception is that the Persons of the Son and Spirit do not originate themselves.

24. Thomas is saying in effect that the objection is resting content with the assertion that the Spirit is different from the Son because the Spirit proceeds differently than the Son, without there being any need to specify *how* that procession is different. But for Thomas, reason—without in any way comprehending the mystery of the Trinity—can probe further into that mystery so as to gain some insight into the nature of the difference between these processions.

Question 39:

The Persons in Relation to the Essence

1.39.7[1]
Are attributes of the essence appropriated to the Persons?

It would seem that the words used for the attributes of [God's] essence should not be appropriated to the Persons [of the Trinity].[2]

1. Whatever might incline toward an error in faith should be avoided in divine matters, because, as Jerome says, "disordered words bring up the risk of heresy."[3] Now to appropriate to any one Person those terms that are common to the three Persons may incline to an error in faith, for it might be thought either that such things are suited only to the Person to whom they are appropriated or that they are suited more to that one than to the others.[4] Therefore attributes of the essence should not be appropriated to the Persons.

---

1. On this article, see Emery (2007, 312–37).

2. Thomas distinguishes between "essential attributes" of God (such as power, reason, goodness, eternity, etc.), which are truly predicated of all three Persons of the Trinity, and the "notions" that identify the Persons of the Trinity (see 1.36 note 11). Strictly speaking, only these notions belong "properly" to the Persons—i.e., identify what is particular to each Person (see 1.32.2–3). But the Christian tradition has employed a number of triadic formulations by which terms that identify essential attributes of God—such as "power, wisdom, and goodness" or "unity, equality, and concord"—are used in such a way that each of the terms is associated with one of the Persons of the Trinity. Certain other terms not found in triadic formulations, such as "the book of life," likewise come to be associated with particular Persons (in this case, the Son). This practice of association comes to be known as "appropriation"—i.e., using a term that refers to something common to all three Persons as if it were proper to one of them.

3. This is ascribed to Jerome in the Ordinary Gloss on Hosea 2:16 and in Peter Lombard's *Sentences* bk. 4, dist. 13, ch. 2, but is nowhere found in the extant works of Jerome.

4. The objection suggests that whatever advantage there might be to the practice of appropriation, it is outweighed by the disadvantage of potentially leading people into heresy. So, for example, to appropriate "power" or "unity" to the Father might suggest that only the Father is powerful or one, when in fact these are attributes of all the Persons of the Trinity by virtue of their identity with the divine essence. Likewise, if we appropriate "creator" to the Father, this could suggest that only the Father creates, when

2. The attributes of the essence, expressed in the abstract, signify in the manner of a form.[5] But one Person is not related to another as a form, since a form is not distinguished from that of which it is the form in terms of its subject.[6] So the attributes of the essence, especially when expressed in the abstract, ought not to be appropriated to the Persons.

3. What is proper is prior to what is appropriated, for what is proper is included in the meaning [*ratio*] of the appropriated.[7] The attributes of the essence are, to our way of understanding, prior to the Persons, in the way that what is common is prior to what is proper.[8] Thus the attributes of the essence ought not to be appropriated to the Persons.

On the contrary: The Apostle says in 1 Corinthians (1:24): "Christ the power of God and the wisdom of God."

I answer: In order to show forth what we hold on faith, it is fitting that attributes of the essence should be appropriated to the Persons. For although the Trinity of Persons cannot be proved by demonstration, as was said above (1.32.1), it is nevertheless fitting that it be made known by things that are clearer to us.[9] Now according to reason, God's essential attributes are clearer to us than the personal properties, because beginning with creatures, from which we take our knowledge, we can come to certain knowledge of the essential attributes, which we cannot obtain regarding the personal properties, as was said above (1.32.1). Therefore, just as we make use of the likeness of

---

in fact the act of creation, like all of the acts of God in our world, is shared in by all of the Persons of the Trinity (see 1.32 note 11).

In expressing a concern about heresy, Thomas perhaps has in mind here Peter Abelard, who made the triad "power, wisdom, goodness" central to his trinitarian theology and was accused on this basis of heresy.

5. That is, God's being powerful is spoken of abstractly as the possession of "power," just as God's being one is spoken of as the possession of "unity," both of which suggest that they are being spoken of along the model of a person being human by possessing "humanity" or an apple being red by possessing "redness."

6. The point of the objection seems to be Aristotle's point (against Plato) that a form is not a subsisting thing, even though it might seem so when we express it abstractly. For example, my humanity is not something really distinct from me; it is simply my being human. Since the Persons of the Trinity are distinct from one another, attributes that are spoken of abstractly, in the way that forms are, cannot be used to identify the Persons of the Trinity.

7. What is proper to the Persons—the "notions" by which they are identified (see 1.36 note 11 and note 2, above)—is prior to the appropriations in the sense that it is only once we grasp these notions that we can make the appropriations. Thus it is only once we have grasped the unbegottenness of the Father and his fatherhood in relation to the Son that we can see *why* "power" or "unity" should be appropriated to him and *what* "power" and "unity" mean when so appropriated.

8. What is proper to the divine essence—the essential attributes—is prior to the Persons because it is shared by them, in the same way that "humanity" in general is grasped prior to grasping the particular humanity of Tom, Dick, or Harriet. This seems to introduce a contradiction, inasmuch as what are being appropriated, the essential attributes, seem to be both prior and posterior to the Persons at the same time.

9. We have seen this same principle invoked before by Thomas as a central tenet in our knowing and naming of God—see 1.2.2 and 1.13.5, above.

the trace or image found in creatures for showing forth the divine Persons, so too do we make use of the essential attributes.[10] This showing forth of the divine Persons through the attributes of the essence is called "appropriation."

The divine Persons can be shown forth in two ways by the essential attributes. In one way by the path of likeness, and thus things that pertain to understanding are appropriated to the Son, who proceeds by way of understanding, as the Word.[11] In another way by way of unlikeness, in the way that power is appropriated to the Father because, as Augustine says, our fathers are sometimes feeble on account of old age, and no such thing should be suspected of God.[12]

Reply to 1: The essential attributes are not appropriated to the Persons as if they were alleged to belong to them alone, but to show forth the Persons by way of likeness or unlikeness, as above explained. Thus no error in faith follows, but rather the showing forth of the truth.[13]

Reply to 2: If the essential attributes were appropriated to the Persons as belonging exclusively to them, then it would follow that one Person would be related to another in the manner of a form. Augustine excludes this in *De Trinitate* (7.2), showing that the Father is not wise by the wisdom he brought forth [*genuit*], as if only the Son were wisdom, so that only the Father and the Son together, but not the Father without the Son, could be said to be wise.

10. Thomas sees here two distinct ways in which we apply our minds to the Persons of the Trinity, in both cases using something better known to us to think about something less known to us. One is how we draw from what we know of ourselves as intellectual creatures—particularly the processions of knowledge and love in the mind (see 1.27.1, 3, above)—in seeking analogies for the relations of origin within the Trinity, and this is how we derive the notions of the Persons. The other is how, drawing from what we know of the divine essence, we can appropriate, in light of the insight we have gained into the divine Persons via our analogy drawn from the intellect, essential attributes to the Persons to gain further insight into their identity.

11. Thomas is not saying that this can be done only in the case of the Son but is simply offering one example of how, based on the insight we have into a divine Person via analogy with the intellect, we can appropriate an essential attribute to that Person.

12. This point is not found in the extant works of Augustine but is made in Hugh of St. Victor, *De Sacramentis* 1.2.8, from whence it passes into Peter Lombard, *Sentences* bk. 1, dist. 34, chs. 3–4. According to this "way of unlikeness," the essential attributes are appropriated to the Persons precisely *because* of how those attributes are found deficiently in creatures. So "power" is appropriated to the Father because the human name "father" might imply one who has grown enfeebled with age. In the following article (1.39.8) Aquinas gives a fuller account of Hugh's argument, in which he notes that "wisdom" is appropriated to the Son because human sons are, especially when young, often unwise, and "goodness" is appropriated to the Spirit because, in human beings, being "spirited" might denote a violent disposition.

13. All human language about God fails to some degree, and in the case of our speaking about the Trinity it perhaps fails most of all. But if this is borne in mind then one can avoid falling into heresy by constantly seeking to see *how* our language fails. In the case of our practice of appropriation, it fails inasmuch as it implies that the association of, for example, the Father with power might imply any lack of power in the Son or Spirit. If we are careful to negate this implication, then the practice of appropriation need not lead us into heresy.

Rather, the Son is called the wisdom of the Father because he is wisdom from the wise Father; for each is wisdom in himself and together both are one wisdom. Hence the Father is not wise by the wisdom brought forth, but by the wisdom which is his own essence.[14]

Reply to 3: Although "essential attribute" is prior to "person," according to its proper meaning [*secundum rationem propriam*] as we understand it [*secundum modum intelligendi*], nevertheless, inasmuch as "essential attribute" has an appropriated meaning, nothing prevents the property of a Person from being prior to what is appropriated.[15] In this way the concept "color" follows the concept "body" inasmuch as it is a body, but is naturally prior to "white body," inasmuch as it is white.[16]

14. If we think of an essential attribute as a subsisting thing, after the manner of a Platonic form, then we might be led to think, for example, that the Son as wisdom is a kind of subsisting form by which the Father is wise, which would imply that the Father is not himself wise but is wise only because of the Son. But this is rejected on the authority of Augustine. On an Aristotelian model, on the other hand, persons are not wise by virtue of a subsisting form of wisdom but by virtue of their possession of a wise nature. The Son and the Father both possess a wise nature because they both possess the divine nature, which is wisdom itself. Thomas is too polite to point out that Augustine's unquestionably correct view on the Trinity is better supported by the Aristotelian approach Thomas favors than by the Platonic approach characteristic of Augustine.

15. Thomas here seems to be saying that the essential attribute is prior in one way and posterior in another. It is prior inasmuch as, for example, we must have some sense of what "divine power" means before we can see why we should appropriate it to the Father, but it is posterior inasmuch as, once we have appropriated it to the Father, our understanding of the divine power of the Father is modified in light of the personal notions of "unbegottenness" and "paternity." Hence there is no contradiction in the essential attribute being both prior and posterior.

16. One final note on appropriation. This practice has been criticized by a number of modern theologians, most notably Karl Rahner (1904–84). The essence of their criticism is that the "theory" or "doctrine" of appropriation is a kind of rescue operation necessitated by an approach to the Trinity that diminishes the distinctiveness of the Persons such that Father, Son, and Spirit are not really distinct from one another but only distinct in our understanding of them. In this view, Augustine and Thomas resort to appropriations in an (inadequate) attempt to maintain the distinctness of the Persons. Such criticisms seem to me to miss the mark entirely. Apart from the fact that Thomas explicitly says that the Persons are really and not only logically distinct from one another, appropriation is best thought of neither as a theory nor as a doctrine, but as a practice of speaking whereby we associate things that are true of all three Persons in a particular way with one of them. Thomas's reflections on this practice of associating essential properties with particular Persons are not intended to establish the distinctness of the Persons; the relations of origin do that (i.e., the Son is distinct from the Father because the Son comes forth from the Father; the Father does not come forth from the Son), and this is expressed in the "notions." Rather, Thomas seeks to illuminate how language that names the attributes of creatures ("power," "wisdom," "goodness") can be borrowed and applied to God not only to name the divine essence but also to illuminate (i.e., *manifestare*) the distinctiveness of the Persons. As Jean-Pierre Torrell (2003, 158) puts it, appropriated terms offer "one of our rare chances to mumble something about the unsayable."

Question 43:

The Sending of the Divine Persons

1.43.2[1]

Is sending eternal or only within time?

It would seem that sending [*missio*] can be eternal.[2]

1. Gregory says (*Sermon 26, 2*, in *Homilies on the Gospels*) that the Son is begotten and for that reason sent. But the Son's begetting [*generatio*] is eternal and so his sending is as well.[3]

2. Everything that has something temporal attributed to it undergoes change. A divine Person, however, is not changed. The sending of a divine Person is therefore not in time but eternal.[4]

1. On this article, see Emery (2007, 360–412).
2. The language of "sending" runs throughout the New Testament. We see it in connection with Jesus, who is "sent . . . to the lost sheep of the house of Israel" (Matt. 15:24) and "sent . . . to proclaim release to the captives" (Luke 4:18). God "sends" Jesus into the world "not . . . to condemn the world, but in order that the world might be saved through him" (John 3:17). Jesus's "food is to do the will of him who sent" him (John 4:34), and he is sent in the "likeness of sinful flesh" (Rom. 8:3). We also see it in connection with the Holy Spirit: the "power from on high" that Jesus promises will descend upon his apostles (Luke 24:49); the "Advocate" whom the Father sends in Jesus's name (John 14:26) and whom Jesus himself sends (John 15:26; 16:7); the one whom "God has sent . . . into our hearts, crying, 'Abba! Father!'" (Gal. 4:6). At least since Augustine (and, arguably, since the Gospel of John), this biblical language of "sending" had been linked to the notion of the eternal procession of the Son and Spirit in the Godhead. Augustine writes, "The Word of God . . . is sent by him of whom it was born. He sends who begot; that is sent which was begotten" (*De Trinitate* 4.20.28). Peter Lombard speaks of the missions as "temporal processions" (*Sentences* bk. 1, dist. 14, ch. 1, no. 45), a notion that influences what Thomas has to say in this article.

In a sense, this discussion of the "missions" both brings what has preceded to a culmination and opens out into everything that will follow in the *Summa*: the creation of human beings in the image and likeness of God; the activity of human beings as knowers and lovers to whom God has given the gifts of faith, hope, and charity; the taking flesh of the eternal Son of God for us and for our salvation. In all of this, the Son and the Spirit are at work, and the mission upon which the Father sends (*missit*) them is the presence in time of the eternal processions and relations that Thomas has been discussing in the previous fifteen questions.

3. If the Son's eternal generation is the basis or cause of his sending, then it seems that his sending should be eternal as well.

4. Sending in the context of time implies change: if I am sent by my wife to the grocery store to buy milk, I change from being at my starting point, comfortably seated in my chair, to being at my destination,

3. Sending implies procession.[5] But the procession of the divine Persons is eternal—and so, therefore, is sending.

On the contrary: It is said in Galatians (4:4): "When the fullness of time had come, God sent his Son."[6]

I answer: A certain distinction is to be noted in the words that convey the origin of the divine Persons. Some words—such as "procession" [*processio*] and "going forth" [*exitus*]—convey in their meaning only a relation to a source [*principium*]. Other words, however, designate the destination [*terminus*] of the procession along with the relation to the source. Of these, some words—such as "begetting" [*generatio*] and "breathing forth" [*spiratio*]—designate an eternal destination, for begetting is the coming forth of the divine Person in the divine nature, and breathing forth, taken passively, conveys the coming forth of subsistent love. Other words—such as "sending" [*missio*] and "giving" [*datio*]—convey a destination in time along with a relation to a source.[7] For something is sent so that it may be in something else, and something is given so that it may be possessed. But for a divine Person to be possessed by a creature, or exist in it in a new way, is an event within time.[8]

---

standing in a line waiting to pay. But such change would be unfitting for a divine Person, such as the Son or the Spirit. Their sending, therefore, must be eternal.

5. That is, if I am sent I must "come forth" (see 1.27.1 note 2, above) in order to fulfill the mission I have been given.

6. Thomas's choice of this verse from Paul's Letter to the Galatians for the *sed contra* is singularly apt because it sums up how the Son, who comes forth from God in eternity, is also sent to be in the world at a specific moment in time.

7. Thomas maps out a taxonomy of words as they express the origin of the divine Persons:

   1. Words conveying relation to a source (*processio, exitus*)
   2. Words conveying relation to a source and designating a destination that is
      a. eternal (*generatio, spiratio*)
      b. in time (*missio, datio*)

The difference between only conveying a relation to a source and both conveying a relation to a source and designating a *terminus* or destination might be thought of as the difference between those terms that indicate only *that* something is coming forth and those terms that indicate both *that* and *how* something is coming forth. If I say, "I come from Canada," I am identifying only my source and leaving unspecified whether I have recently been in Canada and have now arrived somewhere else or whether I am a native of Canada, born and bred—I am specifying a point of origin without specifying *how* it is my origin (and thus in a sense not identifying myself as, say, Canadian).

There is an obvious oddness to speaking of an "eternal destination." The English word "destination," implying as it does movement through space, is in some sense metaphorical, though the Latin *terminus* also includes such meanings as "purpose" and can even be used as a synonym for *definitio* (even in English we speak of defining our "terms"). In speaking of words that designate an eternal *terminus*, Thomas seems to mean those (such as "begetting" or "breathing forth") that identify not only *that* a thing comes forth but also *how* it comes forth, and thus in some way identify *what* it is that comes forth, while also indicating that this coming forth is an "intransitive" action (see 1.27 note 8, above) and thus does not imply an event in time.

8. Words like "sending" (*missio*) or "giving" (*datio*) do imply an event it time, because I am sent from point A to point B in order to newly begin to be in point B; and X is given to Y in order that Y might newly begin to possess X.

Therefore "sending" and "giving" in God are only spoken of as events in time; "begetting" and "breathing forth" are solely eternal; but "procession" and "coming forth" in God are spoken of both eternally and as events in time.[9] For the Son proceeds eternally so as to be God, but also in time so as to be a human being, in accord with his visible sending, or again in order to dwell in a human being, in accord with his invisible sending.[10]

Reply to 1: Gregory speaks of the begetting in time of the Son not from the Father but from his mother. Or it may mean that it is because he is begotten from eternity that the Son is capable of being sent.[11]

Reply to 2: A divine Person might be in someone in a new way, or might be possessed by someone in time, not as a result of a change on the part of the divine Person, but of a change on the part of the creature, just as God is called "Lord" in time as a result of a change in the creature.[12]

Reply to 3: "Sending" not only conveys procession from a source but also designates the destination of the procession within time. Hence "sending" is only within time. Or we may say that "sending" includes the eternal procession along with something in addition: an effect in time. For the relation of a

9. Because words like "process" or "come forth" do not specify a destination, they may be used for either eternal acts or events that occur within time. This would allow for Peter Lombard's identification of "sending" as "procession in time," which underscores the close link between the procession of the Son and Spirit in eternity and their sending in time. We might say that the sending of the Son and Spirit is the manifestation in time of the eternal life of the Trinity. What Jesus does in his life, death, and resurrection simply *is* what it means to be the eternal Word present in time for us and for our salvation; the Spirit's work of making holy simply *is* what it means to be the bond of love in the midst of human history.

10. Thomas here gestures at the various *missiones* that he will sketch in the remaining six articles of this question. The Son and the Spirit are sent both invisibly and visibly. The invisible sending of the Son and Spirit causes in us the gift of sanctifying grace, by which God is present to us as known through faith (the sending of the Word) and loved through charity (the sending of the Spirit) (1.43.3, 5). This invisible sending is not reserved for extraordinary events but is in everyone who shares in God's grace—not just in one's initial turning to God but also in one's ongoing growth in the life of grace (1.43.6). The visible sending of the Son is, of course, his incarnation, in which he is the source of our salvation; the visible sending of the Spirit refers to those particular moments in the lives of Jesus and the apostles when a sign is given of the power of God to make holy—e.g., the dove at Jesus's baptism and the tongues of fire at Pentecost (1.43.7).

11. Thomas's first suggestion in this reply is not particularly plausible, especially if one looks at the actual quotation from Gregory, which says, "The Son is sent from the Father from the fact that he is begotten by the Father," clearly indicating that he is speaking of the Son's eternal begetting. Thomas's second suggestion is much truer to Gregory's point: it is because God is already a dynamic process of begetting and breathing forth that this dynamism can be extended into time in the sending of the Son and Spirit. This also accounts for why the Father, who is neither begotten nor breathed forth, cannot be sent (1.43.4).

12. Thomas uses the distinction between "logical" and "real" relations (see 3.1 note 10, below) to make the point that what we call the "sending" of the Son and Spirit involves no change in the divine Person sent, but only in the rational creature to whom they are sent: a man begins to exist who is God, a sinner passes from unrighteousness to righteousness, etc.

divine Person to his source must be eternal. We therefore speak of a twofold procession—eternal and in time; not that there is a twofold relation to the source, but a twofold destination—in time and in eternity.[13]

13. We see here how closely Thomas ties the eternal coming forth and the sending in time: for both the Son and the Spirit, their eternal procession and temporal procession have a single, identical relationship to their source. Thus the Son both proceeds from and is sent by the Father, and the Spirit both proceeds from and is sent by the Father and Son together.

Question 45:

How Things Come Forth
from the First Principle

1.45.5¹

Does it belong to God alone to create?

It would seem that it does not belong to God alone to create.

1. According to the Philosopher (*De anima* 2.4, 415ᵃ), the perfect is that which can make its own likeness. Immaterial creatures are more perfect than material creatures, which can make their own likeness, for fire generates fire, and a human being begets a human being. Therefore an immaterial substance can make a substance similar to itself. Immaterial substance, however, can be made only by creation, since it has no matter from which to be made. Thus a creature can create.²

2. The greater the resistance is on the part of the thing made, the greater the power that is required in the maker. But a "contrary" is more resistant than "nothing," so it requires more power to make something from its contrary—which a creature can do—than to make a thing from nothing, and hence it is even more the case that a creature can do this.³

---

1. On this article, see Gilson (1960, 179–221); McCabe (1987, 2–9); Bauerschmidt (2013, 107–23); Tanner (2016).

2. Thomas has already specified that he is using "creation" to indicate not simply the giving of a new structure to matter but specifically the act of giving something its entire existence. The way theologians put this is to say that creation is *ex nihilo* (from nothing). Carving a statue is not, properly speaking, an act of creation since it is involves giving already-existing matter (e.g., rock or wood) a new form (e.g., that of a person or cow). Likewise, animal or plant reproduction would not be an act of creation, since this too is a matter of giving form (in this case a soul) to preexisting matter. However, the objection argues, if a nonmaterial being (e.g., an angel) could engender another nonmaterial being, then this *would* be an act of creation, since it would not be simply the imparting of form to matter.

3. If one can do something, it follows that one can also do a lesser thing: if I can jump three feet, it follows that I can also jump two feet. The objection says that it is a greater thing to make something from preexisting matter than to make something from nothing, since the matter offers resistance to the activity

3. The power of the maker is judged by the measure of what it makes. Created being is finite, as we proved earlier when discussing the infinity of God (1.7.2–4), and therefore only a finite power is required to create something created. But to have finite power is not contrary to the idea of a creature, and so it is not impossible for a creature to create.

On the contrary: Augustine says in *De Trinitate* (3.8.13) that neither good nor bad angels can create anything. It is therefore even less the case with other creatures.

I answer: At first glance, according to what precedes (1.45.1), it is evident enough that creation cannot be the action of anyone except God alone.[4] For more universal effects must be traced back to more universal and prior causes. Among all effects the most universal is existence itself, and so it must be the proper effect of the first and most universal cause, which is God.[5] For this reason also it is said in the *Book of Causes* (proposition 3) that neither an intelligence nor a noble soul gives existence, except inasmuch as it works by divine operation.[6] But to produce existence absolutely and not as this or that being is part of the meaning of "creation." Therefore it is clear that creation is an act belonging to God alone.

It happens, however, that something shares the action properly belonging to something else[7] not by its own power but instrumentally, inasmuch as it acts

---

of the maker: it is easier to come up with the idea of a work of art or a structure than to actually execute it. Therefore, since creatures can make things out of matter (e.g., statues, houses, boats), they certainly can do the lesser thing of making something from nothing.

4. Here Thomas is referring back to the first article in the question (1.45.1), where he has argued that "creation" means to make something from nothing.

5. The most fundamental (or "most universal") activity of anything is the very act of existing (see 1.3 note 18). Whatever causes that act must therefore be the most fundamental cause. As Thomas argued in the first three of the five ways, this is what people call "God."

6. The *Book of Causes* is the work of an unknown author, who was probably Muslim or Jewish, writing at some point prior to the twelfth century. In Thomas's day it was commonly thought to be a work by Aristotle, even though it clearly reflects a much more Platonic viewpoint. In fact, much of it is taken from the *Elements of Theology*, written by the fifth-century pagan Neoplatonist Proclus, though the author has subtly altered Proclus's thought to accommodate a view of the universe as the intentional creation of God, rather than a necessary emanation. In his earlier writings, Thomas seemed unsure of Aristotle's authorship of this work. When William of Moerbeke's translation of Proclus's *Elements* appeared in 1268, Thomas quickly realized that this was the ultimate source of the *Book of Causes*. He was apparently the first to make this identification, and in his own commentary on the *Book of Causes* (1272) he made use of Proclus's work to interpret it.

In the *Book of Causes*, the author posits—in addition to the first cause, which is "higher than eternity and before it"—other causes that he calls "intelligences" (identified by Thomas with angels), as well as "souls." In Thomas's interpretation of the *Book of Causes*, both intelligences and souls can be causes by virtue of their sharing in the first cause, which is God.

7. "Shares" is a translation of the Latin *participare*, which means both "imparting" and "sharing in," not unlike our word "share." If I say to you that "I want to share power," it could mean that I want to receive a share for myself from another, or it could mean that I want to share it with others.

by the power of another, in the way that air, by the power of fire, can heat and ignite. Based on this, some have supposed that, even though creation is the proper act of the universal cause, some lesser cause, inasmuch as it acts by the power of the first cause, can create.[8] And so Avicenna (Ibn Sina) asserted that the first separate substance, created by God, then created another after itself, along with the substance of the world and its soul, and that the substance of the world creates the matter of inferior bodies. In the same way the Master says,[9] in his book of *Sentences* (bk. 4, dist. 5), that God can communicate to a creature the power of creating, so that it creates ministerially, not by its own power.[10]

But this is not possible. For a secondary, instrumental cause does not share in the action of a superior cause except inasmuch as it acts by something proper to itself to prepare for the effect of the principal agent. If it has no effect on the basis of what is proper to itself, it is used to no purpose. Nor would there be any need of particular instruments to carry out particular actions. Thus we see that a saw, in cutting wood, which it does based on the special character of its own form, produces the form of a bench, which is the effect properly belonging to the principal agent.[11] Now the proper effect of God creating is what is presupposed by all other effects—that is to say, existence in the absolute sense [*esse absolute*]. Therefore, nothing else can act as a preparation and instrument for this effect, since creation is not from anything presupposed that could be prepared by the action of an instrumental agent.[12]

8. Here Thomas is introducing something like an objection into the body of his argument. He sketches an opinion that he will go on in the next paragraph to refute.

9. I.e., Peter Lombard.

10. To use the example Thomas uses in the next paragraph, we can say "A carpenter cuts a piece of wood," or we can say "A saw cuts a piece of wood." Both statements can be true at the same time. Therefore (so this argument goes) a creature could be used by God in the act of creation in such a way that we could truly say the creature creates. Thomas seems to accept this view in his early theology (e.g., *Commentary on the Sentences* bk. 2, dist. 1, q. 1, a. 3; *Disputed Questions on Truth* 5.9). In his mature theology, however, while still accepting the distinction between primary and secondary causality (see 1.2 note 61), he no longer thinks that the act of creation itself can be delegated to secondary causes.

11. In other words, a tool or "instrument" shares in the action of the one who wields it by making a unique contribution to the wielder's purpose. This contribution is "dispositive," meaning that it prepares for what the tool wielder wants to do (e.g., the carpenter wants to build a bench, and the saw prepares the wood for this purpose).

12. "Creation" names that relation by virtue of which something exists. Because creation is *ex nihilo*, prior to creation there is nothing to be prepared by a tool; there is simply nothing. We might say that instrumental causality presumes a context in which the thing brought about will exist, whereas creation brings the context into existence.

Thomas's understanding of creation as a relation of creature to creator underscores the fact that God does not simply bring things into existence, but at every moment sustains that existence. Peter Geach writes, "In one respect the use of the word ['made'] when applied to God is more like 'the minstrel made music' than 'the blacksmith made a shoe'; for the shoe is made out of pre-existing material, and, once made, goes on existing independently of the smith; whereas the minstrel did not make the music out of pre-existing

Thus it is impossible for any creature to create, either by its own power or instrumentally or ministerially.

It is particularly unfitting to say that it is something bodily that creates, since no body acts except by touching or moving, and so requires in its action some preexisting thing that can be touched or moved, which is contrary to the meaning of creation.

Reply to 1: A perfect thing imparting [*participans*] a nature makes a likeness of itself,[13] not by producing that nature in an absolute sense but by applying it to something else. For a particular human being cannot be the cause of human nature absolutely, because he would then be the cause of himself. Rather, he is the cause by which human nature is in the person who is begotten.[14] So he presupposes in his action particular matter, by which this particular human being exists.[15] But just as a particular human being shares in human nature, so every created being shares, so to speak, in the nature of existing [*naturam essendi*], for only God is his own existence, as we have said earlier (1.7.1, 2).[16] Therefore no created being can produce being absolutely, except in the sense that it causes existence "in this particular thing." Thus the action by which something makes its own likeness necessarily presupposes that by which a thing is "this particular thing."[17] In an immaterial substance, however, it is not possible to presuppose anything by which it is "this particular thing," because, being a subsisting form, it is what it is by its form, by which it has existence. For this reason an immaterial substance cannot produce another immaterial substance like itself in regard to its existence, but only in regard to some added perfection, as when we say, following Dionysius (*The Celestial Hierarchy*

---

sounds, and the music stops if he stops making it; and similarly God did not make the world out of anything pre-existing, and its continued existence depends upon his activity" (Anscombe and Geach 1961, 110).

13. Thomas means "perfect" in the sense of a thing having actualized its potential. Thus any actual human person is in this sense a "perfect" human nature, as any fire is a "perfect" fiery nature. Also, note that for Thomas things are what they are because they share or "participate" in a particular nature (see 1.3 note 13). Thus Tom, Dick, and Harriet are all human beings because they share in human nature. In this view of things, Thomas follows both Plato and Aristotle, though they disagreed with each other on the exact nature of this participation.

14. When humans reproduce, they do not produce "human nature" but a particular instance of human nature. If human nature did not already exist, then there would be no humans to engage in reproduction. Note that neither Thomas nor Aristotle has the evolution of species in view.

15. See 1.36 note 13; 1.50 note 12; 1.75 note 8.

16. To say that human beings share in human nature is to say that they *have* human nature; it is not to say that they *are* human nature. Likewise, every created thing that exists participates in the act of existing but is not itself that act of existing; we say it *has* existence, not that it *is* existence. Even though existence is "proper" to (i.e., truly belongs to) existing things, only God *is* his own act of existing (see 1.3.4, above); everything else must have its existence imparted to it by God.

17. A creature can make *this* or *that* being, but cannot make *being* itself, for, in the case of material beings, a creature's act of making presupposes what differentiates *this* from *that*—namely, matter.

8.2), that a superior angel illuminates an inferior one.[18] In this way, even in heaven there is fatherhood, as the words of the Apostle in Ephesians (3:15) make clear, "from whom all fatherhood in heaven and on earth is named." From this it appears evident that no created being can cause anything unless something is presupposed, which is contrary to the meaning of "creation."

Reply to 2: A thing is made from its contrary coincidentally [*per accidens*], as is said in the *Physics* (1.7, 190^b), but something is made directly [*per se*] from the subject that is in potentiality.[19] And so the contrary resists the agent to the degree that it prevents the potentiality from attaining the actualization that the agent intends to bring about. For example, fire seeks to bring the matter of water to an actualization like itself, but it is blocked by the form and contrary dispositions [of water], which prevent the potential from being brought to actualization.[20] The more the potentiality is impeded, the more power is required in the agent to bring about its actualization of the matter.[21] Therefore, much greater power is required in an agent if no potentiality pre-exists.[22] For this reason it is apparent that it is an act of much greater power to make a thing from nothing than from its contrary.

Reply to 3: The power of an agent is reckoned not only from the substance of the thing made but also from the way it is made: a greater heat not only heats more but heats more quickly. So, although creating some finite effect does not show an infinite power, creating it from nothing *does* show an infinite power, as is clear from what has been said (reply to obj. 2). For if a greater power is required in an agent in proportion to the distance of potentiality from actuality, it follows that the power of that which produces something from no presupposed potentiality is infinite, because there is no proportion between "no potentiality" and "some potentiality" (which the power of a natural agent presupposes), just as there is no proportion between "nonbeing" and "being."[23] And because no creature has absolutely infinite power, any more than it has infinite being, as was proved earlier (1.7.2), it follows that no creature can create.

---

18. With regard to immaterial beings (e.g., angels), no matter can be presupposed; what is presupposed is the very existence of the other immaterial being that is acted upon.

19. We make fire from wood because the matter per se is apt for that purpose (wood burns well); if the wood is coincidentally ("accidentally") wet, it is opposed to burning. Wet wood can eventually be made to burn, given a hot enough fire, because it can lose the accidental property (wetness) that is contrary to its burning.

20. On "act" (or "actualization") and "potency," see 1.2 note 36.

21. What we might call "contrariness" works by making the matter less apt to receive a particular structure ("form"). Thus, being wet impedes wood's potential to be fire, and a hotter fire is needed to make it burn.

22. In creation from nothing, there is not simply a "blocked" potential but no potential whatsoever.

23. We should not think that we can have a continuum, with "existence" at one end and "nonexistence" at the other, not least because there are no intermediary stages between existing and not existing: you either are or you are not. To bring something into existence where once there was nothing is an act so radical that only infinite power (i.e., God's) can bring it about.

Question 50:

The Substance of the Angels

1.50.1[1]

Is there any entirely spiritual creature, completely nonbodily?[2]

It would seem that an angel is not entirely nonbodily.

1. That which is nonbodily only in relation to us, but not in relation to God, is not absolutely nonbodily. John of Damascus says in *On the Orthodox*

1. On this article, see Bonino (2016, esp. 111–30).

2. Thomas's identification as the "Angelic Doctor" probably has more to do with his reputation for possessing a purity that approached that of the holy angels than it does with his teachings on angels themselves. Still, he does discuss angels in some detail, devoting fourteen questions in the *Summa theologiae* to their nature (1.50–64) and another nine to their role in God's guidance of the universe (1.106–14). However, Thomas is not notably *more* interested in angels than other theologians of his day—Peter Lombard, for example, devoted ten distinctions of the second book of his *Sentences* to angels.

Medieval theologians were interested in angels for several reasons. Angels are pervasive in the Scriptures of the Old and New Testaments, serving as messengers of God (the Greek word *angelos* means "messenger") and agents of God's will, as well as worshiping God in heaven. Angels feature prominently in the early Christian tradition: in the writings of Augustine and Gregory the Great and particularly Dionysius the Areopagite. Also, Thomas, like other medieval Christian theologians, as well as various Jewish and Muslim thinkers, associated angels with the "intelligences" that Aristotle and later Neoplatonic philosophers thought were responsible for the movement of the heavenly bodies. Angels therefore also provided theologians with an opportunity to address certain philosophical questions concerning the structure of reality and human nature, since angels represented beings that are like humans in possessing intelligence yet are at the same time different from human beings, somehow less bodily and more "spiritual."

This article addresses this final point, focusing on what exactly it means for angels to be "spiritual beings." The fact that Thomas addresses this question at the outset of his discussion of angels indicates that much of what Thomas will go on to say regarding angels—their modes of knowledge, communication, and activity—will be shaped by the position that he stakes out in this article that angels are entirely nonbodily (*omnino incorporeus*).

To my knowledge, no medieval theologians ever discussed how many angels could dance on the head of a pin, and they would have found it as silly a question as we would. But the question of how many angels could dance on the *point* of a pin (though, again, to my knowledge none of them ever discussed this question) would not have struck them as similarly foolish, since a point takes up no space and so the question addresses whether or not angels are bodily and how they are related to points in space.

Faith (2.3) that "an angel is said to be nonbodily and nonmaterial as regards us, but compared to God it is found to be bodily and material." Therefore it is not absolutely nonbodily.[3]

2. Nothing is moved except a body, as Aristotle shows in the *Physics* (6.4, 234[b]). John of Damascus says in the place cited above that an angel is "an ever-mobile intellectual substance."[4] Therefore, an angel is a bodily substance.

3. Ambrose says in the book *On the Holy Spirit* (1.7): "Every creature, circumscribed within its nature, is limited." Since being limited is a feature of bodies, every creature is therefore bodily.[5] But angels are God's creatures, as is clear from Psalm 148 (v. 2): "Praise the Lord, all his angels"; and, farther on (v. 5), "For he spoke, and they were made; he commanded, and they were created." Therefore, angels are bodily.

On the contrary: It is said in Psalm 104 (v. 4): "Who makes his angels spirits."

I answer: It is necessary to posit some nonbodily creatures. For what God chiefly aims at in created things is the good, which consists in assimilation to God. The perfect assimilation of an effect to a cause is seen when the effect imitates the cause with regard to that by which the cause produces the effect, in the way that heat in one thing makes heat in another.[6] Now God produces

3. Most medieval theologians seemed to vacillate between a denial that angels are bodily in the same sense that we are (which seems clear from the stories of angels in the Bible) and an insistence that they cannot be nonbodily in the same sense that God is. The quotation from John of Damascus in this objection captures that vacillation: compared to us, angels seem nonbodily, but compared with God they seem bodily.

The reason for this vacillation is the desire to make clear that angels, however exalted their manner of existence, are still creatures. Thomas's contemporary Bonaventure argues that since only God is "pure act"—a point with which Thomas agrees (see 1.2 note 39, above)—and all creatures are a combination of unrealized potentiality and actuality, and since potentiality and actuality correspond to matter and form, angels must be composed of matter and form (Bonaventure, *Commentary on the Sentences* bk. 2, dist. 3, pars. 1, a. 1, q. 1). Thomas, with the distinction between essence and existence that he posits in creatures, has a different way of accounting for how angels can be immaterial and yet still not be pure act (see 1.3, above).

4. If we wish to distinguish angels from God, and if God is an unmoved mover, then angels must be "moved movers," which is why John of Damascus defines them as "ever-mobile" (or "ever-movable"). But, the objection argues, only something occupying space—that is, something bodily—can be moved. Therefore, angels must be bodily.

5. This objection is also worrying about properly distinguishing angels from God. One way to do so is to say that angels, like all other creatures, are finite or limited, whereas God is infinite or unlimited. But to be limited seems to be connected with being bodily, since bodies have clear boundaries. If angels are creatures and therefore limited, it would seem that they have to be in some sense bodily.

6. By "assimilation" Thomas does not mean anything like "absorption," as if God intends that creatures be united to him in such a way that they lose their individual identities. Rather, the good that God intends for creatures is that they be perfectly fulfilled as the kind of thing that they are, just

a creature by intellect and will, as was shown earlier (1.14.8; 1.19.4). Hence the perfection of the universe requires that there be intellectual creatures. But intellectual acts cannot be actions of a body, nor of any bodily power, because every body is delimited by the "here" and the "now." In order that the universe be perfect, therefore, it is necessary to posit the existence of some nonbodily creature.[7]

The ancients, however, being ignorant of the power of understanding, and not distinguishing between sense and intellect, supposed that nothing existed in the world except that which the senses and the imagination could grasp. And because only bodies are contained in the imagination,[8] they supposed that there were no beings except bodies, as the Philosopher recounts in the *Physics* (4.6, 213[a]; 4.7, 213[b]). From this came the error of the Sadducees, who said there was no spirit (Acts 23:8).[9] But the very fact that the intellect

---

as God is perfectly fulfilled as the source from whom all perfection flows. In other words, creatures are "perfect" to the degree that they let the creative power of God make them be actually what they are potentially.

7. Thomas's argument here is a bit hard to follow, in part because it seems to presume his earlier argument that if effects in some way resemble their causes, then the best way for a finite universe to reflect its infinite Creator is by the creation of a diversity of creatures. As he puts it succinctly in his *Compendium of Theology* (1.102): "It was impossible that one thing perfectly represent the divine goodness because of the remoteness of each creature from God. Therefore, it was necessary that many things represent him, so that one thing supplied what another lacked." No single finite creature could ever reflect God as well as the entire ensemble of finite creatures that make up the world.

With this in mind we can understand Thomas to be saying that if God creates the world by means of the divine intellect and will, then the diversity of the world should include creatures possessed of intellect and will. But don't human beings have intellect and will? Here we need to bear in mind the distinction Thomas makes between "intellect" and "reason" (in the context of discussing the angels; see 1.58.3). Reason is what we might call a "thought process"—as when we move from premises to a conclusion. Intellect, on the other hand, is something more akin to "intuition"—as when we grasp the truth of something in an instant without going through a reasoning process. Reason depends at least in part on our senses: when we reason that, because Socrates is a man and all men are mortal, then Socrates must be mortal, we derive our knowledge of the humanity of Socrates and the mortality of humans from what we can see and hear. But intellect does not depend on the senses: when we grasp that a whole is greater than its parts or that something cannot be both true and false at the same time, this is not knowledge derived from observing the world but knowledge derived directly from the fact of our being intelligent. God, who is without a body and therefore has no senses, knows entirely through intellect.

The final step of Thomas's argument is that the perfect goodness of the universe would seem to require that it contain not only beings that employ both reason and intellect, the way that humans do, but also beings that, like God, are purely intellectual and therefore entirely nonbodily. To put it simply, a universe that includes nonbodily creatures of pure intellect is more perfect, and therefore a better reflection of God's power, than one that does not.

8. On Thomas's use of "imagination" see 1–2.9 note 3.

9. Thomas has to account not only for the fact that some ancient philosophers, as well as figures from Scripture such as the Sadducees, did not believe in nonbodily creatures; he also has to account for the fact that quite a few Christian theologians thought that angels were in some sense material. His explanation of this seems to be that because we humans know primarily through our senses, we simply assume that all knowledge must be of this sort.

is above the senses shows rationally that there are some nonbodily things, comprehensible only to the intellect.

Reply to 1: Nonbodily substances are in between God and bodily creatures. But the midpoint compared to one extreme appears to be the other extreme, in the way that something lukewarm seems to be cold when compared to something hot. And it is for this reason, and not because there is anything of a bodily nature in them, that it is said that angels are material and bodily compared to God.[10]

Reply to 2: "Movement" in this case is understood in the sense in which it is said with regard to understanding and willing. So an angel is called an ever-mobile substance because it is always actually understanding, and not as if it were sometimes actually understanding and sometimes potentially understanding, as is the case with us. Thus it is clear that the argument is based on an equivocation.[11]

Reply to 3: Circumscription by location is a property only of bodies; but circumscription by the limits of what a thing is [*terminis essentialibus*] is

10. In his response Thomas is indirectly acknowledging the legitimacy of the concern that if angels were thought to be nonbodily then they would seem to be pure act, just as God is. As he understands it, however, angels are "in between" God and bodily creatures in the sense that they have something in common with both: they share with bodily creatures a nature composed of possibility (essence) and actuality (existence), while they share with God a nonbodily or purely intellectual form of existence. Thus an angel seems "bodily" in comparison with God in the same way that room-temperature water seems "cold" in comparison with hot water.

11. On the fallacy of equivocation, see 1.13 note 22. In this case, the equivocation involves the word "move." As we saw in looking at Thomas's first way of demonstrating God's existence, "move" can sometimes mean specifically a change of location and can sometimes mean any change in which a potential is actualized (see 1.2 notes 34 and 36, above). To say that angels are "ever-mobile" according to the first meaning would seem to imply a constant motion from place to place, something that could only be true of a body. But to say that angels are "ever-mobile" according to the second meaning is to say that their intellects are always in a state of actuality with regard to knowledge. Thomas will later clarify that this means that angels know what they know without learning and not that angels are always actually thinking about everything that they know (1.58.1). One should also note that this regards the natural knowledge of angels. Just as with human beings, there is also a supernatural knowledge bestowed upon the angels by which they know mysteries exceeding created intelligence (1.57.5).

The issue of angelic knowledge occupies Thomas at some length in the *Summa*. He devotes five questions, a total of twenty-three articles, to the topic. This is because in Scripture one of the significant roles of angels is as messengers of divine revelation (as opposed to the "intelligences" of Greek philosophy, which primarily influence affairs on earth by moving heavenly bodies). This prompts Thomas to explore how and from where angels derive their knowledge. The picture is a somewhat elaborate one, in which, in addition to their natural knowledge, angels behold supernatural truth through their vision of the divine Word. But each angel stands in a relationship of superiority and inferiority to other angels, and the higher in the angelic hierarchy an angel is, the more perfectly it perceives the Word (1.55.3). So each angel has the role of receiving illumination from the angels above it and in turn illuminating the angels below it. As elaborate (and sometimes confusing) as it is, Thomas's picture of angels depicts a vast world of spiritual beings engaged in an unceasing process of receiving and imparting enlightenment so that God's glory may be extended by becoming more widely known.

something common to all creatures, whether bodily or spiritual. This is why Ambrose says in the book *On the Holy Spirit* (1.7) that although some things are not contained in a bodily location, they are nevertheless not without circumscription by their substance.[12]

12. Earlier in the *Summa* Thomas notes that just as a form or nature is "contracted" (i.e., made a particular individual) by matter, so too existence is "contracted" by a form or nature. That is to say, Bossie and Flossie are different cows because Bossie's bovine form is embodied in a particular bit of matter and Flossie's bovinity is embodied in a different bit of matter; likewise in the case of angels, though angels have no matter to contract their natures, Gabriel and Michael still have distinct acts of existence because Gabriel's existence is contracted by the form of Gabriel and Michael's by the form of Michael (see 1.7.2). In the case of material things, their individuality is a result of matter "dividing up," as it were, different instances of the same nature or species. In the case of angels, Thomas says, because they are immaterial, each angel must be its own nature or species, since a species can only be divided by matter (1.50.4).

Question 75:

The Nature of the Soul Itself

1.75.4[1]
Is the soul the human being, or is the human being something composed of soul and body?[2]

It would seem that the soul is the human being.

1. It is said in 2 Corinthians (4:16): "Though our outer person is corrupted, yet that which is inner is renewed day by day." But that which is within a human being is the soul. Therefore the soul is the inward human being.[3]

2. The human soul is a kind of substance. Because it is not a universal substance, it is therefore a particular substance. And if this is so, then it is a "hypostasis" or a person.[4] But it can only be a human person. The soul is thus a human being, for a human person is the human being.[5]

1. On this article, see Gilson (1960, 222–40); Kenny (1993, esp. 129–59); Pasnau (2012).

2. Here Thomas displays his Aristotelian commitments, preferring Aristotle to Plato not only in terms of philosophical cogency but also with regard to his compatibility with traditional Christian theology. Plato tended to speak of the self as equivalent to the soul, and of the body as a vehicle moved by the soul but not intrinsic to the self's identity. Aristotle, with his understanding of human beings as "rational animals," emphasized the inherently embodied nature of human beings and the relationship of soul to body as one of form to matter (on form and matter, see 1.12 note 2).

The Christian tradition, true to its Jewish roots and despite the debt owed by the fathers of the early church to Platonic philosophy, takes with great seriousness the proposition that human beings are created by God not simply as souls that make use of bodies but as composite unities of body and soul. From this proposition flows much else in Christian theology: the importance and nature of God's incarnation in Christ, the sacramental economy of salvation, and the resurrection of the body. It was in connection with an exposition of Paul's discussion of the resurrection of the body in 1 Cor. 15 that Thomas had occasion to put his view most pointedly: "Soul is not the whole human being, but only part of one; my soul is not me [*anima mea non est ego*]" (*Commentary on 1 Corinthians* 15.2.924 [my trans.]).

3. The objection interprets Paul's language of the "inner human being" in a Platonic way, implying that within the shell of the body (the "outer human being") there is an "inner self" that, as it were, is inhabiting the body but is a self quite distinct from the outer human being.

4. On "hypostasis" and "person" see 1.29 note 2.

5. This objection trades on Boethius's definition of "person" as "an individual substance possessing a rational nature" (see 1.29 note 5, above). Since the soul fits this definition, it must be a person, and since it

On the contrary: Augustine, in *The City of God* (19.3), commends Varro's view "that a human being is not merely a soul, nor merely a body, but both soul and body."

I answer: The statement "the soul is a human being" can be understood in two ways. In one way, it can be understood to be saying that what it means to be a human being is identical with what it means to be a soul, though this particular human being (Socrates, for instance) is not a soul, but rather is composed of soul and body. I say this because some have suggested that the form alone constitutes the species, while matter is part of the individual and not of the species.[6] But this cannot be true, for what pertains to the nature of the species is what the definition signifies, and in physical things the definition does not signify the form only, but the form and the matter. Hence in physical things the matter is part of the species:[7] not, of course, particular bits of matter [*materia signata*], which is what makes things discrete individuals, but matter in general [*materia communis*]. For just as it belongs to the notion of this particular human being to be composed of this soul, of this flesh, and of these bones, so it belongs to the notion of humanity as a whole to be composed of soul, flesh, and bones.[8] This is because whatever belongs in common to the substance of

---

is a human soul, it couldn't be any other sort of person than a human person. Therefore, a human person is simply his or her soul.

6. In this context, "species" means something like "kind" or "class of things," the way the term is used in biological classification (for other uses of the Latin *species*, see 1.12 note 11 and 3.63 note 4). According to the view Thomas is discussing, when we are discussing the human species, the meaning of "human" is "a soul," and not "a soul joined to a body"—even though, in individuals, souls are joined to the bodies through which they exist as individuals. Thus in order to define what human beings are, one does not need to include embodiment in one's definition. This is the view put forward by Averroes in his commentary on Aristotle's *Metaphysics* 7 (comm. 21; comm. 34); Thomas discusses this further in his own commentary on the *Metaphysics* (7.9).

7. I have translated *in rebus naturalibus* as "in physical things," since context suggests that Thomas is talking here about those sorts of things discussed in Aristotle's *Physics*—i.e., bodies undergoing change. Also, in the context of this article, "part of the species" might be understood to mean "part of the definition of a class of things."

8. As mentioned earlier (1.36 note 13; 1.50 note 12), Thomas's view is that what makes individual members of a species distinct from one another is that each individual within the species instantiates that species' form in a distinct quantity of matter (what Thomas calls here *material signata*); thus Tom, Dick, and Harriet all share the identical form "human" but are distinct because that form occurs in different matter. To fully appreciate Thomas's position, it helps to remember that matter, as Thomas understands it, occupies a certain segment of space and time. Thus Harriet's possession of "matter" amounts to her having lived out her humanity in a particular time and place—that is, to her having a particular history—and this is what differentiates her from all other human beings.

This individual matter is something different from matter in general (*material communis*) or what we might call "the notion of matter," which forms part of the definition of "human being." The view of Averroes, which Thomas is criticizing, seems to take account only of *material signata* and to ignore the *material communis* that enters into the definition of "human being."

all the individuals contained under a given species necessarily belongs to the substance of the species.[9]

The statement "the soul is a human being" may also be understood in another way: *this* particular soul is *this* particular human being. It would, in fact, be possible to hold this if one were to suppose that the soul's activity of sensing[10] belonged to it apart from the body, because in that case all the activities that are attributed to the human being would belong to the soul alone. For that which performs the activities specifically belonging to a thing *is* that thing.[11] Therefore, whatever performs the activities of a human being *is* a human being. But it has been shown above that sensation is not the activity of the soul by itself.[12] Since, then, sensation is an activity of a human being (though not only of human beings),[13] it is clear that a human being is not merely a soul, but rather something composed of soul and body. Plato, because he held that sensation belonged to the soul by itself, could also hold that a human being is a soul simply making use of a body.[14]

Reply to 1. According to the Philosopher in the *Ethics* (9.8, 1168[b]), something is seen to be chiefly what is primary in it; thus what the ruler of a state does, the state as a whole is said to do. In this way, what is primary in humans is sometimes said to be the human being: indeed, sometimes the intellectual aspect of the soul is, in accordance with the truth of things, called the "inward" human being. Sometimes the sensing aspect of the soul, along with the body, is called the human being by those whose observation does not go beyond the senses. And this is called the "outward" human being.[15]

9. Thomas's argument seems to be that if every single being that is included in the class of things called "human beings" is necessarily embodied, then embodiment must form part of the definition of a human being. We might complicate this a bit by noting that there are some things, like the capacity for laughter, that are generally found in human beings but do not enter into the definition of "human being" (i.e., do not belong to the "substance" of humanity), being instead "proper accidents" (see 1.3 note 7). So it cannot simply be the ubiquity of embodiment that makes it definitional of the human species as a whole, but rather the fact that it is definitional of each member of the species.

10. Literally, "the operation of the sensual soul."

11. Here again the influence of Aristotle shows itself: Thomas conceives of the "nature" of something not as a hidden element within it, but rather as the source of its characteristic activity. A nature is not a "thing," but rather a capacity to act in a certain way.

12. In 1.75.3 Thomas notes that sensation is invariably accompanied by bodily changes, such as the dilation of the pupil in the act of seeing (or, we might add, the vibration of the ear drum in the act of hearing), concluding from this that the soul by itself cannot be the subject of sensation.

13. I.e., it is also the activity of nonhuman animals.

14. The characteristic activity of human beings is not simply thinking (which God and angels do as well), but specifically thinking based on sense data, which depends on bodily organs of sense. Thus the body, which is the locus of sensation, is necessarily included in what it means to be human.

15. The first objection has cited a passage of Scripture that seems to identify the soul as the "inward self." Though Thomas doesn't use the term, his reply in essence identifies the use of synecdoche

Reply to 2. Not every particular substance is a *hypostasis* or a person, but only one that has the complete nature of its species. Thus a hand or a foot cannot be called a *hypostasis* or a person, and, similarly, neither can the soul, since it forms only a part of the definition of "human."[16]

(allowing a part to stand for the whole) in the passage. At the same time, the soul is not simply any part of the human being; it is the primary part, because the soul is the source of life and thought for the body.

16. The soul is not a "part" of a human being in exactly the way that a hand or foot is, since separation from one's hand or foot does not make one cease to be a human being, while the separation of soul from body does precisely that, making one into a different sort of thing (actually, two things: a corpse and a "separated soul"). But Thomas uses the language of soul as "part" in numerous places (see the quotation from his commentary on 1 Cor. 15 in note 2 above) and consistently describes human beings as "composites" of body and soul. In this way he seeks to acknowledge the duality of body and soul while maintaining that both are integral to making up a human being.

Question 93:

The Image and Likeness of God

1.93.4[1]

Is the image of God in each human being?

It would seem that the image of God is not found in every human being.

1. The Apostle says in the First Letter to the Corinthians (11:7) that "man is the image of God, but woman is the image of man."[2] Therefore, since a woman is an individual of the human species, not every individual is suited to be an image of God.

2. The Apostle says in the Letter to the Romans (8:29), "Those whom God foreknew to be conformed [*conformes*] to the image of his Son, these he predestined." But not all human beings are predestined, so not all people have the conformity [*conformiatem*] of the image.[3]

3. Likeness belongs to the meaning of "image," as explained above (1.93.1).[4] But by sin human beings were made unlike God. Therefore, they lose the image of God.[5]

---

1. On this article, see Pelikan (1978); Merriell (2005).

2. The Vulgate actually reads, "Woman is the *glory* of man." The misquotation in the objection will be silently corrected by Thomas in his response. The larger context of the quotation from Paul is a discussion of whether women should cover their heads in Christian worship and, if so, why. And though Paul's discussion might presume certain things about the nature of human beings as male and female, Thomas recognizes that it is not really intended by Paul as a statement of whether or not the image of God is in women.

3. The language of "conformity" is, in this context, another way of speaking about likeness.

4. In the first article Thomas argues that an image is a kind of "likeness" [*similitudinem*], distinguished from other sorts of likeness in that it has its source in that which it resembles. Two eggs might be "like" each other, but one is not the image of the other, since "image" implies an original or "exemplar" of which the image is a reflection. Thus for Thomas the idea of "image" is tied up with the notion of God as the source of all things.

5. The notion that through sin human beings lose the image of God can be found in the writings of Augustine, though in his later writings he abandoned this view, holding that while sin obscures God's image in us, it does not erase it. Compare *On the Literal Meaning of Genesis* 6.27 and *City of God* 22.24.

On the contrary: It is written in the psalm (39:6): "Surely a human being passes as an image."[6]

I answer: Since a human being is said to be the image of God on account of the intellectual nature, one is thus maximally in the image of God inasmuch as one is maximally able to imitate God in one's intellectual nature.[7] But the intellectual nature maximally imitates God in this way: God understands and loves himself.[8] And so the image of God in a human being can be thought of in three ways. In one way, inasmuch as human beings have a natural inclination [*aptitudinem*] to understanding and loving God. This aptitude consists in the nature of the mind itself, which is common to all

---

6. A more literal translation of the original Hebrew would be that the human being "passes like a shadow."

7. Thomas distinguishes the image of God as found in human beings from that image as found in other beings. He notes that *all* creatures can be called images of God in a minimal sense, inasmuch as, by virtue of their existence, they are like God, who is Being itself. Living creatures are even more images of God inasmuch as they are like God, who is Life itself. But it is intelligent beings that are most properly spoken of as "images of God" because they share with God a similarity not only in their life or existence but also in possessing a spiritual nature (1.93.2). This is why in the book of Genesis it is said only of human beings, among all the things that God has made, that they are made in the image of God (though Thomas thinks angels are likewise in the image of God and, absolutely speaking, more so than humans; see 1.93.3).

Yet there is also a sense in which the maximal image of God is Christ, who is, as the Letter to the Colossians puts it, "the image of the invisible God" (1:15) in a perfect sense: a true image, having his source in the Father, but possessing equal divinity with the Father. For this reason, Thomas says, Christ is said simply to *be* the image of God, whereas the book of Genesis (1:27) says that human beings are made *to* or *toward* the image of God [*ad imaginem Dei*]. Thomas, following earlier commentators, sees this as indicating the relative imperfection of human beings with regard to how they image God (1.93.1 ad 2).

8. In locating the image of God in the intellect, and specifically in the capacity to know and to love, Thomas follows the general drift of early and medieval Christian interpretation. As discussed above (1.27), Thomas employs Augustine's "psychological analogy" of the Trinity to speak of how the processions of the Son and Spirit might be thought of by comparison with the immanent activities of knowing and loving in the human soul. Here Thomas looks at the psychological analogy from the opposite end, as it were: it is precisely in their activities of knowing and loving—specifically, knowing and loving *God*—that human beings are maximally in God's image.

Thomas goes on to say later, "Since the uncreated Trinity is distinguished according to the procession of a word from a speaker, and by the procession of love from both of these, . . . it is possible to say that there is an image of the uncreated Trinity in the rational creature, in whom there is a procession of a word with regard to the intellect and a procession of love with regard to the will, achieving a sort of representation of kind [*quandam repraesentationem speciei*]" (1.93.6). By this last phrase, Thomas seems to mean that the thinking and loving of the rational creature, as immanent acts of the soul, together form a representation of the *kind* of activity that is the immanent life of God. Thus for Thomas human beings are made to the image of God in terms of similarity both to the one divine nature and to the three Persons of the Trinity.

It should also be noted that Thomas thinks of the trinitarian image of God not in terms of a static feature, but of activity. He says, "Primarily and chiefly the image of the Trinity is to be found in the mind on account of its acts—that is, from the knowledge that we possess, we form an internal word by thinking, and from this we burst forth into love" (1.93.7). By the time Thomas writes the *Summa*, his view is that it is not just any acts of knowing and loving that make us the image of God, but the acts of knowing and loving *God*—which are present in all people, though sometimes only in an incipient way. See the following note.

human beings.[9] In another way, inasmuch as a person actually or habitually knows and loves God,[10] although imperfectly. This is the image through the conformity of grace.[11] In a third way, inasmuch as a person actually knows and loves God perfectly. This image consists in the likeness of glory.[12]

Therefore, regarding the words of Psalm 4, "The light of your countenance, O Lord, is signed upon us" (v. 6), the gloss[13] distinguishes a threefold image: of "creation," of "re-creation," and of "likeness." The first is found in all human beings, the second only in the just, the third only in the blessed.

Reply to 1: The image of God, in its principal meaning—namely, the intellectual nature—is found both in man and in woman.[14] Therefore, the book of Genesis, after saying, "to the image of God he created him," adds, "male and female he created them" (1:27). It says "them" in the plural, as Augustine remarks (*On the Literal Meaning of Genesis* 3.22), so that it should not be thought that both sexes were conjoined in one individual.[15] But in a secondary way the image of God is found in man in a way that it is not found in woman. For man is the source and goal [*principium et finis*] of woman, just as God is

9. This would be the broadest sense in which human beings are made to the image of God. Simply by being creatures who know and love, we have some sort of inclination or predisposition to knowing and loving God, since it is only in this that we find perfect fulfillment. However, this inclination remains more potential than it is actual and, as Thomas makes clear elsewhere (see 1–2.109.2, below), does not suffice to unite us with God.

10. I can be said to speak French "habitually" when I have the ability to speak French, but I only speak French "actually" when actively engaged in speaking French. Similarly, I know and love God "actually" when I am actively engaged in thinking about and desiring God, and I know and love God "habitually" when I possess the capacity to do so but am not currently exercising that capacity (e.g., I might be engrossed in weeding my garden and not thinking about God).

11. It is through grace that human beings become capable of fulfilling their inclination to be united to God through knowledge and love, but they do so imperfectly in this life due in part to the limitations of the body and in part to the wounds that sin has inflicted upon human nature.

12. The saints and angels in heaven know God because their minds are illuminated by the light of glory, which perfects the image of God within them. Note that these three ways of possessing God's image follow a pattern Thomas uses throughout the *Summa*: nature, grace, and glory. Thus we possess the image in one way by virtue of having a human nature, we possess it in a different and more perfect way when those natures are elevated and healed by grace, and we will bear that image in the most perfect way when we behold God's glory in the beatific vision (see 1–2.3 note 10).

13. On "glosses," see 1.12 note 10.

14. Though Thomas's view on the sexes might not seem particularly enlightened by modern standards, the bottom line for Thomas, as for Augustine, whom he follows on this score, is that the image of God is in the soul, not the body, and, as regards their possession of a rational soul, men and women are fundamentally equal, both made in the image of God.

15. Some of the church fathers had speculated that prior to the fall human beings were asexual, with sexual differentiation coming only once the mortality brought by sin made it necessary for humans to reproduce in order to preserve the human race (this is perhaps the view expressed by Gregory of Nyssa in *On the Making of Man* 16–17, though his views are not without their ambiguity). Thomas rejects this view, following instead the view of Augustine that sexual difference is original to the human race and will persist in the afterlife.

the source and goal of every creature.[16] So after the Apostle says that "man is the image and glory of God, but woman is the glory of man,"[17] he shows why he has said this, adding, "for man is not from woman, but woman from man; and man was not created on account of woman, but woman on account of man" (1 Cor. 11:8–9).

Reply to 2 and 3: These arguments refer to the image according to the conformity of grace and glory.

16. Here we see that Thomas, despite his acceptance of a fundamental equality of man and woman as regards the rational soul, still regards woman as in some sense subordinate to man, at least in terms of "accidents" that do not reflect the core identity of humans as rational animals. Here he specifically points to the view that man is the "source and goal" of woman. Presumably this claim is partly drawn from the story in Gen. 2 of Eve being fashioned from Adam's rib, with the goal of providing the man with a companion. It probably also reflects the view of Aristotle that the male, as providing the active principle of human reproduction, is in at least one sense the norm of the human species and that females, who provide only the passive, material element in the generation of new human beings, are the result of the active principle failing to reproduce itself perfectly (1.92.1 ad 1). Thomas's Franciscan counterpart in Paris, St. Bonaventure, seems to have disagreed, holding that the woman was "an equal co-producer" (*Breviloquium* 2.10.6; cf. *Commentary on the Sentences* bk. 3, dist. 4, a. 3, q. 1).

17. In his commentary on 1 Corinthians Thomas explicitly notes that Paul does *not* say of the woman (as the objection would have it) "that she is the image and glory of man, but only that she is the glory of man. This gives us to understand that it is common to man and woman to be the image of God" (*Commentary on 1 Corinthians* 11.2.607).

The First Half of

THE SECOND PART

PROLOGUE TO THE
First Half of the Second Part

John of Damascus states (*On the Orthodox Faith* 2.12) that the human being is said to be made to the image of God, in which "image" signifies "an intelligent being endowed with free will and having its own power."[1] Therefore, now that we have spoken of the exemplar—that is, God[2]—and of those things that came forth by divine power in accordance with his will,[3] it remains for us to consider his image—that is, the human being—insofar as we too are the source of our actions, in the sense of having free choice and control of our actions.[4]

---

1. As we saw earlier (see 1.93 note 8), Thomas associates the image of God with the capacity for knowing and willing. Here he alludes to the trinitarian nature of that image, quoting John of Damascus saying that the image involves power, intelligence, and free will, which are often appropriated to the Father, Son, and Spirit (see 1.39.7, above).

2. 1.1–43.

3. 1.44–119.

4. Thomas links the first two parts of the *Summa* in terms of God as the exemplar of human beings, who are God's image. Just as God is the source from which all creatures come forth by the divine will (discussed in part 1), so too human beings are the source of their own free actions (discussed in part 2), and in this way they image God. Part 2 then divides into (1–2) a discussion of the principles of human action—the end, the will, virtue, law, and grace—and (2–2) a discussion of how those actions divide up into various species of good and bad actions—virtues and vices.

Question 1:

The Final Goal for Human Beings

1–2.1.1[1]
Do human beings act because of an end?

It would seem that it is not fitting for human beings to act because of an end [*propter finem*].[2]

1. A cause is naturally first. But "end" conveys the idea of something that is last, as the word itself indicates. Therefore "end" does not convey the idea of a cause. But that because of which a person acts is the cause of human action, since this phrase "because of which" indicates a relationship of causation. Therefore, it is not fitting that human beings act because of an end.[3]

2. What is itself a final end is not something that is on account of an end. But in some cases actions are a final end, as the Philosopher makes clear in the *Ethics* (1.1, 1094[a]).[4] Therefore not everything a person does is for the sake of an end.

---

1. On this article, see Wieland (2002); McCabe (2008, 41–50); Williams (2012).

2. Literally, "according to an end," which might mean "because of an end" or "for the sake of an end" or "on account of an end," where "end" means not so much the termination of activity as it does the goal or purpose of the action (though, as we shall see, Thomas also recognizes the former meaning). As is apparent from Thomas's fifth way of demonstrating God's existence, his worldview is "teleological," meaning that he thinks in terms of the activity of things being accounted for by their "ends" or "goals" (in Greek, *telos*). Here, as he begins his inquiry into human action, he is specifically asking whether human activity is properly thought of in these terms.

3. If I say that Bob lost his job *because of* Betty, I am saying that Betty is the cause of Bob's unemployment. In such a case it might seem natural to presume that Betty did something first (perhaps giving him a poor performance evaluation) that brought about the subsequent loss of Bob's job. But, the objection claims, the word "end" itself implies something that comes at the conclusion of a series of actions, and therefore an end cannot be a cause, since a cause must be prior in time to its effect.

4. Servais Pinckaers notes that "the objection puts its finger on a profound difference between Aristotle and Christian thought regarding how beatitude [i.e., perfect happiness] is conceived" (2001, 215). For Aristotle, action can be an end in itself, whereas for Christians the last end—that which is not for the sake of some further end and which makes one supremely happy—can only be God, an object that stands outside of us.

3. It would seem that one acts on account of an end when one deliberates. But many people act without deliberating, sometimes not thinking of anything at all, as when one moves one's foot or hand or scratches one's beard while focused on something else.[5] Human beings, therefore, do not do everything because of an end.

On the contrary: All things that are within a genus are derived from the source [*principium*] of that genus. But the end is the source in human actions, as the Philosopher makes clear in the *Physics* (2.9, 200ª).[6] It is fitting, therefore, that a human being do everything for the sake of an end.

I answer: Among the actions done by a person, only those that belong to human beings inasmuch as they are human [*quae sunt propriae hominis inquantum est homo*] are properly called "human." Now human beings differ from nonreasoning creatures by being in control of their actions. Therefore, only those actions that a person is in control of are properly called human. People are in control of their actions through their reason and will; on this account the free will is said to be "the faculty and will of reason."[7] Therefore those actions are properly called human that come forth from a deliberate act of will. If any other actions belong to a human being they can be called actions "of a human," but not properly "human actions," because they do not belong to human beings by virtue of their being human [*non sint hominis inquantum est homo*].[8] Now it is clear that all actions that come forth from a

5. What Thomas means by "deliberation" is the thought process that leads up to an action, which makes us characterize it as "deliberate." I can say that I am acting *for the sake of* an end or goal only if my action to attain that goal is deliberate. But, the objection notes, we engage in many actions that are not deliberate but rather instinctual, as when we scratch an itch. It simply doesn't make sense to say that I thoughtlessly dragged my nails across my skin for the sake of scratching, since "for the sake of" implies that my action is deliberate. And an action that has no "for the sake of" is one that has no end or goal.

6. The end or goal is the source of our actions because we chose our actions in light of the end that we wish to attain: I will act differently with regard to a piece of wood depending on whether building a fire or building a house is my end goal. In this sense the end determines our actions in a way analogous to how, in the realm of abstract reasoning, our premises determine our conclusion in an argument (see 1.1 note 18).

7. Peter Lombard, *Sentences* bk. 2, dist. 24, ch. 3. Here again we see reason and will invoked as distinctive human faculties, those which make us creatures *ad imagem Dei* (see 1.93 note 8). Thomas's point is that if we want to speak of *human* actions, we should speak of those actions that are particular to us as human, which are those that involve reason and will. Similarly, if we wanted to speak of "fiery" action or "watery" action, we would speak of those actions, such as heating or making wet, that are particular to fire and water.

8. Thomas does not deny the point made by the third objection that human beings engage in all sorts of actions without deliberating (i.e., without using their reason and will). We scratch, we breathe, we digest food, we trip and fall down, etc. But for Thomas it is important to distinguish these, which he calls "actions of a human being," from "human actions" strictly speaking. This is because, as we shall see, it is only human actions that are subject to moral evaluation. That is, only deliberate actions can be praised as virtuous or criticized as vicious. Though I might have good respiration or digestion, that goodness is not a *moral* goodness, meaning that while they may make me a well-functioning animal, they do not make me a good human being. Likewise, if I trip and fall down and break a valuable vase, this might be an unfortunate event,

power are caused by that power in accordance with the nature of its object. The object of the will, however, is the end and the good.[9] Therefore, all human actions must be for the sake of an end.

Reply to 1: The end, although it is the last thing to be done, is first in the intention of the doer. And it is in this way that it has the nature of a cause.[10]

Reply to 2: If any human action is the final end, it must be voluntary; otherwise it would not be human, as stated above. Now an action can be said to be voluntary in two ways: in one way because it is commanded by the will, as in the cases of walking or speaking; in another way because it comes forth [*elicitor*] from the will, as in the case of the act of willing itself.[11] It is impossible for the act itself that the will calls forth to be the last end, for the object of the will is the end, just as the object of sight is color.[12] Hence, just as it is impossible for the first visible thing to be the act of seeing itself, since every act of seeing is of some visible object, so too it is impossible for the first thing desired [*primum appetibile*], which is the end, to be the act of willing itself.[13] It follows, therefore, that if a human action is the last end, it must

---

but I am not to blame in a moral sense since the action was not deliberate (provided that my tripping is not the unintended result of something that I *did* do deliberately, such as drinking a fifth of whiskey). In this sense, Thomas's distinction between human actions and the actions of a human being is fundamental to everything that will follow in the second part.

9. Having distinguished human action as that which involves reason and will, Thomas goes on to note that the will is defined by its "object." The object of the will is the goal that is desirable, not unlike the way that sight is defined by having visible things as its object and the sense of hearing is defined by having audible things as its object. It is because they have different objects—the visible and the audible—that sight and hearing are distinguished from each other, and likewise the intellect and will are distinguished by their different objects—the knowable and the desirable.

10. If I say that Bob lost his job *because of* Betty, I might be saying that Betty did something that brought it about that Bob lost his job, such as giving him a poor performance evaluation. But I might also be saying that Bob lost his job because of actions he himself took out of his desire for Betty (perhaps, mistakenly thinking that love can be bought, he embezzled money to buy her diamonds and furs). The chain of events that leads to Bob's unemployment is launched because he intended something with regard to Betty (winning her love). Thus even though it is only at the end of the series of actions that Bob can obtain what he desires, he must intend to obtain it from the beginning of his actions; otherwise he would never act (Bob swears that he would never have embezzled were it not for his love of Betty). Thus there is a sense in which the "end" *is* "first"—at least in the sense that I must first intend to gain the end before I am motivated to act.

11. Thomas here distinguishes two sorts of voluntary acts (i.e., acts of the will): (1) the "commanded" actions that we do because of the will and (2) the "elicited" act of willing itself. In the first instance, I might act, under the direction of my will, to get up and walk across the room to get a drink of water; in the second instance, I might act simply in the sense of willing, of engaging in the activity of desiring water. We might call the first sort "a willed act" and the second sort "an act of will"; we might also call the first an "exterior" act and the second an "interior" act.

12. See note 9 above.

13. Just as we cannot see sight, so we cannot desire willing for its own sake. This would seem to separate Thomas from thinkers like Friedrich Nietzsche (1844–1900), for whom willing itself could be the end: what the will wants, according to Nietzsche, is ultimately not to attain this or that end, but simply to increase the power of its act of willing. This "will to power" is rejected by Thomas as incoherent, in the same way

be an action commanded by the will. In that case, some action of a human being, at least the act of willing itself, is for the sake of an end. Therefore, whatever a person does, it is true to say that a human being acts for the sake of an end, even when doing an action that is a last end.[14]

Reply to 3: Such actions are not properly human actions because they do not come forth from rational deliberation, which is the proper source of human actions. They therefore have something like an imaginary end,[15] but not one that is determined in advance by reason.

---

that "seeing sight" is incoherent. The act of will always has an object that calls it forth, and the will's desire ceases when that object is attained.

14. Thomas's argument becomes a bit difficult to follow here. What he seems to be saying is that every external "willed act" involves an internal "act of will" and, as he has just argued, an act of will always has some end or goal as its object. Therefore, every willed act also has an end, borrowed, as it were, from the act of will.

15. By "imaginary" Thomas most likely means an end or goal that is grasped on the level of the senses (and, thus, through "images"), in the way that a nonhuman animal might perceive a certain food to be desirable or a physical threat something to be avoided. He does not mean that such actions have an end or goal that is somehow unreal.

Question 3:

What Happiness Is

1–2.3.8[1]
Does perfect human happiness consist in the vision of the divine essence?

It would seem that the perfect human happiness [*beatitudo*] does not consist in the vision of the divine essence.[2]

1. Dionysius says in the *Mystical Theology* (1.3) that what is highest in the intellect unites a human being to God as to something completely unknown. But what is seen in its essence is not altogether unknown. Therefore the highest perfection of the intellect—namely, happiness—does not consist in God being seen through his essence.[3]

2. The higher the nature, the higher its perfection. But to see his own essence is the perfection proper to the divine intellect. Therefore the final perfection of the human intellect does not reach to this height, but consists in something less.[4]

On the contrary: It is written in 1 John (3:2), "When he shall appear, we shall be like him; and we shall see him as he is."

I answer: Final and perfect happiness cannot consist in anything other than the vision of the divine essence. To make this clear, two points must be

---

1. On this article, see Wieland (2002); Pinckaers (2005, 115–29); Porter (2016).

2. I typically translate *beatitudo* as "happiness," though it might also be translated as "blessedness." It is important to see that Thomas is not referring to a feeling or emotion, but to a state of fulfillment, which I shall occasionally express with the translation "perfect human happiness." Also, with regard to "vision," remember that for Thomas "vision" equals "knowledge," and the "essence" of something is its distinctive nature—that which makes it *this* kind of thing rather than *that* kind of thing. So to have vision of something's essence is to know its nature.

3. Earlier (1–2.3.5) Thomas argued that because it is our intellect (our capacity to know) that makes us distinctive as human animals, our ultimate happiness or fulfillment as human beings must be one that engages this distinctiveness—that is, our capacity to know. In other words, it must be a "human act" (see 1–2.1 note 8).

4. The force of the objection is that if knowledge of the divine essence pertains to the perfection of God, then it cannot pertain to human perfection.

considered. First, a human being is not perfectly happy as long as something remains for one to desire and seek. Second, the perfection of any power is judged according to the nature of its object. Now the object of the intellect is *what a thing is* [*quod quid est*]—that is, the essence of a thing, as said in *De anima* (3.6, 430ᵇ);[5] for this reason the intellect attains perfection insofar as it knows the essence of a thing.[6] If therefore an intellect knows the essence of some effect, by which it is not possible to know the essence of the cause (i.e., to know of the cause *what it is*), that intellect cannot be said to reach that cause in an absolute sense, although it may be able to gather from the effect the knowledge *that* the cause is [*an sit*].[7] Consequently, in knowing an effect and knowing that it has a cause, there naturally remains in a human being the desire to know about the cause *what it is*. This desire belongs to wondering and causes inquiry, as is stated in the beginning of the *Metaphysics* (1.2, 982ᵃ).[8] For instance, if someone, knowing the eclipse of the sun, considers that it comes from some cause and does not know what that cause is, he wonders about it, and from wondering proceeds to inquire. Nor does this inquiry cease until he arrives at a knowledge of the essence of the cause.

If therefore the human intellect, knowing the essence of some created effect, knows no more of God than *that he is*, its perfection does not yet reach the first cause in an absolute way, but there remains in it a natural desire to seek the cause. For this reason it is not yet perfectly happy. Consequently, for perfect happiness the intellect needs to reach the very essence of the first cause.[9] Thus it will have its perfection through union with God as with that

5. The intellect is fulfilled—reaches its goal—when it possesses the definition of a thing, when it can answer the question *Quid est?* (What is it?). One might say that Thomas envisions human beings as animals who are different from other animals in that they constantly ask *Quid est?*

6. The language of the intellect attaining perfection may sound more exalted to us than Thomas intends (see 1.45 note 13). For a human being, to attain perfection in knowing is not to become omniscient but simply to function properly as a human intellect—that is, to actually be what a human intellect is. So our intellects attain a certain kind of perfection all the time; for example, when we look at a four-legged beast that gives milk and say, "That's a cow."

7. Though we may know the essence of some effect, if what we know about its cause is simply *that* it is but not *what* it is, our desire to know remains unsatisfied, since we do not yet know *why* the effect has the essence that it does.

8. As with "perfection," so too "wonder" (*admiratio*) should not be given an overly exalted interpretation: here "wonder" seems simply to mean being puzzled. Given that human beings are fulfilled by knowing what something is, so long as we do not know what something is, we are puzzled and keep inquiring. Our intellects are "perfected" with regard to something when we cease being puzzled and stop our inquiry because we know fully what the thing is, which seems to include knowing its cause.

9. The *perfect* happiness or ultimate fulfillment (i.e., *beatitudo*) of human beings occurs when we cease being puzzled about and inquiring after the cause of *everything*, not simply of this or that thing. In other words, our intellects are ultimately perfected when we can answer, if only partially, the question *Quid est?* with regard to God.

object in which perfect human happiness alone consists,[10] as stated earlier (1–2.1.7; 1–2.2.8).

Reply to 1: Dionysius speaks of the knowledge of those who are on the road [*in via*], journeying toward happiness.[11]

Reply to 2: As stated earlier (1–2.1.8), "end" can be taken in two ways. In one way, it can be taken with regard to the thing itself that is desired, and in this way the same thing is the end of the higher and lower natures, and indeed of all things, as stated earlier. In the other way, it can be taken with regard to the attaining of this thing, and in this way the end of the higher nature is different from that of the lower, according to their respective relationships to that thing. So the happiness of God—who, in understanding his essence, comprehends it—is higher than that of a human being or an angel, who sees it but does not comprehend.[12]

10. For Thomas "vision of the divine essence"—what is commonly called the "beatific vision"—is not simply having a bit of information about God; rather, it actually brings us into *union* with God. In 1.12.5 Thomas says that the "light of glory" (*lumen gloriae*) makes those who see God "*deiform*—that is, like to God." This description fits with Thomas's general views on how we know things (see 1.12 note 11). One way to put it is that "knowing" something amounts to possessing that thing's "form" without actually *being* that thing. The cow Bossy possesses the form of "cowness" by virtue of actually being a cow. When I know that Bossy is a cow, I am in possession of the "form" of "cowness" through the intelligible species (i.e., the essence of the thing as grasped by the mind) of the cow being imprinted on my mind. In the case of the vision of God, the "light of glory" fulfills the function in the mind that the intelligible species fulfills in knowing created things. This vision is "beatific" both because it is the vision possessed by the blessed (i.e., the saints and angels) and because by this act of seeing we become blessed—i.e., partakers of perfect happiness.

11. Dionysius is referring to human beings in this life. Thomas, like Augustine, sees human life as a journey or pilgrimage toward God.

12. Thomas says that human beings (and angels) can "see" God's essence but cannot "comprehend" it. This is an important, though potentially obscure, point. We might say that there are three kinds of knowledge of God: (1) that of "wayfarers," who can know *that* God is but not *what* God is (see 1.12 note 6); (2) that of the angels and the saints in heaven, who can know *what* God is but cannot have an exhaustive or comprehensive knowledge of God; and (3) God's own knowledge of himself. So the knowledge in creatures of the divine essence is not the same as God's knowledge of the divine essence, not least because God possesses the divine essence simply by being God (not unlike the way that Bossy possesses cowness by being a cow).

Question 4:

Those Things That Are Required for Happiness

1–2.4.6[1]

Is perfection of the body necessary for perfect human happiness?

It would seem that perfection of the body is not necessary for perfect human happiness.[2]

---

1. On this article, see Leget (2005); Dillard (2012).

2. Thomas's conviction that human beings are a composite unity of soul and body (see 1.75.4, above) has as a correlate the conviction that perfect happiness involves not simply the immortality of the soul but also, as the Apostles' Creed puts it, "the resurrection of the flesh" (*carnis resurrectionem*). If a human being is to have hope, it must be hope for the whole person, body *and* soul. Like other Christians, Thomas holds that the resurrection of the body will occur at the second coming of Christ. But some problems arise.

First, if it is the whole person who is fulfilled by the vision of God's essence, as Thomas has argued, would it not make more sense to say that the vision of God awaits the reunion of body and soul at the second coming and that prior to this the soul exists in some sort of interim state that does not involve either reward or punishment? This is a view that Thomas, in various places (e.g., *Summa contra Gentiles* 4.91; *On Reasons for the Faith* 1), associates with some "Greeks" (i.e., Eastern Orthodox Christians). The view that souls do not possess the beatific vision prior to the resurrection of the body also seems to have been a position held, at least for a while, by Pope John XXII (ca. 1244–1334), though it was subsequently condemned by his successor, Pope Benedict XII (1285–1342) in his decree *Benedictus Deus* (1336). Thomas argues against this view on the basis of various scriptural passages, such as Luke 23:43, where Christ tells the good thief, "Today you will be with me in paradise." What, Thomas argues, could paradise be but the proper reward of the self: the vision of God? Thomas also argues that since the soul is capable of being rewarded or punished as soon as it is separated from the body, it is fitting that its reward or punishment not be delayed.

Second, even if the vision of God is possessed by the souls of the saints prior to the reunion of body and soul, does this reunion somehow enhance their enjoyment of God? Having defined perfect human fulfillment (*beatitudo*) in 1–2.3.8 as the vision of God's essence, which is an activity of the mind, Thomas is left with this question: Are the currently disembodied souls of the saints somehow less happy now than they will be when they are reunited with their bodies? In his *Sentences*, Peter Lombard had, in essence, answered affirmatively: the happiness of the souls of the blessed is increased by their reunion with their

1. Perfection of the body is a bodily good. But it has been shown earlier (1–2.4.2) that happiness does not consist in bodily goods. A perfect condition of the body, therefore, is not necessary for perfect human happiness.

2. Perfect human happiness consists in the vision of the divine essence, as shown above (1–2.3.8). But the body has no role in this operation, as was also shown earlier (1–2.4.5). Therefore no particular condition of the body is required for perfect happiness.

3. The more the intellect is withdrawn from the body, the more perfectly it understands.[3] But happiness consists in the most perfect operation of the intellect.[4] Therefore the soul should be withdrawn from the body in every way. In no way, therefore, does perfect happiness depend on some condition of the body.[5]

On the contrary: Perfect happiness is the reward of virtue; thus it is written in John (13:17): "You shall be blessed, if you do them." But the saints are promised, as a reward, not only that they shall see and enjoy God but also the well-being of their bodies, for it is written in Isaiah (66:14): "You shall see and your heart shall rejoice, and your bones shall flourish like the grass." Therefore a good condition of the body is necessary for happiness.

---

bodies; and in his own commentary on Lombard's *Sentences*, Thomas agreed. But in the present article we see Thomas modifying his view.

For Thomas's mature position, a key consideration is whether the vision of God is somehow insufficient for human fulfillment, such that human beings require the addition of some created thing—the body—for complete happiness, in which case final human happiness would depend, at least in part, on a creature. But in 1–2.2.8 Thomas argues the general point that ultimate happiness cannot depend on a creature; and in 1–2.4.5 he argues the specific point that the union of body and soul cannot be an essential requirement for seeing God, since we see God not through sense images but through the light of glory, though the union of body and soul might still have a role to play in the "well-being" (*bene esse*) of our seeing God.

All of this is a backdrop for Thomas's discussion in this article, which deals not simply with the soul's union with the body but also with the perfection or fulfillment of that body (in thinking about the perfection of the body, it is good to keep in mind the sense of "perfection" as actualization or completion; see 1.45 note 13). Thomas is not simply asking whether the body is some sort of external aid to the soul's fulfillment (as if the soul alone constituted the "self"), but rather whether the body itself is "saved" by having some sort of share in the vision of God.

3. For Thomas's account of knowledge, see 1.12 note 11. In this case, the objection focuses on how our knowledge of what something is depends on "abstracting" its form from the material particularity of what we perceive through our senses. Thus when I know the animal in front of me to be a dog, it is by setting aside the particularity of the animal so as to see what it has in common with all other animals called "dogs."

4. On the perfection of the intellect, see 1–2.3 note 6.

5. The first two objections argue for the non-necessity of the perfection of the body for human happiness. This objection raises the stakes, arguing that since knowledge involves a process of "abstraction" or withdrawal of the mind from the body, the perfect knowledge that is involved in the vision of God would require a correspondingly perfect separation of mind and body; thus the union of body and soul actually *hinders* the perfect happiness of the soul.

I answer: If we speak of the human happiness one can have in this life,[6] it is clear that a good bodily condition is necessarily required for it, for this happiness consists, according to the Philosopher (*Ethics* 1.13, 1102ª), in "an activity according to perfect virtue." It is clear that a person can be hindered from every virtuous activity by physical disability.[7]

But if speaking of perfect happiness [*beatitudine perfecta*], some have maintained that happiness does not require any particular condition of body—indeed, it requires that the soul be completely separated from the body. Augustine, in *The City of God* (22.26), quotes the words of Porphyry, who said that "for the soul to be happy, everything physical must be fled." But this is unfitting. Since it is natural to the soul to be united to the body, it is therefore impossible for the perfection of the soul to exclude the body's natural perfection.[8]

Consequently, we must say that the perfect condition of the body is required for happiness that is in every way perfect, and this is the case both as a condition for and as a result of happiness.[9]

It is a *condition* for perfect happiness because, as Augustine says in his *On the Literal Meaning of Genesis* (12.35), "If a body is such that it is difficult and burdensome to govern, like the flesh that is corruptible and weighs upon the soul, the mind is turned away from that vision of the highest heaven." From this he concludes that "when this body will no longer be 'animal,' but

6. Thomas distinguishes between the happiness that can be had in this life (which he elsewhere calls "imperfect happiness"—see 1–2.5.4, below) and the perfect happiness of the next life. What Thomas means by "imperfect happiness" has been the subject of much discussion, not least because Thomas is not entirely clear. Is he referring to the happiness that is attainable by human beings purely by their natural powers, or is he referring to the happiness attainable by Christians through grace, which remains imperfect until it is fulfilled in divine glory? Depending on which passage in Thomas one is reading, either understanding is possible. Cf. 1–2.5 notes 7 and 8.

7. Thomas does not mean, of course, that a physically disabled person cannot be moral. Rather he holds that our attainment of complete human excellence (which is another way of translating the Greek word *aretē*, normally translated as "virtue") involves excellence of body as well as of soul, since human beings are unities of body and soul. So attainment of the imperfect happiness afforded by this life might be impeded by various kinds of physical weakness; in particular, given the dependence of the intellect on sense data, our capacity to reason might be hindered by a bodily defect.

8. This argument presumes that the union of body and soul is "natural" (see 1.75.4, above). Here we run up against a fundamental philosophical disagreement between Thomas and those whose views he would oppose. Thomas is well aware of the argument that the union of body and soul—or, perhaps, the "imprisonment" of the soul in the body—is something profoundly *un*natural. It was held by ancient Platonists like Porphyry and, in Thomas's day, was held by those Christian heretics known as Albigensians or Cathars, who argued that matter was evil and that the soul was a divine spark held captive in the body. To a Cathar, it would be all too obvious that *only* the separation of body and soul could lead to blessedness.

9. Or, as a more literal translation of Thomas would have it, it is necessary "both antecedently and consequently." In other words, perfection of the body comes (logically speaking) both "before" (as a condition for its possibility) and "after" (as a result of its attainment) the final perfection of the soul.

'spiritual,' then it will be made equal to the angels, and that which formerly was its burden will be its glory."[10]

It is a *result* of perfect happiness because there will be an overflow from the happiness of the soul into the body, so that this, too, will attain its own perfection. Therefore Augustine says in the letter to Dioscorus (*Epistle 118*, 3) that "God gave the soul such a powerful nature that from its exceeding fullness of happiness the strength of incorruption overflows into the lower nature."[11]

Reply to 1: Happiness does not consist in bodily good as its object, but bodily good can add a certain beauty [*decorem*] and perfection to happiness.[12]

Reply to 2: Although the body contributes nothing to that function of the intellect by which the essence of God is seen, nevertheless it might prove a hindrance. Consequently, perfection of the body is required so that it does not hinder the lifting up of the mind.

Reply to 3: The perfect operation of the intellect requires that the intellect be withdrawn from this corruptible body that weighs upon the soul, but not from a spiritual body, which will be completely subject to the spirit. This will be discussed in the third part of this work.[13]

10. In common with the whole Christian tradition, Thomas holds that the resurrected bodies of the just, like Christ's resurrected body, will not simply be reanimated (i.e., reunited with the soul) but will be fundamentally transformed. In the Middle Ages qualities—described as *dotes* or "dowries"—such as "clarity," "invulnerability," "subtlety," and "agility" were typically ascribed to such transformed bodies (these are largely drawn from the Gospel accounts of Jesus's resurrected body). The key point, however, is that the transformed human body is no longer a burden that hinders the soul's enjoyment but rather the perfect medium through which the soul's glory is manifested. Note, however, that it does not seem to be a medium for knowledge, as it is currently, since God will be known directly through the light of divine glory (see 1–2.3 note 10).

11. Thomas habitually speaks of the perfection of the body as something that is a kind of "excess" or "overflow" from the perfection of the soul. Here he is clear that the perfection of the soul, absolutely speaking, has priority over the perfection of the body.

12. *Decorem* implies a kind of ornamentation or adornment. Thomas's use of this term suggests a way out of what can seem to be the circular claim that the perfection of the body both is prior to and follows upon the perfection of the soul. The perfection of the body is not of the essence of human fulfillment, because this fulfillment is nothing other than knowing or "seeing" God, which is done through the soul by the light of glory and in which all human desire is satisfied. However, the full glorification of the person also involves the glorification of the body to which the soul is naturally united, and thus, in a qualified sense, the soul still wishes to be united with its body. As Thomas puts it in 1–2.4.5 ad 5, in the vision of God the soul already possesses the highest good that can be desired, but it does not possess it in every possible way, since it does not possess it through bodily perfection: "After the body is taken up again, perfect happiness does not become more intensive, but more extensive." This is a shift from his earlier position, in his commentary on Lombard's *Sentences*, where he claimed that both the extent and the intensity of beatitude increased upon the soul's reunion with its body.

13. The discussion in question can be found in the so-called *Supplementum*, questions 82 and following. Thomas never finished writing the *Summa*, breaking off a few months before his death while in the midst of treating the sacrament of penance. Thus he never wrote the sections dealing with the sacraments of anointing of the sick, marriage, and ordination—nor the sections that would have treated the "four last things"—death, judgment, heaven, and hell. Thomas's followers assembled the *Supplementum* out of his early commentary on Peter Lombard's *Sentences*, in order to round out the original plan of the *Summa*.

Question 5:

The Attainment of Happiness

1–2.5.4[1]

Can perfect happiness be lost after it has been acquired?

It would seem that perfect happiness can subsequently be lost.[2]

1. Happiness is a kind of perfection. But every perfection is in the thing perfected in a manner that is suited to it. Since a human being is by nature changeable, it seems that happiness is shared in by human beings in a changeable manner.[3] And consequently it seems that a person can lose happiness.

2. Perfect happiness consists in an act of the intellect, which depends upon the will. But the will can be directed to things that are the opposite of one another. It seems, therefore, that it can cease the operation by which a human being is made happy, and thus that person will cease to be happy.[4]

3. The end corresponds to the beginning. But the happiness of human beings has a beginning, since humans were not always happy. Therefore, it seems that it has an end.[5]

On the contrary: It is said of the just in Matthew (25:46) that "they shall go into life eternal," which, as stated above (1–2.5.2), is the happiness of the

---

1. On this article, see Gaine (2003, 87–136).

2. This article, particularly in the second half of Thomas's reply, addresses an issue raised by the view that Origen of Alexandria was alleged to have held (though firsthand evidence is lacking) that, after the restoration of all things, beatified souls might fall again, having grown bored with God. This view was widely rejected, though the question remained open as to how to reconcile the impossibility of a second fall with a belief in human free will: If the souls and heaven cannot turn away from God, in what sense are they still free?

3. This might be seen as an extension of the principle that "grace does not take away nature but perfects it" (see 1.1 note 34). Since it is the nature of human beings to be changeable, even grace cannot make their happiness be unchangeable.

4. The objection, interpreting the will's freedom as its ability to choose between different things, claims that the very nature of the will necessitates that it could turn from happiness to choose its opposite.

5. This objection might be thought of as a variation of the first objection: since it is the nature of human beings to have a finite existence, their happiness must likewise be finite, having a beginning and an end.

saints. But what is eternal does not pass away.[6] Happiness, therefore cannot be lost.

I answer: If we are speaking of imperfect happiness, such as we can have in this life, it *can* be lost.[7]

This is clear in the case of the happiness of the contemplative life, which is lost either through forgetfulness (for instance, when knowledge is lost through sickness), or through certain occupations, by which one is entirely distracted from contemplation.[8] This is also clear in the case of the happiness of the active life, since the human will can be changed so as to fall from virtue (in whose act happiness principally consists) into vice.[9] Even if virtue remains intact, outward changes can still disturb such happiness, inasmuch as they get in the way of many acts of virtue, even though they cannot take virtue away altogether, because there still remains the act of virtue by which a person bears these adversities in a praiseworthy manner.[10] And since the happiness of this life can be lost, which seems to be contrary to the nature of happiness, the Philosopher says in the *Ethics* (1.10, 1101ᵃ) that some are happy in this life, not absolutely speaking, but "in the manner of human beings," whose nature is subject to change.[11]

6. The *sed contra* points us to the fact that the Gospels use the term "eternal life" to speak of perfect human happiness, and it notes that what is eternal does not come to an end.

7. We see here again the distinction between perfect and imperfect happiness (*beatitudo*) that Thomas draws (see 1–2.4 note 6). As noted earlier, at least at times Thomas identifies imperfect happiness with the kind of life described in Aristotle's *Nicomachean Ethics* (see 1–2.3.2 ad 4 and 1–2.3.6 ad 1). Aristotle is therefore still useful to Christians, since the happiness he speaks of can be true happiness while still being imperfect. So we might contrast a false happiness, such as the pleasure we might experience committing adultery or pulling off a really good bank caper, with a true happiness that yet remains imperfect, such as a life of moral virtue lived out in human community or a life devoted to contemplation of what reason can discern of God. Both of these, however good, are still imperfect—or, we might say, "incomplete"—compared to the happiness associated with the vision of God's essence, which is a complete happiness leaving nothing to be desired.

8. Does Thomas mean by "contemplative life" the specifically Christian state of graced contemplation of God, or something broader, such as any life given over to thought and study (see 2–2.182.1, below)? In either case, his basic point is the same: in this life our thinking is often interrupted, as when illness causes us to forget or our train of thought is interrupted by having to cook a meal or wash our clothes, and therefore the happiness of the life of thought and study cannot be perfect in this life.

9. Thomas sees the happiness of the active life as consisting in our doing those actions that spring from a virtuous disposition. But virtuous people often lose their virtue, and their character becomes corrupted; therefore, the happiness of the active life cannot be perfect in this life.

10. Even if a person remains virtuous, his or her happiness might be diminished by changed circumstances. Thus falling into poverty might keep one from acting generously, or a crippling disease might keep one from engaging in an act of bravery. Part of the happiness of possessing virtue is the opportunity to act on those virtues, but sometimes circumstances that prevent us from acting can reduce our virtuous action to the level of simply patiently suffering those circumstances. To put it in terms Thomas has used earlier (see 1–2.1 note 11), even if the exterior willed act is prevented by circumstances, the interior act of will can suffice as an exercise of virtue. But the impeded exercise of virtue could still result in diminished happiness.

11. Thomas thinks Aristotle gestures toward perfect, eternal happiness when he makes this passing remark in the *Nicomachean Ethics* about those who are happy in this life being happy *ut homines* (as human beings),

But if we speak, on the other hand, of that perfect happiness that we await after this life, it must be noted that Origen, following the error of certain Platonists, suggests that a person, after attaining final happiness, can become unhappy again.[12] This, however, is clearly false for two reasons.

First, based on the general idea of "happiness" itself.[13] Being a perfect and sufficient good,[14] happiness must quiet human desire and exclude every evil. Now one naturally desires to retain the good that one has and to be sure that it will be retained; otherwise one is necessarily afflicted by the fear of its loss or by the sadness of knowing for certain that it will be lost. It is therefore required for true happiness that one have a sure belief [*opinionem bonum*] in never losing the good that one possesses. If this belief is true, it follows that one will never lose happiness. If false, this itself is something evil—i.e., having a false belief—for falsity is an evil for the intellect, just as truth is its good, as stated in the *Ethics* (6.2, 1139ᵃ). Consequently, such a person will no longer be truly happy since some evil is in him.[15]

Second, the same thing is apparent if we consider the specific nature of happiness.[16] It has been shown (1–2.3.8, above) that perfect human happiness consists in the vision of the divine essence. Now it is impossible for anyone seeing the divine essence to wish not to see it. This is because every good that one possesses and yet wishes not to have is either insufficient, so that something sufficient is desired in its place, or else has something disagreeable connected to it, on account of which it becomes unpleasant.[17] But the

---

implying that there is a kind of supernatural happiness beyond this life. Many modern interpreters of Aristotle are not as convinced as Thomas is that Aristotle is suggesting a supernatural happiness beyond this life.

12. Thomas is perhaps thinking of *On First Principles* 2.3, though it is not clear what writings of Origen he had access to. Thomas had little direct knowledge of Plato, and his understanding of Platonist views on this question may be derived from Augustine, *City of God* 10.30. See also note 2, above.

13. Thomas argues here from the very meaning of the term *beatitudo* in general—specifically, its perfection and completeness.

14. See Aristotle, *Ethics* 1.7, 1097ᵃ.

15. Since blessedness, being by definition perfect, would seem to exclude anything negative, and since anxiety is a negative emotion, one who experiences anxiety over losing happiness is not, by definition, happy. So if we are confident that we will never lose our happiness, and this is in fact true, then we are perfectly happy. If we are confident that we will never lose our happiness and we are deceived about this, then we are not perfectly happy, since we are suffering the negative quality of being deceived. In either case, truly perfect happiness excludes the loss of that happiness. Here it helps to bear in mind that Thomas does not mean by *beatitudo* simply a subjective, emotional state, but rather something more like "complete fulfillment."

16. Thomas now makes an argument based on the specific nature of *human* happiness as the vision of God's essence.

17. So, for example, I might desire french fries, but because french fries alone do not make for a balanced diet, I eventually desire (as scurvy sets in) to eat something other than french fries. Or, I desire a romantic relationship with someone despite his or her personality flaws simply because the person is so physically attractive, but over time those flaws that I thought I could overlook loom larger and larger until I cease to desire that person, no matter how beautiful he or she might be.

vision of the divine essence fills the soul with all good things by joining it to the source of all goodness. For this reason, it is written in the Psalms, "I will be full when your glory shall appear" (17:15), and in the book of Wisdom it is said, "All good things came to me with her" (7:11)—that is to say, with the contemplation of wisdom. Similarly, the vision of the divine essence has nothing disagreeable connected to it, for it is written of the contemplation of wisdom, "Her conversation has no bitterness, nor her company any tediousness" (Wis. 8:16). It is thus evident that one who is happy cannot abandon happiness by his own will.[18]

Similarly, one cannot lose happiness by God taking it away, because the taking away of happiness is a kind of punishment; it therefore cannot be withdrawn by God, the just judge, except for some fault, which one who sees God's essence cannot fall into, since, as was shown earlier (1–2.4.4), the uprightness of the will necessarily results from that vision.[19]

Nor again can any other agent take it away, for the mind that is joined to God is raised above all other things, and thus no other agent can hinder the mind from such a union.[20] It seems therefore unfitting that a human being should, over time, pass from perfect happiness to misery, and vice versa,

18. The vision of God, unlike french fries or a physically attractive person, is both a complete good, satisfying every desire, and a perfect good, containing no flaws.

A different argument is made by Thomas in the *Summa contra Gentiles*: "Nothing that is contemplated with wonder [*cum admiratione*] can be tiresome, since as long as the thing remains in wonder it continues to stimulate desire. But the divine substance is always viewed with wonder by any created intellect, since no created intellect comprehends it. So, it is impossible for an intellectual substance to become tired of this vision" (3.62.9). Because God's essence cannot be comprehended by any creature, even in the beatific vision, there is always more to discover about God, so it is not possible for God to ever cease being an object of fascination for us. This seems to be in conflict with Thomas's discussion in 1–2.3.8, above, which suggests that when one beholds God's essence, "wondering" [*admiratio*], and therefore desire, ceases. The cessation of wondering and desire in the beatific vision, and their replacement by enjoyment (*delectatio*), seem to represent Thomas's more typical position. The view he expresses in the *Summa contra Gentiles* can also be found in the writings of the Dominican tertiary Catherine of Siena (1347–80), who writes of God saying of the souls in heaven: "They desire me forever, and forever they possess me, so their desire is not in vain. They are hungry yet satisfied, satisfied yet hungry" (*Dialogue* 41).

19. Having addressed the question of whether the soul enjoying *beatitudo* could willingly turn from the vision of God, Thomas now turns to the question of whether such a soul could be unwillingly turned from that vision. He first asks whether God could take the vision from us, and he replies that God could only do this as a punishment for some fault, since God is supremely just. But the soul that sees the divine essence clings to God and thus can incur no fault for which a just God would punish it.

20. Thomas next asks whether something other than God could ever cause the soul enjoying *beatitudo* to turn from God. His answer is that the union of the mind with God makes it impossible for anything to tempt the mind away from God. This implies that the soul enjoying *beatitudo* is more stable in its happiness than were Adam and Eve, who could be tempted away from God. Here Thomas shows the influence of Augustine, who argued that before sinning, human beings were "able not to sin" (*posse non peccare*), but also able to sin (*posse peccare*), and in their fallen state are "not able not to sin" (*non posse non peccare*), but in heaven will be "not able to sin" (*non posse peccare*). See Augustine, *Admonition and Grace* 33.

because such temporal changes are not possible except for things that are subject to time and motion.[21]

Reply to 1: Happiness is complete perfection, which excludes every defect from the blessed. Therefore, it comes without change to one who has it, brought about by divine power, which elevates the human being to participation in an eternity that transcends all change.

Reply to 2: The will can be directed to things that are the opposite of one another in things that are means to the end, but it is oriented toward the last end by natural necessity. This is clear from the fact that a human being is not able not to wish to be happy.[22]

Reply to 3: Happiness has a beginning due to the condition of the one who shares in it, but it has no end on account of the condition of the good, sharing in which makes one blessed.[23] Therefore, it is from one cause that happiness has a beginning and from another that it has no end.

21. In concluding his argument, Thomas suggests that the soul that is perfectly happy cannot turn from God because it is no longer "subject to time and motion." He goes on to say in the reply to the first objection that this is because it participates or shares in God's own eternity. He says elsewhere in the *Summa* that "the happiness of the saints is called eternal life because through enjoying God they become partakers, as it were, of God's eternity, which surpasses all time, so that the continuation of happiness does not differ in respect of present, past, and future" (2–2.18.2 ad 2).

22. For Thomas, the objection has misunderstood the nature of free will. In Thomas's view, the will is free with regard to its choice of means by which to attain its ultimate end, but not with regard to the end itself, since the will is necessarily drawn to what it sees as good (see 1.83.4 as well as 1–2.6.1, below). In the vision of God's essence, the means by which we see God is no created thing but, rather, the light of glory, which is not something distinct from the divine essence itself (see 1–2.3 note 10). So you might say that in the beatific vision we are joined to the end without any means. Since freedom of choice has to do with means and not ends, human free will is not compromised by the impossibility of the soul enjoying *beatitudo* turning away from its final end.

23. Happiness has a beginning because of the kind of being *we* are (temporal), but it has no end because of the kind of being *God* is (eternal).

Question 6:

The Voluntary and Involuntary

1–2.6.1[1]
Is anything voluntary found in human acts?

It seems that nothing voluntary can be found in human acts.

1. The voluntary is "what has its principle within itself," as is clear from Gregory of Nyssa,[2] John of Damascus (*On the Orthodox Faith* 2.24), and Aristotle (*Ethics* 3.1, 1111ª). But the principle of human acts is not in the human being himself or herself but rather outside, for human desire [*appetitus hominis*] is moved to act by a desirable object [*appetibili*] that is external and is like an unmoved mover, as it says in *De anima* (3.10, 433ᵇ).[3] Nothing voluntary, therefore, is found in human acts.

---

1. On this article, see Gallagher (2002); Williams (2012).

2. The quotation is actually from *On the Nature of Human Beings* 31, a work by the late-fourth-century Christian writer Nemesius of Emesa, which was widely attributed to Gregory in both the East and the West during the Middle Ages. The section of John of Damascus's *On the Orthodox Faith* that deals with the voluntary and the involuntary and to which the objection appeals is heavily indebted to Nemesius.

3. The objection brings together two seemingly contradictory claims. The first claim is that an action is free if and only if it has its *principium* or source within the doer of the action. So if I choose to walk down a flight of stairs, my descent is a free action. But if I am shoved down the stairs by someone else, my descent is not a free action. This claim is also presumed by the other two objections. The second claim is the one that Thomas makes in the very first article of the second part (see 1–2.1.1, above), that we act if and only if we are moved or motivated by a desire for some good thing that we do not possess (e.g., I move my hand to bring a glass to my lips because of the goodness of the wine that the glass contains). But this second claim locates the source of our act outside of us, in the good thing that we do not possess. Therefore, it would seem, our actions cannot be free.

Note that Thomas calls this good thing that motivates our action an "unmoved mover"—a term he also applies to God—because it moves us by no action other than the very act of being good; it does not itself need to move in order to move us by its attractive power; indeed, it need not even be aware of our existence. This, it should be noted, is not how Thomas thinks of God as an unmoved mover, since God is not only the goal that motivates us but also the active cause of our existence, though it is likely that this *is* how Aristotle thinks of God.

2. In the *Physics* (8.2, 253ª) the Philosopher proves that no new motion is found in animals that is not preceded by an exterior motion.[4] But all human acts are new, since no human act is eternal. Consequently, the principle of all human acts is external and therefore there is nothing voluntary found in them.

3. One who acts voluntarily is able to act from oneself [*per se agere potest*]. But this is not fitting for human beings, for it is written in John (15:5): "Without me you can do nothing."[5] And so there is nothing voluntary found in human acts.

On the contrary: John of Damascus says (*On the Orthodox Faith* 2.24) that "the voluntary is an act consisting in a rational operation." But this is true of human acts.[6] Therefore, there is something voluntary found in human acts.

I answer: There must be something voluntary in human acts. In order to make this evident, we might note that the principle of some acts or movements is in the thing acting—that is, within the thing that moves—but the principle of other movements or acts is external. When a stone moves upward, the principle of this movement is external to the stone, but when it moves downward, the principle of this movement is in the stone itself.[7]

Of those things that move by an intrinsic principle, some move themselves and some do not. Since everything that acts or moves does so for an end, as stated earlier (1–2.1.2),[8] things that are perfectly moved by an intrinsic principle are those in which there is an intrinsic principle not simply for movement but for movement toward an end. In order for something to be done for the sake of an end, some knowledge of the end is required.[9] Therefore, whatever acts or is moved by an intrinsic principle in this way, such that it has some

4. By "exterior motion" the objection means the action of something outside the animal, which Aristotle identifies as its "environment" (in the Latin translation Thomas used, *ambit*). The argument seems to be that the actions of all animals, including humans, are shaped by their environment to such a degree that the actions of the animal are not truly free. This perhaps anticipates certain modern forms of behavioristic determinism, according to which all of our actions are caused by a set of physical or historical or cultural or environmental forces, rather than by the will.

5. Here the objection shifts from philosophical to theological grounds: if without God we can do nothing, then all our actions are determined by something outside of us, and we are not truly free.

6. Note here the distinction between a "human act" and the "act of a human being" (see 1–2.1 note 8, above).

7. Thomas, lacking any theory of gravitational forces, thinks of material objects as having inherent directional tendencies due to their elemental composition. Thus a stone, in which the element of earth predominates, has an intrinsic tendency to move downward. Left to its own natural tendency, a stone will fall, without the need for anything else moving it downward; if a stone rises, this must be because of something else acting upon in (such as a person throwing it upward).

8. On what it means to act for an end, see 1–2.1 notes 2, 6, and 10, above.

9. Thomas makes this same point in the initial article of the *Summa* in arguing for why we need the discipline of theology (see 1.1 note 9).

notion of the end, has within itself the principle of its action, so that it not only acts, but acts for the sake of an end.

But if something has no notion of the end, even if there is a principle of action or movement within it, the principle of its acting or moving for the sake of an end is nevertheless not in that thing but in something else, by which the principle of its movement toward an end is imprinted on it. For this reason, these sorts of things are not said to move themselves, but to be moved by others. But those things that have a notion of the end are said to move themselves because there is a principle in them not only for acting but also for acting for the sake of an end. Consequently, since both the fact that they act and the fact that they act for the sake of an end are from an intrinsic principle, the actions and movements of these things are said to be voluntary, for the word "voluntary" implies that movements and acts are from their own inclination. And so, according to the definition of Aristotle, Gregory of Nyssa, and Damascene, the voluntary is defined not only as having "a principle within" but also as having "knowledge." Therefore, since human beings most of all know the end of their actions and move themselves, in their actions the voluntary is most of all to be found.[10]

Reply to 1: Not every principle is a first principle.[11] Therefore, although what is voluntary, by its very nature, has its principle within [the doer of the action], it is nevertheless not contrary to the nature of what is voluntary to have this intrinsic principle caused or moved by an external principle. For it is not of the very nature of what is voluntary that its intrinsic principle be a first principle. Nevertheless, it must be noted that it can be the case that a principle of movement be first in terms of the kind of thing it is, but not first absolutely; for example, among those things that are subject to change, the primary source of such change is a heavenly body, which is nevertheless not

---

10. Merely having an internal source of movement, in the way that a falling stone does, is not sufficient to warrant saying that something moves itself for the sake of its end. Even though all things have a goal or end to their action (something that they are moving toward), not all things know that they have a goal. Despite the fact that the elemental constitution of the stone is a source of its downward movement, the end or goal of the stone remains external to it, and so the rock can only be said to move itself "imperfectly." A thing moves itself "perfectly" when it has knowledge of the end or goal for the sake of which it is acting; in the act of knowing, it, as it were, takes the end or goal into itself so that that goal becomes something like the elemental constitution of the stone—i.e., an intrinsic principle or source of activity. In this way, something that not only has an end but is capable of knowing that end (as is the case with human beings) has that end as a principle within itself and thus acts in a perfectly free manner. This, Thomas says, is why the authorities cited in the first objection do not say that something acts voluntarily simply when it acts from a principle within, but only when it also acts with knowledge of its end.

11. This is a point that is central to Thomas's whole understanding of how the world is put together: something can be a secondary cause of activity without ceasing to be a genuine principle or "source" of activity (see 1.2 note 61).

the first mover absolutely speaking, but is moved with regard to place by a higher mover.[12] And so the intrinsic principle of voluntary action, which is the capacity for knowing and desiring, is the first principle within the class of those movements that comes from desire [*in genere appetitive motus*], even though it is moved by something external with respect to other kinds of movement.

Reply to 2: A new movement of an animal is preceded by an exterior motion in two ways. In one way, inasmuch as an animal's senses are confronted by means of an exterior motion with something that can be sensed and, when apprehended, moves desire. For example, a lion, on seeing a deer drawing near, begins to move toward it. In another way, inasmuch as a physical change in an animal's body is brought about by some external movement—for example, through cold or heat. The body being affected by the motion of an external body, the desire of the senses, which is the power of a bodily organ, is also moved indirectly [*per accidens*]. In this way, in conjunction with some alteration in the body the appetite is roused to desire something. But this is not contrary to the nature of voluntariness, as stated above (in the reply to 1), for such movements from an exterior source [*principio*] are of a different kind.[13]

Reply to 3: God moves a human being to act not only by offering to the senses something desirable or by making a change in the body but also by moving the will itself. For all movement, whether of the will or of nature, comes forth from God as the first mover.[14] And just as it is not contrary to the

12. Thomas's basic point is that something might be the primary source of change within a certain class of things without being the primary source of change absolutely. His example, however, is not much help to a modern reader, who may not think in terms of movement on earth as being caused by the planets (though the persistent popularity of horoscopes might also make us think otherwise). Today we might be more inclined to say that the "Big Bang," as something like the first movement to occur in the universe, is the ultimate source of all motion in the universe; but this does not mean that the Big Bang itself does not have a source that is not contained within the category of motion. So we might say that the Big Bang is the first principle of the universe with regard to motion, but not the first principle simply speaking. This sort of thinking underlies Thomas's "five ways" of demonstrating God's existence (see 1.2.3, above).

13. Here Thomas notes that there are two ways in which we might talk about an animal (including a human animal) having its action shaped by its environment. On the one hand, the movement of a desirable object brings it to my attention and incites my desire: as the deer comes into view, the lion sees it, desires it, and then moves to hunt it down and eat it. On the other hand, some factor in the environment such as temperature or humidity or the brightness of the sun might indirectly lead my desire to be incited: cold weather increases my appetite; high humidity makes me want to lie in a hammock and drink beer; bright sun makes me seek out shade. As Thomas noted in his reply to the previous objection, in the case of human beings, neither of these sorts of environmental influences takes away the reality of the will as a principle of action.

14. In this reply, Thomas moves beyond the problem of "natural determinism" posed by the first two objections to the potentially more difficult issue of what we might call "supernatural determinism"—i.e., the idea that God determines our every action. Not afraid to grasp the nettle, Thomas begins by noting that there is a unique way in which God is involved in our actions, not only by influencing the will through

concept of nature that the movement of nature be from God as the first mover (inasmuch as nature is a kind of instrument of God as mover), so too it is not contrary to the concept of a voluntary act that it be from God, inasmuch as the will is moved by God. Nevertheless, a natural movement and a voluntary movement share this essential feature: they are from an intrinsic principle.[15]

---

the senses or by the environment but by actually moving the will itself, a view that follows necessarily from the position Thomas argued in the five ways (1.2.3, above) that God is the first mover of all things.

15. Just as God, as the creator of its nature, is the ultimate source of the downward motion of the falling rock, so too God, as the creator of the will, is the ultimate source of the will's choosing. Yet just as the rock's falling is not contrary to, but actually in accord with, its nature as a heavy object, so too the will's willing is not contrary to, but actually in accord with, its nature as the voluntary power of the soul. This is what Thomas means in saying that both natural and voluntary movement are from an intrinsic principle. For Thomas, however, acting from an intrinsic principle not only *does not* but *cannot* mean acting independently of God; it is God who makes our acts to be free acts by making us to be free creatures. For more on this issue, see 1–2.9.6.

Question 9:

The Mover of the Will

1–2.9.1[1]
Is the will moved by the intellect?

It would seem that the will is not moved by the intellect.

1. Regarding the psalm that says, "My soul passionately wanted to desire your ways of justice [*tuas justificationes*]" (119:20), Augustine says that the intellect flies ahead, while the feelings follow sluggishly, if at all; we know the good, but doing it does not delight us (see *Exposition 8 of Psalm 118*, 4). But this would not be the case if the will were moved by the intellect, for the movement of what can be moved is a result of the motion of the mover. The intellect, therefore, does not move the will.[2]

2. In presenting what is to be desired, the intellect is related to the will in the same way that the imagination is to the sensory appetite.[3] But in presenting what is to be desired, the imagination does not move the sensory appetite; indeed, sometimes we relate to what we imagine in the same we do to a picture that is shown to us, which does not move us at all, as it says in *De anima* (3.3, 427[b]). Therefore, neither does the intellect move the will.[4]

1. On this article, see Gallagher (2002); Williams (2012).
2. In the sermon that Thomas cites, Augustine addresses the question of how it is that we can want to desire something without actually desiring it. In the course of his discussion, Augustine distinguishes between, on the one hand, knowing that something is good and wanting in a theoretical way to desire it and, on the other hand, actually desiring it. The objection's point is that if the intellect moved the will, then simply knowing that we ought to desire something would suffice to make us actually desire it.
3. For Thomas, "imagination" is not the creative cognitive capacity that we today mean by this term, but rather more the storehouse of images derived from the senses that human beings accumulate over time. It is what allows me to call to mind a particular object even when I am not directly perceiving it. The analogy is that just as our faculty of image retention and retrieval is what presents objects to the part of our mind that grasps sense images, so too our intellect is what presents objects to the part of our mind (namely, the will) that grasps the goodness of things.
4. We can conjure up an image of a tiger without recoiling in fear or of a ripe peach without salivating. Following on the analogy between the imagination and the intellect, we should be able to think of something good without desiring it.

3. Something is not both the mover and the thing moved with regard to the same thing. But the will moves the intellect, for we exercise the intellect when we will to do so. Therefore, the intellect does not move the will.[5]

On the contrary: The philosopher says in *De anima* (3.10, 433[b]) that a thing understood as desirable is an unmoved mover, whereas the will is a moved mover.[6]

I answer: Something needs to be moved by something else inasmuch as it has potential with respect to many things; for that which is potential needs to be actualized by something actual, and to do this is to make something move.[7] Now a power of the soul is understood to have potential to different things in two ways: in one way with regard to acting and not acting, and in another way with regard to this action or that action. It is like how the power of seeing sometimes actually sees and sometimes does not, and sometimes sees white and sometimes black. It therefore needs a mover in two respects: with regard to the exercise or use of the act, and with regard to the determining of the act.[8] The first concerns the subject, which is found sometimes to act and sometimes not to act, while the other concerns the object, by which the act is specified.[9]

Now the motion of the subject itself is from some agent. And since every agent acts for the sake of an end, as was shown above (1–2.1.2), the source of this motion is from the end. It is for this reason that the skill [*ars*][10] that pertains to the end moves by its command the skill that pertains to the means to the end, just as the skill involved in navigation rules over the skill involved in shipbuilding, as it says in the *Physics* (2.2, 194[b]).[11] Now goodness in general,

---

5. Since I can will myself to think or not think about something, the will is clearly capable of moving the intellect. But something cannot be moved by something that it moves, so the intellect must not be able to move the will.

6. On this use of the term "unmoved mover" see 1–2.6 note 3.

7. See 1.2 note 36.

8. Here Thomas distinguishes between the choice of acting or not acting, on the one hand (what he elsewhere calls the "exercise" of the act), and the choice of acting in this way or that way, on the other (what he elsewhere calls the "determination" of the act). To his example of the power of sight, we might add that of the difference between my deciding to get up out of my chair rather than not and my deciding to get up out of my chair to get a beer rather than to pet my dog.

9. By "specified" Thomas means that it makes the act be the kind of act it is. So someone can cut wood and hammer nails, but these are only acts of "shipbuilding" if the "object" or point of this collection of actions is to build a ship. With a different object, our acts of cutting and hammering might be housebuilding rather than shipbuilding. Likewise, my getting up out of my chair is an act of thirst relieving if the beer is my object and an act of dog rewarding if petting my dog is the object.

10. See 2–2, prologue note 10.

11. Since the point of building a ship is to be able to sail it somewhere, it is the one who sails the ship who determines whether the shipbuilder builds the ship. If there is no sailor who desires to go somewhere, there is no motive for the shipbuilder to build the ship.

which has the nature of an end, is the object of the will. Therefore, in this respect the will moves the other powers of the soul to their acts, for we make use of the other powers when we will.[12] For the end and perfection of every other power is included under the object of the will as some particular good; and it is always the art or power directed toward the universal end that moves to action the arts or powers directed toward particular ends included in the universal. Thus the leader of an army, who intends the common good—that is, the order of the whole army—moves by his command one of the officers, who intends the order of one company.

On the other hand, by determining the act the object moves in the manner of a formal principle, by which in natural things actions are specified, the way the act of heating is specified by heat. But the first formal principle is being [*ens*] and truth in general, which is the object of the intellect. And so it is by this kind of motion that the intellect moves the will by presenting its object to it.[13]

Reply to 1: From this passage we should take the point not that the intellect does not move [the will], but that it does not move [it] from necessity.[14]

Reply to 2: Just as imagining a form without evaluating its fittingness or harmfulness does not move the sensory appetite, so neither does the apprehension of what is true without the thought of its goodness and desirability (*sine ratione boni et appetibilis*). Hence the speculative intellect does not move, but rather the practical intellect, as is said in *De anima* (3.9–10, 432^b–433^a).[15]

12. That is, I get up from my chair when I will to do so, my will being moved by something that is good (whether this be drinking a beer or petting a dog).

13. On "form," see 1.12 note 2. Heating is distinguished from cooling because it involves bringing about the form "heat" in things. The end, not as goodness-in-general but as this or that particular good, is like a form in relation to our actions, and form is grasped by the intellect. It is because my intellect grasps the difference between the goodness involved in drinking a beer and the goodness involved in petting a dog that I will, in rising from my chair, be doing one of these things rather than the other. We might say that it is the intellect that gives to will its character as either dog-petting-desire or beer-drinking-desire.

In terms of Thomas's basic distinction in this article (note 8), the will moves the intellect in terms of the exercise of its act (I will myself to engage in thinking), and the intellect moves the will in terms of determining its act (I desire this rather than that because of my intellect's judgment of a particular thing's goodness).

14. If we were forced to will any good that we perceived, then our will would not be free. Thomas says that Augustine's point is that while the intellect *can* move the will by presenting it with a good object, it does not *inevitably* move the will when it does so.

15. The objection is correct that the will is not moved simply by thinking of a good object. Rather, we must think of a good object precisely as *good*—i.e., as desirable. It is the intellect's judgment of goodness (which is the act of the "practical intellect" in accordance with the disposition that Thomas calls *synderesis*—see 1.79.12) that moves the will, not simply its intellectual grasp of the object's existence (which is the act of the "speculative intellect").

Reply to 3: The will moves the intellect with regard to the exercise of the intellect's act, for the true, which is the perfection of the intellect, is itself included in the universal good as a particular good. But with regard to the determination of the act, which derives from the object, the intellect moves the will. For the good itself is apprehended according to a special concept as included under the universal concept of the true. It is thus clear that something is not both the mover and the thing moved with regard to the same thing.[16]

---

16. Because the will *moves* the intellect with regard to its exercise—its thinking or not thinking—and is *moved by* the intellect with regard to its determination—its willing this or that thing—it is clear that the will is something moved in a way that is quite distinct from how it is a mover, such that there is no contradiction between the two claims. It is not unlike how I, as the one pressing my car's accelerator and putting it into gear, can be said to be the cause of my car's motion, even while my car, as that which transports me from point A to point B, can be said to be the cause of my motion. I am both mover and moved, but not in the same sense.

Question 18:

Good and Bad in Human Acts in General

1–2.18.4[1]
Is a human action good or bad on account of its end?

It would seem that the good and bad[2] in human actions are not from their end.

1. Dionysius says in *On the Divine Names* (4) that "nothing acts with a view to evil."[3] If therefore an action were good or bad [*mala*] from its end, no action would be evil [*mala*]. Which is clearly false.

2. The goodness of an action is something existing in the action. But the end is an extrinsic cause. Therefore, it is not on account of its end that an action is said to be good or bad.[4]

3. Something that is a good action may happen to be directed toward a bad end, as when someone gives alms on account of a desire for empty glory; on the other hand, something that is a bad action may happen to be directed toward a good end, as when a theft is committed in order to give something to the poor. It is not, therefore, from its end that an action is good or bad.[5]

---

1. On this article, see Westberg (2002).

2. In most cases I have translated *malum* in this article as "bad" rather than "evil" because we tend to think of the latter term as implying a moral fault, which in Thomas's discussion is only one of the ways in which an action might be judged to be *malum*. The act of striking out in baseball, for example, is "bad," but it is not "evil."

3. Though the objection is quoting Dionysius, the notion that "the good is what all things desire" is central also to Aristotle (*Ethics* 1.1, 1094[a]).

4. Thomas distinguishes between causes that are "intrinsic"—namely, matter and form—and those that are "extrinsic"—namely, the agent and the end (on Thomas and Aristotle's account of causes in general, see 1.2 note 41; on final causes, see 1.2 note 58). The objection's point is that since "goodness" or "badness" is a feature of a thing, it must be there on account of an intrinsic cause and therefore not on account of an end.

5. The end does not justify the means; stealing is still wrong, even if it is done for a good purpose. Likewise, the end doesn't vitiate the means: a bad ultimate goal does not make a good action done as a means of attaining that goal into a bad action in itself. Giving to the poor is still, in itself, a good action, even when done by celebrities who simply want to distract the public from their most recent DUI.

On the contrary: Boethius says in *On Topical Differences* (bk. 2) that "if the end is good, the thing itself is also good, and if the end is bad, the thing itself is also bad."

I answer: The disposition of things with regard to goodness is the same as their disposition with regard to being.[6] Now the being of some things does not depend on something else, and in these it suffices to consider their being itself, in an absolute sense.[7] There are, however, things whose being does depend on something else; it is necessary, therefore, when considering them to consider their being also in its relation to the cause on which it depends. Now just as the being of a thing depends on the agent and the form, so the goodness of a thing depends on its end.[8] Thus in the divine Persons, who do not have a goodness that depends on another, the reckoning of their goodness is not taken from the end.[9] But human actions, and other things whose goodness depends on something else, have the reckoning of their goodness from the end on which they depend, besides that goodness that exists in them in an absolute sense.

Therefore, in human action a fourfold goodness can be considered.[10] First, it has goodness according to the kind of thing it is [*secundum genus*]—that is, an action; for inasmuch as it has action and being, to that degree it has goodness, as stated above (1–2.18.1).[11] Second, it has goodness according to its species, which is taken from its having a fitting object.[12] Third, it has

6. See 1.1 note 3 on the "unity of the transcendentals." In this instance, this principle is used to justify the view that what is true of things in terms of their being (i.e., that we can distinguish between dependent and nondependent existence) is also true of them in terms of their goodness (i.e., we can distinguish between dependent and nondependent goodness).

7. This nondependent sort of being is found, of course, only in the case of God. All other beings have dependent existence.

8. Here Thomas seems to correlate formal and efficient causality with being and final causality with goodness. Of course, the form and agent can also be thought of as causes of the goodness of a thing: the design of a building and the skill of the builder might be the reason why we call it a "good building." However, the end or purpose of something has, as we shall see, a distinctive role in evaluating its *moral* goodness.

9. Just as God's existence is nondependent, so too is God's goodness.

10. Here Thomas is summarizing his conclusions from the previous three articles.

11. In 1–2.18.1 Thomas argues that in actions, as in things, "each one has as much good as it has being." This is what Thomas refers to in the previous paragraph as "goodness in an absolute sense." Thus one aspect of the goodness of an action is simply whether it is a successfully realized action. My action of swinging a wooden bat is good in this sense if I swing with a smooth arc, with power, etc. The fact that I am swinging this bat in order to bash in someone's skull (i.e., the end of my action) is irrelevant to its goodness in this sense.

12. For Thomas the "object" of the action is "matter about which" [*materia circa quam*] an action is concerned (1–2.18.2), not unlike the "subject matter" of an academic discipline. Just as the subject matter of biology (life) "specifies" it and distinguishes it from physics (which studies bodies in motion), so too our actions are "specified" by their object (see also 1–2.9 note 9). We might say that the object of our action gives it its distinctive "shape," not unlike the way form gives shape to matter. For example, the act

goodness according to its circumstances—as it were, with respect to certain accidents.[13] Fourth, it has goodness according to its end—as it were, in relation to a cause of its goodness.[14]

Reply to 1: The good to which one looks in acting is not always a true good: sometimes it is a true good and sometimes an apparent good. In the latter case, a bad action results from the end.[15]

Reply to 2: Although the end is an extrinsic cause, due proportion and relation to the end are nevertheless inherent to the action itself.[16]

Reply to 3: Nothing prevents an action from having one of the previously mentioned forms of goodness while lacking another.[17] And thus an action that is good according to species or according to its circumstances can be directed to a bad end, or vice versa. However, an action is not good simply speaking unless *all* these forms of goodness occur together—for "every single defect causes evil, but good is caused from the complete cause," as Dionysius says (*On the Divine Names* 4).[18]

---

of swinging a bat is not, in itself, *about* anything; it only becomes a meaningful act once it is seen in terms of its object: Am I intending to drive in a home run (and therefore playing baseball) or crack a skull (and therefore perhaps assaulting someone, or defending myself, or trying to perform primitive brain surgery)?

It can be difficult to distinguish between the object of a human action and its end, and this is because in the moral evaluation of an act, object and end are identical. The cracking of a skull with a bat cannot be understood as the particular kind of moral act that it is without inquiring into the purpose for which the skull is being cracked.

13. Just as the object of an action is like the substantial form of a thing, making it the action that it is, so the circumstances in which an action is done are like the accidents of a thing. Thomas notes (1–2.18.3) that the goodness of a thing is not simply a matter of a thing's substantial form but can also depend on its accidents. So a human being who lacks the capacity for laughter is still a human being (i.e., possesses the substantial form of a human being) but realizes that humanity less fully because of lacking the accidental property of a sense of humor. In the same way, an action (such as using a bat to drive in a home run) might still be good in terms of its object, but that goodness can be diminished by when or where or how the action is done (such as doing it while in the middle of a crowd of people).

14. Two actions that seem identical in all other ways—swinging a bat while standing at home plate in the process of playing a baseball game—might receive very different moral evaluations depending on the purpose for which they are done: achieving fame and glory versus raising money for charity.

15. What matters in the capacity of something to draw the will is not the goodness of the thing in itself but rather the intellect's apprehension of the thing as good. This accounts for the fact not only that we might be attracted to something evil but also that we might fail to be attracted to something good.

16. What determines the goodness or badness of the action is not the end itself, but the relationship or "fit" between the action and the end, and this relationship is something intrinsic to the doer of the action.

17. That is, one of the four ways mentioned at the end of the body of the article.

18. A morally good action must be, in a sense, comprehensively good; a failure to be good in one respect leads to the badness of the action as a whole. We might think of this in terms of a complete description of an action. For example: In the Jerusalem temple (circumstance), the priest cut (act) the throat of a sheep (object) as a sacrifice to honor YHWH (end). If we change one of these elements—so that, for example, the priest is at a birthday party, or drops the knife, or cuts the throat of a child, or seeks to honor Baal—then the action may fail to be morally good.

Question 55:

The Essence of the Virtues

1–2.55.4[1]
Is "virtue" suitably defined?[2]

1. On this article, see Kent (2002); Bauerschmidt (2013, 258–64).

2. Thomas's discussion of "virtue" follows upon his discussion of *habitus*, which I translate here as "disposition." For Thomas, a *habitus* is not a habit in the way that chewing your nails is; rather, it is more like a skill. Human beings are born with certain capacities for action, such as mobility, thinking, and willing. In addition to these capacities with which they are born, human beings can also develop new capacities for action, as when one acquires an ability to shoot a bow or play a musical instrument or be courageous or prudent or just in one's dealings with others. When these abilities become a settled disposition or capacity, they are what Thomas calls a *habitus* and contribute to the perfection or completeness of a person. Some kinds of *habitus*, such as a bow-shooting *habitus* or a violin-playing *habitus*, perfect a person with regard to a particular activity. Other kinds of *habitus*, such as a capacity to act bravely or prudently or justly, perfect persons in a more general way, making them not simply better bow shooters or violin players but better human beings. These sorts of *habitus* are what Thomas calls "virtues" and are what he is seeking a definition for here.

Thomas might have organized his discussion of the Christian moral life in the second half of the second part around the Ten Commandments (something not uncommon in the Middle Ages), but he chose instead to use the virtues to structure his discussion, not least because he thought that human moral excellence was a better way of displaying how it is that human beings are led to blessedness. Those who think of morality primarily in terms of rule following, rather than virtue cultivation, might initially find much of what Thomas says puzzling. On the other hand, those who think of morality in terms of not inflicting harm on others, as is common in modern societies, might find Thomas equally puzzling. The key for modern readers is to see that for Thomas the moral evaluation of an act rests primarily not on its effect on others but on its effect on the doer of the act. Those acts are good that constitute me as a good person. While rules and consequences have a role to play in evaluating an action, these are subordinated to what the action says about the doer of the action.

Two other points should be noted about virtue and how Thomas departs from the Aristotelian tradition. First, Aristotle holds that the way we acquire virtue is through repeated practice; this is as true of being brave or just as it is of violin playing (see *Nicomachean Ethics* 2.1, 1103ᵃ–1103ᵇ). Thomas agrees that this is true of what he calls "human" or "acquired" virtue, but he also holds that there are other virtues that are not acquired through practice but are "infused" in us—i.e., received as a gift from God (Thomas discusses the cause of *habitus* in general in 1–2.55.3–4 and of virtue in 1–2.63).

Second, Aristotle holds that the essence of a virtue is that it is the "mean" (*meson*) or midpoint between two different vices, which can be understood in relation to the virtue in terms of excess and deficiency (see *Nicomachean Ethics* 2.6, 1106ᵇ). For example, the virtue of fortitude (i.e., courage) is the

It would seem that this customary definition of virtue is not a fitting one: "Virtue is a good quality of the mind, by which we live uprightly, of which no one makes bad use, which God works in us without us."[3]

1. Virtue is the goodness of a person, since it is virtue "that makes its subject good" (Aristotle, *Nicomachean Ethics* 2.6, 1106[a]). But it seems that goodness is not good, just as whiteness is not white. It is therefore unsuitable to describe virtue as a "good quality."[4]

2. No difference is more general than its genus, since it is what divides the genus.[5] But "good" is more general than "quality," because it is convertible with being.[6] Therefore "good" ought not to be put in the definition of virtue as differentiating quality.

3. As Augustine says in *De Trinitate* (12.8): "When we come across anything that is not common both to us and to cattle, it is something pertaining to the mind." But some virtues also belong to the irrational parts [of the soul], as the Philosopher says in the *Ethics* (3.10, 1117[b]). Every virtue, therefore, is not a good quality "of the mind."[7]

4. "Uprightness" [*rectitudo*][8] seems to pertain to justice, on account of which the upright are called "just." But justice is a kind of virtue. It is there-

---

mean between cowardice and recklessness. Thomas again partially agrees that some virtues are defined as a mean, but he holds that some infused virtues do not follow a middle path between vices. For example, Thomas holds that whereas one might, in the case of courage, fear death too little or too much, one cannot believe in God or hope in God or love God too much (Thomas discusses virtue as a mean in 1–2.64).

3. This definition is from Peter Lombard (*Sentences* bk. 2, dist. 27, ch. 1), cobbled together by him, as Thomas notes, primarily from phrases and ideas found in Augustine's *On Free Choice of the Will* (cf. *Retractions* 1.9).

4. The objections take up the various elements of the Augustinian definition of virtue. In this case, the phrase "a good quality" is criticized for treating virtue as if it were a thing rather than a quality of a thing. Just as "whiteness" is not itself something white (for this would require that "whiteness" possess the quality of "whiteness," which would in turn need to possess a further quality of "whiteness," and so on ad infinitum), so too "goodness" is not good; rather, it is a quality of a person who is good.

5. A genus or general category is subdivided into less general categories by differences: thus "animal" is subdivided by different sorts of animals: dogs, cats, horses, earthworms, etc. These differences must have a narrower range of application than the general category in order to subdivide it.

6. On the "convertibility" of the transcendentals, see 1.1 note 3, above. The argument here is that in the phrase "good quality" the term "good," which is supposed to subdivide the genus "quality," is more rather than less general in scope than what it is supposed to divide, because "good" is coextensive with "being."

7. Things like emotions, which are rooted in our bodily natures rather than our rational nature, can be subject to shaping by virtue. Moreover, one virtue, moderation, is specifically directed to the moderation of bodily pleasures (which is the context in which Aristotle mentions "virtues of the irrational parts"). Therefore, the objection concludes, virtue is not found only in the mind, as the phrase "a good quality of mind" seems to suggest, but also in the body.

8. *Rectitudo* might also be translated as "righteousness," but the translation "uprightness" underscores how *rectitudo* is the state of being able to stand in God's presence, freed from the burden of sin, as well as how *rectitudo* involves a certain "straightness" of our intentions through their being oriented toward God, our final goal.

fore unfitting to put "righteous" in the definition of virtue, as when we say that virtue is that "by which we live uprightly."[9]

5. Whoever is proud of something makes bad use of that thing. But many are proud of virtue; for Augustine says in his *Rule* that "pride lays an ambush for good works in order to destroy them" (*Epistle 211, 6*). It is therefore untrue "that no one makes bad use of virtue."[10]

6. Further, one is justified by virtue. But Augustine, commenting on John (14:12), "He shall do greater things than these," says: "He who created you without you will not justify you without you" (*Sermon 169, 11.13*).[11] It is therefore unfitting to say that "God works virtue in us without us."[12]

On the contrary: There is the authority of Augustine, from whose words—principally in *On Free Choice of the Will* (2.19)—this definition is gathered.

I answer: This definition perfectly comprises the complete notion of virtue, for the perfect notion of anything is gathered from all of its causes, and the definition stated above includes all the causes of virtue.[13]

The formal cause of virtue, as of anything, is taken from its genus and difference when it is said to be "a good quality," for the genus of virtue is "quality" and the difference is "good." But it would be a more fitting definition if in place of "quality" we substituted "disposition" (*habitus*), which is the immediate genus [*genus propinquum*].[14]

9. In essence the objection argues that if we use a virtue—"justice"—to define virtue, then our definition becomes a circular one.

10. A key part of Augustine's critique of Roman virtue is that it was vitiated by pride in those very virtues.

11. Different forms of this quotation from Augustine are cited by numerous medieval writers (see, e.g., Bonaventure, *Breviloquium* 5.3.6; Catherine of Siena, *Dialogue* 119) to argue for some degree of human cooperation in God's work of making us upright (i.e., the work of "justification").

12. Along with the technical question regarding the definition of virtue, this objection points to a tension mentioned earlier (see note 2, above) between Aristotle's account of virtue, which sees it as a quality acquired by human beings through repeated practice, and the Augustinian account of virtue, which sees it as a quality infused in the soul by God. Thomas's account of virtue can be thought of as a delicate attempt to negotiate this tension.

13. Thomas here is reflecting Aristotle's view that to know *what* something is involves knowing *why* it is: knowing the definition of "harmony"—the existence of a ratio between musical tones—is the same as knowing the cause of harmony—that there is a ratio between tones (see *Posterior Analytics* 2.2, 90^a). Thomas justifies the adequacy of this definition by showing how it gives an account of virtue in terms of Aristotle's four causes (on the four causes, see 1.2 note 41).

14. In his *Commentary on Aristotle's "Physics"* (4.23.637) Thomas clarifies what he means by "immediate genus." As noted, things within a genus are distinguished from one another by differences; these differences might themselves serve as genera that are further differentiated. Thus in geometry the genus "shape" is differentiated into "circle," "square," "triangle," etc. "Triangle," in turn, might serve as a genus within which we might differentiate "scalene," "equilateral," etc. If our goal is to define an equilateral triangle over and against a scalene one, then the best genus for that purpose will be "triangle" and not "shape," since this is the genus that immediately contains the relevant difference, and this is what Thomas calls the "immediate genus." His point here is that if what we want is to define virtue over against other

Like any other accident, virtue has no matter out of which it is formed.[15] But it does have matter about which [it is concerned] and matter in which [it exists]—namely, the subject.[16] The matter about which [it is concerned] is virtue's object, which could not be included in the definition given above because the object determines a specific kind of virtue, whereas here we are giving a definition of virtue in general.[17] Therefore, we have the subject [in which virtue exists] in the place of the material cause, when it is said that virtue is a good quality "of the mind."[18]

Since it is a settled disposition toward action [*habitus operativus*], the final goal of virtue is the activity [*operatio*] itself.[19] It should be noted that some dispositions to action are always directed toward evil, as in the case of vicious habits; others are sometimes directed toward good and sometimes toward evil, in the way that regards both the true and the false; but virtue is a settled disposition that is always directed toward good.[20] So, in order to distinguish virtue from those [dispositions] that are always directed toward evil, it is said, "by which we live uprightly"; and to distinguish it from those [dispositions] that are sometimes directed toward good and sometimes toward evil, it is said, "of which no one makes bad use."

---

acquired capacities, such as bow shooting or violin playing, then the immediate genus is *habitus* rather than "quality," since "quality" includes—along with *habitus*, which is an acquired capacity for action—such things as color, position, etc.

15. Note that Thomas identifies virtue as an "accident." This means that it is an incidental quality that does not change the nature of the thing of which it is a quality. This excludes the possibility of it having matter from which it is made, for while a statue might be made out of marble, one would not say that its whiteness was made out of marble. It also means that virtue does not change the fundamental nature of the person who is virtuous—a human being can lose or gain virtue without ceasing to be a human being (just as a white statue can be painted red without ceasing to be a statue).

16. Since there is no matter out of which virtue is made, Thomas looks for things that are analogous to matter. The first of these is what we might call the "object" that the virtue concerns (e.g., "justice" is about fairness) and the second is what we might simply call the "subject" (i.e., the one who possesses that virtue).

17. There is no subject matter to virtue in general because it is a virtue's subject matter—or what Thomas calls its "object"—that distinguishes one virtue from another. Thus justice, which has to do with fairness to others, is different from moderation, which has to do with controlling bodily desires.

18. Virtue has no matter out of which it is made or with which it is particularly concerned, but it does have a subject that it modifies, just as whiteness or redness modifies a statue. In the case of virtue, its subject is the mind, by which Thomas means the higher capacities of the soul.

19. The point of having a virtue is not simply to possess that virtue, but to act in accordance with it, just as the point of the *habitus* of bow shooting is to shoot a bow. A virtue that was possessed but never acted upon (were such a thing imaginable) would be pointless—i.e., lacking an end.

20. In addition to virtue, there are both vices (which are defined by their orientation toward evil action) and those *habitus* (such as the capacity for bow shooting) that might be good or bad, depending on whether the further goal they are given is good (such as shooting at a target) or evil (such as shooting at a noisy neighbor). What makes virtue different from both of those is that it causes good action and cannot even potentially be used for an evil end.

The efficient cause of infused virtue, which is what is being defined here, is God. For this reason it says, "which God works in us without us." If this part is omitted, the remainder of the definition will be common to all virtues, both acquired and infused.[21]

Reply to 1: That which first falls under the intellect is being; for this reason we attribute to everything that we apprehend that it is a being, and consequently that it is one and is good, which are convertible with being. We therefore say that essence is "a being" and is "one" and is "good," and that oneness is "a being" and is "one" and is "good," and similarly concerning goodness. But there is no place for this in regard to special forms, such as whiteness and health, for not everything that we grasp is grasped through the notions "white" and "healthy."[22]

We must, however, note that just as accidents and nonsubsistent forms are called beings not because they themselves have being but because things are by them, so also are they called good or one not by some other goodness or oneness but because by them something is good or one. Likewise, virtue is called good because by it something is good.[23]

Reply to 2: The "good" that is included in the definition of virtue is not good in general, which is convertible with being and is more extensive than quality, but the good of reason, according to what Dionysius says in *On the Divine Names*: the good of the soul is to be in accord with reason (4.32.733a).[24]

Reply to 3: Virtue cannot be in the irrational part of the soul, except insofar as it participates in reason, as it says in the *Ethics* (1.13, 1102^b–1103^a). And therefore reason, or the mind, is the proper subject of human virtue.[25]

---

21. As mentioned above (see note 2), Thomas holds that, in addition to those virtues that are acquired through our own actions, there are virtues that are present in us by divine gift, which Thomas calls "infused." Thomas notes here that the Augustinian definition is specific to infused virtues, which are solely the work of God, but that with the omission of the final phrase ("which God works in us without us"), the definition could apply to acquired virtues as well.

22. The first part of Thomas's reply is to point out the dis-analogy between an accidental quality, such as whiteness, which is possessed by some things and not others, and a transcendental property of all things that exist, such as "goodness."

23. The second part of Thomas's reply is that while we would not say that whiteness is white, we might say it is good or one to the degree that it makes that which possesses this quality good or one by making it white (for example, whiteness makes a piece of cloth good if you are looking to make a flag to surrender with, so in that case we would say that whiteness is good). Likewise we can say that a quality, such as virtue, is good to the degree that it makes its possessor courageous or temperate or prudent or just.

24. The kind of goodness that virtue possesses is not the transcendental property applicable to all beings, but the specific goodness of being a quality of the soul that brings the acts of the soul into harmony with reason.

25. The irrational part of the soul shares in virtue to the extent that it is made subject to the rational part of the soul. Thomas will go on to specify that the seat of virtues "can only be the will, or some power [of the soul] insofar as it is moved by the will" (1–2.56.3). This is because a virtue is what allows us to act well, and it is the will that moves us to action.

Reply to 4: The uprightness that is proper to justice is constituted in relation to those external things that come into human use, which are the proper matter of justice, as will be shown later (1–2.60.2; 2–2.58.8). But the uprightness that signifies being oriented toward a suitable end and to the divine law, which is the rule of the human will, as stated above (1–2.19.4), is common to all the virtues.[26]

Reply to 5: One can make bad use of virtue as an object—for instance, by thinking about a virtue badly, either by hating it or by being proud of it—but not as a principle of action, that is to say, so that an act of virtue would be bad.[27]

Reply to 6: Infused virtue is caused in us by God without our acting, but not without our consent. This is how we should understand the words "which God works in us without us." As to those things which are done by us, God causes them in us, but not without us acting, for he works in every will and nature.[28]

---

26. The term "justice" can be used specifically to refer to the virtue that concerns our dealings with others, or it can be used more generally to refer to how any of the virtues directs us to our true end. In the case of the Augustinian definition, it is this latter, more general, sense that is meant.

27. If I stop and think about my courage or moderation or justice—if I "objectify" it—then it is possible for me to make bad use of my possession of that virtue by becoming arrogantly proud of it; but insofar as I am the one who possesses that virtue—if I "subjectify" it—then it is impossible for that virtue to make me act badly. So if I truly possess the virtue of courage, I cannot help but act well when I act courageously.

28. The "natural movement" of the will is to move freely toward the good, not unlike the way that the natural movement of the rock is to move downward. Therefore, the only thing outside the will that could cause that free movement would be that which gave the will its nature in the first place—namely, God. See 1–2.6 note 15.

Question 61:

The Cardinal Virtues

1–2.61.2[1]
Are there four cardinal virtues?

It would seem that there are not four cardinal virtues.[2]

1. Prudence directs the other moral virtues, as is clear from what was said earlier (1–2.58.4).[3] But that which directs other things has priority over them. Prudence alone, therefore, is a principal virtue.

2. The principal virtues are in some way moral virtues. But we are directed to moral actions both by practical reason and by a correct appetite, as is said in the *Ethics* (6.2, 1139^a). Therefore, there are only two cardinal virtues.[4]

3. Among other virtues, one likewise has priority over another. But in order for a virtue to be called "principal," it is not required that it have priority over all virtues, but only above some. It seems, therefore, that there are many more principal virtues.[5]

On the contrary: Gregory says in his *Moral Reflections on the Book of Job* (2.49.76), "The entire structure of good works is built on four virtues."

1. On this article, see Kent (2002); Mattison (2010).

2. The virtues of prudence (*prudentia*), justice (*iustitia*), moderation (*temperentia*), and fortitude (*fortitudo*) occur as a distinct group both in Greek philosophy (e.g., Plato's *Republic* 4) and in the Bible (Wis. 8:7). The term "cardinal" (literally, "hinge") in this connection seems first to have been used by Ambrose of Milan in the fourth century. Aristotle neither speaks of "cardinal virtues" nor singles out these four amid the other virtues for any type of special role.

3. While the virtue of moderation, for example, might give us balance with regard to bodily pleasure, it is the virtue of prudence that guides us as to what this means in particular circumstances, so the other virtues cannot function properly without prudence, and in this sense prudence would seem to be *the* principal or cardinal virtue.

4. The image of God in human beings is found in their two distinctively human powers: knowing and willing (see 1.93 notes 9 and 10); therefore it would seem that the key virtues should be only two in number: one directed toward knowing (practical reasoning) and the other toward willing (right desiring).

5. Given that there are many virtues that can be seen as subdivisions of other virtues, it seems that there are more "principal" virtues than the four traditional cardinal virtues.

I answer: Things may be enumerated either according to their formal principles or according to the subjects [in which they are found], and by either means we find that there are four cardinal virtues.

For the formal principle of these virtues is the good of reason,[6] which we can think about in two ways. In one way, inasmuch as it consists in reason's consideration itself, and in this way there will be one principal virtue, called "prudence."[7] In another way, inasmuch as the order of reason is laid down with regard to something else: either regarding actions, and in this way we have "justice," or regarding emotions, and then we need two virtues. For it is necessary to lay down the order of reason regarding the emotions in consideration of their very repugnance to reason. This can occur in two ways. First, inasmuch as emotion urges us to something contrary to reason, and then it is necessary for it to be restrained, and this we call "moderation." Second, inasmuch as emotion holds us back from what reason dictates—for example, through fear of danger or hard work—and then it is necessary that one be strengthened to do what reason dictates, in order not to retreat, and this is called "fortitude."[8]

Similarly, the same number is found if we consider the subjects [in which the virtues are found]. For we find four subjects of these virtues: what is rational through its essence (and this is perfected by prudence) and what is rational by participation, which is subdivided into three—the will (which is the subject of "justice"), the concupiscible power (which is the subject of "moderation"), and the irascible power (which is the subject of "fortitude").[9]

6. That is, they all enable us to act in a reasonable way.

7. Exercising prudence is itself a reasonable action (which is why it is "practical reasoning"). The other cardinal virtues are directed to making other actions reasonable.

8. Virtues need to regulate both *actions* and *reactions*. If it is a matter of *actions*, things that affect others, then we need the virtue of justice. If it is a matter of our *reaction* (which is one way we might translation Thomas's term *passio*), this might be a case where we have to reasonably direct our being drawn to something we find desirable, in which case we need the virtue of moderation, or it might be a case where we have to reasonably direct our wanting to flee from something we find undesirable, in which case we need the virtue of fortitude.

9. Thomas is quite happy to consider alternative reasons for why there might be four cardinal virtues. In this case, he sees the different cardinal virtues as have different "subjects"—i.e., as perfecting different human faculties. Prudence perfects reason with regard to knowing how to act, and justice perfects the will with regard to acting equitably toward others. Moderation perfects the "concupiscible faculty," which is the instinctual desire rooted in the senses by which we desire bodily things (see 1.81.2), and fortitude perfects the "irascible faculty," which is the fight-or-flight instinct by which we respond to danger.

Earlier Thomas had identified the will, or a faculty moved by the will, as the subject of virtue (see 1–2.55 note 25, above). This fits easily with what he says here about justice (the subject of which is the will) as well as moderation and fortitude (by which the concupiscible and irascible faculties are moved by the will). But what about prudence? That which is "rational through its essence" would seem to be the intellect, not the will. Thomas notes later that the subject of prudence is indeed the "cognitive faculty" and not the desiring

Reply to 1: Prudence is the principal of all the virtues, speaking absolutely. But each of the others is put forward as having priority within its own genus.

Reply to 2: What is rational by participation is subdivided into three, as was said above.

Reply to 3: All the other virtues among which one has priority over another can be traced back to the four that have already been spoken about, both regarding the subject and regarding the formal principles.[10]

---

faculty, but it is that aspect of the cognitive faculty that is concerned with action, and therefore the will. We might say, speaking loosely, that with regard to reasoning and willing, prudence has a foot in both camps.

10. One of the questions that occupied medieval thinkers concerning the virtues was whether the cardinal virtues simply named categories into which virtues are gathered (e.g., under "justice" we group the virtues of religion, piety, truthfulness, gratitude, etc.) or whether they themselves name actual virtues. Thomas's view is that they are actual virtues and not merely the names of categories, but they are "principal" virtues—those aimed at the most comprehensive end, to which other virtues are related as "parts" because they share a formal principle or reside in a common subject. Thomas divides these parts of virtue into (1) integral parts (the things that need to work together for a perfect act of virtue), (2) subjective parts (different virtues that relate to a cardinal virtue in the way that species relate to a genus), and (3) potential parts (those virtues that approximate the cardinal virtues in related, though less comprehensive, areas, often referred to by Thomas as "annexed" virtues) (see 1–2.48.1).

Question 62:

The Theological Virtues

1–2.62.3[1]
Is it fitting to posit faith, hope, and charity as theological virtues?

It would seem that it is not fitting to posit faith, hope, and charity[2] as three theological virtues.[3]

1. Theological virtues are possessed in relation to divine happiness in the way that a natural inclination is possessed in relation to the end that is in accord with human nature [*ad finem connaturalem*].[4] Among the virtues related to the end that is in accord with human nature there is only one natural virtue

1. On this article, see Mattison (2010); Wawrykow (2012).

2. The Latin tradition translates the Greek word *agapē* as *caritas*. One might simply translate *caritas* as "love," but Thomas uses other words (*dilectio, amor*) that could also be translated in this way. Moreover, *caritas* is not simply synonymous with these other terms. Like the Latin tradition as a whole, Thomas uses *caritas* to name our love of God and neighbor, a love that is possible only because of God's prior gift of love. To mark Thomas's use of this term, therefore, I have used the somewhat obsolete word "charity."

3. Thomas earlier defines "theological virtues" as those "additional principles by which one may be oriented to supernatural happiness, just as one is oriented by natural principles to the end that is in accord with human nature, though not without divine assistance" (1–2.62.1). He says these virtues are called "theological" because (1) they have God as their object (i.e., we have faith in *God*, we hope in *God*, we love *God*), (2) they are infused in us by God, and (3) we know of them through Scripture.

As Thomas notes in the *sed contra*, the triad of faith, hope, and charity comes from Paul's First Letter to the Corinthians, though the three crop up elsewhere in Paul's writings as well (e.g., 1 Thess. 1:3; 5:8). It was only shortly before Thomas's day that the term "theological virtues" seems to have come into use (see, e.g., William of Auxerre, *Summa Aurea* 3.18).

4. At the outset of question 62, Thomas notes that human blessedness is twofold: a happiness that is "proportioned to human nature," which we can attain by our natural powers, and a happiness that "exceeds human nature," which "can be had only by divine power, by a kind of sharing in divinity" (1–2.62.1). The first sort of happiness he describes as being *connaturale*, or in accord with human nature. At the same time, he elsewhere describes this sort of happiness as "imperfect" (1–2.5.5), suggesting something perhaps paradoxical about human beings: it is only by exceeding human nature that human beings can be perfectly happy.

posited—the understanding of principles. Therefore, one ought to posit only one theological virtue.[5]

2. Theological virtues are more perfect than intellectual and moral virtues. But faith is not placed among the intellectual virtues, for it is something less than a virtue, since it is imperfect knowledge. Likewise, hope is not placed among the moral virtues, for is something less than a virtue, since it is an emotion. Much less therefore should they be posited as theological virtues.[6]

3. Theological virtues orient the human soul to God. But it is impossible to orient the human soul to God except by means of its intellectual aspect, where the intellect and will are found. Therefore, there should only be two theological virtues: one that perfects the intellect, the other that perfects the will.

On the contrary: The Apostle says in 1 Corinthians (13:13), "Now there remain faith, hope, charity, these three."

I answer: As stated above (1–2.62.1), theological virtues orient a human being to supernatural happiness in the same way that a human being is oriented by natural inclination to the end that is in accord with human nature. Now the latter happens in two ways. First, according to the reason or intellect, inasmuch as it contains the first universal principles, known to us by the natural light of the intellect, from which reason sets out in both theoretical and practical matters. Second, through the uprightness of the will, which tends naturally to the good as defined by reason.[7]

But these two fall short of the level of supernatural happiness, as it says in 1 Corinthians (2:9), "Eye has not seen, nor ear heard, nor has it entered into the human heart, what God has prepared for those that love him." Consequently, it is necessary with regard to both that something supernatural be imparted to human beings to orient them to a supernatural end. First, with regard to the intellect, certain supernatural principles are imparted to human beings, which are grasped by means of divine light; these are things to be

---

5. The objection seems to be stating that just as the knowledge of natural truth, which is the natural end of human beings, is rooted in a single natural "virtue" or *habitus*—the grasp that we have of self-evident first principles (see Aquinas, *Commentary on the Nicomachean Ethics* 6.5.1179)—so too the supernatural end of human beings should be likewise rooted in a single virtue.

6. If what distinguishes supernatural happiness from natural happiness is that the latter is imperfect, then it would seem unfitting that things that are imperfect, such as faith (which is an imperfect form of knowledge) and hope (which is a mere emotion), should have a role in bringing us to a more perfect happiness.

7. Having drawn a parallel between, on the one hand, the theological virtues and supernatural happiness and, on the other hand, the natural inclination of the person and natural happiness, Thomas goes on to further specify that our natural inclination involves both our intellect, which identifies the true and the good, and our will, which draws us to the good that the intellect identifies.

believed [*credibilia*], which is done through *faith*.[8] Second, the will is oriented to this [supernatural] end, both with regard to the movement of intention, which tends toward that end as something attainable—which pertains to *hope*[9]—and with regard to a certain spiritual union, by which the will is in some sense transformed into that end—which is done through *charity*.[10] For the appetite of each thing is naturally moved and tends toward the end that is in accord with its nature, and this movement is from a certain conformity of that thing with its end.

Reply to 1: The intellect needs intelligible species, by which it understands, and so one must posit in it some natural disposition over and above its power.[11] But the nature of the will itself suffices for its natural orientation to the end, whether with regard to tending toward the end or with regard to conformity with it. But in relation to things above nature, its natural power is not sufficient in either of these respects. And for this reason it was necessary for a supernatural disposition to be added with respect to both.[12]

Reply to 2: Faith and hope imply a certain imperfection, for faith is of those things that are not seen, and hope of those things that are not possessed. To have faith and hope, therefore, in those things that are under human power falls short of the definition of virtue. But to have faith and hope in those things that are above the capacity of human nature surpasses all virtue that

---

8. The natural light of the intellect is insufficient for identifying truths that exceed reason's grasp; therefore, there must be a disposition to believe truths that are revealed by God. And this is the virtue of faith.

9. Aquinas's language of "intention" is important here, since it indicates not mere desire, but a desire for something seen as attainable. We might recognize and desire some good—e.g., the desire to inflate oneself like a pufferfish so as to frighten off potential predators—but we could not intend that good since it is not within the capacities of human nature. Likewise, even if the intellect, by the virtue of faith, comes to know truths that are beyond natural reason, and even if the will desires the supernatural good, the will cannot "intend" that good—i.e., desire it as a good that can be attained—since it exceeds our natural human capacities. There must therefore be a disposition that enables the will to intend such a good, and this is the virtue of hope.

10. As Thomas indicates in his reply to the third objection, below, the will (or appetite) can be thought of in terms both of the desire that impels it toward a good and the love that unites it to the good once it is attained. Therefore, in addition to the virtue of hope, there must also be in the will the virtue of charity, which enables us to delight in and be united with the good that is God.

11. In order for thought to take place the mind needs, in addition to the power of thought itself, something to think about (i.e., the "intelligible species," which Thomas holds are derived from our senses—see 1–2.3 note 10).

12. Thomas's response to the objection shows that he thinks that the deficiency of our nature is not simply an intellectual one—we lack knowledge of God—but also a problem of the appetite. The objection suggests that if something were added to our intellect to perfect it in such a way that we could know God more perfectly, then the will would naturally desire to be united with God. However, the necessity of the virtues of hope and love, in addition to faith, suggests that our natural appetites are imperfect as well and need to be disposed by God to intending and being united to God.

is in proportion to human being, according to what is said in 1 Corinthians (1:25): "The weakness of God is stronger than human beings."[13]

Reply to 3: Two things pertain to the appetite: movement to the end and conformity to the end through love. And thus there must be posited two theological virtues in the human appetite: hope and charity.

---

13. It is one thing to have knowledge gained from hearsay (natural "faith") or to have an optimistic outlook (the emotion of hope), but it is another thing to believe what God reveals (the theological virtue of faith) and to intend the supernatural good (the theological virtue of hope). The objection, Thomas suggests, confuses these two.

Question 65:

The Connection of the Virtues

1–2.65.2[1]
Can there be moral virtues without charity?

It would seem that there can be moral virtues without charity.[2]

1. On this article, see Porter (1995); Shanley (1999); Marenbon (2015, 160–87).
2. This article brings together a number of key concerns in Thomas's understanding of virtue, which the reader should keep in mind while reading this article:

The connectedness of the virtues: Is it possible to have one virtue in isolation from the rest? For example, can you be courageous without being just, or moderate in your appetites without being prudent? The view Thomas develops in the article prior to this one (1–2.65.1) is that while *imperfect* virtues (i.e., mere inclinations to do a good act) do not need to be connected, *perfect* virtues (i.e., virtues in the full sense of the term) do. Thomas thinks virtues, properly speaking, cannot exist in isolation from one another: a terrorist might have a kind of inclination that leads him to ignore danger, which might superficially resemble courage, but he cannot have the virtue of courage unless he also possesses justice, moderation, and prudence. This is the consensus view of the vast majority of ancient and medieval thinkers. Modern thinkers tend to be more skeptical about this point.

The relation of infused charity to the moral virtues: When Thomas refers to "perfect" virtues in this article, he means the *infused* moral virtues. Thomas holds that in addition to the naturally acquired moral virtues and the supernaturally infused theological virtues, there are also supernaturally infused moral virtues that are received when we receive the theological virtues. Thomas discusses these at 1–2.63.3-4, suggesting that while the acquired moral virtues orient us toward natural goods, and theological virtues orient us toward God as our supernatural end in a general way, the infused moral virtues orient us to that end with regard to specific actions. Thus, the virtue of charity might direct me to love God above all other things, but I need the infused virtue of moderation in order to fulfill a vow of celibacy or the infused virtue of fortitude to submit to martyrdom as specific ways of loving God above all other things.

The status of the virtues of unbelievers: One tradition of interpreting Augustine (not without textual support in Augustine himself) is to see all the virtues of non-Christians as "splendid vices," meaning that they are all tainted by a self-seeking pride that makes them, from a Christian perspective, not really virtues at all. Thomas does not think that this is the case, but still wishes to distinguish the virtues of nonbelievers from those of believers by noting their "imperfection." What is not clear is whether the "imperfection" of the acquired virtues of nonbelievers means that these virtues are mere inclinations—disconnected from one another, and so not true virtues at all—or that these virtues are true virtues, but ones that are still insufficient for achieving the final end of human beings (i.e., the vision of the divine essence). See note 11, below, as well as 1–2.109.2, below.

1. It is stated in the book of *Sentences* of Prosper (7) that "every virtue apart from charity can be common to the good and the bad." But, as it says in the same book, "Charity cannot exist except in the good." Therefore, it is possible to have the other virtues without charity.[3]

2. Moral virtues can be acquired by means of human acts, as stated in the *Ethics* (2.1, 1103^{a-b}). But charity cannot be had except by being infused, according to Romans (5:5), "The charity of God is poured into our hearts by the Holy Spirit, who is given to us." Therefore, it is possible to have the other virtues without charity.

3. The moral virtues are mutually connected inasmuch as they depend on prudence.[4] But charity does not depend on prudence—indeed, it exceeds prudence, according to Ephesians (3:19): "The charity of Christ surpasses all knowledge."[5] The moral virtues, therefore, are not connected with charity and can exist without it.

On the contrary: It is written in 1 John (3:14), "Anyone who does not love remains in death." But the spiritual life is perfected by the virtues, for they are "that by which we live rightly," as Augustine says in *On Free Choice of the Will* (2.19). They therefore cannot exist without the love of charity.

I answer: As stated above (1–2.63.2), insofar as moral virtues are productive of good deeds oriented to an end that does not exceed the natural capacities of a human being, it is possible to acquire them by means of human works.[6] Acquired in this way, they can exist without charity, as was the case with many of the gentiles. But insofar as they bring about good acts oriented to a supernatural final end, they fit the definition of virtue truly and perfectly and cannot be acquired by human acts but rather are infused by God. These sorts of moral virtues cannot exist without charity.[7] For it is stated above (1–2.58.4–5)

---

3. If bad people can have any or all of the virtues except charity, then obviously one does not need to have charity to possess the other virtues (this, of course, presumes that bad people *can* have virtues).

4. Thomas has argued earlier (1–2.58.4; 1–2.65.1) that the other moral virtues, which orient us toward appropriate ends, cannot function apart from prudence. See note 8, below.

5. Elsewhere Thomas describes the virtue of prudence as "wisdom about human affairs" (2–2.47.2 ad 1) and therefore a kind of knowledge, which (according to the Letter to the Ephesians) charity surpasses.

6. As noted earlier (1–2.55 note 2, above), Thomas agrees with Aristotle that virtues that aim at the good as defined by human reason are formed in us by repeated actions (i.e., practice makes perfect).

7. Thomas willingly grants that acquired moral virtues exist in "many" non-Christians (i.e., "gentiles"). However, he goes on to say that the term "virtue" is applied "perfectly and truly" only to those moral virtues that help us attain our supernatural goal, and these, infused in us by God, necessarily require the gift of charity. This might be taken to suggest that the virtues of non-Christians are false virtues, a mere pretense. But Thomas's discussion and defense of the Augustinian definition of virtue (1–2.55.4, above) seems to speak more positively of acquired virtues, nowhere implying that they are false virtues, and stating that they conform to the definition of virtue, except for the phrase "which God works in us without us." Perhaps Thomas's point here is that only infused virtues conform *completely* to the Augustinian definition, and so by comparison are virtues most truly and perfectly, without implying that acquired virtues, even as

that the other moral virtues cannot exist without prudence and that prudence cannot exist without the moral virtues inasmuch as the moral virtues make one well disposed to certain ends, from which prudential reasoning proceeds.[8] For the right functioning of prudential reasoning, it is much more necessary that one be well disposed concerning one's ultimate end (which is accomplished through charity) than that one be well disposed concerning other ends (which are accomplished through the moral virtues), in the same way that right reason in speculative matters needs above all else the indemonstrable first principle that contradictories cannot simultaneously be true.[9] It is therefore clear that neither can infused prudence exist without charity, nor consequently the other moral virtues, which cannot exist without prudence.[10]

It is therefore clear from what has been said that only infused virtues are perfect and ought to be called virtues absolutely [*simpliciter*], for they rightly orient human beings to the ultimate end, absolutely speaking. The other virtues (namely, the acquired) are virtues not absolutely but in a restricted sense, for they orient one well regarding a final end of some particular sort, but not regarding the final end absolutely speaking.[11] Thus in connection with the words of Romans (14:23), "All that is not of faith is sin," the gloss quotes Augustine, saying, "Where the truth is not acknowledged, virtue is false even in good behavior."[12]

---

found in non-Christians, are false virtues. Indeed, when Thomas uses the term "virtue" without any sort of modifier (e.g., "infused" or "theological"), he often seems to mean acquired moral virtue (see 1–2.61.1), which would be an odd thing to do if he did not think that they were true virtues.

8. Here Thomas briefly summarizes his argument for the unity or connection of the moral virtues based on the role of prudence in directing our choice of means to attain the ends of the other virtues. The other moral virtues need prudence because, while they orient us toward a good, it is prudence that guides us in making right choices regarding our pursuit of that good. Likewise, prudence needs the other moral virtues, or else it has no good to pursue.

9. Having established the importance of prudence for the proper functioning of the other virtues, Thomas goes on to discuss what we need for prudence to function well. In theoretical or speculative reasoning (i.e., our quest to know what is true), we begin from the first principles of reason; in prudential or practical reasoning (i.e., our quest to know how to act) we begin from the end that we are seeking. Since charity is that which unites us to our ultimate end, prudence is most perfect when joined to charity.

10. Thomas's way of putting this in 2–2.23.8 is that charity is the "form" of the virtues. Note that Thomas here is concerned with infused prudence, not acquired prudence. Thus when he says that (infused) prudence cannot exist without charity, he is not denying the possibility of someone without charity having acquired prudence.

11. As noted earlier, Thomas distinguishes between imperfect happiness, which we can attain in this life, and perfect happiness, which is only attained in the next life (see 1–2.5 note 15, above). Acquired virtues are imperfect because they orient us toward an imperfect or incomplete happiness, and therefore are virtues *secundum quid* ("in a restricted sense"), whereas infused virtues are perfect because they orient us toward perfect or complete happiness, and therefore are virtues *simpliciter* (absolutely speaking).

12. The quotation in the gloss (see 1.12 note 10) is actually from Prosper of Aquitaine's *Sentences* (106), not from Augustine. Thomas's point here is a subtle one. An unbeliever's good action might be truly good if

Reply to 1: "Virtues" here is being taken in the sense of imperfect virtue. Otherwise, if moral virtue is taken in its perfect sense, it "makes its subject good" (Aristotle, *Nicomachean Ethics* 2.6, 1106ᵃ) and consequently cannot exist in someone evil.

Reply to 2: This argument works for acquired moral virtues.

Reply to 3: Though charity exceeds knowledge and prudence, yet prudence depends on charity, as I have said, and so consequently do all the infused moral virtues.

---

it is done for a good reason (e.g., an atheist buying ice cream for his child simply because the child likes ice cream). But an unbeliever's action that is good in and of itself might still be evil if it is done for the sake of that unbelief (e.g., an atheist buying ice cream for his child on a Sunday morning instead of taking the child to church in order to make the point that atheism is more fun than Christianity and thereby to inculcate unbelief in his child). So not every action of the unbeliever is sinful, but only those motivated by unbelief. But even the truly good actions of the unbeliever do not earn the unbeliever salvation. Thomas writes in his *Commentary on Romans*, "When an unbeliever does something good from the dictate of reason and does not refer it to an evil end, he does not sin. However, his deed is not meritorious [of salvation], because it was not enlivened by grace" (14.3.1141).

Question 68:

The Gifts

1–2.68.1[1]
Do the gifts [of the Holy Spirit] differ from the virtues?

It seems that the gifts are not distinguished from the virtues.[2]

1. Gregory—explaining Job (1:2), "Seven sons were born to him"—says in *Moral Reflections on the Book of Job* (1.27.38): "Seven sons were born to us, because the conception of a good causes the seven virtues of the Holy Spirit to be born in us." And he quotes what is said in Isaiah (11:2–3), "the Spirit of understanding will rest upon him," and so on, where the seven gifts of the Holy Spirit are enumerated. The seven gifts of the Holy Spirit are therefore virtues.

2. Augustine—explaining what is found in Matthew (12:45), "Then he goes and takes seven other spirits," and so forth—says in *Questions on the Gospels* (1.8): "The seven vices are contrary to the seven virtues of the Holy Spirit"—that is, the seven gifts. But the seven vices are contrary to what are

---

1. On this article, see O'Connor (1974); Jordan (2016, 137–51).

2. The sevenfold enumeration of the "gifts of the Spirit" is derived from Isa. 11:1–3: "A shoot shall come out from the root of Jesse, and a flower shall grow out of his roots. The spirit of the Lord shall rest on him, the spirit of wisdom and understanding, the spirit of counsel and might, the spirit of knowledge and reverence, and he shall be filled with the spirit of the fear of the Lord" (my trans., following the Vulgate). These are rendered in the Latin tradition as *sapientia* (wisdom), *intellectus* (understanding), *concilium* (right judgment), *fortitudo* (might), *scientia* (knowledge), *pietas* (reverence), and *timor Domini* (fear of the Lord). As is typical of Thomas, he accepts this list of gifts as part of the theological tradition but still seeks to understand why there would be these seven (and not others), how they are related to one another, and how they relate to other ways of talking about how God works in the lives of Christians—such as infused virtues, the fruits of the Spirit (listed by Paul in Gal. 5:22–23), and the beatitudes that preface Jesus's Sermon on the Mount in Matthew's Gospel. In this article, Thomas focuses on how the gifts of the Spirit differ from the virtues. Of particular note is how he surveys a range of different approaches that were current in thirteenth-century Paris, seeking one that would adequately distinguish gifts and virtues.

commonly called virtues. Therefore, the gifts are not distinct from what are commonly called virtues.[3]

3. Things whose definitions are the same are themselves the same. But the definition of "virtue" also fits the gifts, for each gift is "a good quality of the mind by which we live uprightly," and so on. Likewise the definition of "gift" fits the infused virtues, for a gift is "an act of giving without repayment" [*datio irreddibilis*], according to the Philosopher (*Topics* 4.4, 125ᵃ). The virtues and gifts are therefore not distinct.[4]

4. Several of those things listed among the gifts are virtues. For as stated above (1–2.57.2), wisdom, understanding, and knowledge are intellectual virtues; right judgment pertains to prudence, reverence [*pietas*] to a kind of justice, and fortitude is one of the moral virtues. It seems, therefore, that the gifts are not distinct from the virtues.[5]

On the contrary: Gregory, in *Moral Reflections on the Book of Job* (1.27.38), distinguishes the seven gifts, which he says are signified by the seven sons of Job, from the three theological virtues, which he says are signified by the three daughters of Job. And later in the *Moral Reflections* (2.49.76) he distinguishes the same seven gifts from the four cardinal virtues, which he says are signified by the four corners of the house.

I answer: If we speak of "gift" and "virtue" according to the meaning of the words themselves, there is in this sense no opposition to each other. For the definition of "virtue" is taken from the fact that it perfects a human being for good action, as was said earlier (1–2.57.2), while the definition of "gift" is taken from its relation to the cause from which it comes. But nothing prevents that which is from one as a gift from being the perfection of another in terms of acting well, especially since we have already said (1–2.63.3) that some virtues are infused in us by God. In this sense, therefore, it is not possible to distinguish gift from virtue.[6] For this reason

3. When Thomas speaks of what are "commonly called" (*communiter dictis*) virtues, he could be speaking of what are called virtues in everyday speech, or he could mean what is common to all the different kinds of virtues, whether intellectual or moral, acquired or infused. The parallelism with the seven vices might mean that he is thinking of the four cardinal virtues combined with the three theological virtues.

4. Things that share a definition belong in the same category. As the objection notes, not only does the definition of "virtue" discussed earlier (1–2.55.4, above) fit with the meaning of "gift," but also the definition of "gift" (taken from Aristotle) fits with the meaning of "virtue," specifically if we are thinking of the infused virtues.

5. The objection points out that the names of some of the gifts of the Spirit overlap either with intellectual virtues, cardinal virtues, or other virtues that are related to the cardinal virtues.

6. Up to this point in his response, Thomas has partially conceded the third objection's point: the definition of "virtue" and that of "gift" in no way contradict each other, and so both could apply to the same thing. But the meanings of terms cannot be thought of solely in terms of definitions; they must also

some[7] have suggested that the gifts are not to be distinguished from the virtues. But there remains a not-insignificant difficulty: What reason can be given for why some virtues are called gifts and not others, and why some things are numbered among the gifts that are not numbered among the virtues, as is clear in the case of fear?

Because of this, others have said that the gifts are to be distinguished from the virtues,[8] but they have not assigned a fitting cause for this distinction— that is to say, one that would apply to all the virtues and in no way to the gifts, or vice versa.[9] Some, observing that among the seven gifts four pertain to reason (wisdom, knowledge, understanding, and counsel) and three to the power of appetite (fortitude, piety, and fear), held that the gifts perfect the free will inasmuch as it is a capacity of reason, but the virtues perfect it inasmuch as it is a capacity of the will. For they found only two virtues in the faculty of reason or understanding—namely, faith and prudence— but the others in the power for desiring or being affected [*vi appetitiva vel affectiva*]. But it would have been necessary, if this distinction were to be fitting, that all the virtues would have to be in the power for desiring, and all the gifts in the reason.[10]

But others, observing that Gregory says in *Moral Reflections on the Book of Job* (2.49.77) that "the gift of the Holy Spirit, which forms prudence, moderation, justice, and fortitude in the mind subject to it, strengthens that same mind against every temptation by the seven gifts," said that the virtues are oriented toward acting well, but the gifts toward resisting temptation. But this distinction is also insufficient. For the virtues also resist those temptations that lead to sins that are contrary to the virtues, for everything naturally resists its contrary. This is especially clear with charity, of

---

take account of how words are actually used in human discourse. So, he goes on to note, the church has not treated those things listed as virtues and those listed as gifts interchangeably; some things that are virtues are not found among the sevenfold gifts (e.g., justice or hope), and at least one of the gifts—fear of the Lord—has not traditionally been the name of a virtue. This suggests that even when there is an overlap in names, there can be a distinction in the things that bear those names.

7. Among others, Peter Lombard, *Sentences* bk. 3, dist. 34, ch. 2 (citing a text from Ambrose of Milan as his authority).

8. The clear distinction between the virtues and the gifts seems to appear first in the Parisian theologian Philip the Chancellor (ca. 1160–1236). Most of the different options for distinguishing them that Thomas surveys here are drawn from those discussed in Philip's *Summa de bono*, which Thomas seems to have encountered via either his teacher Albert the Great or his fellow student Bonaventure.

9. Thomas sets out his standard for what would count as properly distinguishing the virtues from the gifts: one would need to find something that is true of all of the virtues but none of the gifts, or true of all of the gifts but none of the virtues.

10. While it is true that *most* of the virtues relate to the will (i.e., "the power of desiring"), not *all* of them do, so this approach fails to meet the standard Thomas has set out.

which it is written in the Song of Songs (8:7), "Many waters cannot quench charity."[11]

Still others, seeing that these gifts are recounted in Scripture as having been in Christ, as is clear in Isaiah (11:2–3), said that the virtues are oriented toward acting well in general, but the gifts are oriented to conforming us to Christ, principally in terms of what he suffered, for it was above all in his passion that these gifts shone forth.[12] But even this does not seem sufficient [to distinguish the gifts from the virtues]. For the Lord himself leads us to be conformed to him especially in terms of humility and meekness (Matt. 11:29: "Learn from me, because I am meek and humble of heart") and in terms of charity (John 15:12: "Love one another, as I have loved you"). And these virtues were especially resplendent in Christ's passion.[13]

Therefore, in order to distinguish the gifts from the virtues, we ought to follow the way of speaking that we find in Scripture, where they are presented to us not under the term "gift" but under the term "spirit." For thus it is said in Isaiah (11:2–3): "There shall rest upon him the spirit of wisdom and of understanding," and so on, from which words we are clearly given to understand that these seven are enumerated there inasmuch as they are in us by divine inspiration.[14] For inspiration signifies motion from outside.[15] For it is seen that there is in a human being a twofold source [*principium*] of movement: one that is interior, which is reason, and another that is exterior, which is God, as stated above (1–2.9); the Philosopher also says this in the chapter "On Good Fortune."[16]

11. The approach that would see the virtues as orienting us to the good and the gifts as helping us resist temptation fails to meet the standard Thomas has set out because not only the gifts but also the virtues help us to resist temptation. If I possess the virtue of fortitude, for example, I have the capacity to resist the temptation to both cowardice and foolish bravado, which are the vices opposed to fortitude.

12. This view rightly notes that the passage in Isaiah from which the list of seven gifts derives has been interpreted by Christians as a messianic prophecy, which brings out the role of the Holy Spirit in conforming Christians to Jesus Christ—i.e., it is the role of the Spirit and the Spirit's gifts to make us like Jesus.

13. Thomas says that "even this" approach fails to meet the standard he has set out, because while the gifts *do* make us like Christ, the virtues do as well, particularly the virtues of humility, meekness, and charity shown in his suffering on the cross.

14. Faced with a range of ways of distinguishing the virtues and the gifts, none of which meets the standard he has set out, Thomas returns to the biblical text. And what he notices is that Isaiah does not speak of "gifts" at all, but rather "spirits" that are given to the one who will come forth from the root of Jesse (i.e., the Messiah). So it is from this term "spirit" that Thomas begins his interpretation.

15. *Inspiratio* is from the verb *inspirare*—literally, "to breathe into"—and, Thomas says, indicates the act by which something is moved by something external to it.

16. This is a work made up of extracts from Aristotle's *Eudemian Ethics* and a work known as the *Magna Moralia* (Great ethics), which may or may not have been written by Aristotle. The particular part of this work that Thomas is referencing here is taken from *Eudemian Ethics* 7.14, 1248^a. It should be noted that the way in which Thomas conceives of this divine movement of the soul is in fact quite alien to Aristotle, for whom God moves the soul *only* by being the object of the soul's desire.

Now it is evident that whatever is moved must be proportioned to its mover, and the perfection of the movable thing, precisely as something movable, is the disposition by which it is inclined to be moved well by its mover.[17] The higher the mover, the more perfect must be the disposition by which the movable thing is proportioned to it; thus we see that a student must have a more perfect disposition in order to be able to receive a higher teaching from his teacher.[18] Now it is clear that human virtues perfect a person on account of humans naturally being moved by reason in their internal and external acts. Therefore, it is necessary that higher perfections be in a human being, by which one is disposed to being moved divinely. And these perfections are called gifts, not only because they are infused by God but also because by them a person is disposed to be readily moved by divine inspiration; as it says in Isaiah (50:5): "The Lord has opened my ear, and I have not denied him, have not turned back."[19] The Philosopher too, in the chapter "On Good Fortune," says that for those who are moved by divine prompting [*instinctus*] there is no need to consult according to human reason, but only to follow their inner prompting, for they are moved by a principle better than human reason. This then is what is said by some—that the gifts perfect a human being for acts higher than acts of virtue.[20]

Reply to 1: Sometimes these gifts are called virtues, according to the general definition of "virtue." But they have something in addition to the general definition of "virtue," inasmuch as they are certain divine virtues, perfecting a

17. I.e., in an appropriate way.

18. Thomas here is thinking of teaching and learning on analogy with physical change: just as a fire imparts to wood the form that the fire possesses, making it a burning thing, so too a teacher imparts to a student the form of knowledge that the teacher possesses, making the student a knower (we sometimes even speak of teachers "kindling" a love of knowledge in students). And just as some wood will burn more or less hot due to its capacity to receive the form of fire (e.g., damp wood will not burn as hot as dry wood), so too some students will learn more or less advanced knowledge due to their capacity to receive knowledge (e.g., a hungover student will likely grasp differential equations less quickly than one who is sober and well rested).

19. Human virtues (by which Thomas here seems to mean both acquired and infused virtues—see 1–2.65 note 2) move us through reason, and in this way they are "internal" to the person; gifts, on the other hand, because they come from *inspiratio*, are our being moved by an "external" force—the Holy Spirit. It is here that Thomas finds something that distinguishes all the gifts from all the virtues: the virtues make us amenable to internal movement by reason, whereas the gifts make us amenable to external movement by God.

20. At this point Thomas shifts from the language of *inspiratio* to the language of *instinctus* (prompting/instigation/impulse), which he tends to use from here on when speaking of the gifts of the Spirit, perhaps because it better expresses what he sees as distinctive about the gifts: they are the God-given disposition by which God makes us responsive to the "prompting" of the Holy Spirit, so that we can engage in acts that go beyond human nature, which are necessary for human salvation. Thomas will note in the next article (1–2.68.2) that "in [the person's] orientation to the ultimate supernatural end, to which reason is formed only somewhat and imperfectly by the theological virtues, the motion of reason alone is insufficient unless it receives the prompting and motion of the Holy Spirit from above."

person insofar as one is moved by God.[21] This is why the Philosopher (*Nicomachean Ethics* 7.1, 1145ᵃ) posits, above ordinary virtues, certain virtues that are "heroic" or "divine," according to which some are called "divine men" [*divini viri*].

Reply to 2: Vices, inasmuch as they are contrary to the good of reason, are contrary to the virtues; but inasmuch as they are contrary to divine prompting, they are contrary to the gifts. For the same thing is contrary both to God and to reason, whose light derives from God.[22]

Reply to 3: This definition is given to virtue taken in a general way. Thus, if we wish to restrict the definition to virtues as distinguished from gifts, we say that the phrase "whereby we lead a good life" ought to be understood as referring to uprightness of life as this is understood according to the rule of reason. Similarly, the gifts, as distinct from infused virtue, may be said to be that which is given by God in relation to his motion—which is to say that it makes a person follow God's promptings well.[23]

Reply to 4: Wisdom is called an intellectual virtue insofar as it comes forth from the judgment of reason; but it is called a gift insofar as it works from divine prompting. And similar things are said of the other virtues.

---

21. We use the term "virtue" somewhat loosely, and while the gifts *do* in fact fit the definition of "virtue," they also go beyond that definition by including the notion of an *external* movement by God.

22. Just because vice is contrary to the rule of reason does not mean that it cannot *also* be contrary to the promptings of the Spirit, especially since the promptings of the Spirit, while exceeding reason, are not, for Thomas, contrary to reason.

23. Even the infused virtues, "which God works in us without us," involve a movement "internal" to the soul because they cause us to follow the rule of reason, while the gifts cause us to follow the promptings of the Spirit.

Question 71:

Vices and Sins Considered in Themselves

1–2.71.6[1]
On the definition of sin proposed by Augustine.

It appears that sin is defined unfittingly by saying: "Sin is a word or deed or desire contrary to the eternal law" [*peccatum est dictum vel factum vel concupitum contra legem aeternam*].[2]

1. "Word" or "deed" or "desire" involves an action. But not every sin involves an act, as stated earlier (1–2.71.5). This definition, therefore, does not include every sin.[3]

2. Augustine says in the book *On the Two Souls*: "Sin is the will to retain or obtain what justice forbids" (11.15). But the will is included under desire (*concupiscentia*), insofar as "desire" can be taken in a broad sense to mean any appetite. Therefore, it would have sufficed to say, "Sin is a desire contrary to the eternal law," and it was not necessary to add "word or deed."[4]

3. It appears that sin consists specifically in turning away from the end, for good and evil are considered chiefly with regard to the end, as explained above (1–2.18.6). Therefore Augustine, in *On Free Choice of the Will* (1.11), defines sin in relation to the end, saying that "sin is nothing else than neglecting

---

1. On this article, see Sweeney (2002); Bauerschmidt (2016b).

2. This definition is drawn from Augustine's *Against Faustus the Manichaean* (22.27) and, like the Augustinian definition of "virtue" (1–2.55.4, above), commanded widespread acceptance because of its use in Peter Lombard's *Sentences* (bk. 2, dist. 35, ch. 1).

It is worth noting that this article occurs within a question concerning "vices and sins." A "vice" is the disposition to act badly (just as a virtue is a disposition to act well), while a "sin" is the bad action itself.

3. In speaking of "deeds," Augustine seems to exclude "sins of omission," in which we fall short not because of what we do, but because of what we fail to do.

4. If the previous objection argues that the Augustinian definition says too little (not covering sins of omission), this objection argues that it says too much, since sin is really a matter of what we will more than a matter of what we do or say. As Jesus teaches in the Sermon on the Mount (Matt. 5:21–22), if I am angry with someone, this is as much a sin as actually killing them.

eternal things and pursuing temporal things"; and in the book *Eighty-Three Questions* (30) he says that "all human evil is a matter of using what we should enjoy and enjoying what we should use." But the proposed definition makes no mention of turning away from our appropriate end. Therefore, it is an insufficient definition of sin.[5]

4. Something is said to be prohibited because it is contrary to the law. But not all sins are evil because they are prohibited; some are prohibited because they are evil. Therefore, sin in general should not be defined as being against the law of God.[6]

5. "Sin" denotes a bad human act, as is clear from what has been said (1–2.71.1). But "the evil of humans is to be against reason," as Dionysius states in *On the Divine Names* (4). Therefore, it would have been better to say that sin is against reason than to say that sin is contrary to the eternal law.[7]

On the contrary: The authority of Augustine is sufficient.

I answer: As is clear from what was said before (1–2.71.1), sin is nothing other than a bad human act. But, as was also said earlier (1–2.1.1), an act is human based on the fact that it is voluntary, either in the sense of coming forth [*elicitus*] from the will (e.g., willing or choosing) or in the sense of being commanded by the will (e.g., the exterior actions of speech or deeds).[8] But a human act is evil if it lacks its due measure, and every measure of something is attained through a comparison to some standard [*regula*], and if the thing deviates from that measure, it will be incommensurate.

The standard of the human will is twofold. One is proximate and homogeneous: human reason itself. The other, however, is the primary standard: the eternal law, which is, as it were, God's reason.[9] Therefore, Augustine puts two

---

5. The objection brings out the importance of an action's end or goal in thinking about its rightness or wrongness (see 1–2.18.4, above). The quotation from Augustine's *Eighty-Three Questions* also introduces the terms "use" (*uti*) and "enjoyment" (*frui*), which are key categories in Augustinian ethics: to live rightly we must properly distinguish between the means, which we "use" to reach the end, and the end itself, which we "enjoy" and in which our desire finds rest.

6. The objection betrays a concern that sin not be understood *simply* as a kind of "legal violation"—as wrong only because God has declared it wrong. This reflects an ancient debate—extending back at least to Plato's *Euthyphro*—as to whether certain actions are good because the gods love them, or whether the gods love certain actions because they are good.

7. This objection is concerned with the same issue as the previous one: the mention of divine law might seem to make vice and virtue arbitrary, based solely in God's will. This objection focuses on actions being virtuous due to their accord with the rule of reason.

8. On what makes an act done by a human being a "human act," see 1–2.1 note 8. On the distinction between an act flowing or "elicited" from the will and a "commanded" act of will see 1–2.1 note 11. Either sort of act might be good or bad.

9. Thomas does not think of sins primarily as a matter of rule breaking, as if God had more or less arbitrarily set up laws and we sinned when we broke them. Still, the notion of a "rule" or "standard" does play a role in his thinking. Human reason itself sets the standard for human action, such that an action that

things in the definition of sin. One pertains to the substance of a human act, which is something like the "matter" of sin, and this is when he says, "word or deed or desire." The other pertains to the idea of evil, which is something like the "form" of sin, and this is when he says, "contrary to the eternal law."[10]

Reply to 1: Affirmation and negation are traced back to a single genus. For example, in the Godhead "begotten" and "unbegotten" are traced back to the genus "relation," as Augustine states in *De Trinitate* (5.6–7). And so what is "said" and "unsaid," what is "done" and "undone," should be taken in the same way.[11]

Reply to 2: The first cause of sin is in the will, which commands all voluntary acts, for it is only in these kinds of acts that sin is to be found. This is why Augustine sometimes defines sin in terms of the will alone. But, as has been said (1–2.20.1–3), because external acts also pertain to the substance of sin when they themselves are evil, it was necessary in defining sin to include something pertaining to external action.[12]

Reply to 3: The eternal law first and foremost orients a human being to his or her end, but as a consequence of this it makes one well disposed concerning things that are means to the end. Therefore, when he says, "contrary to the eternal law," he includes both turning away from the end and all other forms of disorder.[13]

---

is unreasonable fails as a human action. Thomas calls this "homogeneous" because it is not something alien to us, and he calls it "proximate" because it is the immediate standard to which our actions ought to conform. But the standard for human reason itself is divine wisdom, which Thomas here calls "the eternal law"; this is "primary" because it is, we might say, the standard by which our standard is judged, so that our reason becomes itself unreasonable when it fails to conform to divine reason.

10. Just as a piece of bronze is potentially a cup or a statue, depending upon what form it receives, so a human action is potentially good or evil, depending upon whether or not it conforms to divine reason.

11. Thomas's response to the issue of why Augustine's definition doesn't include sins of omission is slightly obscure. His essential point is that in order to grasp a negation, such as "unbegotten" or "unsaid," we must first grasp the corresponding affirmation. So what is crucial in providing a definition is to include the affirmative terms, leaving the negations to be understood by implication. It is not entirely clear that this really addresses the issue, since the definition could intentionally be excluding the negations, rather than including them by implication.

12. Thomas affirms the Augustinian view that the will is primary in determining the goodness or badness of an action. But he does not think that the will is the *only* thing that matters, for this would lead to the counterintuitive conclusion that wanting to commit adultery is the exact same sin as actually committing adultery, a view that was proposed by Peter Abelard (1079–1142). To put it in terms discussed earlier (1–2.1 note 11), for Thomas sin includes not only the act of will but also the willed act. It is worth bearing in mind that Thomas's purpose in the *Summa* was to train Dominican friars for the carrying out of their ministry, which included hearing confessions. So in thinking about sin, Thomas is concerned not simply with a theoretical definition of sin but with one that would be useful for confessors in assessing the severity of one's sins. A recognition that the act of will must be assessed in light of the willed act is crucial for properly administering the sacrament of penance.

13. Thomas's immediate reply is that "the eternal law" includes both the end and all the means that lead to that end. He also uses this as the occasion to note that sin does not always involve willing the wrong

Reply to 4: In saying that not every sin is evil because it is forbidden, this must be understood of a prohibition made by positive law.[14] But if one speaks with reference to the natural law, which is contained primarily in the eternal law but secondarily in the natural judgment of human reason, then *every* sin is evil because it is forbidden, for it is precisely because it is disordered that it conflicts with natural law.[15]

Reply to 5: Theologians consider sin chiefly in terms of it being an offense against God; moral philosophers consider it in terms of it being contrary to reason.[16] Therefore, Augustine more fittingly defines sin in terms of its being "contrary to the eternal law" than in terms of its being contrary to reason, especially since we are ruled and guided by the eternal law in many things that exceed human reason, as in the case of those things that are matters of faith.

---

end; it can sometimes involve willing the wrong means to a correct end (e.g., I will to give alms, which is praiseworthy, but I seek to obtain the funds by robbing banks).

To reject our final end is always what the tradition calls a "mortal" (i.e., deadly) sin. But to act in a disordered way without actually turning away from our final end is what has been called, at least since the time of Augustine (see *On the Spirit and the Letter* 48), "venial" sin (see 1–2.72.5). A key difference between these two is that mortal sin, because it severs our relationship with God, brings with it an eternal penalty, which can ordinarily only be remedied through baptism or sacramental penance, whereas venial sin brings only temporal penalty, which can be remedied through various pious acts.

14. By "positive law," Thomas means humanly enacted laws, and he concedes that things are not wrong simply by virtue of being outlawed.

15. Violating the eternal law is not like violating a positive law, because the eternal law is the primary standard against which human actions are measured (see note 9, above). For the meaning of "natural law," see Thomas's discussion in 1–2.91.2, below.

16. Or, to put it in terms Thomas uses earlier in this article, philosophers judge morality in terms of its "proximate" measure, and theologians judge morality in terms of its "primary" measure.

Question 91:

The Various Kinds of Law

1–2.91.2[1]

Is there any natural law?[2]

It would seem that there is no natural law in us.

1. Human beings are governed sufficiently by the eternal law, for Augustine says in *On Free Choice of the Will* (1.6) that the eternal law "is that by which

---

1. On this article, see Westberg (1992); Kerr (2002, 97–113); Sokolowski (2004); McDermott (2007, 49–63).

2. Thomas prefaces his discussion of law (1–2.90.prologue) by noting that, in addition to the "intrinsic" or internal sources of human action (i.e., the natural powers of the soul, such as our capacities for motion and reproduction, thought and willing, along with the acquired dispositions of the soul, such as knowledge and virtue and vices), there is an "extrinsic" or external source moving us toward good: God. And God moves us in two ways: through *law*, which tells us what is good, and through *grace*, which assists us in doing good. (Thomas also mentions that the devil can be an external source of action, influencing us toward evil through temptations, though not moving the will in the way that God can; see 1–2.55 note 28.) So in the remainder of this part of the *Summa*, Thomas discusses these external sources moving us toward good.

In 1–2.90.1 Thomas begins with a definition of "law" as "something that is a standard and measure of actions" (*quaedam regula est et mensura actuum*). By 1–2.90.4 Thomas has elaborated this definition so as to define "law" as "something set up by reason for the sake of the common good, made by whoever is responsible for the care of the community, and which is publicly proclaimed" (*quaedam rationis ordinatio ad bonum commune, ab eo qui curam communitatis habet, promulgata*). We might think of this by breaking the definition of law down into Aristotle's four causes (see 1.2 note 41). First, reason, as *formal cause*, gives law its structure; a law that is not in conformity with reason is deformed, perhaps to the point of not being a law at all. The common good—i.e., the good of human beings taken as a whole, and not of one person as an individual—is the *final cause* of law, its goal or purpose; laws are for the sake of a community, not an individual. The people as a whole or, more commonly, the duly constituted individual or group that represents the people, is the *efficient cause* of law, that which enacts or brings about the law; private citizens on their own cannot put laws into effect. Finally, the act of making the law publicly known, of putting it down in writing or publicly proclaiming it in words, is something like a *material* cause—what gives the law material embodiment; people must be made aware of the rules that bind them. Something that fails to fulfill all four of these criteria fails to be a genuine law.

Thomas is aware, however, that "law" is a term that is used analogously, and in this article and those that follow we find him exploring different ways in which the term is used.

it is just that everything should be most orderly."³ But nature does not abound in superfluous things, just as it does not fail in necessary things. Therefore there is no law that is natural to human beings.⁴

2. By the law one is oriented in one's actions to a goal [*ad finem*], as stated above (1–2.90.2). But the orientation of human acts to their goal is not by nature, as happens in nonrational creatures, which act to attain their end only on the basis of their natural appetite. Rather, human beings act to attain their end on the basis of reason and will. Therefore there is no law that is natural to human beings.⁵

3. The more one is free, the less one is under the law.⁶ But human beings are freer than any other animal on account of free choice [*liberium arbitrium*], which they have, unlike other animals. Since other animals are not subject to a natural law, neither therefore are human beings subject to any natural law.⁷

On the contrary: Regarding the statement in Romans (2:14), "When the Gentiles, who do not have the law, do by nature those things that are required by the law," the gloss comments:⁸ "Although they have no written law, they

3. We have encountered the notion of "eternal law" in Thomas's discussion of sin (see 1–2.71 note 9). In the present question, Thomas has discussed eternal law in the article prior to this one, and he goes on to discuss it in more detail in 1–2.93. He defines it in 1–2.93.1 as "nothing other than the pattern [*ratio*] of divine wisdom as it directs every action and movement" and goes on to say in 1–2.93.4 that God's will, which is identical with God's essence, *is* the eternal law. We might say that what Thomas means by "eternal law" is the radical orderliness of God inasmuch as it gives order to creation.

4. If the eternal law is that which orders creatures, then there is no need for a different law by which human beings are governed, thus making any law in us by nature superfluous. The superfluity of such a form of law would itself seem to be a violation of divine order.

5. The objector is taking "natural law" to be something akin to what we might mean by a "law of nature" and argues that only things that lack intelligence are ruled by laws of nature; human beings, having intelligence and free will, are not ruled by the laws of nature—at least not with regard to distinctively human actions (presumably they are still subject to gravity and such).

6. This seems to be a questionable premise: i.e., the purest freedom possible is really a freedom from *all* law. In his reply, however, Thomas does not call this view into question, as one might expect him to. Perhaps it never occurred to him that one would aspire to a freedom from *all* law, and so he takes this premise to be the rather obvious statement that one is, in specific cases, free if one is not bound by law: if I am not required by law to drive on the left side or the right side of the road, then I am presumably free to drive on whichever side strikes my fancy (or seems safest).

7. The third objection seems to employ a different definition of natural law than the second objection. As mentioned (see note 5, above), the second objection seems to understand "natural law" to mean something like the modern notion of a law of nature, and so nonrational animals, acting out of instinct, are bound by natural law; but rational animals (i.e., humans), possessing a free will grounded in the intellect, are not. The third objection, like Thomas, sees law as tied to rationality (see note 2, above) and so takes it as obvious that nonrational animals are free from natural law. The objection then argues that if human beings are to have free will, then they must be even *more* free of natural law than nonrational animals. At least in one respect, therefore, the third objection is using a notion of "natural law" that fits more closely with Thomas's own understanding of law.

8. On "gloss," see 1.12 note 10.

still have the natural law, by which everyone understands and is conscious in themselves of what is good and what is evil."

I answer: As stated above (1–2.90.1 ad 1), law, since it is a standard [*regula*] and measure, can be in someone in two ways: the way it is in the one ruling and measuring and the way it is in the one that is ruled and measured, since a thing is ruled and measured to the degree that it shares in the standard or measure.[9] Because all things under divine providence are ruled and measured by the eternal law, as is clear from what was said above (1–2.90.1), it is evident that all things share in some way in the eternal law—that is to say, they have an inclination toward their proper activities and goals from its imprint [*impressione*] upon them.[10]

Now, among all creatures, a rational creature is under divine providence in the best possible way, inasmuch as it shares in providence by providing for itself and for others. Thus it shares in eternal reason, by which it has a natural inclination to the activity and goal it ought to have. Such sharing in the eternal law by a rational creature is called "natural law."[11] For this reason the psalmist (Ps. 4:6), after saying, "Offer up the sacrifice of justice," adds (as though someone had asked what the works of justice are), "Many say, 'who shows us good things?'" He responds to this question, saying, "The light of your face, O Lord, is signed upon us"—as if to say, "the light of natural reason, by which we discern what is good and evil." This pertains to the natural law, which is nothing other than an imprint of divine light in us.[12]

It is therefore clear that the natural law is nothing other than a sharing in the eternal law by a rational creature.

9. If, say, I decide to arrange the furniture in my living room in a particular way, for a particular purpose, that design is "my design" in a fundamental way, because I am the source of the arrangement, and it is "the room's design" in a derivative way, by virtue of it being arranged according to my design.

10. *Impressione* can mean "imprint" or "influence"—either of which would be a plausible translation. God, as the universal arranger of things, is the source of their order in a fundamental way (this is what Thomas means by the "eternal law"); creatures, as the things arranged, bear the imprint of this order and thus possess it by sharing or "participating" in God's eternal law.

11. Human beings are subject to God's providence in a unique way that makes them different from nonrational beings. They are not arranged in the way that I might arrange furniture in a room, placing it here or there. Rather, there is a real sense in which rational creatures arrange themselves by pursuing the good to which their will, informed by reason, draws them. This does not mean, however, that they are somehow independent from God's providential guidance, for the rational nature by which they are drawn to the good shares in the eternal reason of God. We might say that nonrational creatures share in the eternal law simply by being guided to fulfillment, whereas rational creatures share in the eternal law by guiding themselves to a fulfillment that is in accord with their God-given natures. This way of sharing in the eternal law that we find in rational creatures is what we mean by "natural law."

12. This verse from the Psalms is a favorite of Thomas's for talking about natural law (see *Commentary on Job* 33.2; *Commentary on Romans* 2.3.216; *Commentary on the Gospel of John* 1.5.128).

Reply to 1: This reasoning would work if natural law were something different from eternal law. It is, however, nothing except a sharing in it, as was said.[13]

Reply to 2: Every operation of reason and will is derived in us from what is in accord with nature, as stated above (1–2.10.1). For every act of reasoning is derived from principles that are naturally known, and every act of desiring things that are for the sake of a goal is derived from the natural appetite for the ultimate goal. And so the initial orientation of our acts to their goal must be done through natural law.[14]

Reply to 3: Nonrational animals share in eternal reason in their own way, just as a rational creature does. But because a rational creature shares in it intellectually and rationally, the act of sharing in eternal law by a rational creature is properly called a law, for law is something related to reason, as stated above (1–2.90.1).[15] Nonrational creatures, however, do not share in the eternal law rationally; therefore, this cannot be called "law" except by way of a kind of similarity.[16]

1–2.91.3[17]
Is there any human law?

It would seem that there is no human law.

1. The natural law is a sharing in the eternal law, as was said (1–2.91.2, above). But through the eternal law "all things are most orderly," as Augustine says in *On Free Choice of the Will* (1.6). Therefore natural law suffices for ordering all human affairs, and there is no need for any human law.[18]

2. As was said before (1–2.90.1), law by its nature is the measure of other things. But human reason is not a measure of things, but vice versa, as stated

13. The mistake of the objection is to treat natural law as if it were a different sort of law than eternal law, when in fact it is simply the eternal law as this is shared in by rational creatures.

14. Both for human beings and for other creatures, what is good for us to desire is determined not by what we *choose* but by what we *are*. Being human, we cannot flourish if we seek the kind of perfection that would be fitting for a rock or an oak tree or an antelope. Where we differ from other creatures is in our ability to choose how we pursue that perfection.

15. Thomas largely agrees with the objection that nonhuman animals do not, strictly speaking, follow the natural law because they do not share in the eternal law via reason. He does not think, however, that being under the natural law makes us less free, since it is the same reason by which we are subject to natural law that makes us capable of free action.

16. For Thomas, any talk of a "law of nature" by which nonrational animals are ruled is really a metaphorical way of talking about their subjection to providence.

17. On this article, see Westberg (1992).

18. Given the universal scope of God's eternal law and the reality of natural law as the way in which human beings share in that eternal law, it would seem superfluous (and perhaps even arrogant) for human beings to create their own laws.

in Aristotle's *Metaphysics* (10.1, 1053ᵃ; cf. 10.6, 1157ᵃ).[19] Therefore no law can proceed from human reason.

3. A measure ought to be completely certain, as stated in the *Metaphysics* (10.1, 1052ᵇ–1053ᵃ). But the dictates of human reason about matters of conduct are uncertain, according to Wisdom (9:14): "The thoughts of mortals are fearful, and our designs [*providentiae*] uncertain." Therefore no law can proceed from human reason.

On the contrary: Augustine, in *On Free Choice of the Will* (1.6), posits two laws, one eternal and the other temporal, and the latter he calls "human."[20]

I answer: As stated above (1–2.90.1 ad 2), a law is a kind of dictate of practical reason. Now the same process is found in practical as in speculative reason: each proceeds from specific premises to specific conclusions, as stated above (1–2.90.1 ad 2).[21] Thus we say that in speculative reason we proceed from unprovable premises known by nature to the conclusions of the different sciences, the knowledge of which is not imparted to us by nature but discovered by the labor of reason. So too it is from the precepts of natural law, as from general and unprovable premises, that human reason must proceed to

19. Aristotle is quite dismissive of those who, like Protagoras, claim that "man is the measure of all things." He notes that this means not that human beings are themselves some standard of truth, but simply that our capacity for knowledge and perception allows us to take the measure of things. He concludes, "They are saying nothing, then, while appearing to say something remarkable" (*Metaphysics* 10.1, 1053ᵇ).

20. The medieval notion of the "temporal" is not precisely what people today would call the "secular." Earthly events within the flow of time were considered, as the term implies, "temporal" matters, and these were generally seen as under the purview of rulers, who, if they were just, were guided by human reason. Those matters that concerned the eternal destiny of humans were considered "spiritual" and were generally under the purview of ecclesiastical rulers, who were guided by divine law (see 1.91.4). This distinction sounds much neater in principle than it proved to be in practice, not least because both temporal and spiritual rulers were seen to derive their authority from God and to exercise roles with regard to the care of the Christian community. Thomas himself says, "The king is indeed the minister of God in governing the people" (*On Kingship* 1.8). Moreover, temporal matters, no less than spiritual matters, were to be oriented to the ultimate end of human beings, which is eternal life with God. So for medieval people there was no neat division of labor between temporal and spiritual rulers, and much of the eleventh and twelfth centuries were taken up by questions of where to draw a line between these two. For example, should appointment to offices in the church, such as bishop and abbot, which were financially supported by lands within the realm of a king or an emperor, be under the control of a temporal ruler or a spiritual ruler? Kings and emperors tended to argue that since this concerned a temporal affair—the control of income-generating property—it should be determined by temporal authorities, whereas popes tended to argue that since this concerned the appointment of those charged with the eternal welfare of Christ's flock—bishops and abbots—it should be determined by spiritual authorities.

21. On speculative and practical reason, see 1–2.9 note 15. Here Thomas points out what these two uses of reason have in common: both begin from premises or principles and move through the process of reasoning to conclusions regarding, in the case of speculative reason, what is true or, in the case of practical reason, what is to be done.

more particular ways of ordering of things.[22] Provided that the other essential conditions of law described earlier (1–2.90.2–4) are observed, these particular ways of ordering things devised by human reason are called "human laws."[23] Therefore Cicero says in his *Rhetoric* (*De inventione* 2.53) that "the beginning of justice was in nature; then certain things became customary on account of their usefulness; afterward things that came from nature and were approved by custom were ratified by fear and reverence [*metus et religio*] for the law."

Reply to 1: Human reason cannot share fully in the command of divine reason, but only in its own way and incompletely. Therefore, just as with speculative reason there is in us, through a natural sharing in divine wisdom, a knowledge of certain general principles, but not proper knowledge of every truth contained in divine wisdom, so too with practical reason human beings have a natural sharing in the eternal law with regard to certain general principles, but not with regard to specific guidance in individual cases, even though these are contained in the eternal law. And so it is necessary additionally that human reason proceed to certain specific legal sanctions.[24]

Reply to 2: Human reason is not itself the standard by which reality is measured [*regula res*]. Rather, the principles imparted to it by nature are the general standard and measure of all things that humans do, of which natural reason is the standard and measure, even though it is not the measure of things that come from nature.[25]

22. Just as speculative reason draws specific conclusions from general principles, so too practical reason makes specific determinations concerning good actions beginning from the general principles of natural law. Thomas will go on to argue in a later article (1–2.95.2) that this making-specific of the natural law might occur in two ways: one in which a human law flows directly from the natural law as a conclusion flows from its premises (such as outlawing murder as a way of implementing the natural law's prohibition of unjust killing) and another in which a human law determines parameters of action for the sake of a consistent and harmonious living-out of the natural law within society (such as setting the time for children beginning school at age five as one way in which the natural law's injunction that parents educate their children is enacted). The latter sort of human law admits far more variability (some societies might set the age at four and others at six) than the former (no society can allow murder and remain a truly human society).

23. For the "other essential conditions of law" see 1–2.91 note 2.

24. Human beings "share" or "participate" in God's wisdom (i.e., "eternal law") but do not possess it in the way that God does. In this sense our possession of that wisdom is imperfect and must be supplemented by human reason, not because something is lacking in God's wisdom, but because we are finite in our possession of that infinite wisdom. In discerning truth, our participation in God's wisdom allows us to know general principles of thinking (such as the principle that something cannot be both true and false at the same time) without knowing each and every particular fact about the world. These are things we must discover through our own investigative labor. Likewise, in discerning how human beings should act, our participation in divine wisdom (i.e., "natural law") gives us general principles of action without telling us how we ought to act in every particular instance. This is something we discover through our own investigative labor, and when we are not just thinking about our own actions but seeking to guide a society, we then codify the fruits of our labors into laws.

25. This response poses some difficulties with regard to interpretation. It could be taken to be saying that although human reason is not the measure of natural things, it *is* the measure of human actions. Or,

Reply to 3: Practical reason is concerned with matters of action [*opera-bilia*], which are singular and contingent, but not, as speculative reason is, with matters of necessity [*necessaria*]. Therefore human laws cannot possess that infallibility that the demonstrated conclusions of the sciences possess.[26] Nor must every measure be in every way infallible and certain, but only with regard to what is possible for the kind of measure it is.[27]

---

and this I think is more likely, it could be saying that while human reason is the measure of human action, it is so only because of the principles imparted to it by its participation in eternal law (i.e., by natural law), and of these principles it is in no sense the measure.

26. Speculative reason grasps the Pythagorean theorem as something necessary: there is no right triangle for which $a^2 + b^2 \neq c^2$, no matter whether it is a triangle in thirteenth-century Paris or one in nineteenth-century Prague. But practical reason and the laws it generates deal with particular actions that are variable according to circumstances. This is true when these human laws are necessary entailments of natural law (unjust killing is always wrong, but you still need to determine what counts as unjust) and even more true when human laws are simply giving specificity to the natural law (parents must educate their children, but the timing and amount of schooling will vary from culture to culture and from child to child). One of the challenges of legislating is the need to frame laws that are general enough to be applied to the widely varied circumstances of particular cases, but not so general as to be useless.

27. The kind of measurement that a pollster might make of public opinion will necessarily be less precise than the kind that an engineer makes with a micrometer. But a micrometer, while in one sense more precise than a poll, would not be particularly useful in measuring public opinion.

Question 109:

The Necessity of Grace

1–2.109.2[1]

Can human beings wish and do good without grace?

It would seem that human beings can wish and do good without grace.[2]

1. Something is in one's power if one has mastery over it. But human beings have mastery over their acts, and especially of their willing, as stated earlier (1–2.1.1; 1–2.13.6). Therefore, human beings, left to themselves and without the help of grace, can wish and do good.

2. One has more power over what is in accord with one's nature than over what is beyond one's nature. But sin is against a human being's nature, as John of Damascus says (*On the Orthodox Faith* 2.30), whereas deeds of virtue are in accord with that nature, as stated earlier (1–2.71.1). Therefore, since one can sin from one's own power, it appears to be even more the case that one can likewise wish and do good.

1. On this article, see Shanley (1999); Kobusch (2002); Wawrykow (2005); McCosker (2016).

2. For Thomas, "grace" (*gratia*) is an analogical term, having a variety of related but not identical meanings, that operates within a picture of the world in which God shows favor to human beings by giving them what they need in order to attain fulfillment through eternal life with God. Thus, it can refer either to God's favorable disposition toward humanity (what later theologians called "uncreated grace") or to those gifts that God gives so that we may attain eternal life (what later theologians called "created grace").

Although Thomas distances himself from some of the rhetorical excesses committed by Augustine in the midst of the Pelagian controversy, his teaching on the need for grace, particularly in his mature works, remains profoundly indebted to Augustine. This indebtedness is not always obvious to readers who focus on Thomas's fundamentally "optimistic" account of human nature (i.e., sin does not destroy the goodness of our nature) and who therefore do not see the rather strict limits Thomas places on the good we can accomplish without special divine assistance that goes beyond what God as creator imparts to human nature. What becomes clear in this article is that Thomas sees human beings as incapable of doing anything to earn salvation, or even to *will* to do good, apart from God's gift of grace. At the same time, he thinks there is a meaningful sense in which we can speak of human beings "meriting" salvation by their good actions.

3. Truth is the good of the intellect, as the Philosopher says in the *Ethics* (6.2, 1139ᵇ). But the intellect can know truth by itself, just as every other thing can do its own natural activity by itself. Therefore, it is even more the case that human beings can, left to themselves, do and wish good.³

On the contrary: The Apostle says in Romans (9:16), "It is not of him who wills" (namely, to will) "nor of him who runs" (namely, to run) "but of God who shows mercy." And Augustine says in *On Rebuke and Grace* (2.3) that "without grace human beings do nothing truly good, whether thinking, or wishing and loving, or acting."

I answer: Human nature may be looked at in two ways: first, in its integrity, as it was in our first parents before sin; second, as it is corrupted in us after the sin of our first parents.⁴ Now in both states human nature needs the help of God as first mover in order to do or wish any good whatsoever, as stated earlier (1–2.109.1). But in the state of integrity, in terms of the sufficiency of the power of acting, human beings by their natural endowments could wish and do the good that was in proportion to human nature, such as the good of acquired virtue, though they could do no good that surpassed human nature, such as the good of infused virtue.⁵ In the state of corrupt nature, however,

3. All three of the objections share the presumption that an action in accord with a rational being's nature is somehow "possessed" by that being. There is certainly truth in this presumption, since it makes sense to speak of "my" actions only if they in some sense belong to me. The second objection also makes the valid point that if I am to be blamed for my sins, it is only right that I be praised for my good actions, which is possible only if they are in a real sense "mine." The objections also share the presumption that in order for these actions to be mine, I must be capable of doing them apart from divine grace.

4. For Thomas, human nature in its "integrity" is what he calls the state of "original justice," a term that originates with Anselm of Canterbury. It is a condition of "integrity" because it is a state in which the various aspects of the human person—intellect, senses, and body—are harmoniously integrated with one another on account of the harmonious relation of the human person as a whole to God. The state of corruption caused by sin is a state of dis-integration, in which intellect and sense are at war with each other.

Note that Thomas understands Adam and Eve to be historical individuals. However, his understanding of human nature's states of integrity and corruption does not depend on the historicity of the details of the story of Adam and Eve. The most important point is that human nature is not inherently sinful (thus we may speak of its state of integrity), but in actual fact no human is born without the wound of sin (the state of corruption). These claims can be maintained without appeal to Adam and Eve as historical figures. The difficult question is whether these claims can be maintained without appealing to the "state of integrity" as a historical period (even if it is only a moment in duration) at the beginning of human history, when an individual or group of human beings were in fact without sin, or whether, instead, it is sufficient to maintain that this is simply a logical possibility that was never realized historically. Because Thomas presumes Adam and Eve as historical figures, he never considers the second possibility, and consequently neither accepts nor rejects it.

5. Here Thomas distinguishes two ways in which human beings need God's assistance in order to do or wish any good. First, all action must ultimately be traced back to God as the first mover; thus, even prior to the fall of humanity, Adam and Eve needed this sort of general divine assistance to do any good—although they needed nothing beyond God's ever-present activity as the source of creation in order to do "the

human beings fall short of what is in accordance with human nature, so that they are unable to fulfill it by their own natural powers.[6] Yet because human nature is not completely corrupted by sin, so as to be deprived of every natural good, even in the state of corrupted nature it can, by virtue of its natural endowments, work some particular good, such as building dwellings, planting vineyards, and other such things. Yet it cannot do all the good natural to it, so that it falls short in nothing. It is like a sick person who can make some movements by himself yet cannot move fully as a healthy person can, unless cured by the help of medicine.[7]

And thus in the state of nature in its integrity, one needs a strength from grace that is added to natural strength for one reason—namely, in order to do and wish supernatural good. But in the state of corrupted nature one needs this grace for two reasons: in order to be healed and, beyond this, in order to

---

good that was in proportion to human nature." Second, human beings need a special and additional divine assistance ("infused grace") because they have been called by God to a destiny that exceeds what human nature can do. Even in the state of original justice, human beings required this special assistance; indeed, the state of original justice was itself a special gift of divine grace and not a natural endowment of human nature, since it involved submission of the intellect to God, which is a good that exceeds human nature.

What exactly Thomas means by "the good that was in proportion to human nature" is somewhat unclear. Apparently this good does not include the submission of the intellect to God, since Thomas denies this in 1.100.1, where he says that original justice was not something that flowed from human nature itself, but was "a gift conferred by God on the entire human nature." Therefore, the good Thomas has in mind must entail something more modest, such as an ad hoc ability to follow God's law.

6. Whereas prior to the fall human beings were able to do "the good that was in proportion to human nature" with only the general assistance of God as the first mover, the disintegration brought about by sin makes it impossible to live and act in a fully human manner apart from the special assistance of God's grace.

7. The difficulties of the position Thomas is attempting to map out on the human need for grace are manifest in these last two sentences. Thomas is unwilling to say that human beings cannot do *any* good apart from grace, since there are certain undeniably good things that human beings, even sinful human beings, accomplish without any special divine assistance. It does seem absurd, for example, to think that a special act on God's part is required every time a person succeeds in building a house or raising a crop. Such a view would seem to imply that God's creation has been so thwarted by sin that it has virtually ceased to function.

At the same time, one should attend to the modesty of the kinds of things Thomas lists as possible for fallen human beings without grace: building and planting, neither of which implies a moral good, but only a sort of technical accomplishment. The picture becomes a bit muddier in the fifth article of this same question, where (quoting a spurious work attributed to Augustine) Thomas offers a similar list of "works conducive to a good that is natural to human beings" and includes "having friends" among them. This muddies the picture because friendship among human beings, unlike building and planting, *is* a moral achievement—at least in the case of friendships based on virtue. Indeed, there is a sense in which such friendships are for Thomas the penultimate moral achievement, exceeded only by friendship with God.

We might sort out this matter by observing that Thomas describes the things that human beings can do apart from grace as "particular" things, and not as the complete good of which human nature was capable in the state of integrity. Taking the difficult case of friendship, we might say that for fallen human nature it is possible to have friends, but that apart from grace such friendships cannot characterize our lives in their totality. Sin has fragmented our lives in such a way that, apart from grace, the goods we can accomplish can never make us good people in any absolute sense.

carry out works of supernatural virtue, which are meritorious.[8] Furthermore, in both states human beings need divine help in order to be moved to act well.

Reply to 1: Human beings are in control of their actions, and of their willing or not willing, because of the deliberation of reason, which can be bent to one side or the other. But if they are in control of their deliberating or not deliberating, this can be only by virtue of a previous deliberation. And since this cannot go on to infinity, we must finally arrive at this conclusion: the free will of human beings is moved by an external principle that is above the human mind—that is, by God, as the Philosopher proves in the chapter "On Good Fortune" (*Eudemian Ethics* 7.14, 1248[a]).[9] Therefore, even when it was unweakened by sin, the human mind was not master of its activity to such a degree that it did not need to be moved by God;[10] this is even more the case with the free will of human beings weakened by sin, since by sin's corruption of its nature the will is hindered from willing good.

8. Because the language of "merit" has been controversial, particularly between Roman Catholics and Protestants, it is worth saying briefly what Thomas means by it. To say that an action "merits" a reward is to say that the reward is a fitting response to that act; to say that someone merits salvation is to say that their use of their freedom, as expressed in their actions, is such that salvation is a fitting response on God's part. In discussing merit, Thomas distinguishes between meriting something according to a strict measure of justice, such that a denial of the reward would be unjust (i.e., meriting something *de condigno*), and meriting something in the sense that it is fitting that a reward be given, but the denial of the reward would not in itself be unjust (i.e., meriting something *de congruo*). We might think of this as the difference between paying your bill and leaving a tip (provided the tip is not, as it is in the United States, something that is de facto payment for the waiter). The tip is not something justice requires, but neither is it *unjust*, since it is a fitting response to the service given. But whether we are speaking of merit *de condigno* or merit *de congruo*, we should note certain peculiarities that indicate the caution we must use in speaking of merit.

Thomas himself notes in 1–2.114.1 that we use the word analogically when we speak of God "rewarding" human action, since we can act in the first place only because God has given us the capacity to act: "A human being obtains from God, as a reward for his doing, what God gave that person the power to do in the first place." Further, even when Thomas speaks of Christ as a human being meriting on our behalf, it is in the context of speaking of the grace that was bestowed on Christ as the head of the church and that Christ shares with us. In other words, merit always, even in the case of Christ, presumes the gift of God's grace. We might say that merit is a matter of "fittingness" or *convenientia* (see 3.1 note 2): although God is never compelled to reward human action, it is "fitting" all the same for God to reward certain actions in certain ways; thus we can say that those actions merit their reward. In the case of Christ, however, Thomas pushes this point further. Because the grace by which Christ merits salvation for himself and others is not simply the grace of "adoption" but that of "union" (i.e., he is not simply an adopted son of God, but God the Son, the second Person of the Trinity), Thomas says in 1–2.114.3 that the reward God gives Christ is not simply "fitting" (*de congruo*) but a matter of justice (*de condigno*).

9. Most modern scholars would not agree with Thomas's suggestion that Aristotle himself recognized a need for God to move the will by a special act.

10. To extend the analogy between existing and doing good (which pertains also in the reply to obj. 2), we might say that just as genuine existence does not imply that our existence is somehow independent from God, so too genuine human willing and acting does not imply that either our will or action is accomplished without divine assistance. My action, no less than my existence, is "mine" even if it has God as its source.

Reply to 2: To sin is nothing else than to fail in the good that belongs to any being according to its nature.[11] Now just as every created thing has its existence from another and is nothing considered in itself, so too it needs to be preserved by another in the good that pertains to its nature; for left to itself it can fail in good, just as left to itself it can fall into nonexistence, unless it is upheld by God.[12]

Reply to 3: Human beings cannot even know truth without divine help, as was stated earlier (1–2.109.1).[13] And yet human nature is more corrupted by sin with regard to the desire for good than with regard to the knowledge of truth.

1–2.109.6[14]
Can human beings, left alone and without the external aid of grace, prepare themselves for grace?

It would seem that human beings, left to themselves and without the external aid of grace, can prepare themselves for grace.

1. Nothing impossible is laid upon human beings, as stated earlier (1–2.109.4 ad 1). But it is written in Zechariah (1:3), "Turn to me [*convertimini ad me*]. . . and I will turn to you." But to prepare for grace is nothing more than to turn to God. Therefore it seems that human beings, left to themselves and without the external aid of grace, can prepare themselves for grace.[15]

2. One prepares oneself for grace by doing what lies within oneself to do, since if human beings do what is in them to do, God will not deny them grace;[16]

11. On Thomas's understanding of sin, see 1–2.71 note 9.

12. Thomas's point is not entirely clear. The kind of divine assistance—being "upheld by God"—that he refers to here seems to be not the general action of God as first mover, by which things are held in existence, but the supernatural gift of grace. Again, we see the paradoxes of human nature: we can live as fully human only by virtue of a gift that exceeds our humanity.

13. This "help" referred to here is not the gift of grace but the action of God as first mover, at least as regards those things that are within human beings' natural capacity to know.

14. On this article, see Kobusch (2002); Wawrykow (2005); McCosker (2016).

15. The objection suggests that Scripture requires, as a precondition for God turning to us in grace, our prior turning to God, which constitutes our preparation for the reception of grace.

16. The idea that "to do that which lies within oneself" (*facere quod in se est*) is sufficient preparation for grace can be traced back to the anonymous fourth-century writer known as Ambrosiaster. In the medieval period this phrase, understood in the sense that doing one's moral best was sufficient preparation to receive God's grace, was widely embraced by theologians, including the young Thomas Aquinas (e.g., *Commentary on the Sentences* bk. 1, dist. 48, q. 1, a. 3), even though, as he came to recognize later in life, it sits uneasily with Augustine's idea of the role of grace in conversion. The young Thomas tried to mitigate this conflict by arguing that our moral best did not, of itself, merit grace, such that God was constrained to give us grace, but rather grace was given because God had promised to do so. The *facere quod in se est* is a principle that would become extremely important for theologians later in the Middle Ages, such as William of Ockham and Gabriel Biel, and is something against which Martin Luther reacted.

for it is written in Matthew (7:11) that God gives his good Spirit "to those who ask him." But something is said to be in us if it lies within our power. Therefore it seems to lie within our power to prepare ourselves for grace.

3. If a person needs grace in order to prepare for grace, that person will likewise need grace to prepare for the first grace, and so on to infinity, which is impossible.[17] Therefore it seems that we must not go beyond what was said first—that is, that human beings, left to themselves and without grace, can prepare themselves for grace.

4. Proverbs (16:1) says, "It belongs to a human being to prepare the soul." But something is said to belong to a human being when one can do it by oneself. Therefore it seems that human beings, left to themselves, can prepare themselves for grace.

On the contrary: It is written in John (6:44), "No one can come to me unless the Father, who has sent me, draws him." But if human beings could prepare themselves, they would not need to be drawn by another. Therefore human beings cannot prepare themselves without the help of grace.

I answer: The preparation of the human will for the good is twofold. First it is prepared to operate well and to enjoy God, and such preparation of the will cannot take place without the gift of habitual grace,[18] from which flow

---

17. Note how the objection, by employing the specter of an infinite regress, sets up the human will as a kind of "first mover" in the process of salvation.

18. What Thomas means by "habitual grace" or, we might say, "grace as a lasting disposition" (on *habitus*, see 1–2.55 note 2) is perhaps most evident in the various contrasts according to which medieval theologians spoke about grace. The most important of these contrasts for Thomas (which he discusses in 1–2.111) are as follows:

1. Gratuitous grace (*gratia gratis data*) versus sanctifying grace (*gratia gratum faciens*), the latter of which is further subdivided into (a) habitual grace and (b) actual grace. Gratuitous grace refers to those gifts that God gives us not for the sake of our own holiness but for the good of others. In his commentary on Paul's First Letter to the Corinthians, Thomas identifies these with the charismatic gifts Paul discusses in 1 Cor. 12, and he makes the point that these gifts are given for the building up of the church. Sanctifying grace is the act of God that makes us holy by (a) giving us a disposition to act lovingly (habitual grace) and (b) moving us to act lovingly (actual grace). For more, see 1–2.110, below.

2. Operating grace (*gratia operans*) versus cooperating grace (*gratia cooperans*). Operating grace is the first movement of grace, in which God works within us to heal our souls so that we both are disposed to act in a good way and will to act in that way. This grace in no sense involves an action on our part; as Thomas puts it, "Our mind is moved and does not move" (1–2.111.2). Cooperating grace, on the other hand, follows upon operating grace and does involve actions that flow forth from the soul that has been healed. But even in the case of cooperating grace, the soul does not act as if it were an independent source of action working parallel to God's action; its action is always dependent upon the cooperating movement of grace. Cooperating grace is the action of grace on those occasions when, Thomas says, "our mind both moves and is moved" (1–2.111.2).

3. Prevenient grace (*gratia praeveniens*) versus subsequent grace (*gratia subsequens*). Because grace brings about a change in human beings, it operates within history and the flow of time. In other words, it first brings about one effect and then another. In 1–2.111.3 Thomas lists five effects of grace, each

works worthy of reward, as stated earlier (1–2.109.5). In a second way, it is possible to think that the human will is prepared for the gift of habitual grace. In order to prepare oneself to receive this gift, it is not necessary to presuppose the gift of any further lasting disposition of the soul; otherwise we would go on to infinity. Rather, we must presuppose some gratuitous help from God, moving the soul from within or inspiring the good we propose to do,[19] for we need divine assistance in these two ways, as stated earlier (1–2.109.2–3).

It is clear that we need the help of God to move us. Since everything that acts does so on account of a goal, every cause must direct its effect toward its goal, and since the order of agents or movers corresponds to the order of goals, human beings must be directed to their ultimate goal by the motion of the first mover, and to their immediate goal by the motion of any of the subordinate movers.[20] This is like the way in which the spirit of a soldier is turned toward seeking victory by the motion of the leader of the army and toward following the flag by the motion of the flag bearer. Since God is, absolutely speaking, the first mover, it is by his motion that everything is turned toward him on account of the general tendency toward goodness by which everything seeks to be made like God in its own way. Therefore Dionysius says in the book *On the Divine Names* (4) that "God turns all to himself."[21]

But God directs the righteous to himself as to a particular goal that they seek, and to which they wish to cling. According to the psalm (73:28), "It is good for me to cling to my God." And the fact that they are turned to God can be only from God's having turned them. But to prepare oneself for grace is, as it were, to be turned to God, just as one who has his eyes turned away from the light of the sun prepares himself to receive the sun's light by turning his eyes toward the sun. It is therefore clear that human beings cannot prepare

---

one leading to the other: (1) the healing of the soul, (2) the desiring of good, (3) the doing of good, (4) perseverance in doing good, and (5) attaining glory. When we speak of one of these effects as preceding the other, we speak of prevenient (i.e., "coming before") grace; when we speak of one of these effects as following upon the other, we speak of subsequent or consequent (i.e., "following upon") grace. Thus, the action of grace causing the soul to desire good is prevenient with regard to our doing the good, and the action of grace causing us to do the good is consequent upon our desiring the good.

19. We might mean two different things when we speak of "preparation to receive grace." We might be speaking of what is necessary in order for us to will and act well, and this requires that we be prepared by being given the disposition called habitual grace. We might also be speaking of what is necessary in order for us to receive the gift of habitual grace, and this requires nothing but the action of God.

20. Timothy McDermott's free translation of this sentence perhaps makes Thomas's point a bit clearer: "For when agents are acting in subordination to one another, their goals are correspondingly subordinated, the initial agent acting toward the ultimate goal and the secondary agents to the nearer goals." See McDermott (1989, 310).

21. Up to this point, Thomas is not speaking of grace but of God's providence, by which God guides and governs the world.

themselves to receive the light of grace except by the gratuitous help of God moving them inwardly.[22]

Reply 1: A person's turning to God is by free will, and for this reason one is commanded to turn oneself to God. But free will cannot be turned to God unless God himself turns it, according to Jeremiah (31:18), "Turn me [*converte me*] and I shall be turned, for you are the Lord, my God," and Lamentations (5:21), "O Lord, turn us [*converte nos*] to you, and we shall be turned."[23]

Reply to 2: A person can do nothing unless moved by God, according to John (15:5), "Without me, you can do nothing." Therefore when one is said to do what lies within oneself to do, this is said to be in that person's power inasmuch as he or she is moved by God.[24]

Reply to 3: This objection holds true for grace as a lasting disposition, for which some preparation is required, since every form requires a suitableness in that which is to be its subject. But no additional motion need be presupposed for a human being to be moved by God, since God is the first mover.[25] Therefore we need not go to infinity.

Reply to 4: It belongs to human beings to prepare their souls, since they do this by their free will. And yet they do not do this without the help of God moving them and drawing them to himself, as was said above.

22. The logic of Thomas's point may not be immediately apparent. He is positioning grace as a special instance of God's providence. In the general case of God's providence, nothing moves without being moved by God—so too in the special case of grace. If preparation for grace involves a "movement," then, like all movement, it cannot be done independently of God's action. Thomas then asserts that the preparation of the soul for grace *is* in fact a kind of movement—one that Scripture describes as "turning." Thus such preparation cannot be done apart from God's gracious action.

Here we can see clearly the influence on Thomas of St. Augustine, who argued against the followers of Pelagius that no action on the part of human beings could prepare them to receive grace. Even when we do that which is within us (see obj. 2 and Thomas's reply), we do it under the action of grace.

23. This reply might seem baffling unless one realizes that for Thomas freedom is not defined by our independence from divine action; rather, our actions are free when God wills them to be such. See 1–2.55 note 28.

24. Thomas here rejects his own early position (see note 16, above), which understood *facere quod in se est* as suggesting an action that is in some sense independent of God's grace. One might well wonder why Thomas seeks to save this phrase at all, since its plain meaning seems quite at odds with his developed position.

25. No infinite regress is involved if we understand the turning of the will to be a matter of actual grace and not habitual grace (see note 19, above).

Question 110:

The Grace of God as Regards Its Essence

1–2.110.1[1]
Does grace posit something in the soul?

It would seem that grace does not posit anything in the soul.[2]

1. One is said to have God's grace in the same way one is said to have another person's grace. Thus it is said in Genesis (39:21) that the Lord gave Joseph "favor [*gratiam*] in the sight of the head of the prison." Now when we say that one person has the grace of another person, nothing is posited in the one who has the favor of the other. Rather, a kind of acceptance is implied in the person whose favor one has. Therefore, when it is said that a person has the grace of God, nothing is implied in the soul; rather, divine acceptance alone is being signified.[3]

1. On this article, see Kobusch (2002); Wawrykow (2005); McCosker (2016).

2. As discussed earlier (see 1–2.109 notes 18 and 19), Thomas distinguishes between "actual grace" (the action of God upon the person receiving grace) and "habitual grace" (a *habitus* or stable disposition created in the soul of the person receiving grace by which that person is able to love God above all other things). This article seeks to justify this distinction. The issue of whether grace necessarily creates a stable disposition within the recipient or whether grace is better thought of simply as the action of God upon a person is relevant both to debates prior to Thomas and those that would come after him. Theologians earlier in the thirteenth century, and Thomas himself in his early commentary on Peter Lombard's *Sentences*, tended to emphasize grace as a disposition created in the soul of the recipient. As his views developed, however, Thomas came to emphasize more the notion of grace as the action of God, though never denying grace as a *habitus*. During the sixteenth century, many of the Protestant Reformers, influenced in part by certain late-medieval scholastic speculations, were highly suspicion of the idea of habitual grace, preferring an understanding of grace as "forensic"—i.e., God's act of declaring sinful human beings to be righteous. In their view, theologians like Thomas who accepted the idea of habitual grace turned God's favor into a human possession.

3. The Latin word *gratia* can mean either "grace" or "favor," an ambiguity reflected in English when we speak of being in someone's "good graces," meaning that they are favorably disposed to us. The argument here turns on that dual meaning of *gratia*, pointing out that when someone is favorably disposed to me, it implies something in them (i.e., their favorable disposition) and not anything in me. Likewise, grace, as God's favorable disposition toward us, implies something in God, not something in us.

2. As the soul gives life to the body, so too God gives life to the soul. Thus it is said in Deuteronomy (30:20): "He himself is your life." But the soul enlivens the body immediately. And therefore nothing lies as an intermediary between God and the soul. Grace, therefore, does not posit any created thing in the soul.[4]

3. Commenting on Romans (1:7), "Grace to you and peace," the gloss says: "Grace—that is, the forgiveness of sins." But the forgiveness of sins does not posit anything in the soul, but only in God, who does not impute the sin; according to the psalm (32:2): "Blessed is the man to whom the Lord has not imputed sin." Therefore, neither does grace posit anything in the soul.[5]

On the contrary: Light posits something in what is illuminated.[6] But grace is a kind of light of the soul; thus Augustine says in the book *On Nature and Grace* (22): "The light of truth rightly deserts the transgressor of the law, who thus deserted becomes blind." Therefore grace posits something in the soul.

I answer: According to the common way of speaking, grace is usually taken in three ways. In one way, for anyone's love, in the way we are accustomed to say that a soldier is in the good graces [*habet gratiam*] of the king—that is, the king looks on him with favor. Second, it is taken for any gift freely given [*dono gratis dato*], as when we customarily say, "I do you this favor" [*hanc gratiam facio tibi*]. In a third way, it is taken for gratitude returned for a gift given freely [*pro recompensatione beneficii gratis dati*], according to which we are said to give thanks [*agere gratias*] for benefits.[7] Of these three, the second depends on the first, for it is from the love by which one has favor toward another that one bestows something on that other. And the third comes from the second, for acts of gratitude arise from benefits freely bestowed [*ex beneficiis gratis exhibitis gratiarum actio consurgit*].[8]

---

4. The objection sets up this analogy: as the soul gives life to the body, so God's grace gives life to the soul. Since the soul gives life to the body in the way that a form actualizes matter, without any kind of intervening factor, even more is it the case that God's grace gives life to the soul directly, without any intervening factor (such as a created disposition) within the soul.

5. Not unlike the first objection, this objection anticipates some of the arguments of the Protestant Reformers (who would come some 250 years later). The forgiveness of sins is a matter of God not "imputing" them to us—i.e., not holding us responsible. This does not require anything of us, but only of God. Thus there is no need to posit anything in us.

6. That is, when something is illuminated, it possesses a quality—luminosity—that it did not have before and without which it could not be said to be illuminated.

7. In English we refer to thanks given over food as "saying grace."

8. As mentioned earlier (1–2.109 note 2), "grace" is a word that is used analogically. And just as we describe both a urine sample and a diet as "healthy" based on the primary use of "healthy" as a term describing a body (see 1.13 note 24), so too we speak of grace as a disposition of the soul based on the primary use of "grace" as the favor God shows us in creating such a disposition in us. Likewise, we speak of the "grace" (i.e., thanks) that we render to God based on the disposition or habitual grace from which that thanks flows.

As regards the last two, it is clear that grace posits something in one who receives grace: first, the gift itself that is freely given, and second, the acknowledgment of this gift. But as regards the first, there is a difference to be noted between God's favor [*gratiam Dei*] and human favor [*gratiam hominis*]. For because the good of the creature comes from the divine will, any good in the creature flows from God's love as willing the good of the creature. But the human will is moved by a good already existing in things, and thus human love does not cause the entire good of the thing, but presupposes it, whether in part or totally.[9] Therefore it is clear that any love on God's part is followed by some good caused at some time in the creature, though not coeternal with [God's] eternal love.[10]

And the love of God toward creatures is considered differently on account of such differences of goodness. For one [sort of love] is general, by which God "loves all things that are," as it says in the book of Wisdom (11:24), and in accord with which natural existence [*esse*] is lavished on created things. But the other is a special love, by which he draws the rational creature above the condition of its nature to a sharing in the divine good. According to this love God is said to love someone in an absolute sense, for according to this love God wills absolutely the eternal good of the creature, which is God himself. If, therefore, one is said to have the grace of God in this sense, there is signified something supernatural in that person that comes from God.[11]

9. Here Thomas notes an absolutely crucial distinction between God and creatures. We love something or someone because we are drawn to a goodness that exists in them: I love beer because of its malty goodness; I love my friend because of the goodness of his character. We might say that I love something or someone in reaction to the action of its goodness upon us. But because God is *actus purus*, fully actualized, God's love is nonreactive. God does not love in response to a lovable goodness already in the creature; rather, God's love creates the lovable goodness of the creature. We might note that there is a similar difference with regard to knowledge of truth: we know things as true because they exist, whereas it is because God knows things as true that they exist.

If God's love is not reactive to a good existing in a thing but actively creates that goodness, then God's grace must be not only God's favor toward us but also that which creates in us a disposition by which we become favorable.

10. Though God's eternal love is creative of the good in us, that good is not on this account itself eternal. Rather, God wills eternally that a particular being will possess some lovable goodness at some determinate point in time, just as God wills eternally that some particular creature will begin to exist at a determinate point in time.

11. Thomas is distinguishing here between the general providence God shows in providing for creatures—the way in which God creates their natural goodness—and the special favor that we call "grace"—the way in which God creates in us a supernatural goodness. The principle that grace perfects nature (see 1.1 note 34) suggests that grace is not an additional layer placed upon a purely natural foundation, but rather involves a kind of renovation of nature. At the same time, Thomas's reference here to "grace" signifying "something supernatural" in us suggests that the perfection of nature by grace is not the realization of any natural potential in us, the way that the child is potentially an adult and will become an adult if no obstacle comes in the way. The child's capacity to become an adult is something

But sometimes "the grace of God" is said in reference to God's eternal love, as when we speak of the grace of predestination, inasmuch as God freely [*gratuito*], and not on the basis of merits, predestines or chooses some. As it says in Ephesians (1:5–6), "He has predestined us for adoption as children, to the praise of the glory of his grace."[12]

Reply to 1: Even when someone is said to have the favor of a human person, there is understood to be in that one something that is favored by the person—just as in the case of someone who is said to have God's favor. But there is this difference: what is favored by a human being in another human being is presupposed by the former's love, but whatever is favored by God in a human being is caused by divine love, as was said.

Reply to 2: God is the life of the soul as an efficient cause, but the soul is the life of the body as a formal cause. No intermediary lies between form and matter, because the form itself gives form to [*informat*] the matter or subject. But the agent gives form to the subject not by its substance but by the form that it causes to be in the matter.[13]

Reply to 3: Augustine says in his *Retractions* (1.25): "When I said grace to be the forgiveness of sins, but peace is in reconciliation with God, this should not be taken to mean that peace and reconciliation do not pertain to general grace, but that the special name 'grace' signifies the forgiveness of sins."

---

natural in it, a result of God's general providential care for creation. But our capacity for eternal life with God is not a result of that general providence, but a specific act of God lifting us, as it were, above nature.

12. In the last part of this paragraph Thomas returns to the distinction between grace as God's favor and grace as a disposition. Thus "the grace of God" might refer to the supernatural disposition in those whom God chooses, or it might refer to God's act of choosing.

This section also raises the issue of predestination. The term "predestination" is somewhat misleading, since Aquinas's understanding of God's eternity involves no "before" or "after" (see 1.10.1), so predestination cannot mean a decision God reached at some earlier point in time. The "pre" in predestination refers not to time, but to the priority of God's eternal willing of salvation. Like Paul and Augustine, Thomas holds that God's providence involves God's eternal "election" or choosing of those who would be saved. For Thomas, this choice in no way circumvents human freedom, any more than the action of a primary cause circumvents the activity of a secondary cause (see 1.2 note 61). At the same time, this choice is not caused by any goodness existing in the creature; rather, it is the choice that causes the creature's goodness (see note 9, above). In the end, any reason for the choice of some individuals and not others is hidden within the mystery of God's will. See 1.23 for Thomas's discussion of this.

13. God is the efficient cause of grace in the soul, not the formal cause, and an efficient cause works through the medium of a form. For example, while the form "table" directly shapes the matter of which the table is composed, the carpenter who makes the table does so by giving the matter the form of a table, not by imparting his own form to the matter. If God were the formal cause of grace in the soul, then the soul in a state of grace would become God, just as matter that receives the form of a table becomes a table. Thomas is willing to speak of the soul in glory becoming "deiform" through the vision of God (see 1–2.3 note 10), but he does not see grace working in this way.

Therefore, not only forgiveness of sins pertains to grace, but many other of God's gifts.[14] And therefore forgiveness of sins does not take place without some effect divinely caused in us, as will become clear later.[15]

14. Thomas thinks of the work of grace not simply as removing sin but also as advancing us in goodness, a goodness that exceeds our natural endowments. This is why even apart from sin humans would have needed the help of grace to attain eternal life with God. As Thomas develops his account of human salvation through Christ, he will consistently speak of the work of Christ not only in terms of forgiveness of sin but also in terms of growth in love (see 3.1 note 20).

15. Thomas discusses this in 1–2.113.2.

The Second Half of

THE SECOND PART

PROLOGUE TO THE
Second Half of the Second Part

After a general consideration of virtues and vices and other things pertaining to moral matters, it is necessary to consider each one specifically. For talking about morals in a general way is less useful, given that actions concern particular things.[1] Now things concerning morals can be considered specifically in two ways: in one way on the part of moral matters themselves, as when one considers this virtue or that vice, and in another way as regards people's specific states of life [*speciales status hominum*], as when one considers subjects and prelates, the active and the contemplative, or whatever different states belong to people.[2] Therefore, we will first give specific consideration to what pertains to all the human states of life,[3] and second, we will consider specifically what is relevant to particular states of life.[4]

However, as regards the first topic, if we were to treat virtues, gifts,[5] vices, and commandments separately, we would have to say the same thing many times. For instance, if you wanted to adequately treat the commandment "You shall not commit adultery," you would have to inquire into adultery, which is a particular sin, knowledge of which depends upon knowledge of the opposite virtue. Therefore, our path of explorations will be shorter and less

---

1. Thomas here reminds us, lest we forget, that the *Summa* is intended to be, at least in part, a work of "practical theology." In particular, it is to help in training Dominican friars to hear confessions. As such, it needs to address not only general moral principles but also specific virtues and vices and the acts that flow from them.

2. There are two sets of specifics we might consider in considering the morality of the act. First are the particular acts themselves. Second are the particular contexts in which those acts take place. The latter is what Thomas means by "states of life," which we might think of as one's "public identity." For example, what might be a virtuous act for someone in authority might be a vicious act for someone not in authority; likewise, a lifestyle that might befit a contemplative might be highly unfitting for someone with public responsibilities.

3. Questions 1–179.

4. Questions 180–89.

5. That is, the sevenfold gifts of the Holy Spirit. See 1–2.68.1, above.

cumbersome if in the same treatment we examine a virtue, its corresponding gift, its opposite vices, and the relevant affirmative and negative commandments.[6] This way of examining the matter will be most appropriate for the vices themselves in terms of their proper species, for it was shown above (1–2.72) that vices and sins are divided into different kinds [*diversificantur specie*] by their matter or object and not by other differentiations among sins, such as those of thought or word, or deed,[7] or those that are on account of weakness or ignorance or malice, or other things of this sort. In contrast, it is the same matter upon which both a virtue acts rightly and the vice opposed to that virtue departs from rightness.

Hence, just as all moral matters are traced back to an examination of the virtues, so all the virtues are further traced back to seven, of which three are the theological, which we will deal with first,[8] and the other four are the cardinal, which we will deal with afterward.[9] Of the intellectual virtues, one is prudence, which is included and numbered among the cardinal virtues. Skill [*ars*], to be sure, which has to do with things that can be made, does not pertain to morals, as was said above.[10] The other three intellectual virtues— that is, wisdom, understanding, and knowledge—share names with certain gifts of the Holy Spirit; therefore, they will be treated within the examination of the gifts that correspond to the virtues. The other moral virtues are all in some way traced back to the cardinal virtues, as is clear from what was said above.[11] Therefore, in examining each cardinal virtue, all the virtues and the corresponding vices that are in any way relevant to it will be examined. And thus nothing about morals will be overlooked.

6. Thomas here describes how he uses the three theological virtues and the four cardinal virtues as general headings under which he groups not only discussions of those virtues but also the vices that are their opposites, as well as the gifts of the Spirit and the beatitudes that tradition has associated with each of those virtues. In this way, Thomas attempts to bring order to what he sees as the disorder of his predecessors' discussions of moral matters, giving primacy to the virtues as providing the architectonic structure for his own discussion.

7. Literally, "of heart, of mouth, and of deed" (*cordis, oris, et operis*).

8. Questions 1–46.

9. Questions 47–179.

10. 1–2.57.3–4. In Aristotelian terms, "craft" or "skill" has to do with *poiēsis*, or production, while morality has to do with *praxis*, or action. We judge someone a good craftsperson based on what he or she produces, regardless of *how* they produce it, whereas we judge someone a moral person not on the basis of what their action produces, but based on how they act. We might say that in skill the goodness lies in the thing produced by the action, while in moral virtue the goodness lies in the one doing the action.

11. 1–2.61.3. On the question of the relationship of other virtues to the cardinal virtues, see 1–2.61 note 10.

Question 2:

The Act of Faith

2–2.2.3[1]

Is it necessary for salvation to believe anything above natural reason?

It would seem unnecessary for salvation to believe anything above natural reason.[2]

1. What befits a thing according to its nature seems to be sufficient for its well-being and perfection. But matters of faith surpass natural human reason, since they are things unseen, as was said earlier (2–2.1.4). Therefore believing seems unnecessary for salvation.[3]

2. It is dangerous for a person to assent to matters when one cannot judge whether what is proposed is true or false; according to Job (12:11), "Does not the ear discern words?" But we cannot make this kind of judgment in matters of faith, since we cannot trace them back to first principles, by which we make all our judgments. Hence it is dangerous to bring faith into such matters.[4] Therefore believing is not necessary for salvation.

---

1. On this article, see Brown (2002); McCabe (2007, 1–16); Niederbacher (2012).

2. The first virtue Thomas discusses is the virtue of faith. Hebrews 11:1, in the Vulgate translation Thomas used, defines faith as "*sperandarum substantia rerum, argumentum non apparentium*" (the substance of things to be hoped for, the evidence of things that appear not). Drawing on this canonical definition but recasting it in an Aristotelian way, Thomas says that faith is "a disposition of the mind [*habitus mentis*] by which eternal life is begun in us, making the intellect assent to what is not apparent" (2–2.4.1; cf. *Commentary on Hebrews* 11.1.558).

We should note that in this definition Thomas spells out that faith (1) is a virtue by which (2) the vision of God that is eternal life is present inchoately (3) by an intellectual act (4) that is distinguished by having as its object something that is not apparent to the intellect. Another way in which he attempts to locate faith as a human act is to situate it between *scientia* and "opinion" (see 1.12 note 14).

3. The objection's first premise, borrowed from Aristotle, is that the goal of a thing (that which fulfills its nature) must be within the grasp of its nature. The second premise is twofold: (1) faith, as Thomas has maintained, concerns things that are "unseen" and, (2) as Aristotle teaches, the natural object of the human intellect is a material substance apprehended through the senses. Therefore, since it is contrary to human nature, faith cannot be required for the perfection of that nature.

4. In matters of faith, we "borrow" our first principles from God's own self-knowledge (see 1.1 note 21). The objection seems to be saying that this is a shaky basis for knowledge.

3. Humanity's salvation rests on God, according to the psalm (37:39), "But the salvation of the just is from the Lord." According to Romans (1:20), "The invisible things of God . . . are clearly seen, being understood by the things that are made, even his eternal power and divinity." Those things that are clearly seen by the understanding, however, are not an object of belief. It is therefore not necessary for salvation that one should believe certain things.[5]

On the contrary: It is written in Hebrews (11:6), "Without faith it is impossible to please God."

I answer: Wherever natures have a relationship with regard to one another, we find that two things come together for perfection of a lower nature: one that is in accord with that nature's own movement, while the other is in accord with the movement of a higher nature. Thus water, in accord with its own motion, moves toward the center [of the earth], while, in accord with the movement of the moon, it moves around the center according to its ebb and flow.[6] Similarly, the planets have their own motion from west to east, while in accord with the movement of the first heaven they have a movement from east to west.[7]

Now only the created rational nature has an unmediated orientation toward God. This is because other creatures do not attain to something universal, but only to something particular, sharing in the divine goodness either only by existing (as in the case of inanimate things) or also by living and knowing individual things (as in the case of plants and animals).[8] However, a rational nature, inasmuch as it knows the universal meaning of "good" and "being," is immediately related to the universal principle of existence.[9]

Consequently, the perfection of a rational creature consists not only in what belongs to it according to its nature but also in what is attributed to it on account of a supernatural sharing in divine goodness.[10] Therefore it was

5. Not unlike in the second objection in the opening article of the *Summa*, here it is argued that nature, investigated by philosophy, gives us a clear knowledge of God sufficient for salvation.

6. On the inbuilt direction of material objects, see 1–2.6 note 7. Despite the obsolete physics of his example, Thomas's point remains fairly clear: when one thing is under the sway of another, you must take two things into account in order to understand its movement: both the natural inclination of the thing and the influence of that which is acting upon it. Thus even after Newton, it remains the case that the weight of water explains why the ocean stays on the earth, but one cannot explain the tides without taking the moon into account.

7. The cosmology of this example is even less useful than the previous one.

8. Inanimate things have being. In addition to being, plants have life (or a "vegetative soul") and animals have knowledge of particular things (or a "sensual soul").

9. Only creatures with intellect (humans and angels) have an immediate relation to God, because their intellect allows them to apprehend or "grasp" abstractions ("good-in-general," "existence-in-general") and thus to grasp God as the universal cause of existence.

10. Humans are under the sway of God somewhat as the ocean is under the sway of the moon. The moon gives the ocean an ability (and thus a purpose) that it otherwise would not have. Hence in talking about human purpose, we must take into account not simply what human beings can do but also what God can do.

said above (1–2.3.8) that ultimate human happiness consists in a supernatural vision of God. A human being cannot attain this vision unless taught by God, according to John (6:45): "Every one that has heard from the Father and has learned comes to me." However, a person does not acquire a share of this learning instantly, but little by little, according to the ways of human nature.[11] And everyone who learns in this way needs to believe in order to come to perfect knowledge [*scientia*]. In this way, the Philosopher as well remarks that "a learner ought to believe" (*On Sophistical Refutations* 2, 165[b]).

Therefore in order to come to a perfect vision of heavenly happiness, one must first of all believe God, as a disciple believes the master who is teaching him.[12]

Reply to 1: Since human nature is dependent on a higher nature, natural knowledge does not suffice for its perfection, and some supernatural knowledge is necessary, as stated above.[13]

Reply to 2: Just as a person assents to first principles by the natural light of the intellect, so too a virtuous person has, by the stable disposition of a virtue, right judgment concerning things that are befitting that virtue. In this same way, a person assents to the things of faith and rejects what is contrary to faith, by the light of faith that God bestows. Therefore, there is no danger or "condemnation to those who are in Christ Jesus" (Rom. 8:1) and whom he has enlightened by faith.[14]

---

11. In this, humans differ from angels, who attain supernatural knowledge instantly (see 1.50 note 7) and so have no need for faith.

12. Because it is through our intellects that we are directly under God's sway, Thomas uses the analogy of a teacher to explore how God's influence over us is exercised. He makes the point that at the outset of the student–teacher relationship the teacher sees more of the educational goal than does the student, and therefore the student must take much on trust. In 1–2.2.2, Thomas distinguishes this sort of trust in God from a mere belief in things about God by using a distinction borrowed from St. Augustine (found in, e.g., *Sermon 29, 6*, in *Homilies on the Gospel of John*). One might "believe in God" (*credere Deum*) in the sense of believing that God exists or that certain things are true about God. Or one might "believe God" (*credere Deo*) in the sense of trusting in God. The distinction is fairly obvious: it is the distinction between believing, for example, that the president of the United States exists and believing that what the president of the United States tells you is true. One can certainly do the former without the latter. Augustine and Thomas also distinguish a third form of belief—*credere in Deum*—that we might (awkwardly) translate as "believing toward God," which is to say that we make God the end or goal of our faith, and consequently the object of our love.

In his *Commentary on the Gospel of John* (6.3.901), Thomas notes that according to the first two understandings of "belief" we can believe in a creature: I can believe that the president exists, and I can trust in what he says. But in the third sense, only God can properly be the object of my belief, because it is only by being united to God through love that I find the perfect happiness that Thomas calls *beatitudo*. Thus, Thomas says, "To believe in God as our goal belongs to faith that is given shape by charity [*credere in Deum ut in finem, est proprium fidei formatae per caritatem*]."

13. That is, in the body of the article.

14. In his response, Thomas draws an analogy between faith and moral virtue, inasmuch as each is a *habitus* (on what Thomas means by a *habitus*, see 1–2.55 note 2). The analogy makes the point that just

Reply to 3: In many respects, faith perceives the invisible things of God in a higher way than natural reason does, in proceeding from creatures to God.[15] Therefore it is written in Sirach (3:23), "Many things are shown to you above human understandings."

2–2.2.7[16]
Is it necessary for salvation to believe explicitly in the mystery of Christ?

It would seem that it is not necessary for the salvation of all that they should believe explicitly in the mystery of Christ.

1. A human being is not bound to believe explicitly in something the angels are ignorant of, since the unfolding of faith is through divine revelation, which reaches human beings by means of the angels,[17] as stated earlier (2–2.2.6; 1.111.1). But even the angels were ignorant of the mystery of the incarnation, and thus they ask in the psalm (24:8), "Who is this king of glory?" and in Isaiah (63:1), "Who is this that comes from Edom?" as Dionysius explains in *The Celestial Hierarchy* (7.3). Therefore human beings were not required to believe explicitly in the mystery of Christ's incarnation.

2. Everyone agrees that blessed John the Baptist was one of the great ones [*maioribus*], and nearest to Christ,[18] who said of him in Matthew (11:11) that "among those who are born of women, there has not arisen one greater." But John the Baptist does not appear to have known the mystery of Christ explicitly, since he asked Christ, "Are you he that is to come, or should we look for another?" as it is put in Matthew (11:3). Therefore even the greatest were not required to have explicit faith in Christ.

3. Many gentiles obtained salvation through the ministry of the angels, as Dionysius states in *The Celestial Hierarchy* (9.3). It would seem, however, that

---

because something is not given with human nature, it is not for this reason "unreliable." Indeed, virtues, far from being unreliable, give our natures the stability needed for us to act well in a consistent way. So too, faith is not unreliable, but rather necessary for us to know the truth about God.

15. Although there can be a "natural" knowledge of God, this knowledge is both quantitatively and qualitatively different from the knowledge that comes through faith. Quantitatively, there are some things that can be known through faith (e.g., the doctrine of the Trinity) that cannot be known through reason. Qualitatively, the things we know about God through natural reason are known *better* through supernatural faith.

16. On this article, see Marenbon (2015, 160–87).

17. On angels as agents of revelation, see 1.50 note 11.

18. The term *maiores*, as well as the distinction in the body of the article between *maiores* and *minores*, carries the implication of wisdom and learning, perhaps as we might use the term "elder" to speak of the leaders in certain cultures. The term *minores*, which I translate as "lowly," carries the implication of intellectual unsophistication, though it also has the implication of low social status. This distinction and its terminology are drawn from Peter Lombard, *Sentences* bk. 3, dist. 25, ch. 2, and are found in many thirteenth-century theologians.

the gentiles had neither explicit nor implicit faith in Christ, since no revelation was made to them. It seems, therefore, that believing explicitly in the mystery of Christ was not necessary for everyone for salvation.[19]

On the contrary: Augustine says in *On Rebuke and Grace*, "Our faith is sound if we believe that no one, whether old or young, is delivered from the contagion of death and the bonds of sin except by the one mediator of God and human beings, Jesus Christ."[20]

I answer: As stated earlier (2–2.2.5; 2–2.1.8), that through which human beings obtain perfect happiness belongs, strictly speaking and in itself, to the object of faith.[21] But the mystery of Christ's incarnation and passion is the way by which people come to perfect happiness, for it is written in Acts (4:12) that "there is no other name given to human beings by which we must be saved." Therefore belief of some kind in the mystery of Christ's incarnation was necessary at all times and for all persons, but this belief differed according to differences of times and persons.[22]

Prior to the state of sin the [first] man believed explicitly in Christ's incarnation insofar as it was intended for the consummation of glory, but not insofar as it intended to free us from sin by the passion and resurrection, since the man had no foreknowledge of his future sin. Apparently he did, however, have foreknowledge of the incarnation of Christ, from the fact that he said in Genesis (2:24), "For this reason a man shall leave father and mother and shall cleave to his wife." Of this passage, the Apostle says in Ephesians (5:32) that this "is a great sacrament . . . in Christ and the church," and it is not believable that the first man was ignorant about this sacrament.[23]

19. Dionysius speaks of the "gentiles"—i.e., pagan non-Jews—being saved through the ministry of angels, but not through revelation.

20. Though the view expressed can be found in ch. 7 of Augustine's *Admonition and Grace*, the actual quotation comes, more or less, from Augustine's letter to the bishop Optatus (*Epistle 190*, 2.5).

21. Put differently, *what* we believe in when we have faith (i.e., the object of our faith) is that thing by which we gain eternal happiness (*beatitudo*).

22. The reference to belief of "some kind" means either explicit belief or implicit belief. Thomas says (2–2.1.7) that "all the articles of faith are contained implicitly in certain primary matters of faith, such as God's existence and his providence over the salvation of humanity." So the explicit belief that God provides for the salvation of human beings contains the implicit belief in salvation through Christ—provided, of course, that one does not explicitly reject salvation through Christ. In 2–2.2.5 Thomas says that to believe certain things implicitly is "to be ready to believe them."

With regard to "times," Thomas proposes a threefold division: before sin, after sin, and after grace (i.e., the incarnation). One might compare this with the historical scheme Thomas uses in his remarks on the human need for grace in 1–2.109.2. With regard to "persons," Thomas distinguishes between what the learned [*maiores*] should know and what the uneducated [*minores*] should know. On the whole, much more explicit belief is expected of the learned.

23. Thomas seems to be saying that Adam (and Eve) understood their union to be a sacrament—that is, a sacred sign (see 3.61 note 9)—and therefore must have known the reality toward which, according

After sin, however, the mystery of Christ was believed in explicitly, not only with regard to the incarnation but also as to the passion and resurrection, by which the human race is freed from sin and death. Otherwise they would not have foreshadowed Christ's passion by certain sacrifices both before and under the Law.[24] The meaning of these sacrifices was known explicitly by the great ones [*maiores*], while the lowly [*minores*], under the veil of those sacrifices, believed them to be intended by God in reference to Christ's coming, and thus their knowledge was in a way "veiled."[25] And, as stated earlier (2–2.1.7), the nearer they were to Christ, the more distinct was their knowledge of Christ's mysteries.

Since grace has been revealed, however, both the great ones and the lowly are required to have explicit faith in the mysteries of Christ, particularly those that the whole church celebrates and publicly proclaims, such as the articles that refer to the incarnation, of which we have spoken earlier (2–2.1.8). But regarding other subtle considerations referring to the articles about the incarnation, people are bound to believe them more and less explicitly, according to what is fitting to one's status and role.[26]

Reply to 1: The mystery of the kingdom of God was not entirely hidden from the angels, as Augustine observes in the *On the Literal Meaning of Genesis* (5.19), yet certain aspects of it were more fully known to them when Christ revealed these things.

Reply to 2: It was not out of ignorance that John the Baptist inquired about Christ's coming in the flesh, since he had clearly professed his belief in [the incarnation], saying in John (1:34), "I saw, and I gave testimony, that this is the Son of God." Therefore he did not say, "Are you he that has come?" but "Are you he that is to come?" asking about the future, not about the past. Likewise, one should not believe that he was ignorant of Christ's future suffering, both because he had already said, "Behold the Lamb of God, who takes away the sins of the world" (John 1:29), foretelling Christ's future sacrificial

---

to Paul, it pointed: the union of Christ and the church (see Eph. 5:32). This indicates a knowledge of the incarnation as advancing us in goodness, though not as forgiving sins.

24. That is, both prior to and following the giving of God's Law to Moses on Mt. Sinai.

25. The animal sacrifices of the Old Testament are a typological foreshadowing of the death of Jesus on the cross (on the notion of "typology," see 1.1 note 39). According to Thomas, the *maiores*—such as the prophets—had explicit knowledge that these sacrifices pointed toward the death and resurrection of Christ as the source of our salvation, whereas the *minores* held this belief as an implication of their explicit belief that the sacrifices were provided by God as a means of forgiving sins.

26. Who you are and what your position is in the church determine how explicitly you must believe the finer points of doctrine. It is no great matter if a butcher cannot tell you whether the union of humanity and divinity in Christ takes place in his person, but it does matter if a teacher of theology cannot tell you.

offering, and because other prophets had foretold it, as may be seen especially in Isaiah 53. We may therefore say with Gregory (*Sermon 26*, in *Homilies on the Gospels*) that he asked this question because he did not know whether Christ would descend into hell in his own person. He knew that the power of Christ's passion would be extended to those who were detained in limbo—according to Zechariah (9:11), "You also, by the blood of your testament, have sent forth . . . prisoners out of the pit, in which there is no water"—but he was not bound to believe explicitly, before its fulfillment, that Christ was to descend there himself.[27]

It may also be said, as Ambrose observes in his commentary on Luke (7:19), that he did not make this inquiry from doubt or ignorance, but from devotion. Or one can say, with Chrysostom (*Sermon 36*, in *Homilies on Matthew*), that he did not inquire as though he himself were ignorant, but so that his disciples would be satisfied on that point by Christ. Therefore Christ directed his answer to the disciples, pointing to the signs of his works.[28]

Reply to 3: Many gentiles received revelations of Christ, as is clear from their predictions. Thus we read in Job (19:25), "I know that my Redeemer lives."[29] The Sibyl, too, foretold certain things about Christ, as Augustine states in *Against Faustus the Manichaean* (13.15).[30] Moreover, we read in the history of the Romans that[31] at the time of Constantine Augustus and his mother Irene, a tomb was discovered in which a man lay on whose breast was a golden plate with the inscription, "Christ shall be born of a virgin, and in him, I believe. O sun, during the lifetime of Irene and Constantine, you shall see me again."[32]

If, however, some were saved without receiving any revelation, they were not saved without faith in a mediator. Though they did not have faith explicitly,

---

27. On Christ's descent into limbo, see 3.65 note 21.

28. As he does in a number of places, Thomas considers many possible literal meanings of a difficult text without feeling compelled to settle on one. In this case the difficult text is a story from Matthew's Gospel: John the Baptist, who is in prison, sends a messenger to Jesus to inquire about whether he is the expected Messiah. The difficulty arises because other texts, particularly in the Gospel of John, indicate that John knows who Jesus is. Thus in John 1:29–30 we read that John the Baptist sees Jesus and says, "Here is the Lamb of God who takes away the sin of the world! This is he of whom I said, 'After me comes a man who ranks ahead of me because he was before me.'" Thomas presents several attempts by previous writers to deal with this difficulty without giving *the* definitive solution.

29. Though Job appears in the Old Testament, he is nowhere identified as an Israelite, and he often features in medieval discussion of the possibility of salvation for people outside the Old Covenant.

30. Sibyls were prophetesses in pagan Greek literature.

31. This story is found in the *Chronographia* of the ninth-century Byzantine historian Theophanes the Confessor.

32. To this point in his reply, Thomas is presuming that various pre-Christian pagans *did*, in fact, receive revelation, so as to believe *explicitly* in Christ. Though not part of the public record of revealed truth, these one-off divine interventions made salvation possible for certain individuals.

they nevertheless had implicit faith in divine providence, believing God to be the liberator of humanity in whatever way was pleasing to him and in accordance with what he himself revealed to those who knew the truth, as stated in Job 35:11: "[God] teaches us more than the beasts of the earth."[33]

2–2.2.10[34]
Does reason influencing us in matters of faith lessen faith's merit?

It would seem that reason influencing us in matters of faith lessens faith's merit.[35]

1. Gregory says (*Sermon 26*, in *Homilies on the Gospels*) that "there is no merit in believing what is shown by reason." If human reason, in providing sufficient proof, totally excludes the merit of faith, then it would seem that any kind of human reasoning influencing us in matters of faith diminishes the merit of believing.[36]

2. Whatever diminishes the amount of virtue diminishes the amount of merit, since "happiness is the reward of virtue," as the Philosopher states in the *Ethics* (1.9, 1099b). But human reasoning seems to diminish the amount of the virtue of faith, since it is essential to faith to be about the unseen, as stated earlier (2–2.1.4, 5).[37] But the more a thing is prompted by reasons, the less is it unseen. Therefore human reasoning influencing us in matters of faith diminishes the merit of faith.

3. Contrary things have contrary causes. But an incentive contrary to faith increases the merit of faith, whether it be persecution pushing one to renounce

---

33. Thomas says that one cannot be saved without belief in Christ, but this may be an implicit belief rooted in the explicit belief that God in his goodness would provide the means for human salvation. So Thomas's ultimate answer to this question suggests that the need for explicit faith is not absolute, that particular circumstances are taken into account. In some circumstances—where God's revelation has not been given (i.e., pagan contexts) or where it has been given under a "veil" that cannot be penetrated by the unlearned (e.g., by the simple folk of the Old Testament)—implicit faith suffices. However, now that grace has appeared in Christ, all who have access to the truth of the incarnation are bound to believe it explicitly, whether they are learned or unlearned.

34. On this article, see Marshall (2005); McCabe (2007, 1–16).

35. For Thomas, something's "merit" is the degree to which it is deserving of reward (see 1–2.109 note 8). As mentioned earlier (note 2, above), in the act of faith the intellect is moved by the will to assent to what God reveals. Because it is an act of the will moved by grace, faith's assent is meritorious, since we merit a reward when we willingly do a good action (such as believing God). Reason, however, is not meritorious, since the intellect cannot help but assent to a truth that it sees, so no act of will is involved. The question at hand is whether, by mixing reason into our life of faith, we dilute or diminish the merit we would derive from believing.

36. If a complete proof eliminates faith's merit, then reasoning that falls short of proof would at least lessen faith's merit.

37. On knowledge, faith, and seeing, see 1.1 note 17.

the faith, or an argument persuading one to do so. Therefore reason aiding faith diminishes the merit of faith.[38]

On the contrary: It is written in 1 Peter (3:15), "Always be prepared to satisfy everyone that asks you a reason for that faith and hope that is in you."[39] But the apostle would not urge this if the merit of faith were diminished by it.[40] Reasoning, therefore, does not diminish the merit of faith.

I answer: As stated earlier (2–2.2.9 ad 2), the act of faith can be meritorious to the extent that it is subject to the will, not only regarding use but also regarding assent.[41]

Human reasoning that influences us in matters of faith can be related to the will of the believer in two ways. In one way as *prior*—for example, when one would not have the will to believe, or to believe promptly, unless moved by human reasoning. Here the influence of human reasoning diminishes the merit of faith, in the same way that, as was said earlier regarding moral virtues, an emotion [*passio*] that precedes choice makes the virtuous act less praiseworthy.[42] For just as a person should perform acts of moral virtue on account of the judgment of reason and not on account of emotion, so a person should believe matters of faith on account of the divine authority and not on account of human reason.[43]

In a second way, human reason can be *consequent* to the will of the believer. When a person has a will that believes promptly, one loves the truth believed and ponders it, embracing whatever reasons one can find for it.[44] In this sense, human reasoning does not exclude the merit of faith but is a sign of greater

---

38. The objection draws an analogy between the persecution of a martyr and the "intellectual persecution" one undergoes when an unbeliever tries to argue you out of your faith. Drawing out the analogy, we might say that using reason in the latter case would be like the martyr taking a sword into the arena to fight off the lions.

39. The Vulgate reads simply, "of that hope that is in you." Thomas typically quoted Scripture from memory, and not always precisely.

40. Normally "the Apostle" refers to Paul, but here it refers to Peter.

41. See note 35, above. The act of faith merits not only through the uses to which it is put but in the very act of assent itself.

42. For example, a teenager who simply *likes* Disney movies is less deserving of reward for having seen *Snow White* twenty-five times with his little sister than he would have been had he performed this feat because reason told him it was a good thing to do in order to attain the goal of loving his little sister as a creature of God. For the various meanings of *passio*, see 3.46 note 7.

43. Many of us would hold that it is better to believe something because we have thought it out for ourselves than to believe it on the authority of someone else. In the case of divine truths, however, Thomas thinks it is better to believe them on God's authority than it is to believe them on the authority of our own reason, both because God's reason far surpasses our reason and because such belief testifies that we love and trust in God. This sets up the following, perhaps surprising analogy—reason : divine authority : act of faith :: emotion : reason : act of moral virtue.

44. One might call this the "exploratory" use of reason: we not only use reason to demonstrate things about God but also to explore the truth about God already assented to out of love for that truth (see 3.1

merit. Again, it is like the case of moral virtues, in which a consequent emotion is the sign of a will that is more ready to act, as stated earlier (1–2.24.3).[45] This is the meaning of John (4:42), where the Samaritans say to the woman [at the well], who symbolically represents human reason, "Now we believe not on account of your words."

Reply to 1: Gregory is speaking of the case of a person who has no will to believe unless prompted by reason. But when one has the will to believe matters of faith solely on the authority of God, the merit of faith is not destroyed or diminished, even if one has demonstrative arguments for some of them (e.g., the existence of God).

Reply to 2: Reasons pointing to the authority of faith are not demonstrations that can lead the human intellect to intellectual vision, and so matters of faith do not cease to be unseen.[46] But reasons do remove obstacles to faith by showing that what faith proposes is not impossible.[47] Therefore, such reasons do not diminish the merit or the distinctive nature of faith. In the case not of the articles of faith but of the preambles to the articles, demonstrative reasons in support of them take away from the distinctive nature of faith because they make apparent that which is proposed; nevertheless such reasons do not take away from the distinctive nature of charity, which makes the will prompt to believe them even if they are unseen, and so the measure of merit is not diminished.[48]

Reply to 3: Whatever is contrary to faith, whether a person's thoughts or an external persecution, increases the merit of faith, insofar as the will is shown to be readier and more firm in believing. The martyrs, therefore, had more of faith's merit for not renouncing faith on account of persecution, and in a similar way the wise have faith's merit for not renouncing their faith on

---

note 2 on *convenientia*). This is what St. Anselm means by his famous phrase *fides quaerens intellectum* (faith seeking understanding).

45. Although we should not do virtuous things simply because we associate them with pleasant emotions, a person for whom virtuous action brings with it no joy is less virtuous than a person who enjoys being good. Likewise, a person who is prompted by faith to try to understand what he or she believes has attained a worthier faith than one who *simply* accepts things on authority.

46. In other words, such reasons are not demonstrative proofs.

47. See 1.1 note 31, regarding the ad hoc strategy of answering objections.

48. The "preambles to faith" are those things that reason can grasp about God without divine aid (see 1.2 note 25). They should not, however, be thought of as preliminary steps of pure reason that one *must* take before one can believe. One may well hold the preambles on the basis of faith rather than reason. For example, one does not need to be able to use reason to prove God's existence before one can accept the rest of the Christian faith. Indeed, *most* Christians hold to the preambles on the basis of faith rather than reason. But even if one does assent to a preamble of faith based on a rational demonstration, one deserves a reward for faith so long as one's assent to that truth would not cease in the absence of this proof.

account of the arguments against the faith brought forward by philosophers or heretics. On the other hand, things that are agreeable to faith do not always diminish the readiness of the will to believe, and therefore they do not always take away from the merit of faith.[49]

49. In the end, Thomas's view on this question seems to be that reason does not diminish the merit of faith so long as one would believe the matter even if one could not reason one's way to it. And in the case of the "exploratory" use of reason (see note 45, above), it can *increase* the merit of faith.

Question 11:

Heresy

2–2.11.3[1]
Should heretics be tolerated?

It seems that heretics should be tolerated.[2]

1. The Apostle says in 2 Timothy (2:24–26), "The servant of the Lord ought to be gentle . . . admonishing with modesty those who resist the truth, in case God would at some time give them repentance to know the truth, and they might recover themselves from the snares of the devil." Now if heretics are

---

1. On this article, see Garrigou-Lagrange (1965, 423–56); Novak (1995).

2. Though the idea of heresy is an ancient one in Christianity, and the fourth and fifth centuries saw considerable upheaval over the teachings of figures such as Arius and Nestorius, the suppression of heresy was not of prime concern in the West in the early Middle Ages, presumably because of more pressing matters, such as famine and invasion. Concern about heresy, not simply as individual erroneous opinions but as connected to large-scale movements, undergoes a revival beginning in the twelfth century—in large part because of the Cathar movement, which Thomas's own religious order, the Dominicans, was founded to combat. Indeed, after 1231 and the founding of the Roman Inquisition, Dominicans often had a prime role in investigating and rooting out heresy.

Thomas has earlier defined "heresy" as a type of unbelief [*infidelitas*] "pertaining to those who profess the Christian faith but corrupt its defined doctrines [*dogmata*]" (1–2.11.1). He holds heresy to be a worse form of unbelief than the unbelief of pagans and of Jews (the other two forms of unbelief he identifies): "Someone who resists the faith after having accepted it sins more grievously than someone who resists it without having accepted it, just as someone who fails to fulfill a promise sins more grievously than one who has promised nothing" (1–2.10.6). This distinction has significant practical consequences for Thomas. Pagans and Jews ought never to be compelled to accept the Christian faith, though they can be compelled not to hinder its proclamation and practice, while heretics *can* be compelled, since they are being held accountable for fulfilling a past promise (1–2.10.8).

It should be noted that simply holding a heretical opinion on a matter of defined faith does not in itself make one a heretic. Any number of uneducated people might hold erroneous views on any number of Christian doctrines. Even theologians (including Thomas himself, on the immaculate conception; see 3.27.2, below) have held opinions contrary to what would later become official dogma and not been deemed heretics on that account. As the term "heresy" itself implies (from the Greek *hairesis*, meaning "choice"), in order to be a heretic in the full sense, one must choose to persist in holding on to one's erroneous belief even after the error has been made clear. See 1–2.11.2 ad 3.

not tolerated, but handed over to death, the chance to repent is taken from them. This, therefore, seems contrary to the Apostle's command.

2. Whatever is necessary in the church is tolerated. But heresies are necessary in the church, since the Apostle says in 1 Corinthians (11:19), "There must be heresies so that they who are tested may be manifest among you." Therefore it seems that heretics are to be tolerated.[3]

3. In Matthew (13:30) the Lord commanded his servants to let the weeds grow until the harvest—that is, the end of the world, as is explained there. Now the saints explain that the weeds signify heretics.[4] Therefore heretics are to be tolerated.

On the contrary: The Apostle says in Titus (3:10–11): "After the first and second admonition, avoid a person who is a heretic, knowing that someone like this has been overthrown."

I answer: Concerning heretics, two points should be considered: one on the part of the heretics, the other on the part of the church.

On their part there is sin, for which they deserve not only to be separated from the church by excommunication but also to be severed from the world by death. For it is a much more serious matter to corrupt faith, which is the life of the soul, than to forge money, by which earthly life is supported.[5] Therefore if forgers of money and other evildoers are immediately handed over to death by secular rulers, much more may heretics, as soon as they are convicted of heresy, not only be excommunicated but even justly killed.[6]

3. The argument reflects Thomas's view that not only has heresy served to identify (by their resistance to heresy) those who are truly faithful, but heresy has also had a key role in the development of Christian doctrine. This can be seen in how Thomas will often describe a Christian doctrine by means of showing how it falls between opposite heretical views—as in his use of Arius and Sabellius in 1.27.1, above. For other doctrinal issues, Thomas offers similar pairings, such as Nestorius and Eutyches for the hypostatic union (see 3.2 note 2, below). In chapter 9 of his work *On the Reasons for Faith* (1264), Thomas writes, "The holy, catholic, and apostolic church proceeds carefully between contrary errors. It distinguishes the Persons in the Trinity against Sabellius, yet without falling into the error of Arius, but rather professes only one essence of the three Persons; in the mystery of the incarnation, on the other hand, it distinguishes the two natures against Eutyches, but does not separate the persons in the manner of Nestorius." In other words, pairs of heretical positions serve to indicate what is *not* meant by doctrines such as the Trinity or the hypostatic union without overdefining something that is ultimately rooted in the mystery of God.

4. Matthew's story of weeds that are sown among wheat is a locus classicus for discussions of the toleration of heretics. See, for example, John Chrysostom, *Sermon 46*, in *Homilies on Matthew*, or Augustine, *Seventeen Questions on Matthew* 11. The objection is suggesting that the obvious interpretation of this parable is that heretics should be tolerated until the final judgment.

5. In other words, if we are looking solely at the evil of heresy itself, then it surely merits not only excommunication but even death, since it involves a corruption of something of supreme value.

6. One should note the typical medieval division of labor: it is the church that judges whether or not someone is a heretic and imposes the penalty of excommunication, which cuts one off from the sacramental life of the church; it is the civil authorities that impose and carry out the death penalty for the civil crime of heresy. Thomas holds that it is always wrong for the clergy to kill anyone (see 2–2.64 note 7), and so it

But on the church's part there is mercy, which aims at the conversion of those who stray. Therefore she condemns not immediately, but after the first and second admonition, as the Apostle directs.[7] After that, if a heretic is found still to be stubborn, the church, no longer hoping for his conversion, provides for the salvation of others by separating the heretic from the church by a sentence of excommunication and, further, gives him up to the secular authorities to be banished from the world by death.[8] For Jerome is quoted in *Decretals* 24.3 saying, "Cut off putrid flesh, expel the mangy sheep from the fold, so the whole house, lump of dough, body, and flock will not burn, rot, putrefy, die. Arius was one spark in Alexandria, but because it was not immediately put out the whole earth was devastated by its flame."[9]

Reply to 1: It pertains to this modesty that a heretic should be admonished a first and second time. If he is unwilling to retract, he is to be taken to have been overthrown, as is clear from the words of the Apostle, quoted above.[10]

Reply to 2: The usefulness that comes from heresy is not intended by heretics—for, as the Apostle says, it consists in the perseverance of the faithful being tested, and it is allowed, as Augustine says (*On Genesis against the Manichees* 1.1), so "that we cast off our laziness and search the divine Scriptures more carefully." What heretics directly intend is the corruption of the faith, which inflicts very great harm. Therefore we should consider more what they directly intend and banish them, rather than what is unintended and tolerate them.[11]

---

was not the role of the church to carry out executions. But because, in Thomas's view, *religio* is a moral virtue that is a part of justice, the divisions caused by heresy undermine not only the church but society as a whole, and thus heresy is of concern to secular rulers and is fittingly punished by them.

In order for modern readers to have some sense of the perceived danger of heresy for medieval people, it is important to appreciate how interwoven religious belief and social cohesion were in most traditional societies. In the medieval Christian West, the bonds of shared Christian faith were seen as crucial for the peace and well-being of society.

7. Though heresy in itself is deserving of immediate excommunication and death, the church, being merciful, allows heretics a second, and even third, chance to repent.

8. Note that the justification for both excommunication and execution of heretics is the need to attend to the spiritual well-being of others. From Thomas's perspective, cutting off a heretic from the church, or even from life itself, is a drastic but sometimes necessary measure, not unlike cutting off a diseased arm or leg. This again runs counter to modern sensibilities, which tend to see religious views as matters of private opinion, having little or no bearing on the common good.

9. This quotation is taken from Jerome's *Commentary on Galatians*, bk. 3, on Gal. 5:9.

10. It is true, as it says in 2 Tim. 2:24–26 (cited in the objection), that a heretic should be tolerated so as to have a chance to repent, but there are limits to this toleration.

11. As is generally the case, the goodness or badness of an action depends on the intention with which it is done (see 1–2.18 note 12, above). Since heretics do not intend the good result that happens to occur because of their action (that Christian faith is strengthened), that good result in no way makes their action good.

Reply to 3: According to *Decretals* 24.3, "Excommunication is one thing and uprooting [*eradicatio*] is another." One is excommunicated, as the Apostle says, so that "his spirit may be saved in the day of the Lord" (1 Cor. 5:5). Yet if a heretic is completely uprooted by death, this is not contrary to the command of the Lord, which is to be understood as referring to the case when the weed cannot be pulled up without pulling up the wheat, as explained above (2–2.10.8 ad 1) when discussing unbelievers in general.[12]

12. Thomas packs a lot into this brief reply. He distinguishes excommunication (which is done for the good not only of the community of believers but also of the heretics themselves, in hope that it might bring them to their senses) from "eradication" or death (which is done solely for the benefit of the religious and civil community). Thomas suggests that after admonishing a heretic twice, the church should proceed with excommunication. But the heretic should not always be handed over to the civil authorities for execution. He notes that the point of the parable of the wheat and the weeds is that you should forgo pulling up the weeds in order to preserve the wheat until harvest time. But, he notes, if one *can* pull up the weeds without harming the wheat, why would one not do so? So heretics should be tolerated in civil society when acting against them would harm public order, but they need not be tolerated in other circumstances. In 1–2.10.8 ad 2 he quotes Augustine's *Contra Epistolam Parmeniani* to give an idea of the kind of circumstances under which one might chose not to tolerate a heretic: "when a man's crime is so publicly known, and so hateful to all, that he has no defenders, or none such as might cause a schism" (3.2). Of course, one might ask why a heretic who has no following whatsoever would pose any threat to the body politic.

Question 17:

Hope

2–2.17.2[1]
Is eternal happiness the proper object of hope?

It would seem that eternal happiness is not the proper object of hope.[2]

1. A person does not hope for something that exceeds every movement of the soul, since the act of hope is a kind of movement of the soul. But eternal happiness exceeds every movement of the human soul, for the Apostle says in 1 Corinthians (2:9) that it has not "entered into the human heart." Therefore perfect happiness is not the proper object of hope.[3]

2. Petitionary prayer is an expression of hope, for it is written in the psalm (37:5), "Commit your way to the Lord and trust in him, and he will do it." Now human beings legitimately ask God not only for eternal happiness but also for the goods, both temporal and spiritual,[4] of the present life, and also to be delivered from the evils that will no longer be in eternal happiness, as is clear from the Lord's Prayer. Therefore eternal happiness is not the proper object of hope.[5]

---

1. On this article, see Cessario (2002).

2. In reading this article it is helpful to bear in mind that for Thomas, something we hope for must be a future good that is difficult yet possible to obtain (see 1–2.40.1). Thus the object of hope is (1) *good*, not evil (distinguishing hope from fear); (2) *future*, not present (distinguishing hope from enjoyment); (3) *difficult*, not easy (distinguishing hope from desire); and (4) *possible*, not impossible (distinguishing hope from despair).

In asking about the "proper object" of hope, Thomas is asking what thing it is directed toward that distinguishes it from other virtues. On the way in which acts and virtues are specified by their objects, see 1–2.9 note 9; 1–2.18 note 12; and 1–2.55 note 17.

3. The first objection can be taken as pressing the final feature of the object of hope: that it must be something that is possible to attain. Even if eternal happiness is possible through God's grace, it is not possible through the soul's own movements, in which hope is included.

4. On "temporal" in this context, see 1–2.91 note 20.

5. The objection is simply pointing out that we ask for many things from God apart from eternal happiness. On the whole we see nothing wrong with saying to God things such as "I hope I get that job" or

3. The object of hope is something difficult. But in relation to human beings, many other things besides eternal happiness are difficult. Eternal happiness is therefore not the proper object of hope.

On the contrary: The Apostle says in Hebrews (6:19) that we have hope "that enters in"; that is, it makes us enter "within the veil"—namely, into the happiness of heaven, according to the interpretation of a gloss on these words.[6] Therefore the object of hope is eternal happiness.

I answer: As stated earlier (2–2.17.1), the hope of which we speak now reaches out to God by leaning on his help in order to seek after the hoped-for good.[7] But an effect must be in proportion to its cause, and therefore the good that we should especially and above all hope for from God is an infinite good, which is in proportion to the power of our divine helper, since it belongs to an infinite power to lead to an infinite good. Eternal life, which consists in the enjoyment of God himself, is such a good;[8] for from him we should hope for nothing less than himself, since his goodness, by which he imparts good things to a creature, is no less than his essence.[9] Therefore the proper and principal object of hope is eternal happiness.

Reply to 1: Eternal happiness does not enter into the human heart perfectly—that is, so that it would be possible for a wayfarer to know what it is and what it is like.[10] Yet according to its broad outlines—namely, as "the perfect good"—it can fall within human understanding. It is in this way that the movement of hope toward it arises.[11] Therefore the Apostle specifically says in Hebrews

---

"I hope my mother gets better." Thus while eternal happiness might be *an* object of hope, it cannot be *the* object of hope.

6. On "glosses," see 1.12 note 10.

7. In 1–2.40 Thomas has already spoken about hope as a *passio* or emotion (one that, according to 1–2.40.6, abounds in young men and drunkards). But the hope Thomas speaks of here is not simply a feeling but a theological virtue (see 1–2.62). Though hope-as-emotion and hope-as-theological-virtue have their objects defined in similar ways (see note 2), they are distinguished precisely by the virtue's object being specified as eternal life.

8. Since hope as a theological virtue is something that is instilled in us by God, it must reflect the infinite power of its cause. Therefore hope's proper object must be something infinite—namely, God's eternity itself.

9. In speaking of the feeling of hope, we can normally discern two "objects." For example, if I hope that you will give me twenty dollars, then my hope might be articulated in two ways: (1) I hope that you will give me *twenty dollars* (*what* I hope for), and (2) I hope that *you* will give me twenty dollars (*in whom* I hope). Now in the case of the theological virtue of hope, these two merge into one, since *what* I hope for (eternal life—i.e., a sharing in God's own nature) is identical with the one *in whom* I hope (God). This is why hope is a *theological* virtue: God is its object.

10. A "wayfarer" (*viatores*—literally, "those on the road") is someone in this life, as opposed to those in heaven (the blessed—often called by Thomas *comprehensores*, or "those who attain") and those in hell (the damned).

11. As so often with divine realities, in this life we grasp just enough of our eternal reward, veiled in the vague notion "supreme good," to provide our hope with an object.

(6:19) that hope enters in, "even within the veil," because what we hope for is as yet veiled to us.

Reply to 2: We should not pray to God for any other goods unless they are directed toward eternal happiness. Hence hope primarily looks to eternal happiness. The other things for which we pray to God, hope looks to as secondary and as oriented toward eternal happiness. In the same way, faith regards God principally and regards secondarily those things that are oriented toward God, as stated earlier (2–2.1.1).[12]

Reply to 3: To one who longs for something great, all lesser things seem small. For this reason, to one who hopes for eternal happiness, nothing else appears difficult compared to that hope. But compared to the abilities of the one who hopes, other things may also be difficult for him. In these cases, one may have hope for such things in relation to hope's principal object.[13]

---

12. As Christians we have many different beliefs, but these are secondary to or derivative of the principal object of our belief: God himself, who reveals these things to us. Likewise, we may hope for many different things, but we exercise the virtue of hope only when we ask for these things as desired for our journey toward eternal life with God. I may hope to meet someone and fall in love and marry because I would find this personally fulfilling. But such hope is only a feeling, not the theological virtue. On the other hand, I may hope to find a spouse who will help me love God and thus obtain eternal life. This would be the theological virtue of hope, not merely the feeling of hope.

13. For example, while withstanding torture is difficult, its difficulty is nothing compared to the difficulty of attaining eternal life, since the former is possible for brave infidels, but the latter is only possible through God's grace. Still, if one hopes to withstand torture in order to attain eternal life, as in the case of martyrdom, then the hope of bearing up under torture is included within one's hope for eternal life and is therefore the act of the theological virtue.

Question 19:

The Gift of Fear

2–2.19.11[1]

Does fear remain in the heavenly homeland?

It would seem that fear does not remain in the heavenly homeland [*in patria*].[2]

1. It is written in Proverbs (1:33), "He shall enjoy abundance, without fear of evils," which is to be understood as referring to one who already enjoys wisdom in eternal happiness. But every fear is about some evil, since evil is the object of fear, as stated earlier (1–2.42.1).[3] Therefore there will be no fear in the heavenly homeland.

2. Human beings will be conformed to God in the heavenly homeland, according to 1 John (3:2), "When he shall appear, we shall be like him." But God fears nothing. Therefore human beings in the heavenly homeland will have no fear.

3. Hope is more perfect than fear, since hope looks to the good and fear looks to evil. But there will be no hope in the heavenly homeland. Therefore there will not be fear there either.

---

1. On this article, see Miner (2017).

2. In speaking of heaven as our *patria* or "homeland," Thomas is invoking the Augustinian image of God as our true homeland and God incarnate in Christ as the way to that homeland. In *De doctrina christiana* (1.11), Augustine writes, "Cum ergo ipsa sit patria, viam se quoque nobis fecit ad patriam" (Although God himself is our homeland, he also made himself the way to that homeland [my trans.]). Human beings are wayfarers in exile from our true home because of sin, and we seek to return (see 2–2.17 note 10). During our time of exile, we experience the "restlessness" or *inquietudo* of which Augustine wrote in his *Confessions* (1.1): "Fecisti nos ad te et inquietum est cor nostrum donec requiescat in te" (You have made us for yourself, and our heart is restless until it rests in you [my trans.]). For Augustine, it is because we are in exile that we suffer such things as fear: it is part of the restlessness or disturbance from which we will be freed when we rest in God. In using the term *patria* in this article, Thomas is alluding to Augustine's understanding of this promised rest, and he is asking if there is any sense in which fear of God, which is spoken of positively in Scripture, can be a part of that rest.

3. Just as hope has some future good as its object, so fear has some future evil as its object.

On the contrary: It is written in the psalm (19:9), "The fear of the Lord is holy, enduring forever."

I answer: Servile fear, or fear of punishment,[4] will be in no way present in the heavenly homeland, since such fear is excluded by the security of eternal happiness, which is part of the very idea of happiness, as stated earlier (1–2.5.4, above).[5] But with regard to filial fear, just as it grows as charity grows,[6] so too is it perfected when charity is made perfect. Therefore, in the heavenly homeland it will not have quite the same act as it has now.[7]

In order to make this clear, it is necessary to understand that the proper object of fear is a possible evil, just as the proper object of hope is a possible good. Since the movement of fear is a kind of fleeing, fear implies fleeing from a possible difficult evil, since small evils do not inspire fear. Now just as a thing's good consists in retaining its proper place in the order of things, so too a thing's evil consists in forsaking its proper place. The proper place of a rational creature, however, is that it should be below God and above other creatures.[8] Therefore, just as it is bad for a rational creature to submit

---

4. In 2–2.19.2 Thomas distinguishes between four kinds of fear (distinctions he borrows from Peter Lombard; see *Sentences* bk. 3, dist. 34): worldly, servile, initial, and filial. Thomas calls fear that turns us *away* from God "worldly fear" (*timor mundanus*); this might include such things as a fear of pain or loss of property or reputation. On the other hand, fear may turn us *toward* God in several ways. We may turn toward God out of fear of punishment, and this is what Thomas calls "servile fear" (*timor servilis*). Or we may turn toward God out of fear of offending God's goodness and thereby alienating ourselves from God, much as we may fear hurting the feelings of someone we love; Thomas calls this "filial fear" (*timor filialis*) or, when quoting Augustine in this article, "chaste fear." Thomas also recognizes that we may have a mixed motivation for our fear: Maria may fear failing her introductory theology course both because she does not want to disappoint her parents (not to mention her teacher) *and* because she does not want to lose her scholarship. This is what Thomas calls "initial fear" (*timor initialis*), which is located between servile and filial fear. "Initial fear" is characteristic of those who are just beginning to love God. As such, it is closer to filial fear than it is to servile fear, since it fears most committing an offense against God, though fear of sin's punishment is not absent.

5. See 1–2.5 note 15.

6. The more we love someone, the less we are motivated by a desire to avoid punishment for our misdeeds and the more we are motivated by a desire to avoid hurting or offending that person.

7. "Quite the same act as it has now" translates Thomas's Latin accurately, but it does not necessarily help us understand what he is saying, in part because of the flexibility of the term *actus*. The term can mean "action," but it can also mean a perfected state of existence, as in the case of *actually* being something rather than *potentially* being something (see 1.2 note 36). Here Thomas seems to be saying simply that "fear" in heaven will be a fundamentally different kind of thing than "fear" in this life. As the rest of the article shows, he seems to have some doubts whether there is really any point in even using the word "fear" to describe those in heaven. But since Scripture speaks of "fear of God" as "everlasting" (see the text cited in the *sed contra*), Thomas has a stake in arguing that although it might be *misleading* in some cases to speak of the fear that remains in the blessed, it is not *improper* to do so (since Scripture never speaks improperly).

8. There are two opposite ways in which created beings with minds (i.e., human beings and angels) can become morally disordered: (1) by placing created beings without minds above themselves (e.g., by becoming enslaved to material goods) and (2) by placing themselves—mere creatures—above God, who is the uncreated source of creation.

to a lower creature through love, so too is it bad for it not to submit to God but to presumptuously rise up against him or treat him with contempt. This evil is possible to a rational creature considered according to its nature, on account of the natural flexibility of the free will. But in the blessed it becomes impossible, on account of the perfection of glory.[9] Therefore the act of fleeing the evil of not being subject to God will exist in the heavenly homeland as something possible in terms of nature, although impossible given the state of bliss. But on our journey [to that homeland] this evil is fled as something altogether possible.[10]

Therefore Gregory—interpreting Job (26:11), "The pillars of heaven tremble and quake at his command"—says in his *Moral Reflections on the Book of Job* (17.29), "The very powers of heaven that gaze on him without ceasing, tremble while contemplating. But this awe, far from being a punishment, is not from fear but from wonder," because, that is to say, they are in wonder at God's transcendent existence and incomprehensibility. Augustine, in *The City of God* (14.9), also admits fear in heaven in this sense, although he leaves the question doubtful. He says, "If this chaste fear that endures for ever and ever is to be in the future life, it will not be a fear that is afraid of an evil that might possibly occur, but a fear that holds fast to a good that we cannot lose. For when we love the good that we have acquired with an unchangeable love, without doubt our fear is secure—if one may put it this way—in avoiding evil. 'Chaste fear' signifies the will that cannot consent to sin and by which we avoid sin, not with concern for our weakness, for fear that we might sin strongly, but with the tranquility born of charity. But if no sort of fear at all is possible there . . . perhaps fear is said to endure for ever and ever because that to which fear leads us is everlasting."

Reply to 1: The passage quoted excludes from the blessed the fear that denotes concern and anxiety about evil, but not the fear that is accompanied by security, as Augustine said.

Reply to 2: As Dionysius says in his *On the Divine Names* (9), "The same things are both similar and dissimilar to God. They are similar on account of a contingent imitation of what cannot be imitated"—that is, inasmuch

---

9. See 1–2.5.4, above.

10. If we take avoidance of evil as the key element in fear, then we *can* say that the blessed have fear in that they avoid evil. However, this is a peculiar kind of avoidance. In the state of blessedness, humans remain human, and thus they possess a nature that in itself is capable of sinning, yet sinning has de facto become impossible for them because they are so enraptured by God's glory. So we might say that whereas the fear of wayfarers is with regard to a possible future evil, the fear of the blessed is simply an aversion to an evil that, while possible given human nature taken in itself, is impossible given human nature as sharing in the light of glory.

as they imitate, so far as they can, God, who cannot be imitated perfectly—
"and they are dissimilar because they are the effects of a cause of which they
fall infinitely and immeasurably short." Therefore, if there can be no fear in
God, since there is none above him to whom he may be subject, it does not
follow that there is none in the blessed, whose happiness consists in perfect
subjection to God.[11]

Reply to 3: Hope implies a kind of defect that is removed when happiness is
present—namely, that happiness lies in the future. But fear implies a natural
defect in a creature, according to which it is infinitely distant from God, and
this defect will remain even in the heavenly homeland. Therefore fear will
not be cast out altogether.[12]

---

11. Here fear is linked to subjection; that is, it is a kind of filial fear.

12. What is essential to fear is some sort of "defect"—which in this context means not a lack of something a thing should have (e.g., a car lacking an engine) but simply a falling short of some perfection (e.g.,
a car lacking the ability to think). The "defect" of the absence of a future good is an essential part of the
definition of hope, but it is not an essential part of the definition of fear. For fear the "defect" is simply
the infinite distance between the creature and God, which remains in heaven, and so something properly
called "fear" can likewise remain in heaven.

Question 23:

Charity

2–2.23.1[1]
Is charity friendship?

It would seem that charity is not friendship.

1. Nothing is more characteristic of friendship than to live together with friends, as the Philosopher says in the *Ethics* (8.5, 1157ᵇ).[2] But human beings have charity toward God and the angels, "whose fellowship [*conversatio*] is not with mortals," as Daniel (2:11) says.[3] Therefore charity is not friendship.

2. There is no friendship without reciprocal love [*reamatione*], as it says in the *Ethics* (8.2, 1155ᵇ). But charity extends even to one's enemies, according to Matthew (5:44): "Love your enemies." Therefore charity is not friendship.[4]

---

1. On this article, see Schockenhoff (2002); Torrell (2011, 45–64).

2. Noteworthy in this article is Thomas's constant dialogue with Aristotle on the subject of friendship. Though the theme of divine friendship hardly originates with Thomas, being found in previous writers ranging from the Gospel of John (15:15) to Gregory of Nyssa (ca. 335–ca. 395) to Aelred of Rievaulx (1110–67), Thomas's account is innovative in the way that it draws on Aristotle's *Nicomachean Ethics* for a rigorous analysis of human friendship in order to clarify what it means to speak of "friendship with God." However, as becomes obvious, Thomas does not simply adopt Aristotle's views on human friendship and apply them to God. Rather, Thomas argues that all true human friendships are grounded in friendship with God, an argument that leads to some rather dramatic revisions of what "friendship" means—revisions that would probably have baffled Aristotle (e.g., the notion of loving one's enemies).

3. The citation is from Daniel, but the objection is essentially Aristotelian. In the *Nicomachean Ethics* (2.7, 1158ᵇ–59ᵃ), Aristotle says that if two parties are greatly unequal in terms of virtue or wealth or anything else, "then they are no longer friends and do not even expect to be so." He continues, "And this is most manifest in the case of the gods; for they surpass us most decisively in all good things. . . . Much can be taken away and friendship remain, but when one party is removed at a great distance, as is God, the possibility of friendship ceases." In Thomas's commentary on this section of the *Nicomachean Ethics*, he identifies the "gods" as "separated substances"—i.e., angels—thus accounting for the objection's reference to God *and* angels.

4. While it might make sense to say that you love someone who does not love you back, it does not make sense to say that you are friends with someone who does not consider themselves your friend in return. It's just pathetic and creepy and stalkerish. So if we are commanded to have charity toward our enemies, who by definition are not our friends, then charity must be something different from friendship.

3. According to the Philosopher in the *Ethics* (8.3, 1156ᵃ), friendships are of three sorts—that is, friendship for pleasure, friendship for usefulness, and honorable friendship.⁵ But charity is neither friendship for usefulness nor for pleasure, for Jerome says in his letter to Paulinus, which is to be found at the beginning of the Bible (*Epistle 53*),⁶ "True affinity joined by the glue of Christ depends not on household interests, nor on mere bodily presence, nor on crafty and cajoling flattery, but is when people are drawn together by the fear of God and the study of the divine Scriptures." Neither is charity the friendship of the honorable, since by charity we love even sinners, whereas the friendship of the honorable is only for the virtuous, as it says in the *Ethics* (8.4, 1157ᵃ).⁷ Therefore charity is not friendship.

On the contrary: It is said in John (15:15), "Now I will not call you servants . . . but my friends." But this was not said to them except on account of charity. Therefore charity is friendship.

I answer: According to the Philosopher in the *Ethics* (8.2, 1155ᵇ), not every love has the character of friendship, but only the love that is accompanied by wishing someone well [*benevolentia*]—that is, when we love someone in such a way that we wish good [*bonum velimus*] to them. If, however, we do not wish good to what we love but wish its good for ourselves, as when we say that we love wine or a horse or something similar, it is not the love of friendship but a kind of desire [*concupiscentiae*], for it would be ridiculous to speak of someone being friends with wine or with a horse.⁸

5. Aristotle says that in useful friendship (*amicitia utilis*) and pleasurable friendship (*amacitia delectabilis*), the friend is not loved for his or her own sake, but because they can provide us with something we need or simply because we find that person's presence enjoyable (e.g., because they are beautiful or funny). In honorable friendship (*amicitia honesti*), on the other hand, the friend is loved for his or her own sake—that is, because of the virtues (which are more than simply pleasing qualities, such as beauty or wit) he or she possesses. As Aristotle puts it, "Perfect friendship is the friendship of men who are good and alike in virtue; for these wish well alike to each other *qua* good, and they are good in themselves" (*Ethics* 8.3, 1156ᵇ). So these friendships are "honorable" in that both parties are virtuous, and what they desire and rejoice in is the friend's virtue.

6. The reference is to Jerome's letter as forming a sort of preface to the Vulgate.

7. The objection's point seems to be that useful and pleasurable friendships do not rise to the level of Christian charity, while honorable friendship seems too narrow to encompass the love we should have toward the wicked.

8. Thomas acknowledges that the fact that charity is a type of love does not by itself mean that charity is friendship, because not all love involves friendship. Although we might say that we "love" a particular food, that food does not thereby become our friend, in part because we do not desire that the food flourish—in other words, we do not have "benevolence" toward it. Rather, the goodness that the food already possesses incites our desire, the desire to possess that the Western Christian tradition calls "concupiscence." While concupiscence is not necessarily sinful—it is an ordinary part of our animal existence, one pole of what we might call our "desire-avoidance instinct"—it is also not the same thing as benevolence, since we might seek to fulfill our desire for food by consuming it and thereby destroying it. So if charity is to be friendship, it must fulfill certain other criteria: in this case, it must involve well-wishing. Thomas's introduction of the

But well-wishing is not sufficient to identify friendship, for a certain mutual love is required, since a friend is a friend to a friend,[9] and such mutual well-wishing is founded on a certain communion [*communicatione*].[10]

Accordingly, because there is communion between humanity and God inasmuch as he communicates his perfect happiness to us, some kind of friendship must be based on this same communication. This sort of communion is spoken of in 1 Corinthians (1:9): "the faithful God, by whom you are called into the fellowship of his Son."[11] The love based on this communion is charity. Therefore it is evident that charity is the friendship of human beings toward God.[12]

Reply to 1: The life of human beings is twofold. On the one hand, there is the outward life of the senses and the body, and with regard to this life there is no communion or fellowship between us and God or the angels. On the other hand, there is the spiritual life of human beings according to the mind. And with regard to this life there is fellowship between us and both God and the angels.[13] This is incomplete in this present state of life; hence it is written in Philippians (3:20), "Our common life is in heaven." But this common life will be completed in our heavenly homeland—when "God's servants shall serve

---

example of the horse seems to muddy his point, for it seems that we *can* desire that a horse be good, because horses, as animate creatures, grow and develop.

Thomas's discussion raises a difficult point. How can a creature have benevolence toward God? How can a creature wish that God be good, or that good things accrue to God? In 2–2.28.1, Thomas speaks of "the love of benevolence, by which someone rejoices on account of the friend's prospering." This is certainly a kind of "benevolence" that humans could exercise toward God: to rejoice in God's goodness.

9. Beyond well-wishing, friendship also involves mutuality. This is another reason that one cannot be friends with an inanimate object: it cannot consider you its friend. In the case of other people, mutuality is possible, but not inevitable.

10. On *communicare*, see 3.1 note 8. Because of the flexibility of the term *communicatio*, which Thomas trades on in his response here, I have translated it sometimes as "communion" and sometimes as "communication." To say that friendship depends on *communicatio* covers two points that Aristotle makes about friendship: it must be based on a something shared in common (whether this be a matter of usefulness, pleasure, or goodness), and the parties must actually be in communication with one another (see *Ethics* 8.2, 1155ᵇ).

11. Thomas's quotation of this verse from 1 Corinthians indicates his fundamental departure from Aristotle: because God becomes incarnate in Christ, there is communion/communication between God and humanity (see 3.1.1, below), and therefore friendship is possible between God and humanity.

12. Here it should be underscored that the charity Thomas is speaking of is a theological virtue (see 1–2.62.3, above), which means that it is instilled in us by God. As 1 John 4:19 says, "We love because he first loved us." The initiative is always on God's part. Nothing we do wins God's friendship; it is a gift freely bestowed. As Thomas says in his *Commentary on the Gospel of John* (15.3.2012), "Keeping the commandments is not the cause of divine friendship but the sign, the sign both that God loves us and that we love God."

13. Even apart from our communion with God in Christ, through the simple fact of our creation as rational beings we share something with God (and the angels). This sharing is, as Thomas goes on to note, incomplete in this life but will be perfected in the next life, through the grace of Christ.

him, and they shall see his face," as it says in Revelation (22:3–4).[14] Therefore charity is imperfect here, but will be perfected in heaven.

Reply to 2: Friendship extends to someone in two ways. First, with regard to the specific person, and in this way friendship extends only to one's friends. Second, it extends to someone with regard to someone else, as in the case when someone is friends with a certain person, and for his sake loves everyone with some connection to him, whether they are children, or servants, or related in any way whatsoever. Indeed so much do we love our friends that for their sake we love all who belong to them, even if they hurt or hate us. In this way, the friendship of charity extends even to our enemies, whom we love because of charity toward God, to whom the friendship of charity is chiefly directed.[15]

Reply to 3: The friendship of the honorable is directed only to one who is virtuous as the principal person, but for that person's sake we love those who belong to him, even if they are not virtuous. In this way charity, which above all is the friendship of the honorable, is extended to sinners, whom we love out of charity for God's sake.

14. The quotation from Philippians, with its reference to our "common life" (in Latin, *conversatio*; in Greek, *politeuma*), indicates another way in which Thomas departs from Aristotle in his account of friendship. For both Thomas and Aristotle, friendship is essentially "political," inasmuch as it depends on friends sharing a common life. For Aristotle, the common life upon which friendship is based is that of the *polis* or city-state: it would be unthinkable for a citizen of Athens to be friends with a citizen of Sparta, because it is in the life of the *polis* that the diverse interests of individuals are coordinated so as to form a common good. Of course, even within the *polis* the possibility of friendship is limited; those who do not share fully in the "common life" of the city—women, slaves, children, foreigners—cannot be friends in the fullest sense of the term.

For Thomas, however, the common life of Christians is not that of some earthly city-state, with its attendant limitations; it is rather the common life of the heavenly Jerusalem, in which all those who will be saved share equally without regard to status. Thus friendship is possible across boundaries that seemed unbreachable in the ancient world—ultimately even across the boundary that separates the divine and the human.

15. If we love someone, we love all those who are connected with them. But because all creatures exist only by virtue of their relatedness to God, in loving God we are called to love all creatures. This does not, however, lessen the paradox of having charity toward our enemies, such that our enemies are our friends. A similar argument is used in the reply to the next objection.

Question 24:

Charity in Relation to Its Subject

2–2.24.9[1]
On the different degrees of charity.

It would seem unfitting to distinguish three degrees [*gradus*] of charity—that is, beginning, progressing, and perfected [*incipiens, proficiens, et perfecta*].[2]

1. Between the beginning of charity and its ultimate perfection there are many degrees intervening. Therefore it is not right to posit only one intermediary.[3]

2. Charity begins to progress as soon as it begins to be. Therefore we ought not to distinguish progressing charity from beginning charity.

3. However perfectly one has charity in this world, it is possible for one's charity to increase, as was said (2–2.24.7). But for charity to increase is for

---

1. On this article, see Garrigou-Lagrange (2002); Torrell (2003, 359–62).

2. Thomas's language of "infused" virtue might give the impression that faith, hope, and love, along with the infused moral virtues (see 1–2.65 note 2), are given to people by God in such a way that they possess them perfectly. This would, however, be an extraordinarily unrealistic picture of the Christian life, one in which people are "zapped" by God with virtues and are suddenly capable of living perfect Christian lives. Thomas knows that even those in a state of grace typically continue to struggle as Christians. At the same time, he wants to clearly distinguish the infused virtues from the acquired virtues. One cannot come to possess the virtues of faith, hope, and love simply by means of one's own efforts; they remain God's free gifts. Thomas seeks to maintain the gratuitous character of the infused virtues and yet account for how our ability to exercise those virtues can increase or decrease over the course of a life.

Thomas notes that we can distinguish between the possession of a disposition for action and the ease with which we can engage in that action. In the case of virtues acquired through practice, the process of acquiring the virtue tends to bring with it a certain ease of action. But in the case of virtues infused in us by God, there is a need subsequent to the infusion of the virtue for acquiring a facility in exercising that virtue. Thomas writes earlier in the *Summa* (1–2.65.3 ad 2), "Sometimes the [infused] habits of moral virtue experience difficulty in their works on account of certain contrary dispositions remaining from previous acts. This difficulty does not occur in the case of acquired moral virtue, because the repeated acts by which they are acquired remove the contrary dispositions as well." Even in the case of infused charity, contrary dispositions remain that must be overcome.

3. This first objection argues that three degrees are insufficient to properly measure the increase of charity, which calls for a more finely grained account.

213

it to progress. Therefore perfected charity should not be distinguished from progressing charity. Therefore the three degrees of charity spoken of above are not fittingly assigned.[4]

On the contrary: Augustine says in his *Tractates on the First Letter of John* (5.4), "As soon as charity is born it takes food"—which pertains to beginners— "after having taken food, it grows strong"—which pertains to those making progress—"after having grown strong, it is perfected," which pertains to the perfect. Therefore there are three degrees of charity.

I answer: The spiritual growth of charity can be considered as somewhat similar to the growth of the human body.[5] For though the latter growth can be divided into many parts, it has certain fixed divisions according to the particular actions or endeavors to which one is led by this growth, as when we speak of the age of infancy before one has the use of reason, after which we distinguish another human state when one begins to speak and to use reason, and then a third state, which is puberty, when one begins to be able to reproduce, and so on until one arrives at perfection.[6]

In the same way the different degrees of charity are distinguished according to the different endeavors to which one is brought by the growth of charity. For at first it is incumbent on a person chiefly to work at avoiding sin and resisting one's sinful desires, which move in opposition to charity. This pertains to beginners, in whom charity must be nourished or kept warm in order not to be destroyed. The second thing one must work at is aiming to progress in good. This endeavor pertains to those who are progressing, whose primary intention is that their charity be strengthened by growth. The third endeavor is that one aim primarily at being united with God and enjoying him. This pertains to the perfect, who "desire to be dissolved and be with Christ" (Phil. 1:23). We observe the same thing in bodily change: first there is moving away from one term, second, drawing near to the other term, and, third, rest in this term.[7]

4. The second and third objections both argue that at least one of the degrees of charity is superfluous. The second argues that since charity progresses as soon as it is possessed, there is no need to distinguish the beginning of charity from its progress. The third argues that since charity can always grow greater, there is no need to distinguish the perfection of charity from its progress.

5. Thomas often draws parallels between the physical (which is better known to us) and the spiritual (which we know less readily). See, for example, his use of human physical development and flourishing as a model for understanding why there are seven sacraments (3.65.1, below).

6. We distinguish "stages" of bodily life by the acquisition of new capacities: infancy precedes the acquisition of language, which inaugurates childhood, which in turn precedes puberty, which inaugurates adolescence, and so forth. The "perfection" to which the process of development leads does not necessarily refer to moral perfection but is simply Thomas's way of speaking of our full maturation as a human—i.e., adulthood.

7. The initial stage in the development of charity is the work of resisting sin so as to be purged of sinful desires that move us in ways that are contrary to charity. Once purged of sin, we begin to work at growing in love. Such growth makes possible a third endeavor: being united with God. The threefold process of

Reply to 1: All these distinct degrees that can be grasped in the growth of charity are included in the three discussed above, just as every division of a continuum is included in these three: the beginning, the middle, and the end, as the Philosopher states in *On the Heavens* (1.1, 268ᵃ).[8]

Reply to 2: Those in whom charity is beginning may progress, yet the chief concern that besets them is to resist sins, which disturb them by their attack. But afterwards, feeling this attack less and being somewhat more secure, they undertake to move toward perfection, yet with one hand doing the work and the other holding a sword, as it is said in Esdras (Neh. 4:17) about those who built Jerusalem.[9]

Reply to 3: The perfect too make progress in charity, but this is not their chief concern; rather their endeavor is principally directed toward union with God. And though this is also sought by both the beginner and those making progress, yet they feel other concerns more: avoiding sin in the case of beginners, advancing in virtue in the case of those making progress.[10]

---

development from purgation from sin through spiritual growth to union with God that Thomas describes bears some resemblance to what is sometimes called the *triplex via* or "threefold path" of purgation, illumination, and union, which is found in various spiritual writers. Garrigou-Lagrange (see note 1) in particular seeks to integrate Thomas's account of charity with the mystical writings of John of the Cross, producing an account that is significantly more elaborate than what Thomas sketches here.

It should be borne in mind that although Thomas speaks of different "endeavors" (*studia*) demarcating the stages of growth in charity, he sees all of these actions by the human person as a flowering of the divine gift of charity infused in the soul. What Thomas charts here is not a plan for spiritual self-improvement but rather a way of registering the fact that people grow and develop spiritually.

8. Variations on the threefold pattern of spiritual growth are found not only throughout the history of Christianity but also in many non-Christian religious traditions. In some thinkers these stages can be further subdivided and highly elaborated. Thomas's version is by comparison fairly simple, though his response here seems to acknowledge that one might elaborate upon his basic scheme.

9. Thomas, like spiritual masters of many traditions, does not see these "stages" as strictly successive. One does not, for example, complete a purgative initial stage and then move on to growth with no looking back. He knows that we need to be purged of sin throughout our lives, no matter how spiritually advanced we may seem to be. Likewise, we can experience some growth in charity even when, as beginners in the life of grace, we are primarily concerned with resisting sin.

10. In Thomas's view, those who are perfected in charity do not for that reason cease to be concerned with avoiding evil and doing good, as some of the more dramatic statements of mystical writers might lead some to suppose. But the focus of their attention shifts from vices to be avoided or the virtues to be developed to being united with God through love and knowledge. An athlete or a musician must initially focus on avoiding bad habits and acquiring technical skills in order to play their sport or instrument, but eventually one reaches a point where it is the game or the song that becomes the focus, and not the mechanics. Likewise, one who is perfected in love and knowledge needs to focus less on the mechanics of avoiding vice and cultivating virtue and more on God.

Question 40:

War

2–2.40.1[1]
Is any kind of war licit?

It would seem that waging war is always a sin.[2]

1. A penalty is not inflicted except for sin. But a penalty is declared by the Lord on those who wage war, according to Matthew (26:52): "All that take the sword will perish by the sword." Therefore all war is illicit.

2. Whatever is contrary to a divine rule is a sin. But war is contrary to a divine rule, for it is said in Matthew (5:39), "I say to you, do not resist evil";

---

1. On this article, see Russell (1975); Reichberg (2010).
2. In the early church, service in the military was, along with being an actor or a pimp, widely seen as a profession forbidden to Christians. The church was not committed to pacifism in the abstract; rather, the waging of war was seen as so wrapped up in Roman idolatry of the emperor and so contrary to the teachings of Jesus that military service was considered morally perilous. Once Christians began to be tolerated by the empire under the emperor Constantine and more and more citizens of the empire sought entry into the church, the Christian position on military service softened. Augustine had a significant role in sketching the possibilities and limits of Christian participation in war.

Though Thomas is sometimes identified as one of the chief architects of what today is called "just war theory"—which is a set of criteria for determining whether it is just to go to war as well as how one justly conducts oneself in the context of war—what he says about war is relatively minimal and scattered in various places in his writings. This article deals almost exclusively with the issue of when the decision to go to war might or might not be sinful. The issue of what actions are or are not licit *during* a war is not particularly well developed, and one must gather hints from various places in Thomas's writings (see, for example, what Thomas says about the use of disproportionate means of self-defense in 2–2.64.7, below).

What is clear from what Thomas does say here about war is that he sees killing in war as sometimes not only licit, but even demanded by the need to preserve the common good. As his many references in this article make clear, he is heavily indebted to Augustine for his thinking. Yet unlike Augustine, who saw even morally licit war almost entirely as a sign of the misery of fallen human existence, Thomas sees the defense and preservation of the common good (a notion he gets from Aristotle, not Augustine) as a positive good achieved through just wars. At the same time, the way in which he locates this discussion of war in the *Summa*—not in his discussion of justice or of fortitude but in his discussion of vices that are contrary to peace, which is an effect of *caritas*—suggests that he has not left Augustinian ambivalence toward war entirely behind.

and in Romans (12:19), "Not defending yourselves, beloved, but giving room for the wrath [of God]." Therefore waging war is always sinful.

3. Nothing is contrary to an act of virtue except sin. But war is contrary to peace. Therefore war is always a sin.

4. Training for anything permissible is itself permissible, as is evident from training in matters of *scientia*. But the training for war that takes place in tournaments is forbidden by the church, for those dying in these sorts of warlike exercises are deprived of ecclesiastical burial.[3] Therefore war seems to be a sin absolutely.

On the contrary: Augustine says in a sermon on the son of the centurion, "If Christian teaching found fault with all war, those [soldiers] in the Gospel who asked for counsel concerning salvation would have been better advised to throw down their arms and withdraw from military service entirely. But they were told, 'Harass no one . . . and be content with your pay.' If he taught them to be content with their pay, he did not forbid military service."[4]

I answer: For a war to be just, three things are required.

First, the authority of the prince by whose command war is to be waged.[5] For it is not the role of private persons to start a war, because such can pursue their rights in the tribunal of a superior. Likewise, it is not the role of a private

---

3. Note that courtly tournaments served as training for combat as much as forms of entertainment. Note also that the church frowned on such tournaments. See, e.g., the Second Lateran Council (1139), canon 14: "We entirely forbid, moreover, those abominable jousts and tournaments in which knights come together by agreement and rashly engage in showing off their physical prowess and daring, and which often result in human deaths and danger to souls. If any of them dies on these occasions, although penance and viaticum are not to be denied him when he requests them, he is to be deprived of a church burial."

4. This quotation is actually from Augustine's *Letter 138*, to Marcellinus. The Gospel story referred to is from Luke 3:14, where soldiers, among others, come to John the Baptist and ask what they should do in response to his proclamation of the kingdom. Augustine presumes that if all war were sinful, then John would have told the soldiers this.

5. The term *princeps* might also be translated simply as "leader" or "ruler," but I translate it as "prince" as a reminder of the very different nature of political authority in Thomas's world, an authority that was thought to derive not simply from the will of the people but from the choice of God. At the same time, Thomas was not a monarchial absolutist who saw the power of rulers as unfettered. He combines two principles from Aristotle—that political communities are (1) guided best when either one or a small number of people have final authority and (2) are most peaceful when everyone has *some* role in governing them—to advocate what we might call a "mixed polity," combining elements of monarchy, aristocracy, and democracy. Thus the best political order is one in which "there is a single person who is placed in command on the basis of virtue and presides over everyone, and in which there are others under him who rule in accord with virtue, and yet in which ruling pertains to everyone, not only because the rulers can be chosen from among everyone, but also because they are chosen by everyone" (1–2.105.1). Note that Thomas seems to suggest an elected rather than hereditary monarchy. Thomas's support for this sort of governance might have been influenced by the model of Italian city-states or even by the structure of his own Dominican Order, whose governing documents enshrine the kind of "mixed polity" that Thomas seems to advocate.

person to call together a multitude, which has to be done in war.[6] Since the care of public matters belongs to princes, it pertains to them to watch over the public affairs of the city, kingdom, or province subject to them.[7] And just as it is permitted for them to defend it by the sword against internal disturbances when they punish evil-doers—according to the Apostle in Romans (13:4): "He does not bear the sword in vain, for he is God's minister, an avenger to execute wrath upon one who does evil"—so too it pertains to them to defend the republic by the sword of war against external enemies.[8] Hence in the psalm (82:4) it says to princes, "Rescue the poor: and liberate the destitute from the hand of the sinner." Therefore Augustine says in *Against Faustus the Manichaean* (22.75): "The order of nature suited to peace among mortals requires that the authority to undertake and plan for war be in the hands of princes."

Second, a just cause is required—namely, that those who are attacked deserve to be attacked on account of some fault.[9] Therefore Augustine says in his *Quaestiones in Heptateuchum* (q. 10, on Josh. 8:2): "Just wars are usually described as those that avenge wrongs when the nation or city has to be punished either for refusing to make amends for what was done unjustly by its subjects or to restore what was wrongly taken."

Third, it is necessary that those fighting should have a proper intention—namely, that they intend either that good be advanced or that evil be avoided. Thus Augustine says in the book *On the Words of the Lord*,[10] "In the eyes of true worshipers of God, those wars are peaceful that are waged not from lust or cruelty but carried on with a zeal for peace, that evil be restrained and the good assisted." For it can happen that the war is declared by the legitimate

6. Thomas gives two reasons why a private citizen cannot declare a war: (1) the wrongs that a private citizen suffers can be addressed in a court of law, and (2) a private citizen does not have the authority to assemble other citizens, which you need to have if you are going to gather an army with which to fight a war. Note that Thomas does not seem to envision a standing army that fights wars, but rather a fighting force that has to be raised on each occasion that a people is going to war.

7. Even a ruler could not go to war to address a private grievance, but only in his capacity as a "public person"—i.e., one who is charged with protecting the common good.

8. Thomas sees the war-making authority of the ruler as rooted in the same principle as the "policing" function of the ruler: protection of the common good.

9. Thomas's account of what constitutes a "just cause" is frustratingly brief, since this would seem to be the crux of the matter. Thomas clearly thinks you cannot attack an enemy who is in no way at fault, but what exactly constitutes fault is not made clear. For example, is a particular degree of harm needed to constitute a just cause? Is a mere insult sufficient reason to go to war, or must there be an existential threat posed by an attacker? The subsequent quotation from Augustine suggests that an unatoned-for past bad act by an opponent who poses no immediate threat might suffice as a just cause. In this sense, Thomas does not seem to distinguish between defensive and offensive wars.

10. The quotation of Augustine is taken from Gratian's *Decretum* 2.23.1, canon 6, and though Thomas cites the eighth-century collection of Augustine's sermons known as *De verbis Domini*, the quotation cannot be found in any of Augustine's extant works. The sentiment expressed, however, is not alien to Augustine.

authority and for a just cause and nonetheless is rendered illicit on account of a faulty intention. Hence Augustine says in *Against Faustus the Manichaean* (22.74), "The desire to harm, the cruelty of vengeance, an insatiable and relentless spirit, the savagery of revolt, the lust of power: all these and other similar things are rightly condemned in war."[11]

Reply to 1: As Augustine says in the second book against the Manichees (*Against Faustus the Manichaean* 22.70), "One who 'takes the sword' is one who arms himself in order to spill the blood of someone without the command or permission of a superior or legitimate authority." Conversely, one who wields the sword either as a private person by the authority of a prince or judge or as a public person through zeal for justice and by the authority, so to speak, of God is not said to "take the sword" but to use it as commissioned by another. Therefore it does not deserve punishment.[12] Yet even those by whom the sword is used sinfully are not always slain by the sword. But they still always perish with their own sword, for they are punished eternally for the sin of the sword, unless they should repent.[13]

Reply to 2: Such precepts, as Augustine observes in *The Lord's Sermon on the Mount* (1.19), should always be kept in the preparedness of the mind—namely, that one be always ready to not resist or not defend oneself, if necessary. But sometimes it is necessary to act otherwise on account of the common good, or even for the good of those against whom one is fighting.[14] Hence Augustine says in his letter to Marcellinus (*Epistle 138*, 2), "Many things are done against the will of those whom we have to punish with a kindly severity. . . . For the person from whom the freedom of iniquity is taken benefits in being vanquished, since nothing is more truly a misfortune than that good

11. A just cause does not suffice to make a war itself just. Again, the quotation from Augustine fills out somewhat the kind of things that might constitute a faulty intention. It is not entirely clear whether Thomas sees the criterion of right intention as applying to the prince's intention in declaring war or to the individual combatant's intention in fighting. If a prince leads his people to war simply to attain glory so as to gain advantage for himself, then even if the war is being fought for a just cause (i.e., the opponent is guilty of some wrongdoing), the war would seem to be unjust. In the case of an individual warrior, if his intention is to engage in sadistic acts of violence, then the warrior is unjust even if the war is just.

12. Thomas, following Augustine, is distinguishing between what we might call the "public violence" of policing or warfare (what Paul in Rom. 13 would call "wielding" the sword) and the "private violence" of carrying out a vendetta (what Jesus condemns as "taking" the sword—a term that to Augustine suggested the seizing of the sword for one's own personal purposes).

13. Jesus's statement in Matthew's Gospel is not a prediction of the manner in which those who unjustly take up the sword will die but a warning of the eternal consequence of their action.

14. Thomas here again sounds the theme of war as preserving the common good. Nonresistance to evil may be required of an individual under certain circumstances, but for one who has charge of public affairs, the preservation of the common good through waging war is not only forgivable; it is commendable. Indeed, it may even be a moral obligation that we bear toward our opponents, so that through the punishment of war they might be brought back to the right path.

fortune of sinners, by which punishing impunity is nourished and the evil will, like an inner enemy, is strengthened."

Reply to 3: Those who wage just wars aim at peace. So peace is not opposed except the evil peace, which the Lord "came not to send upon the earth," as it says in Matthew (10:34). Therefore Augustine says to Boniface (*Epistle 189*), "We do not seek peace in order to practice war, but we wage war to procure peace. Be peaceful, therefore, in warring, so that, subduing those whom you conquer, you bring them to the benefits of peace."[15]

Reply to 4: Human exercises in matters of war are not universally forbidden, but only disordered and dangerous exercises, which are the source of slaughter or plundering. In ancient times warlike exercises were without such danger, and thus they were called "the practice of arms" or "wars without blood," as Jerome makes clear in a letter.[16]

15. This is a basic element of Augustine's account of war that Thomas takes over: the goal of war is the restoration of peace. It is in part from this presumption that much of the later just war tradition's account of the actual conduct of war is derived: war must be fought in such a way as to make possible the restoration of peace. Observing such principles as the prohibition on the intentional killing of noncombatants facilitates the ultimate restoration of a state of peace between nations. It should be noted that while Thomas believes that it is always wrong to intentionally kill the innocent, it is not entirely clear whether he considers all noncombatants innocent. At least in the case of the wars fought by ancient Israel, he argues that it was not wrong for the Israelites to kill all the inhabitants of the cities God had promised to them, including women and children, "on account of their former crimes" (though he does not specify what those crimes were; see 1–2.105.3 ad 4). Whether Thomas thought this applied beyond the specific case of Israel's wars of conquest is not clear. One certainly hopes not.

16. The source of these phrases is actually the *Epitoma Rei Militaris*, a text on military organization by Vegetius, a late fourth-century Roman Christian writer.

Question 47:

Prudence in Itself

2–2.47.4[1]
Is prudence a virtue?

It would seem that prudence is not a virtue.[2]

1. Augustine says in *On Free Choice of the Will* (1.13) that prudence is "the knowledge [*scientia*] of things to be desired and to be avoided." But knowledge is contrasted with virtue, as is clear in [Aristotle's] *Categories* (8, 8ᵇ). Therefore prudence is not a virtue.[3]

2. There is no virtue that belongs to a virtue. But "there is a virtue of skill [*artis*]," as the Philosopher states in the *Ethics* (6.5, 1140ᵇ). Therefore skill is not a virtue. But there is prudence involved in skill, for it is said concerning Hiram in 2 Chronicles (2:14) that he knew how "to carve all sorts of sculpture, and to devise prudently everything needed for the work." Therefore prudence is not a virtue.[4]

1. On this article, see Westberg (1994); McCabe (2002, 152–65).

2. We have already encountered the virtue of prudence in Thomas's discussions of whether there are four cardinal virtues (see 1–2.61, above) and whether the virtues are "connected" (1–2.65, above). For Thomas, *prudentia* is "right reason" or "thinking straight" [*recta ratio*] about things to be done. It does not establish the end of the virtues—that is done by what Thomas calls *synderesis* (2–2.47.6)—but directs us in choosing the means by which the end is attained. It does this by establishing the "mean" or midpoint that the other virtues observe (2–2.47.7; on the notion of virtue observing the mean between opposed vices, see 1–2.55 note 2). Therefore, it is necessary to have prudence in order to have any other virtue.

The specific question Thomas is asking in this article is multifaceted: whether prudence is a disposition (*habitus*) rather than a power of the soul, whether it is a virtue or simply an aspect of other virtues, and whether it is a moral virtue as opposed to an intellectual one.

3. The force of the objection seems to be that by describing prudence as *scientia*, Augustine is assigning it to the speculative power of reason, which discerns truths that are both necessary and certain, rather than to practical reason. On Thomas's understanding of *scientia*, see 1.1 note 17.

4. On "skill" [*ars*], see the prologue to the second half of the second part, note 10. The upshot of the objection seems to be that if skill in making things is not a virtue, and such skill involves prudence, then neither is prudence a virtue.

3. No virtue can be immoderate.[5] But prudence is immoderate; otherwise what is said in Proverbs (23:4) would be refuted: "Be moderate in your prudence." Therefore prudence is not a virtue.

On the contrary: Gregory says in his *Moral Reflections on the Book of Job* (2.49) that prudence, moderation, fortitude, and justice are four virtues.

I answer: As stated above (1–2.55.3; 1–2.56.1), when virtue in general was dealt with, "Virtue is that which makes one who has it good and renders his or her work good."[6] But "good" can be used in two different ways: in one way materially, for the thing that is good, and in another way formally, on account of the reason why it is good [*secundum rationem boni*].[7] Good of this second sort is the object of our capacity for desire [*appetitivae virtutis*].[8]

Therefore if there are any settled dispositions [*habitus*] that make the assessment of reason correct without regard to the correctness of desire, they have less of the nature of a virtue since they orient one toward good materially—that is, to a thing that is good, but not on account of *why* it is good. But those dispositions that are concerned with the correctness of the appetite have more of the nature of virtue because they are concerned with the good not only materially but also formally—that is, they are concerned with what is good in terms of why it is good.[9]

Now, as stated above (2–2.47.1 ad 3), it pertains to prudence to apply correct reason to action, which is not done without correct desire. Therefore prudence has the nature of virtue not only in the way that the other intellectual virtues do but also as the moral virtues have it, among which it is numbered.[10]

---

5. Because, that is, virtue involves a mean between two vices.

6. This definition is specifically of *moral* virtue. Intellectual virtues, such as understanding (*intellectus*) or knowledge (*scientia*) or skill (*ars*), perfect the one who has them in particular ways—one who is skilled at cooking is perfected with regard to food preparation—but not as a human being per se. One can be an excellent chef while still being a lousy human being.

7. The distinction here is between the goodness of something in itself and the goodness of something seen in the context of human beings journeying to their final end. Thus skill in food preparation is, materially speaking, good. However, particular instances of cooking must be evaluated morally in terms of the wider context of our lives as fulfilled by the vision of God. So if I choose to bake a pie rather than save a person from drowning, the materially good act of skillful cooking cannot be, formally speaking, declared to be good (no matter how tasty the pie), because it has diverted me from the greater good of loving my neighbor.

8. For rational beings like us, the proper object of our capacity for desire is our final end: God. And all other things should be seen as leading us to that end.

9. Acquired skill at pie making, which makes me reason correctly about how not to overwork the dough or how to blind-bake the crust, is not a "virtue" in the full sense because it cannot connect this activity to a larger narrative of a fulfilled human life. As noted, it only makes me a good pie-maker and not a good person. A "virtue" in the full sense of the term must be not only a capacity to know how to do something but also a capacity to know *why* this thing is good in terms of my final end.

10. As an intellectual virtue, prudence is an acquired capacity that perfects our thinking, making us think correctly. Along with skill, and unlike the other intellectual virtues, prudence perfects our capacity for thinking correctly not about what is true, but about how to act. Unlike skill, however, prudence perfects

Reply to 1: In this quotation Augustine is taking "knowledge" [*scientia*] in a broad sense to mean any kind of correct reason.[11]

Reply to 2: The Philosopher says that there is a virtue of skill because skill does not itself require correct desire [*rectitudinem appetitus*], so that in order for a person to make correct use of a skill, it is necessary to have a virtue that makes the appetite properly directed.[12] Prudence, however, has no place in matters of skill, both because skill is directed to a particular end and because it has predetermined means for arriving at that end. Still, someone is said to act "prudently" in matters of skill by a kind of resemblance. Moreover, with some skills deliberation is needed on account of uncertainty regarding how they arrive at their end, as in the case of medicine and navigation, as it says in the *Ethics* (3.3, 1112b).[13]

Reply to 3: This saying of the wise man[14] should not be understood as saying that prudence itself should be moderate, but rather that moderation must be imposed on other things in accordance with prudence.[15]

---

our thinking about what is to be done not in the restricted sense that a skill does but in the unrestricted sense of moving us toward the ultimate goal of our life. In this way prudence straddles the line between intellectual and moral virtue. Like an intellectual virtue, it perfects our capacity for thinking correctly; like a moral virtue, it does not simply make us good at something, but makes us good absolutely. So we might say that prudence is the acquired disposition that allows us to reason well with regard to those actions that fulfill us as human beings.

11. Augustine is not referring to the particular intellectual virtue *scientia* but is speaking loosely of any intellectual virtue, which would include prudence.

12. Thus, for example, the ability to make good pies is not enough for good pies to exist; we must also have the desire to make good pies. That desire will be regulated by some virtue or vice. If we have acquired, say, the vice of sloth, we may well not use our pie-making skill, even though the members of our family are hungry. If we have the virtue of moderation, we will employ our pie-making skill, but only to make as many pies as are fitting for us (and others) to consume.

13. While we do not need prudence in the strict sense to make pies well, since the steps of pie making are capable of being put down in a recipe, the activity of pie making is sufficiently complex (given, for example, the changeability of the environment in which we are making pies with regard to temperature, humidity, etc.) that skill in pie making does involve a prudence-like capacity to adjust our means to the particular end of a delicious pie in light of circumstances. So if we are speaking loosely, we might speak of the prudence of a craftsperson.

Note the further implication that Thomas does not think of the moral life as something like following a recipe. He recognizes that there are a multitude of variables in moral action that require ongoing prudent adjustment of our course of action depending on circumstances. A set of instructions—whether a recipe or a law code—is no substitute for thinking straight about what one is doing.

14. I.e., Solomon.

15. In other words, it is by means of prudence that we discern the mean that other virtues must observe.

Question 58:

Justice

2–2.58.1[1]
What is justice?

It would seem justice is unfittingly defined by jurists as "the stable and perpetual willingness to give to each person what is right for that person" [*constans et perpetua voluntas ius suum unicuique tribuens*].[2]

1. According to the Philosopher in the *Ethics* (5.1, 1129ª), justice is "an abiding disposition [*habitus*] by which people are disposed to do what is just and by which they are and will to be just." But "will" denotes a power, or also an act. Justice, therefore, is unfittingly said to be "willingness."[3]

2. The uprightness of the will is not the will itself; for if the will were its own uprightness, it would follow that no will is ever perverse. But according to Anselm, in the book *On Truth* (12), justice is uprightness [*rectitudo*]. Therefore justice is not "willingness."[4]

---

1. On this article, see White (1956, 133–44); Porter (2002).

2. This is the definition given by the Roman jurist Ulpian in the third century. It acquired a kind of authoritative status among Christians by being included in the sixth-century Eastern Roman emperor Justinian's *Digest,* a collection of Roman legal writings. As he often does when confronted with a definition that has achieved canonical status among theologians or canon lawyers, Thomas seeks to show how it is compatible with other approaches to the same topic (one sees Thomas doing this, for example, with the Augustinian definition of "virtue" and the definition of "faith" drawn from Heb. 11:1; see 1–2.55.4, above; 2–2.2 note 2). Here Thomas is looking at Ulpian's definition of "justice" in light of both Aristotle and a Christian tradition of reflection on justice stemming most immediately from Anselm, but finding its roots in St. Paul, that focuses on the notion of *rectitudo* or "uprightness." See 1–2.55 note 8, as well as note 13, below.

3. The main thrust of the objection is that Ulpian's definition disagrees with Aristotle's, particularly by defining the virtue of justice not as a *habitus* but as a power (i.e., the will) or an act (i.e., the act of willing). Furthermore, if "willingness" is taken to mean the power of will, it seems inadequate, since the mere capacity to act justly could hardly be considered the virtue of justice.

4. The objection notes that unless the quality of "uprightness" is added to "willingness," it is left unclear that justice involves a will that has been rightly ordered by the disposition to act justly.

3. Only God's will is perpetual. So if justice is "perpetual willingness," then justice would be in God alone.

4. Everything perpetual is stable, since it is unchangeable. It is therefore superfluous in defining justice to say that it is both "perpetual" and "stable."

5. It pertains to a ruler to render what is right to each person. If justice gives each one what is his or her right, then it follows that it is found only in rulers, which seems unsuitable.

6. Augustine says in the book *On the Morals of the Catholic Church* (15) that "justice is love serving God alone." It therefore does not render to each person what is due.[5]

I answer:[6] The definition given above of justice is fitting if it is rightly understood. For since every virtue is a settled disposition that is the source of a good act, a virtue must be defined by means of the good act concerning the subject matter belonging to that virtue.[7] But the subject matter belonging to justice consists of what involves another, as shall be shown later (2–2.58.2).[8] Therefore the act of justice in relation to its own subject matter and object is touched on in the words "to give to each person what is right [*ius*]," since, as Isidore says in his *Etymologies* (10.1.124), "One is said to be just who keeps the laws [*ius*]."[9]

Now in order for an act concerning any subject matter whatsoever to be virtuous, it is required both that it be voluntary and that it be stable and firm, for the Philosopher says in the *Ethics* (2.4, 1105ᵃ) that for an act to be virtuous it needs first of all to be done knowingly, second to be done by choice and

---

5. "Alone" is taken here as implying that justice is concerned only with our relationship with God and not "each person" as the definition says.

6. Note the absence of a *sed contra* paragraph; it is as if the authoritative definition given at the outset of the article serves as the *sed contra*.

7. A virtue is defined both by its subject matter and its act. For example, the subject matter of prudence is human action (2–2.47.5), and its act is the rational discerning of the mean between opposed vices (2–2.47.7), and so Thomas defines prudence as "right reason applied to action" (2–2.47.2).

8. Thomas argues that justice, strictly speaking, directs our actions in relation to others and not to ourselves. This is because it is concerned with a certain kind of equality, which is necessarily a relationship between things that are distinct (the connection between justice and equality is reflected in our language even today when we speak of the margins of a text being "justified" when the lines of text are all of equal length). Thus I cannot act justly or unjustly toward myself, but only toward another; those who commit suicide are guilty not of injustice against themselves, but against the political community, which is thereby deprived of citizens (see his *Commentary on the Nicomachean Ethics* 5.17.1094). Thomas does acknowledge that we sometimes speak loosely or metaphorically of justice with regard to ourselves; for example, we might say it is an act of justice when our reason gives our bodies what is due to them, such as deciding on an adequate amount of food or sleep.

9. The Latin term *ius* has a wide range of meanings: it can mean "law" (as in the quotation from Isidore of Seville) or "what is right in relation to others" or even "jurisprudence," in the sense of the philosophy of law. With regard to the definition under scrutiny here, Thomas notes that it properly identifies both the subject matter (our relationship to others) and the act (doing what is right [*ius*]).

with regard to an appropriate end, and third to be done firmly. The first of these is included in the second, since that which is done through ignorance is involuntary, as it says in the *Ethics* (3.1, 1111ᵃ). For this reason, the definition of justice proposes first the "will," to show that an act of justice ought to be voluntary. "Stable" and "perpetual" are then added in order to indicate the firmness of the act.[10]

Therefore the definition given above is a complete definition of justice, except that the act is mentioned instead of the lasting disposition that is specified by that act, since a disposition is spoken of in terms of the act.[11] If one wanted to put it in the proper form of a definition, it could be said that justice is a lasting disposition by which someone by a constant and perpetual will gives to each person what is right for that person [*iustitia est habitus secundum quem aliquis constanti et perpetua voluntate ius suum unicuique tribuit*]. This is more or less the same definition as proposed by the Philosopher in the *Ethics* (5.5, 1134ᵃ), saying that "justice is a lasting disposition by which someone is said to operate in accordance with the choice of a just person."[12]

Reply to 1: "Will" here names the act, not the power. It is, however, customary among authorities to define dispositions by their acts; thus Augustine says in his sermons on John (tractate 40) that "'faith' is having faith in what is not seen."

Reply to 2: Justice is the same as uprightness not in its essence but rather in its causality, for it is a disposition that makes one operate and will in an upright way.[13]

Reply to 3: The will can be spoken of as perpetual in two ways. In one way, on the part of the will's act, which lasts forever. In this sense only God's will is perpetual. In another way, on the part of the subject—that is, because one

---

10. Justice, like any virtue, involves actions that are done consciously (thus the presence of "willingness" in the definition) and done with a kind of accomplished ease (thus the presence of "stable and perpetual" in the definition). In the same way that someone who knows enough French to order off the menu in a French restaurant does not yet have the disposition of French-speaking, so too someone who only occasionally wants to act justly does not yet possess the virtue of justice.

11. That is to say, justice is a *habitus* or disposition, but the definition given by Ulpian names the act flowing from this disposition (the willingness to give each person his or her due) and not the disposition itself. This forms the basis of Thomas's response to the first objection.

12. One can almost hear Thomas breathe a sigh of relief once he gets Ulpian's definition aligned with Aristotle's.

13. "Uprightness" is not identical to "justice" because an action can be an upright action without being a just one. For example, I might pay my workers a living wage in order to enhance my reputation for generosity, not because it is what I owe them. While my action, considered in itself, would be "upright," I would not thereby be just, because I was not willing the right end in my actions. As Anselm says in *On Truth* 12, "Every will has a what and a why" (*omnis voluntas sicut uult aliquid, ita uult propter aliquid*), and we must consider both in seeking to define justice. Justice can be called uprightness because it causes us to will in a correct manner, not because all doers of upright acts are just.

wills to do something always. This is required by the very idea of justice. For it does not fulfill the meaning of "justice" that one wishes to preserve justice for a period of time in some particular transaction, since one could hardly find someone willing to act unjustly in *every* case. Rather it is required that a person should have the will to preserve justice always and in all cases.[14]

Reply to 4: Since "perpetual" is not taken to imply the perpetual duration of the act of the will, it is not superfluous to add "stable," so that just as "perpetual will" is said in order to indicate that someone has the purpose of observing justice always, saying "stable" indicates firm perseverance in this intention.

Reply to 5: A judge renders to each one what belongs to him or her by way of command and direction, because a judge is the "living embodiment of justice" [*iustum animatum*][15] and the ruler is "the guardian of justice," as it says in the *Ethics* (5.4, 1132ᵃ; 5.6, 1134ᵇ). But those subject to them render what belongs to each person by way of execution.[16]

Reply to 6: Just as love of God includes love of neighbor, as said above (2–2.25.1), so too a person's service of God includes rendering to each person what is owed.

14. The distinction here is between (1) actively willing for a period of infinite duration to act justly, which only God can do, and (2) willing to always act justly. Even though I am not at every moment engaged in willing to be faithful to my spouse, since sometimes I am not thinking about my spouse at all and so cannot be willing to be faithful to her, this does not prevent me from willing to always be faithful to her. It is in this second sense that the definition speaks of justice involving a "perpetual willingness."

15. Literally, "the soul of justice."

16. In the background of Thomas's reply is his awareness of the different ways in which we speak of justice. Thus, for instance, we speak of "distributive justice" in connection with what share individuals have in the common good, and it is the role of judges and rulers to determine this share and ensure that such sharing takes place, not in their capacity as individuals but precisely as embodiments of the community. In connection with the obligations of individuals to the common good we speak of "legal justice," and in connection with the obligations that individuals have to one another we speak of "commutative justice." Thus justice is a virtue reserved for judges and princes if we are speaking of distributive justice, but not if we are speaking of justice in a legal or commutative sense.

Question 64:

Homicide

2–2.64.7[1]
Is it licit to kill someone in self-defense?

It would seem that nobody may licitly kill someone in self-defense.[2]

1. Augustine says to Publicola (*Epistle 47*, 5), "As to killing others in order to defend one's own life, I do not approve of this unless one is a soldier or holds a public office, so that one does it not for oneself but for others, having legitimately accepted power, provided it is in keeping with one's role [*personae*]." But one who kills someone in self-defense kills in order not to be killed. This would therefore seem to be illicit.[3]

2. In [Augustine's] *On Free Choice of the Will* (1.5) it says, "How are those who are stained with human blood for the sake of these things that ought to be held of little worth free from sin before divine providence?" Now among the things he says should be held to be of little worth are those things that people can forfeit unwillingly, as appears from the context.[4] The chief of

---

1. On this article, see Foot (2002); Boyle (1978).

2. Thomas describes this question as being concerned with *homicidio*, which literally means the "killing of a human being." After an article discussing the legitimacy of *any* killing—including the killing of plants and animals—Thomas considers various circumstances in which human life might be taken and the legitimacy of such taking. For Thomas "homicide" is a morally neutral description of the taking of human life, and not necessarily a crime; therefore the context in which life is taken (e.g., *whose* life is taken or *by whom* life is taken) plays a role in determining the licitness of that taking.

Here Thomas looks at the taking of life in the particular circumstance of self-defense. As becomes clear, even within this specific circumstance the intention of the doer of the action plays an important role in determining the nature of the act.

3. This objection distinguishes between killing to defend oneself, which Augustine considers illegitimate, and killing to defend the common good, which is legitimate. Soldiers or public officials, in killing to defend themselves, are in fact defending the common good, since they have a public role as defenders of the community. See note 15, below.

4. Augustine defines "lust" (*libido*) as the love of goods that can be gained or lost through fortune and that therefore cannot be the ultimate good. He writes, "Evil people desire to live without fear, just

these, however, is the life of the body. Therefore it is illicit for anyone to take the life of another for the sake of one's own bodily life.[5]

3. Pope Nicolas says in the *Decretals* (1.50.6: *De his clericus*), "Concerning the clerics—namely, those who have killed a pagan in self-defense—about whom you have asked, as to whether through penance they may afterward return to their former state or rise to a higher one, know that in no case do we allow or grant any license for them to kill any person under any circumstances."[6] But clerics and laity are similarly bound to observe moral laws. Therefore it is illicit for the laity as well to kill anyone in self-defense.[7]

4. Murder is a more grievous sin than simple fornication or adultery. But no one may licitly commit simple fornication or adultery, or any other mortal sin, in order to save one's own life, since the life of the spirit is to be preferred to that of the body. So it is not licit for anyone, in defending oneself, to take the life of another in order to save one's own life.[8]

5. If the tree is evil, so too the fruit, as it says in Matthew (7:17). But self-defense itself seems to be illicit according to Romans (12:19): "Not defending yourselves, beloved." Therefore what comes from it—the killing of a person—is also illicit.[9]

On the contrary: It is written in Exodus (22:2), "If a thief is found breaking into a house or digging under it and is wounded so as to die, the killer will not be guilty of blood." But it is much more licit to defend one's life than one's house. Therefore neither is someone guilty of murder in killing another in defense of one's own life.

I answer: Nothing prohibits one act from having two effects, of which only one is within the [agent's] intention, while the other is outside of the [agent's]

---

as good people do. But the difference is as follows: good people pursue this by turning their love away from things that cannot be possessed without the risk of losing them; evil people, on the other hand, try to remove hindrances so that they may securely attach themselves to these things to be enjoyed" (*On Free Choice of the Will* 1.4).

5. Augustine's argument runs as follows: (1) it is sinful to kill for a trivial reason; (2) among the trivial reasons for killing are any trivial goods (i.e., transitory things that can be gained or lost through fortune); (3) the chief trivial good is bodily life itself; therefore (4) it is sinful to kill to preserve one's own bodily life.

6. From a letter sent by Nicholas I to Bishop Osbald of Regensburg in 867.

7. In an earlier article of this question (a. 4), Thomas discussed the prohibition on clerics shedding blood, even in self-defense. He gives two reasons for this prohibition: (1) clerics are ordained to minister in the liturgy of the Eucharist, which is a representation of the self-sacrificial death of Christ, who made no defense of himself, and (2) clerics minister the New Law of Christ, which, in contrast to the Old Law of Moses, prescribes no penalty of death. The objection argues that the moral law is the same for all people, no matter their state in life, and therefore what is forbidden to clerics should be forbidden to laypersons as well.

8. If a lesser sin, such as fornication, is forbidden under the circumstance of saving one's life, then a greater sin, such as homicide, would even more be forbidden under the same circumstance.

9. This objection raises the stakes in arguing not only that is it forbidden to *kill* in self-defense but that, according to Scripture, *any* form of self-defense is forbidden.

intention [*praeter intentionem*]. But moral acts are of a particular kind based on what is intended and not according to what is outside the intention, since this is incidental, as is clear from what is said above (1–2.72.1; 2–2.43.3).[10]

From the act of defending oneself, therefore, two effects may follow: one is the saving of one's own life, but the other is the killing of the aggressor. Because one's intention is the preservation of one's own life, an action of this sort does not have the nature of something illicit since it is natural to everything to preserve itself in existence to the extent that it can.[11]

Nevertheless, an act proceeding from a good intention may be rendered illicit if it is out of proportion to the end. Therefore if someone uses more violence in defending one's own life than is required, it will be illicit.[12] But

10. Here we see sketched what later comes to be called the "principle of double effect." Having earlier argued that the moral "species" of an act (i.e., its goodness or badness) relates directly to the intention of the one doing the act and only incidentally to the nature of the act itself, Thomas here notes that a single act might have multiple effects, but it is only the intended effect that determines the goodness or badness of the act; other effects do not figure into the moral evaluation of the act because they are "outside" the intention.

To use an example suggested by the philosopher Philippa Foot that became famous in the twentieth century as "the trolley problem," if a trolley car were hurtling out of control toward a group of five people tied to the track, would it be acceptable for me to divert it onto another track where it would hit only a single person? According to the principle of double effect, it would. The act of diverting the trolley onto the other track is a single action with two effects: one intended (saving the five) and one unintended (killing the one). The effect of killing the one person is undoubtedly a bad thing, but it is morally acceptable for me to divert the trolley because that death is not the intended effect; it is, as it were, a "side-effect." One important point that this example makes clear is that "unintended" does not mean "unforeseen." In the proposed scenario, I see that there is a person on the track, but I still choose to divert the trolley with the intention of saving the five. The killing of the one person is not "accidental" in the sense of being a result of unforeseen chance, but is "incidental" in the sense of not being what is sought by my action.

Double effect reasoning should be distinguished from means-end reasoning. The permissibility of killing one person to save the five is not a case of the means of killing being justified by the positive end of securing a greater good for a greater number. Thomas is resolute in maintaining that we can never intend an objective evil as the means to a good end. What needs to be noted, in the case of the trolley problem, is that the means by which the saving of the five is accomplished is not the death of the one person; it is the diversion of the trolley onto the other track. I would divert the trolley whether or not it involved the death of the one person. If the death of the one *were* in fact the means—say I diverted the trolley by throwing a very large person in front of it—then my action would not be morally acceptable.

11. Thomas here gives a fairly direct application of double effect reasoning to the question of killing in self-defense. An act of incapacitating an attacker can have two effects: saving one's life and killing the aggressor. The former is the intended effect, not the latter. Because the intended effect is not only permissible but laudable, since it is natural for something to want to continue existing, the unintended effect is allowable.

12. Thomas introduces a further consideration into double effect reasoning: the act must not be disproportionate to the good end sought. So, for example, if I sought to divert the trolley by detonating a thermonuclear device and killing hundreds of thousands of people, this would not be an acceptable means of saving the five people, even if I were to claim that the death of those thousands was outside of my intention. Indeed, the detonation of a thermonuclear device to divert a trolley might itself speak to the nature of my intention. "Intention" is not, as some have supposed, a purely interior act—like flexing a mental muscle—by which one gives moral meaning to one's actions. Intentionality is manifest *in the action*

if one repels force with moderation, it will be a legitimate defense, because according to the law, "it is permitted to repel force by force within the limits of a restrained defense."[13] Nor is it necessary for one's salvation that a person forgo an act of moderate self-defense in order to avoid killing another, since one is bound to provide more for one's own life than for another's.[14]

But because killing a person is prohibited except by the public authority acting for the common good, as stated above (2–2.64.3), it is not licit for a person to intend killing someone in self-defense, except for those that have public authority.[15] These, while intending to kill a person in self-defense, refer this to the public good, as seen in the case of a soldier fighting against an enemy and in the case of one who administers justice fighting against criminals. Even these sin, however, if they are moved by disordered private desires [*privata libidine*].[16]

---

and in the description given to the action, such that certain intention descriptions are simply implausible when attached to certain actions (e.g., detonating a thermonuclear device to divert a trolley). Thus the considerations of intention and of proportionality are not entirely unrelated to each other.

13. Thomas is drawing on a decision made by Pope Innocent III in 1210, which subsequently entered canon law, regarding a priest who struck a thief who was stealing church goods (*Letter 12*, 59). But the notion of a "moderate" or "restrained" defense stretches back at least to the late third century, where it appears in a ruling made by the Roman emperors Diocletian and Maximian.

14. In 2–2.25.12 Thomas, drawing on Augustine, identifies four objects of love: God, ourselves as both soul and body, and our neighbor. In question 2–2.26 he sketches a schema of how these objects of love should be properly prioritized: we should love God above all other things, since God is the source of all goodness; then we should love our own souls; then we should love our neighbor, with whom we hope to enjoy eternal happiness; finally, we should love our own bodies. By giving priority to love of one's own soul over love of neighbor, Thomas rejects any sort of strictly altruistic standard for love. As he sees it, we cannot help but love ourselves more than others. At the same time, because we love our neighbor more than our own body, we must, when acting as private citizens, only have recourse to a "moderate" self-defense.

15. It might seem at first glance that Thomas is retracting everything that he has just said. But his point is that while one commits no sin in killing someone in the process of defending oneself, one cannot intend to defend oneself *by* killing the aggressor. One might foresee that a certain use of force will result in the aggressor's death, but that death must be incidental with regard to one's intention. One might judge whether or not this is the case by asking if one would be willing to use a nonlethal force if this were possible. One might also look at the degree of force applied, asking whether it is proportionate to the end of self-defense or exceeds the demands of that end in such a way as to become lethal.

Of course, such reasoning is not likely to take place in the moment one is repelling an attack. It might be helpful if one has time to plan how one might repel an aggressor, but would not be much use in responding to a sudden attack. Remember that Thomas's discussion in the *Summa* has as its purpose helping Dominican friars in hearing confessions and discerning the penitent's degree of moral culpability. One can see how the principle of double effect might be useful in this retrospective task.

16. The principle that in self-defense one cannot intend, even if one foresees, the death of the attacker does not apply, according to Thomas, in the case of public officials who are protecting the common good. When a judge passes a death sentence, the intention is to protect society precisely *by* the killing of the criminal (just as one might divert a trolley by throwing a very large person in front of it). Thomas therefore understands Jesus's teaching on nonretaliation to speak only to the case of defending oneself and not to the case of defending society. Thomas goes on to note that the rendering of such judgments and

Reply to 1 and 2: The quotation from Augustine should be understood in reference to the case when one intends to kill a person in order to save oneself from death.

The quotation from *On Free Choice of the Will* should be understood in the same sense. This is why he says explicitly, "for the sake of these things," by which he indicates the intention. This makes clear the response to the second objection.[17]

Reply to 3: [In the case of clerics,] irregularity[18] results from the act of killing a person, even if it is not a sin, as is clear in the case of a judge who justly condemns someone to death.[19] For this reason a cleric, even if he kills someone in self-defense, is irregular, though he intends not to kill, but only to defend himself.

Reply to 4: The act of fornication or adultery is not directed to the preservation of one's own life by necessity, as is the act that sometimes results in the taking of a person's life.[20]

Reply to 5: Here the defense forbidden is that which comes from vengeful spite. For this reason a gloss on this passage says: "Not defending yourselves—that is, not thirsting to strike your enemy."[21]

---

the carrying out of such sentences must be completely dispassionate—one cannot be settling personal scores or indulging a personal bloodlust.

17. The objections are correct, Thomas says, but only with regard to what is directly intended.

18. When Thomas speaks here of the "irregularity" of clerics killing in self-defense, he is saying that the wrongness of the action is not the killing per se, but the violation of the cleric's particular *regula* or rule of life, which forbids killing for the reasons outlined above (note 7). So even killing that is in itself nonsinful involves, in the case of clerics, a sinful violation of the cleric's *regula*.

19. Thomas seems to mention the case of a judge here to say that even in cases where directly intending someone's death is not sinful, clerics are prohibited from doing so. Thus it is the secular powers, rather than the church, that have the task of executing heretics (see 2–2.11 note 6).

20. The relevant difference between killing and fornication is that the latter is, in Thomas's estimation, never a life-saving measure.

21. This explanation is found in Peter Lombard's *Magna Glossatura* (Great gloss). What is being forbidden is not killing itself but killing out of bloodlust. On "glosses" see 1.12 note 10.

Question 77:

Cheating That Is Committed in Buying and Selling

2–2.77.1[1]
Is it licit to sell something for more than it is worth?

It would seem that someone can licitly sell a thing for more than it is worth.[2]

1. Justice in the transactions of human life is determined by civil laws. But according to these it is licit for a buyer and a seller to deceive each other, which happens inasmuch as the seller sells a thing for more than it is worth, and the buyer buys a thing for less than it is worth.[3] Therefore it is licit for someone to sell a thing for more than it is worth.

2. That which is common to all would seem to be natural and not sinful. But as Augustine reports in *De Trinitate* (13.3), the saying of a certain comedic actor was accepted by all, "You wish to buy low and sell high," which simply echoes what is said in Proverbs (20:14): "Every buyer says, 'Bad, bad,' and

---

1. On this article, see Baldwin (1959); Franks (2009, 84–104); Koehn and Wilbratte (2012).

2. Thomas's thinking on economic matters draws from a rich array of sources, including Aristotle, the Bible, the church fathers, more recent theologians of the twelfth and thirteenth centuries, Roman law and its medieval interpreters, and canon (i.e., church) law. Modern discussions of Thomas's view on "just price" tend to divide between those who see it as focused on the cost of labor in producing the thing to be sold and those who see it focused on the current market price. Particularly if one takes Thomas's commentary on Aristotle's *Nicomachean Ethics* into account, both factors seem to be of concern to Thomas.

3. The objection may have in mind the statement of Pomponius (ca. AD 130) quoted by Ulpian that "it is naturally permitted to parties to circumvent each other in the price of buying or selling" (Justinian, *Digest* 4.4.16.4 [my trans.]). See also the Code of Justinian 4.44 (*De rescindenda venditione*), 8, 15. As Thomas will clarify in his response, Roman law provided for a legal remedy when there was a dramatic difference between the selling price and the true value of what was sold, but not for lesser differences. The force of the argument here seems to be that secular law allows for buyers and sellers to deceive one another up to a point, which undermines the principle that the price must be according to strict justice.

then goes away and boasts." It is therefore licit to sell something for more and buy it for less than it is worth.[4]

3. It does not seem illicit if something that ought to be done because of the demands of integrity [*ex debito honestatis*] is done instead by contractual obligation [*ex conventione*]. But according to the Philosopher (*Nicomachean Ethics* 8.13, 1163ª), in a friendship based on usefulness, compensation [for a favor] ought to be done based on how useful it was to the receiver, which sometimes exceeds the value of the thing given, as happens when someone is in great need of something, either to avoid danger or to derive some benefit. It is therefore licit in contracts of buying and selling to provide something for a higher price than it is worth.[5]

On the contrary: It is said in Matthew (7:12), "Whatever you wish people would do to you, you should also do to them." But no one wants to buy a thing for more than its worth. Therefore no one should sell a thing to another for more than its worth.[6]

I answer: To employ fraud so that something is sold for more than a just price is altogether sinful, inasmuch as one deceives one's neighbor in an injurious way. Therefore Cicero says in *De officiis* (3.15), "Contracts should be entirely free from dishonesty: the seller will not engage a bidder [to run prices up] nor the buyer someone to bid low against himself [to keep them down]."[7]

If, however, fraud is absent, we can then speak of buying and selling in two ways. In one way, we can speak of them in terms of themselves, and from this point of view buying and selling are seen to be established for the common advantage of both parties, one of whom needs what belongs to the other, and vice versa, as the Philosopher makes clear in the *Politics* (1.3, 1257ª). But that which is established for common advantage should not be more of a burden

4. The logic of the objection is that if something is widespread then it is natural, and if it is natural then it is not sinful. Both Augustine and Scripture are invoked in support of the widespread nature of the desire to buy low and sell high.

5. The argument of this objection is somewhat obscure. It begins by establishing an analogy between how one acts in a friendship and how one acts in a contractual relationship. It then notes that in friendships rooted in usefulness (on the various sorts of friendship in Aristotle, see 2–2.23 note 5), an exchange of gifts or favors is based on the usefulness to the receiver, which might be at variance with the actual value of the favor or gift from the perspective of the giver. If I give to someone an old piece of clothing that I no longer want but that they want very much because of their retro fashion sense, then their desire to repay me in some way for that gift should be judged in terms of the value of the piece of clothing to them, not to me. Therefore, the argument seems to go, in contracts of buying or selling we don't need to observe strict equity either.

6. The *sed contra* makes a simple application of the Golden Rule.

7. Out-and-out fraud, Thomas notes, is clearly forbidden. What he seems to envision, drawing on Cicero, is a case where a seller hires someone to bid against other buyers in order to drive up the price, or a buyer somehow arranges for others to make artificially low offers. It is not entirely clear how the latter sort of fraud would work.

to one party than to another. Therefore all contracts should be established between them according to the equality of the things involved.[8] The value [*quantitas*][9] of a thing that comes into human use, however, is measured by the price given for it, which is the reason money was invented, as it says in the *Nicomachean Ethics* (5.5, 1133ᵃ).[10] Therefore the equality of justice is taken away if either the price exceeds the amount of the thing's value or, conversely, the [value of the] thing exceeds the price. Consequently, to sell a thing for more than it is worth or to buy it for less than it is worth is in itself unjust and illicit.[11]

8. For Thomas, commerce in itself—in which one exchanges what one has for what one needs—is directed to the common good and therefore ought to be of equal benefit to both parties, such that neither of them suffers loss in the transaction. The question is how one determines such equality of benefit. It clearly can't be done on a purely numerical basis—since, to take the example of a cobbler and a builder, an exchange of one shoe for one house hardly seems fair. There needs, rather, to be a proportional exchange, which requires some way to determine the relative value of the goods exchanged: How many shoes equals how many houses? This is done not according to the nature of the goods exchanged (Thomas notes that we value a pearl more highly than a mouse even though, in itself, the nature of a mouse is greater than that of a pearl, since it is a living being) but according to human need for those goods: in order for the shoes to have any value for the builder, he must have some need for shoes; the more need he has of them the greater their value (see *Commentary on the Nicomachean Ethics* 5.9.981). Thomas also suggests that the more needful something is for human existence in general, the greater its value—thus we must exchange a large number of shoes (which humans can live without) in order to obtain a single bushel of wheat (which is necessary to sustain human life).

Though Thomas does not mention it explicitly, both Roman and canon law and other theologians at times appealed to the current price that goods fetch (i.e., their market value) as an indicator of their value as determined by need. In a letter addressing certain specific cases of potentially corrupt economic practice, Thomas mentions in passing how one ought not to charge more for something than its price in the market (*secundum communem forum*) (see *On Buying and Selling* 2). Some have suggested that Thomas's tacit acceptance of the identification of "just price" with "market price" anticipates the economic theories of Adam Smith.

In his commentary on Aristotle's *Nicomachean Ethics*, Thomas also discusses, in addition to need, a second basis for value: the labor and expense involved in production (see *Commentary on the Nicomachean Ethics* 5.9.980, 983). For example, if a farmer were to accept a bushel of wheat in exchange for a single pair of shoes, there would be, Thomas says, a "surplus of labor" (*superabundantiam laboris*) in the farmer's wheat, since more work went into producing the wheat than into producing the shoes. Some have suggested that in this Thomas anticipates the economic theories of Karl Marx.

9. I am presuming that by *quantitas* Thomas means the amount of the thing's value.

10. Money is instituted as a medium for measuring need and easing the process of exchange (for example, in those cases where the cobbler has no need for a house but can use the money with which the builder buys shoes to buy something that he actually *does* need). See Aquinas, *Commentary on the Nicomachean Ethics* 5.9.989.

11. So the "just price" of a thing would be the monetary amount that properly measures the value of the good offered for sale in terms of (1) the need that the buyer has and (2) the labor and expense that went into its production. To my knowledge, Thomas offers no formula for how one integrates these two factors, and it is not clear that such a formula is possible. Determining the just price of something offered for sale involves a number of contingent and highly particular factors—and therefore, in Thomas's reckoning, is a matter not of speculative reasoning but of practical wisdom. Thomas likely agreed with most of his contemporaries that disputes over the just price of something were to be settled by appeal to the

The other way we can speak of buying and selling is with regard to their incidentally resulting in the advantage of one party and the disadvantage of the other—for instance, when someone has great need of a certain thing and someone else will be annoyed by being without it. In such a case a just price will be one that takes into consideration not only the thing being sold but also the loss that the seller incurs from the sale. And thus it can be licit to sell something for more than it is worth in itself, though it cannot be sold for more than it is worth to the owner.[12]

Yet if one derives a great advantage from obtaining the other's property, and if the seller incurs no loss through not having that thing, then the latter ought not to raise the price, because the advantage accruing to the buyer comes not from the seller but from the circumstances of the buyer. No one should sell another what is not his, though one can charge for a loss that is suffered.[13] Still, one who is greatly delighted by the thing he has bought may voluntarily pay the seller something extra, and this pertains to the buyer's moral integrity.

Reply to 1: As stated above (1–2.96.2), human law is given to people, among whom there are many deficient in virtue; it is not given only to the virtuous. For that reason human law was unable to forbid everything contrary to virtue, but it suffices that it prohibit whatever is destructive of human life together, while it treats other matters as if they were licit not because it approves of them but because it does not punish them.[14] In this way, the law treats as licit, in the sense of providing no punishment, cases where, without employing deceit, a seller sells his goods for more than their worth or a buyer buys them for less than their worth—unless the excess is too great, since then even human law

---

judgment of a good man (*arbitrium bonus vir*). In other words, the just price was the price determined by a just person—one who by the virtue of justice could weigh the various incommensurable factors to arrive at a price that would give both buyer and seller their due.

12. At least part of what Thomas is getting at here is the legitimacy of a seller charging more for a product than he or she paid for it, even though the product has not undergone any change. The marketing of the product—its transportation or preservation—has not brought about any change in the item itself, yet it has cost the seller time and labor and therefore increased its value, and so the vendor can charge more for it. See 2-2.77.4 ad 2.

13. A seller ought not to charge a higher price for something simply because it will greatly benefit a particular buyer, because what would seem to justify the price hike—the potential benefit to the buyer—is something that does not, as it were, "belong" to the seller but to the buyer. For example, if I, an illiterate seller, know that selling you, a budding young scholar, a copy of the *Summa theologiae* will allow you to go on to a lucrative career as a theologian, I ought not to jack up the asking price beyond the just price simply for that reason. However, as Thomas goes on to note, the buyer might voluntarily pay a premium, but is not required to by justice.

14. Thomas here is restating his view that human law cannot forbid everything that is evil, but he focuses primarily on those evils that subvert human societies. From the perspective of human law, a thing is "licit" not because it is morally acceptable but because it is not punished, because such punishment might cause more harm than good to the peace of human societies.

requires that restitution be made (for instance, if someone is deceived about the amount of the just price of a thing by more than half).[15]

But divine law leaves nothing unpunished that is contrary to virtue. Therefore, according to divine law it is reckoned illicit if, in buying and selling, the equality of justice is not observed. One who has received more must make compensation to one that has suffered loss, if the loss be considerable.[16] I add this last point because sometimes the just price of things is not precisely determined, but consists more in a kind of estimate, so that a slight addition or subtraction does not seem to take away the equality of justice.[17]

Reply to 2: As Augustine says in the passage referred to, "This comedic actor, either by looking into himself or by his experience of others, thought that all are inclined to wish to buy low and sell high. But since in reality this is a defect, everyone can acquire that justice by which one can resist and overcome this inclination." He then gives the example of someone who gave the just price for a book to one who on account of ignorance asked a low price for it. Hence it is clear that this common desire is not from nature but from vice, and therefore it is common to many who walk along the broad road of vice.[18]

Reply to 3: In commutative justice, the equality of things is the primary consideration. But in useful friendships, the equality of usefulness is considered, so that recompense should be made according to the usefulness gained, whereas in buying it should be according to the equality of things.[19]

---

15. This is the principle, derived from Roman law, of what medieval jurists would call *laesio enormis* (abnormal harm), which states that if a father sells land for less than half its worth, then his son has the right to buy it back for the selling price or, if the buyer wishes to keep the land, to receive the difference between the selling price and the just price (see the Code of Justinian 4.44 [*De rescindenda venditione*], 2, 8). In the Middle Ages this principle was extended to cover items bought for more than half again their just price. Thomas's point here is that human law seeks not to enforce strict justice in buying and selling, but only to prevent abnormal harm.

16. Things that human law leaves unpunished might very well still be contrary to divine law and therefore need to be confessed, and penance done for them. At least in this context, Thomas is concerned less with economic theory and more with penitential practice leading to growth in virtue.

17. Thomas again notes the ambiguity entailed in determining the just price. Slight variations in price among different sellers is not in itself an indication of injustice.

18. Thomas rejects the implication that something is in accord with nature (and therefore virtuous) just because it is widespread. Indeed, he alludes to Jesus's contrast between the wide and narrow gates (Matt. 7:13) to suggest that vice is actually quite common and that the excuse "that's just human nature" is no excuse at all.

19. Just as the objection is somewhat obscure, so too is Thomas's response. Whereas the objection trades on the analogy of exchanges between friends and commercial exchanges, Thomas underscores the *disanalogy* between the two. Thomas's point seems to be that exchanges between friends have directly in view the usefulness of what is given, whereas commercial exchanges are focused on the price being a proper measure of the need, labor, and expense that gives the goods their value.

Question 123:

Fortitude

2–2.123.3[1]
Is fortitude about fear and daring?

It seems that fortitude is not about fear and daring.[2]

1. Gregory says in his *Moral Reflections on the Book of Job* (7.21.24): "The fortitude of the just is to conquer the flesh, to oppose its delights, and to extinguish the pleasures of the present life." Therefore fortitude seems to be more about pleasures than about fear and daring.[3]

2. Cicero says in his *Rhetoric* (*De inventione* 2.163) that it pertains to fortitude to take on dangers and to endure toil. But this does not seem to pertain to the emotions of fear and daring, but more to a person's strenuous actions or external dangers. Therefore fortitude is not about fear and daring.

3. Fear is opposed not only to daring but also to hope, as stated above (1–2.45.1 ad 2) in discussing the emotions. Therefore fortitude should not be about daring any more than about hope.[4]

---

1. On this article, see Houser (2002).

2. Medieval Latin speakers generally translated Aristotle's term *andreia*—literally, "manliness"—by the word *fortitudo*. One might in turn translate *fortitudo* as either "strength" or "courage" depending on context. Objections 1 and 3, in particular, seem to turn on this ambiguity, so I have translated *fortitudo* in this article by the somewhat archaic word "fortitude" in order to preserve the ambiguity. In the notes, however, I often use the term "courage."

As noted above, Thomas generally follows Aristotle in seeing virtues as observing the "mean" or midpoint between opposed vices (see 1–2.55 note 2). Here he is seeking to determine the vices between which the virtue of courage is poised, arguing (again, following Aristotle) that they are fear (*timor*) and daring (*audacia*). Thomas discusses these as emotions earlier in the *Summa* (1–2.41–45).

3. In the passage quoted, Gregory brings up courage in the context of ascetic discipline, suggesting that the strength denoted by *fortitudo* is principally concerned with regulating concupiscence.

4. It is good to bear in mind that this objection is talking not about the theological virtue of hope but about hope as an emotion (see 2–2.17 note 7).

In a sense, this objection and the one preceding it reveal the somewhat messy tradition of talking about the virtues that Thomas has inherited, which draws on Greeks like Aristotle and Romans like Cicero as

On the contrary: The Philosopher says in the *Ethics* (2.7, 1107ᵇ; 3.9, 1115ᵃ) that fortitude is about fear and daring.

I answer: As stated above (2–2.123.1), it pertains to the virtue of fortitude to remove any obstacle that holds the will back from following reason. But someone being held back from doing something difficult is part of the meaning of fear, which connotes shrinking from an evil that entails difficulty, as stated above (1–2.42.5) in discussing the emotions. Thus fortitude is principally about fear of difficult things, which can hold the will back from following reason.[5] But it befits fortitude not only to steadfastly endure the blows of these difficulties by curbing fear but also to be moderate in attacking them—when, that is, one must eliminate them altogether so as to have security in the future, which seems to pertain to the idea of daring.[6] Therefore fortitude is about fear and daring—curbing fear and moderating daring.

Reply to 1: Gregory is speaking here of the fortitude of the just, as it is had commonly by all the virtues. Thus he puts forth first things pertaining to temperance, as in the words quoted [in the objection], and then adds what pertains properly to fortitude seen as a special virtue, saying: "To love the rough places of this life for the sake of an eternal reward."[7]

Reply to 2: Dangerous situations and strenuous toil only hold the will back from following reason to the extent that they are feared. Therefore it is proper that fortitude be immediately about fear and daring, but indirectly about dangers and toils as being the objects of those emotions.[8]

---

well as on Christian Scripture. All of these talk about fortitude, but not all in the same way or according to the same overall conception of virtue.

5. Though courage is a mean between fear and daring, it is primarily related to fear, since fear implies a lagging behind or shrinking from pursuit of the good, and this underscores the idea of virtue as overcoming what holds us back from excellence.

6. Thomas is making a couple of different points in this sentence. One is that courage involves both endurance and action: the ability both to hold steadfast in the face of danger and to act so as to overcome the cause of the danger. The other is that what allows us to act to overcome a source of danger—daring—is something that needs to be moderated as much as fear does, so that we do not act in a reckless way that unnecessarily increases the threat posed to us.

7. Gregory is talking not about fortitude as a specific virtue, but as a general quality of steadfastness that is found in all the virtues due to their quality as *habitus* or stable dispositions (see 1-2.55 note 2). Thomas notes that if one reads a bit further in Gregory, it becomes clear that he first applies this general quality of steadfastness to temperance and then to courage.

8. The immediate object of courage is the regulation of our inner states of fear and daring, and it is by regulating these that it is related to external threats and difficult situations. This fits with Thomas's general view that virtues are not simply about *acting* well but about *being* good; one might endure a particular difficult situation without necessarily possessing the virtue of courage. People might act in ways that seem to us bravely heedless of danger if they are unaware of the danger, or if they have faced similar danger before and escaped and so are hopeful that this will happen again, or if they are so skilled in fighting that what seems dangerous to us does not seem dangerous to them. In none of these cases is the virtue of courage required. Likewise, someone who, in a fit of rage, attacks a large group of opponents does not

Reply to 3: Hope and fear are opposites in terms of their objects, for hope is about good and fear is about evil. Daring, however, is about the same object [as fear] and is the opposite of fear in terms of the one advancing and the other shrinking back, as stated above (1–2.45.1).[9] And since fortitude properly considers those worldly evils that hold one back from virtue, as is clear from Cicero's definition, fortitude is thus properly about fear and daring and not about hope, except inasmuch as hope is connected with daring, as stated above (1–2.45.2).[10]

---

need the virtue of courage, but only the emotion of anger. Emotions are passing things, while virtues are settled dispositions, so someone who acts bravely on account of anger in one situation (if, say, their child is being menaced) would not necessarily act bravely in a different situation (if, say, a stranger is being menaced), whereas someone with the virtue of courage acts bravely in *all* situations. See 2–2.123.1 ad 2.

9. The emotion of hope and the virtue of courage are both opposed to fear, but in different ways: hope in terms of its object (it is drawn by a potential good, whereas fear is repelled by a potential evil) and courage in terms of how it reacts to a potential evil (moving toward it rather than shrinking from it).

10. Since courage is about overcoming evils, it is directed primarily at regulating fear and daring, which are our responses to danger, and is related to the emotion of hope only indirectly, inasmuch as hope might increase daring.

Question 124:

Martyrdom

2–2.124.2[1]
Is martyrdom an act of fortitude?

It seems that martyrdom is not an act of fortitude.[2]

1. In Greek, "martyr" means "witness." Now witness is rendered to faith in Christ; according to Acts (1:8), "You will be witnesses to me in Jerusalem," and so forth. And Maximus [of Turin] says in a sermon, "The mother of martyrs is the catholic faith, which those glorious athletes have signed with their blood" (*Sermon 88*). Therefore martyrdom is more an act of faith than of fortitude.[3]

---

1. On this article, see Clark (2010).

2. While here Thomas addresses the question of what sort of virtue is involved in martyrdom, the article immediately preceding this one addresses whether martyrdom is a matter of virtue at all. The objections in that article focus on issues of the role of the will in virtue and whether courting death is lawful, but what is perhaps the more fundamental difficulty is left implicit by Thomas: the Aristotelian approach to ethics, focused as it is on happiness and human flourishing, seems irreconcilable with the martyr's willing embrace of suffering and death. Aristotle famously says in the *Nicomachean Ethics* (7.13, 1153[b]), "Those who say that, if a man be good, he will be happy even when on the rack, or when fallen into the direst misfortune, are intentionally or unintentionally talking nonsense." This reflects Aristotle's general position that one needs certain material conditions to be met in order for one to attain happiness and that certain of those conditions—being healthy, not being physically unattractive, being male, not being enslaved—might be beyond one's control. The Christian view of happiness, with the Beatitudes of Jesus (Matt. 5:3–12) as their *magna carta*, seems comprehensively at odds with Aristotle's view, proclaiming happy those who mourn and are meek and, above all, those who are persecuted for righteousness's sake. Indeed, Thomas cites Jesus's words "Blessed are they that suffer persecution for justice's sake" in the *sed contra* of this article.

From an Aristotelian perspective, the Christian exaltation of martyrdom as a way in which people are conformed to Christ would seem to be, as the Philosopher says, nonsense. For Thomas, however, it is only in conformity to Christ that supernatural happiness is found. It may be on the question of martyrdom that Thomas's differences from Aristotle appear most clearly. Yet while his view of human flourishing differs radically from Aristotle's (a difference that, it is true, he tends to underplay), Thomas still employs the conceptual tools of Aristotle's metaphysics and ethics to engage in reasoned reflection on the Christian quest for happiness.

3. Drawing on the root meaning of the word "martyr," this objection argues that at the heart of martyrdom is the act of bearing witness to Jesus, which springs not from courage but from faith.

2. A praiseworthy act belongs primarily to the virtue that inclines one to it, is manifested by it, and without which it avails nothing. But charity above all inclines one to martyrdom. Thus Maximus says in a sermon, "The charity of Christ is victorious in his martyrs" (*Sermon 16*). Also, the greatest charity is manifested in the act of martyrdom; according to John (15:13), "no one has any greater love than this: to lay down one's life [*animam*] for ones friends." Also, without charity martyrdom is worthless; according to 1 Corinthians (13:3), "If I should hand over my body to be burned, and do not have charity, it gains me nothing." Therefore martyrdom is more an act of charity than of fortitude.[4]

3. Augustine says in a certain sermon on St. Cyprian: "It is easy to honor a martyr by celebration, but it is a great thing to imitate his faith and patience" (*Sermon 311*). But in any act of virtue praise is rendered principally for the virtue of which it is the act. Therefore martyrdom is more an act of patience than of fortitude.[5]

On the contrary: Cyprian says in his letter *To the Martyrs and Confessors* (*Epistle 8*), "O blessed martyrs, with what praise shall I acclaim you? Warrior most brave, by what proclamation shall I announce your bodily strength?" Now one is praised for the virtue whose act one performs. Therefore martyrdom is an act of fortitude.[6]

I answer: As is clear from what is stated above, it pertains to fortitude to strengthen a person in the good of virtue against perils (2–2.123.3, above), and chiefly against the perils of death (2–2.123.4), and most of all against those that occur in battle (2–2.123.5).[7] It is evident that in martyrdom one

---

4. The objection marshals various authorities to argue that the virtue most associated with martyrdom in Scripture and tradition is not courage but charity. Charity motivates martyrdom, is manifest in martyrdom, and makes martyrdom meritorious.

5. Apparently in Aquinas's day (as in ours) it was more common to hear someone praised for having "the patience of a martyr" than "the courage of a martyr," perhaps because "courage" implies a more active stance than does "patience."

6. The *sed contra* sets up the comparison of martyrdom and combat, which will be Thomas's principal reason for connecting martyrdom with fortitude.

7. Thomas argues in 2–2.123.4 that if fortitude strengthens us to do the good of reason in the face of physical peril, it is defined by its capacity to do so in the face of the greatest physical peril, which is the peril of death. Death is the greatest physical peril because if we are not alive then we cannot share in any bodily goods whatsoever. But fortitude is more specifically about physical peril on the battlefield, since, Thomas argues, it is on the battlefield that one faces peril for the sake of the common good. In contrast, Thomas claims, "the dangers of death arising out of sickness, storms at sea, attacks from robbers, and other such things do not seem to come upon someone through pursuing some good" (2–2.123.5). It seems that here Thomas is simply being influenced by the long Greek and Roman association of *aretē/ virtus* in general and *andreia/fortitudo* in particular with the excellence of the warrior. It is difficult to see how someone who faces a dangerous sea crossing in order to secure food for a city facing famine is not facing peril for the sake of the common good. It is also difficult to see how martyrdom, at least as it is

is firmly strengthened in the good of virtue, not deserting faith and justice despite the imminent danger of death, an imminence due to a certain kind of unique combat with one's persecutors.[8] Cyprian says in a discourse (*Epistle 8*): "The throng of bystanders watched in wonderment this heavenly combat, and Christ's servants standing while in peril with voice unfettered, mind uncorrupted, and strength divine." Therefore it is evident that martyrdom is an act of fortitude. For this reason, the church says of martyrs that they "were made strong in battle" (Heb. 11:34).[9]

Reply to 1: Two things must be considered in the act of fortitude. One is the good in which the brave person is strengthened, and this is the goal of fortitude. The other is the strength itself, by which one does not fall to the opponents that hinder one from achieving that good, and the essence of fortitude consists in this. Just as civic fortitude strengthens a person's soul in human justice, so that in order to preserve it one would face the danger of death, so too the fortitude that comes from grace strengthens one's soul in the good of God's justice, which is "through faith in Christ Jesus," as it says in Romans (3:22). So martyrdom is linked to faith as the goal for which one is strengthened, but to fortitude as the disposition from which it comes forth.[10]

understood within Christianity, can be seen as a form of courage as long as a tight association with the Greek notion of *andreia* is maintained.

8. One of the ways in which Thomas goes about loosening the association between courage and the battlefield is by the distinction he makes in 2–2.123.5 between "general warfare" (*bello communi*) and "singular combat" (*particularis impugnatio*). The former is what we would normally think of as battle, while the latter would include, for example, "a judge or even private individual [who] does not refrain from giving a just judgment because of fear of an impending sword or any other danger, even if it threatens death." Thomas further loosens the association by going on to note in the same article that someone who possesses the virtue of courage, and therefore does not abandon the good in either general warfare or singular combat, would also not abandon the good when faced with other sorts of threats to life: "for example, someone not failing to care for a sick friend on account of fear of deadly infection, or not refusing to undertake a journey for some pious purpose on account of fear of shipwreck or robbers." At this point Thomas has considerably widened the scope of acts of fortitude.

Martyrdom finds a place among the acts of fortitude as a kind of "singular combat," because it, like war, involves clinging to the good in the face of opponents who seek one's life precisely because of one's adherence to the good. In this way it is more clearly an act of fortitude than undertaking a dangerous voyage or tending to a sick friend, since storms and infections do not threaten one *because of* one's adherence to the good; rather one's adherence to the good simply provides the occasion for facing such dangers.

9. Citing Cyprian and the Letter to the Hebrews, Thomas invokes both Scripture and tradition to show that martyrdom has been understood as a kind of warfare, and thus unambiguously an exercise of the virtue of fortitude.

10. Thomas sets up an analogy between "civic fortitude"—by which he seems to mean the acquired virtue of fortitude—and fortitude as an infused moral virtue. The former causes one to risk one's life for the sake of political justice, and the latter causes one to risk one's life for the sake of the justification that comes through faith. Witnessing to faith in Christ is the end or goal of martyrdom, but fortitude is the virtue from which the martyr's action springs, so both virtues are involved in the martyr's act.

Reply to 2: Certainly charity inclines one to the act of martyrdom as its primary and principal motive, since it is the virtue commanding it, but fortitude does so as being martyrdom's specific motive, being the virtue from which it comes forth. Thus martyrdom is the act of charity as commanding, and of fortitude as that from which it comes forth.[11] And thus it is that it manifests both virtues. But it is due to charity that it is meritorious, as is the case with any act of virtue.[12] For this reason it is worthless without charity.

Reply to 3: As stated above (2–2.123.6), martyrdom pertains to endurance, which is the most basic act of fortitude, and not to aggression, which is its secondary act. And since patience comes to the aid of fortitude with regard to its chief act, which is endurance, martyrs are also praised for their patience.[13]

11. On the distinction between "commanded" and "elicited" acts, see 1–2.1 note 11. The act of dying for the Christian faith is commanded by (i.e., done because of) the virtue of charity, but it is elicited by (i.e., flows from) the virtue of fortitude.

12. Thomas consistently holds that virtues have no merit for salvation apart from charity. See 1–2.65.2, above.

13. By identifying endurance, rather than aggression, as the principle act of fortitude (see 2–2.123.6), Thomas decisively shifts the exemplar of courage from the "manly" warrior on the battlefield to the physically passive martyr, who actively wills to witness to faith, hope, and charity.

Question 141:

Moderation

2–2.141.4[1]
Is moderation only about desires and delights of the sense of touch?

It would seem that moderation [*temperantia*] is not only about desires and delights of the sense of touch.[2]

    1. Augustine says in his *On the Morals of the Catholic Church* (19.35) that "the job of moderation is to restrain and settle the desires that make us covet the things that draw us away from the laws of God and the fruit of his goodness." A little further on (19.36) he adds that "it is the duty of moderation to disdain all bodily enticements and popular acclaim." But it is not only by coveting pleasures of the sense of touch that we are withdrawn from God's laws, but also by desire for pleasures of the other senses, which also pertain to bodily enticements, and likewise by lust for riches or for worldly glory.[3] Therefore it is said in 1 Timothy (6:10), "Greed [*cupiditas*] is the root of all

---

1. On this article, see Cates (2002); Elders (2018).

2. I translate Thomas's term *temperantia* (the medieval Latin rendering of the Greek *sōphrosynē*) as "moderation" in part because modern English speakers might associate "temperance" with the Temperance Movement of the nineteenth and early twentieth centuries, which sought to promote abstention from alcohol. While Thomas considered drunkenness a vice and a failure of *temperantia* (see 2–2.150), he did not generally seek to promote abstention as a solution. Because for Thomas *temperantia* is not about eschewing pleasurable things, but about making right use of them, "moderation" is a better translation.

    Thomas associates moderation, among all the other virtues, with beauty (2–2.141.2 ad 3). This is because, for Thomas, "proportion" (along with "clarity" or brightness) is a key criterion for something being beautiful (see 1.5.4 ad 1; 2–2.145.2). He likewise notes that moderation preserves human beings from ugliness (*turpitudo*) resulting from overindulgence of their animal nature. We might say that moderation does not seek to make human beings into bodiless angels (Thomas considers *insensibilitas*—a total rejection of bodily enjoyment—to be a vice; see 2–2.142.1), but rather strikes the fitting "balance" between rationality and animality in human beings, a balance that brings out the full beauty of our humanity.

3. It would seem that not just touch but *all* the senses need moderation, as does the will's attraction to material things.

evils." So moderation is not only about desires for the pleasures of the sense of touch.

2. The Philosopher says in the *Ethics* (4.3, 1123ᵇ) that "one who is worthy of small things and judges himself worthy of them is moderate, but he is not magnanimous."⁴ But honors, whether small or great, of which he is speaking there, are enjoyable not according to touch but according to the soul's perception.⁵ Therefore moderation is not only about desires for the pleasures of the sense of touch.

3. Things that are in the same genus would appear for that same reason to belong to the matter of a particular virtue. But all the pleasures of the senses appear to be in the same genus. Therefore, for the same reason, they all belong to the matter of moderation.⁶

4. Spiritual pleasures are greater than bodily ones, as noted above (1–2.31.5) in discussing the emotions.⁷ But sometimes people forsake the law of God and the state of virtue because of a desire for spiritual pleasures, as in the case of curiosity in matters of knowledge. This is why the devil promised knowledge to the first human, saying in Genesis (3:5), "You will be like gods, knowing good and evil." Moderation, therefore, is not only about pleasures of the sense of touch.⁸

5. If pleasures of the sense of touch were the proper matter of moderation, it would follow that moderation is about all pleasures of touch. But it is not about all—for example, those that occur in games. Therefore pleasures of the sense of touch are not the proper matter of moderation.⁹

4. For Aristotle, "magnanimity" (in Greek, *megalopsychia*—literally, being "great-souled") identifies one who is worthy of the great honor he receives and knows that he is worthy of it. He writes that this "seems to be a sort of crown of the virtues; for it makes them greater, and it is not found without them" (*Nicomachean Ethics* 4.3, 1124ᵃ). Aristotle's specific point here is that those who receive a small measure of honor and know themselves worthy of small honors cannot be called magnanimous, because the term implies greatness, and so such persons are called "temperate" because of the appropriate fit of their worthiness and the honor they receive.

5. The objection notes Aristotle's use of "temperate" to refer to the enjoyment of being held in esteem by others rather than one's enjoyment of bodily pleasures.

6. The "matter" of a virtue can be understood as the human capacity that is brought under the rule of reason by that virtue. The objection argues that since the various senses are simply different kinds within the same genus, they all constitute the same matter (since different kinds relate to their genus in the way that forms relate to matter; see Aquinas, *On Being and Essence* 6) and are therefore perfected by the same virtue. For this reason, the sense of touch should not be singled out as the subject of this virtue.

7. By "spiritual pleasures" Thomas does not mean pleasures associated with what modern people would call "spirituality," but simply those that result from the activity of the mind rather than of the body.

8. Another way to put the objection is that what tempted Adam and Eve was not the sensual pleasure of the apple, but the desire for God-like knowledge—a spiritual good, not a material one.

9. While a golfer feels a certain pleasure when the club solidly connects with the ball, it would seem strange to say that this pleasure needs to be moderated so as to be subjected to reason.

On the contrary: The Philosopher says in the *Ethics* (3.10, 1118ª) that "the domain of moderation concerns the desires and delights of the sense of touch."

I answer: As stated above (2–2.141.3), moderation is about desires and pleasures in the way that fortitude is about fear and daring. Fortitude is about fear and daring regarding the greatest evils, by which nature itself is extinguished—dangers associated with death.[10] Similarly, moderation must be about desires for the greatest pleasures. Since pleasure results from an activity that is in accord with nature, it is consequently more powerful to the extent that it results from a more natural activity. What is most natural to animals are those activities that preserve the nature of the individual through food and drink and that preserve the nature of the species by the joining of male and female. Therefore moderation is specifically concerned with the pleasures of food and drink and with sexual pleasures.[11] But these pleasures result from the sense of touch, so it follows that moderation is about pleasures of touch.[12]

Reply to 1: Here Augustine seems to understand moderation not as a special virtue having a particular matter but as pertaining to reason's moderation in any matter whatsoever, which is a general condition of virtue.[13] But we can also say that if one is able to curb the greatest pleasures, even more can one curb minor pleasures. It therefore pertains principally and properly to moderation to govern the desires and pleasures of the sense of touch, and secondarily other pleasures.[14]

Reply to 2: The Philosopher here takes the word "moderation" to refer to the moderation of external things—that is to say, when someone tends to

10. See 2–2.124 note 7.

11. As Aquinas sees it, moderation is needed in the most physically pleasurable activities and those that are most necessary for sustaining human nature, whether in an individual or in the species. These activities are eating and drinking, by which the individual is sustained, and procreation, by which the species is sustained.

12. While it may be plausible that sexual pleasure is primarily a matter of the sense of touch, it seems less plausible in the case of eating and drinking, since the flavor and aroma of food and drink seem to play a more significant role in our desiring them than does the tactile sensation of eating and drinking. But Thomas is thinking not about the aesthetics of food and drink as much as about their role in sustaining life. We might say that he is thinking about food and drink in terms of the filled belly and slaked thirst, something that we desire on a more basic, animal level than we do a tasty meal.

13. Augustine, Thomas says, is using the term *temperantia* in a general way to speak of how virtue seeks the midpoint between two vices, not as the name of the virtue he is discussing.

14. Thomas offers a second explanation for Augustine's words: if we develop the capacity to moderate our strongest desires—those associated with touch—then we will be able to moderate the weaker desires associated with smell, taste, etc. In this way we can say that moderation applies, either directly or indirectly, to all the senses.

what is proportionate to him or her—but not as referring to moderation in the soul's affections, which pertains to the virtue of moderation.[15]

Reply to 3: The pleasures of the other senses [apart from touch] are possessed differently in humans and in other animals. In other animals pleasures are not caused by the other senses except in relation to things sensed through touch, in the way that a lion is pleased to see a deer, or to hear its voice, in relation to his food. A human being, however, is delighted by the other senses not only for this reason but also on account of the fittingness of the thing sensed.[16] So moderation is about the pleasures of the other senses, inasmuch as they are referred to the pleasures of touch not principally but consequently. Insofar as the things sensed by the other senses are delightful because of their fittingness, as with a person being pleased at a well-harmonized sound, this pleasure does not pertain to the preservation of nature.[17] Therefore these kinds of feelings do not have such preeminence that moderation can be said of them antonomastically.[18]

Reply to 4: Spiritual pleasures by their nature are greater than bodily pleasures, but they are not so perceptible to the senses. Consequently they do not so powerfully affect the appetite, against whose impulse the good of reason is preserved by moral virtue.[19] Or it may be said that spiritual pleasures, strictly speaking, are in accord with reason; therefore they are not curbed except

15. The objection misreads Aristotle's point. The modest person of modest acclaim is "moderate" not on account of the degree of pleasure taken in his acclaim, but simply because the degree of acclaim is in proportion to his degree of achievement.

16. A lion feels pleasure at the sight of a deer not because of the beauty and grace of the deer's movement or because of its impressive array of antlers, but merely because the sight is a precursor to the satisfying sensation of deer meat sliding down its gullet. Human beings can take pleasure in the sight of a deer in the way that a lion does (perhaps hunters feel this kind of joy at spotting a deer), but they can also take pleasure in the beauty of a deer in a way that is unrelated to the deer as a source of food.

17. When sight or sound or smell might prompt us to seek immoderate pleasure in food or sex, we need the virtue of moderation to subordinate that desire to reason. So, for example, moderation is involved in the smell of food, but not of flowers; it is involved in the sight of a beautiful human body, but not a beautiful landscape. Our enjoyment of the odor of flowers and the sight of landscapes is so distant from the desire for self-preservation that they rarely if ever break free from the rule of reason.

18. This refers to a figure of speech in which the term for a general class of things is used as the name for a particular thing that is preeminent in that class (see 2–2.141.2)—something Thomas does repeatedly in referring to Aristotle as "the Philosopher." Here Thomas is acknowledging that the senses are all members of the same genus, but because only touch is associated with the preservation of human nature, it, and not the other sensations, is preeminent, and only the virtue that regulates it can antonomastically be called "moderation."

19. Just as the existence of God might be self-evident in itself but not evident to us (see 1.2.1, above), so too the pleasures of the mind might be in themselves greater than the pleasures of the body, but this is something we might easily miss because of the way in which bodily pleasures overwhelm our senses and cloud our minds.

incidentally—for example, in cases where one spiritual pleasure holds back another that is more important and more binding.[20]

Reply to 5: Not all pleasures of the sense of touch pertain to the preservation of nature. Consequently it is not necessary that moderation concern all pleasures of touch.[21]

20. Pleasures of the mind are by their nature reasonable and so only need to be moderated when a lesser spiritual pleasure conflicts with a greater one (if, say, I let my reading of Aristotle get in the way of my reading of sacred Scripture).

21. In this response, Thomas simply reiterates his main point: the virtue of moderation is not, as the objection claims, about *all* pleasures of touch, but specifically about the pleasures of touch associated with the preservation of human nature: i.e., the pleasures of food and sex. It never occurs to Thomas that someone might find a game—golf, say—to be as pleasurable as food or sex.

Question 153:

Lust

2–2.153.2[1]
Is there no sexual act that is without sin?

It would seem that no sexual act can be without sin.[2]

1. Nothing would seem to impede virtue except sin. But every sexual act greatly impedes virtue, for Augustine says in his *Soliloquies* (1.10.17), "I consider that nothing so casts down the male mind from its height as the charms of a woman and those bodily contacts."[3] Therefore it seems that no sexual act is without sin.

2. Wherever there is an excess that makes one retreat from the good of reason, this is vicious, because virtue is corrupted by excess and deficiency, as is said in the *Ethics* (2.2, 1104ᵃ). But in every sexual act there is excess of pleasure, which absorbs the mind to such a degree that, as the Philosopher says in his *Ethics* (7.11, 1152ᵇ), "it is incompatible with the act of understanding."[4] Also, as Jerome states, during that act the hearts of the prophets were ren-

---

1. On this article, see Nolan (1992); Cates (2002).

2. Christianity in general and medieval Christianity in particular have a reputation for being anti-sex. But it was in fact Christian theologians, both in antiquity and in the Middle Ages, who were the most vociferous defenders of the goodness of marriage and sex against various religious and philosophical systems that saw anything involving the body as inherently sinful. Augustine defended the "goods of marriage" against both Manichaean dualist and overly enthusiastic Christian advocates of celibacy, such as Jerome. Thomas, likewise, defends the goodness of sexual acts within marriage against dualist Cathars, a concern he makes explicit in his *Sentences* commentary: "It is impossible to say that the act by which children are procreated is universally illicit . . . unless it were argued, according to the insanity of certain people, that bodily things were caused by an evil God" (bk. 4, dist. 26, q. 1, a. 3). While neither Augustine nor Thomas would be considered "sex-positive" by the standards of Western society today, their views were not as unrelievedly negative as is sometimes claimed.

3. Since virtue is a disposition to act in accord with reason, and since one cannot reason during the sexual act, then sex makes virtue impossible and so must be vicious.

4. This essentially repeats the first objection, but uses Aristotle rather than Augustine as an authority and invokes the notion of virtue as the midpoint between opposed excesses.

dered insensible to the spirit of prophecy.[5] No sexual act, therefore, can be without sin.

3. A cause is more powerful than its effect. But original sin in children is transmitted by concupiscence, without which the sexual act is impossible, as Augustine declares in the book *On Marriage and Concupiscence* (1.24).[6] Therefore no sexual act can be without sin.

On the contrary: Augustine says in *On the Good of Marriage* (25.33), "This is a sufficient answer to heretics . . . if only they will grasp that there is no sin in what is against neither nature . . . nor custom . . . nor a commandment." And he refers to the sexual acts that the ancient patriarchs enjoyed with their several wives. Therefore not every sexual act is a sin.

I answer: In human acts, sin is that which is against the order of reason. But the order of reason consists in the fitting ordering of everything to its end. Therefore it is not a sin if a person makes reasonable use of certain things, in a fitting manner and order, for the end to which they are adapted, provided that this end be something truly good.[7] But just as it is truly good that the bodily nature of one individual be preserved, so too it is a most excellent good that the nature of the human species be preserved. And just as the use of food is aimed at preserving the life in the individual, so too the use of sexual acts is aimed at preserving the human race as a whole.[8] Thus Augustine says in *On the Good of Marriage* (16.18): "What food is to the well-being of a person, such is sexual intercourse to the well-being of the race." Therefore just as the use of food can be without sin if done in an appropriate manner and order, so that it agrees with the well-being of the body, so also the use of sexual acts can be without sin if done in an appropriate manner and order, as fitting with the end of the procreation of humans.[9]

---

5. Not only does the sexual act impede the acquisition of virtue in accord with natural reason; it also impedes the workings of the Holy Spirit within prophets. The text Thomas refers to is actually not from Jerome but from Origen, *Homilies on Numbers* 6.3.7. One might note that Origen makes clear in this text that sexual acts within marriage are not sins, even though they impede the prophetic spirit.

6. Augustine writes in the place cited, "Whenever it comes to the actual process of generation, the very sexual intercourse that is lawful and honorable cannot be effected without the ardor of lust, in order to accomplish what pertains to the use of reason and not of lust. . . . From this concupiscence whatever comes into being by natural birth is bound by original sin" (my trans.). In other words, as the objection understands the matter, sexual intercourse, which is caused by concupiscence and is the cause of sin's transmission, must itself be sinful.

7. For Thomas's general account of what makes a human act good or bad, see 1–2.18, above.

8. See 2–2.141 note 11, above.

9. Thomas argues for the goodness of sexual acts based on their role in reproducing the species. He sees sexual acts that are not by their nature susceptible to human reproduction—such as acts between two men or two women or certain acts between a man and a woman—as illicit, though he does allow for sexual acts to have ancillary purposes apart from reproduction. His thinking here is shaped by Augustine's reflections on three "goods" of marriage: procreation; faithfulness (which for Thomas includes

Reply to 1: Something can be said to impede virtue in two ways. In one way, as regards the common state of virtue, and in this sense nothing impedes virtue except sin. In another way, as regards the state of perfect virtue, and in this sense virtue can be impeded by something that is not a sin, but simply less good. In this way sex with a woman causes the soul to fall not from virtue but from the height—that is, from the perfection of virtue. Thus Augustine says in *On the Good of Marriage* (8), "Just as what Martha did when occupied with serving the holy ones was good, but what Mary did in hearing the word of God was better, so too we praise the good of Susanna's marital chastity, but we prefer the good of the widow Anna, and even more that of the Virgin Mary."[10]

Reply to 2: As stated above (2–2.152.2 ad 2; 1–2.64.2), the midpoint of virtue is discerned not according to quantity but according to how it fits with right reason. Therefore an abundance of pleasure in a sexual act that is directed according to reason is not opposed to virtue's midpoint. Further, the quantity of external sensation enjoyed, which depends on the disposition of the body, does not pertain to virtue; rather what matters is how much the interior appetite is affected by that enjoyment.[11] From the fact that the free act of reason in considering spiritual things cannot be had simultaneously with this pleasure, it does not follow that the act in question is contrary to virtue. For it is not contrary to virtue if the act of reason is sometimes interrupted by something that is reasonable to do; otherwise it would be contrary to virtue

---

the "marriage debt," which is the obligation of spouses to be sexually available to each other, so that their partner is not tempted by sin); and the bond of marriage itself, which signifies the love of Christ for his church. In his early commentary on Lombard's *Sentences*, Thomas argues that sexual acts within marriage are entirely free from sin if they are engaged in for the purpose of fulfilling either or both of the first two goods of marriage: procreation and payment of the marriage debt. He does not think sexual acts are licit if engaged in solely for the purpose of signifying Christ's bond to the church, since this is signified by the relationship of marriage in its entirety and not simply by sexual acts (to argue otherwise might seem to risk turning Christianity into some sort of fertility cult). Apart from procreation and payment of the marriage debt, Thomas holds that sexual intercourse, even within marriage, "is always a sin, at least venially" (see *Commentary on the Sentences* bk. 4, dist. 31, q. 2, a. 2; on venial sin, see 1–2.71 note 13, above). While Thomas sees sexual intercourse between spouses as a source of intimacy—"the act of fleshly copulation . . . produces a kind of sweet communion [*suavem societatem*] even among wild animals" (*Summa contra Gentiles* 3.123)—he does not, at least in his early work, seem to have seen this intimacy as in itself sufficient to make a sexual act licit.

10. Like Augustine, and unlike Jerome, Thomas sees sexual acts within marriage not as the lesser of two evils (with fornication being the greater evil) but as the lesser of two goods (with celibate chastity being the greater good), not unlike the way in which the active life is a lesser good by comparison with the contemplative life (see 2–2.182.1, below).

11. Thomas notes earlier in the *Summa* that the human body prior to the fall was actually *more* susceptible to sexual pleasure because of the greater sensitivity of the body (1.98.2 ad 3). The pleasure of intercourse, however, would not have diverted unfallen humans from love of God, because in the state of original justice the senses were perfectly subject to reason.

for a person to go to sleep.[12] That concupiscence and sexual pleasure are not subject to the command and moderation of reason comes from the punishment of the first sin,[13] inasmuch as reason, rebelling against God, deserved to have its body rebel against it, as is clear from Augustine (*City of God* 13.13).

Reply to 3: As Augustine says in the same place (*On Marriage and Concupiscence* 1.24), "From the concupiscence of the flesh, as it were the daughter of sin, which is not imputed as sin to the regenerate, a child is born bound to original sin." Therefore it does not follow that this act is a sin, but that in this act there is some sort of penalty resulting from the first sin.[14]

12. While an act is good if it is in accord with reason, that act itself does not have to involve the exercise of reason. So, for example, even though sleeping involves the suspension of our capacity to reason, it is still in accordance with reason to get sufficient sleep, since reason tells us that human flourishing requires adequate periods of rest. So the reasonableness (and therefore moral goodness) of an action is determined not by the act itself but rather by how the act fits into the overall intention of human flourishing.

13. That is, the loss of original justice.

14. Sexual intercourse is not itself a sin, but any disordered pleasure that we experience during it is an effect of original sin in us.

Question 182:

The Active Life Compared to the Contemplative Life

2-2.182.1[1]

Is the active or the contemplative life superior or more worthy?

It would seem that the active life is superior to the contemplative.[2]

1. The Philosopher says that it seems that what is best is that which belongs to those who are better (*Topics* 3.1, 116[a–b]). But the active life belongs to those of higher rank—namely, prelates,[3] who are established in a position of honor

---

1. On this article, see Bonino (2002); Jordan (2016, 152–62); Van Nieuwenhove (2017).

2. This article falls within the final section of Thomas's vast *Secunda Pars*. Having considered principles of action and virtues and vices that pertain to all human beings, Thomas offers a brief discussion of particular spiritual gifts, forms of life, and roles within the church. Among these particular ways of living a Christian life, two forms of life stand out as fundamental: the active life and the contemplative life. As is apparent in the present article, Thomas is stepping into a long-running discussion that also has relevance in his own day, not least because of controversy over the new mendicant religious orders, which seemed to blur the distinction between these two forms of life. This issue comes up again in Thomas's discussion of Jesus's manner of living (see 3.40.1, below).

Thomas weaves together traditional Christian discussions of action and contemplation with Aristotelian reflections on the relative value of the "theoretical" and the "practical" (see 2–2.179.2). As mentioned earlier (see 1–2.5 note 8), Thomas is somewhat flexible in his use of "contemplative life"—using it sometimes in connection with a divinely given knowledge associated with prayer and other times as a broad term encompassing what we might call "the intellectual life." Likewise, the term "active life" could mean either ascetic practice, which might serve as a prelude to contemplative life, or the life of active charity directed toward one's neighbors. What might seem at first a certain lack of precision in using these terms is in fact a result of a comprehensive vision, in which our natural desire to know is intrinsically related to our desire for the vision of God (see 1–2.3.8, above), and our capacity to act justly and charitably toward others is inseparable from our inner life being rightly ordered through acquired and infused virtue.

3. The Latin *praelatus* refers to those holding high church office, typically bishops or those who had analogous roles, such as the abbots of monasteries. In his discussion of different "states of life" (i.e., one's *status* or permanent role in the church), Thomas asks which is most "perfect." After noting that Christian perfection in general involves perfection through charity (2–2.184.1), he goes on to argue that this sort of perfection is different from the perfection of one's "state," which involves not one's

and power, which is why Augustine says in *The City of God* (19.19) that "in our actions we must not love honor or power in this life." It would seem then that the active life is superior to the contemplative.

2. In all dispositions and actions, it pertains to what is superior to give guidance, in the way that the art of war, being superior, guides the making of bridles.[4] But it pertains to the active life to order and guide the contemplative, as is clear from the words addressed to Moses in Exodus (19:21): "Go down and charge the people, lest they should have a mind to pass the limits that have been fixed, so as to see the Lord."[5] Therefore the active life is superior to the contemplative.

3. No one ought to be taken away from a greater thing in order to be occupied with lesser things, for the Apostle says in 1 Corinthians (12:31), "Be zealous for the better gifts." But some are taken away from the state of the contemplative life to be occupied with the active life, as we see in those who are transferred to the state of prelate.[6] It would seem, therefore, that the active life is superior to the contemplative.

On the contrary: Our Lord said in Luke (10:42), "Mary has chosen the best part, which shall not be taken away from her." Through Mary, however, the contemplative life is signified. Therefore the contemplative life is superior to the active.[7]

---

subjective holiness but the role to which one is bound by a solemn vow (2–2.184.4). Men and women who make vows of poverty, chastity, and obedience are therefore in a state of perfection, even though they might be less perfect in charity than a layperson. Thomas also argues that prelates such as bishops are in the highest state of perfection, because they are not simply seeking perfection for themselves, as those who take religious vows do, but are engaged in bringing others to a state of perfection through their pastoral and sacramental ministries (2–2.184.7). This, we might note, makes their role inherently more "active" than that of those who simply take vows of perfection; thus the objection's argument that the active life is superior.

4. Thomas appears to be alluding to *Nicomachean Ethics* 1.1, 1094ᵃ. His point is simply that a general who is skilled in the art of war gets to tell horse riders how to ride into battle, and riders skilled in the art of riding get to tell bridle-makers the sort of bridles they need in order to ride well, so that military skill determines bridle-making skill.

5. How this biblical verse supports the objection's claim is a bit obscure. It seems that Thomas may be drawing upon a notion, found in Origen, that Moses represents the active life, whereas his brother Aaron represents the contemplative life. Thus it is the active life that sets the limit beyond which human beings may not pass in their contemplative quest.

6. The objection is envisioning a situation in which a monk, living a contemplative life, becomes a bishop—a not uncommon occurrence in the Middle Ages, when such luminaries as Gregory the Great, Gregory VII, and Anselm of Canterbury were all drawn from the ranks of the monasteries.

7. The tradition of Martha, who is "busy about many things," representing the active life and Mary, who sits at the feet of Jesus, representing the contemplative life is an ancient one, perhaps originating with Origen of Alexandria (see fragment 171 on Luke 10:38 in his *Homilies on the Gospel of Luke*). The same interpretation is found in John Cassian's *Conferences* (1.8) and Gregory the Great's *Moral Reflections on the Book of Job* (6.18). Augustine offers a variation on this theme, seeing Martha as the present church

I answer: Nothing prevents something from being more excellent in itself while being surpassed by another in some respect. Therefore we must reply that the contemplative life is, speaking absolutely, better than the active. The Philosopher, in his *Ethics* (10.7, 1177ᵃ–1178ᵃ) proves this by eight arguments.[8]

The first is because the contemplative life is fitting to human beings according to what is best in them (i.e., according to the intellect) and concerning its proper objects (i.e., knowable things [*intelligibilium*]) while the active life is occupied with external things.[9] Thus, as Gregory says in his *Moral Reflections on the Book of Job* (6.37), [the name of] Rachel, by whom the contemplative life is signified, is interpreted as "the vision of the principle," but the active life is signified by Leah, who was "bleary-eyed."[10]

Second, because the contemplative life can be more continuous, though not as regards the highest degree of contemplation, as stated above (2–2.180.8 ad 2; 2–2.181.4 ad 3).[11] For this reason Mary, by whom the contemplative life is signified, is described as constantly "sitting at the Lord's feet."

Third, because the pleasure of the contemplative life is greater than that of the active. As Augustine says in the book *On the Words of the Lord* (*Sermon 103*, 2), "Martha was troubled, but Mary feasted."[12]

---

militant on its pilgrimage through history and Mary as the future church triumphant in its heavenly rest (see *Questions on the Gospels* 2.20).

8. The body of the article weaves together Aristotelian and Christian elements, taking Aristotle's discussion of the contemplative life from the *Nicomachean Ethics* and reinterpreting it along Christian lines. We might ask ourselves whether Aristotle would have been able to recognize his own views once Thomas is done reinterpreting them.

9. Contemplation is superior not only because it engages the highest human faculty (the capacity to know) but also because it concerns the highest sorts of things (those that are knowable). For Aristotle, humans grasping material substances in a nonmaterial way—i.e., intellectually—raises them to a higher order of existence. He writes in the *Nicomachean Ethics*, "This [contemplative] activity is the best . . . since not only is intellect the best thing in us, but the objects of the intellect are the best knowable objects" (10.7, 1177ᵃ).

10. Though less common than Martha and Mary, Leah and Rachel, the two wives of Jacob (see Gen. 29), also appear in the Christian tradition as types of the active and contemplative lives, perhaps most famously in canto 7 of Dante's *Purgatorio*. The suggestion—based on the etymology of Rachel's name—that the contemplative life involves a "vision of the principle" gives a more theological spin to Aristotle: the proper object of contemplation is not merely intelligible truths but God as First Truth (see 2–2.180.1 ad 2).

11. Aristotle's point seems to be that physical activity is subject to interruption, if for no other reason than sheer physical fatigue, while thinking is less subject to such interruption. In his earlier discussion of this aspect of contemplation (2–2.180.8), Thomas notes that the highest form of contemplation, in which the intellect grasps God nondiscursively (see note 15, below), can be had only momentarily in this life. As Augustine describes it in *Confessions*, "So in the flash of a trembling glance [my intelligence] attained to that which is. At that moment I saw your invisible nature understood through the things which are made. But I did not possess the strength to keep my vision fixed. My weakness reasserted itself, and I returned to my customary condition. I carried with me only a loving memory and a desire for that of which I had the aroma but which I had not yet the capacity to eat" (7.17.23).

12. Thomas, along with Aristotle, sees pleasure (*delectatio*) as following upon the fulfillment of desire. He clarifies that the superlative pleasures of the contemplative life, which Aristotle says are notable for "their

Fourth, because in the contemplative life one is more self-sufficient, since one needs fewer things for it. Thus it is said in Luke (10:41), "Martha, Martha, you are worried and troubled about many things."[13]

Fifth, because the contemplative life is loved more for its own sake, but the active life is directed to something else. Thus in Psalm 27 (v. 4) it is written, "One thing I have asked of the Lord, one thing I require, that I may dwell in the house of the Lord all the days of my life, that I may see the will of the Lord."[14]

Sixth, because the contemplative life consists in a kind of leisure [*vacatione*] and rest, according to Psalm 46 (v. 10), "Be still [*vacate*] and see that I am God."[15]

Seventh, because the contemplative life accords with divine things, while the active life accords with human things. Thus Augustine says in the book *On the Words of the Lord* (*Sermon 104, 2*): "*In the beginning was the Word:*

purity and their enduringness" (*Nicomachean Ethics* 10.7, 1177ᵃ), are a function of the excellence of what is sought: "The purity of these pleasures is because they are about immaterial things; their enduringness is because they are about unchangeable things" (*Commentary on the Nicomachean Ethics* 10.10.2090). The quotation from Augustine suggests not only that the active life is less pleasant but that it is to some degree, at least by comparison with the contemplative life, *unpleasant*.

13. Aristotle explains that "self-sufficiency" in this context does not mean that contemplatives are in any less need of food and shelter and other physical necessities. But while a just person needs other people upon whom and with whom to exercise the virtue of justice, and likewise with fortitude and moderation, contemplation itself does not need the presence of others to be carried out (*Nicomachean Ethics* 10.7, 1177ᵃ). Thomas picks up on Aristotle's further remark that, even in contemplative pursuits, one can sometimes be aided by companions: "It is better for the wise person to have coworkers in the study of truth, because sometimes one sees what does not occur to another, who is perhaps wiser" (*Commentary on the Nicomachean Ethics* 10.10.2096). Perhaps because here Thomas is not thinking of purely philosophical or "scientific" contemplation, but rather the contemplation of prayer, this observation seems less germane.

14. Thomas states here, in a direct and compressed way, a point that he made over the course of the eight articles that make up 1-2.2. There, having asked whether the final end—that which is sought for its own sake—could consist in wealth or honor or glory or power or any bodily good or pleasure, Thomas concludes, "Nothing can quiet the human will except the universal good, which is not found in any created thing, but only in God" (1-2.2.8). The good that is God is never sought for the sake of something else, and contemplation, which is the seeking of this God, is pursued for its own sake, never for the sake of something else.

15. As Aristotle puts this point, while the diverse forms of the active life—whether pursued in warfare or politics—are all characterized by busyness, the life of the scholar (as students tell their professors on occasion) seems to be one of leisure. Thomas seems to be making a different point: not that the contemplative life is pursued because it both requires and affords leisure, but that what we are pursuing in the contemplative life is a kind of intellectual and spiritual rest, found in the contemplation of God. Thomas writes that in the highest moments of contemplative thought, "discoursing ends and the soul's gaze is fixed in contemplation of the one simple truth" (2-2.180.6 ad 2). The busy running around of thought, as we construct propositions and arguments, comes to an end in the highest beholding of God. We do not simply cultivate stillness in order to contemplate, but in contemplating the mind achieves a kind of stillness that mirrors, albeit dimly, the eternal stillness of God.

behold whom Mary heard; *the Word was made flesh*: behold to whom Martha ministered."[16]

Eighth, because the contemplative life accords with what is most characteristic of a human being—that is, the intellect—while in the works of the active life the lower powers, which are common to us and other animals, also play a role. Therefore in the psalm (36), after the words "Both humans and beasts you will save, O Lord" (v. 6), that which is special to human beings is added (v. 9): "In your light we shall see light."[17]

A ninth reason is added by the Lord in Luke (10:42) when he says: "Mary has chosen the better part, which shall not be taken away from her." Augustine, in the book *On the Words of the Lord* (*Sermon 103*, 4), explains this, saying: "Not *you have chosen badly*, but *she has chosen better*. Hear why it was better: because it shall not be taken away from her. The burden of necessity will someday be taken from you, while the sweetness of truth is eternal."[18]

Yet in a restricted sense and in specific cases it is better to choose the active life on account of the needs of the present life. As the Philosopher says in *Topics* (3.2, 1118ª), "It is better to philosophize than to be rich, but for one who suffers need, it is better to be rich."[19]

16. In his *Commentary on the Nicomachean Ethics,* Thomas does not treat this or the following reason as among the arguments Aristotle gives for the priority of contemplation. And, indeed, they seem somewhat different from what precedes.

While Aristotle's account of contemplation is on the whole more "secular" than Thomas's, at this point Aristotle seems to point to a connection between contemplation and the divine. He says that such a life seems too exalted for a mere human being and is possible only "in so far as something divine is present in him." The contemplative calling invites us, "so far as we can, [to] make ourselves immortal and strain every nerve to live in accordance with the best thing in us" (*Nicomachean Ethics* 10.7, 1177ᵇ). Thomas's quotation of Augustine, however, seems to bend Aristotle's words to make them apply not to something divine in *us* but to the divinity of Christ. Martha served the humanity of Christ, while Mary contemplated his divinity.

17. In both Aristotle and in Thomas, this eighth reason is more a kind of summing up of what has come before than its own distinct reason. Contemplation uniquely fits the specific kind of animals that we are. Thomas goes on to add, by way of contrast, that physical activity is something that we share with other animals.

18. In discussing earlier the "continuous" nature of contemplation (2–2.180.8), Thomas adds to Aristotle's claim that contemplation is less prone to interruption (see note 11, above) the point that since it is an activity of the soul, which is not subject to corruption, it can continue beyond this life. It is not clear that Aristotle himself would agree with this, and it is noteworthy that Thomas does not here attempt to attribute this view to Aristotle.

19. Thomas adds an important caveat: though the contemplative life is better in principle, in practice there might be good reason to engage in aspects of the active life. Indeed, Thomas tends to treat these forms of life as "ideal types," noting that in practice most lives are a blend of these two types. Even a philosopher might need to worry about money on occasion. In his discussion of Jesus's own manner of living (3.40.1, below), Thomas will explore the religious reasons why one might take up a form of life that contains both contemplative and active elements.

Reply to 1: It is not only the active life that pertains to prelates, but they should also excel in the contemplative life. For this reason Gregory says in the *Book of Pastoral Rule* (2.1) that a leader should be "foremost in action . . . more uplifted than others in contemplation."[20]

Reply to 2: The contemplative life consists in a certain liberty of the soul. For Gregory says in his *Homilies on Ezekiel* (1.3) that the contemplative life "passes over into a certain freedom of mind, thinking not of temporal things but of eternal." And Boethius, in *The Consolation of Philosophy* (5.2), writes, "The human soul must be more free while it remains gazing upon the Divine mind, but less so when stooping down to bodily things." Thus it is clear that the active life does not directly command the contemplative life, but rather prescribes certain works of the active life in order to dispose one to the contemplative life, by which it more serves the contemplative life than rules it.[21] Gregory refers to this when he says in the *Homilies on Ezekiel* (1.3) that "the active life is bondage, but the contemplative life is called freedom."

Reply to 3: Sometimes someone is called away from contemplation to the works of the active life on account of some necessity of the present life, yet not in such a way as to be compelled to completely abandon contemplation. As Augustine says in *The City of God* (19.19), "Love of truth seeks holy leisure; the demands of charity take up an honest toil"—that is, the active life. "If no one imposes this burden, we can devote ourselves to sifting and contemplating truth, but if it is imposed, it must be taken up, on account of the demands of charity. Yet even then we need not completely abandon the enjoyment of truth, so as to be deprived of its sweetness and crushed by this burden." And so it is clear, when a person is called from the contemplative life to the active life, that this is done not by way of subtraction but by addition.[22]

20. While undoubtedly recognizing that many fall short of this, Thomas thinks that church leaders should not simply be efficient managers but should be people of deep prayer.

21. Passing over in silence the objection's appeal to an allegorical interpretation of Moses, Thomas underscores the freedom associated by authors like Gregory the Great and Boethius with the contemplative life, which implies its nonsubordination to the demands of the active life. Thomas notes that the relationship that the active life has with the contemplative life is not like that of a general who commands, but more like that of a servant who aids in preparation. Thus the active life, particularly understood in terms of ascetic practice, can provide assistance to the contemplative life.

22. Whenever Thomas discusses spiritual perfection, the matter always comes down to charity. Though the contemplative life is in itself superior to the active life, if charity requires one to leave off contemplation for a time so as to engage in the spiritual or corporal works of mercy, then the call of charity must be answered. For a true contemplative, Thomas notes, such acts of charity should enhance and not diminish one's contemplative enjoyment of God as First Truth.

THE THIRD PART

PROLOGUE TO
the Third Part

Because our Savior the Lord Jesus Christ, in order to "save his people from their sins" (Matt. 1:21), as the angel bore witness, showed to us in himself the way of truth, by which we can come to the bliss of eternal life by rising again, it is necessary, in order to complete the work of theology, that after consideration of the ultimate goal of human life and the virtues and vices, there should follow a consideration of the Savior of all and the benefits bestowed by him on the human race.

Concerning this there comes to mind for consideration, first, the Savior himself; second, his sacraments by which we gain salvation; third, the goal of immortal life to which we come by rising again through him.

Concerning the first, a double consideration comes to mind: the first is about the mystery of the incarnation itself, by which God was made human for our salvation; the second, about such things as our Savior himself—that is, God incarnate—did and suffered.[1]

---

1. Thomas here makes clear his projected plan for the third part of the *Summa*:
   1. Jesus Christ
      a. The incarnation: Jesus's constitution as divine and human
      b. The work of Christ: what Jesus did and suffered
   2. The sacraments: signs of Christ's saving work
   3. Resurrection and eternal life: the consummation of all things in Christ

   We should note that Thomas stopped writing in the middle of his discussion of the sacrament of penance and never began his treatment of eternal life.

   Thomas's reference to what Jesus "did and suffered" (*acta et passa*) refers to the entire narrative of the Word's visible mission, which, like any narrative, is composed of both what he undertakes and what he undergoes.

Question 1:

The Fittingness of the Incarnation

3.1.1[1]
Was it fitting that God should become incarnate?

It would seem that it was not fitting [*conveniens*] for God to become incarnate.[2]

1. Since God from all eternity is the very essence of goodness, it is therefore best for him to be as he had been from all eternity. But from all eternity God was without flesh. Therefore, it is most fitting for him not to unite himself to flesh, and thus it was not fitting for God to become incarnate.[3]

2. Things that are infinitely distant are not fittingly joined, in the way that it would not be a fitting union if one were to paint a figure in which "the neck of a horse was joined to the head of a man."[4] But God and flesh are

---

1. On this article, see Garrigou-Lagrange (1950, 44–54); Kerr (2002, 162–80); Bauerschmidt (2013, 160–75, 180–87).

2. In the first sentence of the first article of the third part of the *Summa*, we encounter the term *conveniens*. In this translation it is generally rendered as "fitting" or, sometimes, "suitable." Though Thomas has used it earlier in the *Summa*, its use proliferates in the third part, in part because it identifies a kind of reasoning—distinct from the deductive, syllogistic logic associated with *scientia*—that is suited to thinking about the things that flow forth from the saving will of God, which are the particular focus of this section of the *Summa*. In this part, Thomas repeatedly inquires after the *convenientia* of various things that Christians hold to be revealed truth. For example, Thomas sees the incarnation of God in Jesus Christ as a truth given to us in revelation. It is not something that we can "prove" through the use of reason, not least because it regards a contingent fact of history (see 1.1 note 22). However, there is still a role for reason here, not in proving the incarnation, but in manifesting or showing forth how it fits together (*convenire* means literally "to come together") with other things that Christians hold true about God. Thomas discusses *convenientia* and its relationship to "necessity" in more detail at 3.46.1, below.

We should note that this term, as well as the kind of reasoning it denotes, is hardly unique to Thomas. It plays a major role in the writings of Anselm, for whom it is linked with the notion of *rectitudo* or "rightness" (see 1–2.55 note 8), and in the works of Thomas's contemporary Bonaventure.

3. If God is unchanging (as Thomas believes), how can we speak of God *becoming* human without admitting that God has changed? In terms of the notion of *convenientia*, how can the beliefs (1) that God is unchanging and (2) that God became incarnate "come together" in a coherent way?

4. This quotation is from the opening line of the *Ars poetica* of the Roman poet Horace, where he uses it as an example of the kind of incongruity that might provoke laughter.

infinitely distant, since God is most simple and flesh is composite—especially human flesh.[5] Therefore it was not fitting that God should be united to human flesh.

3. A body is as distant from the highest spirit as malice is from the highest goodness. But it would be completely unfitting that God, who is the highest goodness, should take on malice. Therefore, it is not fitting that the highest uncreated spirit should take on a body.

4. It is not fitting that the one who surpasses what is greatest should be contained in what is least and that he who has care of great things should shift his concern to unimportant things. But God, who takes care of the whole world, cannot be contained by the whole universe.[6] Therefore it would seem unfitting that "within the small body of a squalling infant should lie hidden the one in comparison with whom the whole universe is accounted as little; . . . and that this ruler should leave his throne for so long, and transfer the government of the whole world to so frail a body," as Volusianus writes to Augustine.[7]

On the contrary: It would seem to be most fitting that the invisible things of God should be made known by visible things, since it was for this purpose that the whole world was made, as is clear from the what the Apostle says in Romans (1:20): "The invisible things of God . . . are clearly seen, being understood through the things that are made." But, as John of Damascus says at the beginning of his third book (*On the Orthodox Faith* 3.1), by the mystery of incarnation "are made known simultaneously God's goodness, wisdom, justice, and power" or virtue: "his goodness, for he did not despise the weakness of his own handiwork; . . . his justice, because . . . he did not snatch humanity forcibly from death, but caused the tyrant to be defeated by no other; . . . his wisdom, for he found a suitable solution for a most difficult problem; his infinite power" or virtue, "for nothing is greater than for God to become a human being." Therefore it was fitting for God to be incarnate.

I answer: A thing is "fitting" [*conveniens*] if it belongs to something because of its very nature, in the way that it is fitting for human beings to reason, since this befits them inasmuch as they are rational by nature. But

5. On "simplicity," see 1.12 note 2. Medieval people thought of material objects as composed of four basic elements—earth, air, fire, and water—so a body was by its very nature nonsimple, just as God was by his very nature simple.

6. The argument here is both metaphysical and moral: it would be incongruous for God's immensity to be contained in a human body, and it would be irresponsible for the power that governs the universe to abandon his post to take on the form of powerlessness.

7. Numbered as *Epistle 135* among Augustine's letters.

God's very nature is goodness, as is clear from Dionysius in *On the Divine Names* (1.5). Therefore, whatever pertains to the idea of goodness befits God.

It pertains to the idea of goodness to communicate itself to others, as is plain from Dionysius in *On the Divine Names*.[8] Which means that it pertains to the idea of the highest good to communicate itself in the highest manner to the creature, which is done above all by "so joining created nature to himself that one person is made up of these three: the Word, soul, and flesh," as Augustine says in *De Trinitate* (13.17). Therefore it is clear that it was fitting for God to become incarnate.[9]

Reply to 1: The mystery of the incarnation was not brought about through God being changed in any way from the state in which he had been from eternity, but through his having united himself in a new way to a creature or, rather, through having united it to himself.[10] It is fitting that creation, which is by its very definition mutable, should not always be in one way. Therefore, just as creation began to be even though it had not been before, so likewise it is fitting that creation, not having been previously united to God, was later united to him.[11]

8. In *On the Divine Names* 4.1 Dionysius (i.e., Pseudo-Dionysius) writes, "[The sacred writers] call the divine subsistence itself 'goodness.' This essential Good, by the very fact of its existence, extends goodness into all things." Thomas is exploiting the dual meaning of *communicare*, which can mean both to pass along information (what we usually mean by "to communicate") and to "share." So when Thomas speaks of the good as "communicating" itself, this means not so much that it makes itself known as that goodness shares itself, just as fire shares its fiery actuality with something flammable. In the specific case of God, God shares the goodness of his existence with us by bringing us into existence.

9. Here Thomas explains the incarnation in terms of God's desire to "share" himself with us. Since God is the highest goodness, it is only fitting that God would share himself in the highest way possible—by actually becoming one of us. Note how Thomas's argument highlights the continuity between creation and incarnation: just as God shares himself with creatures in creating them, God shares himself in an even higher way by becoming incarnate, but both are instances of the nature of good as self-communicating. Note also how this argument *ex convenientia* (see note 2, above) works: Thomas does not think he is proving that God *had* to become incarnate, but rather showing that the incarnation fits with our understanding of God as the highest goodness.

10. Here Thomas employs a distinction that he made earlier (1.13.7) between a "logical" (or "notional") relation and a "real" relation. To use a rough analogy, if I teach you to speak French, *you* will have changed (you can now speak French), but *I* will remain unchanged (I could speak French before, and I can speak French now), even though now you can say something about me that you could not say before (i.e., "You taught me French"). Thus I would have a logical relation to your acquisition of French, whereas you would have a real relation to it. To use another analogy, if you are standing on my right and then move around to my left, your position relative to me has changed, but I have not undergone any change, even though you can say something about me that you could not say before (i.e., "You are standing on my right").

11. The incarnation *would* be *inconveniens* (unfitting) if it involved a change on God's part, but it is entirely fitting for creatures to change. To put it somewhat cryptically, what is "new" in the incarnation is not that God begins to exist as a creature but that a creature begins to exist who is God.

Reply to 2: To be united to God in unity of person was not fitting to human flesh according to its natural condition, since this was above its dignity. Nevertheless, it was fitting that God, by reason of the infinite excellence of his goodness, should unite it to himself for the salvation of humanity.[12]

Reply to 3: Whatever condition by which any creature whatsoever differs from the Creator has been established by God's wisdom and in relation to God's goodness. For God according to his goodness—being uncreated, immutable, and nonbodily—produced mutable and embodied creatures. And in a similar way, the evil of penalty [*malum poenae*] was established by God's justice for God's glory.[13] But the evil of fault [*malum culpae*] is committed by withdrawing from the plan of the divine wisdom and from the order of the divine goodness.[14] And therefore it is fitting that God could have taken on a created, mutable, and embodied nature subject to penalty; but it was not fitting that he take on the evil of fault.[15]

Reply to 4: As Augustine replies in the letter to Volusianus (*Epistle 137*, 2), "Christian teaching nowhere holds that God was so poured into human flesh as either to desert or lose—or to transfer and, as it were, contract within this frail body—the care of governing the universe. This is how people think who are unable to conceive of anything but bodily things . . . God is great not in mass but in might. For this reason the greatness of his might feels no confinement in confining spaces. If the transitory word of a person is heard simultaneously by many, and completely by each of them, then it is not incredible that the abiding Word of God should be everywhere at once." Therefore nothing unfitting follows from God becoming incarnate.

12. Human nature could in no way merit (see 1–2.109 note 8) the incarnation; it is a pure gift of God's grace.

13. The "evil of penalty" refers to the occurrence of bad things, such as illness, which for Thomas are a result of sin's entry into the world and yet are somehow (perhaps in ways not obvious to us) a part of the way in which God provides for creatures. Were God somehow to forestall the evil consequences that flow naturally from sin, we might fail to understand our proper relationship as creatures to God our creator. The "evil of penalty" shows that turning away from God, who is the source of our existence, results in a diminishment of that existence. The evils we suffer give us knowledge of ourselves, so that, as Catherine of Siena (1347–80) wrote, "We see our own nothingness, that our very existence is ours by grace and not because we have a right to it, and every grace beyond our existence as well—it is all given to us with boundless love. Then we discover so much of God's goodness poured out on us that words cannot describe it" (2001, 208). On "penalty" or *poena* in general, see 3.65 note 4.

14. The "evil of fault" refers to the willing of evil, which for Thomas is something that God is not responsible for and that people do by turning away from God's will. On the difference between *poena* and *culpa*, see 3.65 note 4.

15. Thomas's point is that, in a sense, it is not as good to be bodily as it is to be pure spirit, and it is even less good to be embodied in fallen flesh that is subject to sickness and death. But this deficiency of goodness can be willed by God as part of a greater overarching good: the self-communication of God and the salvation of humanity. However, there is another sort of deficiency of goodness—that is, the evil of fault—that cannot be willed by God in view of a greater good because it involves the will itself being evil, which is contrary to God's nature.

3.1.2[16]
Was it necessary for the restoration of the human race that the Word of God should become incarnate?

It would seem that it was not necessary for the restoration of the human race that the Word of God should become incarnate.

1. Since the Word of God is perfect God, as has been said in the first part (1.27.2 ad 2; cf. 1.4.1, 2), no power was added to him by taking on flesh. If, therefore, the incarnate Word of God restored [human] nature, he could also have repaired it without taking on flesh.[17]

2. Nothing more would seem to be required for the restoration of human nature, which had fallen through sin, than that humanity should repay for sin. Because God cannot require from human beings more than they can do, and because he is more inclined to be merciful than to punish, it seems that just as God imputes the act of sin to humanity, he should likewise impute the opposite act of destroying sin.[18] It was not, therefore, necessary for the repair of human nature that the Word of God should become incarnate.

3. It pertains especially to the salvation of humanity that God be revered. Thus it is written in Malachi (1:6), "If I am Lord, where is my fear? If Father, where is my honor?" But people revere God more by considering him raised above all and far removed from the senses. Thus in Psalm 113 (v. 4) it is said, "The Lord is high above all nations, and his glory above the heavens," and farther on, "Who is like the Lord our God?" (v. 5), which pertains to reverence. Therefore, it would seem unfitting to human salvation that God should become like us by taking on flesh.

On the contrary: What frees the human race from destruction is necessary for human salvation. But such is the divine mystery of the incarnation, according to John (3:16): "God so loved the world that he gave his only begotten Son, that whoever believes in him may not perish, but have life everlasting." Therefore it was necessary for human salvation that God should become incarnate.

I answer: Something is said to be necessary to some goal in two ways. In one way, when something cannot be without it, in the way that food is necessary for the preservation of human life. In another way, when a goal is arrived at

16. On this article, see Garrigou-Lagrange (1950); Kerr (2002, 54–76, 162–80); Bauerschmidt (2013, 180–87); Jordan (2016, 21–31).

17. Because God is pure act (see 1.3 note 12), the divine nature cannot have its power increased by being joined to human nature; therefore nothing is possible to God incarnate that is not possible to God apart from the incarnation, so the incarnation cannot be necessary for salvation.

18. Since it is by God's decree that we are condemned for sin, by God's decree our condemnation can be lifted, without any need for the incarnation.

in a better and more fitting [*convenientius*] manner, in the way that a horse is necessary for a journey. In the first way, the incarnation of God was not necessary for the restoration of human nature, for God with his omnipotent power could have repaired human nature in many other ways. In the second way, however, the incarnation of God *was* necessary for the restoration of human nature. Hence Augustine says in *De Trinitate* (13.10), "We shall also show that other ways were not lacking to God, to whose power all things are equally subject, but that there was not a more fitting way of healing our misery."[19]

The incarnation may be considered with regard to our furtherance in good.[20] First, with regard to faith, which is made more certain from believing God himself, who speaks. For this reason Augustine says in *The City of God* (11.2) that, in order that humanity "might journey more trustfully toward the truth, the Truth itself, the Son of God, having assumed human nature . . . , established and founded faith." Second, with regard to hope, which is thereby greatly raised up. As Augustine says in *De Trinitate* (13.10), "Nothing was so necessary for raising our hope as to prove to us how much God loved us. And what could afford us a stronger proof of this than that the Son of God should deign to be a sharer in our nature?" Third, with regard to charity, which is greatly stirred up by this. Thus Augustine says in *On the Instruction of Beginners* (4), "What greater cause is there of the Lord's coming than to show God's love for us?" And afterward he adds, "If we have been slow to love, at least let us not be slow to love in return."[21] Fourth, with regard to

19. Here Thomas distinguishes two ways in which a means might be thought of as necessary to a given end. First, as a sine qua non with regard to the end: you must have food in order to live. Second, as the most "fitting" means among a number of possible means for obtaining the end, either because it allows the end to be obtained more easily or because the means brings along with it a variety of other goods in addition to the specific purpose sought. Thomas argues that the first sort of necessity does not apply to the incarnation; because of God's omnipotence, God is free from any absolute necessity except that which attaches to the divine nature itself (e.g., God, the highest good, cannot will to be evil). We might think of this as a "weak" form of necessity, but it is sufficient to launch a line of inquiry into why the means chosen by God are the most fitting.

20. Here Thomas begins introducing what serves as a key structuring device for his discussions of human salvation: our salvation involves both our "furtherance in good" and our "removal from evil." As one contemporary theologian puts it, salvation for Thomas is fundamentally a matter of our possession of the image of God, which, after the fall, involves both "image perfection" and "image-restoration" (see Cessario 1990, 128). In other words, salvation is not simply a matter of God forgiving human sin; it is a more comprehensive process of our being drawn beyond our natures so as to become "sharers of the divine nature" (2 Pet. 1:4). On the soul becoming "deiform," see 1–2.110 note 13. Grace both "elevates" and "heals" our nature; salvation does involve the lifting of the burden of sin, but it also involves the lifting up of human nature through participation in divine goodness.

21. Note that in these first three reasons we find the triad of faith, hope, and charity—the theological virtues, which are the key to human participation in divine goodness (see 1–2.62 note 3).

right action, of which Christ provides us an example. As Augustine says in a sermon on the Lord's birth (*Sermon 371*), "A human being, who *could* be seen, was *not* to be followed; God, who could *not* be seen, *was* to be followed. And therefore, so that we might be shown one who could be both seen and followed by human beings, God was made a human being." Fifth, with regard to the full sharing in divinity, which is true human blessedness and the goal of human life. This is bestowed upon us by Christ's humanity, for Augustine says in a Christmas sermon, "God became a human being, that human beings might become God."[22]

The incarnation was likewise useful for our withdrawal from evil. First, because one is taught by it not to prefer the devil to oneself, nor to honor him who is the author of sin. Thus Augustine says in *De Trinitate* (13.17), "Since human nature is united to God so as to become one person, do not let these proud spirits dare to prefer themselves to human beings simply because they have no bodies."[23] Second, because we are taught by this the greatness of human dignity, so that we should not stain it with sin. Thus Augustine says in the book *On True Religion* (16), "God has proved to us how high a place human nature holds among creatures, inasmuch as he appeared to us as a true human being." And Pope Leo says in a sermon on the nativity (*Sermon 21, 3*), "O Christian, acknowledge your worth and, having been made a partner of the divine nature, refuse to return to your former worthlessness through evil deeds."[24] Third, because in order to take away human presumption, "the grace of God is shown to us in the man Christ, though no merits went before," as Augustine says in *De Trinitate* (13.17). Fourth, because "human pride, which is the greatest stumbling block to our clinging to God, can be refuted and cured by such humility on the part of God," as Augustine says in the same place. Fifth, in order to free humanity from slavery. Indeed, as Augustine says in *De Trinitate* (13.13), this "should be done in such a way that the devil should be overcome by the justice of a human being, Jesus Christ," and this

---

22. The phrase Thomas quotes is not found in the authentic sermons of Augustine, though it is found in sermon 128 in Migne, Patrologia Latina 39, among the sermons that have in the past been ascribed to Augustine but that are now thought not to be authentic. The phrase is more commonly associated with Eastern Christian thought and is first found in Athanasius's *On the Incarnation* 54.

23. The incarnation shows us that immaterial beings are not necessarily "higher" than human beings by virtue of their immateriality. Thus, humans should not subject themselves to demonic forces simply because of their immateriality.

24. We can once again note the fundamentally positive account that Thomas gives of human salvation. In these first two points, even when discussing salvation under the heading of our removal from evil, Thomas focuses on how the incarnation shows us the dignity and worth of human nature. Only after addressing the false "humility" that leads us to *under*value ourselves, and so subject ourselves to sin, does Thomas turn to the pride that leads us to *over*value ourselves. Of course, Thomas does see human pride as a major source of sin, but not as the only source.

was done by Christ making repayment for us. A mere man could not have made repayment for the whole human race, but God was not bound to repay; therefore, it was proper for Jesus Christ to be both God and a human being. For this reason Pope Leo says in the same sermon on the nativity (*Sermon 21*, 2), "Weakness is received by strength, lowliness by majesty, mortality by eternity, in order that one and the same mediator of God and humanity might die in one and rise in the other—for this was our fitting remedy. Unless he was God, he would not have brought a remedy; and unless he was human, he would not have set an example."[25]

And there are very many other advantages that followed, beyond the perception of human comprehension.

Reply to 1: This reason follows from the first kind of necessity, without which we cannot reach the end.[26]

Reply to 2: A repayment can be said to be sufficient in two ways.[27] In one way, perfectly, inasmuch as it is condign—that is, compensation equal to the fault committed. In this way repayment sufficient for sin cannot be made by one who is merely human because the whole of human nature was corrupted by sin, so that neither the goodness of any one person nor even of many people could make up adequately for the harm done to the whole of the nature. Further, a sin committed against God has a kind of infinity, derived from the infinity of the divine majesty; for the greater the person we offend, the more serious the offense. Thus for equivalent repayment [*condignam satisfactionem*] it was necessary that the act of the one repaying should have an infinite efficacy— namely, the act of one who is both God and a human being.

In the other way, repayment may be termed sufficient even though it is imperfect—that is, the one accepting it may be content with it, even though it is not compensation equal to the fault committed. In this way the repayment

25. It is in this fifth point that Thomas introduces the notion of "repayment" or "satisfaction" (*satisfactio*), which he will develop at greater length in 3.48.2, below. Here we might note that *satisfactio* is the key image by which Thomas understands the significance of Christ's suffering and death, but it by no means exhausts the significance of his death for human salvation. Even here, this image seems to blend with another interpretation of Christ's death that is also characteristic of Thomas: that of Christ as the example for human beings to imitate.

26. The incarnation does not increase God's saving power, but rather is the fitting means chosen by God for human salvation.

27. In speaking of merit, Thomas distinguishes between a reward that one is owed in justice (meriting *de condigno*) and a reward that is fitting but not owed in justice (meriting *de congruo*); see 1–2.109 note 8. In this response, Thomas makes a similar distinction with regard to repayment—between one that is equivalent to what is owed (*condigna*) and one that is imperfect yet sufficient (*satisfactio sufficiens imperfecte*) because it is graciously accepted by the one to whom recompense is due. These two distinctions are related because on the cross Christ merits *de condigno* because he makes equivalent repayment (*satisfactio condigno*).

of one who is purely human is sufficient. And because every imperfect thing presupposes something perfect by which it is sustained, the repayment of everyone who is merely human has its efficacy from the repayment of Christ.[28]

Reply to 3: God, taking flesh, did not diminish his majesty, and consequently he did not lessen the reason for revering him, which is increased by the increase of knowledge of him. On the contrary, inasmuch as he wished to draw near to us by taking flesh, he drew us to know him better.[29]

3.1.3[30]
If humanity had not sinned, would God have become incarnate?

It seems that if humanity had not sinned, God nonetheless would have become incarnate.[31]

1. As long as the cause remains, the effect remains. But as Augustine says in *De Trinitate* (13.17), "Many other things are to be considered in the incarnation of Christ" beyond absolution from sin, as was said earlier (3.1.2).[32] Therefore, even if humanity had not sinned, God would have become incarnate.

---

28. Here again Thomas's discussion of repayment connects to his discussion of merit. On the cross Christ makes an equivalent repayment for human fault and therefore receives merit in strict justice. This perfect repayment and reward forms the basis upon which human beings receive reward *de congruo* for the imperfect repayment they make through acts of love toward God and their neighbors. To adapt the analogy of the bill and the tip I used earlier to talk about merit (1–2.109 note 8), we might say that it is only because Christ has satisfied justice by paying the bill (that is, making adequate repayment to God) that the tip we leave (that is, our good deeds) constitutes something praiseworthy. One hardly expects praise if one leaves a tip but walks away from the check.

29. In the case of God, familiarity does not breed contempt.

30. On this article, see Garrigou-Lagrange (1950, 76–104); Hunter (2020, esp. 111–61).

31. This is an issue that does not arise in this form until the early thirteenth century with Robert Grosseteste (1175–1253), so when Thomas is writing there is no consensus among theologians as to how the question should be answered (indeed, there is still no consensus among theologians on this question).

Thomas's answer to this question is often contrasted with that of the Franciscan John Duns Scotus (ca. 1266–1308), who argued (in a way not found in any of the objections in this article) that the motive for the incarnation was not first and foremost the salvation of fallen humanity but the glorification of Christ's human soul through its sharing in the beatific vision (i.e., "the vision of the divine essence"; see 1–2.3.8, above). Therefore, Scotus argued, Christ would have become incarnate even if there had been no need to save humanity from sin (see *Ordinatio* bk. 3, dist. 7, q. 3).

But answers to the question did not fall on a neat divide between Franciscans and Dominicans. In answering this question, Thomas agrees with the Dominican Guerric of Saint-Quentin (died ca. 1243) but disagrees with his Dominican teacher Albert the Great (ca. 1200–1280); he disagrees with the Franciscan Alexander of Hales (ca. 1186–1245) but agrees with his Franciscan colleague Bonaventure (1221–74). It is only later that the battle lines between Dominican Thomists and Franciscan Scotists on this issue get clearly defined (for some sense of this, see Garrigou-Lagrange 1950), and Thomas's view is a good deal more tentative than is often thought.

32. Thomas says that Christ came both to withdraw us from evil and to advance us in goodness (see note 20, above). Christ advances us in goodness in a variety of ways—for example, by strengthening faith,

2. It pertains to the omnipotence of divine power to perfect its works and to show itself by some infinite effect. But no mere creature can be said to be an infinite effect, since it is finite by its very essence. It seems that only in the work of incarnation is an infinite effect of the divine power shown in a special manner, inasmuch as things infinitely distant are joined, since it has been brought about that a human being is God. And in this work especially the universe would seem to be perfected by the last creature—namely, humanity—being united to the first principle—namely, God. So even if humanity had not sinned, God would have become incarnate.[33]

3. Human nature is not made more capable of grace through sin.[34] But after sin it is capable of the grace of union, which is the greatest grace. Therefore, if humanity had not sinned, human nature would have been capable of this grace; nor would God have taken away from human nature any good it was capable of.[35] Therefore, if humanity had not sinned, God would have become incarnate.

4. God's predestination is eternal. But it is said in Romans (1:4) of Christ that he "was predestined the Son of God in power." Therefore, even before sin it was necessary that the Son of God should become incarnate, so that God's predestination might be fulfilled.[36]

5. The mystery of the incarnation was revealed to the first human, as is clear when he says, "This now is bone of my bones," and so on (Gen. 2:23), which the Apostle says is "a great sacrament . . . in Christ and in the church," as is plain from Ephesians (5:32).[37] But a human being could not have foreknowl-

---

hope, and charity; by giving us an example of doing good; and by bestowing upon us a full participation in divinity.

33. This objection suggests that the perfection of the universe requires the existence of some creature who can draw the finite and the infinite together into a unity; in other words, God must become a creature. A form of this argument was made by Robert Grosseteste in his *On the Cessation of the Laws* 3.1.26–28.

34. Grosseteste makes a version of this argument in *On the Cessation of the Laws* 3.1.4, but the unstated authority in the background is Paul in his Letter to the Romans, who asks rhetorically, "What then are we to say? Should we continue in sin in order that grace may abound?" and answers with an emphatic "By no means!" (Rom. 6:1–2).

35. The argument of this objection is as follows: (1) Human nature can be joined with divine nature; (2) sin cannot bring about anything good; (3) sin is not responsible for the capacity of human nature to be joined with divine nature; (4) this capacity would exist apart from sin; (5) God would not leave a human capacity unfulfilled; (6) therefore Christ would have become incarnate to join human and divine nature, even apart from sin. This argument raises an issue (i.e., no. 5) that would become important later in Roman Catholic theology: the question of whether God is obliged to give human beings the beatific vision (i.e., "the vision of the divine essence"; see 1–2.3.8, above) for the completion of their natures. See Thomas's response to this objection below.

36. This objection, based on the predestination of Christ, was addressed by Thomas's Dominican predecessor at the University of Paris, Guerric of Saint-Quentin (died ca. 1243). See Guerric's *Quodlibetal Questions* 7.1.

37. See 2–2.2 note 23. Grosseteste gives a version of this argument in his *On the Cessation of the Laws* 3.1.20–21.

edge of his fall, for the same reason that the angels could not, as Augustine proves in *On the Literal Meaning of Genesis* (11.18). So even if humanity had not sinned, God would have become incarnate.

On the contrary: Expounding what is set down in Luke (19:10), "For the Son of Man has come to seek and to save that which was lost," Augustine says in *On the Words of the Lord* (*Sermon 174*, 2), "If humanity had not sinned, the Son of Man would not have come." And regarding 1 Timothy (1:15), "Christ Jesus came into this world to save sinners," a gloss says,[38] "There was no cause of Christ's coming into the world except to save sinners. Take away sicknesses, take away wounds, and no medicine is needed."

I answer: There are different opinions about this question. For some say that even if humanity had not sinned, the Son of God would have become incarnate, but others assert the contrary. It seems that our assent should be given more to this latter assertion. For things that spring solely from God's will, beyond all that is owed to the creature, cannot be made known to us except insofar as they are handed on in Holy Scripture, through which the divine will is made known to us. Therefore, since everywhere in the Holy Scripture the sin of the first human being is assigned as the reason of incarnation, it is more fittingly said [*convenientius dicitur*] that the work of incarnation was appointed by God as a remedy for sin,[39] so that if sin had not existed, the incarnation would not have been. The power of God, however, is not limited to this; for even had sin not existed, God could have become incarnate.[40]

38. On "glosses," see 1.12 note 10.

39. On *convenientia*, see note 2, above.

40. Thomas is stating his view with considerable care here. He is not saying that God *could not* become incarnate apart from sin, nor is he saying, as is sometimes thought, that God *would not* have become incarnate if humans had not sinned. What he is saying is that this question is rooted in the mystery of the divine will and goes beyond the natural scope of human knowledge. The only basis we have for addressing such questions is divine revelation, as recorded in Scripture, and if we look at Scripture we see that "Christ Jesus came into the world to save sinners" (1 Tim. 1:15). Of course, Thomas is not basing his answer on a single verse; the entire story of God incarnate in Christ has the particular shape that it does because it is the story of incarnation as a remedy for sin. To ponder what the story would have been if humans had never sinned is simply to indulge in idle speculation. It is worth remembering, however, that those who say that God would *not* have become incarnate if humans had not sinned are also indulging in idle speculation that goes beyond what God has revealed.

What Thomas is establishing in this article is an approach to the incarnation that will shape his whole discussion. He begins with what God has *in fact* done in Christ, not with what God *might* have done; he is concerned about our actual history with God, not about a possible alternative history. This is an approach that might be called "reasoning *from* revelation": given what God has in fact done, how does this fit with other things that we hold to be true about God? So Thomas will not ask, "Should Christ have been born in Bethlehem?" (much less "Was Christ *really* born in Bethlehem?"), but rather, "Why was it fitting for Christ to be born in Bethlehem?"

Reply to 1: All the other causes that are assigned [in the preceding article] pertain to the remedy for sin.[41] For if human beings had not sinned, they would have been flooded with the light of divine wisdom and made perfect by God with the righteousness of justice, in order to know everything necessary. But because human beings, deserting God, fell to the level of bodily things, it was fitting that God should take on flesh and, by means of bodily things, should provide them with the remedy of salvation.[42] Therefore, regarding John (1:14), "And the Word was made flesh," St. Augustine says, "Flesh had blinded you; flesh heals you. For thus Christ came and overthrew by flesh the vices of the flesh" (*Sermon 2, 16*, in *Homilies on the Gospel of John*).

Reply to 2: The very way in which things are produced from nothing shows the infinity of divine power.[43] Also, for the perfection of the universe it is sufficient that the creature be oriented in a natural way to God as to its goal. But it exceeds the limits of the perfection of nature that a creature should be united to God in a person.[44]

Reply to 3: A double capacity can be seen in human nature. One is according to the order of natural power, which is always fulfilled by God, who fulfills everything according to its natural capability. The other is according to the order of the divine power, which all creatures obey instantly, and the capacity we speak of pertains to this. But God does not fulfill all such capacities of nature; otherwise, God could do in creatures only what he has in fact done, and this is false, as stated in the first part (1.105.6).[45]

41. Thomas seems to be saying that both the "removal from evil" and the "advancement in good" need to be seen in light of the salvation of fallen humanity.

42. Apart from human sin, God could have simply advanced human beings in good through the infusion of the light of divine wisdom. But sin involves a turning from spiritual things to material things (literally, "collapsing into" them); therefore, because of sin, it is fitting for God to advance human beings in good by material means—i.e., incarnation.

43. Though creation is a finite effect of God's infinite power, the act of bringing forth creation from nothing is something no finite power could do; therefore creation is an adequate manifestation of God's infinite power.

44. It is difficult to know what Thomas means when he speaks of human beings having God as their goal or purpose "in a natural way," since he also says that union with God exceeds the capacities of human nature (1.1.1). But whatever he means by the "natural way" for creatures to be oriented to God, his main point here is that the perfection of human nature does not require the kind of union of humanity and divinity that occurs in Christ, which he will later characterize as a "hypostatic" or "personal" union (see 3.2.2, below).

45. Thomas is raising an issue that will be much debated both in the late sixteenth century (in the controversy over the teachings of Michel Baius) and in the twentieth century (in the controversy between traditional Thomists and the so-called *Nouvelle Théologie*). As noted earlier, one can argue that for Thomas there is no purely "natural" fulfillment for human beings; human existence is in some sense thwarted apart from its supernatural fulfillment. Thomas maintains repeatedly that fulfillment is impossible apart from God's grace. But the question is whether God is somehow "obligated" to give grace to human beings, since he has created them such that they cannot be fulfilled without it. If God is obligated, then in what sense is grace a "gift" (which is the meaning of the word "grace")? Thomas's answer is clear:

But nothing would prohibit human nature from being raised to something greater after sin; for God allows evils to happen in order to bring from them something better. Therefore it is written in Romans (5:20), "Where sin abounded, grace did more abound." Therefore, too, in the blessing of the Paschal candle, we say, "O happy fault, that merited such and so great a redeemer!"[46]

Reply to 4: Predestination presupposes foreknowledge of future things. Therefore, just as God predestines that a person will be saved by the prayers of others, so also he predestined the work of incarnation to be the remedy of human sin.[47]

Reply to 5: Nothing prevents an effect from being revealed to someone to whom the cause is not revealed. Therefore the mystery of incarnation could be revealed to the first human being without his being conscious of his fall ahead of time, for not everyone who knows an effect knows the cause.[48]

God is in no sense obligated by the human capacity for supernatural fulfillment. Here Thomas describes this capacity for supernatural fulfillment as the ability to "obey instantly" or, put in a different way, the ability to respond to God's gracious initiative. This capacity is something that goes beyond what human nature requires, though apart from exercising this capacity, humans in fact do not reach their fulfillment.

With regard to the specific issue at hand, Thomas takes it as a given that God could act in human history in ways different from the ways God has in fact acted, but Thomas is unwilling to say much about such matters, beyond stating this very general principle.

46. The phrase "happy fault" or *felix culpa* comes from the text of the *Exultet*, the chant sung by the deacon at the beginning of the Vigil of Easter. This notion of *felix culpa* is sometimes used to argue that God's fulfillment of human nature *requires* the fall of humanity. Thomas, however, would not subscribe to this interpretation of *felix culpa*. What we see from the history of God's dealings with humanity is not the necessity of evil, but rather God's ability to bring good out of evil, turning that evil (against our intentions) into a happy fault.

47. Just as Christ's incarnation is foreknown by God, so too the fact that "Christ Jesus came into the world to save sinners" was also foreknown by God. Indeed, since *everything* is foreknown by God, it is impossible to distinguish *on this basis* between one thing being necessary and another thing being contingent. Such distinctions must be based on *how* something is foreknown by God. The things that God knows do invariably occur, but if God knows them as occurring freely, then their invariable occurrence will still be free occurrence. If God knows them as occurring necessarily, then their occurrence will be necessary. This strikes many people as extremely counterintuitive, though it may help to keep in mind that God is outside the flow of time, so that divine "foreknowledge" is no different from any other sort of divine knowledge. What God knows is in the future for us, but it is in the eternal present for God. On predestination see 1–2.110 note 12.

48. On Adam's faith in the incarnation, see 2–2.2 note 23. The objection argues that since Adam did not have foreknowledge of his sin, foreknowledge of the incarnation is something distinct from foreknowledge of sin. Again, Thomas agrees, but adds that the distinction is that of cause and effect. Just as we can know an effect without knowing the cause (we can recognize a fire without knowing who lit it), so too Adam could know of the incarnation without knowing that it was occasioned by sin.

Question 2:

The Mode of Union of the Word Incarnate

3.2.2[1]
Did the union of the incarnate Word take place in the person?

It would seem that the union of the incarnate Word did not take place in the person.[2]

1. On this article, see Coakley (2016); Gorman (2017, 35–52).
2. This article is one slice of Thomas's extended reflection on how we might best speak and think about the union of humanity and divinity in Christ. Thomas takes as his starting point the definition of the Council of Chalcedon (AD 451): Jesus Christ is "one and the same Christ, Son, Lord, Only-begotten, recognized in *two natures, without confusion*, without change, without division, without separation; the distinction of natures being in no way annulled by the union, but rather the characteristics of each nature being preserved and *coming together to form one person* and subsistence, not as parted or separated into two persons, but one and the same Son and Only-begotten God the Word, Lord Jesus Christ" (emphasis added). Thomas is not trying to prove this definition but to make sense of it, to suggest why it is important, and to indicate what it allows us to say about God incarnate.

In the council's definition and in this section of the *Summa*, the key terms are "nature" (the *particular kind* of thing something is) and "person" (the *thing* that is of some particular kind). In brief, we can understand "nature" and "person" as corresponding to two different questions: "*What* is it?" (the nature) and "*Who* is it?" (the person). The question of the proper use of these terms was the source of much uninspiring rancor over the course of the fourth and fifth centuries. At one extreme were those who said that because Jesus was one "who" (a divine person), he could be only one "what" (i.e., his nature was solely divine). These folks are usually represented in Thomas by the Egyptian monk Eutyches. At the other extreme were those who said that since Jesus was two "whats" (divine and human), he must in some sense be two "whos" (a divine being and a human being), which are somehow conjoined by the divine being indwelling the human being. In Thomas, this view is usually represented by Nestorius.

The claim of Chalcedon, which Thomas will attempt to explain and explore, is that God incarnate is only one "who" (the Person of the Son) but two "whats" (a human nature and a divine nature). This particular article explores the claim that "one" should go with "person" rather than "nature," while at the same time maintaining that the unity of Christ's person does not entail that he have only one nature. Part of what makes this terminology potentially confusing is that "person" and "nature" are also employed in the theology of the Trinity (see 1.29 note 2), in which it is said that God has "one nature" (the divine essence) existing as "three Persons" (Father, Son, and Spirit). So in the case of the Trinity, plurality is ascribed

1. The person of God is not something other than his nature itself, as we said in the first part (1.39.1). If, therefore, the union did not take place in the nature, it follows that it did not take place in the person.[3]

2. Christ's human nature has no less dignity than ours. But personhood pertains to dignity, as was stated in the first part.[4] Therefore, since our human nature has its own personhood, even more so should Christ's have its own personhood.[5]

3. Boethius says in *On the Two Natures* (3) that a person is an individual substance of a rational nature.[6] But the Word of God took on an individual human nature, for "universal human nature does not exist of itself, but is the object of pure thought," as John of Damascus says (*On the Orthodox Faith* 3.11). Therefore human nature has its own personhood. Therefore it does not seem that the union took place in the person.[7]

On the contrary: We read in the Council of Chalcedon, "We confess that our Lord Jesus Christ is not partitioned or divided into two persons, but is one and the same only begotten Son and Word of God."[8] Therefore the union of the Word is made in the person.

---

to the Persons and unity to the nature, whereas in the case of Christ, plurality is ascribed to the natures and unity is ascribed to the Person. Thomas wants to show that this may indeed be confusing, but not because the terminology itself is confused; rather, confusion arises because we do not always adequately grasp the proper use of the terminology.

3. This objection identifies a key problem in the claim that Jesus Christ is one person subsisting in two natures: granted that God is "simple" (see 1.3 note 2), God's nature (*what* God is) is not a different thing from God's person (*who* God is). Indeed, the fundamental trinitarian claim for Thomas is that while the three Persons are really distinct from one another, they are each identical with the divine nature. So, the claim here goes, whatever is true of the nature must be true of the person, and so if the union is not in the nature, neither can it be in the person.

4. See 1.29.3 ad 2.

5. If our human nature possesses some positive feature that Christ's humanity lacks—in this case, "personhood"—then it would seem that his humanity is inferior to ours, which would be unfitting. So Christ's humanity must have its own personhood, such that his human and divine natures could not be united in a single person.

6. See 1.29 note 5.

7. The objection makes the point that God became incarnate not by taking on or "assuming" human nature in the abstract, but by taking on a particular, individual human nature—the human nature of Jesus of Nazareth. What normally makes a human nature particular or, as Boethius puts it, "an individual substance" is personhood. Therefore Jesus's human nature must have its own personhood.

8. Thomas's theology of the incarnation is notable for his careful rereading of the documents of the early Christian councils that forged the mainstream Christian articulation of the relationship of humanity and divinity in Christ. Much thirteenth-century Christology took as its framework the "three opinions" identified by Peter Lombard in his *Sentences* (bk. 3, dist. 6, chs. 2–4) as to how the union of humanity and divinity in Jesus was to be understood: the *homo-assumptus* view, the "subsistence" view, and the *habitus* view (for a discussion of the first and third opinions, which Thomas rejects, see 3.16 note 10). Thomas, unsurprisingly, follows this approach in his *Commentary on the Sentences*, as well as in various other works. By the time he writes the *Summa*, he makes explicit mention of these views only briefly (3.2.6),

I answer: "Person" has a different meaning from "nature"; namely, "nature" designates the essence of the species, which is signified by the definition.[9] And if nothing was found to be added to what pertains to the concept of the species, there would be no need to distinguish the nature itself from its *suppositum*, which is the individual subsisting in this nature, because every individual subsisting in a nature would be completely identical with its nature.[10] Now in certain subsisting things, we happen to find things that do not belong to the concept of the species—that is, accidents and individuating principles—which appear chiefly in those things that are composed from matter and form. Therefore, in these things the nature and the *suppositum* really differ, not as if they were wholly separate, but because the *suppositum* itself includes the nature of the species, and in addition certain other things besides the concept of the species.[11] Therefore the term *suppositum* indicates

their significance as a framework for Christology having been eclipsed by his deep engagement with the councils of the fourth and fifth centuries.

9. See Aristotle, *Physics* 2.1, 193ª.

10. It will be helpful at this point to clarify the relation of the terms *suppositum*, "person," and "nature." Roughly speaking, for Thomas a *suppositum* (or the equivalent Greek term, *hypostasis*) is the individual entity about which a statement is made. Thus in the proposition "Socrates is a human being," the *suppositum* is Socrates. A "nature" (which is the same thing as "the concept of the species") indicates that which makes a thing the kind of thing it is. In the proposition "Socrates is a human being," the term "human being" designates the "nature" of Socrates, a nature that corresponds to the definition "rational animal." The term "person" simply indicates a *suppositum* whose nature is rational.

This distinction between *suppositum* and "nature" helps us understand why a statement such as "The husband of Xanthippe is the teacher of Plato" is true. A seemingly similar true statement, "All bachelors are unmarried men," is true because "bachelor" and "unmarried" have the same meaning (or, in technical terms, "signification"); put differently, "bachelors" and "unmarried men" indicate the same nature. But this is clearly not the case with "The husband of Xanthippe is the teacher of Plato." One cannot be an unmarried man without being a bachelor (presuming that "widower" is simply a kind of bachelor), but one can certainly be the teacher of Plato without being the husband of Xanthippe. Rather, "The husband of Xanthippe is the teacher of Plato" is true because the phrases "husband of Xanthippe" and "teacher of Plato" refer to the same *suppositum*—Socrates.

Thomas says that if an individual entity were nothing but its nature, then there would be no distinction between *suppositum* and nature. In the case of Socrates, however, this is not the case, since in addition to being a rational animal, he is also the husband of Xanthippe and the teacher of Plato, and many other things besides. Thomas will go on to argue that a distinction between *suppositum* and nature characterizes *any* material being, since in addition to its nature it has its particular matter (see 1.12 note 2). Indeed, this distinction applies even to nonmaterial creatures (such as angels), since in addition to their natures they possess something else: the fact of having been created (see 1.3 note 2). It does not, however, apply in the case of God, which is why the Persons of the Trinity as distinct *supposita* are identical with the divine nature.

11. Thomas argues that in material creatures there is a real difference between *suppositum* and nature, but there is not a separation. At least in the case of material beings, Thomas bases his argument on Aristotle's view that natures exist only as adhering in some subject or *suppositum*. Just as one never finds matter without it being some specific *kind* of matter, so too one never finds an identity without it being some particular *instance* of that identity.

a whole that has a nature as its "formal" and perfecting part.[12] Consequently, in things that are composed of matter and form the nature is not predicated of the *suppositum*, for we do not say "this human being is his humanity."[13] But if there is a thing in which there is nothing outside the species or its nature, as in the case of God, the *suppositum* and the nature are not really distinct in it, but only in our way of thinking. Then it is called "nature" inasmuch as it is an essence, and a *suppositum* inasmuch as it is subsisting.[14] And what is said of a *suppositum* is understood of "person" in the case of rational or intellectual creatures, for a person is nothing other than "an individual substance of rational nature," according to Boethius.

Therefore, whatever is in any person is united to him in person, whether it pertains to his nature or not.[15] And so, if the human nature is not united

12. On "form," which is here identical with "nature," see 1.12 note 2. The form is "perfecting" because it makes a thing what it is.

13. What Thomas says here is initially a bit puzzling since, in the proposition "Socrates is a human being," it certainly seems to be the case that a nature ("human being") is being predicated of a *suppositum* ("Socrates"). Thomas's concern is that we not let grammatical predication in a proposition (on predication, see 1.3 note 3) lead us to think of a person as an empty point of reference to which a nature can be attached. I am not an "x" that possesses human nature; I just simply *am* a concretely existing instance of human nature. There is no Socrates apart from his possession of a human nature. Socrates is a human in a different way than he is a husband to Xanthippe or a teacher to Plato. Presumably we could imagine that were Socrates a single student instead of a married teacher he would nonetheless still be Socrates (indeed, we do in fact think that he was Socrates before his marriage and while still in school); but we cannot imagine that if Socrates were to possesses the nature of a cow he would be the same *suppositum*. The upshot of this discussion is that, as noted before, nature and person are distinguishable, but not separable: a human nature is always found only in a particular person.

14. If we should be wary of separating nature and person in the case of human beings, we should be even more wary in the case of God, since God's simplicity (see 1.3 note 2) requires that the words "divinity" and "God" signify the same thing (the same *res significata*), though they do so in different ways (according to a twofold *modus significandi*). Thus "divinity" signifies as if it were an essential quality belonging to God, and "God" signifies as if it were that to which the essential quality of "divinity" belongs. The reason for this dual way of signifying is the problem that is inherent in *all* theological language: we want to speak about the uncreated God, but our language and conceptual apparatus is designed to speak about creatures (see 1.13 notes 8 and 9). Thomas consistently attempts to find the least inadequate use of the human way of speaking, so that human speech can point to the mystery of God.

15. At this point, it is helpful to step back and see where Thomas has led us. The basic problem is how to reconcile the notion of divine simplicity with the single *suppositum* and the dual natures of Christ. Thomas does not want to retreat from his strong affirmation of the identity of God's essence (nature) and existence (*suppositum*). At the same time, he wants to say something about Christ's *suppositum* (namely, that it is one) that he does not want to say about his nature. For Thomas, this difficulty hardly comes as a surprise, since our creaturely language is woefully inadequate to the theological task. On the other hand, it is the only language we have available. So when speaking of God we must attend carefully to the *way* in which our language embodies meaning (the *modus significandi*), while realizing that our language never adequately says *what* we mean (the *res significata*).

When we attend to the way in which our language embodies meaning, we see that "person" or *suppositum* is the subject of which things are predicated. If we conceive of this along the lines of a grammatical analysis, what Thomas wants to alert us to is how in our ordinary speech it is the subject (or person) that

to God the Word in person, it is not united to him in *any* way, and thus belief in the incarnation is altogether done away with, which subverts the entire Christian faith.[16] Therefore, since the Word has united a human nature to himself—which does not, however, pertain to his divine nature—it follows that the union took place in the person of the Word, and not in the nature.

Reply to 1: Although in God nature and person are not really different, the words still differ in their ways of signifying God, as was said above, since "person" signifies in the manner of something that subsists. And because human nature is united to the Word in such a way that the Word subsists in it,[17] yet neither in such a way that anything is added to the definition of his [divine] nature nor in such a way that his nature would be changed into something else, it follows that the union took place in the person, not in the nature.

Reply to 2: Personhood is necessarily related to the dignity and perfection of a thing, insofar as it is part of the dignity and perfection of that thing to exist by itself (which is understood by the word "person"). But it is a greater dignity to exist in something nobler than oneself than to exist by oneself. Therefore the human nature of Christ has a greater dignity than ours, because in us human nature, being existent by itself, has its own personhood, but in Christ it exists in the person of the Word.[18] In the same way, it pertains to the

---

unites different predicates; for example, "Socrates" unites "the husband of Xanthippe" and "the teacher of Plato." When we say "Jesus Christ is divine and human," two distinct predicates ("divine" and "human") are said of the same *suppositum*. Of course, there remains a certain asymmetry, since the divine nature is predicated of the person of the Son from all eternity, whereas the human nature comes to be predicated of him in time. For more on the logic of the statement "God is a human being," see 3.16.1, below.

16. This might seem a rather dire statement to make about rather technical theological terms, but it indicates that for Thomas the technicalities of the incarnation are crucial; indeed, it is the unity of the *suppositum* or person that allows us to ascribe to God certain things concerning the human nature of Jesus Christ such that the human story of Jesus becomes truly the story of God. Thus we can say "God was born of the Virgin Mary" and "God died on the cross" not as mere metaphor, but as literally true. In Thomas's view, the truth of such statements is the whole point of the incarnation.

17. *Verbum in ea subsistat*: this wording seems at first as if it must be a mistake on Thomas's part, since it sounds as if the human nature is the subject or *suppositum* in which the Word is found. However, everything else Thomas has said indicates the opposite: the Word, and not the human nature, is a subsisting thing; it is in this way that Thomas makes "the Word" the subject of the verb *subsistere*. To make Thomas's point clearer, we might translate this clause as follows: "Human nature is united to the Word in such a way that the Word subsists as human."

18. Following the teaching of the Council of Chalcedon, Thomas does not conceive of the person that unites humanity and divinity as some neutral *suppositum*; rather, it is the second Person of the Trinity, the divine Word. Thus, although Christ has a genuine human nature, this nature exists in the divine *suppositum* of the Word. Strictly speaking, therefore, although Christ has a human nature, he is not a human "person." However, we must remember that for Thomas "person" means the subject to which things are attributed; it does not carry our modern notion of "personality." For many people today, the denial that Jesus was a human person is tantamount to saying that he was not truly human. Thomas, however, clearly maintains that Christ has a fully human psychology, because he possesses a fully human soul (in Greek, *psychē*). See 3.9.4, below. So in the denial of human "personhood" to Jesus, one must be clear that "person" is being

dignity of a form to fulfill a species, yet the capacity for sensation is nobler in humans than in nonrational animals, where it is itself the form that perfects, because of its union with the nobler form that perfects it.[19]

Reply to 3: As John of Damascus says (*On the Orthodox Faith* 3.11), "The Word of God . . . did not assume human nature in general, but in particular [*in atomo*]"—that is, in an individual—otherwise every human being would be the Word of God, just as Christ was. Yet we must bear in mind that not every individual in the genus "substance" is a person, even in the case of rational natures. Rather, this is the case only with that which exists by itself, and not that which exists in some more perfect thing.[20] Therefore the hand of Socrates, although it is a kind of individual, is not a person, because it does not exist by itself, but in something more perfect—that is, in the whole. The same thing is signified by the designation of a person as "an individual substance," for the hand is not a complete substance, but part of a substance. So although the human nature is a kind of individual in the genus of substance, it does not have its own personhood, because it does not exist separately but in something more perfect—namely, in the person of the Word. Therefore the union took place in the person.

---

used in a particular semantic and metaphysical sense, not in our everyday sense, according to which we might well say that Jesus is a human person.

19. Both human beings and other animals have the capacity for sensation; in animals this capacity comes from the "sensual soul," which is their substantial form (i.e., that which makes them what they are), whereas in humans this capacity comes from the "rational soul." Thus in human beings the capacity for sensation has greater "nobility" than it does in animals, because it is the capacity of a more noble substantial form.

Thomas alludes in passing here to what was, in his day, one of his most controversial teachings: the unity of substantial form in human beings. Many of Thomas's contemporaries, like Bonaventure, held that human beings possessed three souls (and therefore three substantial forms) corresponding to the three levels of life: the capacity for life and generation (as with plants); the capacity for sensation (as with nonrational animals); and the capacity for thought (as with human beings and angels). Thomas, in contrast, held that in order for a human being to be one thing, he or she could have only one substantial form, and this was the rational soul. It is perhaps difficult for people today to fully appreciate the heat generated by this debate.

20. In other words, not every "thing" or "substance" is an individual entity in the same sense that a "person" is. Some things exist as parts of larger wholes. The analogy Thomas goes on to use is in some ways unfitting, since Jesus's humanity is not a "part" of him in the same way that Socrates's hand is a part of him. In particular, Thomas wants to speak of Christ's humanity as "a kind of individual in the genus of substance," but he has already denied that Socrates's hand is an individual substance (it is, rather, a part of a substance). Thomas is aware of how feeble his analogy is; so, as with all analogies, we have to recognize both how it is fitting and how it is unfitting for what he wants to say. Christ's humanity is like a part of an individual inasmuch as it receives its existence from that to which it is joined (i.e., the divine person of the Word). However, it is unlike a part of a whole inasmuch as it is a kind of individual substance. He thinks the part-whole analogy, for all its problems, is preferable to other analogies that were on offer, such as the accident-substance analogy, which would give a weaker sense of the unity of Christ.

Question 9:

Christ's Knowledge in General

3.9.4[1]
Did Christ have any knowledge acquired through experience?

It would seem that in Christ there was no knowledge acquired through experience.[2]

1. On this article, see Madigan (1997); Gaine (2015); Gaine (2018).

2. Thomas, along with every orthodox theologian up to his day, believed that, as the second Person of the Trinity, Christ had "divine" knowledge—that is, all the knowledge that properly belongs to God, possessed in the way that God possesses it. Twelfth-century theologians differed, however, on whether Christ also possessed "created" knowledge—i.e., the kind of knowledge proper to a creature. Hugh of St. Victor said no, seeing Christ's human soul as participating in the perfect wisdom of the eternal Word and having no separate, created knowledge (see On the Sacraments 2.1.6). Peter Lombard, on the other hand, said that Christ's true humanity entailed his possession of truly human knowledge (Sentences bk. 3, dists. 13–14), and most thirteenth-century theologians followed him on that point. However, most theologians conceived of this created knowledge along the lines of the beatific vision, leaving little if any room for Christ to acquire knowledge in the normal way that human's do—i.e., through experience.

In Summa theologiae 3.9 Thomas gives his mature account of the different kinds of knowledge that Christ possessed. After affirming Christ's uncreated, divine knowledge as the Word, he goes on to sketch three kinds of created, human knowledge that Christ had: (1) Beatific knowledge (as the blessed in heaven have), which arises from the vision of the divine essence. Thomas says that if Christ is to be the cause of this knowledge in us, then it must be something that he himself possesses. (2) Infused knowledge, which is imprinted directly on the passive intellect by God—the sort of knowing-by-divine-gift that the angels possess (and, in a different way, the prophets). (3) Acquired knowledge, which is obtained in the ordinary human way, through sense experience. We might note here that these three forms of knowledge correspond to Thomas's triad of nature (acquired knowledge), grace (infused knowledge), and glory (beatific knowledge) (see 1.93 note 12).

In this article Thomas argues for Christ's possession of acquired knowledge and, in doing so, departs from the typical view of medieval theology, and indeed from his own earlier view (see notes 6 and 12, below). He is not particularly bothered, as we might be today, by the question of what it would be like for one human being to possess these three forms of knowledge—that is, by the question of what the "experience" of God incarnate would have been. Rather, he is concerned with showing what must be affirmed of Christ's human knowledge if Christ is to be both truly human and truly divine. The modern question may be a good one, but it is not the question that provoked the answers Thomas gives here.

Before reading the rest of this article, it is important to understand Thomas's views on the normal apparatus of human knowledge. For that, see 1.12 note 11.

1. Whatever was fitting for Christ, he had in the most perfect way. But Christ did not have acquired knowledge in the most perfect way, since he did not devote himself to the study of books [*studio litterarum*], by which knowledge is acquired most perfectly, for it says in John (7:15), "The Jews marveled, saying, 'How does this man know letters, having never learned?'" It seems, therefore, that there was no acquired knowledge in Christ.[3]

2. Nothing can be added to what is full. But the potential of Christ's soul was filled with divinely infused intellectual species, as was said earlier (3.9.3).[4] Therefore no acquired species could be added to his soul.

3. One who already has the disposition of knowledge [*habitum scientiae*] acquires no new disposition through what is received from the senses;[5] otherwise two forms of the same species would be in the same thing together. Instead, the disposition that previously existed is strengthened and increased.[6] Therefore, since Christ had the disposition of infused knowledge, it does not seem that he acquired any new knowledge through what he perceived by the senses.[7]

On the contrary: It says in Hebrews (5:8), "Since he was the Son of God, he learned obedience by the things that he suffered"—that is, "experienced," says a gloss. There was, therefore, in Christ some knowledge from experience, which is acquired knowledge.

I answer: As is plain from what was said earlier, "nothing that God implanted in our nature was lacking" in the human nature assumed by the Word

---

3. The objection presumes that (1) if Christ had acquired knowledge, it would be knowledge acquired in the most perfect way, and that (2) formal instruction—"book learning"—is the most perfect way of acquiring knowledge. However, Christ did not have formal instruction; therefore, it supposes, Christ did not have acquired knowledge.

4. In the previous article, Thomas argues that the "passive" or "receptive" part of Christ's human intellect was actualized when God directly imprinted upon it the intellectual conceptions by which he knows things. Put more plainly, but less precisely, Christ as a human being possessed by divine gift knowledge of all things. The objection argues that if this were the case, then there would be no need for Christ to gain knowledge of things in the ordinary human way—in other words, through experience.

5. On *habitus* in Thomas, see 1–2.55 note 2.

6. When I encounter a cow for the first time, I gain a new intellectual conception: "cowness." When I encounter a cow for the second or third or fourth time, I do not acquire a second or third or fourth conception of "cowness." Rather, my already existing conception of "cowness" is strengthened, perhaps because I now see that certain features that I thought were essential to being a cow (e.g., being brown) are in fact incidental.

The view that Christ's experientially acquired knowledge was simply an enhancement of knowledge already imprinted by God was the common view of Thomas's contemporaries. His teacher Albert the Great wrote in his commentary on Lombard's *Sentences* (3.13.10) that sense experience did not "create" (*faciens*) a *habitus* but only "stimulated" (*excitans*) one that already existed.

7. Since Christ already had a full set of intellectual conceptions by divine gift, he could not, strictly speaking, learn anything. When he encountered a cow for the first time he already possessed the concept "cow," so at no point in his human life did he ever learn what a cow was.

of God.[8] It is clear that God implanted in human nature not only a possible but an active intellect; therefore, one must necessarily say that in the soul of Christ there was not merely a possible intellect but also an active intellect. But if in other things "God and nature make nothing superfluous," as the Philosopher says in *On the Heavens and the Earth* (1.4, 271^a), still less is there anything superfluous in the soul of Christ. Something that does not have its own function is superfluous, since "all things exist for the sake of their functions," as is said in *On the Heavens and the Earth* (2.3, 286^a). Now the proper function of the active intellect is to make intellectual species actual by drawing them from sense images; therefore, it is said in *De anima* (3.5, 430^a) that the active intellect is that "by which [the soul] is made all things."[9] So it is necessary to say that in Christ there were intellectual species received into the possible intellect by the action of the active intellect. This means that there was acquired knowledge in him, which some call knowledge "from experience" [*experimentalem*].[10]

And for this reason it is said, although I wrote differently earlier,[11] in Christ there was acquired knowledge, which truly is knowledge in a human way, not

8. The specific reference is a bit unclear, but one might look, for example, at the fifth question of the third part. Thomas also appears to be silently quoting a phrase from John of Damascus (*On the Orthodox Faith* 3.6).

Along with the mainstream of the Christian tradition, Thomas held that Christ was human in every normal sense of the term. Specifically, there was no power or faculty of human nature that was lacking in him, usurped, as it were, by a divine power or faculty. So if human beings have a faculty for acquiring knowledge through sense experience, Christ, too, must possess that faculty, or else he would be something less than human. We might think of this aspect of Thomas's theology of Christ as informed by his conviction that "grace does not take away nature but perfects it" (see 1.1 note 34). On the other hand, it is possible that this conviction is itself informed by the church's teaching on the integrity of Christ's humanity. In other words, because we see in Christ the perfection and not the destruction or supplanting of his humanity, we come to see that God's characteristic way of acting in the world is to bring natures to perfection and not to supplant them.

9. The active intellect draws the form of the thing perceived from the sense image and imprints it on the possible intellect (see 1.12 note 11); by taking on the form of the thing it knows, the rational soul becomes that thing "virtually." Since the soul has the capacity to know anything that is knowable, it is (virtually) all things.

The Latin term Thomas uses here, *abstractio*, is often translated as "abstracts," but I generally render it as "draws," since in contemporary English the word "abstract" carries connotations of being removed from reality, whereas for Thomas it is the mind's act of *abstractio* that connects it to reality, as the mind draws more general conceptions from specific sense images.

10. If Christ is to have a complete humanity, he must have both the capacity to receive conceptual knowledge (the passive or possible intellect) and the capacity to derive concepts from sense experience (the active intellect). But there would be no point in having these capacities if he did not exercise them, because a capacity exists in order to carry out its "proper operation" or characteristic activity. If Christ had an active intellect, then it must have engaged in its characteristic activity, which is to derive concepts from sense experience.

11. This is a question on which Thomas, somewhat famously, changed his mind. Not surprisingly, in his early *Commentary on the Sentences* (bk. 3, dist. 14, q. 1, a. 3, qa. 5; bk. 3, dist. 18, q. 1, a. 3 ad 5) he follows the

only as regards the subject receiving it but also as regards the active cause. For such knowledge is posited in Christ according to the light of the active intellect, which is natural to human nature.[12] Infused knowledge, on the other hand, is attributed to the soul on account of a light infused from on high, and this manner of knowing is suited to the angelic nature. But beatific knowledge, by which God's essence itself is seen, is proper and natural to God alone, as was said in the first part (1.12.4).

Reply to 1: Since there is a twofold way of acquiring knowledge—by discovery and by being taught—the way of discovery is the higher, and the way of being taught is secondary.[13] Therefore it is said in Aristotle's *Ethics* (1.4, 1095^b), "He indeed is best who knows everything by himself; yet he is good who obeys him that speaks well." And so it was more fitting for Christ to possess knowledge acquired by discovery than by being taught, especially since he was given by God to be the teacher of all, according to Joel (2:23): "Be joyful in the Lord your God, because he has given you a teacher of justice."

Reply to 2: The human mind has two relations. One is to higher things, and in this respect the soul of Christ was full of infused knowledge. The other relation is to lower things—that is, to sense images [*phantasmata*], which naturally move the human mind by the power of the active intellect. It was necessary that even in this respect the soul of Christ should be filled with knowledge, not because the first fullness was not in itself sufficient for the human mind, but because it was proper for it also to be perfected by being conformed to sense images.[14]

---

view of his teacher Albert the Great. Even as late as his *Compendium of Theology*, written not long before this section of the *Summa*, he still seems hesitant to ascribe any genuine acquired knowledge to Christ.

12. This is Thomas's mature position: Christ possessed genuine knowledge acquired through experience. What was it that caused Thomas to change his view, running counter to the theological current of his day? No doubt in part he saw this view as a fitting consequence of the affirmation of the full humanity of Christ. If, as the Letter to the Hebrews (2:17) would have it, Christ "had to become like his brothers and sisters in every respect, so that he might be a merciful and faithful high priest in the service of God," then he must have acquired knowledge through experience. Also in play, however, is a growing commitment to Aristotle's account of knowledge in terms of the possible and active aspects of the intellect as the best and truest account of how a human being knows.

13. Thomas simply denies the premise of the objection—namely, that book learning is the best way of acquiring knowledge. Indeed, Thomas later (3.12.3) goes on to deny that Jesus ever learned anything from anyone; rather he gained all his acquired knowledge on his own. This idea somewhat diminishes the sense that Jesus was "like his brothers and sisters in every respect." However, it is entirely consistent with Thomas's view that *scientia* is superior as a way of knowing to simply memorizing facts: it is one thing to parrot back $a^2 + b^2 = c^2$, and it is another to grasp the Pythagorean theorem. While Jesus may have learned certain facts from his parents—like the Aramaic word for "bird" or what the capital of the province of Judea was—his knowledge of the whys and wherefores of the world came by his own discovery.

14. With respect to *what* Christ knows, infused knowledge is certainly sufficient, and acquired knowledge can add nothing. But with respect to *how* Christ knows, acquired knowledge adds to infused knowledge the operation of the active intellect. However, this reply seems to skirt the issue of whether, to put it crudely,

Reply to 3: The nature of an acquired disposition is one thing, and that of an infused disposition is another. For the disposition of knowledge is acquired by the relation of the human mind to sense images; therefore, another disposition of the same kind cannot be acquired repeatedly. But the disposition of infused knowledge is of a different nature, coming down to the soul from on high, without any recourse to sense images. And therefore these dispositions are each defined differently.[15]

---

there is any "room" for experientially acquired concepts in an intellect that has been "filled" with divinely imparted concepts. In part, Thomas's answer to this question is found in the reply to the third objection.

15. To address the question of how one can have the same knowledge from two different sources (e.g., knowledge of "cowness" through a divinely imprinted concept and knowledge of "cowness" through encountering a cow), Thomas simply denies that these two bits of knowledge are the same *habitus*, since they come from different sources. However, Thomas does not go on to spell out exactly how this distinction works. Indeed, his reply seems more an assertion than any sort of argument.

Question 16:

What Is Fittingly Said of Christ

3.16.1[1]
Is this statement true: "God is a human being"?[2]

It would seem that this is false: "God is a human being."

1. Every affirmative proposition uniting matter remote in some way [*materia aliqua remota*] is false.[3] But this proposition, "God is a human being," is of remote matter, since the forms signified by the subject and predicate are

---

1. On this article, see O'Neill (1965); McCabe (2002, 107–14).

2. This may strike us as an odd question to ask, and Thomas addresses it in a highly technical way that draws upon certain views on the logic of predication. But in terms of Thomas's overall discussion of Jesus Christ the question actually makes a lot of sense. In the *Summa*, this article is framed within a larger question concerning what we can and cannot say about God given the Christian belief that Jesus is God incarnate: one person (or, what is more important in this article, one *suppositum* or "logical subject") who possesses two natures, divine and human. Within the context of this larger question Thomas also has articles asking such things as whether one can truly say that "a human being is God" or that "Christ is a creature."

Thomas's point here is that because Jesus was both divine and human—because two natures are united in one logical subject—we can make certain statements about God that we could not make otherwise, such as "God was born of the Virgin Mary" or "God died on the cross." Our ability to say such things about God stems from what is known as the *communicatio idiomatum* or "exchange of properties" (a term Thomas does not use in the *Summa* but does use in his commentary on Lombard's *Sentences*—e.g., bk. 3, dist. 5, q. 2, a. 2). In Jesus, God took on a human nature and thus identified himself with such humble human activities as birth and death.

Note that the claim Thomas is inquiring about, *Deus est homo*, can be translated as either "God is human" or "God is a human being"; in the context of this question, the second translation is likely the better one.

3. In this context, the term *materia* means the "subject matter" of the proposition—that is, the subject and predicate contained in the proposition. Thomas, drawing on Aristotle's *On Interpretation*, holds that there are three possible relations of the subject and predicate (see *Commentary on Peri hermeneias* 1.13): (1) if the predicate forms all or part of the definition of the subject, then the "matter" is said to be "necessary" or "natural" (e.g., "A human being is a rational animal"); (2) if the predicate is something that may or may not be true of the subject, then the "matter" is said to be "possible" or "contingent" (e.g., "The woman is laughing" or "The table is blue"); (3) if the predicate cannot be properly joined to the subject, then the "matter" is said to be "remote" (e.g., "The table is laughing"). Often statements of the last sort seem to us not so much wrong (the way "The woman is laughing" might be wrong if the woman is in

---

as far apart as they can be. Therefore, since the proposition in question is affirmative, it would seem to be false.

2. The three divine Persons are in greater mutual agreement than the human nature and the divine. But in the mystery of the incarnation one Person is not predicated of another: we do not say that the Father is the Son, or vice versa.[4] Therefore it seems that we should not predicate human nature of God by saying that God is a human being.

3. Athanasius says that "just as the soul and the flesh are one human being, so God and a human being are one Christ."[5] But this is false: "The soul is the body." Therefore this also is false: "God is a human being."[6]

4. It was said in the first part (1.39.4) that what is predicated of God, not relatively but absolutely, befits the whole Trinity and each of the Persons. But this term "human being" is not relative, but absolute. Therefore, if it is truly predicated of God, it would follow that the whole Trinity and each of the Persons is a human being, which is clearly false.[7]

On the contrary: It is written in Philippians (2:6–7), "who, being in the form of God . . . emptied himself, taking the form of a servant, being made in human likeness and found in the human condition." And so he who is in the form of God is a human being. But he who is in the form of God is God. Therefore God is a human being.

I answer: This proposition "God is a human being" is accepted by all Christians, yet not all with the same meaning. Some grant the proposition, but not according to the proper understanding of the terms.[8] Thus the Manichaeans say the Word of God is a human being, yet not truly human, but only appar-

---

fact crying) as nonsensical. Similarly, the objection argues, the statement "God is a human being" is as nonsensical as "The table is laughing."

4. The objection argues that even though the Father, Son, and Spirit share the *same* divine nature, we still do not say "the Father is the Son" or "the Son is the Spirit." Even less, then, should we be able to say "God is a human being," since we are in this case talking about two *different* natures.

5. On "Athanasius" here, see 1.36 note 8.

6. Though soul and body unite to form one person, this does not warrant claiming that the soul is the body. Even more so, the objection claims, God and humanity forming the one person Jesus Christ does not warrant saying that God is a human being.

7. The objection notes that in speaking of the Trinity we say some things about God "absolutely" (or, as Thomas sometimes says, "essentially")—such as "good" or "wise" or "divine"—that are equally true of all the Persons of the Trinity; we say other things "relatively" (or, as Thomas sometimes says, "notionally") in terms of the relations of origin of the Persons—such as "begotten" or "unbegotten"—that are true only of one of the Persons (see 1.39 note 2). The objection argues that "human being" is an absolute term like "good" or "wise" or "divine," since it identifies a nature, and so would have to be equally true of all the Persons of the Trinity, which it clearly is not, since only the Son is incarnate.

8. According to Thomas, anyone who would call themselves a Christian would be willing to say that "God is a human being." Differences arise either over how the terms "God" and "human being" are understood or over the nature of the union described by the word "is."

ently human, inasmuch as they say that the Son of God took on an imaginary body. In this way, God is said to be a human being in the same way that a bronze statue is called a human being, because it has the appearance of a human being.[9] Similarly, those who held that Christ's body and soul were not united could not say that God is truly a human being; rather, he is figuratively called a human being on account of the parts.[10] Both these opinions were disproved earlier (3.2.5–6; 3.5.1–2).

Some, on the contrary, maintain the reality on the human side but deny the reality on the side of God; for they say that Christ, who is the God-man [*qui est Deus homo*], is God not naturally but by participation—that is, by grace, in the same way as all other holy men are called gods—Christ being more excellently so than the rest, on account of his more abundant grace.[11] And thus, when it is said that "God is a human being," the word "God" does not stand for the true and natural God. This is the heresy of Photinus,[12] which was disproved earlier (3.2.10, 11).

But some grant this proposition, together with the reality of both terms, holding that Christ is truly God and truly a human being, but they do not preserve the truth of the predication;[13] for they say that "human being" is said of God on account of some sort of conjunction, whether of dignity, authority,

9. The Manichaeans were a Christian group in the third and fourth centuries who believed that material reality was inherently evil and who therefore believed that Jesus's material human body was simply an illusion. Their views were similar to those of the Cathars of the thirteenth century.

10. In the twelfth century, Peter Abelard, wishing to maintain the reality of Christ's humanity, had argued that although there was only one *person* in Christ (as Chalcedon taught), the human and divine natures were distinct *hypostases*. This view, called the *homo-assumptus* view, was widely seen in the Middle Ages as a revival of Nestorianism (see 3.2 note 2), since most theologians saw *persona* and *hypostasis* as synonymous in this context (as Thomas himself does). Followers of Abelard, attempting to avoid the charge of Nestorianism, modified this theory in order to explain how the human nature could be a distinct hypostasis while not being a "person." They argued that the body and soul were not united to each other, and so did not form a person, according to the Boethian definition of "person" as "an individual substance of rational nature"; rather, each was independently joined to the person of the Son of God. This latter view, known as the *habitus* theory of the incarnation, is the object of Thomas's criticism here. In Thomas's eyes, those who hold this view are not so much Nestorian (as was Abelard) as something worse: their position is equivalent to Manichaeism inasmuch as, by denying the union of body and soul, it makes the humanity of Christ only an apparent humanity.

11. Christians believe that they are all "adopted" children of God through grace (which is why Christians can pray to God as "our Father"), but only Christ is God "by nature." The position Thomas is arguing against here is one that would deny this distinction and depict Jesus as simply a holy person. He would then be "divine" only in that sense and not in the sense that God the Father and the Holy Spirit are divine. The reference to human beings being called "gods" suggests biblical passages such as Psalm 82:6—"I say, 'You are gods, children of the Most High, all of you.'"

12. Photinus was a fourth-century heretic. Not much is known about his teachings, but he apparently denied that Jesus was truly divine.

13. In other words, they understand "God" and "human being" correctly but do not understand how these two things are joined by "is."

affection, or indwelling. It was in this way that Nestorius held God to be a human being: this means nothing more than that God is joined to a human being by the sort of conjunction in which a human being is indwelled by God and united to him by affection and by a sharing in divine authority and honor. And those who suppose two *supposita* or hypostases in Christ fall into the same error,[14] since it is impossible to understand how, in the case of two things distinct in *suppositum* or hypostasis, one can be properly predicated of the other, unless it is merely by means of a figure of speech, inasmuch as they are united in something. It is as if we were to say that Peter is John because they are somehow mutually joined together.[15] And these opinions also were disproved earlier (3.2.3, 6).

Supposing, therefore, according to the truth of the catholic faith,[16] that the true divine nature is united with a true human nature not only in the person but also in the *suppositum* or hypostasis, we say that this proposition is properly formed: "God is a human being"—not only according to the truth of its terms (i.e., because Christ is truly God and truly human) but also according to the truth of the predication. For a word signifying the common nature in the concrete may stand for whatever is contained in the common nature, as this term "human" may stand for any individual human being.[17] And thus this word "God," from the very way that it signifies, may stand for the person of the Son of God, as was said in the first part (1.39.4). Now we may truly and properly predicate of every *suppositum* of any nature a word signifying that nature in the concrete, as "human" may properly and truly be predicated of Socrates and Plato. Therefore, since the person of the Son of God, for whom this word "God" stands, is a *suppositum* of human nature, this word "human" may be truly and properly predicated of this word "God," on the ground that it stands for the person of the Son of God.[18]

14. Thomas is presumably speaking of Abelard and others who held the *homo-assumptus* view (see note 10, above). On the term *suppositum* (and the roughly equivalent Greek term *hypostasis*), see 3.2 note 10.

15. One might think of the way in which some couples who are expecting a baby will say, "We are pregnant." Such a claim is, of course, "merely . . . a figure of speech," and an unfortunate one at that. The pregnancy cannot be properly predicated of the man, since the man and the woman remain distinct *supposita*. The fact that it is only the woman who is pregnant usually becomes quite clear at the onset of labor, if not earlier.

16. Here Thomas is not trying to prove that Jesus is fully divine and fully human and yet a single *suppositum*; he is, rather, presuming it. He is trying to show what statements are logically possible given this belief.

17. So having identified the nature shared by Tom, Dick, and Harriet as "human," we can also speak of each of them individually as "a human."

18. To grasp what Thomas is saying here, we might compare the statement "God is a human being" to "God is the rock of my salvation." For Thomas these are two distinct kinds of statements: the first is

Reply to 1: When different forms cannot come together [*convenire*] in one *suppositum*,[19] the proposition is necessarily in remote matter, the subject signifying one form and the predicate another. But when two forms *can* come together in one *suppositum*, the matter is not remote, but natural or contingent, as when I say, "Something white is musical."[20] But the divine and human natures, although as far apart as possible, nevertheless come together, by the mystery of incarnation, in one *suppositum*, in which neither exists accidentally but both essentially [*secundum se*].[21] Therefore this proposition is in neither remote nor contingent matter, but in natural matter. "Human being" is not predicated of God accidentally but essentially [*per se*], as of its own hypostasis,[22] not on account of the form signified by this word "God," but on account of the *suppositum*, which is the hypostasis of the human nature.[23]

---

literally true, whereas the second is metaphorically true but literally false. "God" and "human being" are used literally, whereas "rock" is used metaphorically. This is what Thomas means by "the truth of its terms."

But "God is a human being" is also literally true because "is" is used in the way we use it when we make literal statements, which is what Thomas means by "the truth of the predication." So the term "human" can be used in the abstract to refer literally to any individual instance of human nature, and likewise "God" can be used to refer literally to any individual instance of divine nature. These abstract terms also can be applied literally to any concrete individual subject [*suppositum*] possessing that nature. So in the statement "God is a human being," the term "God" is applied literally to Jesus Christ because his *suppositum* is one possessing the divine nature, and the term "human" is applied literally to him because his *suppositum* is one possessing a human nature. So, making explicit the implied *suppositum*, we might unpack the proposition in this way: "[Christ who is] God is [the same Christ who is] a human being."

In the case of "God is the rock of my salvation," the *suppositum* indicated by the term "God" does not in fact possess a mineral nature, and therefore the statement cannot be true in a literal way.

19. Note here how the notion of *convenientia* is insinuated into the discussion (see 3.1 note 2). One might reword the objection to say that the proposition "God is a human being" is an "unfitting" one.

20. Some "natures" [*formae*] *can* be combined in an affirmative proposition, either because one of the natures is an accidental form (i.e., a property of something that is changeable and does not enter into its definition; see 1.3 note 3) or because it is necessary matter.

The example "something white is musical" seems bizarre, but Thomas is thinking here of an example he will mention in the next question (3.17.2, below): Socrates, who is both white and musical. Though being white and being musical are "different forms," they are accidental forms, and thus can be combined in an affirmative proposition.

21. In saying that the divine and human natures are possessed by Jesus "essentially" and not "accidentally" Thomas is saying that Jesus is human in a different way than a chair is blue (which is a changeable property of the chair). Rather Jesus is human in the same way that a chair is something in which one sits (which is part of the definition of a chair, or what a chair is per se). The statement "God is a human being" is said of Jesus essentially because both "God" and "a human being" enter into the definition of who Jesus is (even though "human being" is not part of the definition of "God," nor "God" part of the definition of "human being").

22. That is, we say "God is a human being" because the second Person of the Trinity is the proper *suppositum* of Jesus's human nature.

23. As so often when speaking of divine things, Thomas finds that no single form of normal human discourse is suitable. Rather, we must speak "between" our normal ways of speaking. Thus when speaking of God, we must in some ways speak as if God were a "nature" (a general category of things) and in some ways as if God were a particular concrete instance of a nature. The same sort of speech applies to

Reply to 2: The three divine Persons come together in one nature yet are distinguished in *suppositum*, and therefore they are not predicated of one another.[24] But in the mystery of the incarnation the natures, being distinct, are not predicated of one another when they are signified abstractly, for the divine nature is not human. But because they agree in *suppositum*, they are predicated of each other when signified concretely.[25]

Reply to 3: "Soul" [*anima*] and "flesh" are signified abstractly, in the same way as "divinity" and "humanity." Speaking concretely, we say "something alive" [*animatum*] and "something fleshly" or "something bodily," just as, in the latter case, we say "God" and "human being." Therefore in neither case is the abstract predicated of the abstract, but only the concrete of the concrete.[26]

Reply to 4: This term "human being" is predicated of God because of the union in the Person, and this union implies a relation. Therefore it does not follow the rule of those terms that are predicated absolutely of God from eternity.[27]

---

the incarnation: our language is somewhat like language about accidental properties and somewhat like language about essential natures, but not precisely like either. See 3.2 note 20 and 3.17 note 14.

Perhaps the most significant point Thomas makes in this somewhat difficult reply is that humanity and divinity are not different forms (*formae diversae*). The statement "God is a human being" is not a contradiction like "black is white" because all differences must appear against some common background. "Black" and "white" are both colors—there is a common category of which they are distinct kinds. Cast against this common background, the statement "black is white" appears obviously nonsensical. "Divinity" and "humanity," however, do not share any such background because part of what Thomas means by "divinity" is that which is not contained in *any* category. Thus when we encounter the claim of the Christian faith that "God is a human being," we may disbelieve it, but, according to Thomas, we cannot accuse it of being nonsense.

24. On "predicated," see 1.3 note 3.

25. In other words, we can say "God is a human being," but we cannot say "divinity is humanity," nor can we say "the Son is the Father." In the case of the Son and the Father, we have different *supposita*, since the Persons of the Trinity are distinct hypostases. And in the case of divinity and humanity, we have distinct natures.

26. One could not say that "the soul is flesh" (*anima est caro*), but one *could* say "something alive is something fleshly" (*animatum est carneum*), since being alive and being fleshly are both properties of a single concrete "something."

27. To say that the second Person of the Trinity became incarnate is to speak of a particular relationship between the second Person of the Trinity and the human nature of Jesus. One might say that "incarnate" is a relational term and that, as such, it is more like "begotten" than it is like "good" or "wise." Just as only one Person of the Trinity is the relationship named by the term "begotten," so too only one Person of the Trinity has that relationship to humanity named by the term "incarnate." On the notion of the Persons of the Trinity as relations, see 1.29.4, above.

Question 17:

Christ's Unity with Regard to His Existence

3.17.2[1]
Is there only one existence in Christ?[2]

It would seem that in Christ there is not only one existence [*esse*], but two.[3]

1. On this article, see Garrigou-Lagrange (1950, 427–38); McCabe (2002, 107–14); Coakley (2016); Gorman (2017, 101–25).

2. This is thought by many to be a key article in Thomas's theology of Christ, for several reasons. First, in this article Thomas employs a number of concepts that are distinctively (if not uniquely) his, most especially the notion of *esse*. It is as if in this article Thomas is trying to fuse his mastery of the classical theological vocabulary derived from the church councils of the first five centuries with his metaphysical language of existence.

Another reason this article has excited interest over the centuries is that in another work—*Disputed Question on the Union of the Incarnate Word*—Thomas seems to contradict what he says here. When, in *Disputed Question*, Thomas confronts the question of "whether in Christ there is only one existence [*esse*]," he says that although there is in Christ only a single existence in an absolute sense [*esse simpliciter*], there is, because of his human nature, another existence that is "secondary" [*secundarium*]. In the present article, and indeed in all of his other writings, Thomas nowhere mentions such a "secondary existence."

Some authors (e.g., Cajetan in the sixteenth century), seeing the differences between the two texts as dramatic, have argued that *Disputed Question* must be either an early work by Thomas or not by Thomas at all. More recently, some scholars have claimed that it was written at almost exactly the same time as this article of the *Summa* (the spring of 1272, in Paris). If so, then it would seem Thomas himself did not see any contradiction between the two texts. Indeed, some authors (e.g., the Benedictine theologian Herman-Michel Diepen, in the mid-twentieth century) have argued that the *Disputed Question* represents the "true" position of Thomas.

My own view is that the *Disputed Question* says substantially the same thing as Thomas's other writings: in all texts addressing this issue Thomas's main concern is to maintain that Christ has a single act of existence as a person (i.e., a single *esse*); Thomas nowhere envisions the unity of Christ's person as some sort of combination of two independent acts of existing. However, in all texts the human nature can be spoken of as having the sort of *esse* "by which" something exists as this or that sort of thing, and this is what the *Disputed Question* calls "secondary" *esse*.

3. For some general remarks on *esse*, see 1.3 note 2. It is important to remember that in this article Thomas is not asking whether there are two "beings" or "entities" in Christ, but whether Christ, by virtue of his human and divine natures, possesses two distinct acts of existing (*duo esse*).

1. John of Damascus says in *On the Orthodox Faith* (3.13) that whatever is a consequence of a nature is doubled in Christ. But existence is a consequence of a nature, for existence is from the form.[4] Therefore in Christ there are two existences [*duo esse*].

2. The existence of the Son of God is the divine nature itself, and is eternal. However, the existence of the human being Christ is not the divine nature, but is an existence in time.[5] Therefore there is not only one existence in Christ.

3. In the Trinity, although there are three Persons there is nevertheless only one existence because of the unity of nature. But in Christ there are two natures, although there is one person. In Christ, therefore, there is not only one existence.[6]

4. In Christ the soul gives some existence to the body, since it is its form. But it does not give the divine existence, since this is uncreated. Therefore in Christ there is another existence beyond the divine existence, and so in Christ there is not only one existence.

On the contrary: Each thing is said to be one to the degree that it is said to be a being [*ens*], for "one" and "being" [*ens*] are interchangeable. Therefore, if there were two existences [*duo esse*] in Christ, and not one only, Christ would be two, and not one.

I answer: Because in Christ there are two natures and one hypostasis,[7] it must follow that things pertaining to the nature in Christ are two and that those pertaining to the hypostasis in Christ are only one. But existence pertains both to the nature and to the hypostasis: to the hypostasis as "that which has existence" and to the nature as "that by which something has existence."[8]

---

4. That is, Socrates *is* a human being because Socrates possesses the form of humanity. The identification of "form" or "nature" as that which gives existence is also the basis for objections 3 and 4.

5. This objection makes two distinguishable points: (1) if Christ's human nature does not have its own independent act of existence, then it does not possess a created existence, and therefore is not a creature; and (2) if Christ's human nature is temporal and his divine nature is eternal, then *esse* cannot be predicated univocally of these two natures (see 1.13.5), and hence Christ must have two distinct acts of existence.

6. In the Trinity we have the principle of one nature = one *esse*. Therefore if the person of Christ has two natures, he must have two *esse*.

7. On "hypostasis," see 1.29 note 2.

8. Here Thomas begins by agreeing with John of Damascus, as cited in the first objection, that what belongs to the natures of Christ is twofold. Thus, for example, Thomas will argue in the following question (3.18) that Christ has two wills: divine and human. However, contrary to the first objection, Thomas does not think that this "doubling" settles the question, since *esse* belongs to *both* the natures *and* the person/hypostasis (on "hypostasis," see 3.2 note 10), but in different ways. Thomas characterizes this difference as that between the existence by which something is what it is and the existence that is that thing's act of existing. We can see this difference in the way we use forms of the verb "to be": the difference, for example, between saying "he is happy" or "he is a human being" and saying simply "he is." In the first two statements, I am asserting something about someone, and thus the "is" is a consequence of his happy or human nature; in the third statement, the "is" is an assertion of my judgment that a particular person

For we speak of a nature in the way we speak of a form, which is said to be a being because something is "on account of" it: "on account of" whiteness a thing is white; and "on account of" human nature a thing is a human being.

It must be borne in mind that if something is a form or nature that does not pertain to the existence-as-a-person [*esse personale*] of a subsisting hypostasis,[9] this existence is said to belong to the person not simply, but in some particular respect.[10] Thus to be [*esse*] white is the existence [*esse*] of Socrates not because he is Socrates but because he is white. And there is no reason why one hypostasis or person should not have multiple instances of this sort of existence, for the existence on account of which Socrates is white is distinct from the existence on account of which he is a musician. But that existence that belongs to the hypostasis or person *as such* cannot possibly be multiplied in one hypostasis or person, since it is impossible that one thing should not have one existence.[11]

If, therefore, the Son of God acquired a human nature not hypostatically or personally but accidentally, as some maintained, it would be necessary to assert two existences in Christ: one inasmuch as he is God and the other inasmuch as he is a human being.[12] Thus in Socrates we indicate one existence inasmuch as he is white and another inasmuch as he is a human being, since

---

exists. Statements like the first two can obviously be multiplied, since one can be both a happy being *and* a human being and much else besides. But the third statement cannot be multiplied, since the one who exists as a happy human is only one instance of existing.

9. What Thomas means by *esse personale* is that by which a person exists at all, as opposed to that by which a person exists as this or that *kind* of person. Later in this article I translate *esse personale* as "personal existence" in order to make Thomas's Latin resemble normal English, but the reader should be aware that I am translating the same Latin term.

10. This is the difference between "I am happy" and "I am a human being." I can cease to be happy, but I am still myself; if I cease to be a human being, I cease to be me and become something else—for example, a corpse. Thus being human is integral to my *esse personale*, whereas being happy is an "accident" or nonessential quality of my existence-as-a-person.

11. To schematize what Thomas has said thus far:

1. There is the *esse* of a hypostasis or subject (the *esse personale* or "existence-as-a-person"), which is its act of existing and which cannot be multiple.

2. There is the *esse* of a nature or predicate, which makes a thing exist in this or that particular way (as a human being, as something white, as something happy, as something musical). The *esse* of a nature can be either

   (a) the *esse* of an "accident" (such as being white, musical, or happy or a particular age, height, weight, etc.), of which one subject can possess many, or

   (b) the *esse* that belongs to the subject "simply" and by which it is what it is. This *esse* seems closely related to the *esse* of the hypostasis and, like the *esse* of the hypostasis, can be only singular. An example would be the being of a subject's nature as human or canine. One might be both musical *and* happy, but one cannot be both a human being and a dog.

12. This was in fact the view of most scholars in the thirteenth century (for example, William of Auxerre prior to Thomas and Duns Scotus after him), who held that the best analogy for thinking about the relationship between Christ's humanity and his divinity was to think about the way in which an accident,

"being white" [*esse album*] does not pertain to the personal existence of
Socrates. But being possessed of a head, being bodily, being alive—all these
do pertain to the one person of Socrates, and therefore there arises from these
things only the one existence of Socrates. And if it so happened that, after
the person of Socrates was constituted, he acquired hands or feet or eyes
(as happened to the man born blind),[13] no new existence would be added
to Socrates by these things, but only a certain relation to them. That is, he
would be said to exist not only with reference to what he had previously but
also with reference to what he later acquired.[14]

   Thus, because the human nature is united to the Son of God hypostatically
or personally and not accidentally, as was said earlier (3.2.5, 6), it follows that
in acquiring a human nature he acquired no new personal existence [*esse
personale*], but only a new relation of the already existing personal existence
to human nature, in such a way that the person is said to subsist not only
according to the divine nature but also according to the human nature.[15]

---

or nonessential quality, is related to the subject that has that quality. For Thomas, however, this view
smacked of the heresy of Nestorius.

   13. See chapter 9 of John's Gospel. Note that Thomas is not simply offering this Johannine text as
a decorative proof text for an essentially philosophical argument. The example of the man born blind is
a particularly apt one because the question of whether he is the same person (i.e., has the same *esse
personale*) after the healing as before is raised by the crowd (9:8–9).

   14. The analogy between Christ's human nature and a part of a human being is one Thomas has already used (see 3.2 note 20). Socrates's hand is what it is only because it is a part of the person Socrates.
Similarly, Christ's humanity is what it is only because it is a part of the person of the Son of God. The key
point in this analogy is that when something is a part of a whole, its act of existence is the existence of that
whole.

   Thomas's analogy has been much criticized, not least by Duns Scotus (see *Ordinatio* bk. 3, dist. 6,
q. 1, nos. 4–5). Scotus argued that a part shares in the existence of the whole only because it shares in
the form or nature of the whole. But the human nature of Christ does not share the divine nature; this
would be the opposite heresy from Nestorianism—namely, that of Eutyches (see 3.2 note 2). Therefore
the part–whole analogy is, according to Scotus, simply misleading. In defense of Thomas, one can say
that he must be aware of the failings of this analogy, but he prefers to maintain it rather than take the
path followed by most medievals, who said that Christ's human nature is an accretion to his divine
person that possesses its own act of existence. One might say that Christology is always a balancing
act between Nestorius and Eutyches, and Thomas's own judgment in his context is that it is the former
that is the greater danger.

   15. Despite the seeming complexity of this article, Thomas's argument is in fact quite simple. The *esse*
of Christ's humanity "belongs" to the hypostasis/*suppositum*/person of the Son of God and therefore must
be one, following the principle laid down at the beginning of the response: "Things pertaining to the nature
in Christ are two and . . . those pertaining to the hypostasis in Christ are only one."

   It is important to ask what is finally at stake for Thomas in this article. Certainly he is concerned to
maintain the unity of Christ against the various views that would lead to "Nestorianism," which he believes
disallows such crucial claims as "God is a human being" (see 3.16 note 2). Salvation grows out of the fact
that, in Christ, God's eternal act of existence becomes the act of existence of a human nature (see the
reply to obj. 2 in this article). This view becomes apparent in 3.48.2, below, where salvation turns on the
unity of divine and human natures in one subject in Christ's self-offering on the cross.

Reply to 1: Existence is a consequence of nature, not as "that which has existence" [*habentem esse*] but as "that by which something is" [*qua aliquid est*]. However, it is a consequence of the person or hypostasis as "that which has existence." Therefore it has unity from the unity of hypostasis, rather than duality from the duality of the nature.

Reply to 2: The eternal existence of the Son of God, which is the divine nature, becomes human existence inasmuch as the human nature is assumed by the Son of God in the unity of person.[16]

Reply to 3: As was said in the first part (1.3.3; 1.39.1), since the divine Person is the same as the nature, there is no distinction in the divine Persons between the existence of the Person and the existence of the nature, and, consequently, the three Persons have only one existence.[17] But they would have a threefold existence if the existence of the Person were distinct in them from the existence of the nature.

Reply to 4: The soul in Christ gives existence to the body insofar as the soul makes the body actually alive, which is to give it the fulfillment of its

---

Also, Thomas's desire to associate *esse* with hypostasis/*suppositum*/person reflects his firm metaphysical conviction that it is concrete things, rather than "forms" or "natures" themselves, that are most properly said to exist. Thus, in the case of rational beings, the question of existence is always primarily a question of "personal existence," and when we ask about the existence of Christ, we must speak first and foremost of the single, concrete person Jesus Christ, in whom divinity and humanity are united.

It is also important to remember that for Thomas, God's *esse*—God's eternal act of existence—is something ungraspable by human reason (see 1–2.3 note 12). As Henk Schoot (1993) argues, by positing in Christ a unity of *esse*, Thomas locates the union of humanity and divinity in a realm that is irreducibly mysterious to the mind of creatures, since the divine essence remains incomprehensible even in the beatific vision. All accounts of this union must "limp," because it is a union that reaches "all the way down" to the incomprehensible divine act of existence.

16. God's eternal and uncreated act of existence is the act of existence of a human nature not because that human nature is eternal or uncreated but because at a particular moment in history that nature was "assumed" or "taken on" by the second Person of the Trinity. Thus, Thomas's view is not that of Eutyches. Garrigou-Lagrange (1950, 437) notes that this suggests that we can think of Christ's humanity as "ecstatic"— its existence is, as it were, displaced into God, "just as an ardent lover is attracted to the object loved."

17. Here Thomas invokes the principle of divine simplicity (see 1.3 note 2) to argue that in God nature and person are not distinguished from each other in terms of *esse*. However, he still maintains that the three Persons of the Trinity are distinct, not because their existence as Persons is somehow different from the act of existence of their shared nature (as, for example, three instances of the divine nature in the way that Tom, Dick, and Harriet are three instances of human nature), but because they are distinct from one another by virtue of their relations of origin. Still, they share in the same act of existence, which is the divine nature. See 1.29.4, above.

It is not immediately apparent how this response answers the objection. Perhaps Thomas's point is that the divine act of existence is not a "thing" that can be numbered alongside some other thing and then added to it to make two things. The unity of the divine act of existence is not like a "one" in a series of numbers; rather it is the unity of the utter uniqueness of God's act of existing. In this sense, just as the one divine nature cannot be added to the three Persons to make four things, so too the "one divine act of existence" cannot be added to the human act of existence to make two acts of existence.

nature and species. But if we consider the body thus perfected by the soul apart from the hypostasis possessing them, then this whole composed of soul and body, which we call "humanity," does not signify "what is" [*quod est*] but "whereby it is" [*quo aliquid est*]. This is why existence itself belongs to the subsisting person, since it has a relation to such a nature, and the soul is the cause of this relation, since it perfects human nature by informing the body.[18]

18. With this reply we can return to the difficulty presented by the seeming contradiction between Thomas's view presented here, which firmly maintains that Christ has but one *esse*, and the view presented in *Disputed Question on the Union of the Incarnate Word* 4, which says that Christ's human nature possesses an existence "that is not the principle *esse* of its *suppositum*, but secondary" (see note 2, above). This reply seems to indicate that even here Thomas is willing to speak in a certain, qualified sense of the *esse* that the human nature possesses of itself, though this is *esse* only in the sense that it is by the human nature that Christ exists as a human being. What seems consistent between the two accounts is that the human nature in no way contributes to the "existence-as-a-person" (*esse personale*) of Christ, since Christ's personhood is the divine personhood of the second Person of the Trinity.

Question 27:

The Sanctification of the Blessed Virgin

3.27.2[1]

Was the Blessed Virgin sanctified before animation?

It would seem that the Blessed Virgin was sanctified before animation.[2]

1. As was said (3.27.1), more grace is bestowed on the Virgin Mother of God than on any other saint. But it seems some were granted sanctification before animation,[3] for it is said in Jeremiah (1:5), "Before I formed you in the

---

1. On this article, see Nichols (2004).

2. This article is the subject of some controversy, not least because Thomas appears to deny here what would later (in 1854, with the Apostolic Constitution *Ineffabilis Deus*) become official Roman Catholic dogma—namely, that Mary, from the moment of her conception, was preserved from original sin. This doctrine, the immaculate (i.e., "unstained") conception, is sometimes confused with the virgin birth of Jesus, though in actuality the immaculate conception is one step removed from Jesus's birth, since its specific concern is with what it means for Mary to be "fully of grace," and therefore a suitable mother for Christ.

The claim that Mary was conceived "immaculately" (i.e., without original sin) was rather late in developing, really gaining currency only with Duns Scotus (1266–1308). The views Thomas expresses here were commonly held in his day (by, among others, Bernard of Clairvaux, Peter Lombard, Alexander of Hales, Bonaventure, and Albert the Great). Thomas does hold that Mary was cleansed from original sin in the womb of her mother, but he argues that this cleansing occurred at some point after her conception.

It should be noted, however, that in this article Thomas is not addressing precisely the question of the immaculate conception. His question differs on at least two counts: (1) he is asking whether Mary was "sanctified," not whether she was "preserved" from sin; (2) he is asking whether this could happen before "animation," not "conception" (see the following note).

It should also be noted at the outset that Thomas discusses Mary in the context of Christology, never forgetting that Mary called herself *ancilla Dei* (the handmaid of God), and he treats her as an ancillary topic in his theology of Christ. Thomas devotes four questions, consisting of sixteen articles, to "Mariology," which is quite austere by later standards. Of course, he discusses Mary in other places in the *Summa*, but the fact that he is content to let his discussion of her be lodged in the midst of a variety of christological questions is itself instructive.

3. By "animation" Thomas means the infusion or imparting of the rational soul (*anima*) to the body. Following Aristotle, Thomas held that the fetus became animated only at some period after conception— around forty days for males and fifty days for females—because the soul requires a "due quantity" of matter for its infusion. The one exception he makes is the case of Christ, who received his rational soul at the moment of his conception (see 3.33.2).

womb, I knew you," and the soul is not infused before the formation of the body. Likewise, Ambrose says of John the Baptist in his *Commentary on Luke* (bk. 1, on Luke 1:15), "The spirit of life was not yet in him, and already he possessed the Spirit of grace." It is thus even more the case that the Blessed Virgin could be sanctified before animation.

2. It was fitting, as Anselm says in *On the Virginal Conception* (bk. 18), "that this Virgin should shine with such a purity that none greater can be conceived, apart from God." For this reason it is said in the Song of Songs (4:7), "You are all fair, O my love, and there is not a spot in you."[4] But the purity of the Blessed Virgin would have been greater if she had never been stained by the contagion of original sin. Therefore it was granted to her to be sanctified before her flesh was animated.[5]

3. As it has been stated earlier (3.27.1), no feast is celebrated except that of someone holy. But some keep the feast of the Conception of the Blessed Virgin. It seems, therefore, that in her very conception she was holy, and so it seems that she was sanctified before animation.[6]

4. The Apostle says in Romans (11:16), "If the root be holy, so are the branches." But the roots of children are their parents. Therefore the Blessed Virgin could be sanctified even in her parents, before animation.

4. Advocates for the doctrine of the immaculate conception often point to Anselm's *On the Virginal Conception and Original Sin* as the text that prepared the way for the later work of Duns Scotus. Regarding Mary's holiness, Anselm applies the same sort of logic he uses to prove God's existence in his *Proslogion* (see 1.2 note 3). Anselm's student and biographer, Eadmer, appears to have been the first Western theologian to propose that Mary's purity—"than which none greater can be conceived"—involved her being freed from sin at her conception, in a way distinct from and surpassing those others (e.g., Jeremiah or John the Baptist) who were thought to have been cleansed in the womb (see Eadmer, *On the Conception of Holy Mary* 9).

5. This objection hints at an argument that Scotus would use later to argue for the fittingness of the immaculate conception: since Mary is "full of grace," God would bring about her redemption in the best way possible; it is better to be preserved from sin than to be cleansed from sin; therefore it is fitting that Mary would be preserved from original sin. As it is sometimes put: *Decuit, potuit, ergo fecit*—it was fitting; it was possible; therefore it was done.

6. In the controversy over the immaculate conception, the doctrinal question was accompanied by an equally pressing liturgical one: Should there be a feast of Mary's conception, and should this feast be designated the "Feast of the *Immaculate* Conception"? Though a feast of the conception of Mary was celebrated in Palestine as early as the seventh century, it was not universally observed in Thomas's day. After the time of Scotus the observance of the feast as one celebrating the immaculate conception increased in popularity (though not without controversy). In 1476 Pope Sixtus IV allowed the liturgical celebration of the feast and dedicated a chapel to Mary as Immaculate Virgin in St. Peter's Basilica in Rome.

As the question is framed in the objection, only "saints" (i.e., those who are holy) have feast days; therefore if there is a feast of the conception of Mary, she must have been holy at the time of her conception. In the previous article (3.27.1) Thomas uses this same sort of argument in the *sed contra* to argue that Mary was made holy before her birth: since the church observes the feast of the birth of Mary (in contrast to most other saints, who are commemorated on the date of their death), she must have been holy at the time of her birth.

On the contrary: The things of the Old Testament are prefigurations of the New, according to 1 Corinthians (10:11): "All things happened to them in figure."[7] Now the sanctification of the tabernacle, of which it is written in Psalm 46 (v. 4)—"The most high has sanctified his own tabernacle"—seems to signify the sanctification of the Mother of God, who is called "God's tabernacle," according to Psalm 19 (v. 4), "He has set his tabernacle in the sun." But it is written of the tabernacle in Exodus (40:34), "After all things were completed, the cloud covered the tabernacle of the Testimony, and the glory of the Lord filled it." Therefore the Blessed Virgin was also not sanctified until all in her was completed—that is to say, the body and the soul.

I answer: The sanctification of the Blessed Virgin cannot be understood as having taken place before animation for two reasons.

First, because the sanctification of which we are speaking is nothing other than the cleansing from original sin, for sanctification is a "perfect cleansing," as Dionysius says in *On the Divine Names* (12.2). But moral fault cannot be taken away except by grace, the subject of which is the rational creature alone. Therefore before the infusion of the rational soul, the Blessed Virgin was not sanctified.[8]

Second, since only the rational creature is susceptible to moral fault, before the infusion of the rational soul the offspring conceived is not guilty of a fault. And so, in whatever way the Blessed Virgin would have been sanctified before animation, she could never have incurred the stain of original sin. Therefore she would not have needed redemption and salvation, which is through Christ, of whom it is said in Matthew (1:21), "He shall save his people from their sins." But it is unfitting [*inconveniens*] that Christ not be the "savior of all people," as 1 Timothy (4:10) says.[9] It remains, therefore, that the Blessed Virgin was sanctified after her animation.

---

7. See 1.1 note 39.

8. Here Thomas simply applies the principle that a thing must be something before it can be some *sort* of thing. Thus Mary's rational soul had to exist before it could exist as either sinful or holy. Since only a rational soul can sin or bear the mark of sin, only a rational soul can be freed from sin, and therefore Mary could not have been freed from sin at any point prior to her animation. So, in Thomas's view, Mary must have borne the mark of sin, if only for an instant, after her animation.

Duns Scotus will argue later, in what will eventually be seen as the definitive answer to this difficulty, that Mary's sanctification occurs neither before nor after her animation, but at the very instant when her soul was joined to her body (*Ordinatio* bk. 3, dist. 3, q. 1).

9. This second argument follows from the first. If Mary were to have been "sanctified" prior to her reception of a rational soul, then "sanctified" must mean, in her case, something other than being freed from original sin. But if this were the case, then she would not be redeemed by Christ, who frees us from bondage to sin. This view is unacceptable to Thomas because of its "unfittingness." In other words, it does not cohere with the whole sweep of the story of salvation through Christ. Therefore, Mary must

Reply to 1: The Lord says that he "knew" Jeremiah before he was formed in the womb—that is to say, by the knowledge of predestination. But he says that he "sanctified" him not before formation but before he "came forth out of the womb," and so on.

As to what Ambrose says (that the spirit of life was not yet in John the Baptist when he already had the Spirit of grace), this is not to be understood such that "spirit of life" refers to the life-giving soul, but to the air that we breathe out [*respiratus*]. Or it may be said that the spirit of life—namely, the soul—was not yet in him with regard to its manifest and complete operations.[10]

Reply to 2: If the soul of the Blessed Virgin had never been stained by original sin, this would take away from the dignity that Christ has inasmuch as he is the universal Savior of all. So after Christ, who as the universal Savior did not need to be saved, the purity of the Blessed Virgin is greatest. For Christ did not contract original sin in any way whatever but was holy in his very conception, according to Luke (1:35): "The holy one that shall be born from you shall be called the Son of God."[11] The Blessed Virgin, however, did indeed contract original sin, but was cleansed from it before her birth from the womb. This is what is signified in Job (3:9), where it is said of the night of original sin, "Let it expect light"—that is, Christ—"and not see it" (because "no defiled thing comes into her," as is written in Wisdom [7:25]), "nor the rising of the dawning of the day"—that is, of the Blessed Virgin, who in her birth was immune from original sin.[12]

---

have borne the mark of sin after her animation, if only for an instant, in order that she could receive Christ's redemption.

Again, Scotus will argue later for a different view, which will become part of the dogmatic definition of the immaculate conception. According to Scotus, in Mary's case "sanctified" *does* mean something other than being freed from original sin; it means being *prevented* from contracting original sin in the first place. However, this salvation is still through Christ; Mary's holiness is given to her so that she can be a fitting mother for the redeemer, and it is given on the basis of what Christ will do on the cross. Indeed, Scotus even raises the stakes on Christ as the universal mediator of salvation, arguing that if Christ is the most perfect redeemer, then in at least one instance he would redeem in the most perfect way possible, which would be not simply to cleanse from sin, but to prevent sin's stain entirely, and this he did in the case of the Mother of God. See *Ordinatio* bk. 3, dist. 3, q. 1.

10. The quotation from Ambrose seems to suggest that John the Baptist received grace before he received a rational soul. Thomas offers two possible alternative readings of Ambrose: (1) John possessed a rational soul, but had not yet taken a physical breath; or (2) John possessed a rational soul, but it was not yet manifested through his actions.

11. Note that Thomas holds that Christ, uniquely of all humanity, possesses a rational soul from the moment of his conception (3.33.2) and can therefore be holy from that very moment.

12. We can read this somewhat complicated response as Thomas's preemptive rejoinder to the Scotist solution (see notes 8 and 9, above) to the difficulties outlined in the body of the article: if we locate Mary's sinlessness at the very moment of her conception and see it as a "preventative" sinlessness, then nothing distinguishes her conception from that of Jesus. For Thomas, this view diminishes the honor shown to Christ.

Reply to 3: Although the church of Rome does not celebrate the conception of the Blessed Virgin, it still tolerates the custom of certain churches that do keep that feast. Therefore such celebration is not to be entirely disapproved of. Nevertheless the celebration of this feast does not lead us to understand that she was holy in her conception. But since the time of her sanctification is not known, the feast of her sanctification, rather than of her conception, is celebrated on the day of her conception.[13]

Reply to 4: Sanctification is twofold. One is the sanctification of the whole nature, inasmuch as the whole human nature is freed from all corruption of sin and punishment, which will take place at the resurrection. The other is personal sanctification, which is not transmitted to offspring brought forth by the flesh, because it has to do not with the flesh but with the mind. So though the parents of the Blessed Virgin were cleansed from original sin, nevertheless she contracted original sin, since she was conceived by way of fleshly desire and the intercourse of man and woman; for Augustine says in the book *On Marriage and Concupiscence* (1.12), "All flesh born of sexual intercourse is sinful."[14]

13. Thomas says that since we do not know precisely when in the womb Mary was made holy, some churches commemorate this mystery on the day of her conception, but conception and sanctification are not necessarily linked. Indeed, Thomas says that what is commemorated on that feast day is the sanctification, not the conception. Since, as we have seen, Thomas separates conception and animation, he would no doubt say that one thing we *do* know is that she was not sanctified at her conception.

14. Here Thomas reflects the viewpoint of Augustine that it is the inordinate desire or "concupiscence" of the parents during the sexual act that transmits original sin. The redemption of "the flesh" is something that awaits the resurrection, so the parents of the Virgin Mary, although cleansed of original sin through faith in the redeemer who was to come, would not have been freed from concupiscence. Thus Mary was conceived in the ordinary human way, by two people who experienced bodily desire for each other, and so would have had original sin transmitted to her.

Question 40:

Christ's Way of Living

3.40.1[1]

Should Christ have associated with people or led a solitary life?

It seems that Christ ought not to have associated with people, but should have led a solitary life.[2]

1. It was appropriate for Christ to show by his manner of life not only that he was a human being but also that he was God. But it is not fitting for God to associate with human beings, for it is said in Daniel (2:11), "Except the gods, whose conversation is not with human beings"; and the Philosopher says in the *Politics* (1.2, 1253ᵃ) that one who lives alone is "either a beast" (that is, if one does this on account of ferocity) "or a god" (if one does this on account of the contemplation of truth).[3] Therefore it seems that it was not fitting for Christ to associate with human beings.

2. Christ, while he lived in mortal flesh, should have led the most perfect life. The most perfect life, however, is the contemplative, as we have stated in the second part (2–2.182.1, above), and solitude is most suitable to the contemplative life; according to Hosea (2:14): "I will lead her into the wilderness, and I will speak to her heart." It seems, then, that Christ should have led a solitary life.

---

1. On this article, see Torrell (2003, 131–35); Dodds (2004).
2. The next few articles are from a section of the *Summa* that looks at the actual events of Jesus's life and their *convenientia* (see 3.1 note 2). Thomas is in no sense trying to deduce rationally the way Jesus *had to* live. Rather, given that Jesus *did* live a certain sort of life, can we discern reasons for the way he lived?
3. The full quotation from Aristotle: "He who is unable to live in society, or who has no need because he is sufficient for himself, must be either a beast or a god: he is no part of a state. A social instinct is implanted in all men by nature" (*Politics* 1.2, 1253ᵃ). Aristotle's point is not, as the objection makes it appear, that living as a part of human society would be impossible for one who was divine; rather, human beings are, as Aristotle puts it, "social animals"—it is part of their nature to live in groups. Only a god or a beast could live outside of society.

3. The behavior of Christ ought to have been uniform, because it should have always given evidence of what is best. But at times Christ sought lonely places, avoiding the crowd. Therefore Remigius,[4] commenting on Matthew, says, "We read that our Lord had three places of refuge: the ship, the mountain, and the desert; he went to one or other of these whenever he was pressed by the crowd." He should have always, therefore, led a solitary life.[5]

On the contrary: It is said in Baruch (3:37), "Afterward he was seen upon earth and conversed with human beings."

I answer: Christ's behavior had to be in keeping with [*conveniret*] the purpose of his incarnation, on account of which he came into the world.[6]

He came into the world, first, in order to manifest the truth;[7] thus he says himself in John (18:37), "For this was I born, and for this I came into the world, that I should give testimony to the truth." And so he ought not to have hidden himself, leading a solitary life, but should have appeared openly and preached in public. For this reason in Luke (4:42–43) he says to those who wished to detain him, "I must preach the kingdom of God to other cities also; for that is the reason I am sent."

Second, he came in order to free human beings from sin; according to 1 Timothy (1:15), "Christ Jesus came into this world to save sinners." And therefore, as Chrysostom says,[8] "Although Christ might, while staying in the same place, have drawn all people to himself, to hear his preaching, yet he did not do so;

---

4. Remigius of Auxerre was a ninth-century monk and scholar. The original source of the quotation is unknown, but Thomas quotes the same passage in connection with Matt. 5:1 in the *Catena aurea*, his collection of patristic comments on the Gospels. A similar statement can be found in Isidore of Seville's (ca. 560–636) *Questions on the Old and New Testaments* 36.

5. The objection seems to be that *whichever* was better—action or contemplation—Jesus should have done *only* that thing.

6. Here we see one of the chief ways in which Thomas understands *convenientia*—as a way of describing the suitability of certain means to an end. To take an example he uses elsewhere, it might be possible to go on a twenty-mile journey on foot, but it is more "fitting" to use a horse (provided, of course, that the goal of the journey is to get to a certain destination and not to get exercise). Once one understands the goal of the action—to travel to a distant place—one can understand the fittingness of the means chosen.

7. While the order of these reasons may not imply any sort of ranking of priority, the notion of Jesus's mission of manifesting the truth, both through his preaching and through his actions, is very important for Thomas's Christology. Otto Hermann Pesch (1970) characterizes Thomas's overall theological approach as "sapiential," with his Christology underscoring Jesus as divine wisdom made flesh (note that in the passage from Baruch quoted in the *sed contra*, it is the personified figure of Wisdom who speaks). Perhaps this reflects Thomas's Dominican identity, since the role of the preacher is to convey divine wisdom. To depict Jesus's mission in terms of the manifestation of wisdom, which entails not monastic seclusion but at least intermittent immersion in the crowd, might be seen as a subtle—or not-so-subtle—defense of the Dominican way of life.

8. Like the quotation from Remigius (see note 4, above), this quotation ascribed to Chrysostom is also found in Aquinas's *Catena aurea*, on Luke 4:42, though it is not found in any of Chrysostom's extant works.

he thus gave us the example to go about and seek those who perish, like the shepherd searching for the lost sheep and the physician going to the sick."[9]

Third, he came in order that "by him we might have access to God," as it is written in Romans (5:2). And thus it was fitting that he should give people confidence in approaching him by associating familiarly with them. For this reason it is written in Matthew (9:10), "It came to pass as he was sitting . . . in the house, behold, many publicans and sinners came, and sat down with Jesus and his disciples." Jerome comments on this passage, saying, "They had seen the publican who had been converted from a sinful to a better life, and consequently they did not despair of their own salvation."

Reply to 1: Christ wished to manifest his divinity through his humanity. So he associated with people, since it is proper to a human being to do so, manifesting his divinity to all, preaching and working miracles and leading a blameless and righteous life among people.[10]

Reply to 2: As stated in the second part (2–2.182.1, above), the contemplative life is, absolutely speaking, more perfect than the active life, because the latter is taken up with bodily actions. But that form of active life in which someone delivers to others the fruits of contemplation by preaching and teaching is more perfect than the life that is solely contemplative, because such a life presupposes an abundance of contemplation. And so Christ chose such a life.[11]

Reply to 3: "Christ's action is our instruction."[12] And therefore, in order to give an example to preachers that they should not always be before the

9. One might also note that the second example does not work now that doctors do not make house calls. What Thomas perhaps has in mind is more the way in which the other aspect of Dominican ministry, along with manifesting the truth through preaching, is the care of souls through the sacrament of penance, a ministry that sometimes brought Dominicans into conflict with parish clergy, who were unhappy with members of their flock seeking out Dominicans as confessors. Once again the example of Jesus serves as a defense of Dominican practice.

10. The objection presumes that if Christ were to act like a normal human being—in this case, living with other people—such actions would somehow "mask" his divinity. Thomas, on the other hand, holds that the humanity of Christ, his human words and actions, are the means by which God is manifested. Like the first objection in 3.16.1, this objection presumes that humanity and divinity are *formae diversae* and that Jesus's being and acting fully human must be to the detriment of his being and acting fully divine. But as we have seen, Thomas does not think of humanity and divinity as opposites in this sense (see 3.16 note 23). So Thomas's answer is very carefully worded: he does not speak of Christ doing some human things and some divine things, but rather it is through the human acts of Christ—preaching, working miracles, living justly—that his divinity is manifested.

11. The phrase "delivers to others the fruits of contemplation" (*contemplata aliis tradere*), coined here by Thomas, would become an unofficial motto for the Dominican Order. We might say that Thomas understands the active life of preaching and teaching to be rooted in the life of contemplation: one must through contemplation journey deeply into the mystery of God, and by teaching one retraces one's steps, so as to share with others the mystery one has contemplated.

12. This is a point Thomas stresses repeatedly: Christ teaches by example. In this particular case, he teaches preachers by his example that they ought to seek occasions of contemplative solitude, so as

public, our Lord sometimes withdrew from the crowd. We read three reasons for his doing this.

Sometimes it was for the sake of bodily rest; therefore, in Mark (6:31) it is stated that the Lord said to his disciples, "'Come apart into a deserted place, and rest a little.' For there were many coming and going, and they did not even have time to eat."

Sometimes it was for the sake of prayer; thus it is said in Luke (6:12), "It happened in those days that he went out to a mountain to pray, and he passed the whole night in prayer to God." Ambrose remarks on this passage that "by his example he instructs us in the precepts of virtue" (*Commentary on Luke*, bk. 5).

Sometimes he did so in order to teach us to shun human approval. For this reason, commenting on Matthew (5:1) ("Jesus, seeing the multitude, went up into a mountain") Chrysostom says, "By sitting not in the city and in the marketplace but on a mountain and in a place of solitude, he taught us to do nothing for show and to withdraw from the crowd, especially when we have to speak of important things" (*Sermon 15*, in *Homilies on Matthew*).

3.40.3[13]
Should Christ have led a life of poverty in this world?

It would seem that Christ should not have led a life of poverty in this world.[14]

1. Christ should have taken up the most desirable sort of life. But the most desirable sort of life is one that is midway between riches and poverty,[15] for

---

to make their preaching more effective. Thomas is perhaps quoting Innocent III (1160–1216), *Sermon 22 de tempore*.

13. On this article, see Horst (1998); Dodds (2004); Franks (2009).

14. This may not seem to be a pressing christological question, but it was in fact a controversial issue in the thirteenth and fourteenth centuries. The new "mendicant" or "begging" orders—the Franciscans and Dominicans—both embraced poverty as an important part of their life, which distinguished them from traditional monasticism, for which "poverty" did not mean destitution (many monasteries possessed lands that supported them) but the renunciation of the ownership of individual property coupled with a certain austerity of life. With the rise of the mendicants, this notion of poverty was expanded to mean non-ownership of property not only by the individual members of the order but by the order itself. Thus the houses the early Dominicans lived in were not owned by the Dominican order but by the church; they were then "loaned" to the Dominicans for their use (this practice continued, at least officially, until the fifteenth century).

The radicals among the Franciscans (known as the "Spirituals") held that Christ lived a life of absolute poverty and that complete material poverty, and not simply non-ownership, was required for a perfect life. This view led to controversy within the Franciscan order and within the church as a whole, and in the fourteenth century Pope John XXII condemned the proposition that Christ lived a life of absolute poverty. The Dominicans tended to have a more moderate approach to poverty. As we shall see, Thomas holds that poverty is not a good in itself but is the most "fitting" form of life for one who wishes to be a follower of Christ, in particular for a preacher.

15. Though Thomas goes on to cite the book of Proverbs, the real source behind this objection is Aristotle's notion of virtue as a "mean" (see 1–2.55 note 2).

it is said in Proverbs (30:8), "Give me neither beggary [*mendicitatem*] nor riches; give me only the necessities of life." Therefore Christ should not have led a life of poverty, but of moderation.

2. External wealth is intended for bodily use, with regard to food and clothing. But in food and clothing Christ led an ordinary life, following the way of life of those among whom he lived. It seems, therefore, that he should also have observed the ordinary manner of life as to riches and poverty, and have avoided extreme poverty.

3. Christ invited people to imitate in particular his example of humility, according to Matthew (11:29): "Learn from me, because I am meek and humble of heart." But humility is most commendable in the rich; thus it is said in 1 Timothy (6:17), "Command the rich of this age not to be haughty." So it seems that Christ should not have chosen a life of poverty.[16]

On the contrary: It is said in Matthew (8:20), "The Son of Man has nowhere to lay his head," as if saying, according to Jerome, "Why do you desire to follow me for the sake of riches and worldly gain, since I am so poor that I do not have even the smallest dwelling place, and I am sheltered by a roof that is not mine?" (*Commentary on Matthew*, bk. 1). And regarding Matthew's (17:27) statement, "That we may not scandalize them, go to the sea," Jerome says, "This, understood literally, edifies those who hear it; they are told that the Lord was so poor that he did not have the means to pay the tax for himself and his apostles" (*Commentary on Matthew*, bk. 3).[17]

I answer: It was appropriate for Christ to lead a life of poverty in this world.

First, because this was in keeping with the duty of preaching, which he says in Mark (1:38) is the purpose for which he came: "Let us go into the neighboring towns and cities, that I may preach there also, because that is what I came for." Now in order that the preachers of God's word may be able to give all their time to preaching, they must be absolutely free from care of worldly things, which is impossible for those who possess wealth. For this reason the Lord himself, sending the apostles to preach, said to them, "Do not possess gold nor silver" (Matt. 10:9). And the apostles themselves

16. The humility of the poor is not particularly praiseworthy, because it is imposed on them and not voluntarily chosen. Christ, of course, would have possessed the most praiseworthy form of humility, and so must not have been poor.

17. The relevance of the first example is obvious; the second example is from Matthew's account of how Jesus, needing money to pay a Roman tax and possessing no money himself, sent Peter fishing, whereupon he caught a fish containing a coin with which they could pay the tax. The use of Jerome (ca. 347–420) in this *sed contra* is itself instructive, since he had preached an austerely ascetic form of Christian practice and his phrase *nudus nudum Christum sequi*—"to nakedly follow the naked Christ"—was embraced by many early Franciscans as expressive of their approach to poverty. As we shall see, this Franciscan approach was not quite the same as that of Thomas and his fellow Dominicans.

say in Acts (6:2), "It is not right that we should leave the word [of God] and serve tables."[18]

Second, because just as he took bodily death upon himself in order to bestow spiritual life on us, so too he bore bodily poverty, in order to bestow on us spiritual riches, according to 2 Corinthians (8:9): "You know the grace of our Lord Jesus Christ: that he became poor for our sakes so that through his poverty we might be rich."[19]

Third, because if he had riches his preaching might be ascribed to greed. For this reason Jerome says about Matthew (10:9) that if the disciples had possessed wealth, "they would have seemed to preach in order to gain money, not for the salvation of humankind" (*Commentary on Matthew*, bk. 1). And the same reasoning applies to Christ.[20]

Fourth, so that the power of his divinity might be shown to be greater, to the degree that he seemed by his poverty to be more lowly.[21] Therefore, in a sermon of the Council of Ephesus we read, "He chose all that was poor and despicable, all that was of small account and hidden from the majority, that his divinity may be recognized as having transformed the terrestrial sphere. For this reason he chose a poor maid for his mother, a poorer homeland, and lived in want. Learn this from the manger."[22]

Reply to 1: Both an abundance of riches and beggary, insofar as these are occasions of sin, should be avoided by those who wish to live virtuously, since an abundance of riches is an occasion for being proud, while beggary is an occasion for thieving and lying or even for false oaths. But Christ was not capable of sin, and for this reason he did not have the same motive as Solomon for avoiding these things.[23] Likewise, not every kind of begging is an occasion of theft and false oaths, as Solomon seems to add (Prov. 30:8), but only involuntary poverty, which

18. Here Thomas is considering the practical usefulness of traveling preachers not having possessions. There is no mystique attached to poverty itself; it is simply that if one is constantly worrying about one's investment portfolio, this does not leave much time or energy for preaching the gospel. Thomas sees that wealth, rather than alleviating anxiety, as many people think, actually increases it.

19. Here Thomas seems to be attaching more than simply a practical value to poverty; it also has for him what we might call a symbolic value. The "poverty" that Christ takes on in becoming human—giving up his heavenly status in order to dwell with us on earth—is symbolized by the poverty of his earthly life.

20. One of the things that spurred Dominic to found the Order of Preachers was witnessing how, even though they had better arguments, catholic preachers swathed in rich robes were ineffective in preaching against the Cathar heresy, whose leaders modeled their lives on the communal poverty of the first Christians.

21. This is again what we might call a "symbolic fittingness" of poverty. God's power is better manifested through humble people than through great ones.

22. This is from a sermon by the fifth-century bishop Theodotus of Ancyra, found in the Acts of the Council of Ephesus.

23. King Solomon was traditionally thought to be the author of the book of Proverbs, which is quoted in the first objection.

a person will commit theft and perjury in order to avoid. But voluntary poverty does not have this danger, and it was this sort of poverty that Christ chose.[24]

Reply to 2: One may live an ordinary way of life with regard to food and clothing not only by possessing riches but also by receiving the necessities of life from those who are rich. This is what happened in regard to Christ. For it is said in Luke (8:2–3) that certain women followed Christ and "provided for him from their resources." As Jerome says against Vigilantius,[25] "It was a Jewish custom and not thought wrong, following the ancient tradition of their nation, for women to provide their instructors with food and clothing out of their private means. But because this might give scandal to the gentiles, Paul says that he gave it up" (*Commentary on Matthew*, bk. 4, on Matt. 27:55). Thus their communal living made it possible for them not to possess wealth without their task of preaching being hindered by anxiety.[26]

Reply to 3: Humility is not greatly to be praised in one who is poor because of necessity. But in one who is poor willingly, as Christ was, poverty itself is a sign of great humility.[27]

3.40.4[28]
Did Christ abide by the Law?

It would seem that Christ did not abide by the Law.[29]

24. Thomas makes clear in this reply that the poverty he is talking about is *voluntary* poverty, not the poverty that circumstances might force upon a person.

25. The quotation is from Jerome's commentary on Matthew but addresses more or less the same issue as Jerome's polemical *Contra Vigilantium*: whether ministers of the church should be financially supported by the faithful.

26. Poverty, as Thomas means it here, does not involve necessarily going hungry or naked; rather it involves not possessing the means of obtaining food and clothing. As mentioned (see note 14, above), for several centuries not only did individual Dominicans renounce personal ownership, but the Dominican order as a whole did not own property, having it, as it were, held in trust by the church. So poverty, as Thomas understands it, does not mean going without life's basic necessities. Of course, this system *can* turn poverty into a less-than-convincing facade, in which one owns nothing but lives quite comfortably—even luxuriously. One is reminded of the old joke in which a young man, upon looking at the lavish residence in which members of a religious order lived, commented, "If this is poverty, I can't wait to see chastity!"

27. Again, we see that what Thomas is talking about is voluntary poverty, not destitution. In sum, Thomas's remarks in this article suggest that he thinks it is fitting for Christ to have been poor (1) for practical reasons—he could better accomplish his mission of preaching the kingdom of God if he was not burdened with property—and (2) for "symbolic" reasons—Christ's poverty better manifested how the power of God is defined by Christ's humility. In both cases, we see that for Thomas poverty is not an end in itself. Indeed, poverty that is thrust upon people often causes them to become *less* virtuous. In the case of Jesus, his poverty was willingly taken on for the sake of his divine mission. In the case of Christians, voluntary poverty frees one to be a follower and imitator of Christ, which is the path to holiness.

28. On this article, see Dodds (2004); Marshall (2016).

29. "Law" here refers, of course, to the Old Testament Law, the Torah. Thomas is not asking whether or not Christ was an obedient subject of the Roman Empire (or of any other empire). Indeed, the real issue is

1. The Law instructed that no work be done on the Sabbath (Exod. 20:8; 31:13; Deut. 5:12), since God "rested on the seventh day from all his work that he had done" (Gen. 2:2). But Christ healed a person on the Sabbath and commanded him to take up his bed (John 5:5–9). It seems, therefore, that he did not abide by the Law.

2. Christ did as he taught; according to Acts (1:1), "Jesus began to do and to teach." But he himself taught in Matthew (15:11) that "not everything that goes into the mouth defiles a person," which is contrary to the injunction of the Law that declares that a person is made unclean by eating and touching certain animals, as stated in Leviticus (11). Therefore it seems that he did not himself abide by the Law.

3. One who consents seems to be judged in the same way as one who acts, according to Romans (1:32): "Not only those who do them, but also those who consent to those who do them." But Christ, by excusing his disciples, consented to their breaking the Law by plucking the ears of grain on the Sabbath, as is related in Matthew (12:1–8). Therefore it seems that Christ did not abide by the Law.[30]

On the contrary: It is written in Matthew (5:17), "Do not think that I have come to destroy the Law or the Prophets." Chrysostom explains this, saying, "He fulfilled the Law . . . first, by transgressing none of its legalities; second, by justifying us through faith, which the Law according to the letter was unable to do" (*Sermon 16*, in *Homilies on Matthew*).

I answer: Christ abided by the precepts of the Law in all things. As a sign of this, he even wished to be circumcised, for circumcision is a kind of declaration of one's intention of fulfilling the Law, according to Galatians (5:3): "I testify to every person accepting circumcising, that he is a debtor to do the whole Law."

Christ wished to abide by the Law, first, to show his approval of the Old Law.[31] Second, that by obeying the Law he might perfect it and bring it to an end in himself, so as to show that he was the fulfillment for which it was ordained.[32] Third, to deprive the Jews of an excuse for slandering him. Fourth,

---

not whether Jesus's behavior was "lawful" in either the civil or religious sense, but rather the relationship between the Old Covenant that God established with Israel and the New Covenant established through Christ. Thomas is, in fact, extraordinarily interested in the Law of the Old Covenant, devoting eight questions to it (1–2.98–105) in the *Summa theologiae*.

30. The three objections, taken together, seem to cover all the ways in which one might violate a divine law: in thought (obj. 3), word (obj. 2), and deed (obj. 1).

31. Following Paul's statement in Rom. 7:12, "The Law is holy, and the commandment is holy and just and good," Thomas sees Christ's obedience to the Law as an affirmation of the fundamental rightness of the way of life laid down in the Torah. He says in 1–2.107.1 that both the Old Law and the New Law of Christ have one and the same goal: the subjection of human beings to God.

32. Though Thomas affirms the Law, he also sees it as ultimately inadequate to the goal that it pursues. It can orient us toward obedience to God; but because it can direct only our outward actions, it cannot itself bring us to that obedience. Thus Christ, through his New Law, must "bring it to an end," in the sense

to free people from subjection to the Law, according to Galatians (4:4–5): "God sent his Son . . . made under the Law, that he might redeem those who were under the Law."[33]

Reply to 1: Our Lord excuses himself from any transgression of the Law in this matter in three ways.

First, because the command to keep the Sabbath holy does not forbid divine work, but human work, for though God ceased on the seventh day from the creation of new creatures, yet he always works by preserving and guiding his creatures. But Christ's doing of miracles was a divine work, and so he says in John (5:17), "My Father works until now; and I work."[34]

Second, he excuses himself by the fact that this precept does not forbid works that are necessary for bodily health. Thus he says in Luke (13:15), "Does not every one of you on the Sabbath untie his ox or his donkey from the manger and lead them to water?" And farther on (Luke 14:5), "Which of you has an ass or an ox fall into a pit, and does not immediately draw him out on the day of the Sabbath?" It is clear, however, that the miraculous works done by Christ pertained to health of body and soul.[35]

---

of bringing it to the goal it seeks to obtain, which is the presence of the Holy Spirit in the believer through grace. Christ does this by means of his death and resurrection. Thus Christ is the "end" of the Law, not in the sense of terminating something bad, but in the sense of being himself the goal toward which it aims and in accordance with which it is to be practiced.

For Thomas this means, in practice, that Christians must obey the moral injunctions of the Law, summed up in the Ten Commandments, because these still serve to orient human beings to God. But Christians no longer obey the ceremonial injunctions of the Law, since all of these—including circumcision, the various sacrifices, and the regulations regarding food—served to point toward the coming of Christ. Now that Christ has come, it would be misleading, indeed sinful, to continue to practice these things because it would give the impression that one does not believe the Messiah has come. Likewise the judicial injunctions of the Law—those that regulated the common life of the nation Israel—are no longer binding because with the coming of Christ the distinction between Jew and gentile has been abolished, thus abolishing the need for a law to regulate the life of the Jewish people as a distinctive community.

33. Thomas derives this ambiguity of "subjection" to the Law from Paul. In one sense it is good to be subject to the Law, because through the Law one is subjected to God. In this sense, Christ willingly subjects himself to the Law. In another sense, one can be subject to the Law by being oppressed by it or, more precisely, by being oppressed by fear of it, because one has within oneself a contrary law that Paul calls "the law of sin" and that Thomas identified as the tendency toward sin and away from God that medieval theologians called the *fomes peccati* (the "kindling" or "tinder" of sin). For Thomas, Christ is subject to the Law in the first sense in order to release those who are subject to it in the second sense.

34. For Thomas, Christ's miracles differ from other miracles in that they are direct actions of God, not the actions of a human being who has been empowered by God. Thus he notes in several places that Christ does not pray before he works miracles because he does not need to invoke divine power, being *himself* the power of God. Just as the ceaseless work God does in sustaining the world is not a violation of the Sabbath rest, so too the miraculous works of Christ are not a violation of that rest.

35. In this second "excuse" Thomas defends Christ's healing on the Sabbath from the opposite direction of the first defense (which invoked Christ's divinity): even if Christ were merely a human being, it is still allowable for a human being to do good works on the Sabbath.

Third, because this commandment does not forbid works pertaining to the worship of God. Thus he says in Matthew (12:5), "Have you not read in the Law that on the Sabbath the priests in the temple violate the Sabbath and are without blame?" And in John (7:23) it says that "a man receives circumcision on the Sabbath." Now when Christ commanded the paralytic to carry his bed on the Sabbath, this pertained to the worship of God—that is, to the praise of divine power.[36]

And thus it is clear that Christ did not break the Sabbath. The Jews, however, falsely accused him of this, saying in John (9:16), "This is not a man of God, who does not keep the Sabbath."

Reply to 2: Christ wished to show by those words that one is not made spiritually unclean by the use of any sort of foods considered according to their nature, but only according to some symbolic meaning [*significationem*] they have. Certain foods are called "unclean" in the Law due to some symbolic meaning, and thus Augustine says in *Against Faustus the Manichaean* (6.7), "If one asks about pigs and lambs, both are clean by nature, since 'all God's creatures are good,' but, according to a certain symbolic meaning they have, lambs are clean and pigs unclean."[37]

Reply to 3: The disciples, when hungry, plucked the ears of corn on the Sabbath; but they also are to be excused from transgressing the Law, since they were compelled by hunger. Similarly, David was not a transgressor of the Law when, being compelled by hunger, he consumed the loaves that it was not lawful for him to eat.[38]

36. The connection Thomas draws here between miracles and worship indicates that for him a miracle is not simply a suspension of the ordinary operations of the world (which he certainly thinks it is) but also an occasion of wonder, which is another meaning of the Latin word *miracula*. Christ works his miracles not only to get a job done—like a doctor healing a patient—but also to incite people to praise God—like a priest leading worship.

37. Writing against the Manichaean bishop Faustus, Augustine says that lambs, because they chew their cud, symbolize people who meditate on and "chew over" words of wisdom, regurgitated, as it were, "from the stomach of memory to the mouth of reflection." Pigs, on the other hand, symbolize those who take superficial pleasure in wisdom (pigs do, after all, enjoy eating) but do not later reflect on those words.

Like Augustine, Thomas justifies Jesus's violation of the letter of the Law by a kind of appeal to the spirit: Jesus fulfills the inward intention of the Law in such a way that literal external obedience is no longer necessary. This is particularly the case with the parts of the Law regulating ceremonial and religious practice, though not with those parts regulating moral conduct.

38. This, of course, is the explanation Christ himself gives in Matt. 12:3–4.

Question 42:

Christ's Teaching

3.42.4[1]
Should Christ have committed his teaching to writing?

It would seem that Christ should have committed his teaching to writing.[2]

1. Writing was invented to entrust a teaching to memory for the future. But Christ's teaching was destined to endure forever, according to Luke (21:33): "Heaven and earth shall pass away, but my words shall not pass away."[3] Therefore it seems that Christ should have committed his teaching to writing.

2. The Old Law was a foreshadowing of Christ,[4] according to Hebrews (10:1): "The Law has a shadow of the good things to come." But the Old Law was put into writing by God, according to Exodus (24:12), "I will give you two tables of stone and the Law, and the commandments that I have written." So it seems that Christ also should have put his teaching into writing.

3. It pertained to Christ, who came to "enlighten those who sit in darkness and in the shadow of death," as it is said in Luke (1:79), to remove occasions of error and to open up the road to faith. But by putting his teaching into writing he would have done this, for Augustine says in *On Agreement among the Evangelists* (1.7), "There are some who wonder why our Lord wrote nothing, so that we have to believe what others have written about him. This is asked especially by those pagans who do not dare to blame or blaspheme Christ and who attribute to him a most excellent, although

---

1. On this article, see Dodds (2004); Armitage (2008); Torrell (2011, 159–73).

2. This too may seem like a peculiar question. Part of Thomas's genius is the way in which he can take a peculiar question and make an interesting theological point with it.

3. The objection contrasts the ephemeral nature of the spoken word—which decays immediately upon being uttered—with the relative permanence of the written word.

4. On the Old Law as the foreshadowing or "type" of the New Law, see 1.1 note 39. The objection seems to be arguing that if something is the case in a lesser matter (i.e., the Old Law was written), then it must be the case in a greater matter (i.e., the New Law should be written).

merely human, wisdom. These say that the disciples made out their teacher to be more than he really was when they said that he was the Son of God and the Word of God, by whom all things were made."[5] And after this he adds, "It seems as though they were prepared to believe whatever he might have written of himself, but not what others at their discretion preached about him." It seems, therefore, that Christ himself should have committed his teaching to writing.

On the contrary: No books written by him are found in the canon of Scripture.[6]

I answer: It was fitting that Christ did not write down his teaching.

First, on account of his dignity. For the more excellent the teacher, the more excellent should be his way of teaching. Consequently it was fitting for Christ, as the most excellent of teachers, to adopt that way of teaching that would imprint his teaching on the hearts of his hearers. Thus it is written in Matthew (7:29) that "he was teaching them as one having power." And so even among the gentiles: Pythagoras and Socrates, who were most excellent teachers, were unwilling to write anything. For writings are a means to an end: imprinting a teaching on the hearts of the hearers.[7]

Second, on account of the excellence of Christ's teaching, which cannot be encompassed in a text; according to John (21:25), "There are also many other things that Jesus did, which, if they all were written, the world itself, I think, would not be able to contain the books that would have to be written." Augustine explains this passage by saying, "We are not to believe that the world could not contain them with respect to physical space . . . but that they could not be comprehended by the capacity of the readers" (*Sermon 124*, 8, in *Homilies on the Gospel of John*). But if Christ had committed his

---

5. Still today one finds people who claim that Jesus was simply a wise man and that it was his followers (especially St. Paul) who turned him into a God. Such people usually think they are being quite innovative, though Thomas's quotation from Augustine suggests that this view has a long lineage.

6. Note that Thomas does not explicitly cite an authority here, as is his normal practice. However, the authority he invokes implicitly is that of the church, which gathered together the list or "canon" of the books of Scripture.

The *sed contra* can also give us some insight into the nature of the *ex convenientia* form of argumentation: the initial response to the objection is simply that Jesus did not, in fact, write his teachings down, implying that he must have had good reasons for doing things this way. An argument *ex convenientia* is one that tries to understand those reasons.

7. Why is it "more excellent" to teach orally than through writing? Though Thomas mentions Pythagoras and Socrates, philosophers of immense influence who left no writings, what really seems to form the background here, as becomes clear in the reply to the second objection, is Paul's teaching that the letter kills and the Spirit gives life (2 Cor. 3:3–6), which is itself a gloss on the prophetic notion of a law that is written directly on the heart (Jer. 31:33). The most excellent of teachers is able to imprint his or her teachings directly on the mind and heart, without the alien medium of writing.

teaching to writing, people would have thought of his teaching as no more profound than what appears on the surface of the writing.[8]

Third, so that his teaching might come to all in an orderly manner:[9] that is to say, he himself teaching his disciples directly, who subsequently taught others by speaking and writing. But if he himself had written, his teaching would have come to all immediately.[10] Therefore it is said of wisdom in Proverbs (9:3) that "she has sent her handmaidens to summon to the fortress."

It is to be observed, however, that, as Augustine says, some of the gentiles thought that Christ wrote certain books containing a kind of magic by which he worked miracles, something Christian teaching condemns. "And yet those who claim to have read those books of Christ do none of those things that they marvel at his doing according to those same books. Indeed, it is by a divine judgment that they are so far mistaken as to assert that these books were letters addressed to Peter and Paul, because they saw them depicted in many places accompanying Christ. No wonder that the inventors were

8. Consider the difference between the place of sacred writings in Christianity and in Islam. Muslims believe the Qur'an to be a direct dictation in Arabic to the prophet Muhammad from God, through an angel. As such it is quite *literally* the word of God. For Christians, on the other hand, it is Jesus who is the Word of God, and Scripture is what bears witness to that Word. Scripture—which in Latin simply means "writing"—is always secondary. Thomas seems to be saying that if Jesus had written his teaching down, we might be tempted to think that the written text is what is of primary importance, rather than Jesus himself.

Thomas implies that the "personal" character of divine revelation in Christ is part and parcel of God's incomprehensibility. Since revelation is first and foremost the person of Christ and not a text, and since the act of existence of Christ's person is the divine act of existence (see 3.17.2, above), and since the divine act of existence cannot be comprehended by human beings (see 1–2.3 note 12), God's self-revelation is in fact a revelation that we can never fully grasp. At the end of his *Commentary on the Gospel of John*, Thomas says, "To write about each and every word and deed of Christ is to reveal the power of every word and deed. Now the words and deeds of Christ are also those of God. Thus, if one tried to write and tell of the nature of every one, he could not do so; indeed, the entire world could not do this. This is because even an infinite number of human words cannot equal the one Word of God" (21.6.2660).

9. Note Thomas's typical emphasis on hierarchical order. As always, however, the point of hierarchy is not for the higher to dominate the lower but, to use a modern term, for the higher to empower the lower, to dignify and elevate them. Christ entrusts the writing-down of his teaching to his apostles not because it is a menial task that he delegates to subordinates but because the apostles are ennobled by being given this role in the imparting of divine revelation. They are, as it were, given the dignity of being "secondary causes" of revelation. Thomas brings this out clearly in his *Commentary on the Gospel of John* (1.4.119), where he writes in reference to John the Baptist, "God wanted to have certain witnesses, not because he needed their testimony, but to ennoble those whom he appointed witnesses. Thus we see in the order of the universe that God produces certain effects by means of intermediate causes, not because he is himself unable to produce them without these intermediaries, but he deigns to confer on them the dignity of causality because he wishes to ennoble these intermediate causes. Similarly, even though God could have enlightened all men by himself and led them to knowledge of himself, yet to preserve due order in things and to ennoble certain men, he willed that divine knowledge reach men through certain other men."

10. The response to the first objection helps clarify Thomas's point here. Jesus relates to us not simply as individuals, but as members of a community—his body, the church. The fact that we depend on the writings of the apostles bears witness to this communal character of the Christian faith.

deceived by the painters; in fact, as long as Christ lived in the mortal flesh with his disciples, Paul was not a disciple of his" (*On Agreement among the Evangelists* 1.9–10).[11]

Reply to 1: As Augustine says in the same book (*On Agreement among the Evangelists* 1.35), "All of his disciples are, as it were, members of the body of which Christ is the head. Consequently, when they wrote what he showed and said to them, we must by no means say that he himself wrote nothing. For his members put forth that which they knew from his speaking as their head. Indeed, at his command they wrote whatever he wished us to read concerning his deeds and words, as if they were his hands."[12]

Reply to 2: Since the Old Law was given under the form of perceptible figures, it was also therefore fittingly written with perceptible signs. But Christ's teaching, which is "the law of the Spirit of life" (Rom. 8:2), ought to be "written not with ink, but with the Spirit of the living God, not on tablets of stone, but on the fleshly tablets of the heart," as the Apostle says in 2 Corinthians 3:3.[13]

Reply to 3: Those who were unwilling to believe what the apostles wrote of Christ would not have believed the writings of Christ himself, whom they thought to have worked miracles by magical means.[14]

---

11. This passage from Augustine refers to pagan writers who claimed that Jesus wrote letters to Peter and Paul, thinking mistakenly that Paul had been a disciple of Jesus during his earthly life. These writers made the mistake because they had seen pictures that, according to early Christian practice, depicted Paul standing alongside Christ.

12. Here we see Thomas taking over from St. Augustine a quite literal understanding of the church as a body of which Christ is the head. This view finds its ultimate origin in St. Paul (see Col. 1:18: "He is the head of the body, the church"). For Augustine and Thomas there is a real sense in which we can say that Christ *did* write down his teaching, because the church, which is his body, wrote down those teachings.

13. Here Thomas reiterates what he sees as the fundamental distinction between the Old Law of the Torah and the New Law of the gospel: the former prescribes outward actions, whereas the latter is a new, internal principle of action (i.e., grace).

14. This seems to refer back to the concluding paragraph of the body of the argument: those gentiles who thought Christ *had* written down his teachings still did not have authentic faith in him, seeing him as no more than some sort of magician.

Question 46:

The Suffering of Christ

3.46.1[1]
Was it necessary for Christ to suffer for the liberation of the human race?

It would seem that it was not necessary for Christ to suffer for the liberation of the human race.[2]

1. The human race could not be delivered except by God, according to Isaiah (45:21): "Am not I the Lord, and there is no God else besides me? A just God and a savior, there is none besides me." But no necessity can befall God, for this would be contrary to his omnipotence. Therefore it was not necessary for Christ to suffer.

2. What is necessary is opposed to what is voluntary. But Christ suffered in accord with his own will, for it says in Isaiah (53:7), "He was offered because it was his own will." It was therefore not necessary for him to suffer.

3. As it says in the psalm (25:10), "All the ways of the Lord are mercy and truth." But it does not seem necessary on the part of the divine mercy that he should suffer, for as it freely bestows gifts, so it would seem to forgive debts without repayment. Nor is it necessary on the part of divine justice, according to which humanity deserved everlasting condemnation. Therefore

---

1. On this article, see Nichols (1990); Healy (2016).

2. This article does not begin, as do so many in this section of the *Summa*, by inquiring into the *convenientia* of some aspect of the story of Jesus (see 3.1 notes 2, 19). Rather, Thomas is asking about the *necessitas* of Jesus's suffering, though, as we shall see, this is not unrelated to fittingness. Thomas has already discussed the sense in which the incarnation of God the Son is "necessary" (see 3.1.2, above); here he takes up the more specific topic of the necessity of the specific *form* in which the Son becomes incarnate: that of the Suffering Servant of God.

This article and the one following are important for examining the particular kind of necessity that is associated with "fittingness," which is discussed explicitly in the third article of this question (3.46.3, below). It is also important to note that these articles are inquiring into the relationship between the suffering of Christ and human deliverance or "liberation" from sin. Thomas has already indicated (3.1.2, above) and will indicate again (3.46.3, below) that more is involved in human salvation than simple liberation from sin.

it does not seem necessary that Christ should have suffered for humanity's liberation.

4. The angelic nature is more excellent than the human, as is clear from Dionysius's *On the Divine Names* (4.2). But Christ did not suffer to repair the angelic nature that had sinned. It seems, therefore, that neither was it necessary for him to suffer for the salvation of the human race.[3]

On the contrary: It is said in John (3:14–15), "As Moses lifted up the serpent in the desert, so must the Son of Man be lifted up, that whoever believes in him may not perish, but may have eternal life."

I answer: As the Philosopher teaches in the *Metaphysics* (5.5, 1015ᵃ), the word "necessary" is used in several ways. In one way it means anything that by its nature cannot be otherwise, and in this way it is evident that it was not necessary for Christ to suffer, either on the part of God or on the part of humanity.[4]

In another way, a thing is said to be necessary on account of something quite apart from itself. If this is either an efficient or a moving cause, then it brings about the necessity of compulsion—for example, when someone cannot get away due to the force of someone else holding him.[5] If, however, the external factor that induces necessity is a goal, then something will be said to be necessary on account of presupposing a goal—that is to say, when some particular goal either cannot exist or cannot exist in a fitting manner unless such an end be presupposed.[6]

---

3. The point of this objection seems to be that if Christ did not have to suffer to save the sinful angels, then he *certainly* could have saved human beings without suffering.

4. We might call this "intrinsic necessity." For example, a human being *must* be a rational animal, because that is the nature of a human being. For Thomas, even God is subject to this sort of "necessity" inasmuch as God cannot be weak (since his nature is to be omnipotent) or ignorant (since his nature is to be all-knowing) or evil (since he is goodness itself). Thomas does not see such necessity as a limitation on God; rather it is simply a matter of God's perfection, which we try to grasp by denying him creaturely imperfections.

In the case of God's action in history, however, we cannot say that God is by nature a being who redeems the world through the suffering of his Son, nor is being redeemed by the sufferings of Christ something due to human beings on account of their nature.

5. On "efficient" or "moving" causality, see 1.2 note 42.

6. The crucial difference Thomas notes here concerns the kinds of necessity entailed in efficient (or "moving") and final causality (see 1.2 note 58). We might say that the necessity imposed by compulsion involves my action being subject to another's will, while the necessity imposed by an end involves my action being subject to my own will. Thomas also mentions a difference in the way that various means might be "necessary" to a particular end or goal. This distinction, between existing at all and existing in a fitting manner, is discussed in 3.1.2, above.

An efficient cause makes something necessary in the sense of "compulsory," whereas a final cause makes something necessary because certain means fit with certain ends. Take this example: "You must pay taxes." This statement could refer to the fact that the IRS would throw me in jail if I did not pay my taxes. In that case, the IRS would be an efficient cause compelling me to pay taxes. However, the statement could also refer to the fact that if we want our government to provide certain services to its citizens, then we should

It was not necessary, then, for Christ to suffer from the necessity of compulsion, either on the part of God, who determined that Christ should suffer, or on the part of Christ himself, who suffered voluntarily.

Yet it was necessary from necessity of the goal. This can be understood in three ways. First of all, on our part, who have been delivered by his suffering [*per eius passionem*],[7] according to John (3:14–15): "The Son of Man must be lifted up, that whoever believes in him may not perish, but may have eternal life." Second, on the part of Christ himself, who through the lowliness of his suffering merited the glory of being exalted. This pertains to what is said in Luke (24:26): "Was it not necessary for Christ to suffer these things, and so to enter into his glory?" Third, on the part of God, whose decree regarding the suffering of Christ—foretold in the Scriptures and prefigured in the observances of the Old Testament—had to be fulfilled. And this is what is said in Luke (22:22): "The Son of Man is going his way according to that which is determined"; and (24:44), "These are the words that I spoke to you while I was still with you, that all the things that are written in the Law of Moses and in the Prophets and in the Psalms concerning me must be fulfilled"; and (24:46), "Thus it is written and thus it was necessary for Christ to suffer and to rise again from the dead."[8]

Reply to 1: This reasoning is based on the necessity of compulsion on God's part.

---

pay taxes. In that case, the goal of having certain services provided would be the final cause, and paying taxes would be a fitting means to that goal. The necessity in this second case is different from that in the first, since it is not a matter of absolute compulsion. One could conceivably seek to reach the desired end by some other means: the government could raise money with an annual nation-wide bake sale, or the U.S. Navy could take up piracy and steal what we need from other countries. Levying taxes is simply the most "fitting" (*conveniens*) way for a government to fund itself (see 3.1 note 19).

7. There is no single English word that captures the Latin term *passio*. Most generally, *passio* is something that happens to us rather than to something that we do; a passion is the antithesis of an action. It therefore includes anything that might befall someone (typically something detrimental), including physical suffering (thus we speak of the passion of Christ). It can also mean emotion, and from the examples of *passio* given in this article—hatred, anger, pity, unhappiness—that seems to be the meaning it has here. In general I try to translate *passio* in a psychological context as "emotion"; in the soteriological context of what Christ experienced on the cross as "suffering"; and in reference to the events surrounding the death of Christ as "the passion." Here I translate *passio* as "suffering" rather than "passion" since it is all very well and true to say that the events of Good Friday are key to human salvation, but Thomas's point is, I think, more specific. It is the *suffering* of Christ, his *pathos*, that is key. If this sense of *passio* is lost, then much of the offense is removed from what Thomas has to say, and one might well wonder why he has to wrestle so with the notion of Christ's *passio*. But if we keep in focus that Thomas is trying to understand the necessity and fittingness of God incarnate *suffering* for us, then his teaching can regain some of its shocking vividness.

8. Thomas thinks that there are three different goals we might think of for which Jesus's suffering served as the means: (1) our salvation, (2) his own glorification, and (3) the fulfillment of God's plan as revealed in the rituals and prophecies of the Old Testament. Here we see again the logic of *conveniens*—these different goals "come together" in being served by the single means of Christ's suffering.

Reply to 2: This reasoning is based on the necessity of compulsion on the part of Christ as a human being.[9]

Reply to 3: That humanity should be freed by his suffering was fitting to both Christ's mercy and his justice. Justice, because by his suffering Christ made repayment for the sin of the human race, and so the human race was set free by Christ's justice. Mercy, indeed, for human beings could not themselves repay for the sin of all human nature, as was said earlier (3.1.2, above), and therefore God gave his Son to repay on behalf of the human race, according to Romans (3:24–25): "Being justified freely by his grace, through the redemption that is in Christ Jesus, whom God has set forth as a reconciling offering, through faith."[10] And this came from a mercy more abundant than if he had forgiven sins without repayment. Hence it is said in Ephesians (2:4–5), "God, who is rich in mercy, on account of his immeasurable charity by which he loved us, even when we were dead in sins, made us alive together in Christ."

Reply to 4: Unlike human sin, the sin of the angels was irreparable, as is clear from what was said earlier, in the first part (1.64.2).[11]

3.46.2[12]
Was there any other possible means of human liberation?

It would seem that there was no other possible way of human deliverance besides Christ's suffering.[13]

1. The Lord says in John (12:24), "Unless the grain of wheat falling into the ground dies, it remains alone; but if it dies, it brings forth much fruit," concerning which Augustine says, "Christ called himself the seed" (*Sermon*

---

9. In his replies to objections 1 and 2 Thomas says, in essence, that the objections are correct if one is speaking of necessity in the sense of compulsion—i.e., being subject to another's will. However, they are inadequate inasmuch as neither God nor Christ is compelled in this matter, and inasmuch as the objections fail to recognize that there is another meaning that can be given to the statement "Jesus had to suffer"—namely, that the suffering of Jesus was the most fitting means to an end that he himself, as both divine and human, willed.

10. Here Thomas argues that Jesus's suffering was in fact a fitting means to the goal of human salvation (the first of the three goals Thomas identifies with regard to Jesus's suffering; see note 8, above). The objection argued that to save humanity in this way would seem to be something like a bribe offered to God, an attempt to buy his mercy or to get him to overlook the strictness of his justice. How the suffering of Christ fits with both God's mercy and justice is discussed further in 3.48.2, below.

11. Christ does not suffer for the angels who sinned because, Thomas holds, they are beyond redemption. So the objection seems to miss the point entirely (something rare in the *Summa*).

12. On this article, see Nichols (1990); Healy (2016).

13. Thomas now takes up the question of the "necessity" of Christ's suffering from the opposite direction. Having argued in the previous article that there is a sense in which Christ's suffering *was* necessary (in the sense of the best means to an end), he asks here whether this sense of "necessity" means that there was absolutely no other way for God to redeem humanity.

51, 9, in *Homilies on the Gospel of John*). Consequently, unless he suffered death, he would not have produced the fruit of our liberation.

2. In Matthew (26:42) our Lord says to the Father, "My Father, if this cup cannot pass me by without my drinking it, your will be done." But he spoke there of the cup of suffering; therefore Christ's suffering could not be bypassed. Thus Hilary says (*Commentary on Matthew*, 31), "Therefore the cup cannot pass unless he drinks of it, because we cannot be restored except through his suffering."

3. God's justice required that Christ should repay by suffering in order that humanity might be delivered from sin. But Christ cannot disregard his justice, for it is written in 2 Timothy (2:13), "If we do not believe, he remains faithful; he cannot deny himself." But he would deny himself were he to deny his justice, since he is justice itself. Therefore, it seems impossible for humanity to be delivered in any way other than by the suffering of Christ.[14]

4. There can be no falsehood underlying the faith. But the ancient fathers believed that Christ would suffer.[15] Consequently, it seems that it had to be that Christ should suffer.

On the contrary: Augustine says in *De Trinitate* (13.10), "The way in which God deigns to deliver us through the mediator between God and humanity, the human being Jesus Christ, is both good and appropriate to the divine dignity; but let us also show that other possible means were not lacking on God's part, to whose power all things are equally subject."[16]

I answer: Something may be said to be possible or impossible in two ways: in one way, simply and absolutely; in the other way, based on an assumption.[17]

Therefore, speaking simply and absolutely, it was possible for God to free humanity by some way other than the suffering of Christ, for "no word is impossible with God," as is said in Luke (1:37).

Yet once a certain assumption is granted, it *was* impossible. Since it is impossible for God's foreknowledge to be mistaken and his will or decree to be annulled, it was not possible, supposing God's foreknowledge and prior

14. The logic of this objection underlies what are sometimes called "penal" accounts of salvation: justice demands punishment for sin; God cannot be unjust and so must inflict punishment for sin; therefore Christ by suffering accepts God's just punishment on behalf of humanity. See 3.48 note 12.

15. By "ancient fathers" Thomas means the holy people of the Old Testament.

16. This passage from Augustine, included by Lombard in his *Sentences* (bk. 3, dist. 20, ch. 1), seems to have offered the definitive answer for thirteenth-century scholastics: whatever necessity one assigned to Christ's suffering could not compromise the freedom and power of God. Cf. Anselm, *Cur Deus Homo?* 2.5.

17. To use a somewhat weak analogy, it may not be necessary, absolutely speaking, for me to return home by 6:00 p.m., but if one adds the assumption that I have promised my wife that I will be home for dinner, there is a real sense in which I *have to* be home by 6:00, or else be untrue to my word. God, of course, cannot be untrue to his word because this would be a defect, and God is perfect.

decree regarding Christ's suffering, for Christ not to suffer and, at the same time, for humanity to be freed in some way other than by his suffering. And the same reasoning holds for all things foreknown and foreordained by God, as was shown in the first part (1.14.13).[18]

Reply to 1 and 2: The Lord here speaks presuming God's foreknowledge and prior decree, according to which it was determined that the fruit of humanity's salvation should not follow unless Christ suffered.

We must understand what is quoted in the second objection in the same way [as in the first]. "If this cup cannot pass me by without my drinking it"—that is to say, because you have so ordained it—therefore he adds, "your will be done."

Reply to 3: Even this justice that requires from the human race repayment for sin depends on the divine will, for if God had willed to free humanity from sin without any repayment, he would not have acted against justice. For a judge cannot dismiss a wrong without penalty while still preserving justice, if his task is to punish wrongs committed against another—for instance, against another person, or against the state, or any leader in higher authority. But God has no one higher than himself, for he is himself the supreme and common good of the whole universe. So if he forgives sin, which has the character of wrongdoing because it is committed against him, he injures no one, just as anyone else acts mercifully and not unjustly in overlooking an offense committed against them without any repayment.[19] And so David said when he sought mercy, "Against you only have I sinned" (Ps. 51:4), as if to say, "You can pardon me without injustice."

Reply to 4: Both human faith and the divine Scriptures upon which faith is built are based on the divine foreknowledge and plan. And the same reasoning

---

18. Thomas's basic point here is that nothing *compels* God to save us through the sufferings of Christ—this is his freely chosen means of saving us. However, it is an *eternal* choice, not one that God makes at some point in world history. For us, "choosing" to do something involves a process of deliberation that issues in an act of will at a particular moment. But since God exists outside of time, this cannot be the case with God's choosing. On predestination, see 1–2.110 note 12.

19. Judges are normally under an obligation to serve the needs of another, whether this be the ruler or, as in the case of democracies, the people themselves. So a judge cannot simply let a robber go free because she or he is feeling particularly merciful at that moment. To do so would violate the duty that the judge has to the robber's victims, as well as to society. God, however, is under no such obligation, since God is the one against whom the sin has been committed. Thus God can justly have mercy upon the sinner, since God is the "victim."

There is a deeper point underlying what Thomas says here. Human judges are always beholden to something that stands above them and by which their own actions can be judged—the law, and ultimately justice itself. However, God is not like a human judge, because he is himself the standard by which we judge justice and injustice. Therefore his mercy could never violate his justice, because God is justice itself.

holds for that necessity that comes from holding something on faith and for the necessity that arises from the divine foreknowledge and will.[20]

3.46.3[21]
Was this means the most fitting?

It would seem that there was some other more suitable way of freeing the human race than by Christ's suffering.

1. Nature in its operation imitates the divine work, since it is moved and regulated by God. Nature, however, never does anything with two things that could be done with one. Therefore, since God could have freed humanity solely by his own will,[22] it does not seem fitting that Christ's suffering should have been added for the liberation of the human race.

2. That which is done through nature is accomplished more fittingly than that which is done through force [*per violentiam*], because force is a kind of severing or lapse from what is according to nature, as is said in the book *On the Heavens*.[23] But Christ's suffering brought about his death by violence. Therefore it would have been more fitting if, instead of suffering, Christ had died a natural death for humanity's liberation.

3. It seems most fitting that whoever keeps something by force and unjustly should be deprived of it by some superior power. Therefore Isaiah (52:3) says, "You were sold for nothing, and you shall be redeemed without money." But the devil possessed no right over humanity, which he had deceived by fraud and held subject in slavery by a sort of force.[24] Therefore it seems most fitting

20. Recall that Thomas sees faith as a kind of sharing in God's own knowledge (see 1.1 note 21). So when the holy people of the Old Covenant knew by faith that Christ would suffer, this was based on God's foreknowledge, and so only imposed the kind of necessity that such foreknowledge implies. On divine foreknowledge, see 3.1 note 47.

21. On this article, see Nichols (1990); Conrad (2014); Healy (2016).

22. See 3.46.2, above, especially the reply to obj. 3.

23. See Aquinas's commentary on Aristotle's *On the Heavens* (2.23), commenting on 2.13, 294[b]–295[a] in Aristotle.

Thomas's term *violentia* has a much broader meaning than our modern word "violence." Any force that makes something go against its natural inclination—that is, "a severing or lapse from what is according to nature"—is, in Thomas's terms, "violent." For example, the natural inclination of a stone is to travel downward (see 2-2.2 note 6); therefore, the action of throwing the stone into the air is a "violent" one, in Thomas's sense of the term. A human death is considered violent not because it involves shooting or stabbing but because one does not die a "natural death," such as when one's body simply wears out. If one is killed by a lethal injection and gently drifts off into the Great Beyond, this would still, by Thomas's definition, be a violent death, even if the injection was administered by a compassionate physician in order to end the suffering of a terminally ill patient.

24. The objection attacks a view of the death of Jesus that is sometimes known as the "ransom" theory of the atonement. This view is found in certain early Christian writers who draw upon New Testament texts such as Mark 10:45 ("the Son of Man came not to be served but to serve, and to give his life a

that Christ should have deprived the devil solely by his power and without suffering.

On the contrary: Augustine says in *De Trinitate* (13.10), "There was no other more fitting way of healing our misery" than by the suffering of Christ.

I answer: Among different means to an end, the most fitting one is that by which various things come together that are themselves helpful to the end.[25] Through the freeing of humanity by Christ's suffering, many things came together for humanity's salvation, beyond liberation from sin.[26]

First, human beings know by this how much God loves them, and they are thereby called to love him in return, which is the perfection of human salvation.[27] Therefore the Apostle says in Romans, "God reveals his love toward us, for while we were his enemies, Christ died for us."[28]

Second, through this he gave us an example of obedience, humility, perseverance, justice, and the other virtues that are displayed in the suffering of Christ and that are necessary for human salvation. Therefore it is written in

---

ransom for many") and 1 Tim. 2:5–6 ("For there is one God; there is also one mediator between God and humankind, Christ Jesus, himself human, who gave himself a *ransom* for all"). In speaking of Christ as a "ransom," some of these writers seemed to imply that because of human sin the devil had, as it were, either taken the human race hostage or somehow acquired a "right" to humanity, and Christ was the ransom or price paid to the devil to regain humanity. Prior to Thomas, both Anselm (*Cur Deus Homo?* 1.6–7) and Peter Abelard (*Commentary on Romans*, bk. 2, qq. on Rom. 3:25–26) had criticized this way of interpreting these passages.

25. Here Thomas speaks of "fittingness" as *concurrere*, meaning "to run or flock together." Once again we see *convenientia* in its root meaning of "come [*venire*] together [*con*]": a means to an end is fitting if it can gather a number of different means together. See 3.1 note 2.

26. Thomas does not want to tie the death of Christ to a single meaning; the suffering of Jesus on the cross works in a number of ways, which come together to bring about human salvation. Salvation involves having our sins forgiven, but not *only* that. As he has argued in the previous article, God could simply have forgiven our sins by an act of will. But it is fitting that God saves us through Jesus's suffering, because it accomplishes more than simply the forgiveness of sins.

27. Christ's willingness to suffer tells us something about the depth of God's love for us and inspires us to try to love God in return. This is the significance of the cross that Peter Abelard had focused on. Rejecting the notion that God had to buy humanity back from the devil (see note 24, above), Abelard saw the death of Jesus primarily as a sign of God's love, which worked its effect in the depths of the human heart. Abelard writes, "By the faith that we have concerning Christ, charity is increased in us, because through this to which we hold fast, that God has united our nature to himself in Christ and, by suffering in that nature, has shown us that greatest charity, concerning which he himself says, 'No one has greater love than this,' etc., for his sake we cling both to him and to our neighbor by the indestructible bond of love" (*Commentary on Romans*, bk. 2, qq. on Rom. 3:22).

Oversimplified accounts of medieval theology often portray Abelard and Anselm as having diametrically opposed theories of salvation, with Abelard stressing the subjective moral influence exerted by Christ's death and Anselm stressing its nature as an objective act of "satisfaction" or repayment (see 3.48 note 2). However, Thomas, like most medieval theologians, incorporated elements of both of these approaches, without seeing them as contradictory. Indeed, one can find in Anselm himself, particularly in his prayers, a strong subjective element.

28. Here Thomas is apparently conflating verses 8 and 10 of Rom. 5.

1 Peter (2:21), "Christ has suffered for us, leaving you an example, that you might follow in his footsteps."[29]

Third, Christ by his suffering not only freed humanity from sin but also merited for us justifying grace and the glory of perfect happiness, as shall be shown later (3.48.1; 3.49.1, 5).[30]

Fourth, human beings are all the more bound by this to refrain from sin. As 1 Corinthians (6:20) says, "You are bought with a great price; glorify and bear God in your body."

Fifth, this results in a greater dignity [for humanity]; for just as a human being was overcome and deceived by the devil, so also it should be a human being that defeats the devil; and just as a human being merited death, so also a human being, by dying, should conquer death.[31] Therefore it is written in 1 Corinthians (15:57), "Thanks be to God who has given us the victory through our Lord Jesus Christ."

It was therefore more fitting that we should be freed by Christ's suffering, rather than by God's will alone.[32]

Reply to 1: Even nature uses several things for one purpose in order to do something more fittingly, in the way that two eyes are used for seeing; and the same thing can be observed in other cases.[33]

29. Because he was a Dominican, the notion of following in the steps of Christ was particularly important to Thomas. Both the Dominicans and the Franciscans sought to live their lives in as close an imitation of Christ as possible, and they took literally the idea that Christ said to his apostles "follow me." In suffering on the cross Jesus shows us the virtues he wishes his followers to have: obedience, humility, constancy, and justice. As Thomas says in his sermons on the Apostles' Creed, "Whoever wishes to live perfectly need do nothing but disdain what Christ disdained on the cross and desire what Christ desired" (*Sermon 6*).

30. Simply being freed from sin is inadequate for human salvation. Thomas understands salvation to be the vision of God, something that we, by our created nature, are not able to attain. So even if we were sinless, we could not be saved without the additional gift of God's grace, which transforms us so as to make us fit for eternal life with God. By his suffering—and, more importantly, by the virtues displayed in that suffering—Christ "merits" that grace for us. In other words, Christ acts on behalf of humanity to make God's favor something that can really belong to humanity.

31. Following St. Anselm, Thomas wants to stress here that Jesus's suffering and death on the cross are human acts, which is important because *God* does not need to win any victory over Satan; *humanity* does. So Jesus acts as human on behalf of humanity to win the victory over sin and death, a victory that God has no need to win, since God is not subject to sin and death.

32. Notice that in these five points Thomas speaks not about why *God* needs the suffering of Christ, but about why *we* do: to convince us of God's love, to give us an example of virtue to follow, to merit grace for us, to help us refrain from further sin, and to endow our human nature with the dignity of having triumphed over Satan, our ancient foe. This alignment of necessity with humanity is significant, because it indicates that for Thomas what is involved in human salvation is not a change on *God's* part—as if God were angry with us, but with the death of Christ this anger is somehow mollified—but a change on *our* part—we are transformed into the kinds of creatures who can live in God's presence. Given Thomas's conviction that God is unchanging, it would be impossible for him to claim that the death of Christ brings about a change in God.

33. That is, the objector is simply wrong in saying that nature never uses two things where one would suffice. We could certainly see with only one eye, but we see *better* with two.

Reply to 2: As Chrysostom says, "Christ had come in order to destroy death, not his own (for since he is life itself, death could not be his), but the death of human beings. Therefore it was not by reason of his being bound to die that he laid his body aside, but because the death he endured was inflicted on him by human beings. But even if his body had sickened and dissolved in the sight of all people, it was not fitting that he who healed the infirmities of others should have his own body afflicted with the same. And even had he laid his body aside without any sickness, and had then appeared, people would not have believed him when he spoke of his resurrection. For how could Christ's victory over death appear, unless he endured it in the sight of all, and so proved by the incorruption of his body that death was destroyed?"[34]

Reply to 3: Although the devil attacked humanity unjustly, nevertheless humanity was justly left by God under the devil's bondage on account of sin. And therefore it was fitting that Christ should free humanity from the devil's bondage through justice, by making a repayment on their behalf through his suffering. This was also a fitting means of conquering the pride of the devil—who is "a deserter from justice" and "a lover of power"—inasmuch as Christ should defeat the devil and free humanity not merely by the power of his divinity but also by the justice and lowliness of suffering, as Augustine says in *De Trinitate* (13.13, 14).[35]

34. The quotation is actually not from Chrysostom but from Athanasius, *On the Incarnation of the Word* 22–23.

35. Thomas deals with the ancient notion of the "rights" of the devil by reinterpreting it such that there is no suggestion either that God negotiates with kidnappers or that the devil had just title to humanity; he focuses, rather, on the notion of the "rightness"—in the sense of "fittingness"—of the devil's injustice and pride being overcome by Christ's justice and humility.

Question 47:

The Efficient Cause of Christ's Suffering

3.47.1[1]

Was Christ killed by someone else or by himself?

It would seem that Christ was not killed by someone else, but by himself.[2]

1. He himself says in John (10:18), "No one takes my life from me, but I lay it down." But someone is said to kill someone else who takes away that person's life. Consequently, Christ was not killed by others, but by himself.

2. Those killed by others fail gradually from a weakened nature, and this is especially apparent in those who are crucified. As Augustine says in *De Trinitate* (4.13), "Those who were crucified were tormented with a lingering death." But this did not happen in Christ's case, since "crying out, with a loud voice, he yielded up the spirit," as is said in Matthew (27:50). Christ was not, therefore, killed by others but by himself.

3. Those killed by others die by violence and therefore die unwillingly, because "violent" is the opposite of "voluntary."[3] But Augustine says in *De Trinitate* (4.13) that "Christ's spirit did not desert the flesh unwillingly, but because he willed it, when he willed it, and in the way that he willed it." Therefore Christ was not killed by others, but by himself.

On the contrary: It is written in Luke (18:33), "After they have whipped him, they will put him to death."

---

1. On this article, see Murphy (1965).

2. The question this article addresses grows out of the shape of the story of Jesus itself. For example, in Peter's first sermon in the book of Acts, he says that Jesus was "handed over to you according to the definite plan and foreknowledge of God, crucified and killed by the hands of those outside the law" (Acts 2:23). The Gospels portray the death of Jesus simultaneously as part of the divine plan, with which Jesus willingly cooperated, and as an unjust act committed by sinful humanity. So the question, as the objections make clear, is whether and to what degree Jesus gives up his life willingly.

3. On "violence," see 3.46 note 23.

I answer: A thing can be the cause of an effect in two ways. In one way, by acting directly so as to cause something. And in this way Christ's persecutors killed him because they inflicted a sufficient cause of death on him with the intention of killing him, and the effect followed; that is to say, death resulted from that cause.[4]

In another way, someone is said to cause something indirectly—that is, by not preventing it when one can do so (as if one were said to get another wet because one did not close the window through which rain was entering). In this way, Christ *was* the cause of his own suffering and death, for he could have prevented his suffering and death. First, by holding back his enemies, so that they would not have been eager to kill him or would have been powerless to do so.[5] Second, because his spirit had the power of preserving his bodily nature from suffering any injury. Christ's soul had this power because it was united in unity of person with the divine Word, as Augustine says in *De Trinitate* (4.13).[6] Therefore, since Christ's soul did not fend off the injury inflicted on his body, but rather willed his bodily nature to succumb to such injury, he is said to have "laid down his life," or to have died voluntarily.[7]

Reply to 1: When it is said, "No one takes away my life from me," it should be understood as meaning "against my will"; for something is properly said to be "taken away" when one takes it from someone who is unable to resist.[8]

---

4. The various elements Thomas lists here indicate that he is interested particularly in the kind of causality unique to intelligent beings, not in any sort of brute, mechanistic causality (e.g., how a boulder in an avalanche might cause someone's death). He is interested in the crucifixion as what we might call a "moral" act. Thus he notes that Christ's persecutors did not simply cause his death by their actions but committed those actions with the intention of causing his death. One of the important points here is that those who killed Christ were not simply puppets, acting out the script that God had written for them. Rather, they were genuine moral agents whose actions flowed from within themselves. See 1–2.6.1, above.

5. As Jesus says in Matthew's account of his arrest, "Do you think that I cannot appeal to my Father, and he will at once send me more than twelve legions of angels?" (Matt. 26:53). Jesus could have countered his persecutors' violence with his own, forcibly restraining them.

6. Even if Jesus had not forcibly restrained his persecutors, he simply could have refused to die, perhaps like St. Denis, who, after having been beheaded, picked up his head and walked into town. The deeper theological point is that all of Christ's bodily weaknesses, including things like hunger and thirst, were things he willingly took on for our sake.

7. Thomas is trying to read the story of the crucifixion in such a way that it displays for us two contrasting instances of human willing: the will of Christ's persecutors, which is the will to destroy him for their own purposes, and the will of Christ himself, which is the will to suffer and redeem for the sake of God. The drama of human salvation is played out in the confrontation between these two fundamental forms of human willing, which might be characterized, respectively, with terms from Augustine's *City of God*, as *amor sui* (love of self) and *amor Dei* (love of God). Both must be genuine acts of will; neither Christ nor his persecutors can be unwilling participants in this drama.

8. Here, and in all the responses, Thomas seems to be agreeing with the objections: Christ caused his own death. But, as usual, Thomas is really rejecting the flat-footedness of the objections. In this instance,

Reply to 2: In order for Christ to show that the suffering inflicted by violence did not take away his life, he preserved the strength of his bodily nature, so that at the last moment he was able to cry out with a loud voice. In this way, his death should be counted among his other miracles. Accordingly it is written in Mark (15:39), "Now when the centurion, who stood facing him, saw that in this way he breathed his last, he said, 'Truly this man was God's Son!'"

It was also a matter of wonder in Christ's death that he died more quickly than the others who were afflicted with the same suffering. Therefore it is said in John (19:32–33) that "they broke the legs of the first, and of the other that was crucified with him," that they might die more speedily. "But when they came to Jesus and saw that he was already dead, they did not break his legs." Mark (15:44) also states, "Pilate marveled that he should be already dead." For just as by his own will his bodily nature kept its strength to the end, so likewise, when he willed, he suddenly succumbed to the injury inflicted.[9]

Reply to 3: Christ died because he suffered violence; at the same time, nevertheless, he died voluntarily, because the violence inflicted on his body prevailed over it only to the degree that he willed it.[10]

---

he wants to say that Christ willingly hands his life over, but that it is also genuinely taken away from him, because his willingness to lay down his life does not affect the motivation of his killers at all.

9. Thomas tends to ascribe to Christ on the cross a measure of equanimity and control that seems to many theologians today to be at best incredible and at worst detrimental to Christ's true humanity, showing him to be more a superhero than one who shared our human condition. Thomas, however, in common with all theologians of his day (and of the centuries prior to him), believed that Christ not only maintained his composure on the cross but even continued to enjoy the beatific vision (see 3.46.8). In other words, the human soul of Christ experienced the highest form of happiness possible during the crucifixion.

Before we dismiss Thomas's view as incredible or even harmful, we should note two things. First, despite Thomas's tendency to stress Christ's composure on the cross, he also clearly maintains that Christ's suffering was intense—indeed, Christ experienced the most intense pain possible (see 3.46.6). Second, this deeply traditional view is not the result of idle speculation about Christ's divinity but grows out of Jesus's teaching in the Beatitudes: "Blessed are those who are persecuted for righteousness' sake" (Matt. 5:10). Christ promises blessedness to his followers in the very moment of their persecution, and not simply as a subsequent reward. On the cross, he embodies the blessedness he promises. Of course, this should imply to us that the blessedness involved in *beatitudo* is something rather different from what we are accustomed to call happiness.

10. In other words, in the case of Christ, "violent" and "voluntary" are not opposed. The question remains, Is this unique in the case of Christ because of the powers conferred on his humanity by union with his divinity? Is the death of a martyr who could have escaped by renouncing her faith also not at the same time violent and voluntary?

Question 48:

What Christ's Suffering Did

3.48.2[1]
Did Christ's suffering bring about our salvation by way of repayment?

It would seem that Christ's suffering did not bring about our salvation by way of repayment.[2]

---

1. On this article, see Cessario (1990, 116–73); Conrad (2014); Spezzano (2017).

2. The Latin word *satisfactio*—from the verb *satisfacere*, meaning literally "to do enough"—indicates a payment or offering of what is owed to a creditor. I have chosen to translate it as "repayment" rather than "satisfaction," not least because in modern English the word "satisfaction" seems to refer to a subjective feeling (as in, "I can't get no . . .") and not to an exchange between two or more parties. At the same time, "repayment" is not an entirely unproblematic translation, since it can imply a purely financial transaction, whereas Thomas wishes to stress *satisfactio* as an act of reparation undertaken to restore a relationship that has been broken.

The term *satisfactio* is first used by Tertullian in the early third century in association with the sacrament of penance. Originally, after having confessed his or her sin, a person would perform some "work of satisfaction" (or "penance," as it is usually called), such as extra praying or fasting or almsgiving, after which God's forgiveness would be pronounced by the priest in the absolution. With the passage of time, the order became reversed, so that absolution was pronounced prior to the penitent performing the work of satisfaction. In many ways, this was a happy development, since it made clear that God's love and mercy is not conditional upon some action that we perform; indeed, God never ceases to love the sinner. But if it is not a means of earning God's love and mercy, then what is the point of the work of satisfaction? The answer lies in the fact that our salvation is not a matter of a change in God's stance toward us, but of a change in our stance before God (see 3.46 note 32). Therefore, in the sacrament of penance the work of satisfaction is the way in which the Holy Spirit brings about a change in the penitent, so as to restore his or her status as an adopted child of God.

The term *satisfactio* is first used in reference to the atoning work of Christ on the cross by Ambrose of Milan in the fourth century, but it is really Anselm of Canterbury, writing some eight hundred years after Ambrose, who works out in detail—in his *Cur Deus Homo?*—an account of Christ's death as an act of satisfaction or repayment, done on behalf of the human race. Thomas's account of *satisfactio* draws heavily on Anselm, but at the same time he does not simply parrot Anselm. As I shall note along the way, Thomas makes several significant changes and shifts in emphasis.

Thinking about the notion of "satisfaction" in general, one might say that the purpose of offering satisfaction in the case of an offense committed against another human being is threefold: (1) to mollify the offended party; (2) to restore the right order of things (e.g., if I have taken two dollars from you,

1. It seems that making the repayment belongs to the one who commits the sin, as is clear in the other parts of penance. For the one who has done the wrong must be sorry over it and confess it.[3] But Christ never sinned, according to 1 Peter (2:22): "who did no sin." Therefore he made no repayment by his personal suffering.[4]

2. No one makes repayment by means of a greater offense. But the greatest of all offenses was perpetrated in Christ's suffering, because those who killed him sinned most severely, as stated earlier (3.47.6). So it seems that repayment could not be made to God by Christ's suffering.[5]

3. Repayment implies equality with the fault, since it is an act of justice. But Christ's suffering does not appear equal to all the sins of the human race, because Christ did not suffer according to his divinity, but according to his flesh, according to 1 Peter (4:1): "Therefore Christ has suffered in the flesh."

I must give you two dollars in order to return matters to their proper state); and (3) to allow the one who committed the offense to engage in a (potentially) transforming act of repayment. In the case of an offense committed against God, God does not need to be mollified. However, the other two purposes of satisfaction still apply: the right order of things must be restored, and those who have committed the offense must engage in the practice of making amends so that their relationship with the offended party (i.e., God) may be restored.

These general features of satisfaction must be kept in mind when speaking of Jesus's suffering and death as a work of satisfaction or repayment. Since Jesus is God's Son by nature and not by adoption (see 3.16 note 11), he cannot lose his status as God's child (i.e., he cannot sin); therefore, the third purpose mentioned above cannot apply to Jesus himself. However, the second purpose still applies: the right order of things must be restored. So we ask, how has the right order of things been distorted? As Thomas (following Anselm) sees it, human sin robs God of our love and obedience, which we owe to him in justice as our creator. What is needed to set things right, then, is for a human being, acting on behalf of humanity as a whole, to give to God the love and obedience that is rightfully God's. This is what Jesus does on the cross. He is a human being who does not withhold from God—even at the cost of his life—any of the love and obedience that God ought to receive. And once Jesus, acting on our behalf, has set things in their proper order, we are enabled to participate in that restored order of things, provided that we are made fit for such participation through being transformed by the Holy Spirit by means of baptism and, after baptism, works of satisfaction (purpose 3).

I should add that Thomas's understanding of Christ's suffering as a repayment for sin is not the whole of his understanding of how Christ saves humanity. There are also the important issues of "merit" (see 1–2.109 note 8) and "sacrifice" and "redemption." But *satisfactio* remains for Thomas the key to understanding how the suffering of Christ reconciles us with God, and it is therefore also the key to understanding the other ways in which Christ's suffering and death operate.

3. The language of *satisfactio* grows out of the sacrament of penance (see previous note), where it was considered one of the three "parts" of the sacrament (the other two being sorrow or contrition and the act of confessing itself). The objection argues that just as acts of contrition and confession must be done by the one who has actually committed the sin, so too must repayment.

4. The implication here is that Christ's sinlessness makes it singularly *unsuitable* to see his death as a kind of "repayment." How can Christ make restitution for sins if he himself is not a sinner?

5. The objection makes the rather obvious point (a point made less obvious, in the case of Jesus's death, by years of pious conditioning) that two wrongs do not make a right: that is, committing an offense that is worse than the original one seems an unlikely way of making amends.

But the soul, where sin resides, is superior to the flesh. Christ did not, therefore, make repayment for our sins by his suffering.[6]

On the contrary: The psalm (69:4) says in the person of Christ,[7] "Then I paid the debt for that which I did not take away." But one has not paid a debt unless one has repaid fully. Therefore it appears that Christ, by his suffering, has fully repaid for our sins.

I answer: One properly makes repayment for an offense by presenting something that the offended one loves as much as, or even more than, he hated the offense. But Christ, by suffering out of love and obedience, presented to God something greater than was required to compensate for the offense of the whole human race. First, because of the greatness of the charity on account of which he suffered.[8] Second, on account of the worth of his life, which he laid down in repayment, for it was the life of God and of a human being. Third, on account of the wide scope of the suffering and the greatness of the sorrows taken on, as stated earlier (3.46.6). And therefore Christ's suffering not only sufficed but was an excess repayment for the sins of the human race; according to 1 John (2:2), "He is the reconciling sacrifice [*propitiatio*] for our sins, and not for ours only but also for the sins of the whole world."

Reply to 1: The head and limbs are like one mystic person; and therefore Christ's repayment extends to all the faithful as being his members.[9] Also,

6. The objection presumes as background Anselm's claim that an offense against God has an "infinite" character (since God himself is infinite). How, then, can something that happens to Christ's human nature, which is finite, make amends for an infinite offense? Moreover, the death of Christ occurs in his body, not his soul, and the body alone is of even less account than the human nature as a whole.

7. Like all medieval theologians, Thomas often reads the Psalms as the voice of Christ speaking prophetically in the Old Testament.

8. It is perhaps significant that this is the point Thomas lists first. His emphasis is consistently on the inner attitude with which Christ takes up his suffering. See note 12, below.

9. Here we see the role of the church in Thomas's thinking on salvation. Because Christ is the head of the body of which Christians are the "members" or "limbs," he can act on their behalf. This same theology of the church as Christ's body is used by Thomas in the article immediately before this one (3.48.1) to discuss how Christ can "merit" on our behalf: his actions are not simply his alone; they in some way belong to all those who are "incorporated" or (to coin a barbarous neologism) "in-bodied" into the community of his followers. Thomas writes: "Christ's works are referred to himself and to his members in the same way as the works of any other person in a state of grace are referred to that person." Thus, as one who suffers persecution for justice's sake, Christ merits salvation (see Matt. 5:10–12); but because Christians form part of the one body of Christ, they merit salvation on the basis of the meritorious act of Christ; they share in his reward.

The effect of Christ's suffering—whether we understand this effect primarily as the meriting of salvation or as the making of repayment—is not applied invisibly, as if by magic, to individuals; rather it operates within the field of force that the Holy Spirit generates through the beliefs and practices of the Christian community—in particular, the sacraments. This integration of his understanding of the church with his understanding of Christ's act of *satisfactio* is one of the ways in which Thomas significantly develops Anselm's account. Anselm never really addresses the question of how Christ's reconciling repayment of love

insofar as any two people are one in charity, the one can make repayment for the other, as shall be shown later.[10] But the same reasoning does not hold for confession and contrition, because repayment consists in an outward action, for which aids [*instrumenta*] may be used, among which friends are to be counted.[11]

Reply to 2: Christ's charity was greater than the malice of his crucifiers. Therefore the value of his suffering as repayment surpassed the murderous offense of those who crucified him: so much so that Christ's suffering was sufficient—and even excess—repayment for the sins of his crucifiers.[12]

---

affects the rest of humanity. Here Thomas indicates that because Christ acts as the head of the body, of which we are members, his offering is our offering, though not in a mechanical way, since becoming one with Christ in his body involves not only outward sacramental actions but also inward transformation, by which the passionate love of Christ becomes our passion (see note 12, below). It is also important to note that Thomas does not restrict the effects of Christ's suffering to the visible members of the church, because (1) all human beings are at least potentially limbs of Christ's body, and (2) "the wind [Spirit] blows where it chooses" (John 3:8).

10. A discussion can be found in *Supplementum* 13.2. On the *Supplementum*, see 1–2.4 note 13.

11. On "instrumental causality," see 1.45 note 11. Here Thomas speaks in terms of Christ being an "instrument" by which humanity makes repayment to God. Thomas sees the unity of the body of Christ as rooted in a kind of friendship between the head and members.

12. People sometimes speak of the sacrificial death of Christ as if God must punish someone for human sin, and so Christ offers himself as a victim to be punished in our place. This view, sometimes called the "penal substitutionary" view of redemption, is not really Thomas's view. In this reply to the second objection, Thomas makes clear that what Christ offers to God is not the external fact of his death, but the "interior" reality of his love and obedience. Although the death of Jesus is a part of God's plan to save humanity, Thomas does not seem to think of it as a punishment that God inflicts upon Jesus (at least not in our modern sense of "punishment"; see 3.65 note 4). Indeed, here the death of Jesus appears to be the result of a sinful human action, which is redemptive only because Christ's love is greater than the hatred of those who killed him.

But *why* does the love of Christ take the form of suffering at the hands of sinful humans? Thomas seems to imply here and elsewhere that Christ's suffering is the result of the fact that the cure must be suitable for counteracting the disease. Thus, on one level, Christ's obedience counteracts human disobedience. But human disobedience to God is rarely if ever outright rebellion; it is more often a misdirected or half-hearted seeking of the good, and it is this misdirection and half-heartedness, no less than explicit malice, for which Christ's suffering or "passion" is the cure.

Here we might return to *passio*, the Latin word Thomas uses for Christ's suffering (see 3.46 note 7). Think of our modern English usage, in which "passion" means being swept up into something or, in the case of love, someone. Christ's passion is both his human soul's wholehearted response to God and the visible manifestation of the Son's eternal act of existence, in which he is swept up, through the Holy Spirit, in love for the Father. We might say that Christ's whole life is his "passion," but, because of sin, such passion must in the end take the form of suffering, for two reasons: (1) because this passion is violently rejected by those who fear that it will mean the end of their illusory independence from God, and (2) because his suffering and death disengage his soul from that which fallen humanity takes as ultimate: bodily life. For these two reasons, the suffering of Christ is a fitting means of undoing the sin of Adam and Eve, in which they turned away from God and turned toward bodily things.

In the end, for Thomas it is "passion"—in the sense of all-consuming love—that makes repayment; but in the context of human sin, the medicine of the passion takes the bitter form of suffering. Thus the "external" fact of Christ's suffering on the cross cannot simply be dispensed with, for the rejection of

Reply to 3: The dignity of Christ's flesh is not to be determined solely according to the nature of flesh, but also according to the person taking it on—that is, inasmuch as it was God's flesh. And from this it had infinite worth.[13]

---

such suffering in favor of the more "spiritual" offering of love could well be just another act of human half-heartedness and misdirection.

13. Thomas's reply presumes what he has said about Christ being a single logical subject (*suppositum*) possessed of two natures, divine and human. The same logic that authorizes one to say "God is a human being" also allows one to say that the flesh that is crucified is God's flesh (*caro Dei*) and is thus of infinite worth. See 3.16.1, above; esp. 3.16 note 18.

Question 53:

Christ's Resurrection

3.53.1[1]
Was it necessary for Christ to rise again?

It would seem that it was not necessary for Christ to rise again.[2]

1. John of Damascus says (*On the Orthodox Faith* 4.27), "Resurrection is the rising again of a living being that was disintegrated and fallen." But Christ did not fall by sinning, nor was his body disintegrated, as is clear from what was stated earlier (3.51.3). It is not, therefore, properly fitting for him to rise again.[3]

2. Whoever rises again is promoted to something higher, since to rise is to be lifted. But Christ's body continued after death to be united with divinity, and so it could not be promoted to anything higher.[4] Therefore, it was not appropriate for it to rise again.

1. On this article, see Crotty (1962); O'Collins (1970); Conrad (2014).
2. During the patristic period, in both the East and the West, writers tended to understand the suffering–death–resurrection of Jesus as a single event by which God redeems the world. In the fifth century, some writers began to speak of the passion of Christ as the unique cause of our forgiveness and thus of our salvation. For these writers, the resurrection was the greatest of miracles, but not directly connected to the mystery of human salvation. Over the course of the Middle Ages, this view came to dominate in the West: the resurrection was not ignored or seen as unimportant, but it was given at best a minor role to play as a cause of our salvation.

In his earlier writings, such as his *Commentary on the Sentences*, Thomas seems to have followed this prevailing view. However, by the time he writes the *Summa theologiae*, he appears to have shifted his position somewhat, as we shall see in this article, so that the resurrection acquires once again its own robust and distinctive role in the event of human salvation.

3. In the previous question, Thomas argues, on the authority of Ps. 16:10 (in Jerome's Vulgate translation, "You will not let your holy one see corruption") as interpreted by John Chrysostom, that Jesus's body did not decay in the tomb. The integrity of Jesus's body was a manifestation of his divine power and a sign that his death was not due to any weakness of his nature (which would have been indicated by the decay of his body) but was something that he accepted willingly. Following up on this argument, the objection seems to be saying that resurrection, as a restoration of bodily integrity, would be a misleading sign.

4. As with the previous one, this objection draws on an argument Thomas makes earlier (3.50.2)—namely, that Christ's body remained united to his divinity, though not to his human soul, while in the tomb.

3. Everything that happened concerning Christ's humanity is directed toward our salvation. But Christ's suffering was sufficient for our salvation, since by it we were freed from guilt and punishment, as is clear from what was said earlier (3.49.1, 3). Consequently, it was not necessary for Christ to rise again from the dead.[5]

On the contrary: It is written in Luke (24:46), "It is proper for Christ to suffer and to rise again from the dead."

I answer: It was necessary for Christ to rise again, for five reasons.[6]

First, for the praise of divine justice, to which it belongs to exalt those who humble themselves for God's sake, according to Luke (1:52): "He has put down the mighty from their seat and has exalted the humble."[7] Consequently, because Christ humbled himself, even to the death of the cross, out of charity and obedience to God, it was proper that he be exalted by God even to a glorious resurrection. Therefore it is said in his person in the psalm (139:2), as the gloss interprets it, "You have known (i.e., approved) my sitting down (i.e., my humiliation and suffering) and my rising up (i.e., my glorification in the resurrection)."[8]

Second, for the building up of our faith,[9] since our belief in Christ's divinity is confirmed by his rising again. According to 2 Corinthians (13:4), "Although

5. Whereas the first two objections indicate ways in which the resurrection of Jesus could be misleading, this third objection argues somewhat differently: since we are freed from sin through Christ's suffering and death, the resurrection serves no saving purpose. Of course, Thomas has already argued (3.46.1, above) that, strictly speaking, God could save us without the suffering of Christ—indeed at the outset of this part of the *Summa* (3.1.2) he argues that God could save us without becoming incarnate at all. But the objection here seems to be making a slightly different point: the resurrection is not simply "unnecessary" in the sense that the incarnation and passion are—that is, what God accomplishes through it *could* be accomplished in some other way; rather, the resurrection in fact accomplishes *nothing* with regard to our salvation.

6. The fact that Thomas offers five different reasons for why it was necessary (*necessarium fuit*) that Christ rise from the dead signals to us that we are dealing with the kind of necessity discerned by arguments *ex convenientia* (see 3.1 note 2). As he has already argued (3.46.1–3), this is not a necessity that imposes any sort of compulsion on God.

7. In presenting the resurrection of Jesus as an act of divine justice, vindicating the cause of Jesus, Thomas seems to anticipate a theme that would be stressed by liberation theologians in the last part of the twentieth century. Like these later theologians, Thomas sees in Mary's song of praise from Luke's Gospel a summary of God's characteristic way of favoring the poor, the weak, and the humble over the rich, the powerful, and the proud. In the resurrection of Jesus, this characteristic "preferential love for the poor" is manifested in an ultimate way.

8. On "glosses," see 1.12 note 10.

9. The Latin reads *ad fidei nostrae instructionem,* which could be translated as "for our instruction in the faith." However, as Jean-Pierre Torrell points out (1999, 543n6), the word *instructio* and the related verb *instruo* carry implications of "building" and "construction." In English this same convergence of meanings is found in the slightly archaic word "edification." So the resurrection is not simply God trying to convey some "fact" about Jesus to us (i.e., that he is divine); rather, it is a means by which we become more sure of Christ's divinity and thus are "built up," adhering more resolutely to this truth.

he was crucified through weakness, yet he lives by the power of God." And therefore 1 Corinthians (15:14) says, "If Christ be not risen again, then our preaching is empty, and our faith is also empty." And in the psalm (30:9), as the gloss explains it, "What benefit is there in my blood (i.e., in the shedding of my blood) while I go down (as if by various degrees of evils) into corruption? (As though he were to answer: 'None; for if I do not rise again at once, but rather my body is corrupted, I shall proclaim to no one, I shall gain no one.')."

Third, to lift up our hope; for in seeing Christ, who is our head,[10] rise again, we hope that we too shall rise again. Therefore it is said in 1 Corinthians (15:12), "If Christ is preached as risen from the dead, how do some among you say that there is no resurrection of the dead?" And it is said in Job (19:25, 27), "I know" (i.e., with certainty of faith) "that my Redeemer" (i.e., Christ) "lives," having risen from the dead; and therefore, "in the last day I shall rise out of the earth. . . . This my hope is held in my breast."

Fourth, to give shape to the lives of the faithful, concerning which Romans (6:4) says, "Just as Christ is risen from the dead by the glory of the Father, so we also may walk in newness of life." And farther on, "Christ, rising from the dead, now dies no more. . . . In this way you also should consider yourselves dead to sin, but alive to God" (Rom. 6:9, 11).[11]

Fifth, to complete our salvation. Just as it was for this reason that, in dying, he endured evil things that he might deliver us from evil, so he was glorified in rising again in order to advance us toward good things; according to Romans (4:25), "He was handed over for our sins, and rose again for our justification."[12]

10. See 3.48 note 9.

11. Since the second reason has to do with faith and the third with hope, we might expect the fourth reason to deal with love or charity (*caritas*), rounding out the trio of "theological virtues" found in 1 Cor. 13:13 (see 1–2.62.3, above), so it seems surprising that Thomas does not mention love here. But a closer reading of the article reveals that our expectation is not in fact misplaced. Thomas says that the resurrection should "shape" or "inform" the lives of those who believe and hope. We should take "form" here in the sense of that which makes something what it is, just as "cowness" is the form of each cow (on form, see 1.12 note 2). Elsewhere (2–2.23.8), Thomas says that charity is the "form" of the virtues—it is that which makes them virtues at all. So, for example, "courage" without charity is not a virtue. When Thomas says that the resurrection was necessary in order "to give shape to the lives of the faithful," he means that for Christians, the fact that Jesus was raised from the dead should "inform" all their actions, such that they may "walk in newness of life" and be "alive to God." The resurrection of Jesus is the key to the Christian moral life because it is the definitive act of God's love in history and is thus a sign of both the Spirit of love shared between the Father and Son and the love of God for all humanity. Lives that are "informed" by this great sign of charity are lives of true virtue. Thus it seems that Thomas is talking about charity after all.

12. Thomas's fifth reason for Christ's resurrection is somewhat different from the first four, in that here (and in the response to the third objection) he makes it clear that the resurrection has a *causal* role in our salvation; it serves to "complete" the process of salvation. Thomas remains rooted in the Western medieval tradition of treating cross and resurrection separately (see notes 2 and 5, above); therefore, here he distinguishes between them and assigns them distinct roles in the process of salvation. He does not seem to think of the resurrection as having a direct causal role in the forgiveness of sins; rather, it is, as he says in

Reply to 1: Although Christ did not fall by sin, he fell by death, because just as sin is a fall from righteousness, so death is a fall from life. Therefore the words of Micah (7:8) can be understood as though spoken by Christ: "Do not rejoice over me, my enemy, because I am fallen; I shall rise again." Likewise, although Christ's body did not disintegrate by returning to dust, yet the separation of his soul from his body was a kind of disintegration.[13]

Reply to 2: Christ's divinity was united with his flesh after death by the personal union, but not by a natural union—that is, the way that the soul is united with the body as its form, so as to constitute human nature. Consequently, by the union of the body and soul, the body was raised to a higher natural condition, but not to a higher state of personhood.[14]

Reply to 3: Christ's suffering brought about our salvation, properly speaking, by removing evils; but the resurrection did so as the beginning and exemplar of all good things.

---

the reply to the third objection, "the beginning and exemplar of all good things." Still, Thomas clearly sees the resurrection of Jesus as a *cause* of our salvation, and not simply as some miraculous add-on to what was accomplished on the cross. Thomas says earlier (see 3.1 note 20) that in thinking of human salvation we need to think in terms of both our "withdrawal from evil" and our "furtherance in good": grace both heals and elevates. Thus the cross, which frees us from sin, and the resurrection, which advances us in goodness, are both genuinely causal factors in the one process of salvation.

13. Here and in the next reply, Thomas's theological purposes are once again well served by his Aristotelian insistence that a human being is not the soul, but the body-soul composite. See 1.75.4, above.

14. Christ's body was a better body after the resurrection than when it lay in the tomb, because body and soul were reunited, which is more in keeping with the natural condition of the body. But it was not the body of a more esteemed person, since it remained the body of the Son of God even while it lay in the tomb.

Question 54:

The Qualities of the Risen Christ

3.54.1[1]
Did Christ have a true body after his resurrection?

It would seem that Christ did not have a true body after his resurrection.

1. A true body cannot be in the same place at the same time with another body. But after the resurrection Christ's body was with another body at the same time in the same place, since he entered among the disciples, "the doors being shut," as is related in John (20:26).[2] Therefore it seems that Christ did not have a true body after his resurrection.

2. A true body does not vanish from a beholder's sight unless it happened to decay. But Christ's body "vanished out of the sight" of the disciples as they gazed upon him, as is said in Luke (24:31). It therefore seems that Christ did not have a true body after his resurrection.

3. Every true body has its fixed shape. But Christ's body appeared to the disciples "in another shape," as is clear from Mark (16:12).[3] Therefore it seems that Christ did not possess a true human body after his resurrection.

On the contrary: It is said in Luke (24:37) that when Christ appeared to his disciples, "being troubled and frightened, they supposed that they saw a spirit"—that is, as if he did not have a true body but an imaginary one. To remove their fears he then added: "Handle and see, for a spirit does not have flesh and bones, as you see me to have" (24:39). Consequently, he did not have an imaginary body but a true one.

---

1. On this article, see Torrell (1999, 561–84).
2. That is, Christ's body and the door would have had to occupy the same space at the same time, which it is impossible for two material objects to do.
3. This reference is to the so-called longer ending of Mark's Gospel, which alludes to the appearance of the risen Jesus to two disciples on the road to Emmaus, which Luke recounts in detail in 24:13–35. Most modern scholars see the Markan passage as a later addition to the Gospel, based on what is found in Luke.

I answer: As John of Damascus says (*On the Orthodox Faith* 4.27), what is said to rise is that which has fallen.[4] But Christ's body fell by death—namely, inasmuch as the soul that was its formal perfection was separated from it.[5] So it was necessary, in order for it to be truly Christ who is risen, for the same body of Christ to be once more united with the same soul. And since the truth of the body's nature is from its form, it follows that Christ's body after his resurrection was both a true body and of the same nature as it was before.[6] But if his body had been an imaginary one, it would not have been a true resurrection, but an apparent one.

Reply to 1: Some say that Christ's body, after his resurrection, entered in among the disciples while the doors were shut—thus existing with another body in the same place—not by miracle but by its glorified condition. But whether it is possible, from some property peculiar to it, for a glorified body to be simultaneously with another body in the same place, will be discussed later when the general resurrection is dealt with.[7] For now let it suffice to say that it was not from any property of the body but rather by the power of the divinity united to it that this body, although a true one, entered in among the disciples while the doors were shut. Accordingly Augustine says in a sermon for Easter (*Sermon 247*) that some argue in this way: "If it were a body, if what rose from the sepulcher were what hung upon the tree, how could it enter through closed doors?" And he answers: "If you understand how, it is

---

4. John of Damascus makes the point that resurrection must involve the body, since it is the body that falls into mortality, not the soul.

5. By "formal perfection" Thomas means that the soul is the form that "perfects" the body by making it the kind of body it is—i.e., a human body (see 1.75, especially note 8).

6. Because a true human body is matter informed by a human soul, Christ's resurrected body must have been a true human body. This leaves some questions unresolved, such as the sense in which the true human body possessed by the risen Christ is said to be *Christ's* body.

One might think, based on Thomas's statement in the first part that "the soul contains the body" (1.76.3)—by which he means that the soul, as the sole substantial form of the body, might be said to "virtually" contain the body—that any matter informed by a person's soul would be that person's body (see 1.119.1). This would suggest that Christ's soul could constitute for itself a new body out of any matter whatsoever. This is not, however, Thomas's view. He clearly believes that Christ's risen body was constituted by the same matter as the body that was laid in the tomb (see 3.50.5), since the scriptural narratives of the empty tomb would seem to require this. So it seems that for Thomas, the continuity of the self in the experience of resurrection, both for Christ and for us, is one that fittingly involves a material continuity. This leads to a number of thorny questions involving dead skin cells that have been sloughed off as well as cannibalism (i.e., who ends up with the consumed body part—see *Summa contra Gentiles* 4.81), which Thomas seeks to resolve by an appeal back to his notion of the soul containing the body.

7. This section of the *Summa* was never written. However, Thomas addresses this question in a number of places (e.g., *Quodlibetal Questions* 1.10.1–2), in which he denies that a glorified body, by its own natural properties, can exist in the same place as another body, on the principle that "glorification does not remove a nature." However, he affirms that it *can* do so through the miraculous power of God, present in Christ by virtue of the hypostatic union.

no miracle; where reason fails, faith is built up." And in his sermons on John (*Sermon 121*) he says: "Closed doors were no obstacle to the mass of a body where divinity was, for if in his birth his mother's virginity remained intact, surely he could enter in by doors not open."[8] And Gregory says the same in a homily for the octave of Easter (*Sermon 26*, in *Homilies on the Gospels*).

Reply to 2: As stated above (3.53.3), Christ rose to an immortal life of glory. But the disposition of a glorified body is such that it is "spiritual"—that is, subject to the spirit, as the Apostle says in 1 Corinthians (15:44).[9] For the body to be entirely subject to the spirit, it is necessary for every action of the body to be subject to the will of the spirit.

Now something being seen is due to the action of the visible object upon the sight, as the Philosopher shows (*De anima* 2.7, 418ª). And so whoever has a glorified body has it in his power to be seen when he wishes to and not to be seen when he wishes not to.[10] Moreover, Christ had this not simply from the condition of his glorified body but also from the power of his divinity, by which it can happen that even bodies not glorified may be miraculously unseen—as was, by a miracle, bestowed on the blessed Bartholomew, that "if he wished he could be seen, and not be seen if he did not wish it."[11]

Christ, then, is said to have vanished from the eyes of the disciples not as though he were decayed or dissolved into invisible elements but because he ceased, of his own will, to be seen by them, either while he was present or while he was departing by the gift of agility.[12]

Reply to 3: As Severian says in an Easter sermon, "No one should suppose that Christ changed his features at the resurrection."[13] This is to be understood in reference to the shape of his bodily members, since there was nothing out of order or deformed in the body of Christ—which was conceived of the Holy

8. That is, just as in his birth Christ could pass through Mary's hymen without breaking it (according to ancient belief in *virginitas in partu*), so too his risen body could pass through the locked door of the upper room.

9. Notice that Thomas understands "spiritual body" not to imply that the body is not material, but that it is perfectly subject to the spirit.

10. Jean-Pierre Torrell points out that Thomas ascribes not only the invisibility but also the visibility of the risen Christ to an act of his will. This indicates that Christ's resurrected body only appears when he wishes it to, such that he chooses to whom he will reveal himself in his risen state. This accords well with the New Testament emphasis on resurrection appearances as revelatory acts of Christ. As Torrell puts it, "The risen Christ retains the initiative in showing himself to whom he wills, when he wills, where he wills" (1999, 569).

11. The reference is to an apocryphal tale found in James of Voragine's *Golden Legend*. Unlike the ability to pass through a door, the ability to appear and vanish, Thomas believes, is a natural property of a glorified body, because of the perfect subjection of such a body to the will. But he also notes that this ability can be miraculously imparted by God to an unglorified body as well.

12. By "agility," Thomas means simply the perfect attunement of the body to the prompting of the spirit. This is one of the four *dotes* or "dowries" traditionally ascribed to glorified bodies; see 1–2.4 note 10.

13. The text is actually from Peter Chrysologus: *Sermon 82*.

Spirit—that had to be set right at the resurrection. Nevertheless, he received the glory of clarity in the resurrection,[14] and so the same writer adds, "but the semblance is changed, when, ceasing to be mortal, it becomes immortal; so that it acquired a glorious appearance, without losing the appearance's substance."

Yet he did not appear to those disciples in glorified beauty, but just as it lay in his power for his body to be seen or not, so too it was within his power to present to the eyes of the beholders his form either glorified or not glorified, or a mixture of the two, or in any fashion whatsoever. Only a slight difference suffices for someone to seem to appear another shape.[15]

14. By "clarity," Thomas envisions a shining quality, due to the overflow of the soul's glory into the body. This too is one of the *dotes* (see 1–2.4 note 10).

15. Thomas seems to be saying that when it suited his purposes, the risen Christ could, by manifesting a small measure of his risen body's glory, make it impossible for those who had known him in his unglorified state to recognize him, without appearing as something other than an unglorified human being. This would account for both Mary Magdalene and the disciples at Emmaus not recognizing him.

Question 59:

Christ's Power as Judge

3.59.5[1]
After the judgment that takes place in the present time, does there remain yet another general judgment?

It would seem that after the judgment that takes place in the present time, there does not remain another general judgment.[2]

1. After the final assigning of rewards and punishments, judgment serves no purpose. But rewards and punishments are assigned in this present time, for in Luke (23:43) the Lord said to the thief on the cross, "This day you shall be with me in paradise,"[3] and also in Luke (16:22) it is said that "the rich man died and was buried in hell." It is pointless, therefore, to expect a final judgment.

2. In an alternate text of Nahum (1:9) it is said, "God shall not judge the same thing a second time."[4] But in the present time God exercises judgment with regard to both worldly and spiritual matters. Therefore, it does not seem that another final judgment is to be expected.[5]

1. On this article, see Torrell (1999, 683–705); Lamb (2004).

2. Thomas is asking whether there will be a final judgment at the end of time, in addition to the judgment that is passed on us at the time of our death. In order to understand the discussion, it is important to keep in mind three things that constrain the argument. First, certain passages in the New Testament, such as those cited later in the first objection, speak of a definitive judgment that is passed at death. Second, based on the New Testament and the creeds, Thomas is committed to the proposition that Jesus will return at some point in the future "to judge the living and the dead," at which time the bodies of the dead will be raised and reunited with their souls. Third, it is a deeply rooted church practice to invoke the prayers of the saints, who were seen as those who were already enjoying the vision of God. Taken together, these three factors seem to leave Christians in the position of saying that there are two judgments, one at the time of death and the other at the time of Christ's return.

3. Note, the emphasis should fall on *"this day."*

4. The "alternative version" in question is the Septuagint, which was the ancient Greek translation of the Hebrew Bible and the basis of the old Latin translation of the Old Testament prior to Jerome's Vulgate translation, which was made directly from Hebrew. The Vulgate version of this verse is quite different: *non consurget duplex tribulatio* (a double tribulation shall not arise).

5. In other words, no double jeopardy.

3. Reward and punishment correspond to merit and blame. But merit and blame do not pertain to the body except inasmuch as it is the instrument of the soul.[6] So neither reward nor punishment is due to the body except through the soul. Therefore, no other judgment is required at the end in order to reward or punish a person in the body, besides that judgment in which souls are now punished or rewarded.[7]

On the contrary: It is said in John (12:48), "The word that I have spoken, the same shall judge you in the last day." There will be, therefore, a judgment at the last day besides that which takes place in the present time.

I answer: Judgment on something changeable cannot be given fully before its consummation. Just as judgment cannot be rendered fully regarding the quality of any action before its completion, both in itself and in its results, because many actions appear to be advantageous which by their effects are shown to be harmful,[8] in a similar way, judgment cannot be fully rendered regarding any person before their life is ended, since one can be changed in many respects: from good to evil, from evil to good, from good to better, or from evil to worse.[9] Therefore the Apostle says in Hebrews (9:27), "It is appointed for mortals to die once, and after that the judgment."

But it must be observed that although a person's earthly life in itself ends with death, it nevertheless remains to some degree dependent on what comes after it in the future. In one way, one's life continues on in people's memories, in which, sometimes contrary to the truth, good or evil reputations linger on.[10]

In another way, one lives on in one's children, who are, as it were, something of their parent. According to Sirach (30:4), "His father is dead, and it is as

6. The body is not, of itself, deserving of either praise or blame. If I save the life of the president because I happen to be standing between the president and an oncoming bullet, it is not a meritorious act; indeed, it is not a human act at all. For a bodily action to deserve praise or blame it must be an action prompted by the soul, such that the soul has intentionally moved the body to act. On "merit" in general, see 1–2.109 note 8.

7. The objection is anticipating an argument like this: the soul is judged at the time of death, and the body is judged when it is raised at Christ's return. This is, in fact, the argument Thomas makes in several of his other works (e.g., *Quodlibetal Questions* 10.1.2). Interestingly enough, this is not the focus of his explanation in this article. Nor does he offer the argument that he employs in his earlier commentary on Peter Lombard's *Sentences* (bk. 4, dist. 47, q. 1, a. 1, qa. 1) that the judgment made at the time of death is an individual one, whereas the judgment made at the end of time is a collective one. As we shall see, Thomas's argument in this article is more complex and, perhaps as a result, less clear.

8. For example, we might make the judgment that Ty Cobb swings the bat beautifully. But we would have to revise our judgment if the bat subsequently connected with the back of an opposing player's head.

9. In *Confessions* 10.36 Augustine writes, "Anyone who could change from the worse to the better can also change from the better to the worse." For Augustine, this mutability of the human person places severe restrictions even on self-knowledge, with the result that we do not have enough information to judge ourselves, much less someone else.

10. The writing of history constitutes a kind of judgment upon the lives of those who are remembered in such histories, even if it is not a true or faithful judgment.

if he were not dead, for he has left one behind him that is like himself." And yet many good people have evil sons, and vice versa.

In a third way, one lives on to a degree in the result of one's actions, as in the case of how, from the deceit of Arius and other false leaders, unbelief continues to flourish down to the end of the world, just as faith will continue to derive its progress until then from the preaching of the apostles.

In a fourth way, one lives on as regards the body, which is sometimes buried with honor and sometimes left unburied, and finally turns completely to dust.

In a fifth way, one lives on in the things on which one's heart is set, such as worldly concerns, some of which are ended quickly, while others endure for a long time.[11]

All these things are submitted to the evaluation of divine judgment. Consequently, a definitive and public judgment cannot be made of all these things during the course of this present time. For this reason, there must be a final judgment at the last day, in which everything concerning every human being in every respect shall be fully and openly judged.[12]

Reply to 1: Some people have held the opinion that the souls of the saints shall not be rewarded in heaven, nor the souls of the damned punished in

---

11. For example, if one devoted one's entire life to a cause, sacrificing other things for the sake of that cause, and after one's death and with the passage of time that cause turned out to be evil or trivial, one's life would be judged accordingly.

12. What Thomas is saying here is, frankly, a little confusing. It may help to take it step by step. First, he notes that, as with an action, a person cannot be judged until a state of completion is attained. In one sense, we attain this completion at our death. Thomas believes, along with most of the Christian tradition, that at death our eternal fate is fixed and we are consigned either to heaven with the saints, to hell with the damned, or to purgatory, where those who have been judged to be among the saved, but whose lives are still marked by sin, are purified. From this moment on there can be no change in our ultimate destination.

However, Thomas notes that in another sense we have a sort of "afterlife" that is purely *natural* and not to be confused with the continued existence of the soul after death. In this "natural afterlife" people live on, for example, through their children or reputation or continuing influence. So there is a sense in which our lives on earth are *not* finished at the time of our death. For Thomas, then, the final judgment is the point at which God offers the final evaluation of our lives, incorporating the "natural afterlife" of our influence on history. However, this judgment is *not*, as Thomas sees it, a second chance, a court of appeals for those who lost the first time around and ended up in hell. That judgment is made at the time of death.

What then is the purpose of this judgment? One of the purposes of judgment is to assign praise and blame; and, as Thomas indicates when he says that the way in which people are remembered is "sometimes contrary to the truth," praise and blame are not always justly apportioned by history. The final judgment is a kind of public manifestation of God's true judgment, correcting and supplementing the imperfect judgment that human beings have made. To use a loose analogy, the final judgment is akin to the hearings of the Truth and Reconciliation Commission in South Africa, whereby both the victims and the perpetrators of decades of violence and deceit were granted a public venue in which to tell the truth about their lives under apartheid (my thanks to David Toole for this example). It is in the final judgment that dictators who may have been revered for their skill in statecraft are revealed as the tyrants that they were, and that the martyrs who died unknown and unburied are shown to be the true heroes of history.

hell, until judgment day.[13] This is clearly false, from what the Apostle says in 2 Corinthians (5:8), "We are confident and would like instead to be absent from the body and to be present with the Lord"—that is, as is apparent from the context, not to "walk by faith" but "by sight." This is to see God in his essence, the vision in which "eternal life" consists, as is clear from John (17:3).[14] It is therefore manifest that souls separated from bodies are in eternal life.

So it must be said, regarding all that concerns the soul, that after death a human being enters into an unchangeable state. Therefore, regarding the reward of the soul, there is no need for postponing judgment. But since there are other things pertaining to a person that go on through the whole course of time and that are not outside of divine judgment, all of these things must be brought to judgment at the end of time. For although one neither merits nor demerits in regard to such things, they still, to a degree, accompany one's reward or punishment.[15] Therefore all these things must be considered in the final judgment.

Reply to 2: "God shall not judge the same thing a second time"—that is, in the same respect. But it is not unfitting for God to judge twice according to different respects.[16]

Reply to 3: Although the reward or punishment of the body depends upon the reward or punishment of the soul, nevertheless, since the soul is changeable only accidentally on account of the body, once it is separated from the body it enters into an unchangeable condition and receives its judgment.[17] But the body remains subject to change down to the close of time, and therefore it must receive its reward or punishment then, in the last judgment.

13. See 1–2.4 note 2.

14. "And this is eternal life, that they may know you, the only true God, and Jesus Christ whom you have sent."

15. This clause might also be translated as "they somehow have something to do with one's reward or punishment." Thomas does not specify *what* exactly. Perhaps what he means is that the revelation of the good or evil wrought in one's "natural afterlife" will be part of one's eternal reward or punishment.

16. To use an example Thomas himself mentions: Arius, at his death, could be judged for his erroneous beliefs about the Trinity; at the final judgment he could also be held accountable for the evil effects of his teachings on later generations, which would also be revealed.

17. The soul by its nature is unchangeable. However, its union with the body makes it changeable, so that, for example, it can acquire good or bad habits. Once it is separated from the body it can no longer change.

Question 61:

The Need for the Sacraments

3.61.1[1]
Are sacraments necessary for human salvation?

It seems that sacraments are not necessary for human salvation.

1. The Apostle says in 1 Timothy (4:8), "Bodily activity is of little use." But the use of sacraments pertains to bodily activity, because sacraments are carried out through the signification of things and words that can be perceived by the senses, as has been said.[2] Therefore sacraments are not necessary for human salvation.

2. In 2 Corinthians (12:9) the Apostle was told, "My grace is sufficient for you." But it would not be sufficient if sacraments were necessary for salvation. So sacraments are not necessary for human salvation.[3]

3. Given a sufficient cause, nothing more seems to be necessary for an effect. But Christ's suffering is the sufficient cause of our salvation, for the Apostle says in Romans (5:10), "If, when we were enemies, we were reconciled to God by the death of his Son, much more surely, being reconciled, shall we be saved by his life." Sacraments therefore are not required for human salvation.[4]

---

1. On this article, see Yocum (2004); Walsh (2005); Holtz (2012); Jordan (2016, 49–61).

2. In 3.60.6 Thomas argues that sacraments are acts of "signification" (or what we might call "acts that convey meaning") involving both words and signs (including gestures, objects, etc.) that can be apprehended through the senses. On the significance of Thomas's developed views on sacraments as signs, see note 9, below.

3. This objection anticipates the argument of the Protestant Reformers of the sixteenth century, who rejected the received understanding of sacraments because they felt that the church had turned them into a kind of "good work" by which one earned one's salvation, instead of relying on God's grace.

4. This objection appears at first glance to be virtually identical to the previous one, with the word "passion" substituted for the word "grace." However, there does seem to be a difference between grace as a cause and Christ's passion as a cause. "Grace" refers to a disposition or quality within the soul, and thus is something like a formal cause; on the other hand, the passion is a historical event, and in this sense more like an efficient cause. On the various types of causality, see 1.2 note 41.

On the contrary: Augustine says in *Against Faustus the Manichaean* (19.11), "It is impossible to keep people together in the name of one religion, whether true or false, unless they are united by means of visible signs or sacraments."[5] But it is necessary for human salvation that people be united together in the name of the one true religion.[6] Therefore sacraments are necessary for human salvation.

I answer: Sacraments are necessary for human salvation for three reasons.[7]

The first is taken from the condition of human nature, which is such that it has to be led by bodily and perceptible things to spiritual and intellectual things.[8] It is characteristic of divine providence to provide for each thing according to the requirements of its condition. And therefore divine wisdom fittingly provides human beings with aids to salvation in the shape of bodily and perceptible signs that are called sacraments.[9]

5. It is noteworthy that Thomas quotes from Augustine's response to the Manichaean bishop Faustus. The Manichaeans held that the material world was inherently evil, and thus that such material things as sacraments could not help one toward salvation. In Thomas's day, criticism of the sacraments was associated with the Cathar heresy, which was thought to be a revival of Manichaeism.

6. Thomas alludes to a point that is central for his thinking about the church and the sacraments: salvation is inextricably tied up with our unity in Christ; the church is a manifestation of that unity; and the sacraments are the "tools" by which God builds up the church. Thomas does not think of the sacraments simply as instruments for imparting grace to individuals but as the ligaments of the mystical body of Christ.

7. In the three reasons that follow, Thomas draws upon a standard medieval notion that sacraments were instituted (1) to instruct human beings, (2) to humble human beings, and (3) to direct human religious activity (see, for example, Hugh of St. Victor, *On the Sacraments of the Christian Faith* 1.9.3).

8. See 1.12 note 11. Sacraments are God's way of accommodating our human way of knowing through the senses.

9. In a previous question (3.60) Thomas discusses the way in which sacraments are "signs" (*signa*). The notion of sacraments as signs derives from Augustine (see *City of God* 10.5) but had fallen under a cloud of suspicion in the eleventh century because it was used by Berengar of Tours to critique an overly "physical" approach to the Eucharist (i.e., that there was something akin to a "chemical" change in the bread and wine by which they became the body and blood of Christ). Berengar's position that the bread and wine were "signs" of Christ's body and blood was widely perceived as a denial that they were truly Christ's body and blood. Theologians such as Hugh of St. Victor went some way toward rehabilitating the category of "sign" but were also careful to note that sacraments "contain by sanctification some invisible and spiritual grace" (*On the Sacraments of the Christian Faith* 1.9.2). This notion of sacraments as "vessels of grace" (*vasa gratiae*)—objects imbued with or "containing" grace—served as a way of securing the causal efficacy of the sacraments, something that the category of sign alone did not seem able to do.

While Thomas in one place (*Commentary on Hebrews* 1.4.64) speaks of sacraments as "vessels of grace" and discusses in several places the notion of sacraments "containing" grace (e.g., *Commentary on the Sentences* bk. 4, dist. 1, q. 1, a. 1, qa. 5), he gives increasing prominence to the category of sign and seeks to underscore that communication of grace by the sacraments of the New Law is not something in addition to their signification, but grows from the specific kind of signification that they involve. In his early *Sentences* commentary he says that sacraments are "in the genus of cause and sign" (bk. 4, dist. 1, q. 1, a. 1, qa. 5 ad 1), while in the *Summa* he says that they are "in the genus of sign" (3.60.1). This location of sacraments as signs allows us to point to four aspects of his mature understanding of sacraments.

First, as John Yocum points out (2004, 160–63), by defining sacraments as "signs" Thomas is able to include the Christian sacraments and the sacraments of the Old Testament (i.e., the rituals enjoined by

The second reason is taken from the state of human beings, who in sinning subjected themselves by their desires to bodily things.[10] Now the healing remedy should be given to a person so as to reach the part affected by disease. Consequently, it was fitting that God should provide human beings with a spiritual medicine by means of certain bodily signs, for if one were offered unveiled spiritual things, one would be unable to apply one's mind to them, because it would be taken up with the material world.

The third reason is taken from the eagerness of human action, which is chiefly toward bodily things. Therefore, so that it should not be too hard for

---

the Law of Moses) under one heading, thus showing the unity of the two covenants and the consistency of God's "sacramental" dealing with humanity. The shift from Thomas's early position can be seen in the fact that in this *Sentences* commentary he denies that the sacraments of the Old and New Testaments were members of a common genus but asserts, rather, that the rituals of the Old Testament are sacraments only in an analogical sense (bk. 4, dist. 1, q. 1, a. 1, qa. 3 ad 5), whereas in the *Summa* he denies that sacraments must necessarily also be causes, thus including the rituals of the Law in a common genus with the Christian sacraments. What distinguishes them within their common genus is that the rituals of the Law of Moses are signs that do not cause grace, whereas the Christian sacraments are signs that do cause grace.

Second, this presses us to ask what kind of sign the Christian sacraments are. Sometimes we think of signs as pointers to something that is absent (as in, "Las Vegas: 450 mi."). We might call this a "sign of" something. But there are also signs that not only point something out but also bring something about, as when the signature of a judge is put on a death warrant: this does not simply point out the convicted person's condemnation and impending death; it brings it about. We might call this kind of sign a "sign for" something. As Thomas sees it, the way in which causality is enfolded within the signifying function of the sacraments suggests that they are more like "signs for" than "signs of." Their signifying brings something about and does not simply point something out, though we should bear in mind that such purely human uses of language are but a pale analogy for the sacraments, which are, as it were, God's language. See McCabe (1987, 165–79).

Third, because for Thomas the Christian sacraments are signs that cause, they are not so much objects imbued with grace as they are actions by which grace is made present. Thus the sacraments are ritual actions that human beings engage in. But if the sacraments are to be the cause of grace, which only God can give, then they must also be the actions of God in Christ. In fact, Thomas thinks that the sacraments are one of the chief ways in which the sanctifying activity of Christ is made present in our own day. As Timothy McDermott puts it (1989, 544), "The [sacramental] rituals are tools the cutting edge of which is their symbolic representation of Christ's sacrifice, tools actually being wielded by Christ to incorporate men into his own life. The sacraments are visible historical gestures of Christ in the present world." For more on sacraments as "tools" or "instruments," see 3.62.1, below.

Fourth and finally, the primacy of the category of "sign" in Thomas's mature theology of the sacraments can help us understand why it is that he says there will be no sacraments in heaven (see 1–2.101.2). As much as Thomas values the sacraments, he sees them as provisional. Just as the rituals of the Old Covenant were sacramental signs pointing toward Christ and the New Covenant, so too the sacraments of the New Covenant are signs pointing toward the marriage of heaven and earth in the new Jerusalem, where there will be "no temple in the city, for its temple is the Lord God the Almighty and the Lamb" (Rev. 21:22). In this way, they are not only signs *for* the presence of grace but also signs *of* our consummation in glory.

10. That is, you have to apply the medicine to the wound. The "wound" that has been inflicted upon human nature, according to Thomas, is the loss of original justice (1–2.109 note 4). In the state of original justice human beings were not led astray by their senses to prefer material things to spiritual things, but with the loss of original justice we have become subject to temptation through the senses. It is therefore fitting that the remedy be applied by sensual means—that is, through the sacraments.

human beings to be drawn away entirely from bodily actions, bodily activity was offered to them in the sacraments, by which they might be trained to avoid superstitious practices (consisting in the worship of demons) and all manner of harmful action (consisting in sinful deeds).[11]

Thus through the institution of the sacraments human beings, in a way befitting their nature, are instructed through perceptible things; they are humbled, through confessing that they are subject to bodily things, seeing that they receive assistance through them; and they are even preserved from harmful bodily acts by the saving use of the sacraments.[12]

Reply to 1: Bodily activity, inasmuch as it is bodily, is not very useful. But activity through the use of the sacraments is not purely bodily, but to a certain extent spiritual—that is, through signification and causality.

Reply to 2: God's grace is the sufficient cause of human salvation. But God gives grace to human beings in a way that is fitting to them. In this way the sacraments are necessary to human beings, so that they may obtain grace.

Reply to 3: Christ's passion is the sufficient cause of human salvation. But it does not follow because of this that the sacraments are not also necessary for human salvation, for they work through the power of Christ's suffering;[13]

11. Thomas is not unduly troubled by the resemblance between Christian sacramental worship and various forms of superstition: both appeal to the human person's need for symbolic, embodied worship. However, he recognizes that ritual activity can be harmful (spiritually, morally, or even physically; one need think only of various modern bacchanalias—fraternity parties come to mind—to see how this might be the case), so God graciously provides us with rituals by which we are led to true human flourishing.

12. All three of Thomas's reasons are linked by his conviction that God provides us with sacraments because he does not expect us to live like the angels. We are bodily creatures, and so God reaches out to us in a bodily way. Here we see again Thomas's view that "grace perfects nature" (see 1.1 note 34). Human beings are by nature embodied creatures who know through their senses. In acting upon us, grace does not need to override our embodied nature.

Although the three reasons Thomas offers here are rooted in *our* nature, not in God's, in *Summa contra Gentiles* 4.56 Thomas offers another reason why sacraments are a fitting means of our salvation, and in this case he is thinking not about us but about God: "Instruments must be proportioned to the primary cause; and the prime and universal cause of human salvation is the Word incarnate; it was fitting therefore that the remedies through which that universal cause reaches human beings should resemble the cause in this, namely, that divine power works invisibly through visible signs." Here, Thomas finds it fitting that the saving work of Christ, the Father's Word—or, we might say, the Father's "Sign"—should be applied to human beings by means of signs. This passage can perhaps provide a fruitful starting point for thinking about the way in which Christ himself is a "sacrament" of God's presence and activity.

13. At first glance, Thomas seems to have involved himself in contradiction here: How can sacraments be necessary to human salvation if something else (i.e., the suffering of Christ) is sufficient for human salvation? However, as Thomas has already pointed out, in addition to absolute necessity, there is a kind of relative necessity, by which something is obtained in the most fitting way possible (see 3.1 note 19; 3.46 note 6). Clearly the necessity of which he speaks here is "necessity" in this second, weaker sense.

and Christ's passion is, so to speak, applied to human beings through the sacraments, according to the Apostle in Romans (6:3), "All we who are baptized in Christ Jesus are baptized in his death."[14]

14. It is one thing to say that we are saved through the death of Christ on the cross. It is another thing to ask *how* that death bears any relationship to us, since we are separated from it by the intervening events of history. For Thomas, the answer to this question is that Christ is the head of the church, and therefore there is a kind of organic unity of the church and Christ: what is true of the head is also true of the body. Moreover, for Thomas the church is essentially a sacramental reality; the sacraments are the tools by which the head builds up the body. So it is chiefly through the sacraments that the saving action of Christ upon the cross is "applied" to human beings.

Question 62:

The Sacraments' Principal Effect, Which Is Grace

3.62.1[1]
Are sacraments a cause of grace?

It seems that the sacraments are not a cause of grace.[2]

1. It seems that the same thing cannot be both a sign and a cause, since the definition of a sign appears to agree more with an effect.[3] But a sacrament is a sign of grace; therefore it is not its cause.

2. Nothing bodily can act on a spiritual thing, since the agent is superior to the patient, as Augustine says in *On the Literal Meaning of Genesis* (12.16).[4]

---

1. On this article, see Yocum (2004); Walsh (2005); Holtz (2012); Jordan (2016, 49–61).

2. As noted earlier (see 3.61 note 9), in the wake of Berengar there was a concern among medieval theologians to underscore the nature of sacraments as causes of grace. Though Thomas comes to place the sacraments under the category of "sign," he does not abandon all talk of causality, and in fact gives a strong account of sacramental causality in this article.

Some modern theologians have seen Thomas's sacramental theology as flawed precisely to the degree that he retains the scholastic emphasis on sacraments as "causes"; see especially Chauvet (1995). According to these critics, an overemphasis on causality grows out of a theology in which God and creation stand over and against each other in a relationship that is essentially that of two distinct entities (this view is generally referred to as "onto-theology"). Sacramental causality then becomes the means by which these two entities seek to "influence" each other. Additionally, the language of "causality" seems to make the workings of the sacraments approach too closely the model of physical change, underplaying their nature as signs or "symbols." One can judge for oneself how well these criticisms fit Thomas's theology. For a Thomist response to Chauvet's criticisms, see Blankenhorn (2006).

3. That is, fire produces smoke, which is a sign of the presence of the fire.

4. The doer of an action ("the agent") is greater than that which receives the action ("the patient"). The statement "the agent is superior to the patient" (*agens est honorabilius patiente*) is found not in Augustine, whom Thomas cites, but in Aristotle, *De anima* 3.5, 4310[a]. What Augustine says in the place Thomas cites is, "For the one that makes surpasses in every possible way the thing out of which it makes something" (*omni enim modo praestantior est qui facit, ea re de qua aliquid facit*), which certainly fits with the thrust of the objection. We can see here how Thomas, perhaps without even noticing it himself, assimilates Augustine and Aristotle (as well as how much Aristotle and Augustine might actually have in common).

But the subject of grace is the human mind, which is something spiritual. Therefore the sacraments cannot cause grace.

3. That which belongs to God should not be ascribed to a creature. But it belongs to God to cause grace, according to the psalm (84:11): "The Lord will give grace and glory." Since, therefore, the sacraments consist in certain words and created things, it seems that they cannot cause grace.[5]

On the contrary: Augustine says regarding John (*Sermon 80*, 3, in *Homilies on the Gospel of John*) that the baptismal water "touches the body and cleanses the heart." But the heart is not cleansed except through grace. Therefore baptism causes grace, and, by a similar process of reasoning, so do the other sacraments of the church.

I answer: It is necessary to say that the sacraments of the New Law cause grace in some way. For it is evident that through the sacraments of the New Law a person is incorporated into Christ. As the Apostle says of baptism in Galatians (3:27), "As many of you as were baptized into Christ have clothed yourselves with Christ." But no one is made a member of Christ except through grace.[6]

Some people, however, say that the sacraments are not the cause of grace by doing something, but because God, when the sacraments are employed, causes grace in the soul. They give as an example someone who presents a lead coin and receives, at the king's direction, a hundred Euro.[7] It is not as though this coin, by any action of its own, caused this person to be given that sum of money; rather, this occurs solely because of the will of the king.[8] Therefore,

---

5. In effect, these objections focus on three different aspects of sacraments that seem to make them unsuitable as causes of grace. First, as signs, sacraments seem unsuitable not only as causes of grace but as causes generally. Second, their material nature seems to make them unsuitable for any kind of spiritual effect, of which grace is one. Third, their nature as creatures seems to make them unsuited as causes of something that God alone can do, which is to give grace.

6. Thomas's initial response depends upon the preceding tradition's nearly unanimous affirmation of the connection between sacramental rituals and incorporation into Christ's body. Since this incorporation is an act of grace, it would seem that there is a close connection between the sacraments and the reception of God's grace. However, as A. M. Roguet (1945, 220) notes, Thomas shows great prudence in recognizing that this conclusion regarding the link between the sacraments and grace does not in itself specify the *way* in which the sacraments cause grace. The tradition of the church is simply that they do so, as Thomas puts it at the beginning of his reply in this article, "in some way" (*per aliquem modem*). Thomas's task as a theologian is to specify further this relationship between the sacraments and grace—that is, to identify the understanding of causality that best accords with and accounts for the shared faith of the church.

7. *Centum libras*: one may substitute here one's favorite form of modern currency.

8. The approach to sacramental causality Thomas discusses here holds that there is nothing in the nature of sacraments themselves that causes grace; they are "causes" only in a manner of speaking, because of God's promise. This approach stresses the promise of God to give grace so as to guarantee that the grace of God is in no way manipulated by human beings. The more extreme versions of this approach see the sacraments as mere "conditions" or "occasions" for God's action; less extreme versions will still speak of

Bernard says in the sermon *On the Lord's Supper* (2), "Just as a canon is invested by means of a book, an abbot by means of a crosier, a bishop by means of a ring, so by the various sacraments various kinds of grace are conferred."

But if one examines this correctly, this way of understanding sacraments does not go beyond the nature of mere signs. For the lead coin is nothing but a sign of the king's direction that this person should receive money. Similarly, the book is a sign of the conferring of the office of canon. According to this, therefore, the sacraments of the New Law would be nothing more than signs of grace; yet we have it on the authority of many holy people that the sacraments of the New Law not only signify but also cause grace.[9]

We must therefore say something different: that an efficient cause can be of two types, principal and instrumental. A principal cause works by the power of its form, and the effect is made similar to the form, in the way that fire, by its own heat, makes something hot.[10] Nothing but God can cause grace in this way, since grace is nothing other than a shared likeness of the divine nature, according to 2 Peter (1:4), "He has given us most great and precious promises, that we may be partakers of the divine nature."

But an instrumental cause does not work by the power of its own form, but only through the motion given to it by the principal agent. So the effect is not made to be like the instrument, but like the principal agent. For instance, the couch is not like the axe, but like the plan that is in the artisan's mind. And it is in this way that the sacraments of the New Law cause grace, for they are directed by God to be used for the purpose of conferring grace.[11] Therefore

---

sacraments causing grace, with the caveat that "cause" is a manner of speaking based on the firmness of God's promise and the efficacy of God's power.

Thomas's Franciscan contemporary Bonaventure inclined toward a less extreme version of this sort of causality, seeing it as more rationally defensible than accounts of sacramental causality rooted in the nature of the sacraments themselves. His final judgment, however, was, "I do not know which is more true, because when we speak of things miraculous, reason is not so much to be relied on" (*Commentary on the Sentences* bk. 4, dist. 1, part 1, a. 1, q. 4, section D).

9. As Thomas sees it, this sort of causality is no causality at all; rather, it reduces the sacraments to "mere signs" that have no intrinsic connection to the gift of grace. Note that Thomas has no argument for why one should find this kind of causality inadequate other than "the authority of many holy ones [*multis sanctorum*]." This seems like a weak argument, until one realizes that by invoking the authority of the saints Thomas is painting a kind of holistic picture of the Christian tradition. The authoritative teaching of the holy people of the past is not to be so much found in books that might be cited, but in the total life of the church down through history. In essence, Thomas is saying that any view that makes the connection between the sacraments and grace an extrinsic one cannot account for the indispensable role that the sacraments have played in the life of the church throughout history.

10. Recall that a form (see 1.12 note 2) is that which makes something the kind of thing it is. So when Thomas says that a principal cause "works by its form" to make an effect similar to its form, he means that it works in such a way that it shares its way of existing with something else; thus fire makes other things fiery.

11. God is the cause of grace, because grace conforms us to God. The sacraments, however, are like tools in God's hands and therefore can in some sense be thought of as causes of grace, just as creatures

Augustine says in *Against Faustus the Manichaean* (19.16), "All these things" (that is, pertaining to the sacraments) "are done and pass away, but the power" (that is, of God) "that works through them remains forever." But something is properly called an instrument when someone works through it. So it is written in Titus (3:5), "He saved us through the washing of regeneration."

Reply to 1: A principal cause cannot properly be called a sign of its effect, even if the effect is hidden and the cause itself is perceptible and manifest.[12] But an instrumental cause, if it is manifest, *can* be called a sign of a hidden effect. The reason for this is that it is not merely a cause but also to a degree an effect, insofar as it is moved by the principal agent.[13] And in this sense, the sacraments of the New Law are both causes and signs. And this is why, to use the common expression, they effect what they signify.[14] From this it is clear that they perfectly fulfill the definition of a sacrament,[15] since they are related to something sacred not only as a sign but also as a cause.

---

can be "secondary causes" (see 1.45 note 10). To use Thomas's analogy of the carpenter: if we ask about the "cause" of a table (i.e., "Why does this table exist?"), the proper answer is, "Because a carpenter made it." In Thomas's terms, the carpenter is the "principal cause" of the table, and it resembles the project that the carpenter has in mind. However, we could also answer truthfully, "Because the axe cut the wood" (though the table does not resemble the axe) because it was through the distinctive form of the axe as a cutting tool that the carpenter acted. Yet it would seem strange to say "The axe made the table," since it is the axe only as wielded by the carpenter that makes a table.

12. A carpenter cannot be a sign of a hidden piece of furniture because we could well have a carpenter without there being any actually existing piece of furniture (e.g., if the carpenter's shop had just burned down, taking his entire stock with it).

13. Thomas appears to be saying that the action of an instrumental cause is itself a sort of effect, since it is acted upon by the principal cause; therefore, it is not excluded from being a sign of a hidden effect. At first, the logic seems a bit askew, since the instrumental cause is an effect—and therefore a sign—of the primary cause, not of the ultimate effect. Certainly an axe just lying around is in no way a sign of a hidden piece of furniture. But we might think of a different example: a doctor using medicine to cure someone. Neither the doctor nor the medicine, in themselves, are signs of the hidden healing taking place, but only the medicine as being used by the doctor. To use Thomas's vocabulary, it is only the medicine "in act" through the doctor's employment of it that is a sign of a hidden healing.

If we apply this analogy to the sacraments, we see why the form (i.e., the words of the ritual) and the matter (i.e., bread and wine, water, oil, etc.) are necessary for there to be a sacrament. The terms "form" and "matter" were used in sacramental theology well before Thomas, but he gives these terms new meaning when he speaks (in, e.g., 3.60.7) of the words and material element of a sacrament in a way that is at least analogous to Aristotle's description of the actualization of matter by form. Only when the matter of the sacrament is given form by the words, and is therefore "in act," does the sacrament become a sign of its effect, just as the axe can be a sign of a table only when it is being wielded by a carpenter whose intention is to craft a table. Dropping the technical scholastic vocabulary, we can say that the material elements must be located within the sacramental ritual in order to become signs of the hidden action of God's grace—that is, in order to be sacraments at all.

14. This claim that sacraments "effect what they signify" is a key phrase in Roman Catholic sacramental theology. Note that Thomas does not say that "they effect *and* they signify," as if the two things are unrelated properties of a sacrament; rather, they cause *by* signifying.

15. That is, a sacrament of the New Law, since the sacraments of the Old Law are signs but not causes.

Reply to 2: An instrument has a twofold action: one that is instrumental—and in this respect it works not by its own power but by the power of the principal agent—and another that is its own action, which belongs to it on account of its own form. Thus an axe cuts something in two by reason of its sharpness, but it makes a couch because it is an instrument employed in a craft. However, its instrumental action is accomplished only by the exercise of its own action, for it is by cutting that the axe makes a couch. Similarly, the bodily sacraments, by their own operation that they exercise on the body, which they touch, accomplish an instrumental operation on the soul by means of divine power. In this way, the water of baptism, cleansing the body by its own power, cleanses the soul inasmuch as it is the instrument of divine power, for soul and body together make a unity. And thus it is that Augustine says that it "touches the body and cleanses the heart."[16]

Reply to 3: This argument considers that which causes grace as principal agent, and this belongs to God alone, as stated above.

---

16. Here Thomas spells out in more detail how his own position differs from an approach that sees the efficacy of the sacraments as dependent only on God's promise and power (see note 8, above). If that were the case, then the specific natural qualities of the sacramental signs would be irrelevant to the operation of grace. But since "grace perfects nature" (see 1.1 note 34), Thomas sees the natural qualities of the signs being taken up and transformed when they are used by God as means of imparting grace. Just as the skilled carpenter, in cutting wood, uses the instrument whose natural qualities are most suited to that task (an axe, say, rather than a hammer), so too God uses the signs whose natural qualities are most suited for the particular action of grace. Thus water is used in baptism for spiritual cleansing, and bread and wine in the Eucharist for spiritual feeding, and so forth (see 3.65.1, below). This natural foundation for the supernatural effect of the sacraments is important to Thomas, as it was for Augustine, who wrote, "If sacraments did not have a resemblance to the things of which they are sacraments, they would not be sacraments at all" (*Epistle 98*, 9 [my trans.]). We might even say that, just as the human person is perfected by attaining the vision of God, so too water is perfected in becoming the means of spiritual washing, and food and drink are perfected by becoming the body and blood of Christ.

Question 63:

The Other Effect of the Sacraments, Which Is a Seal

3.63.1[1]
Does a sacrament imprint a seal on the soul?

It seems that a sacrament does not imprint a seal on the soul.[2]

1. On this article, see Yocum (2004); Walsh (2005); Holtz (2012); Jordan (2016, 49–61).

2. After discussing grace as one effect of the sacraments, Thomas turns to the sacramental "seal" (*character*), which he takes to be the other effect of sacraments. Here, and elsewhere when it is used with regard to the sacraments, I have translated the Latin word *character* as "seal," rather than with the English cognate "character." There are advantages and disadvantages to this choice. Perhaps the main disadvantage is that "character" is the English translation used commonly in sacramental theology (e.g., the English translation of the current *Catechism of the Catholic Church*, 1121, 1272). On the other hand, although the image of a seal impressed in wax is not necessarily any more familiar today than the word "character," it seems to me to have the advantage of better conveying Thomas's meaning, as well as of avoiding confusion with the notion of "character" current in moral philosophy.

The roots of Thomas's understanding of the sacramental seal can be traced back to two main sources: Augustine and Dionysius the Areopagite. In his controversy with the Donatists, Augustine forged a theology of the permanent effects of baptism to which Thomas refers when he quotes Augustine at the end of his response. Though the theological issues in the Donatist controversy were more complex than the single issue of sacramental efficacy (to which the controversy had been reduced in Thomas's day), the practical issue was the question of whether those who had received schismatic baptisms should be baptized upon becoming Catholics. Augustine's rejection of such rebaptism led him to articulate the position that baptism, even baptism by a schismatic group, constitutes a "seal of holiness" and that to rebaptize such a person "is unquestionably a sin" (*Epistle 23*, 2). In other words, baptism places an indelible mark upon a person that cannot be erased by subsequent sin. By the thirteenth century, largely due to the influence of Peter Lombard, the Latin term *character* was used to convey the notion that baptism, along with confirmation and ordination (which, like baptism, were not repeatable), imparted an indelible sacramental seal upon the soul.

The other source for Thomas's theology of the sacramental seal is Dionysius the Areopagite, particularly in *The Ecclesiastical Hierarchy* 5, from whom Thomas derives the idea of a seal that grants one a participation in the priesthood of Christ. The three sacraments that confer this seal make one suited to a particular role in the church, which is essentially a "cultic" community—that is, a community of worship. Thus baptism confers a seal such that the baptized are both suited to worship God through receiving the

1. "Seal" seems to signify some kind of distinctive sign. But Christ's members are distinguished from others by eternal predestination, which does not imply anything in the predestined but only in God as the one predestining, as we have said in the first part (1.23.2). For it is written in 2 Timothy (2:19), "The sure foundation of God stands firm, having this mark: 'the Lord knows those who are his.'" The sacraments, therefore, do not imprint a seal on the soul.[3]

2. A seal is a distinctive sign—for, as Augustine says in *On Christian Teaching* (2.1), a sign "is that which conveys something else to the mind besides the outward appearance that it impresses on the senses."[4] But nothing in the soul can impress an outward appearance on the senses. Therefore it seems that no seal is imprinted on the soul by the sacraments.[5]

3. Just as the believer is distinguished from the unbeliever by the sacraments of the New Law, so also with the sacraments of the Old Law. But the sacraments of the Old Law did not imprint a seal, which is why they are called "justices of the flesh" by the Apostle in Hebrews (9:10); so it seems that the sacraments of the New Law do not either.

On the contrary: The Apostle says in 2 Corinthians (1:21–22), "He . . . who has anointed us is God, who also has marked [*signat*] us, and given the pledge of the Spirit in our hearts." But a seal means nothing else than a kind of marking. Therefore it seems that by the sacraments God imprints his seal on us.

I answer: As is clear from what has been stated already (3.62.5), the sacraments of the New Law are directed toward two things: to remedying sins and to perfecting the soul in what pertains to the worship of God according to the rituals of the Christian life.[6] Now whenever anyone is assigned to some

---

sacraments and obliged to offer worship to the Father along with Christ, the great high priest. Confirmation confers the seal that allows one to honor God by publicly witnessing to God before the world. Ordination confers the seal that grants one the status of worshiping God not only by receiving the sacraments but also by ministering them.

3. The force of this objection is that what distinguishes God's people from other people is something in God—God's eternal choosing of them—and not something in God's people.

4. The word translated here as "outward appearance" is *species*, a Latin word derived from *specere*, meaning "to look," and having a wide range of meanings (see 1.12 note 11 and 1.75 note 6).

5. The somewhat convoluted (but not invalid) logic of this objection is as follows:
   1. A seal (*character*) is a kind of sign.
   2. A sign is something that makes an impression on the senses.
   3. Things that make an impression on the senses must be perceptible, not spiritual.
   4. Things in the soul are spiritual.
   5. Baptism brings about an effect in the soul.
   6. Therefore, the effect of baptism cannot be the imparting of *character*.

6. Here we can see some of the structural similarities between Thomas's thinking about the incarnation and his thinking about the sacraments. Both the incarnation and the sacraments have a twofold purpose: (1) a negative one—to draw us away from sin—and (2) a positive one—to draw us toward the good (see 3.1 note 20). The good toward which Christians are drawn in the sacraments is the worship of God. But

definite purpose, it is normal for that person to receive some outward sign
of this assignment, in the way that soldiers who enlisted in military service
in antiquity used to be signified by certain marks on the body, on account
of being appointed to something bodily. Since by the sacraments people are
appointed to something spiritual pertaining to the worship of God, it follows
that by means of the sacraments the faithful are marked by a certain spiritual seal. For this reason Augustine says in *Against the Letter of Parmenian*
(2.13), "If a deserter from the battle, through fear of the mark of enlistment
on his body, throws himself on the emperor's mercy and, having sought and
received mercy, returns to the fight, is that seal renewed when the man has
been set free and reprimanded, or is it not acknowledged and approved instead? Are the Christian sacraments, by any chance, of a less lasting nature
than this bodily mark?"

Reply to 1: The faithful of Christ are appointed to the reward of future
glory by the mark of divine predestination. But they are appointed to acts
befitting the church in the present by a certain spiritual mark that is marked
on them, and this is called a seal.[7]

Reply to 2: The seal imprinted on the soul is a kind of sign insofar as it is
imprinted by a perceptible sacrament, for we know that someone has received
the baptismal seal because he has been washed by perceptible water. Nevertheless, anything that assimilates one thing to another, or discriminates one
thing from another, even though it is not perceptible, can be called a seal or
a mark on account of a kind of likeness; thus Christ is called "the figure" (in
Greek, *charaktēr*) "of the substance of the Father" by the Apostle in Hebrews
(1:3).[8]

---

to participate in the worship of God is to participate in Christ's priesthood, as Thomas will make clear in
a later article (3.63.3). So it is through the gift of the sacramental sealing of baptism, confirmation, and
ordination that Christians are made capable of receiving and sharing the benefit of worshiping God. Behind this understanding of the sacramental seal is a profoundly biblical understanding of the church as "a
chosen race, a royal priesthood, a holy nation, God's own people" (1 Pet. 2:9). The Christian community has
been chosen and marked by God as a priestly people who offer worship to God on behalf of all humanity.

7. Thomas makes a distinction between that which has to do with our future (divine predestination) and
that which has to do with our present (the sacramental seal by which we participate in Christ's priesthood).
Behind this distinction lies the view that not all people who are sealed by God in baptism or confirmation
or ordination will necessarily be saved. The sacramental seal is indelible, because it is a power deriving from
Christ's eternal priesthood, but grace is not (as Thomas argues in 3.63.5 ad 1), because the human soul is
changeable in this life. Thus an unbelieving person who is baptized does receive the sacramental seal but
does not receive grace (3.68.8). However, with the sacrament of penance, the full effects of baptism can
be received after the fact (3.68.10).

8. Thomas quotes this verse from Hebrews several times in his discussion of the sacramental seal, suggesting that it provides something of a key to his understanding of *character*. The visible rite of baptism
does make an impression on the senses, but this is not the heart of what Thomas means by the sacramental
seal. To stay with the metaphor of "impression," we might say that the sacramental seal is not a matter of

Reply to 3: As stated earlier (3.62.6), the sacraments of the Old Law did not have in themselves any spiritual power for producing a spiritual effect. Consequently, in those sacraments there was no need of a spiritual seal, and bodily circumcision sufficed, which the Apostle calls a "mark" in Romans (4:11).

---

making an impression upon our senses, but of God "impressing" Christ (who is the *charaktēr* of God) upon the soul, like a signet ring making an impression in wax. In this way, Christians are quite literally "conformed" to Christ—spiritually molded and shaped in his likeness.

Thomas is also alluding here to his view that in baptism, confirmation, and ordination the sacramental seal is the *res et sacramentum* (see 3.66 note 5).

Question 65:

The Number of the Sacraments

3.65.1[1]

Should there be seven sacraments?

It seems that there ought not to be seven sacraments.[2]

1. Sacraments have their efficacy from divine power and from the power of Christ's passion. But the divine power is one and Christ's passion is one, since "by one offering he has perfected forever those who are sanctified," as Hebrews (10:14) says. So there ought to be only one sacrament.[3]

2. A sacrament is intended as a remedy for the defect caused by sin, which is twofold: penalty and guilt [*poena et culpa*].[4] Two sacraments would therefore be enough.

3. Sacraments pertain to actions of the ecclesiastical hierarchy,[5] as Dionysius explains. But, as he says, there are three actions of the ecclesiastical

---

1. On this article, see Yocum (2004); Walsh (2005); Holtz (2012).

2. In Thomas's day the official numbering of the sacraments at seven—baptism, confirmation, Eucharist, penance (confession or reconciliation), extreme unction (anointing of the sick), marriage, and ordination—was comparatively recent, being defined by Lateran Council IV in 1215. Various theologians in the twelfth century offered different enumerations; some of them omitted such things as marriage or ordination, whereas others included such things as the use of holy water or the taking of monastic vows (Abelard had five sacraments and Bernard of Clairvaux had ten). Peter Lombard, in his *Sentences*, numbered them at seven (bk. 4, dist. 2, ch. 1), and it was largely because of the influence of this text that seven was accepted as the definitive number of sacraments.

Note that the objections move progressively from arguing for only one sacrament (obj. 1) to arguing for six sacraments, omitting marriage (obj. 5).

3. In some ways the first objection is the most powerful, because it asks why there should be *any* diversification of the sacraments, given that they all have the same effect of imparting grace.

4. In other words, in sinning we both incur a penalty (*poena*) by which our natures are damaged and damage our relationship with God by incurring guilt (*culpa*). The "penalty of sin" or *poenam peccati* is not an "external" punishment imposed by God in an act of retribution. Rather it is the effect of sin upon human nature—the way in which human nature, losing "original justice" (see 1-2.109 note 4), is "disordered" by sin and becomes subject to suffering and death—an effect that is in accordance with God's justice (see 1-2.85.5).

5. That is to say, the priesthood.

hierarchy: to purify, to enlighten, and to perfect (*Ecclesiastical Hierarchy* 5.3). Therefore there ought to be only three sacraments.

4. Augustine says in *Against Faustus the Manichaean* (19.13) that the sacraments of the New Law are less numerous than those of the Old Law. But in the Old Law there was no sacrament corresponding to confirmation and extreme unction. So neither should these be counted among the sacraments of the New Law.

5. Lust is no more serious than other sins, as we have made clear in the second part (2–2.74.5; 2–2.154.3). But there is no sacrament instituted as a remedy for other sins. So neither should the sacrament of marriage be instituted against lust.

On the contrary: It seems that there should be more than seven sacraments.[6]

6. Sacraments are said to be a kind of sacred sign. But many other blessings are done in the church by perceptible signs, such as the blessing of water, the consecration of altars, and other similar things. Therefore there are more than seven sacraments.

7. Hugh of St. Victor (*On the Sacraments of the Christian Faith* 1.12.4) says that the sacraments of the Old Law were offerings, tithes, and sacrifices.[7] But the sacrifice of the church is one sacrament, called the Eucharist. Therefore offerings and tithes also should be called sacraments.

8. There are three kinds of sin: original, mortal, and venial. Baptism is set up as a remedy against original sin, and penance against mortal sin. So there should be another, besides the seven, against venial sin.

I answer: As stated earlier (3.63.1, above), the sacraments of the church were instituted for a twofold purpose—namely, in order to help human beings develop fully [*perficere*] in things having to do with the worship of God according to the rituals of the Christian life[8] and to be a remedy against the defects caused by sin. And in either way it is fitting that there should be seven sacraments.

6. Thomas here deviates from the usual pattern of an article in the *Summa*. After five objections arguing that seven sacraments are too *many*, he now offers three objections—introduced by his usual phrase *sed contra* ("On the contrary" or "On the other hand")—arguing that seven sacraments are too *few*.

7. That is, offerings of nonliving things, offerings of a percentage of one's income (tithes), and offerings of animals (sacrifices).

8. *Perficere* can, of course, be translated as "to perfect," and in other places I have translated it this way. But, as noted above (see 1.45 note 13), for Thomas "perfection" really means "full actualization," which we might also describe as "full development." Since in this article Thomas speaks of the role of the sacraments in terms of the analogy of human physical and social development, it seems that "develop" better conveys his meaning here. It is important, however, to recall that for Thomas something develops in a certain way only under the influence of something else that is already developed in that way.

Spiritual life has a certain resemblance to the life of the body, just as other bodily things have a certain likeness to spiritual things.[9]

In bodily life one develops in two ways: first, in regard to one's own person; second, in regard to the whole community of the society in which one lives, for a human being is by nature a social animal.[10]

With regard to oneself, a person develops in the life of the body in two ways: first, directly [per se]—that is, by acquiring something that brings a certain development to life; second, indirectly [per accidens]—that is, by the removal of hindrances to life, such as sickness or the like.

The life of the body is developed directly in three ways.

First, through generation, by which a person begins to be and to live, and corresponding to this in the spiritual life there is baptism, which is a spiritual regeneration, according to Titus (3:5), "By the washing of regeneration," and so on.

Second, through growth, by which a person is brought to their full size and strength, and corresponding to this in the spiritual life there is confirmation, in which the Holy Spirit is given to strengthen us.[11] For this reason the disciples, who were already baptized, were told in Luke (24:49), "Stay in the city until you are clothed with power from on high."

Third, through nourishment, by which life and strength are preserved in a person, and corresponding to this in the spiritual life there is the Eucharist. Therefore it is said in John (6:53), "Unless you eat of the flesh of the Son of Man, and drink his blood, you shall not have life in you."

And [these three sacraments] would suffice if a person could have a life free from bodily and spiritual suffering; but since people are subject at times both to bodily weakness and to spiritual weakness (i.e., sin), they therefore need a cure for their weakness. This cure is twofold.

One is healing, which restores health, and corresponding to this in the spiritual life there is penance. According to the psalm (41:4), "Heal my soul, for I have sinned against you."

9. Thomas argues for the sevenfold nature of the sacraments as spiritually perfecting human beings by way of analogy with what is required for the bodily perfection of human being. This way of arguing seems to be original to Aquinas and is not found in his early Commentary on the Sentences (bk. 4, dist. 2, q. 1, a. 2), though it appears in the Summa contra Gentiles, completed in the mid-1260s. It would go on to become quite influential as the rationale for the sevenfold sacramental structure, entering official church teaching at the Council of Florence (1439).

10. This precise articulation of the view that human beings are by nature social is one that Thomas takes over from Aristotle, though the view itself was one almost universally accepted in the Middle Ages.

11. Notice that Thomas thinks of confirmation as a sacrament of growth and not, as is common today, as a sacrament that requires some sort of intellectual or spiritual maturity as a prerequisite.

The other is the restoration of one's original vigor by means of suitable diet and exercise, and corresponding to this in the spiritual life there is extreme unction, which removes the remainder of sin and prepares a person for final glory.[12] Therefore it is written in James (5:15), "And if he has sins, they shall be forgiven him."

In relation to the whole community, a person develops in two ways.

In one way, by receiving power to rule the multitude and to carry out public acts. Corresponding to this in the spiritual life there is the sacrament of ordination. Accordingly, it says in Hebrews (7:27) that priests offer sacrifices not for themselves only, but also for the people.

Second, in regard to natural procreation, which is accomplished by marriage, both in the bodily and in the spiritual life, since it is not only a sacrament but also a function of nature.[13]

We may likewise gather the number of the sacraments according to their being intended as a remedy against the defects caused by sin:[14] baptism is

12. In the Middle Ages the anointing of the sick was usually reserved for those at the brink of death—thus the name "extreme unction" (literally, "final anointing"). Thomas therefore thinks of it as a sacrament preparing one for the vision of God, not as a sacrament designed to bring about physical healing; however, he does say in *Summa contra Gentiles* 4.73 that "by this spiritual remedy bodily sickness is sometimes cured, when it is expedient for salvation." In terms of his analogy of health or vigor, penance is like the resuscitation of someone whose heart has stopped, whereas extreme unction is like physical therapy, which restores us to our former (spiritual and, perhaps, physical) strength.

13. One of the hesitations among earlier theologians in numbering marriage among the sacraments was that it was not a rite distinctive to Christians but seemed to be part of the natural fabric of human community. Thomas acknowledges this twofold character of marriage as natural and supernatural and sees the sacramental celebration of marriage as the church's way of directing this natural reality toward the good of God's people—namely, through the nurture of children in the Christian faith—without denying its purely natural function as a way of continuing the human race. See *Summa contra Gentiles* 4.78.

Thomas's discussion in the preceding paragraphs is perhaps easier to grasp in outline form. Remember, he is drawing an analogy between what one needs to develop in bodily existence and what one needs to develop in spiritual existence. Thus we have the following:

I. Fulfillment as an individual
    A. directly (*per se*): by the provision of what aids in fulfillment
        1. birth (baptism)
        2. growth (confirmation)
        3. nourishment (Eucharist)
    B. indirectly (*per accidens*): by the removal of what hinders fulfillment
        4. curing (penance)
        5. recuperation (extreme unction)
II. Fulfillment as a member of a community
        6. receiving power to rule and act publicly (ordination)
        7. propagating (marriage)

14. Here Thomas turns to sacraments as ways of withdrawing from sin. First he looks at them as specific kinds of medicines for specific spiritual ills. Then he draws a connection between the seven sacraments and the three theological virtues (faith, hope, and charity) and four cardinal virtues (prudence, justice, moderation, and fortitude), and the corresponding vices of each.

directed as a remedy against the absence of spiritual life; confirmation, against the weakness of soul found in those of recent birth; the Eucharist, against the soul's tendency to sin; penance, against actual sin committed after baptism; extreme unction, against the remainders of sins—that is, against those sins that are not sufficiently removed by penance, whether through negligence or through ignorance; ordination, against divisions in the community; marriage, as a remedy against sinful desire in the individual and against the decrease in numbers that results from death.

Finally, some incline toward numbering the sacraments according to a certain adaptation to the virtues and to the defects and penalties resulting from sin.[15] They say that baptism corresponds to faith and is intended as a remedy against original sin; extreme unction corresponds to hope and is intended as a remedy against venial sin; the Eucharist corresponds to charity and is intended as a remedy against the tendency toward hatred; ordination corresponds to prudence and is intended as a remedy against ignorance; penance corresponds to justice and is intended as a remedy against mortal sin; marriage corresponds to moderation and is intended as a remedy against sinful desire; confirmation corresponds to fortitude and is intended as a remedy against weakness.

Reply to 1: The same principal agent uses diverse instruments to bring about diverse effects, in accordance with the thing to be done. Similarly, divine power and the passion of Christ work in us through the diverse sacraments as if through diverse instruments.[16]

Reply to 2: There is a diversity of guilt and penalty, both according to what they are—inasmuch as there are various kinds of guilt and penalty—and according to people's various states and conditions. And in this respect it was necessary to have a number of sacraments, as explained above.[17]

---

15. For example, see Alexander of Hales (*Summa universae theologiae* 4.8.7.2) and Bonaventure (*Breviloquium* 6.3.2–3).

16. In this response Thomas does not address directly the question of why there needs to be more than one sacrament, but his answer is implied in the body of the article. Just as the sacraments are for our benefit and not for God's, so too the *diversity* of the sacraments is for our benefit. The single goal of bodily fulfillment requires a diversity of particular goods (birth, nourishment, reproduction, etc.), and likewise the single goal of spiritual fulfillment requires a diversity of "instruments" (on "instrumental causality" in general, see 1.45 note 11; on sacraments as "instruments," see 3.62 note 11). A single carpenter can make a table; the carpenter, however, uses various tools—a saw, a plane, a hammer, and so on—as is required by the material that she is working with. Similarly, although there is a single principal cause of grace—God—there are a diversity of instrumental causes required by the material upon which God is working—namely, the embodied human person.

17. Thomas grants the objection's claim that the sacraments can be diversified according to sin, but the relevant categories are not the effects of sin (guilt and penalty) but the kinds (*species*) of sin, which he addresses in the body of the article.

Reply to 3: In hierarchical actions we must consider the agents, the recipients, and the actions. The agents are the ministers of the church, to whom the sacrament of ordination pertains. The recipients are those who approach the sacraments, who are brought into being by marriage. The actions are purifying, enlightening, and developing [*perfectio*].[18] But purification, considered in isolation, cannot be one of the sacraments of the New Law, which confer grace; rather, it belongs to certain sacramentals—namely, instruction in the faith and exorcism. But purification along with enlightenment, according to Dionysius, belongs to baptism; and for one who falls back into sin, it belongs secondarily to penance and extreme unction. Developing with regard to an ability—which is something like a formal perfection—belongs to confirmation,[19] whereas, as regards the attainment of the end, it belongs to the Eucharist.

Reply to 4: In the sacrament of confirmation the fullness of the Holy Spirit is given for the purpose of strengthening, whereas in extreme unction a person is prepared so that they may take in God's unveiled glory,[20] and neither of these two purposes was suited to the Old Testament. Consequently, nothing in the Old Law could correspond to these sacraments.[21] Nevertheless, the

18. See note 8, above.

19. Thomas speaks here of perfection with regard to a *virtus*, which could be translated as "virtue" or "power" or "capacity," but which I have translated as "ability" in light of his description of it as a *quasi perfectio formalis*. In other words, to acquire an ability is something like acquiring a new form—that is, beginning to exist in a new way. Thus one who acquires skill in archery becomes an archer, and one who acquires skill in pottery becomes a potter. But the word *virtus* also carries a moral connotation, inasmuch as Thomas defines "virtue" as an ability to act well.

20. I have translated *ut recipiat immediate gloriam* loosely, interpreting it as referring to the unmediated nature of the vision of God, not the temporal immediacy of that vision. However, Thomas could be saying that those who receive the sacrament of extreme unction, being cleansed of venial sins, do not need purification in purgatory and thus see God without delay.

21. The fullness of the Holy Spirit is not given until the day of Pentecost, after Jesus's ascension into heaven, and so a sacrament signifying this reception of the Spirit would not be appropriate to the Old Testament. Likewise the attainment of the direct vision of God's glory is possible only after the death of Christ. Until the death of Christ, holy people could not attain the vision of God and awaited Christ's coming in a place of departed spirits. This realm, sometimes called *limbus patrum* (limbo [from the Latin for "edge"] of the fathers), is an ancient Christian belief closely related to the Jewish notion of Sheol, which was the place in which the righteous dead awaited resurrection on the last day. Something like limbo is perhaps alluded to in Eph. 4:9, which says that Christ "also descended into the lower parts of the earth," or in 1 Pet. 3:18–19: "[Christ] was put to death in the flesh, but made alive in the spirit, in which also he went and made a proclamation to the spirits in prison." A similar allusion can be found in Ignatius of Antioch's (ca. 35–ca. 107) *Epistle to the Magnesians* 9.2, and in Irenaeus (ca. 140–200) we find an explicit statement that "the Lord went down under the earth to proclaim to them [i.e., the righteous dead] his coming, the remission of sins for those who believe in him" (*Against Heresies* 4.27.2). The so-called *Gospel of Nicodemus*, probably written in the fourth century, gives a vivid account of Christ breaking down the gates of hell and rescuing Adam, Eve, and all the just from the clutches of Satan.

The *limbus patrum* is distinguished from the *limbus infantium* or *puerorum* (limbo of infants or children), which is the realm of those who were never baptized and never attained the age of reason. There

sacraments of the Old Law were more numerous, because of the various kinds of sacrifices and ceremonies.

Reply to 5: There was need for a special sacrament to be applied as a remedy against sinful sexual desire [*concupiscentiam venereorum*]: first, because not only the person but also the nature is corrupted by this desire;[22] second, because of its intensity, by which it enthralls reason.

Reply to 6: Holy water and other consecrated things are not called sacraments because they do not produce the effect of a sacrament, which is the acquiring of grace.[23] They are, however, a kind of disposition to the sacraments, either by removing obstacles—thus holy water is intended against the snares of the demons and against venial sins—or by making things suitable for the conferring of a sacrament—thus the altar and vessels are consecrated on account of reverence for the Eucharist.

Reply to 7: Offerings and tithes, both in the law of nature and in the Law of Moses, were intended not only for the sustenance of the ministers and the poor but also as prefigurations; and it is for this reason that they were sacraments.[24] But now they no longer remain as prefigurations, and therefore they are not sacraments.

Reply to 8: The infusion of grace is not necessary for the blotting out of venial sin.[25] Therefore, since grace is infused in each of the sacraments of the

---

they enjoy a purely natural happiness, but they are deprived of the supernatural vision of God because they lack the grace of baptism (whether water baptism or baptism of desire; see 3.68 notes 6 and 7). This idea of a special state for unbaptized infants arose as a mitigation of the teaching of Augustine that they were damned to hell (where, he notes, their punishment is lenient; see *Enchiridion on Faith, Hope, and Love* 93). The *limbus puerorum*, which Thomas accepted (see *Commentary on the Sentences* bk. 4, dist. 45, q. 1, a. 2, qa. 3), never became part of official church teaching, despite its nearly universal acceptance by theologians. In recent decades, it has fallen out of theological favor, perhaps because it seems to restrict God's saving will too narrowly.

22. It is not entirely clear what Thomas means here. Perhaps he is referring to the Augustinian view that original sin (i.e., the corruption of human nature) is transmitted through the sinful desire that inevitably accompanies sexual intercourse.

23. Earlier writers, such as Hugh of St. Victor, had used the term *sacramentum* very broadly to speak of all the mysteries of the Christian faith, and for at least the first millennium the use of the term was not fixed (see note 2, above). Thomas is trying to bring greater precision to the term by marking the difference between the seven sacraments of the church and those other rituals of blessing employed by Christians (what he calls *sacramentales*). He makes this distinction in terms of their effect: the seven sacraments are instrumental causes of grace, whereas these other rituals of blessing create the fitting context for the bestowal of grace but are not themselves instrumental causes of grace. To use the example of a carpenter: the carpenter might do better work while listening to music, but we would not normally describe her radio as one of her tools.

24. On prefigurations or "figures," see 1.1 note 43. Thomas calls the rituals commanded by the Old Law "sacraments," though they are in fact more like the *sacramentales* discussed in the previous objection because they are not themselves causes of grace.

25. On venial sins, see 1–2.71 note 13. In contrast to a mortal sin, a venial sin is not a definitive turning away from God; therefore it does not require a new imparting ("infusion") of grace in order for it to be overcome.

New Law, none of them was instituted directly against venial sin, which is taken away by certain sacramentals—for instance, holy water and similar things. Some people, however, hold that extreme unction is intended as a remedy against venial sin; but of this we shall speak in its proper place.[26]

26. Thomas died before actually getting to the discussion of the sacrament of extreme unction in the *Summa*. In his early commentary on the *Sentences* of Peter Lombard (bk. 4, dist. 2, q. 1, a. 1, qa. 4), Thomas holds the view that although the removal of venial sins is not the *principal* effect of extreme unction (i.e., the effect for which it was instituted), it may be, as it were, a "side effect."

Question 66:

The Sacrament of Baptism

3.66.1[1]

Is baptism the act of washing itself?

It seems that baptism is not the act of washing itself.[2]

1. The washing of the body is something transitory, but baptism is something permanent. Therefore baptism is not the act of washing itself but, rather, "the regeneration, the mark, the safeguarding, the enlightenment," as John of Damascus says (*On the Orthodox Faith* 4.9).[3]

2. Hugh of St. Victor says (*On the Sacraments of the Christian Faith* 2.6.2) that "baptism is water sanctified by God's word for the blotting out of sins." Water by itself, however, is not the act of washing; rather, washing involves a certain use of water.[4]

3. Augustine says in his *Homilies on the Gospel of John* (*Sermon 80*, 3), "The word is added to the element, and this becomes a sacrament." But the element is water. Therefore baptism is the water and not the act of washing.

On the contrary: It is written in Sirach (34:30): "One who washes himself [*baptizatur*] after touching the dead, if he touches him again, what does his bathing avail?" It seems, therefore, that baptism is the act of washing or bathing.

---

1. On this article, see Dauphinais (2009).

2. There are two essential points at issue in this question. The first is whether we should think of sacraments as consecrated "objects" (e.g., water, oil, bread) or as "actions." The second point addresses the need for clarity in speaking about the sacramental sign, the reality being signified and brought about, and the ultimate effect at which the sacrament aims.

3. This objection addresses the question of whether the sacrament should be thought of as the transitory sign or as the permanent effect that is brought about. In other words, is baptism about being washed in water, or is it about rebirth, the conferring of a seal, and so on?

4. This objection and the following one raise the issue of sacraments as "objects" versus sacraments as "actions."

I answer: In the sacrament of baptism, three things may be considered—namely, something that is "sacrament only" [*sacramentum tantum*], something that is "reality and sacrament" [*res et sacramentus*], and something that is "reality only" [*res tantum*].[5]

What is sacrament only [*sacramentum tantum*] is something visible and externally existing—namely, the sign of the inward effect—and this pertains to the definition of a sacrament. This external thing that can be perceived by the senses is both the water itself and its use, which is the washing.[6] Therefore some have thought that the sacrament is the water itself, which seems to be the meaning of the passage quoted from Hugh of St. Victor [obj. 2], for in the general definition of a sacrament he says that it is "a material element," and in defining baptism he says it is "water."

But this is not true.[7] Since the sacraments of the New Law bring about a certain sanctification, the sacrament happens where the sanctification happens.

5. It was Augustine, in his *De doctrina christiana*, who introduced the language of "sign" (*signum*) and the "thing" (*res*) to which the sign pointed. In terms of sacramental theology, the sign or sacrament (*sacramentum*) is the visible element of the rite, whereas the "thing" is the effect signified by the sacrament. After the controversy over the teachings of Berengar in the eleventh century (see 3.61 note 9), theologians, seeking to avoid the position that sacraments are "mere signs," began to develop the notion of a middle term between the sacrament itself (*sacramentum tantum*—i.e., the outward sign) and the thing itself (*res tantum*—i.e., the ultimate effect of the sacrament). This middle term was understood as the immediate effect of the sacrament, which linked the sign and its ultimate effect. Hugh of St. Victor and Peter Abelard both spoke of this immediate effect of the sacrament as being both "thing and sacrament" (*res et sacramentum*). At the beginning of the thirteenth century, Pope Innocent III endorsed this terminology.

This set of distinctions became a standard tool in later medieval sacramental theology and in post-Reformation scholasticism. In this article, Thomas applies these distinctions to baptism: the *sacramentum tantum* is the rite of washing with water; the *res et sacramentum* is the sacramental seal that is conferred; and the *res tantum* is the justification or "making righteous" of the sinner. In the Eucharist, the *sacramentum tantum* is the consecration of the bread and wine, the *res et sacramentum* is the body and blood of Christ, and the *res tantum* is unity in and with Christ.

Note that the *res et sacramentum* is unfailingly brought about by the proper performance of the sacramental rite (*ex opere operato*): in baptism the sacramental seal is conferred; in the Eucharist the body and blood of Christ become present. However, the *res tantum*—the ultimate purpose of the rite—is *not* unfailingly brought about. It can be hindered by sin on the part of the one who receives the sacrament. Thus although all who are baptized receive the seal of Christ, they are not all made righteous. And although all who receive the Eucharist receive the body and blood of Christ, they are not all united in and with Christ. Therefore the sacraments do not work mechanically.

6. Thomas employs the notion of *sacramentum tantum* to make clear that what he is speaking of here is the sacramental rite, which includes both the water and its ritual use. Thus for Thomas a sacrament is not a sacred object but a sacred *action* that involves material objects; he therefore seems to have preserved some of the ancient Christian sense of the intimate connection of sacraments and liturgy. Although he does not generally begin his sacramental theology by looking at the rites according to which the sacraments are celebrated, which was common in the patristic period, he often makes appeal to the sacramental rites.

7. For Thomas, this is an unusually bald statement of disagreement with a theological authority. Earlier (3.62.3) he had conceded, on Hugh's theological authority, that the sacraments of the New Covenant can

The sanctification, however, does not happen in the water; rather, a certain instrumental sanctifying power, which is not permanent but transient, flows from the water into the human person, who is the true subject of sanctification. Consequently, the sacrament does not happen in the water itself, but in applying the water to a human being, which is the washing.[8] Therefore the Master in his book of *Sentences* (bk. 4, dist. 3) says that "baptism is the outward washing of the body done together with the prescribed form of words."

The reality and sacrament [*res et sacramentum*] is the baptismal seal, which is both the thing signified by the outward washing and a sacramental sign of the inward justification.[9] This justification is the reality itself [*res tantum*] in this sacrament—namely, the reality signified and not signifying.[10]

Reply to 1: That which is both sacrament and reality—that is, the seal—and that which is reality only—that is, the inward justification—remain: the seal remains and is indelible, as stated earlier (3.63.5); the justification remains, but can be lost. Consequently, John of Damascus defined baptism not with regard to what is done outwardly, which is the sacrament only, but with regard to what is inward. Therefore he posits two things as pertaining to the seal—namely, "mark" [*sigillum*] and "safeguarding," since the seal, which is called a mark, so far as it is concerned in itself, safeguards the soul in good. He also posits two things as pertaining to the ultimate reality of the sacrament—namely, "regeneration," which refers to the fact that a person, by being baptized, begins the new life of righteousness, and "enlightenment," which refers especially to faith, by which a person receives spiritual life, according to Habakkuk (Hab. 2:4; Rom. 1:17; Heb. 10:38): "The just one lives by faith."[11] Baptism is a sort of declaration of faith, and for this reason it is called the "sacrament of faith."

---

be said to "contain" grace. However, Thomas still worries that this view can be taken in too material a sense, as if the material object itself constituted the sacrament. Hugh compares sacraments to jars that contain medicine (*On the Sacraments of the Christian Faith* 1.9.4), an analogy that is somewhat alien to Thomas's way of thinking about sacraments. Here Thomas makes clear that sacraments "contain" grace only inasmuch as they *confer* grace through the use of visible signs in a ritual context.

8. In other words, the purpose of baptism is not to make holy water but to make holy people.

9. It is interesting that Thomas calls the "character" or "seal" conferred by baptism a "sign," since it is not something that is apprehensible by our senses in the normal way. However, because it is something unfailingly brought about by the sign of washing with water, it shares, as it were, in the "sign" qualities of that washing—a kind of sign-at-one-remove. ·

10. That is, in contrast with the *res et sacramentum*, which is both something signified (by the ritual of baptism) and itself a sign (of justification).

11. In Thomas's terms, John of Damascus is speaking of the *res et sacramentum* (the "mark" and the "safeguarding" of the sacramental seal) and the *res tantum* (the "regeneration" and "enlightenment" of being made righteous by God), whereas Thomas himself is speaking of the *sacramentum tantum*. Of course, this is not the conceptual framework within which John worked.

Similarly, Dionysius defined baptism by its relation to the other sacraments, saying in *The Ecclesiastical Hierarchy* (2.1) that it is "like the source of the most holy commands of the sacred action, which forms in the soul the dispositions for their reception"; and again by its relation to heavenly glory, which is the universal goal of all the sacraments, when he adds, "making a path for us by which we rise to a rest beyond the heavens"; and again as to the beginning of spiritual life, when he adds, "the handing on of our sacred and most divine regeneration."[12]

Reply to 2: As already stated [in the reply above], the opinion of Hugh of St. Victor on this question is not to be followed. Nevertheless, the saying that "baptism is water" may be accepted as true insofar as water is the material principle of baptism. This would be a case of "causal predication."[13]

Reply to 3: When the words are added, the element becomes a sacrament, not in the element itself, but in the person to whom the element is applied by being used in washing him. Indeed, this is signified by those very words that are added to the element, when we say, "I baptize you," and so on.[14]

12. Though Dionysius is not mentioned in the objection, Thomas deals with him in the reply. He does so in much the same way as he deals with John of Damascus, by analyzing what he says in terms of the categories of *res et sacramentum* (the seal disposes one to reception of the other sacraments) and *res tantum* (heavenly glory).

13. In other words, a case of speaking of baptism in terms of its causes. In this case, water is the material cause of the sacramental sign. Thomas seems to think that this might be acceptable as a loose way of speaking (thus Hugh's statement is not heretical), but it is ultimately misleading, not unlike the way that the English refer to the marble sculptures stolen in the nineteenth century by the Duke of Elgin from the Parthenon as the "Elgin Marbles."

14. Thomas notes that the words used in the administration of baptism are addressed to the recipient, not to the water. The water is, of course, blessed before it is used, but the sacrament does not take place until that use.

Question 68:

Those Who Receive Baptism

3.68.2[1]
Can someone be saved without baptism?

It seems that no one can be saved without baptism.

1. The Lord said in John (3:5), "Unless one is born again of water and the Holy Spirit, it is not possible to enter the kingdom of God." But only those who enter God's kingdom are saved. Therefore no one can be saved without baptism, by which one is regenerated by water and the Holy Spirit.

2. In the book *De ecclesiasticis dogmatibus* (41),[2] it is written, "We believe that no catechumen,[3] even one who dies with good works, will have eternal life, except in the case of martyrdom, in which everything in the sacrament of baptism is fulfilled."[4] But if someone could be saved without baptism, this would especially be the case with catechumens who are credited with good works, for they seem to have the "faith that works through love" (Gal. 5:6). It seems, therefore, that no one can be saved without baptism.

3. As stated earlier (3.68.1; 3.65.4), the sacrament of baptism is necessary for salvation. But something is necessary if "without it something cannot be," as it is said in the *Metaphysics* (5.5, 1015ª). Therefore it seems that no one can attain salvation without baptism.

1. On this article, see Morerod (2011).

2. A work by Gennadius of Marseilles, who lived in the fifth century. During the Middle Ages it circulated in collections of works by Augustine, and many people attributed it to him. Thomas usually quotes it without ascribing an author, though he ascribes it to Augustine in his *Commentary on the Sentences* (bk. 4, dist. 14, q. 2, a. 5 ad 5).

3. A catechumen is one who is preparing for baptism; the term comes from the Greek word for one who "hears."

4. The idea that martyrs are "baptized in blood" is an ancient one in Christianity. Cyprian (d. 258), for example, speaks of "the most glorious and most sublime blood-baptism" (*Epistle 73*, 22). Thomas himself writes in 3.66.11 that one who is martyred "without baptism of water receives the sacramental effect from Christ's passion, insofar as he is conformed to Christ by suffering for him."

On the contrary: Augustine says regarding the book of Leviticus (*Questions on the Heptateuch* 3.84) that "some have received the benefits of invisible sanctification without visible sacraments; truly it is possible to have the visible sanctification conferred by the visible sacrament without the invisible sanctification, but it will bring no benefit."[5] Since, therefore, the sacrament of baptism pertains to visible sanctification, it seems that someone can attain salvation without the sacrament of baptism by means of an invisible sanctification.

I answer: Someone may lack the sacrament of baptism in two ways.[6]

In one way, both in reality and in desire—as is the case with those who neither are baptized nor wish to be baptized. In the case of those who have the use of the free will, this clearly indicates contempt for the sacrament. Consequently, those who in this sense are unbaptized cannot attain salvation, since they are neither sacramentally nor mentally incorporated into Christ, through whom alone is salvation found.

In another way, someone can lack the sacrament of baptism in reality but not in desire—as when someone desiring to be baptized for some reason dies before receiving baptism. Such a person can attain salvation without being actually baptized, on account of the desire for baptism, which comes from the "faith that works through love." By this love, God, whose power is not tied to visible sacraments, sanctifies a person inwardly.[7] Therefore Ambrose

---

5. In other words, the visible sacrament of baptism does not unfailingly bring about salvation; only the invisible sanctification of grace does so. This distinction between the visible and invisible is important to the Augustinian conception of the church. Augustine says elsewhere, "As long as she is a stranger in the world, the city of God has in her communion, and bound to her by the sacraments, some who shall not eternally dwell in the lot of the saints." Similarly, some citizens of God's city are not yet bound to the church by the visible sacraments but by an invisible sanctification. Thus, "in truth, these two cities are entangled together in this world, and intermixed until the last judgment effects their separation" (*City of God* 1.35).

6. What Thomas says in the following response is based on the scholastic distinction between (1) *sacramentum tantum*, (2) *res et sacramentum*, and (3) *res tantum* (see 3.66 note 5); in baptism, these terms would correspond to (1) the outward washing with water in the name of the Trinity, (2) the conferring of the inward baptismal seal (*character*), and (3) the justification or "making righteous" of the sinner. Thomas's essential argument is that one can have the last without the first—the *res* without the *sacramentum*—because desire for the sacrament is sufficient to bring about its ultimate effect in those cases where the outward sign is, for whatever reason, truly unavailable. However, an explicit refusal of the outward sign would, in Thomas's eyes, make it impossible to receive its ultimate effect, because it would constitute a lack of charity.

When Thomas says that one may lack the sacrament of baptism in two ways, he is not in fact exhausting all of the possibilities available to him. One might, as he will point out, lack both the visible sign *and* its ultimate effect, or one might lack the visible sign but *not* its ultimate effect. However, one might also have the visible sign but still lack its ultimate effect, as in the case of those who place an obstacle in the way of God's grace through receiving the sacrament with insincerity or hard-heartedness.

7. This notion of "baptism of desire" was used by Roman Catholics in former generations who wished to make allowance for the possible salvation of those who were outside the visible bounds of the Roman Church due to a physical or moral impossibility of their obtaining the sacrament. Sometimes this

says of Valentinian,[8] who died while still a catechumen, "I lost him whom I was to regenerate, but he did not lose the grace he prayed for" (*De obitu Valentiniani consolatio* 29–30).

Reply to 1: As is said in 1 Samuel (16:7), "People see those things that appear, but the Lord beholds the heart." But one who desires to be "born again of water and the Holy Spirit" by baptism is regenerated in heart, though not in body. Thus the Apostle says in Romans (2:29) that "circumcision of the heart is spiritual, not literal; whose praise is not from people but from God."[9]

Reply to 2: No one attains eternal life unless free from all guilt and debt of punishment. But this complete absolution is given when one receives baptism or suffers martyrdom; for this reason is it said that in martyrdom "everything in the sacrament of baptism is fulfilled"—that is, with regard to the full liberation from guilt and punishment. Suppose, therefore, that a catechumen has the desire for baptism (otherwise, he could not be said to die with good works, for such works cannot be without "faith that works through love"); such a one, were he to die, would not come immediately to eternal life but would suffer punishment for his past sins; "but he himself shall be saved, but only by fire," as is stated in 1 Corinthians (3:15).[10]

---

phenomenon was also called the "baptism by the Holy Spirit" or "baptism of flames" (*baptismus flaminis*—a kind of patristic pun on *baptismus fluminis* or "baptism in a river"). The latter designation in particular indicated both the fire of the Spirit and the person's burning desire for the sacrament. The possibility of baptism of desire is an official teaching of the church.

Until recently, debates about baptism of desire centered on questions concerning what constituted a "moral impossibility" and how "burning" this desire had to be. For example, if one were raised a Muslim or a Buddhist or an atheist, and if conversion was literally inconceivable given one's cultural background, then was baptism a moral impossibility? Similarly, if one were raised in a non-Christian religion or anti-Christian environment and therefore could not form an explicit desire for baptism, did an implicit desire (i.e., one desires things that comport with baptism—e.g., love of God and neighbor—which one *would have* desired it if one had been raised in different circumstances) suffice?

Historically, those who wished to cast the net of salvation as widely as possible tended to give a positive answer to these questions, and they sometimes cast the net so widely that one might wonder what circumstances would *not* have counted as a moral impossibility and what disposition toward baptism would *not* have counted as an implicit desire. On the other hand, those who wanted the door to salvation all but closed to non-Christians (and non-Catholics) tended to interpret "moral impossibility" and "desire" so strictly as to admit very few. It seems fairly clear that Thomas inclined toward the latter view, though not in an absolutely exclusive way. In recent decades, discussion of the salvation of non-Christians has largely abandoned the framework of baptism of desire.

8. That is, Emperor Valentinian II, who converted from Arianism to catholic Christianity but was assassinated in 371, before he could be baptized.

9. It may not be immediately apparent how this reply answers the first objection, since Thomas does not respond to the specific biblical passage cited. Instead he draws on different passages from Scripture to suggest the spiritual, not physical, effect of baptism. His implicit point is that just as purification of the heart is not tied to visible circumcision, so too it need not be tied to the visible rite of baptism.

10. Both martyrdom and baptism by water free one from the guilt of sin *and* from subsequent punishment (see 3.65 note 4). However, baptism of desire frees one only from guilt. Thus a catechumen who

Reply to 3: The sacrament of baptism is said to be necessary for salvation insofar as a human being cannot be saved without baptism, at least baptism of desire, "which, with God, counts for the deed" (Augustine, *Explanations of the Psalms* 57.3).[11]

3.68.9[12]
Should children be baptized?

It seems that children should not be baptized.[13]

1. The intention to receive the sacrament is required in one who is being baptized, as stated earlier (3.68.7). Children cannot have such an intention, since they do not have the use of free will. Therefore it seems that they cannot receive the sacrament of baptism.

2. Baptism is "the sacrament of faith," as stated above (3.66.1 ad 1, above).[14] But children do not have faith, which consists in an act of the will on the part of the believer, as Augustine says in the *Homilies on the Gospel of John* (*Sermon 26, 2*). Nor can it be said that they are saved through the faith of their parents, since sometimes the parents are unbelievers, and their unbelief would more likely lead to the damnation of their children. It seems, therefore, that children cannot be baptized.

3. It is said in 1 Peter (3:21) that "baptism saves, not as removing the filth of the flesh, but as the questioning of a good conscience toward God." But children have no conscience, whether good or bad, since they do not have the

---

dies must be saved "by fire"—that is, by undergoing purification in purgatory (as do those who incur sins after being baptized in water). Thus Thomas interprets the text cited in the objection as saying that only those who are baptized in water or blood can obtain eternal life *immediately*.

11. Here Thomas simply expands the meaning of "baptism" to include baptism of desire.

12. On this article, see Cunningham (1974).

13. By "children" (*pueri*) Thomas here clearly means infants who cannot profess faith for themselves. The practice of infant baptism seems to have developed in the church over the course of time, perhaps beginning as early as the first generation of Christians. Only with the Radical Reformers or Anabaptists of the sixteenth century did widespread criticism and rejection of the practice emerge. For Thomas, however, the question is not purely theoretical. In the twelfth century, figures such as Arnold of Brescia and Peter de Bruis had argued against infant baptism, and in the thirteenth century the Cathars had rejected baptism by water entirely, substituting for it a "baptism" through the laying on of hands called the *consolatum*, which was performed only on adults (and often not until they were at the point of death).

14. Thomas states repeatedly that baptism is the *sacramentum fidei* (a term first found in Tertullian in the early third century), and most of what he says about baptism seems to presume that the person being baptized is an adult, one capable of making an act of faith. The objection uses Thomas's own approach to baptism against him, as it were, since for Thomas adult baptism seems to be the theological norm. Thus the objection seems to say that Thomas must either disavow the practice of infant baptism or cease calling baptism the "sacrament of faith."

use of reason; nor can they be fittingly questioned, since they do not under-stand.[15] So it seems that children should not be baptized.

On the contrary: Dionysius says in the last chapter of *The Ecclesiastical Hierarchy* (7.3.11), "Our heavenly guides"—that is, the Apostles—"approved of infants being admitted to baptism."

I answer: As the Apostle says in Romans (5:17), "If by the transgression of one, death reigned through that one"—that is, through Adam—"much more will they who receive abundance of grace and gift and justice reign in life through one, Jesus Christ." Now children contract original sin from the sin of Adam, which is clear from the fact that they are subject to death, which "passed upon all" on account of the sin of the first human, as the Apostle says in the same passage (Rom. 5:12). How much more, therefore, can chil-dren receive grace through Christ, so as to reign in eternal life.[16] But the Lord himself said in John (3:5), "Unless one is born again of water and the Holy Spirit, he cannot enter into the kingdom of God." Consequently, it became necessary to baptize children, so that, as they incurred damnation through Adam in birth, so they might attain salvation through Christ in a second birth.

Furthermore, it was fitting that children should receive baptism so that in being nurtured from childhood in things pertaining to the Christian way of life, they might more firmly persevere in them,[17] according to Proverbs (22:6): "A young person, once set on his path, will not depart from it, even when old." This reason is also given by Dionysius in *The Ecclesiastical Hierarchy* (7.3.11).

Reply to 1: The spiritual regeneration brought about by baptism is in some respects like fleshly birth, inasmuch as the child in the mother's womb does not receive nourishment independently but through the nourishment of its mother. Likewise, children before the use of reason—being, as it were, in the womb of their mother the church—receive salvation not by their own act but by the act of the church.[18] Therefore Augustine says in *On the Merits and*

15. This objection reflects the medieval baptismal rite, in which questions were put to the infant being baptized but the godparent answered the questions on the child's behalf. In a sense, the objection points to the incongruity (which persisted until the liturgical reforms following the Second Vatican Council in the 1960s) of using a baptismal rite designed for adults when baptizing infants.

16. The logic here is not immediately apparent. Thomas's point, which he makes more explicitly in the reply to obj. 2, seems to be that salvation is something we *receive*, not something we achieve. Just as in our generation we receive the sin of Adam, so too in our regeneration we receive the grace of Christ.

17. In addition to showing that the baptism of infants is possible, Thomas wants to indicate here that it is good pastoral practice. The idea that young people need the grace of baptism fits well with the importance Thomas places on the role of grace in moral formation and the development of the virtues.

18. Certain metaphors or images of baptism seem to fit better than others with the practice of baptizing infants. For example, to say that baptism is like "fleshly birth" is to say that just as a child is born without giving its consent, so too is it reborn in baptism without its consent. With the help of Augustine, Thomas develops another aspect of the metaphor: just as a child, after conception, is nurtured in the womb, so

Forgiveness of Sins and on Infant Baptism (1.25, 19), "The church, our mother, offers her maternal mouth for her children, that they may be instructed in the sacred mysteries; for they cannot as yet believe with their own hearts so as to gain righteousness, nor confess with their own mouths so as to gain salvation. . . . And if they are rightly said to believe, because in a certain fashion they make their profession of faith by the words of their sponsors, why should they not also be said to repent, since by the words of those same sponsors they show their renunciation of the devil and this world?" For the same reason they can be said to intend [to receive baptism] not by their own act of intention (since at times they struggle and cry) but by the act of those who bring them to be baptized.[19]

Reply to 2: As Augustine says, writing to Boniface (*Against Two Letters of the Pelagians* 1.22), "In the church of our savior little children believe through others, just as they contracted from others those sins that are forgiven in baptism." Nor are they hindered in their salvation if their parents are unbelievers, because, as Augustine says, writing to the same Boniface (*Epistle 98*, 5), "Little children are offered that they may receive grace in their souls, not so much from the hands of those that carry them (yet from these too, if they themselves are good and faithful) as from the whole company of the saints and the faithful. For it is right to understand that they are offered by those who are pleased at their being offered and by whose charity they are united in communion with the Holy Spirit." The unbelief of their own parents, even if after baptism they try to instruct them in the worship of demons, does not hurt the children; for as Augustine says in the same place (*Epistle 98*, 1), "Once

---

too the child reborn in baptism remains sheltered and nourished within the womb of Christ's bride, the church, feeding on the faith of the church.

19. Augustine's argument (which Thomas is adopting) is perhaps difficult for us to grasp, given the pervasive individualism of modern culture. We tend to presume that one cannot intend or believe or answer for another, whereas Thomas seems to think it is obvious that parents and guardians can do these things for their children. We should bear in mind that, in Thomas's day, parents also sometimes offered their children to monasteries as monks and nuns, as well as arranged marriages for them while they were still infants. Of course, he expects that as the capacity for free choice and intention develops in children, they will come to "own" their faith (just as they would eventually have to consent to their entry into religious life or marriage), but he also expects that the faith they profess will be a faith that belongs not to them but to the whole church.

It is instructive to compare what Thomas says here with what he says about the role of intention in adult baptisms. In 3.68.7 he writes that just as "one who has the use of free will must, in order to die to the old life, 'will to repent of his old life' (Augustine, *Sermon 351*), so must he, of his own will, intend to lead a new life, the beginning of which is precisely the receiving of the sacrament." The role of intention is crucial in the case of adults because they can form intentions both for *and against* certain actions; explicit intention is required on the part of an adult precisely because of the possibility of forming a counterintention. Because children cannot form their own intentions, they cannot oppose or inhibit the workings of grace (even though they sometimes struggle and cry when brought to the baptismal font).

the child has been begotten by the will of others, he cannot subsequently be held by the bonds of another's sin so long as he does not consent with his will, according to Ezekiel (18:4): 'As the soul of the father, so also the soul of the son is mine; the soul that sins—that one shall die.' Yet he contracted from Adam that from which he was released by the grace of this sacrament, because he was not as yet an independently living being." But the faith of one—indeed, of the whole church—benefits the child through the operation of the Holy Spirit, who unites the church and communicates the goods of one member to another.[20]

Reply to 3: Just as a child, when being baptized, believes not through itself but through others, so too the child is not questioned itself but by means of others, and the ones asked confess the church's faith in the place of the child, who is included in this faith by the sacrament of faith. The child thus acquires a good conscience in itself—not, of course, a fully realized good conscience, but the disposition to one—by justifying grace.[21]

20. In this reply Thomas makes it clear that it is the faith of the church, not the faith of the parents, that is determinative. Indeed, godparents serve as reminders that baptism is not a family affair but an act of the whole church. At the same time, Thomas says in the next article (3.68.10) that children of unbelievers should not be baptized over the objections of their parents. Although the baptism would be valid, it would be pastorally ineffective and would distort the natural obligation of obedience and respect that children have toward their parents.

21. Baptism is the sacrament of faith, but it is not a sacrament simply conferred on those who already have a fully formed faith; indeed, if one had a fully formed faith (i.e., faith motivated by charity), one would presumably not need the sacrament of baptism, since it is a sacrament whose purpose is to lead to the formation of fully formed faith.

Question 75:

The Conversion of the Bread and Wine

3.75.1[1]

Is the body of Christ in this sacrament truly, or only figuratively or as in a sign?

It seems that the body of Christ is not in this sacrament truly, but only figuratively or as in a sign.[2]

1. It is recounted in John (6:53) that the Lord said, "Unless you eat the flesh of the Son of Man, and drink his blood," and so on. When hearing this, "Many of his disciples said, 'This is a hard saying'" (6:60). The Lord responded, "It is the spirit that gives life; the flesh profits nothing" (6:63), as if saying, as Augustine explains it in connection with Psalm 4 (*Explanations of the Psalms* 98:9), "Give a spiritual meaning to what I have said. You are not to eat this body that you see, nor to drink the blood that they who crucify me are to spill. It is a mystery [*sacramentum*] that I put before you; in its spiritual sense it will give you life, but the flesh profits nothing."

2. The Lord says in Matthew (28:20), "Behold, I am with you all days, until the consummation of the ages." In explaining this, Augustine says (*Sermon 30, 1, in Homilies on the Gospel of John*), "The Lord is on high until the world is ended; nevertheless the truth of the Lord is here with us. For the body, in which he rose again, must be in one place, but his truth is spread abroad everywhere." So the body of Christ is not in this sacrament in truth, but only as in a sign.

---

1. On this article, see Brock (2001); Hütter (2019, 9–17); Salkeld (2019, 57–137).

2. Having argued earlier (see 3.61 note 9) that sacraments are a kind of sign, Thomas asks here whether the sacrament of the Eucharist is *merely* a sign or symbol of Christ's presence. Thomas obviously has Berengar in mind. We might think about this question in this way: Granted that Christ, in instituting this sacrament, said of bread and wine, "This is my body" and "This is my blood," what reason do we have for thinking that he was speaking literally and not figuratively? After all, he also said, "I am the good shepherd," and we do not take this to be a description of his employment, but rather as a figurative expression.

3. No body can be in several places at the same time;[3] indeed, this is not fitting even to an angel, since this would mean that it could be everywhere.[4] But Christ's body is a true body, and it is in heaven. Consequently, it seems that it is not in the sacrament of the altar in truth, but only as in a sign.

4. The church's sacraments are intended for the benefit of the faithful. But according to Gregory in a certain homily (*Sermon 28*, in *Homilies on the Gospels*), the ruler is criticized "for demanding Christ's bodily presence." Furthermore, the apostles were prevented from receiving the Holy Spirit because they were attached to Christ's bodily presence, as Augustine says (*Sermon 94, 2*, in *Homilies on the Gospel of John*) about the statement in John (16:7), "Unless I go, the Paraclete will not come to you." Therefore Christ is not in the sacrament of the altar according to his bodily presence.

On the contrary: Hilary says in *On the Trinity* (8.14), "There is no room for doubt regarding the truth of Christ's body and blood, for now by our Lord's own declaration and by our faith his flesh is truly food and his blood is truly drink." And Ambrose says in *On the Sacraments* (6.1), "As the Lord Jesus Christ is God's true Son, so is it Christ's true flesh that we take and his true blood that we drink."

I answer: Christ's true body and blood being in this sacrament cannot be detected by the senses but only by faith, which rests on divine authority. Therefore, regarding the statement in Luke (22:19)—"This is my body that will be delivered up for you"—Cyril says, "Do not doubt whether this is true, but rather take the Savior's words in faith; for since he is the truth, he does not lie" (*Commentary on Luke*).[5]

3. Part of what it means to be a body is to occupy a particular place. This might be seen as a corollary to the view that two bodies cannot occupy the same place (see 3.54.1 obj. 1, above).

4. The mention of angels in the objection is quite cryptic. The objection seems to be saying that since angels, which are disembodied intelligences, cannot be in multiple locations at the same time, it is even more the case that bodies cannot occupy multiple locations at the same time. Thomas discusses the angels' relation to place in 1.52.

5. In the hymn "Adoro te devote," traditionally ascribed to Thomas, we find a poetic expression of the view he states in this paragraph (from the translation of G. M. Hopkins):

> Seeing, touching, tasting are in thee deceived;
> How says trusty hearing? That shall be believed:
> What God's Son has told me, take for truth I do;
> Truth himself speaks truly or there's nothing true.

Thomas holds that the bread and wine undergo a transformation such that they cease to be bread and wine and become the body and blood of Christ, one substance (bread and wine) ceasing to be present and another (the body and blood of Christ) beginning to be present. However, the appearances (or "accidents" or "species") of bread and wine remain. This view of how Christ is present in the Eucharist is usually known as "transubstantiation," a term Thomas wholly approves of, though he uses it only five times in the *Summa theologiae*.

Contrary to what some people believe, Thomas does not think he can "explain," much less "prove," the transformation of bread and wine into the body and blood of Christ. Indeed, Thomas does not think

This is fitting,[6] in the first place, for the perfection of the New Law. For the sacrifices of the Old Law contained only prefigurations of the true sacrifice of Christ's passion, according to Hebrews (10:1): "The Law has a shadow of the good things to come, not the image itself of the things." And therefore it is necessary that the sacrifice of the New Law instituted by Christ have something more—namely, that it should contain the suffering one himself, not only as a sign or prefiguring, but also in actual truth.[7] And therefore, as Dionysius says in *The Ecclesiastical Hierarchy* (3.1), this sacrament, which really contains Christ himself, "perfects all the other sacraments," in which there is a participation in Christ's power.

Second, this accords with Christ's charity, out of which he took on a true body of our nature for our salvation. And because it is the special feature of friendship to live together with friends, as the Philosopher says in the *Ethics* (8.5, 1157[b]), Christ promises us his bodily presence as a reward, saying in Matthew (24:28), "Where the body is, there shall the eagles be gathered together."[8] Yet in the interim, he does not deprive us of his bodily presence while we are on this pilgrimage, but through the truth of his body and blood unites us with himself in this sacrament.[9] Hence he says in John (6:56), "The one who eats my flesh and drinks my blood abides in me, and I in him."

---

that the transformation of the bread and wine *needs* explaining or proving, since Christ, who is Truth itself, says of the bread, "This is my body," and of the wine, "This is my blood."

6. "*Hoc autem conveniens est.*" Although Thomas does not believe that the transformation of the bread and wine can be explained or proved, he does think that once faith assents to such a transformation, he can show why it is "fitting" (on *convenientia* in general, see 3.1 note 2). In what follows, Thomas offers three reasons that, taken together, offer something like a cumulative case for why one should believe that Christ is speaking literally and not figuratively when he says, "This is my body" and "This is my blood." This cumulative argument seems to be structured according to the three theological virtues, presenting the Eucharist as perfecting hope, love, and faith.

7. The sacrifices commanded in the Old Law were *already* signs of the sacrifice of Jesus on the cross (see 1.1 note 43), and therefore if the Eucharist were meant *only* as a sign or symbol, there would not be much point to it; one might as well continue the animal sacrifices of the Old Law. Moreover, the eucharistic sacrifice of Christians would not be the fulfillment of the hopes of ancient Israel. Note, however, that Thomas does not deny that the Eucharist is a sign; rather, it is something *more* than a sign.

8. In other words, the blessed in heaven will enjoy proximity to Christ's exalted body. Thomas's interpretation of the cryptic statement from Matthew's Gospel seems to be influenced by Gregory the Great's *Moral Reflections on the Book of Job* (31.5): "We may understand this as meaning, 'I who incarnate sit on the throne of heaven, as soon as I shall have loosed the souls of the elect from the flesh, will exalt them to heavenly places'" (my trans.).

9. Following Aristotle, Thomas thinks it is strange to speak of someone as a "friend" when you do not interact with them regularly, and the most fitting mode of interaction for us as human beings is through the medium of our bodies (Zoom and other teleconferencing platforms are a poor substitute for actual face-to-face contact). Therefore, if you think, as Thomas does, that we are called to be Christ's friends (see John 15:13–15), then it is only fitting that Christ provide a way to be present to us bodily, even during the time of our earthly pilgrimage.

Therefore this sacrament is the sign of supreme charity and lifts up our hope, on account of such a familiar union of Christ with us.

Third, this accords with the completeness of faith, which concerns Christ's humanity as much as it does his divinity, according to what is said in John (14:1), "You believe in God, believe also in me." And since faith is in things unseen,[10] just as Christ shows us his divinity invisibly, so too in this sacrament he shows us his flesh in an invisible manner.[11]

Some, not considering these things, have claimed that Christ's body and blood are not in this sacrament except as in a sign. This is a view to be rejected as heretical, since it is contrary to Christ's words. Therefore Berengar, who had been the first inventor of this heresy, was later forced to withdraw his error and to acknowledge the truth of the faith.[12]

Reply to 1: The heretics spoken of before have found in this authority an occasion of error by misunderstanding Augustine's words;[13] for when Augustine says, "You are not to eat this body that you see," he does not intend to exclude the truth of Christ's body, but only that it was not to be eaten in the appearance [*species*] in which it was seen by them.[14] And by the words "It is a

10. See 2-2.2 note 2.

11. Christ's divinity is an object of faith because it is hidden in his humanity. But this humanity itself becomes an object of faith in the Eucharist because it is hidden under the appearances of bread and wine. This is again given poetic expression in "Adoro te devote" (see note 5, above):

> On the cross thy godhead made no sign to men;
> Here thy very manhood steals from human ken:
> Both are my confession, both are my belief,
> And I pray the prayer of the dying thief.

12. Berengar was made to sign two separate oaths. The first, from 1059, said, "The bread and wine that are placed on the altar, after consecration, are not only a sacrament, but also the true Body and Blood of our Lord Jesus Christ and . . . they are sensibly, not only in sacrament but in truth, touched and broken by the hands of the priests and ground by the teeth of the faithful" (Denzinger 2012, 690). Berengar quickly recanted, and one can hardly blame him. This oath prescribes a kind of hyperrealism about the Eucharist that does not fit well with the tradition of the church, making holy communion sound like an act of cannibalism. Thomas himself will reject the claim that, in the breaking of the bread at Mass, the true body of Christ is itself broken (3.77.7).

Twenty years later, at the synod of Rome in 1079, Berengar signed another oath, framed in more moderate language than the first: "I, Berengar, in my heart believe and with my lips confess that through the mystery of the sacred prayer and the words of our Redeemer the bread and wine that are placed on the altar are substantially changed into the true and proper and living flesh and blood of Jesus Christ, our Lord, and that after consecration it is the true body of Christ that was born of the Virgin and that, offered for the salvation of the world, was suspended on the Cross and that sits at the right hand of the Father, and the true blood of Christ, which was poured out from his side not only through the sign and power of the sacrament, but in its proper nature and in the truth of its substance [*substantia*]" (Denzinger 2012, 700).

13. As mentioned before (3.61 note 9), Augustine speaks of sacraments as "signs," and Thomas agrees with Augustine on this point. The heretics (i.e., those who follow Berengar) make their mistake, according to Thomas, in thinking that Augustine believes that sacraments are *merely* signs.

14. See 3.63 note 4.

mystery that I put before you; in its spiritual sense it will give life to you," he intends not that the body of Christ is in this sacrament merely according to mystical signification, but "spiritually"—that is, invisibly, and by the power of the Spirit.[15] Therefore, in commenting on the statement in John (6:63)—"the flesh profits nothing"—he says, "But only in the way that they understood it, for they understood that the flesh was to be eaten in the way that a dead body is torn into pieces, or as it is sold in the meat market, not as it is given life by the spirit. Let the spirit draw near to the flesh, and the flesh profits very much. For if the flesh profited nothing, the Word would not be made flesh so that it might dwell among us" (*Sermon 27*, 5, in *Homilies on the Gospel of John*).[16]

Reply to 2: That saying of Augustine, and all others like it, is to be understood to be about Christ's body as it is seen in its normal outward appearance, in the same way that our Lord himself says in Matthew (26:11), "But you will not always have me." Nevertheless, he is invisibly under the outward appearances of this sacrament wherever this sacrament is brought about.

Reply to 3: Christ's body is not in this sacrament in the same way that a body is in a place, so that its size corresponds to the place, but in a kind of special way that is proper to this sacrament.[17] Therefore we say that Christ's body is upon many altars, not as being in different places, but as being present "sacramentally," and by this we do not understand Christ to be there only as in a sign—even though a sacrament *is* a kind of sign—but that Christ's body is here according to a way proper to this sacrament, as stated above.[18]

15. When Augustine says that Christ's body is "spiritually" present, he is not denying that it is *really* present but only that it is *visibly* present in the way that Christ's body was present to his disciples. Thomas's reply to the next objection makes essentially the same point.

Note as well that Thomas says Christ is present through the power of the Spirit (*per virtutem Spiritus*). In his *Commentary on the Sentences*, Thomas says even more explicitly that "the power of the Holy Spirit alone brings about this conversion" (bk. 4, dist. 8, q. 2, a. 3 ad 1). Western theology, particularly scholastic theology, is sometimes accused of ignoring the role of the Spirit in the Eucharist. But the Spirit was widely held by medieval Western theologians to be the agent of the eucharistic change, even though the Canon (the prayer during which the eucharistic consecration took place, used in the West from at least the time of Gregory the Great) contains no petition for the Holy Spirit to consecrate the bread and wine. For ample documentation, see Congar (1983).

16. For Thomas, as his use of this quotation from Augustine indicates, the logic of objections that say that Christ's words must be understood as "spiritual"—such that the bread is only symbolically Christ's body—can just as easily be applied to the incarnation. In other words, the same mindset that denies eucharistic realism also tends to deny the realism of the incarnation. Here Thomas might have the Cathars in mind more than Berengar.

17. Some manuscripts read "in a kind of *spiritual* way that is proper to this sacrament." In either case, however, Thomas's main concern is to stress the uniqueness of the way Christ is present in the sacrament.

18. Thomas denies that Christ is present only symbolically in the elements of the Eucharist, but he also denies that Christ's presence is a *physical* one—that is, that Christ's body is present, for example, in the same way in which it was present in Mary's womb or on the cross. If this were the case, then Christ's body could not be present on many altars at the same time. Nonetheless, Thomas still wants to claim that

Reply to 4: This argument holds good for Christ's bodily presence as he is present in the manner of a body (that is, as it is in its visible appearance) but not as it is spiritually (that is, invisibly, after the manner and by the power of the Spirit).[19] Therefore Augustine says in his *Homilies on the Gospel of John* (*Sermon 27*, 6), "If you have understood in a spiritual way" Christ's words concerning his flesh, "they are spirit and life to you; if you have understood them in a fleshly way, they are also spirit and life, but not to you."

3.75.8[20]
Is this statement true: "The body of Christ is made out of bread"?

It seems that this is false: "The body of Christ is made out of bread."[21]

1. Everything that something else is made "out of" [*ex quo*] is that which is made into the other; but not the reverse. For we say, "Out of something white, something black is made," and "something white is made black," and we may even say that "a person becomes black," but we still do not say that "a black thing is made out of a person," as is shown in the *Physics* (1.5, 188ᵇ). If it is true, then, that Christ's body is made out of bread, it will be true to say that "bread is made the body of Christ." But this seems to be false, because

---

the body that is present in the Eucharist is the same one that was in Mary's womb and that hung on the cross. This apparent contradiction is resolved by a distinction Thomas makes between *what*—or, better, *who*—is present and *how* this presence occurs. What Thomas wants to say is that Christ's presence in the Eucharist is *neither* purely symbolic *nor* physical; rather it is a way of being present that is unique to the sacrament of the Eucharist.

19. In other words, the objection holds if we are speaking about Christ's body as it was visible, walking around Palestine. So long as the disciples were attached to the visibility of Christ's body, the Spirit—and the way of seeing associated with the Spirit, which is faith—could not come. The presence of Christ is not less real for being spiritual, and "spiritual" should not be taken to mean "purely symbolic."

20. On this article, see Brock (2001); Bauerschmidt (2016a).

21. Much of what Thomas says in this article is a summary and application of what he has said in the seven preceding articles in question 75, and in particular in article 4, which addresses the question of whether bread can be converted into the body of Christ. Here, he draws together all that he has said in this question by inquiring into the acceptability of a particular verbal formulation, an approach that is reminiscent of 3.16.1, above. There, however, the word in question was the copula "is"; here it is the preposition "out of" [*ex*].

As in the case of the earlier, christological discussion, this is more than a matter of simply fretting about words. At issue is the best model to use in understanding the sort of "change" that is involved in transubstantiation. Thomas is sometimes accused of simply grafting Christian theology onto Aristotelian philosophy or of using Aristotle's metaphysics to explain Christian mysteries. This accusation is often supported with reference to Thomas's use of the language of "substance" and "accidents" in his discussion of the Eucharist. This article, however, shows that Thomas's understanding of eucharistic conversion is primarily rooted not in Aristotle's metaphysics but in a Christian metaphysics of creation from nothing, something that is quite alien to Aristotle's philosophy.

the bread is not the subject of the making, but rather its term.[22] So it is not said truly, "The body of Christ is made out of bread."

2. The process of becoming reaches its conclusion in something existing [*esse*], or in something having been made to exist. But this statement is never true: "Bread is the body of Christ"; or "Bread is made the body of Christ"; or again, "Bread will be the body of Christ."[23] It seems therefore that not even this is true: "The body of Christ is made out of bread."

3. Everything that something else is made "out of" is converted into that which is made from it. But this proposition seems to be false: "Bread is converted into the body of Christ," because such conversion seems to be more miraculous than creation, about which we do not say that nonbeing is converted into being.[24] So it seems that this statement is likewise false: "The body of Christ is made out of bread."

4. That out of which something else is made is capable of being that thing. But this statement is false: "Bread is capable of being the body of Christ." Therefore this is likewise false: "The body of Christ is made out of bread."

On the contrary: Ambrose says in the book *On the Sacraments* (4.4), "When the consecration takes place, the body of Christ is made of bread."

I answer: This conversion of bread into the body of Christ has something in common with both creation and natural change,[25] and in some respects differs from both.[26] One thing that is common to all three is the order of the terms—that is, *this* follows after *that*: in creation there is existence after nonexistence; in this sacrament there is Christ's body after the substance of

22. In the statement "The brunette was made into a redhead," both "brunette" and "redhead" are "terms" (i.e., beginning and ending points) of the change, but they are not the subject that undergoes the change (i.e., that "from which something else is made"). We might say, "Jane was made into a redhead," so long as we do not imply that Jane has ceased to exist (being replaced by a redhead), when in fact she is the subject that has undergone the change. The redhead is still Jane. Thus the force of the objection is that the proposition "The body of Christ is made out of bread" treats "bread" as if it were the subject undergoing a change, which would mean that the body of Christ is still bread, just as the redhead is still Jane.

23. The objection seems to be that when we speak of a process of becoming, we can reformulate it as a statement of existence. Thus the statement "The brunette becomes a redhead" entails that "the brunette is a redhead."

24. In 1.45.2 Thomas denies that creation is properly described as a "change," since this would imply that there is some subject that undergoes the change, whereas creation is the bringing of things into existence without a preexisting subject.

25. Under "natural change" [*transmutatione naturali*] Thomas includes both changes of appearance (or "accidental change"), such as Jane changing from a brunette to a redhead, and changes in the kind of thing that something is (or "substantial change"), such as the change in the matter from which Jane is composed when she ceases to be a human being and becomes a corpse.

26. Another way of putting this would be to say that "change" is an analogous term. On analogy, see 1.13.5, above.

bread; in a natural change there is white after black, or fire after air. Also, these terms just mentioned do not exist simultaneously.[27]

The conversion of which we are speaking has this in common with creation: in neither of them is there any common subject belonging to both extremes.[28] This is the opposite of what is seen to be the case in every natural change.[29]

This conversion, however, does have something in common with natural change in two respects, although not in the same way. First, in both cases one of the extremes passes into the other, such as bread into Christ's body, and air into fire, while [in the case of creation] nonbeing is not converted into being.[30] But this change comes to pass differently in the two cases; for in this sacrament the whole substance of the bread passes into the whole body of Christ, while in natural change the matter of the one receives the form of the other, the previous form being laid aside.[31] Second, they have this in common: that in both cases

27. In all three cases you first have A and then B; at no point do you have A and B simultaneously.

28. "Extremes" here is synonymous with "terms." See note 22, above.

29. For Thomas's account of how creation differs from other sorts of change, see 1.45.5, above. Here the key point is that in both creation and the Eucharist there is no X such that "the X that is A" becomes "the X that is B," unlike the case of Jane (see note 22, above), in which "Jane who is a brunette" becomes "Jane who is a redhead." Unlike Aristotle, who understood "creation" as something that happens when God gives form to an eternally existing "prime matter," Thomas holds that creation is simply God bringing things in their totality (both matter and form) into existence (on matter and form, see 1.12 note 2). In other words, there is no "matter that is unformed" that becomes "matter that is formed." Similarly, Thomas holds that in the Eucharist there is no "X that is bread" that becomes "X that is the body of Christ." Yet although we can formulate this matter negatively, by denying the persistence of a subject in both creation and the Eucharist, it is difficult to come up with a positive statement of eucharistic change. As with the mystery of God, so too with the mystery of eucharistic change: what it is not is clearer than what it is (see 1.12 note 7).

30. Part of the problem Thomas confronts is a certain imprecision of language. The Christian tradition has spoken of creation *ex nihilo* (from nothing), but not in the sense of "nothing" as some kind of quasi-thing that is converted into something else; rather, "nothing" is not any kind of thing at all. So in the phrase *creatio ex nihilo*, the preposition *ex* really indicates nothing more than the order of the terms in the proposition. We cannot even really say that in creation we first have nonbeing and then being, since this would seem to ascribe some sort of (albeit shadowy) existence to nonbeing, which is absurd. It would also imply a temporal succession of being following upon nonbeing, which is equally absurd, since there is no time prior to creation, and thus no "before" God's creative act. Thus creation is different from any other sort of change (so much so that it can be called a change at all only improperly), including the eucharistic conversion, in which one first has bread and then has the body of Christ.

31. A substance, in the case of physical realities, is composed of matter and substantial form. When one kind of thing becomes another kind of thing, matter takes on a new form, with the subsequent form replacing the former. For Thomas, this is not the kind of change that occurs in the Eucharist. In this instance (and, seemingly, *only* in this instance), there is a different sort of change: rather than one form replacing another, one entire substance—matter *and* form—replaces the other.

It is worth asking *why* Thomas believes the Eucharist requires a change of the entire substance and not simply a change of form. After all, if wood becomes fire by taking on a new form, why could bread not become the body of Christ in the same way?

Thomas's answer to this question seems circular: it cannot be a natural change because this would not be a change of substance. But *why* must it be a change of substance? Thomas gives something approaching an answer in the *Summa contra Gentiles* 4.61.3, where, in noting (as he does above at 3.65.1) that the

something remains the same (whereas this does not happen in creation). Yet this happens differently in the two cases, for in natural change the same matter or subject remains, whereas in this sacrament the same accidents remain.

From these observations we can gather the various ways of speaking about such matters;[32] for in none of the previously mentioned three things do the extremes exist simultaneously, and therefore in none of them can one extreme be predicated of the other by the substantive verb of the present tense—that is, we do not say: "Nonbeing *is* being," or "Bread *is* the body of Christ," or "Air *is* fire," or "White *is* black."[33]

Yet, on account of the relationship of the extremes, in all of them we can use this preposition *ex* [out of], which denotes order. For we can truly and properly say that "being is made out of nonbeing," and "out of bread, the body of Christ," and "out of air, fire," and "out of white, black."[34]

Eucharist corresponds on a spiritual level to bodily nourishment, he says that "nutriment must be conjoined to the one nourished in substance." Thomas contrasts this with baptism, which corresponds on a spiritual level to physical birth. Birth does not involve my being personally conjoined to my parents—indeed, one might say that birth is precisely the end of that conjunction. However, in order for food to nourish me, its substance must come into contact with mine. But this analogy still does not tell us why the presence of Christ's substance must involve a complete conversion of one substance to another.

We might approach this question using resources borrowed from Thomas, although he himself does not utilize them with regard to this question. In particular, we might emphasize that it is Christ in his personal totality who is present in this sacrament, which means that Christ is present both as human and as divine. Full human presence is bodily presence, because it is my particular matter that differentiates my human nature from that of others (see 1.12 note 2 and 1.75 note 8). So if Christ is to be present in this sacrament in his humanity, this must involve his body in its own proper materiality, though this is the transformed bodily presence of the risen Christ that Paul describes as a "spiritual body." Thomas makes clear that this is an utterly unique sort of bodily presence, since it is not a "local" presence (i.e., it is not a question of occupying a particular place).

32. We might try to envision the array of similarities and differences that Thomas has just mapped out by using a table:

Creation, Natural Change, and Eucharistic Conversion

	A certain order of terms: extremes do not exist simultaneously	A common subject of change	One extreme passes into another	Something remains throughout the change
CREATION	Yes: nothing then something	No	No	No
NATURAL CHANGE	Yes: person then corpse (substantial change) or brunette then redhead (accidental change)	Yes: matter (substantial change) or substance (accidental change)	Yes: a change of form (either substantial or accidental)	Yes: the matter (substantial change) or the substance (accidental change) remains unchanged
EUCHARISTIC CONVERSION	Yes: bread then the body of Christ	No	Yes: a change of substance	Yes: the accidents remain unchanged

33. On "predicated," see 1.3 note 3.
34. See note 30, above.

However, because in the case of creation one of the extremes does not pass into the other, we cannot use the word "conversion" in speaking of creation, so as to say that "nonbeing is converted into being." We can, however, use this word with regard to this sacrament, just as in natural change.[35] But since in this sacrament the whole substance is converted into the whole substance, on that account this conversion is properly termed "transubstantiation."[36]

Again, since there is not any subject of this conversion, the things that are true in natural conversion on account of the subject are not to be granted in this conversion. It is evident, in the first place, that the potential of something to become its opposite is because there is a subject, and for this reason we say that "a white thing can be black," or that "air can be fire." However, the latter statement is not as correct as the former, for the subject of whiteness, in which there is potential to be black, is the whole substance of the white thing, since whiteness is not a part of it, whereas the subject of the form of air is part of it. Therefore when we say, "Air can be fire," it is made true by the part being taken for the whole by means of synecdoche.[37] But in this conversion [i.e., transubstantiation], and similarly in creation, because there is no subject, it is not said that one extreme can be the other, so as to say that "nonbeing can be being" or that "bread can be the body of Christ." And for the same reason it cannot be said properly that "being is made of [de] nonbeing," or that "the body of Christ is made of [de] bread," because this preposition "of" [de] designates a cause that is the same substance as the effect, and, in the case of natural changes, this common substance of the extremes is meant according to something common in the subject.[38] And for the same reason it is not conceded that "bread will be the body of Christ," or that it "becomes the body of Christ," just as it is not conceded in creation that "nonbeing will be being," or that "nonbeing becomes being," because this manner of speaking

35. That is, we use the word "conversion" (conversionis) to speak of both natural and eucharistic conversion because in both cases one thing "passes into another" (transit in alterum): wood becomes fire, and bread becomes the body of Christ.

36. In 3.75.4 Thomas writes, "This conversion is one not of form but of substance. Neither is it a kind of natural motion; rather it can be spoken of by its own special name [proprio nomine]: transubstantiation." One might say that Thomas sees the term "transubstantiation" as a kind of placeholder that distinguishes eucharistic conversion from both creation and natural change.

37. The difference Thomas marks here is between accidental change and substantial change. Strictly speaking, we can say, referring to an accidental change, that "a white table can be a black table" (i.e., by being painted); however, if we were to speak properly, we would not say, in the case of a substantial change, that "air can be fire" but rather that "the matter that constitutes the substratum of air can be the substratum of fire." In other words, in substantial change the substratum is not a "thing" (i.e., a substance) but only part of a thing (i.e., its matter). But, using synecdoche—the form of speech by which a part is taken for the whole—we say "air can be fire" or (perhaps more commonly) "the tree can be a table."

38. That is, it is the common subject shared by the extremes.

is true in the case of natural changes on account of the subject, as when we say that "a white thing becomes black," or "a white thing will be black."

Nevertheless, since after the change something remains the same in this sacrament—namely, the accidents of the bread, as stated earlier (3.75.5)—some of these expressions may be granted in a certain sense.[39] One might say, "Bread is the body of Christ," or "Bread will be the body of Christ," or "The body of Christ is made of [*de*] bread," provided that the word "bread" is not understood as the substance of bread, but in general "that which is contained under the species of bread," under which species there is first contained the substance of bread, and afterward the body of Christ.[40]

Reply to 1: That out of which something is made sometimes implies the subject along with one of the extremes of the change, as is the case when it is said, "A black thing is made out of a white thing."[41] But sometimes it implies only the opposite or the extreme, as when it is said, "Out of morning comes the day." And so it is not granted that *this* becomes *that*—that is, "that morning becomes the day."[42] So likewise in the matter in hand, although it may be said properly that "the body of Christ is made out of bread," yet it is not said properly that "bread becomes the body of Christ," except in a certain sense, as was said above.[43]

Reply to 2: That from which something else is made will sometimes be spoken of in this way because of the subject that is implied.[44] And therefore, since there is no subject of this [eucharistic] change, the comparison does not hold.

Reply to 3: In this change there are many more difficulties than in creation, in which there is only the difficulty that something is made out of nothing,

39. Thomas must do a bit of backpedaling here, since the Roman Canon (the prayer in which the Eucharist is consecrated) asks that the offering of bread and wine "may become for us the body and blood of your most beloved Son, our Lord Jesus Christ" (*nobis corpus et sanguis fiat dilectissimi Filii tui, Domini nostri Iesu Christi*). It is difficult to see how these words differ from those Thomas has just disallowed: "It becomes the body of Christ" (*fiat corpus Christi*).

40. Thomas's answer to the difficulty mentioned in the previous note is that we might sometimes speak of eucharistic conversion as if it were natural change because the "species," which in this context means the outward appearance of bread, functions, at least grammatically, something like a subject that undergoes change. Thus the words of the Roman Canon might be understood as saying, "May that which is contained under the appearances of bread and wine cease being bread and wine and begin to be the body and blood of Christ."

41. This would be the case with the statement "A redhead is made out of a brunette," since Jane is implied as the subject (see notes 22 and 29, above).

42. This would be the case with the statement "Jane replaced John as the head of the company," since there is no independent thing called "the head of the company" that was transformed from John into Jane.

43. That is, when "bread" is understood to mean the outward appearance of bread.

44. "The brunette is a redhead" is a logical (if somewhat confusing) implication of "The brunette becomes a redhead," only because "the brunette" is an oblique way of speaking about Jane (see notes 22 and 29, above).

insofar as this pertains to the mode of production unique to the first cause, which presupposes nothing else. But in this [eucharistic] conversion, not only is it difficult for this whole to be changed into that whole, so that nothing of the former may remain (which is not the ordinary mode of production of any cause); this conversion has the further difficulty that the accidents remain while the substance is destroyed, and many other difficulties with which we will deal later (3.77). Nevertheless, the word "conversion" is accepted in the case of this sacrament, but not in the case of creation, as stated above.[45]

Reply to 4: As was observed above, potentiality pertains to the subject, but there is no subject in this conversion. And therefore it is not granted that bread is capable of being the body of Christ, for this conversion does not come about by the passive potentiality of the creature, but solely by the active power of the Creator.[46]

---

45. Thomas acknowledges with admirable candor the difficulties of understanding the change involved in transubstantiation, compared to which creation is quite easily graspable. He mentions two difficulties here: first, in creation *ex nihilo* there is no prior substance that must be converted; second, the persistence of the appearances of the bread and wine must be accounted for, which presents a problem because they no longer have a substance that they are the appearances of.

46. There is nothing about bread that makes it suited to becoming the body of Christ in the way that wood is suited to becoming a table. Our ability to say "The body of Christ is made out of bread" is not dependent on our ability to say "Bread is able to be the body of Christ" but on our ability to say "God is able to bring it about that the body of Christ is made out of bread." In other words, the eucharistic conversion is in no sense a natural change but is, rather, a miracle wrought by God's power.

Question 80:

Receiving the Eucharist

3.80.1[1]
Should one distinguish two ways of eating Christ's body?

It seems that two ways of eating Christ's body should not be distinguished—namely, spiritually and sacramentally.[2]

1. Just as baptism is spiritual regeneration—according to John (3:5), "Unless one be born again of water and the Holy Spirit," and so on—so also this sacrament is spiritual food. Consequently our Lord, speaking of this sacrament, says in John (6:63), "The words that I have spoken to you are spirit and life." But with regard to baptism we do not distinguish two ways of receiving it—namely, sacramentally and spiritually. Therefore this distinction should not be made regarding this sacrament either.

2. When two things are related such that one exists on account of the other, they should not be divided from each other, because the one derives its species from the other. But sacramental eating is oriented toward spiritual eating as its goal. Hence sacramental eating should not be separated from spiritual eating.

---

1. On this article, see Hütter (2019, 57–65).

2. The distinctions between *sacramentum tantum*, *res et sacramentum*, and *res tantum* form the backdrop for this article (see 3.66 note 5). In his little work *On the Articles of Faith and the Sacraments of the Church*, Thomas spells out succinctly how these terms apply to the Eucharist: "Thus, therefore, there is in this sacrament something that is the *sacramentum tantum* (that is to say, the appearances of bread and wine); something that is *res et sacramentum* (that is, the true body of Christ); and something that is *res tantum* (that is to say, the unity of the mystical body, the church, which this sacrament both signifies and causes)" (part 2 [my trans.]). Cf. *Summa theologiae* 3.73.6.

The remainder of question 80 is composed of eleven articles that are both speculative and practical. Perhaps the most famous speculation appears in 3.80.3 ad 3, where Thomas addresses the question of whether a mouse that eats the consecrated bread receives the body of Christ (see note 8, below). Practically, Thomas addresses questions such as whether the priest should deny communion to a sinner (only if the sinner is notorious and his or her reception of communion would cause scandal). Many of the questions, both practical and speculative, find their resolution in the application of the distinction between spiritual and sacramental eating.

3. Things that cannot exist without one another should not be contrasted with one another. But it seems that no one can eat spiritually without eating sacramentally; otherwise the ancient fathers would have eaten this sacrament spiritually.[3] Moreover, sacramental eating would be pointless if spiritual eating were possible without it. So it is not fitting to distinguish a twofold eating—namely, sacramental and spiritual.[4]

On the contrary: Regarding 1 Corinthians (11:29)—"He that eats and drinks unworthily," and so forth—the gloss says, "We hold that there are two ways of eating: the one sacramental and the other spiritual."[5]

I answer: There are two things to be considered in the receiving of this sacrament—namely, the sacrament itself and its effect. And we have already spoken of both earlier.[6] The perfect way, then, of receiving this sacrament is when one takes it so as to partake of its effect. Now, as was stated earlier (3.79.3, 8), it sometimes happens that someone is hindered from receiving the effect of this sacrament, and such reception of this sacrament is an imperfect

3. The objection presumes that the holy people of the Old Testament did *not* eat Christ spiritually.

4. The three objections all argue against distinguishing or dividing the two forms of eating Christ's body, but they seem to have different interests in doing so. The first objection makes spiritual eating primary, so much so that sacramental eating is not really a way of eating Christ's body at all. The second objection seems to acknowledge a genuine sacramental eating of Christ's body, but its purpose remains the spiritual eating, and so the two forms of eating are bound together so closely that there is no reason to distinguish between them. The third objection emphasizes sacramental eating, as if to say that to eat Christ's body sacramentally is always to eat it spiritually. As usual, Thomas seeks a path between erring alternatives: a solely spiritual understanding of the Eucharist in which the bread and wine are mere symbols (obj. 1) and a hyperrealist account that borders on the mechanical or magical (obj. 3).

5. On glosses, see 1.12 note 10.

6. Thomas here speaks of the twofold division between the sacrament itself (*ipsum sacramentum*) and the effect itself (*effectus ipsius*), which he discusses in questions 73–79 of the third part. It is not immediately apparent how this division relates to the threefold division of *sacramentum tantum, res et sacramentum*, and *res tantum* (see note 2, above). Indeed, Thomas seems to speak about the "effect" in different ways in different places. In *On the Articles of Faith and the Sacraments of the Church*, Thomas speaks of a twofold effect of the sacrament of the Eucharist. The first effect is "the consecration of the sacrament itself"—that is, the changing of bread and wine into the body and blood of Christ. The second effect occurs not in the elements of bread and wine but "in the soul of the one who eats worthily"; this effect "is the joining of that person to Christ." This makes it appear that both the *res et sacramentum* and *res tantum* are grouped together as "effects" and that the "sacrament itself" refers only to the sacramental "species" or appearances of bread and wine (cf. *Summa theologiae* 3.80.4, where he speaks of the twofold *res*, of which the "sacrament" is the sign). If we followed this way of speaking, then we would say that one who ate "sacramentally but not spiritually" would simply eat the *sacramentum tantum*—that is, the accidents of bread and wine. However, Thomas's use of *ipsum sacramentum* in this article (and in those following it) makes it clear that he is referring not simply to the bread and wine but to the *res et sacramentum*—that is, to the true body and blood of Christ. Thus in 3.80.3, arguing against those who would say that sinners do not receive the body and blood of Christ but only the appearances of bread and wine, he states explicitly that "sacramental eating" is the eating of Christ's body and blood, whether it is done by a sinner or a saint.

one.[7] Therefore, as the perfect is contrasted with the imperfect, so sacramental eating, in which the sacrament alone is received without its effect, is contrasted with spiritual eating, in which a person receives the effect of this sacrament so that one is spiritually united with Christ through faith and charity.[8]

Reply to 1: A similar distinction is made regarding baptism and the other sacraments. For some receive the sacrament only [*tantum sacramentum*], whereas others receive the sacrament and the reality of the sacrament. However, there is a difference. Other sacraments are brought about in the use of the material element; the receiving of the sacrament is the completion of the sacrament. But this sacrament is brought about in the consecration of the material element, and both its uses[9] follow from the sacrament. In baptism and in the other sacraments that imprint a seal, those who receive the sacrament receive some spiritual effect—that is, the seal—which is not the case in this sacrament.[10] And therefore, in the case of this sacrament,

---

7. This hindering would normally occur because of mortal sin, which makes it impossible to eat Christ's body spiritually, since this is nothing other than being united to Christ in love. So one in a state of mortal sin would eat Christ's body sacramentally, but would, as Paul says in 1 Cor. 11, eat to his or her own condemnation. As Thomas puts it in his hymn "Lauda Sion" (*Lectionary* 2001):

> Bad and good the feast are sharing,
> Of what divers dooms preparing,
>   Endless death, or endless life.
> Life to these, to those damnation,
> See how like participation
>   Is with unlike issues rife.

8. In 3.80.3 ad 3 Thomas muddies the water somewhat by speaking of a third form of eating: "accidental eating." He notes that although consecrated bread eaten by a mouse or dog would not cease to be Christ's body, we still should not speak of a mouse or dog eating Christ's body "sacramentally," since such animals are "incapable of using it as a sacrament." We should speak rather of a nonhuman animal as eating only the accidents—the *sacramentum tantum*, as it were. He goes on to note that a human being who ate consecrated bread without knowing it was consecrated would also eat only accidentally and not sacramentally.

This third possibility restores the threefold division of *sacramentum tantum, res et sacramentum*, and *res tantum*, but it also presents some confusion because it might appear that Christ's presence is somehow dependent on human understanding. However, Thomas seems quite clear that Christ is present in the sacrament whether a human being (or a mouse) knows it or not. But only when one can "use" the sacrament as a sacrament can one eat "sacramentally," and the ability to "use" the sacrament seems to depend on the ability to know it is a sacrament. As Thomas says in 3.80.3 ad 2, an unbeliever (in this case, one who does not believe that Christ is present in the sacrament) receives Christ in the sacrament but does not feed on him sacramentally.

9. That is, either sacramental or spiritual eating.

10. Some modern authors have criticized Thomas for his view that the sacrament of the Eucharist is brought about (*perficiantur*) through the consecration of the matter and not through its reception. Such authors take this to mean that the real "point" of the Eucharist is to consecrate bread and wine and that holy communion is a sort of optional add-on. One might be forgiven for this criticism, since much late medieval and early modern eucharistic practice proceeded in exactly this way: at most Masses only the priest would receive communion, while lay devotion was focused on the adoration of Christ present

the sacramental use is distinguished from the spiritual use more than in the case of baptism.

Reply to 2: The sacramental eating that attains spiritual eating is not contrasted with spiritual eating, but is included under it. But the sacramental eating that does not secure the effect is contrasted with spiritual eating, just as the imperfect, which does not attain the perfection of its species, is contrasted with the perfect.[11]

Reply to 3: As stated earlier (3.73.3), the effect of the sacrament can be attained by anyone if the sacrament is received through desire, though not received in reality. And so, just as some are baptized with the baptism of flames, on account of their desire for baptism, before being baptized in the baptism of water,[12] so likewise some eat this sacrament spiritually before they receive it sacramentally.

This happens in two ways. In one way, because of a desire to receive the sacrament itself, and in this way those who desire to receive these sacraments once they have been instituted are said to be baptized, and to eat spiritually and not sacramentally.[13] In another way, because of prefiguration: thus the Apostle says in 1 Corinthians (10:2–4) that the ancient fathers were "baptized in the cloud and in the sea," and that "they did eat . . . spiritual food, and . . . drank . . . spiritual drink."[14] Nevertheless sacramental eating is not

---

in the Eucharist. But if one looks at what Thomas has to say as a whole about the Eucharist, it is clear that for him the purpose of this sacrament is the nourishment of Christians through the reception of holy communion.

Thomas's point is simply that the *res et sacramentum* occurs, as it were, in the conversion of the bread and wine, whereas in baptism and the other sacraments in which the *res et sacramentum* is a "character" or "seal" (see 3.63.1) the *res et sacramentum* is accomplished only with the conferral of the seal. Thomas's point is not that after the consecration nothing further is to be done. Thus: "In the sacrament of the Eucharist, what is both *res et sacramentum* is in the matter itself, but what is *res tantum*—namely, the grace bestowed—is in the recipient; whereas in baptism both are in the recipient—namely, the seal, which is *res et sacramentum*, and the grace of pardon of sins, which is *res tantum*" (3.73.1 ad 3).

11. When we speak of those who eat Christ's body "spiritually," we are not distinguishing them necessarily from those who eat his body "sacramentally." Indeed, those who with faith and love eat his body sacramentally most certainly eat it spiritually as well. The distinction is between those who eat spiritually (whether or not this includes sacramental eating) and those who eat it *only* sacramentally.

12. See 3.68 note 7.

13. This sentence refers to what later Roman Catholic tradition would call "spiritual communion," in which someone unable to receive holy communion would seek to unite themselves with Christ through faith in and desire for Christ as he is present in the sacrament. An "act of spiritual communion" might take the following form (this one by St. Alphonsus Liguori): "My Jesus, I believe that you are present in the most holy sacrament. I love you above all things, and I desire to receive you into my soul. Since I cannot at this moment receive you sacramentally, come at least spiritually into my heart. I embrace you as if you were already there and unite myself wholly to you. Never permit me to be separated from you. Amen."

14. "Prefiguration" refers to the way in which the holy people of the Old Testament ate Christ spiritually through faith in God's promised redeemer, a faith that they professed through ritual foreshadowings of

pointless, because the actual receiving of the sacrament produces the effect of the sacrament more fully than the desire for it does, as stated earlier concerning baptism.[15]

Christ, such as the Passover feast (see 1–2.103.3). Thus Thomas simply disagrees with the presumption of the objection that they did not eat spiritually.

15. In 3.69.4 ad 2 Thomas says, "One receives forgiveness of sins prior to baptism inasmuch as one desires baptism, whether explicitly or implicitly, and yet in actually receiving baptism a fuller forgiveness of sins occurs, with respect to being freed of all penalty." One cannot apply this statement to the Eucharist directly, since the ultimate effect of the Eucharist is not forgiveness of sins, as with baptism, but union with Christ. Thomas's point seems to be that a more complete union with Christ is achieved through worthy sacramental eating than through spiritual eating alone.

Also note the more general remarks that Thomas makes about why human beings need sacraments (see 3.61.1, above).

Question 83:

The Rite of This Sacrament

3.83.1[1]
Is Christ sacrificially offered in this sacrament?

It seems that in the celebration of this sacrament Christ is not sacrificially offered [*immoletur*].[2]

1. It is written in Hebrews (10:14) that Christ "by one offering has perfected forever those who are sanctified." But that offering was his sacrificial offering.[3] Therefore Christ is not sacrificially offered in the celebration of this sacrament.

2. Christ's sacrificial offering was made upon the cross, on which "he delivered himself for us, an offering and a sacrifice to God for an odor of sweetness," as is said in Ephesians (5:2). But Christ is not crucified in the celebration of this mystery.[4] Hence, neither is he sacrificially offered.

---

1. On this article, see Marshall (2009).

2. Thomas uses *immolatio* in this article (rather than *sacrificium*), which carries the connotation of an offering that involves the death of that which is offered. Thomas does not use this term because he thinks Christ is killed in the celebration of the Eucharist; rather, the term simply makes clear that the eucharistic sacrifice involves the representation of Christ's death on the cross.

Thomas says in a number of places (e.g., 3.79.7) that the Eucharist "not only is a sacrament but also a sacrifice." Although he has a fairly systematic exposition of how, in the consecration and reception of Christ's body and blood, the Eucharist is a sacrament, his remarks on its nature as a sacrifice are more scattered and unsystematic, in part for historical reasons: the controversy surrounding Berengar of Tours had contributed greatly to the development of the theology of Christ's sacramental presence in the Eucharist, whereas in Thomas's day there had not yet been significant controversy over the sacrificial nature of the Eucharist (though Thomas's contemporary, William Durand, does mention unnamed "perverse heretics [who] think of us as being filled with great presumption because we sacrifice and call the consecration of the host a sacrifice" [*Rationale diviniorum officiorum* 4.30.10]). The sacrificial nature of the Eucharist would, of course, become a major issue in the sixteenth century.

3. The objection here is one that recurs in the sixteenth-century disputes over the sacrificial nature of the Eucharist: the one sacrifice of Christ on the cross makes any further sacrifice unnecessary and therefore precludes the Eucharist from being a sacrifice.

4. The objection is that the ritual actions of the Mass do not represent the particular manner of Christ's death.

3. As Augustine says in *De Trinitate* (4.14), in the sacrificial offering of Christ, the priest and the victim are the same. But in the celebration of this sacrament, the priest and the victim are not the same. The celebration of this sacrament, therefore, is not the sacrificial offering of Christ.

On the contrary: Augustine says, in Prosper of Aquitaine's *Book of Sentences*, "Christ was sacrificed once in himself, and yet he is sacrificed daily in the sacrament."[5]

I answer: The celebration of this sacrament is spoken of as Christ's sacrificial offering for two reasons.

First, because, as Augustine says in *To Simplicianus* (2.3), "the images of things are called by the names of the things of which they are the images, as when, looking upon a picture or a fresco, we say, 'This is Cicero, and that is Sallust.'" But, as was said earlier (3.79.1), the celebration of this sacrament is a sort of image representing Christ's suffering, which is a true sacrificial offering.[6] Therefore Ambrose says, regarding Hebrews (10:1), "In Christ a sacrifice capable of giving eternal salvation was offered up. What then do we do? Do we not offer it up every day in memory of his death?"[7]

In another way, it is called a sacrifice in regard to the effect of his suffering—namely, because by this sacrament we are made partakers of the fruit of our Lord's suffering. Therefore in one of the Sunday Secrets it is said, "Whenever the memorial of this sacrifice is celebrated, the work of our redemption is accomplished."[8]

5. This quotation is not actually in the *Sentences* of Proper of Aquitaine (ca. 390–ca. 455), which was a kind of distillation of quotations from Augustine. It is, however, found in Gratian's *Decretum* (3.2.52), where it is ascribed to Prosper's *Sentences*. The quotation itself is not exactly that of Augustine but is Lanfranc's account of Augustine's view. However, Augustine himself says something very much like this in *Epistle 98*, 9.

6. One might ask exactly *how* the celebration of the Eucharist is an "image" of Christ's suffering on the cross. In 3.83.5 Thomas offers some allegorical interpretations—of the sort typical in medieval expositions of the Mass—of the priest's actions. Thus in the reply to the third objection he says that the various signs of the cross represent various events in Christ's passion, and in the reply to the fifth objection he says that the priest's extending of his arms after the consecration, which was a distinctive Dominican practice, represents Christ's extended arms on the cross. But Thomas means more here than that the Eucharist is a sort of passion play: its representation of the suffering and death of Christ is tied to the very act of eucharistic consecration itself, as the second reason Thomas offers makes clear.

7. The quotation is actually found in John Chrysostom's *Homily 17*, 6, in *Homilies on the Epistle to the Hebrews*. It is ascribed to Ambrose in Gratian's *Decretum* 3.2.53.

8. *Secreta* ("Secret") is the medieval term for the prayer said in the Mass after the bread and wine have been prepared and before the eucharistic prayer begins. In the Dominican rite of Mass of Thomas's day, the particular prayer quoted here was used on the seventh Sunday after the Octave of Trinity; in the current rite of Mass, it is used on the second Sunday in Ordinary Time.

Because a sacrament is both a sign and a cause, the kind of "representation" we speak of with regard to the Eucharist goes beyond merely picturing something absent. Rather, it is a representation that makes present that which it represents. And the Eucharist does not simply represent Christ-in-general, but Christ in his self-offering to God the Father. So just as we might speak of the real presence of Christ

Consequently, according to the first way, it could be said that Christ was sacrificed even in the prefigurations of the Old Testament; therefore Revelation (13:8) speaks of those "whose names are not written in the book of life of the Lamb that was slain from the beginning of the world." But, according to the second way, it is only in this sacrament [of the Eucharist] that Christ is sacrificially offered in its celebration.[9]

Reply to 1: As Ambrose says in the same place, "There is but one victim"— namely, that which Christ offered and which we offer—"and not many victims, because Christ was offered only once, and this latter sacrifice is the pattern of the former; for just as what is offered everywhere is one body, and not many bodies, so also is it but one sacrifice."[10]

Reply to 2: Just as the celebration of this sacrament is an image representing Christ's suffering, so the altar is representative of the cross itself, upon which Christ was sacrificially offered in his own outward appearance.

Reply to 3: For the same reason (cf. reply to obj. 2) the priest also bears the image of Christ, in whose person and by whose power the priest pronounces the words of consecration, as is evident from what was said earlier (3.82.1, 3). And so, in a way, the priest and victim are the same.[11]

---

in the Eucharist, we might speak of the real presence of Christ's sacrifice. Theologians today appeal to the Greek term *anamnēsis* (which in the Gospels is the term Jesus uses at the Last Supper, often translated as "remembrance") to convey this idea of a ritual recalling that makes present.

Thomas appears to hold the view that it is through the separate consecration of Christ's body and blood that Christ's sacrifice is present, because it is a sacramental representation of the separation of Christ's body and blood on the cross. This view is not developed systematically and must be gleaned from scattered remarks. In 3.80.12 ad 3 he says that "the representation of the Lord's passion is brought about in the very consecration of this sacrament, in which one should not consecrate the body without the blood." In 3.76.2 ad 1 he says that the body and blood of Christ are consecrated in the separate species of bread and wine because "this serves the representation of the passion of Christ, in which the blood was separated from the body." The close link Thomas presumes between presence and sacrifice—both being effected through the consecration of the elements—helps make it clear that eucharistic sacrifice, no less than eucharistic presence, is a divine and not a human action.

9. The contrast drawn here parallels what Thomas says generally about the difference between the sacraments of the Old Law and those of the New (see 3.62.1, above).

10. We might say that just as the eucharistic conversion of the bread and wine into the body and blood of Christ is not a new incarnation, so too the eucharistic sacrifice is not a new passion.

11. The priest does not offer Christ; rather Christ offers himself through the instrument of the priest's ministry.

Bibliography

A Note on the Works of Aquinas

Torrell (1996) provides a comprehensive list of all of Thomas's works, along with information on the best editions.

The Leonine edition of Thomas's works is intended to be the definitive edition, but it is not yet complete, in spite of having been launched in 1882. The other major editions of Thomas's complete works are the Piana edition (1570), the Parma edition (1852–73), and the Vives or Paris edition (1871–80). Critical editions of a number of individual works have been published by Marietti in Turin. Thomas's works in Latin are now available online, in the collection originally assembled by R. Busa from a variety of editions, at Corpus Thomisticum, http://www.corpusthomisticum.org.

Many of Thomas's works have been translated into English, and the English translation of Torrell's biography of Aquinas lists them up to 1996. Quite a few have been translated since then. There is an excellent online bibliography of English translations of Thomas's works maintained by Thérèse Bonin of Duquesne University at Thomas Aquinas in English: A Bibliography, http://www.home.duq.edu/~bonin/thomasbibliography.html.

Ancient and Medieval Sources

Abelard, Peter. 2011. *Commentary on the Epistle to the Romans*. Translated by Steven R. Cartwright. Washington, DC: Catholic University of America Press.

Anselm. 1998. *On Truth*. Translated by Ralph McInerny. In *Anselm of Canterbury: The Major Works*. Edited by Brian Davies and G. R. Evans. Oxford: Oxford University Press.

Aquinas, Thomas. 1975. *Summa contra Gentiles*. Translated by Anton C. Pegis. Notre Dame, IN: University of Notre Dame Press.

———. 2010. *Commentary on the Gospel of John*. Translated by Fabian Larcher and James Weisheipl. 3 vols. Washington, DC: Catholic University of America Press.

Aristotle. 1984. *The Complete Works of Aristotle: The Revised Oxford Translation*. Edited by Jonathan Barnes. Princeton: Princeton University Press.

Augustine. 1991. *Confessions*. Translated by Henry Chadwick. Oxford: Oxford University Press.

———. 1993. *The City of God*. Translated by Marcus Dods. New York: Random House.

———. 2010. *On the Free Choice of the Will, On Grace and Free Choice, and Other Writings*. Edited and translated by Peter King. Cambridge: Cambridge University Press.

Catherine of Siena. *The Dialogue*. Translated by Suzanne Noffke, OP. Mahwah, NJ: Paulist Press.

———. 2001. "Letter T241." In *The Letters of St. Catherine of Siena*, vol. 2. Translated by Suzanne Noffke, OP, 208–11. Tempe, AZ: Arizona Center for Medieval and Renaissance Studies.

Irenaeus. 1997. *Irenaeus of Lyons*. Translated and edited by Robert M. Grant. London: Routledge.

Photius. "Patriarch Photius of Constantinople: Encyclical to the Eastern Patriarchs (866)." https://pages.uoregon.edu/sshoemak/324/texts/photius_encyclical.htm.

Pseudo-Dionysius. 1987. *Pseudo-Dionysius: The Complete Works*. Translated by Colm Luibheid and Paul Rorem. Mahwah, NJ: Paulist Press.

Modern Sources

Anscombe, G. E. M., and Peter T. Geach. 1961. *Three Philosophers: Aristotle, Aquinas, Frege*. Oxford: Basil Blackwell.

Armitage, J. Mark. 2008. "Why Didn't Jesus Write a Book? Aquinas on the Teaching of Christ." *New Blackfriars* 89, no. 1021 (May): 337–53.

Baglow, Christopher T. 2004. "Sacred Scripture and Sacred Doctrine in St. Thomas Aquinas." In *Aquinas on Doctrine: A Critical Introduction*, edited by Thomas Weinandy, Daniel Keating, and John Yocum, 1–25. London: T&T Clark.

Baldwin, John W. 1959. "The Medieval Theories of the Just Price: Romanists, Canonists, and Theologians in the Twelfth and Thirteenth Centuries." *Transactions of the American Philosophical Society* 49, no. 4: 1–92.

Bauerschmidt, Frederick Christian. 2013. *Thomas Aquinas: Faith, Reason, and Following Christ*. Oxford: Oxford University Press.

————. 2016a. "'The Body of Christ Is Made from Bread': Transubstantiation and the Grammar of Creation." *International Journal of Systematic Theology* 18, no. 1: 30–46.

————. 2016b. "Thomas Aquinas." In *T&T Clark Companion to the Doctrine of Sin*, edited by Keith L. Johnson and David Lauber, 199–216. London: Bloomsbury T&T Clark.

Blankenhorn, Bernhard. 2006. "The Instrumental Causality of the Sacraments: Thomas Aquinas and Louis-Marie Chauvet." *Nova et Vetera* 4, no. 2 (English edition): 255–94.

Bonino, Serge-Thomas. 2002. "Charisms, Forms, and States of Life." In *The Ethics of Aquinas*, edited by Stephen J. Pope, 340–52. Washington, DC: Catholic University of America Press.

————. 2016. *Angels and Demons: A Catholic Introduction*. Translated by Michael J. Miller. Washington, DC: Catholic University of America Press.

Boyle, Joseph M., Jr. 1978. "*Praeter Intentionem* in Aquinas." *Thomist* 42, no. 4: 649–65.

Boyle, Leonard E. 1982. *The Setting of the "Summa Theologiae."* Toronto: Pontifical Institute of Mediaeval Studies.

Brock, Stephen L. 2001. "St Thomas and the Eucharistic Conversion." *Thomist* 65, no. 4: 529–65.

Brown, Stephen L. 2002. "The Theological Virtue of Faith: An Invitation to an Ecclesial Life of Truth." In *The Ethics of Aquinas*, edited by Stephen J. Pope, 221–31. Washington, DC: Georgetown University Press.

Cates, Diana Fritz. 2002. "The Virtue of Temperance." In *The Ethics of Aquinas*, edited by Stephen J. Pope, 321–39. Washington, DC: Georgetown University Press.

Cessario, Romanus. 1990. *The Godly Image: Christ and Salvation in Catholic Thought from Anselm to Aquinas*. Petersham, MA: St. Bede's Publications.

————. 2002. "The Theological Virtue of Hope." In *The Ethics of Aquinas*, edited by Stephen J. Pope, 232–43. Washington, DC: Georgetown University Press.

Chauvet, Louis-Marie. 1995. *Symbol and Sacrament: A Sacramental Reinterpretation of Christian Existence*. Translated by Patrick Madigan and Madeleine Beaumont. Collegeville, MN: Liturgical Press.

Clark, Patrick. 2010. "Is Martyrdom Virtuous? An Occasion for Rethinking the Relation of Christ and Virtue in Aquinas." *Journal of the Society of Christian Ethics* 30, no. 1 (Spring/Summer): 141–59.

Coakley, Sarah. 2016. "Person of Christ." In *The Cambridge Companion to the "Summa Theologiae,"* edited by Philip McCosker and Denys Turner, 222–39. New York: Cambridge University Press.

Congar, Yves. 1983. "The Holy Spirit and the Eucharist in the Western Tradition." In *I Believe in the Holy Spirit*. Vol. 3, *The River of the Water of Life Flows in the East and in the West*, translated by David Smith, 250–57. New York: Seabury.

Conrad, Richard P. 2014. "St. Thomas on Christ's Passion and Resurrection as Efficient and Exemplar Causes: How This Concept Helps Us Read Scripture and Preach Christ." *Angelicum* 91, no. 1: 167–206.

Crotty, Nicholas. 1962. "The Redemptive Role of Christ's Resurrection." *Thomist* 25, no. 1: 54–106.

Cunningham, James J. 1974. "Appendix 3: The Problem of Infant Baptism." In *Summa Theologiæ*, by Thomas Aquinas. Vol. 57, *Baptism and Confirmation (3a. 66–72)*, 235–38. Cambridge: Cambridge University Press.

Dauphinais, Michael. 2009. "Christ and the Metaphysics of Baptism in the *Summa Theologiae* and the *Commentary on John*." In *Rediscovering Aquinas and the Sacraments: Studies in Sacramental Theology*, edited by Matthew Levering and Michael Dauphinais, 14–27. Chicago: Hillenbrand Books.

Davies, Brian. 2010. "Classical Theism and the Doctrine of Divine Simplicity." In *Language, Meaning, and God: Essays in Honor of Herbert McCabe, with a New Introduction*, edited by Brian Davies, 51–74. Eugene, OR: Wipf & Stock.

Denzinger, Heinrich. 2012. *Compendium of Creeds, Definitions, and Declarations on Matters of Faith and Morals.* 43rd ed. Edited by Peter Hünermann. Translated by Robert L. Fastiggi and Anne England Nash. San Francisco: Ignatius Press.

Dewan, Lawrence. 2012. "The Existence of God: Can It Be Demonstrated?" *Nova et Vetera* 10, no. 3 (English edition): 731–56.

Dillard, Peter. 2012. "Keeping the Vision: Aquinas and the Problem of Disembodied Beatitude." *New Blackfriars* 93, no. 1046: 397–411.

Dodds, Michael. 2004. "The Teaching of Thomas Aquinas on the Mysteries of the Life of Christ." In *Aquinas on Doctrine: A Critical Introduction*, edited by Thomas Weinandy, Daniel Keating, and John Yocum, 91–115. London: T&T Clark.

Elders, Leo. 2018. "St. Thomas Aquinas's Treatise on Temperance and Aristotle." *Nova et Vetera* 16, no. 2 (English edition): 465–87.

Emery, Gilles. 2007. *The Trinitarian Theology of St. Thomas Aquinas.* Translated by Francesca Aran Murphy. Oxford: Oxford University Press.

Foot, Philippa. 2002. "The Problem of Abortion and the Doctrine of the Double Effect." In *Virtues and Vices and Other Essays in Moral Philosophy*, 19–32. Oxford: Clarendon.

Foster, Kenelm, O.P., ed. and trans. 1959. *The Life of Saint Thomas Aquinas: Biographical Documents.* Baltimore: Helicon.

Franks, Christopher. 2009. *He Became Poor: The Poverty of Christ and Aquinas's Economic Teachings.* Grand Rapids: Eerdmans.

Gaine, Simon Francis. 2003. *Will There Be Free Will in Heaven? Freedom, Impeccability and Beatitude.* London: T&T Clark.

———. 2015. "Christ's Acquired Knowledge according to Thomas Aquinas: How Aquinas's Philosophy Helped and Hindered His Account." *New Blackfriars* 96, no. 1063 (May): 255–68.

———. 2018. "Is There Still a Place for Christ's Infused Knowledge in Catholic Theology and Exegesis?" *Nova et Vetera* 16, no. 2 (English edition): 601–15.

Gallagher, David M. 2002. "The Will and Its Acts." In *The Ethics of Aquinas*, edited by Stephen J. Pope, 69–89. Washington, DC: Georgetown University Press.

Garrigou-Lagrange, Réginald. 1950. *Christ the Savior: A Commentary on the Third Part of St. Thomas' Theological Summa*. Translated by Bede Rose. St. Louis: Herder.

———. 1965. *The Theological Virtues I: On Faith*. St. Louis: Herder.

———. 2002. *The Three Conversions in the Spiritual Life*. Gastonia, NC: Tan Books. First published in 1937 as *The Three Ways of the Spiritual Life*, London: Burns, Oates & Washbourne.

Gilson, Étienne. 1960. *The Elements of Christian Philosophy*. New York: Doubleday.

Gorman, Michael. 2017. *Aquinas on the Metaphysics of the Hypostatic Union*. Cambridge: Cambridge University Press.

Healy, Nicholas M. 2016. "Redemption." In *The Cambridge Companion to the "Summa Theologiae,"* edited by Philip McCosker and Denys Turner, 255–68. New York: Cambridge University Press.

Hibbs, Thomas S. 1995. *Dialectic and Narrative in Aquinas: An Interpretation of the "Summa Contra Gentiles."* Notre Dame, IN: University of Notre Dame Press.

Holtz, Dominic. 2012. "Sacraments." In *The Oxford Handbook of Aquinas*, edited by Brian Davies and Eleonore Stump, 448–57. Oxford: Oxford University Press.

Horst, Ulrich. 1998. "Christ, Exemplar *Ordinis Fratrum Praedicantium*, according to Saint Thomas Aquinas." In *Christ among the Medieval Dominicans: Representations of Christ in the Texts and Images of the Order of Preachers*, edited by K. Emery and J. Wawrykow, 256–70. Notre Dame, IN: University of Notre Dame Press.

Houser, R. E. 2002. "The Virtue of Courage." In *The Ethics of Aquinas*, edited by Stephen J. Pope, 304–20. Washington, DC: Georgetown University Press.

Hunter, Justus H. 2020. *If Adam Had Not Sinned: The Reason for the Incarnation from Anselm to Scotus*. Washington, DC: Catholic University of America Press.

Hütter, Reinhard. 2019. *Aquinas on Transubstantiation: The Real Presence of Christ in the Eucharist*. Washington, DC: Catholic University of America Press.

Jordan, Mark D. 2016. *Teaching Bodies: Moral Formation in the Summa of Thomas Aquinas*. New York: Fordham University Press.

Kenny, Anthony. 1969. *The Five Ways: St. Thomas Aquinas' Proofs of God's Existence*. New York: Routledge.

———. 1993. *Aquinas on Mind*. London: Routledge.

Kent, Bonnie. 2002. "Habits and Virtues." In *The Ethics of Aquinas*, edited by Stephen J. Pope, 116–30. Washington, DC: Georgetown University Press.

Kerr, Fergus. 2002. *After Aquinas: Versions of Thomism*. Malden, MA: Blackwell.

Kobusch, Theo. 2002. "Grace." In *The Ethics of Aquinas*, edited by Stephen J. Pope, 207–18. Washington, DC: Georgetown University Press.

Koehn, Daryl, and Barry Wilbratte. 2012. "A Defense of a Thomistic Concept of Just Price." *Business Ethics Quarterly* 22, no. 3: 501–26.

Lamb, Matthew. 2004. "Eschatology." In *Aquinas on Doctrine: A Critical Introduction*, edited by Thomas Weinandy, Daniel Keating, and John Yocum, 224–40. London: T&T Clark.

Lectionary for Mass: For Use in the Dioceses of the United States of America. 2001. 2nd typical ed. Washington, DC: Confraternity of Christian Doctrine.

Leget, Carlo. 2005. "Eschatology." In *The Theology of Thomas Aquinas*, edited by Rik Van Nieuwenhove and Joseph Wawrykow, 365–85. Notre Dame, IN: University of Notre Dame Press.

Madigan, Kevin. 1997. "Did Jesus 'Progress in Wisdom'? Thomas Aquinas on Luke 2:52 in Ancient and High-Medieval Context." *Traditio* 52: 179–200.

Marenbon, John. 2015. *Pagans and Philosophers: The Problem of Paganism from Augustine to Leibniz.* Princeton: Princeton University Press.

Marshall, Bruce. 2005. "*Quod Scit Una Uetula*: Aquinas on the Nature of Theology." In *The Theology of Thomas Aquinas*, edited by Rik Van Nieuwenhove and Joseph Wawrykow, 1–35. Notre Dame, IN: University of Notre Dame Press.

———. 2009. "The Whole Mystery of Our Salvation: Saint Thomas Aquinas on the Eucharist as Sacrifice." In *Rediscovering Aquinas and the Sacraments: Studies in Sacramental Theology*, edited by Matthew Levering and Michael Dauphinais, 39–64. Chicago: Hillenbrand Books.

———. 2016. "Religion and Election: Aquinas on Natural Law, Judaism, and Salvation in Christ." *Nova et Vetera* 14, no. 1 (English edition): 61–125.

Mattison, William. 2010. "Thomas's Categorizations of Virtue: Historical Background and Contemporary Significance." *Thomist* 74, no. 2: 189–235.

McCabe, Herbert. 1987. *God Matters.* London: Geoffrey Chapman.

———. 2002. *God Still Matters.* Edited by Brian Davies. London: Continuum.

———. 2007. *Faith within Reason.* Edited by Brian Davies. London: Continuum.

———. 2008. *On Aquinas.* Edited by Brian Davies. London: Continuum.

McCosker, Philip. 2016. "Grace." In *The Cambridge Companion to the "Summa Theologiae,"* edited by Philip McCosker and Denys Turner, 206–21. New York: Cambridge University Press.

McDermott, Timothy. 1989. *Summa Theologiae: A Concise Translation.* Allen, TX: Christian Classics.

———. 2007. *How to Read Aquinas.* London: Granta Books.

Merriell, D. Juvenal. 2005. "Trinitarian Anthropology." In *The Theology of Thomas Aquinas*, edited by Rik Van Nieuwenhove and Joseph Wawrykow, 123–42. Notre Dame, IN: University of Notre Dame Press.

Migne, J.-P., ed. 1844–55. Patrologia Latina. 217 vols. Paris.

———, ed. 1857–86. Patrologia Graeca. 161 vols. Paris.

Miner, Robert. 2017. "Thomas Aquinas's Hopeful Transformation of Peter Lombard's Four Fears." *Speculum* 92, no. 4 (October): 963–75.

Morerod, Charles. 2011. "'No Salvation outside the Church': Understanding the Doctrine with St. Thomas Aquinas and Charles Journet." *Thomist* 75, no. 4 (October): 517–36.

Murphy, Richard. 1965. "Appendix 3: Causes of Christ's Death (3a.47)." In *Summa Theologiæ*, by Thomas Aquinas. Vol. 54, *The Passion of Christ (3a. 46–52)*, 194–201. Cambridge: Cambridge University Press.

Nichols, Aidan. 1990. "St Thomas Aquinas on the Passion of Christ: A Reading of *Summa Theologiae*, IIIa, q. 46." *Scottish Journal of Theology* 43, no. 4 (April): 447–59.

———. 2004. "The Mariology of St. Thomas." In *Aquinas on Doctrine: A Critical Introduction*, edited by Thomas Weinandy, Daniel Keating, and John Yocum, 241–60. London: T&T Clark.

Niederbacher, Bruno. 2012. "The Relation of Reason to Faith." In *The Oxford Handbook of Aquinas*, edited by Brian Davies and Eleonore Stump, 337–47. Oxford: Oxford University Press.

Nolan, Michael. 1992. "Aquinas and the Act of Love." In *At the Heart of the Real: Philosophical Essays in Honour of the Most Reverend Desmond Connell, Archbishop of Dublin*, edited by Fran O'Rourke, 163–76. Dublin: Irish Academic Press.

Novak, Michael. 1995. "Aquinas and the Heretics." *First Things*, no. 58 (December): 33–38.

O'Collins, Gerald. 1970. "Thomas Aquinas and Christ's Resurrection." *Theological Studies* 31, no. 3 (September): 512–22.

O'Connor, Edward. 1974. Appendices 1–6. In *Summa Theologiæ*, by Thomas Aquinas. Vol. 24, *The Gifts of the Spirit: (1a2ae. 68–70)*, 80–150. Cambridge: Cambridge University Press.

O'Neill, Coleman E. 1965. "Appendix 1: Statements about Christ." In *Summa Theologiæ*, by Thomas Aquinas. Vol. 50, *The One Mediator (3a. 16–26)*, 215–20. Cambridge: Cambridge University Press.

Pasnau, Robert. 2012. "Philosophy of Mind and Human Nature." In *The Oxford Handbook of Aquinas*, edited by Brian Davies and Eleonore Stump, 348–68. Oxford: Oxford University Press.

Pelikan, Jaroslav. 1978. "*Imago Dei*: An Explication of *Summa theologiae*, Part 1, Question 93." In *Calgary Aquinas Studies*, edited by Anthony Parel, 27–48. Toronto: Pontifical Institute of Mediaeval Studies.

Pesch, Otto Hermann. 1970. "Existential and Sapiential Theology—the Theological Confrontation between Luther and Thomas Aquinas." In *Catholic Scholars*

Dialogue with Luther, edited by Jared Wicks, 59–81. Chicago: Loyola University Press.

Pieper, Joseph. 1999. *The Silence of St. Thomas: Three Essays*. Translated by John Murray, SJ, and Daniel O'Connor. South Bend, IN: St. Augustine's Press.

Pinckaers, Servais-Théodore. 2001. *Traduction et commentaire de: S. Thomas d'Aquin, La béatitude (Somme théologique, Ia–IIae, questions 1–5)*. Paris: Cerf.

———. 2005. *The Pinckaers Reader: Renewing Thomistic Moral Theology*. Edited by John Berkman and Craig Steven Titus. Washington, DC: Catholic University of America Press.

Porter, Jean. 1995. "Virtue and Sin: The Connection of the Virtues and the Case of the Flawed Saint." *Journal of Religion* 75, no. 4 (October): 521–39.

———. 2002. "The Virtue of Justice." In *The Ethics of Aquinas*, edited by Stephen J. Pope, 272–86. Washington, DC: Georgetown University Press.

———. 2016. "Happiness." In *The Cambridge Companion to the "Summa Theologiae,"* edited by Philip McCosker and Denys Turner, 181–93. New York: Cambridge University Press.

Prügl, Thomas. 2005. "Thomas Aquinas as Interpreter of Scripture." In *The Theology of Thomas Aquinas*, edited by Rik Van Nieuwenhove and Joseph Wawrykow, 386–415. Notre Dame, IN: University of Notre Dame Press.

Reichberg, Gregory M. 2010. "Thomas Aquinas between Just War and Pacifism." *Journal of Religious Ethics* 38, no. 2 (June): 219–41.

Rocca, Gregory. 2004. *Speaking the Incomprehensible God: Thomas Aquinas on the Interplay of Positive and Negative Theology*. Washington, DC: Catholic University of America Press.

Roguet, Aymon-Marie. 1945. *Traduction et commentaire de: S. Thomas d'Aquin, Les Sacrements (Somme théologique IIIa pars, questions 60 à 65)*. Paris: Cerf.

Russell, Frederick H. 1975. *The Just War in the Middle Ages*. Cambridge: Cambridge University Press.

Salkeld, Brett. 2019. *Transubstantiation: Theology, History, and Christian Unity*. Grand Rapids: Baker Academic.

Schockenhoff, Eberhard. 2002. "The Theological Virtue of Charity." In *The Ethics of Aquinas*, edited by Stephen J. Pope, 244–57. Washington, DC: Georgetown University Press.

Schoot, Henk J. M. 1993. *Christ the "Name" of God: Thomas Aquinas on Naming Christ*. Leuven: Peeters.

Sertillanges, A. D. 1932. *St. Thomas Aquinas and His Work*. Translated by Godfrey Anstruther. London: Burns, Oates & Washbourne.

Shanley, Brian J. 1999. "Aquinas on Pagan Virtue." *Thomist* 63, no. 4 (January): 553–77.

Sokolowski, Robert. 2004. "What Is Natural Law? Human Purposes and Natural Ends." *Thomist* 68, no. 4: 507–29.

Spezzano, Daria. 2017. "'Be Imitators of God' (Eph. 5:1): Aquinas on Charity and Satisfaction." *Nova et Vetera* 15, no. 2 (English edition): 615–51.

Stump, Eleonore. 2012. "God's Simplicity." In *The Oxford Handbook of Aquinas*, edited by Brian Davies and Eleonore Stump, 135–46. Oxford: Oxford University Press.

Sweeney, Eileen. 2002. "Vice and Sin." In *The Ethics of Aquinas*, edited by Stephen J. Pope, 151–68. Washington, DC: Georgetown University Press.

Tanner, Kathryn. 2016. "Creation." In *The Cambridge Companion to the "Summa Theologiae,"* edited by Philip McCosker and Denys Turner, 142–55. New York: Cambridge University Press.

Torrell, Jean-Pierre. 1996. *Saint Thomas Aquinas.* Vol. 1, *The Person and His Work.* Translated by Robert Royal. Washington, DC: Catholic University of America Press.

———. 1999. *Le Christ en ses mystères: La vie et l'oeuvre de Jésus selon saint Thomas d'Aquin.* 2 vols. Paris: Desclée.

———. 2003. *Saint Thomas Aquinas.* Vol. 2, *Spiritual Master.* Translated by Robert Royal. Washington, DC: Catholic University of America Press.

———. 2011. *Christ and Spirituality in St. Thomas Aquinas.* Translated by Bernhard Blankenhorn. Washington, DC: Catholic University of America Press.

Tugwell, Simon. 1988. "The Life and Works of Thomas Aquinas." In *Albert and Thomas: Selected Writings*, translated and edited by Simon Tugwell, 201–66. Mahwah, NJ: Paulist Press.

Van Nieuwenhove, Rik. 2017. "Recipientes per contemplationem, tradentes per actionem: The Relation between the Active and Contemplative Lives according to Thomas Aquinas." *Thomist* 81, no. 1 (January): 1–30.

Walsh, Liam. 2005. "Sacraments." In *The Theology of Thomas Aquinas*, edited by Rik Van Nieuwenhove and Joseph Wawrykow, 326–64. Notre Dame, IN: University of Notre Dame Press.

Wawrykow, Joseph. 2005. "Grace." In *The Theology of Thomas Aquinas*, edited by Rik Van Nieuwenhove and Joseph Wawrykow, 192–221. Notre Dame, IN: University of Notre Dame Press.

———. 2012. "The Theological Virtues." In *The Oxford Handbook of Aquinas*, edited by Brian Davies and Eleonore Stump, 287–307. Oxford: Oxford University Press.

Westberg, Daniel. 1992. "The Relation of Law and Practical Reason in Aquinas." In *The Future of Thomism*, edited by Deal W. Hudson and Dennis Wm. Moran, 279–90. Mishawaka, IN: American Maritain Association.

———. 1994. *Right Practical Reason: Aristotle, Action and Prudence in Aquinas.* Oxford: Clarendon.

———. 2002. "Good and Evil in Human Acts." In *The Ethics of Aquinas*, edited by Stephen J. Pope, 90–102. Washington, DC: Georgetown University Press.

White, Victor. 1956. *God the Unknown*. London: Harvill Press.

———. 1958. *Holy Teaching: The Idea of Theology according to St. Thomas Aquinas*. London: Blackfriars.

Wieland, Georg. 2002. "Happiness." In *The Ethics of Aquinas*, edited by Stephen J. Pope, 57–68. Washington, DC: Georgetown University Press.

Williams, Thomas. 2012. "Human Freedom and Agency." In *The Oxford Handbook of Aquinas*, edited by Brian Davies and Eleonore Stump, 199–208. Oxford: Oxford University Press.

Wipple, John F. 2000. *The Metaphysical Thought of Thomas Aquinas: From Finite Being to Uncreated Being*. Washington, DC: Catholic University of America Press.

Yocum, John. 2004. "Sacraments in Aquinas." In *Aquinas on Doctrine: A Critical Introduction*, edited by Thomas Weinandy, Daniel Keating, and John Yocum, 159–81. London: T&T Clark.

Index to the Introduction and Commentary